Contents

New York architecture color section following p.128

Ethnic New York color section following p.320

Color maps following p.480

3

◄◄ Hudson River ◄ Art installation by Xaviera Simmons

Introduction to

New York City

New York City is everything its supporters and critics claim: an adrenaline-charged, history-laden place that never sleeps, rarely apologizes, and works harder and longer hours than anywhere else. It's also a town of icons, both past and present – you'll find it hard to move about the city without encountering a view of something world-famous, from the lovely green sward of Central Park to the mammoth Brooklyn Bridge to the cathedral-like Grand Central Terminal. The city's boundless energy and spirit will suck you in and make you want to come back again and again.

New York buzzes round-the-clock: not only can you find, buy, or enjoy almost anything 24 hours a day, seven days a week, but there are also enough cultural attractions to fill months of sightseeing. That said, there are some key activities and sights that travelers simply should not miss. Take the city's patchwork of vastly different **neighborhoods**: a stroll from Chinatown through Soho and Tribeca to the West Village reveals the variety of life wedged together in downtown Manhattan. Then there's the city's astonishing **architecture** – you can walk past glorious Art Deco skyscrapers on one block and rows of genteel brownstones on the next – as well as its excellent **museums**, both the celebrated, like the Met and the American Museum of Natural History,

and the less well-known but equally worthy, such as the Frick Collection and the Brooklyn Museum. As if the sights weren't enough, New York has an exhaustive selection of **shops**, and world-class **restaurants** and **bars** that cater to any taste, budget, and schedule. It is justifiably famous for its diverse **theater scene**, with dozens of venues offering everything from high-gloss Broadway musicals to scruffy avant-garde performance pieces. And if it's **nightlife** you're after, look no further: the city's throbbing, jam-packed clubs are known for their cutting-edge parties and music. In other words, just plan on sleeping once you get home.

What to see

Though New York City officially comprises the central island of **Manhattan** and **four outer boroughs** – Brooklyn, Queens, the Bronx, and Staten Island – to many, Manhattan simply *is* New York. Certainly, whatever your interests, you'll likely spend most of your time here. Understanding the intricacies of Manhattan's layout, and above all getting some grasp on its subway and bus systems, should be your first priority. Most importantly, note that New York is very much a city of neighborhoods, and is therefore best explored on foot. For an overview of each district, plus what to see and do there, turn to the introduction of each chapter.

On New York's menu

Don't come to New York on a diet or you'll miss out on one of its greatest pleasures: **food**, and lots of it. There's barely a country in the world whose cuisine isn't ably represented somewhere in the city, so while you should do what you can to experiment with a little from everything, there are some types of cuisine in which New York particularly excels. There is **Jewish-American deli fare** on the Lower East Side, such as overstuffed brisket and pastrami

sandwiches, smoked fish and bagels, latkes, knishes, and chopped liver. All over town (especially in midtown) you can find traditional **steak joints** serving massive porterhouses and tender sirloins. The city is littered with **pizza places** serving pancake-flat pies moist with fresh tomatoes and heaped with home-made mozzarella. You'll find pearlescent **dim sum** in Chinatown and you can't throw a stick without hitting a new **sushi** restaurant. This doesn't even really scratch the surface of the cuisines on offer here, including Ethiopian, Brazilian, Jamaican, and Korean, to name but a few. For more details on our picks, see Chapter 25, "Restaurants."

This guide starts at the southern tip of the island and moves north. **The Harbor Islands** – the Statue of Liberty and Ellis Island – were the first glimpses of New York (and indeed America) for many nineteenth-century immigrants; the latter's history is recalled in its excellent Museum of Immigration. The **Financial District** encompasses the skyscrapers and historic buildings of Manhattan's southern reaches, including Ground Zero, the former World Trade Center site. Immediately east of here is **City Hall**, New York's well-appointed municipal center, and the massive Gothic span of the **Brooklyn Bridge**, while to the west is swanky **Tribeca**, the hub of the city's art scene in the twentieth century but now more of an upscale, outdoor fashion-mall; **Soho**, just to the north, also boasts a large number of shops, as well as some historic cast-iron buildings. East of here is **Chinatown**, Manhattan's most densely populated ethnic neighborhood and a vibrant locale great for Chinese food and shopping. Now more a haven for pasta and red sauce than Italians, **Little Italy** next door is slowly being swallowed by Chinatown's hungry expansion, while the **Lower East Side**, traditionally the city's gateway neighborhood for new immigrants – whether German, Jewish, or, more recently, Hispanic – is being gentrified by young urban professionals. The **East** and **West villages** are known for their bars, restaurants, and shops that cater to students, would-be bohemians, and, of course, tourists. **Chelsea** has displaced the West Village as the heart of Manhattan's gay scene, and scooped Soho for exciting gallery spaces; the area around **Union Square** and **Gramercy Park** features some lovely skyscrapers, including the Flatiron Building, and some of the city's best restaurants. This is where the avenues begin their march north through the busy, regimented blocks of **midtown**, which is punctuated by some of the city's most impressive sights, including Times Square, the Empire State Building, and the **Museum of Modern Art**.

Beyond midtown, the character of the city changes quite rapidly. For more than a dozen blocks, the skyline is relentlessly high-rise, and home to some awe-inspiring architecture; this gives way to first-class museums and appealing stores as you work your way up Fifth Avenue as far as 59th Street. That's where the classic Manhattan vistas are broken by the broad expanse of **Central Park**, a supreme piece of nineteenth-century landscaping. Flanking the park, the **Upper East Side** is wealthier and more

So much to see, so little time...

As noted in our "19 Things not to miss" section (p.11), you can't experience everything New York City has to offer on a single trip. Your best bet is to enjoy the city at your own pace, take in the attractions that interest you most, and remember that you can always come back. The following suggested itineraries are based on what's possible in a day. They're mainly designed around key sights and neighborhoods, and they include suggestions for where to have lunch. Don't be afraid to skip the major attractions, though – just wandering about can be an extremely fulfilling way to see the city.

Three days
- Ellis Island/Statue of Liberty; Financial District (lunch); South Street Seaport; Brooklyn Bridge; Brooklyn Heights.
- East Village; West Village (lunch); Empire State Building; Macy's; Times Square.
- Grand Central Terminal; Rockefeller Center (lunch); St Patrick's Cathedral; Museum of Modern Art; Fifth Avenue shops.

Five days
As above plus...
- Central Park; Metropolitan Museum of Art; Frick Collection; Upper East Side shops.
- Lower East Side; Tenement Museum; Chinatown (lunch); Soho shops.

Seven days
As above plus...
- Lincoln Center; Upper West Side (lunch); Museum of Natural History
- Cathedral of St John the Divine; Columbia University; Harlem; The Cloisters.

grandiose, with many of its nineteenth-century millionaires' mansions now transformed into a string of magnificent museums known as "Museum Mile"; the most prominent of these is the vast **Metropolitan Museum of Art**. The residential neighborhood here is staunchly patrician and boasts some of the swankiest addresses in Manhattan, as well as a nest of designer shops along Madison Avenue in the seventies. On the other side

Getting around in Manhattan

Manhattan can seem a wearyingly complicated place to get around: its **grid-pattern** arrangement looks so straightforward on the map, but can be confusing on foot, and its many subway lines never meet up where you think they should. Don't be intimidated, though – with a little know-how you'll find the city's **streets** easy to navigate and its **subways and buses** efficient and fast. And if you're at all unsure, just ask – New Yorkers are accurate direction-givers and take a surprising interest in initiating visitors into the great mysteries of their city.

There are a few simple terms that are important to learn. Firstly, "downtown Manhattan," "midtown Manhattan," and "upper Manhattan": **downtown Manhattan** runs from the southern tip of the island to around 14th Street; **midtown Manhattan** stretches from about here to the south end of Central Park; and **upper Manhattan** contains the park itself, the neighborhoods on either side of it, and the whole area to the north. Whatever is north of where you're standing is **uptown** (in other words, uptown trains are northbound, even if you're in upper Manhattan), while whatever's south is **downtown** (downtown trains are southbound even from Soho). As for east and west, those directions are known as **crosstown** – hence "crosstown buses."

Downtown Manhattan is tricky to navigate because it was the first part of the city to be settled, and so streets here have names not numbers, and are somewhat randomly arranged. The most fiendishly confusing part of downtown is the **West Village**, where it's essential to have a map at all times – the illogical tangle of streets is quaint but infuriating; for instance, somehow West 4th and West 11th streets, which should run parallel, actually intersect here. Things are much easier above Houston Street on the East Side and 14th Street on the West: the streets are numbered and follow a strict grid pattern like most other American cities. **Fifth Avenue**, the greatest of the big north–south avenues, cuts through the center of Manhattan until it reaches Central Park, whereupon the avenue runs along its eastern flank; crosstown streets are flagged as East or West (eg W 42nd Street, E 42nd Street) from this dividing line, and building numbers also increase as you walk away from either side of Fifth Avenue.

Note that the island of Manhattan is about **thirteen miles long** from base to tip, and around **two miles wide** at its widest point: as a rule of thumb, allow five minutes to walk each east–west block between avenues, and one to two minutes for each north–south block between streets.

of the park, the largely residential young-professional enclave of the **Upper West Side** is worth a visit, mostly for performing-arts mecca Lincoln Center, the American Museum of Natural History, and Riverside Park along the Hudson River. Immediately north of Central Park, **Harlem**, the historic black city-within-a-city, has today a healthy sense of an improving community. Still farther north, past the student enclave of **Hamilton Heights**, home to Columbia University, and **Washington Heights**, a largely Hispanic neighborhood that few visitors ever venture to visit, stands Inwood at the tip of the island. It's here you'll find the Cloisters, a nineteenth-century mock-up of a medieval monastery, packed with great European Romanesque and Gothic art and (transplanted) architecture – in short, one of Manhattan's must-sees.

It's an unfortunate fact that few visitors, especially those with limited time, bother to venture off Manhattan Island to the outer boroughs. This is a pity, because each of them – **Brooklyn, Queens, the Bronx**, and **Staten Island** – has points of great interest, for both historical and contemporary reasons. More than anything, though, some of the city's most vibrant ethnic neighborhoods (and consequently best food) can be found in the outer boroughs: sample the Greek restaurants of the Astoria district in Queens, for example, or the Italian restaurants of the Bronx's Belmont section. If visitors do leave Manhattan, it's usually for Brooklyn, where you can hang out in hip Williamsburg, wander the brownstone-lined streets of Cobble Hill, ride a rickety roller coaster and soak up the old-world charm of Coney Island, or gorge on borscht in the Russian enclave of Brighton Beach.

When to go

◀ Hotel Chelsea

New York's **climate** ranges from sticky, hot, and humid in mid-summer to chilling in January and February: be prepared to freeze or boil accordingly if you decide to visit during these periods. Spring is gentle, if unpredictable and often wet, while fall is perhaps the best season, with crisp, clear days and warmish nights – either season is a great time to schedule a visit. It goes without saying that whenever you're visiting, plan to dress in layers, as it's the only way to combat overheated buildings in winter and overactive, icy air-conditioning come summertime. As noted above, one of the joys of New York City's compact layout is the ease with which you can sightsee by foot, so make sure to pack a pair of comfortable, sturdy shoes, no matter the season.

Average monthly temperatures and rainfall

	Temp °F		Temp °C		Rainfall	
	Max	Min	Max	Min	Inches	mm
January	38	26	3	-3	3.5	89
February	40	27	4	-3	3.1	79
March	50	35	10	2	4.0	102
April	61	44	16	7	3.8	97
May	72	54	22	12	4.4	112
June	80	63	27	17	3.6	91
July	85	69	29	21	4.4	112
August	84	67	29	19	4.1	104
September	76	60	24	16	4.0	102
October	65	50	18	10	3.4	86
November	54	41	12	5	4.4	112
December	43	31	6	-1	3.8	97

19 things not to miss

It's not possible to see everything that New York has to offer in one trip, so what follows is a selective taste of the city's highlights: classic restaurants, engaging museums, stunning architecture, and more. They're arranged in color-coded categories, which you can browse through to find the best things to see and do. All entries have a page reference to take you straight into the Guide, where you can find out more.

01 Empire State Building Page **124** • Still the most original and elegant skyscraper of them all.

02 Grand Central Terminal Page **133** • Take a free Wednesday lunchtime tour of this magnificent building to learn the history of the station's majestic concourse.

03 Halloween Parade Page **421** •
One of the more inventive and outrageous of New York's many annual parades.

04 Central Park Page **152** • The world's most iconic swathe of green: take a boat ride, watch Shakespeare in the Park, or enjoy a Conservatory Garden picnic after a morning spent in a museum.

05 Statue of Liberty Page **44** • There's no greater symbol of the American dream than the magnificent statue that graces New York Harbor.

06 **Brooklyn Bridge** Page **69** • Take the less-than-a-mile walk across the bridge to see beautiful views of the downtown skyline and the Harbor Islands.

07 **Rockefeller Center** Page **128** • If anywhere can truly claim to be the center of New York, this elegant piece of twentieth-century urban planning is it.

08 **Live music** Page **352** • New York's music scene is legendary, and it's undergoing a renaissance: catch anything from garage punk and electro to Afrobeat and jazz.

09 Staten Island Ferry Page **58** • Savor Manhattan's skyline and the Statue of Liberty from a boat's-eye view–absolutely free.

10 Metropolitan Museum of Art Page **161** • You could easily spend a whole day at the Met, exploring everything from Egyptian artifacts to modern masters.

11 Opera at Lincoln Center Page **363** • Put on your glad rags for a night out at New York's spectacular Metropolitan Opera.

12 The Frick Collection Page **175** • Though he may have been a ruthless coal baron, Henry Frick's discerning eye for art and the easy elegance of his collection's setting make this one of the city's best galleries.

14 **St John the Divine** Page **199**
• Still under construction more than a hundred years after its inception, St John's remains the largest and most imposing Gothic-style cathedral in the world.

13 **Fine dining** Page **324** • Nowhere is New York's melting pot more manifest than in its innovative, international food scene, with must-try restaurants like *Aquavit*.

I ACTIVITIES I CONSUME I EVENTS I NATURE I SIGHTS I

15 **Museum of Modern Art** Page **139** • For much of the twentieth century New York was the center of the art universe, and MoMA retains the most comprehensive collection of modern art in the world.

16 **Katz's Deli** Page **314** • A slice of the old Lower East Side, with overstuffed sandwiches served up by a wisecracking counterstaff.

18 **Baseball** Page **403** • It would be a shame not to go to a ball game if you're here between April and October, especially with two teams as iconic as the Yankees and the Mets.

17 **A night on the town** Page **340** • Local brews and native celebrities, romantic hideaways and raucous dive bars, there's always a drink on hand in the city that never sleeps.

19 **Bergdorf Goodman** Page **389** • Department store as art form – even the window – shopping is retail therapy.

Basics

Basics

Getting there

It's pretty easy to get to New York. The city is on every major airline's itinerary, and is also a regional hub for train and bus travel. Expressways surround the city, making driving another viable option.

From North America

From most places in North America, **flying** is the most convenient way to reach New York. There are **three international airports** within close proximity of the city: **John F. Kennedy (JFK;** ☎718/244-4444), **LaGuardia (LGA;** ☎718/533-3400), and **Newark (EWR;** ☎973/961-6000).

By air

All three New York airports provide daily **flights** to and from most major towns and cities on the continent.

Airfares to New York depend on the season and can fluctuate wildly. The highest prices are generally found between May and September; fares drop between March and April and again in October. You'll get the best prices during the low season, November through February (excluding late Nov through early Jan, the holiday season). The lowest **round-trip fares** from the West Coast tend to average around $400–500; from Chicago or Miami it's about $300–250. From Canada, reckon on paying Can$325–400 from Toronto or Montréal and at least Can$500–600 from Vancouver.

By train

New York is connected to the rest of the continent by several **Amtrak train lines** (☎1-800/USA-RAIL, ⏍www.amtrak.com). The most frequent services are along the Boston-to-Washington corridor; there is also one daily train between Montréal and New York. Fares from Boston are about $125 round-trip, or $200 for the *Acela Express*, which saves 35 minutes. DC trains are about $145, considerably more on the *Metroliner* and *Acela Express*. Fares from Canada usually start around Can$165–195. Like

planes, train fares are often based on availability; with the exception of peak travel times (i.e. Christmas), seats are much cheaper months in advance. As more seats are sold, fares increase significantly – book as early as possible.

Although it's possible to haul yourself long-distance from the West Coast, the Midwest, or the South, it's an exhausting trip (three days plus from California) and fares are expensive.

By bus

Going by **bus** is the most time-consuming and least comfortable mode of travel. The only reason to take the bus for more than a few hours is if you're going to make a number of stops en route; if this is the case, you might check out **Greyhound's** (☎1-800/231-2222, ⏍www.greyhound.com) **Discovery Pass**, which is good for unlimited travel within a set period of time.

Unlike most parts of the country, where Greyhound is the only game in town, in the busy northeast corridor there is fierce competition between bus operators. One-way from either DC or Boston to New York can go for as little as $30 on one of the major lines. **Peter Pan Bus Lines** (⏍www.peterpanbus.com) has a $45 Boston–New York round-trip fare. Buses arrive in New York at the Port Authority Bus Terminal, Eighth Avenue and 42nd Street.

The least expensive option by far is the **Fung Wah** bus (☎212/925-8889, ⏍www.fungwahbus.com), which runs nonstop between the Chinatowns of Boston and New York for $15 each way.

From the UK and Ireland

Flying to New York from the UK takes about seven hours; flights tend to **leave Britain** in the morning or afternoon and arrive in New York in the afternoon or evening, though the odd flight does leave as late as 8pm. Coming back, most flights depart in the evening and arrive in Britain early next morning; flying time, due to the prevailing winds, is usually a little shorter.

As far as **scheduled flights** go, British Airways offers the most direct services each day from London's Heathrow to JFK, and also flies from Heathrow to Newark, and to JFK from Manchester. American Airlines, Delta, Continental, United, and Virgin also fly direct on a daily basis; there is not much difference in the prices on the different airlines. Round-trip **fares** generally tend to average £300–400.

Aer Lingus, Continental, and Delta all fly nonstop services to New York from Ireland, but these are always more expensive – expect to pay at least 500 euros.

From Australia and New Zealand

It's not possible to take a nonstop flight between New York and **Australia or New Zealand**, though Qantas offers a direct service from Sydney, with a 2hr layover in Los Angeles (meaning you won't have to change planes). Most Aussies and Kiwis reach the eastern United States by way of LA and San Francisco (flying time is approximately ten hours to the West Coast, with another six-hour flight to New York). The best connections tend to be with United, Air New Zealand, and Qantas.

Fares from eastern Australian state capitals are generally the same: return flights in high season start at around AUS$3000/ NZ$3000 and go up from there (airlines offer a free connecting service between these cities); fares from Perth and Darwin are about AUS$600 more. You might do better by purchasing a direct ticket to either San Francisco or LA, then using one of the domestic flight coupons, or alliance air passes, you can buy with your international ticket (these must be bought before you leave your home country). Average fare per coupon may be as low as $130, depending on season, total number of coupons, and origin of travel. If you intend to take in New York as part of a world trip, a **round-the-world ticket** offers the best value for your

money, working out just a little more than an all-in ticket.

Airlines, agents, and tour operators

Online booking

ⓦ **www.expedia.co.uk** (in UK), ⓦ **www.expedia .com** (in US), ⓦ **www.expedia.ca** (in Canada)
ⓦ **www.lastminute.com** (in UK)
ⓦ **www.opodo.co.uk** (in UK)
ⓦ **www.orbitz.com** (in US)
ⓦ **www.travelocity.co.uk** (in UK), ⓦ **www .travelocity.com** (in US), ⓦ **www.travelocity.ca** (in Canada), ⓦ **www.travelocity.co.nz** (in New Zealand)
ⓦ **www.zuji.com.au** (in Australia)

Airlines

Aer Lingus US & Canada ☎1-800/IRISH-AIR, UK ☎0870/876 5000, Republic of Ireland ☎0818/365 000, New Zealand ☎1649/3083355, South Africa ☎1-272/2168-32838; ⓦwww.aerlingus.com.
Air Canada US & Canada ☎1-888/247-2262, ⓦwww.aircanada.com.
Air New Zealand US ☎1800-262/1234, Canada ☎1800-663/5494, UK ☎0800/028 4149, Republic of Ireland ☎1800/551 447, Australia ☎0800/132 476, New Zealand ☎0800/737000; ⓦwww.airnz .co.nz.
American Airlines ☎1-800/433-7300, UK ☎020/7365 0777, Republic of Ireland ☎01/602 0550, Australia ☎1800/673 486, New Zealand ☎0800/445 442; ⓦwww.aa.com.
British Airways US & Canada ☎1-800/AIRWAYS, UK ☎0844/493 0787, Republic of Ireland ☎1890/626 747, Australia ☎1300/767 177, New Zealand ☎09/966 9777, South Africa ☎114/418 600; ⓦwww.ba.com.
Continental Airlines US & Canada ☎1-800/523-3273, UK ☎0845/607 6760, Republic of Ireland ☎1890/925 252, Australia ☎1300/737 640, New Zealand ☎09/308 3350, International ☎1800/231 0856; ⓦwww.continental.com.
Delta US & Canada ☎1-800/221-1212, UK ☎0845/600 0950, Republic of Ireland ☎1850/882 031 or 01/407 3165, Australia ☎1300/302 849, New Zealand ☎09/9772232; ⓦwww.delta.com.
JAL (Japan Air Lines) US & Canada ☎1-800/525-3663, UK ☎0845/774 7700, Republic of Ireland ☎01/408 3757, Australia ☎1-300/525 287 or 02/9272 1111, New Zealand ☎0800/525 747 or 09/379 9906,

Fly less – stay longer! Travel and climate change

Climate change is perhaps the single biggest issue facing our planet. It is caused by a build-up in the atmosphere of carbon dioxide and other greenhouse gases, which are emitted by many sources – including planes. Already, **flights** account for three to four percent of human-induced global warming: that figure may sound small, but it is rising year on year and threatens to counteract the progress made by reducing greenhouse emissions in other areas.

Rough Guides regard travel as a **global benefit**, and feel strongly that the advantages to developing economies are important, as are the opportunities for greater contact and awareness among peoples. But we also believe in traveling responsibly, which includes giving thought to how often we fly and what we can do to redress any harm that our trips may create.

We can travel less or simply reduce the amount we travel by air (taking fewer trips and staying longer, or taking the train if there is one); we can avoid night flights (which are more damaging); and we can make the trips we do take "climate neutral" via a carbon offset scheme. **Offset schemes** run by climatecare.org, carbonneutral .com and others allow you to "neutralize" the greenhouse gases that you are responsible for releasing. Their websites have simple calculators that let you work out the impact of any flight – as does our own. Once that's done, you can pay to fund projects that will reduce future emissions by an equivalent amount. Please take the time to visit our website and make your trip climate neutral, or get a copy of the *Rough Guide to Climate Change* for more detail on the subject.

www.roughguides.com/climatechange

South Africa ☏ 11/214 2560; ⓦ www.jal.com or www.japanair.com.

JetBlue US ☏ 1-800/538-2583, International ☏ (001) 801/365-2525; ⓦ www.jetblue.com.

Korean Air US & Canada ☏ 1-800/438-5000, UK ☏ 0800/413 000, Republic of Ireland ☏ 01/799 7990, Australia ☏ 02/9262 6000, New Zealand ☏ 09/914 2000; ⓦ www.koreanair.com.

Lufthansa US ☏ 1-800/3995-838, Canada ☏ 1-800/563-5954, UK ☏ 0871/945 9747, Republic of Ireland ☏ 01/844 5544, Australia ☏ 1300/655 727, New Zealand ☏ 0800-945 220, South Africa ☏ 0861/842 538; ⓦ www.lufthansa.com.

Northwest/KLM US ☏ 1-800/225-2525, UK ☏ 0870/507 4074, Australia ☏ 1-300/767-310; ⓦ www.nwa.com

Qantas Airways US & Canada ☏ 1-800/227-4500, UK ☏ 0845/774 7767, Republic of Ireland ☏ 01/407 3278, Australia ☏ 13 13 13, New Zealand ☏ 0800/808 767 or 09/357 8900, South Africa ☏ 11/441 8550; ⓦ www.qantas.com.

Southwest Airlines US ☏ 1-800/435-9792, ⓦ www.southwest.com.

United Airlines US ☏ 1-800/864-8331, UK ☏ 0845/844 4777, Australia ☏ 13 17 77; ⓦ www .united.com.

US Airways US & Canada ☏ 1-800/428-4322, UK ☏ 0845/600 3300, Republic of Ireland ☏ 1890/925 065; ⓦ www.usair.com.

Virgin Atlantic US ☏ 1-800/821-5438, UK ☏ 0870/574 7747, Australia ☏ 1300/727 340, South Africa ☏ 11/340 3400; ⓦ www.virgin-atlantic.com.

Travel agents and tour operators

Amtrak Vacations US ☏ 1-800/654-5748, ⓦ www.amtrakvacations.com. Rail, accommodations, and sightseeing packages.

Contiki US ☏ 1-888/CONTIKI, ⓦ www.contiki.com. 18- to 35-year-olds-only tour operator. Runs highly social sightseeing trips to New York that focus on major tourist attractions.

Delta Vacations US ☏ 1-800/654-6559, ⓦ www .deltavacations.com. Offers packages to New York that include mid-range to upscale accommodations, plus optional sightseeing and airport transfers.

ebookers UK ☏ 0871/223 5000, ⓦ www.ebookers .com; Republic of Ireland ☏ 01/431 1311, ⓦ www .ebookers.ie. Low fares on an extensive selection of scheduled flights and package deals.

International Gay and Lesbian Travel Association US ☏ 1-800/448-8550, ⓦ www.iglta .org. Trade group with lists of gay-owned or gay-friendly travel agents, accommodations, and other travel businesses.

Maupintour US ☏ 1-800/255-4266, ⓦ www .maupintour.com. Luxury tours. Runs trips to New York, with city tours, show tickets, and upscale meals.

New York City.com US ☏1-888/VISITNY, ⊛www
.nyc.com. Touristy group packages, including show
tickets.
New York City Vacation Packages US
☏1-888/692-8701, ⊛www.nycvp.com. All
sorts of short, reasonably priced New York vacations,
from spa weekends to Broadway shows.
North South Travel UK ☏01245/608 291,
⊛www.northsouthtravel.co.uk. Friendly,
competitive travel agency, offering discounted fares
worldwide. Profits are used to support projects in
the developing world, especially the promotion of
sustainable tourism.
STA Travel US ☏1-800/781-4040, UK
☏0871/2300 040, Australia ☏134 782,

New Zealand ☏0800/474 400, South Africa
☏0861/781 781; ⊛www.statravel.com. Worldwide
specialists in independent travel; also student IDs,
travel insurance, car rental, rail passes, and more.
Good discounts for students and under-26s.
Trailfinders UK ☏0845/058 5858, Republic of
Ireland ☏01/677 7888; ⊛www.trailfinders.com.
One of the best-informed and most efficient agents
for independent travellers.
USIT Republic of Ireland ☏01/602 1904, ⊛www
.usit.ie. Student/youth travel specialists, offering
discount flights to North America.
Viator US ⊛www.viator.com. Books piecemeal
local tours and sightseeing trips within New York.

Arrival

Most visitors to New York arrive at one of the three major international airports
that serve the city: John F. Kennedy (JFK; ☏718/244-4444), LaGuardia (LGA;
☏718/533-3400), and Newark (EWR; ☏973/961-6000). All three share a website at
⊛www.panynj.gov. You can find general information about getting to and from the
airports on the website or by calling ☏1-800/AIR-RIDE. Amtrak trains arrive at
Penn Station, and buses at the Port Authority Bus Terminal, both of which are in
Midtown West.

By air

Whichever airport you arrive at, one of the
most efficient ways into Manhattan is by
charter bus. All airport bus services operate
from one of two terminals in Manhattan:
Grand Central Terminal (at Park Ave and
42nd St) and the **Port Authority Bus
Terminal** (Eighth Ave at 34th St, ☏212/564-
8484). Grand Central, in the heart of midtown
Manhattan, is more convenient for the east
side of the island. The Port Authority Bus
Terminal isn't as good a bet for Manhattan
(as it entails carrying luggage from bus to
street level), though you'll find it handy if
you're heading for the west side of the city or
out to New Jersey (by bus). Some airport
buses also stop at **Penn Station** at 32nd St
between Seventh and Eighth avenues, where
you can catch the Long Island Railroad
(LIRR), as well as Amtrak long-distance trains
to other parts of America.

Taxis are the easiest transport option if
you are traveling in a group or are arriving
at an antisocial hour. Reckon on paying
$20–30 from LaGuardia to Manhattan, a
flat rate of $45 from JFK, and $45–55 from
Newark; you'll also be responsible for the
turnpike and tunnel tolls – an extra $5 or so
– as well as a fifteen- to twenty-percent tip
for the driver. Ignore the individual cabs
vying for attention as you exit the baggage
claim; these "gypsy cab" operators are
notorious for ripping off tourists. Any airport
official can direct you to the taxi stand,
where you can get an official New York
City yellow taxi. A few car services have
direct phones near the exits; they're
competitive in price with taxis (they charge
set rates).

If you're not so pressed for time and want
to save some money, it is also possible to
take the **train**, commuter or subway, from

Newark or JFK, connecting via the AirTrain system. Plan on it taking at least an hour to get to Manhattan and costing $7–12.

JFK

The **New York Airport Service** (℡212/875-8200, Ⓦwww.nyairportservice.com) runs **buses** from JFK to Grand Central Terminal, Port Authority Bus Terminal, Penn Station, and midtown hotels every 15 to 20 minutes between 6.15am and 11.10pm. In the other direction, buses run from the same locations every 15 to 30 minutes between about 5.10am and 10pm. Journeys take 45 to 60 minutes, depending on time of day and traffic conditions. The fare is $15 one-way, $27 round-trip; discounts are available.

The **AirTrain** (Ⓦwww.panynj.gov/airtrain) runs every few minutes, 24 hours daily, between JFK and the Jamaica and Howard Beach stations in Queens. The cost is $5 on a MetroCard (see p.26).

The fastest onward connection into Manhattan is to take the LIRR from Jamaica to Penn Station ($5.25 off-peak; 20min); buy tickets at the station, as fares are almost double if purchased on board. You can also take the subway (#E, #J, #Z from Jamaica, and #A from Howard Beach) for just $2 on MetroCard, anywhere in the city. In the daytime or early evening this is a cheap, viable option, although at night it isn't the best choice – trains run infrequently and can be deserted. Travel time to Manhattan is usually a little under an hour.

LaGuardia

The **New York Airport Service** (℡212/875-8200, Ⓦwww.nyairportservice.com) runs **buses** from LaGuardia to Grand Central Station, Port Authority Bus Terminal, and Penn Station every 15 to 30 minutes between 7.20am and 11pm. In the other direction, buses run from Grand Central 5am to 8pm, from Port Authority 5.50am to 7.40pm, and from Penn Station 7.40am to 7.10pm. Journey time is 45 to 60 minutes, depending on traffic. The fare is $12 one-way, $21 round-trip.

You can also travel from the airport by bus. The best bargain in New York airport transit is the #M60 **bus**, which for $2 (exact change

or MetroCard) takes you into Manhattan, across 125th St and down Broadway to 106th St. Ask for a transfer (see p.27) when you get on the bus and you can get almost anywhere. Journey time from LaGuardia ranges from 20 minutes late at night to an hour in rush-hour traffic. Alternatively, you can take the #M60 bus to Astoria Boulevard. There you can transfer to the #N or #W **subway**, which runs through midtown Manhattan and south to Brooklyn.

Newark

Newark Airport Express (℡877/863-9275, Ⓦwww.coachusa.com) runs **buses** to Grand Central Station, Port Authority Bus Terminal, and Penn Station every 20 to 30 minutes between 4am and 12.45am. In the other direction, buses run from the same locations just as frequently (about 5am to 1.30am); service to and from the Port Authority runs 24 hours per day. In either direction, the journey takes 30 to 45 minutes depending on the traffic. The fare is $15 one-way, $25 round-trip.

For train services, take the short AirTrain ride to Newark Liberty International Airport Train Station and connect with frequent NJ Transit or Amtrak trains heading into Manhattan. The AirTrain runs from 5am to midnight and costs $5.50, but if you buy a NJ Transit ticket from machines in the AirTrain terminals before boarding, the AirTrain ticket is included. The fare for NJ Transit is $15 (Amtrak trains are more expensive). If you really want to save a few dollars (and have plenty of time), take a NJ Transit train ($7.75) to Newark Penn Station (not to be confused with Penn Station in Manhattan) and transfer to the PATH system (℡1-800/234-7284, Ⓦwww.panynj.com), with connections to Downtown and midtown Manhattan for just $1.75. The PATH train runs 24 hours per day, but service is limited between midnight and 7am.

By train, bus, or car

Amtrak trains arrive at **Penn Station**, 32nd St between Seventh and Eighth avenues. If you come to New York by Greyhound or any other long-distance **bus** line (with the exception of the Chinatown buses, which

arrive in Chinatown), you arrive at the **Port Authority Bus Terminal** at 42nd Street and Eighth Avenue.

If you're coming from the East Coast (or if you don't mind long journeys), **driving** is an option, but note that you probably won't need (or want) a car once you're in the city. Major **highways** come in from most directions (I-87 and 95 from the north; I-95 from the south; I-80 from the west), and you'll pay a **toll** for any number of bridges and/or tunnels to get into the city.

Getting around

Getting around the city is likely to take some getting used to; public transit here is very good, extremely cheap, and covers most conceivable corners of the city, whether by subway or bus. Don't be afraid to ask someone for help if you're confused. You'll no doubt find the need for a taxi from time to time, especially if you feel uncomfortable in an area at night; you will rarely have trouble tracking one down in Manhattan or on major Brooklyn avenues – the ubiquitous yellow cabs are always on the prowl for passengers. And don't forget your feet – Manhattanites walk everywhere.

By subway

The New York **subway** (☎718/330-1234, Ⓦwww.mta.info) is noisy and initially incomprehensible, but it's also the fastest and most efficient way to get from place to place in Manhattan and to the outer boroughs. Put aside your qualms: it's much safer and user-friendly than it once was, and it's definitely not as difficult to navigate as it seems. Nonetheless, it pays to familiarize yourself with the subway system before you set out. Study the map at the back of this book, or get a free map at any station or information kiosk. Though the subway runs 24 hours daily, some routes operate at certain times of day only; read any service advisories carefully.

The basics

• The subway costs **$2 per ride**, including all subway and most bus transfers (see p.27). In order to ride the subway, you must purchase a **MetroCard**, a card with an electronic strip, from a vending machine (in the subway station) or a subway teller. Vending machines accept all credit and debit cards, but keep some fresh bills on hand in case you have a problem.

• The **MetroCard** is available in several forms. It can be purchased in denominations

---

Safety on the subway

By day the whole train is safe, but don't go into empty cars if you can help it. Some trains have doors that connect between cars, but do not use them other than in an emergency, because this is dangerous and illegal. Keep an eye on bags at all times, especially when sitting or standing near the doors. With all the jostling in the crowds near the doors, this is a favorite spot for pickpockets.

At night, always try to use the center cars, because they tend to be more crowded. Yellow signs on the platform saying "During off hours train stops here" indicate where the conductor's car will stop. While you wait, keep where the token booth attendants can see you if possible. For more information on safety, see "Crime and personal safety," p.35.

between $2 and $80; putting $7 or more on your card will earn you a 15 percent bonus ($20 gives you $23 on your card, or 11 trips for the price of 10, with $1 extra). Unlimited-ride cards – almost always the best deal if you intend to be on the go – allow unlimited travel for a certain period of time: a daily "Fun Pass" for $7.50, 7-day pass for $25, and 30-day pass for $81.

•Most train routes run uptown or downtown in Manhattan, following the great avenues. Crosstown routes are few.

•Trains and their routes are identified by a number or letter (not by their color).

•There are two types of train: the **express**, which stops only at major stations, and the **local**, stopping at every station. Listen to the conductor, who will usually announce the train's next stop.

•**Service changes** due to track repairs and other maintenance work are frequent (especially after midnight and on weekends) and confusing. Read the red-and-white Service Notice posters on bulletin boards throughout the system, and don't be afraid to ask other passengers what's going on. Listen closely to all announcements (though poor sound quality can make them hard to understand); occasionally, express trains run on local tracks.

•Don't hesitate to **ask directions** or **look at a map** on the train or in the station. If you travel late at night, know your route before you set out. Follow common-sense safety rules (see "Crime and personal safety," p.35).

•If you are **lost**, go to the subway teller or phone ☏718/330-1234. State your location and destination; the teller or operator will tell you the most direct route.

By bus

The **bus system** (☏718/330-1234, ⓦwww.mta.info) is simpler than the subway, you can see where you're going and hop off at anything interesting. The bus also features many **crosstown** routes and most services run 24 hours. The major disadvantage is that buses can be extremely slow due to traffic – in peak hours almost down to walking pace.

Anywhere in the city the fare is **$2**, payable on entry with a **MetroCard** (the most convenient way) or with the correct change – no bills. Bus maps can be obtained at the main concourse of Grand Central Terminal or the Convention and Visitors Bureau at 53rd St and Seventh Ave, as well as in subway stations. There are routes on almost all the avenues and major streets. Most buses with an M designation before the route number travel exclusively in Manhattan; others may show a B for Brooklyn, Q for Queens, Bx for the Bronx, or S for Staten Island. The crosstown routes are most useful, especially the ones through Central Park. Also good are the buses that take you to east Manhattan where subway coverage is sparse. Most crosstown buses take their route number from the street they traverse, so the #M14 will travel along 14th Street. Buses display their number, origin, and destination up front.

There are three types of bus: regular, which stop every two or three blocks at five- to ten-minute intervals; limited stop, which travel the same routes but stop at only about a quarter of the regular stops; and express, which cost extra ($5) and stop hardly anywhere, shuttling commuters in and out of the outer boroughs and suburbs.

Bus stops are marked by yellow curbstones and a blue, white, and red sign that often (but not always) indicates which buses stop there. Once you're on board, to signal that you want to get off a bus, press the yellow or black strip on the wall; the driver will stop at the next official bus stop. After midnight you can ask to get off on any block along the route, whether or not it's a regular stop.

Transfers

If you're going to use buses a lot, it pays to understand the **transfer** system. A transfer allows a single fare to take you, one-way, anywhere in Manhattan; they're given free on request when you pay your fare. Because few buses go up and down and across, you can transfer from any bus to almost any other that continues your trip. (You can't use transfers for return trips.) The top of the transfer tells you how much time you have in which to use it – usually around two hours. If unsure where to get off to transfer, consult the map on the panel behind the driver, or ask the driver for help. If you use a MetroCard, you can automatically transfer for free within two hours from swiping the card.

By taxi

Taxis are always worth considering, especially if you're in a hurry or it's late at night.

There are two types of taxis: **medallion cabs**, recognizable by their yellow paintwork and medallion up top, and **gypsy cabs**, unlicensed, uninsured operators who tout for business wherever tourists arrive. Avoid gypsy cabs like the plague – they will rip you off. Their main hunting grounds are outside tourist arrival points like Grand Central. Up to four people can travel in an ordinary medallion cab. Fares are $2.50 for the first fifth of a mile and 40¢ for each fifth of a mile thereafter or for each 60 seconds in stopped or slow traffic. The basic charge rises by 50¢ from 8pm to 6am, and when you take a cab outside the city limits you must agree on a flat fare with the driver before the trip begins (except trips to Newark Airport and Westchester and Nassau counties, for which there are previously determined fare rules).

Trips outside Manhattan can incur toll fees (which the driver will pay through E-Z Pass and which will be added to your fare); the only river crossings that cost money both ways are the Brooklyn-Battery Tunnel and Queens Midtown Tunnel ($5 each). Tolls for the Holland Tunnel, Lincoln Tunnel, and George Washington Bridge (all $8) are paid coming into Manhattan only. All the other bridges are free.

The **tip** should be fifteen to twenty percent of the fare; you'll get a dirty look if you offer less. Drivers don't like splitting anything bigger than a $10 bill, and are in their rights to refuse a bill over $20.

Before you hail a cab, work out exactly where you're going and if possible the quickest route there – a surprising number of cabbies are new to the job and speak little English. If you feel the driver doesn't seem to know your destination, point it out on a map. An illuminated sign atop the taxi indicates its availability. If the words "Off Duty" are lit, the driver won't pick you up.

Certain regulations govern taxi operators. A driver can ask your destination only when you're seated (this is often breached) – and must transport you (within the five boroughs), however undesirable your destination may be. You may face some problems, though, if it's late and you want to go to an outer borough. Also, if you request it, a driver must pick up or drop off other passengers, turn on the air-conditioning, and turn the radio down

or off. Many drivers use a cell phone while driving; this is common but prohibited, and while you can ask him or her to stop, don't expect compliance. If you have a problem with a driver, get the license number from the right-hand side of the dashboard, or medallion number from the rooftop sign or from the print-out receipt for the fare, and file a complaint at ⓦwww.nyc.gov/html/tlc/html /passenger/file_complaint.shtml.

By ferry

Manhattan is connected to New Jersey, Staten Island, and Brooklyn by a web of **ferry** services. These generally serve commuters, but some routes are worth checking out for a relatively cheap opportunity to get onto the water. **New York Water Taxi** (ⓦwww .nywatertaxi.com) runs a weekend-only ferry service around Manhattan, linking West 44th Street with East 34th Street via stops all around the lower half of the island (April–Oct; day pass $20, kids $15). It also runs a handy year-round commuter service to DUMBO, Williamsburg, and Hunters Point in Queens from various points in Manhattan; these tend to operate on weekdays 6.30 to 9am, and 3 to 7pm, and cost $3–5.

None of these options beats the bargain of the free **Staten Island Ferry** (ⓣ718/727-2508, ⓦwww.siferry.com), which leaves from its own terminal in Lower Manhattan's Battery Park and provides stunning views of New York Harbor around the clock. It's also a commuter boat, so avoid crowded rush hours if you can. Departures are every 15 to 20 minutes during rush hours (7 to 9am and 5 to 7pm), every 30 minutes midday and evenings, and every 60 minutes late at night (the ferry runs 24hrs) – weekends less frequently. Few visitors spend much time on Staten Island; it's easy to just turn around and get back on the ferry, although there's plenty to see if you stay. For info on visiting Staten Island, see p.58.

By car

Don't drive in New York. Even if you're brave enough to try dodging demolition-derby cabbies and jaywalking pedestrians, car rental is expensive and parking lots almost laughably so. Legal street parking is nearly impossible to find.

If you really must drive, bear in mind these rules. Seatbelts are compulsory for everyone in front and for children in back. The city speed limit is 35mph. It's illegal to make a right turn at a red light. The use of hand-held cell phones is illegal while driving.

Read signs carefully to figure out **where to park** – if the sign says "No Standing," "No Stopping," or "Don't Even THINK of Parking Here" (yes, really), then don't. Watch for street-cleaning hours (when an entire side of a street will be off-limits), and don't park in a bus stop, in front of (or within several yards of) a fire hydrant, or anywhere with a yellow curb. Private parking is expensive, but it makes sense to leave your car somewhere legitimate. If you park illegally and are towed, you must liberate your vehicle from the impound lot over on the West Side Highway (ⓣ212/971-0770) – expect to pay a $185 cash tow fee and a $70 execution fee (plus $10–15 for each additional day they store it for you) and waste your day.

Car theft and **vandalism** are more of a problem in less-traveled parts of the city, but no matter where you park, never leave valuables in your car.

For **foreign drivers**, any driver's license issued by their country is valid in the US – for more information check the state DMV's website (ⓦwww.nydmv.state.ny.us).

By bike

Cycling can be a viable, if somewhat dangerous, form of transportation. Wear all possible **safety equipment**: pads, a helmet (required by law), and goggles. When you park, double-chain and lock your bike (including wheels) to an immovable object if you'd like it to be there when you return.

Bike rental starts at about $7 per hour or $35 per day (the price goes up to $20/hr in Central Park) – which means opening to closing (9.30am to 6.30pm for instance). You need one or two pieces of ID (passport and credit card will be sufficient) and, in some cases, a deposit, though most firms will be satisfied with a credit-card imprint. Rates and deposits are generally more for racing models and mountain bikes. See Chapter 32, "Sports and outdoor activities," for more information on bicycle rental.

By foot

Few cities equal New York for street-level stimulation. Getting around on **foot** is often the most exciting – and tiring – method of exploring. Footwear is important (sneakers are good for summer; winter and spring often need something waterproof). So is safety: a lot more people are injured in New York carelessly crossing the street than are mugged. The city has a law against jaywalking, and some midtown intersections have cattle gates to prevent crossing at certain corners. Pedestrian crossings don't give you automatic right of way unless the WALK sign is on – and, even then, cars may be turning, so be prudent.

The media

Generally acknowledged as the media capital of the world, New York is the headquarters of just about all the country's major television news organizations and book and magazine publishers. This means that there is a newsstand on just about every corner selling a wonderful variety of newspapers and magazines, as well as frequent opportunities to take part in television-show tapings.

Newspapers and magazines

Although it's still the most vibrant news market in the US, only four newspapers remain: the broadsheets the **New York Times** and the **New York Sun** and the tabloids the **Daily News** and the **New York Post**.

The *New York Times* ($1.25; ⓦwww.nytimes.com), an American institution, prides itself on being the "paper of record" – America's quality national paper. It has solid international coverage, and places much emphasis on its news analysis. The Sunday edition ($4) is a thumping bundle of newsprint divided into a number of supplements that take a full day to read.

It takes serious coordination to read the sizable *Times* on the subway, one reason many turn to the *Daily News* and the *Post*. Tabloids in format and style, these rivals concentrate on local news. The *Daily News* (50¢; ⓦwww.nydailynews.com) is a "picture newspaper" with many racy headlines.

The *New York Post* (25¢; ⓦwww.nypost.com), the city's oldest newspaper, started in 1801 by Alexander Hamilton, has been in decline for many years. Known for its solid city news and consistent conservative-slanted sermonizing, it also takes a fairly sensationalist approach to headlines.

The *New York Sun* ($1; ⓦwww.nysun.com) is not widely read. Only published on weekdays, it's a broadsheet with a determinedly old-fashioned look and a stolid, conservative bent.

The other New York–based daily newspaper is the *Wall Street Journal* ($1.50; ⓦwww.wsj.com), in fact a national financial paper that also has strong, conservative national and international news coverage – despite an old-fashioned design that eschews the use of photographs.

Weeklies and monthlies

Of the **weekly** papers, the *Village Voice* (Tuesdays, free; ⓦwww.villagevoice.com) is the most widely read, mainly for its comprehensive arts coverage and investigative features. It offers opinionated stories that often focus on the media, gay issues, and civil rights. It's also one of the best pointers to what's on around town (including the most interesting, inexpensive cuisine and shopping). Its main competitor, the *New York Press* (ⓦwww.nypress.com), is angrier, much more conservative, and not afraid to

TV-show tapings

If you want to experience American TV up close, there are **free tickets** for various shows. For most shows you must be 16 and sometimes 18 to be in the audience; if you're underage or traveling with children, call ahead.

Morning shows

Good Morning America ☎212/580-5176, ⓦgma.abcnews.com. Show up at the Broadway entrance around 6am for a shot at a standby ticket.

Today There's no way to get advance tickets, just show up at 49th St, between 5th and 8th avenues, as early as possible. Unlike the rest of the morning shows, which run until 9am, *Today* ends at 10am.

Daytime shows

Live with Regis and Kelly ☎212/456-1000. Request online at ⓦbventertainment .go.com/tv/buenavista/regisandkelly/get_tickets.html or send a postcard with your name, address, and telephone number to Live Tickets, PO Box 230777 Ansonia Station, New York, NY 10023-0777. Include your preferred date(s) and number of tickets (limit 4). For standby, go to ABC at 67th St and Columbus Ave as early as 7am Monday through Friday.

Late-night shows

The Colbert Report ⓦwww.comedycentral.com/shows/the_colbert_report/index. jhtml. In theory you can book tickets on the website, but it's almost always sold out. For standby tickets arrive by 4pm at the studio at 513 W 54th Street, between 5th and 6th avenues.

The Daily Show with Jon Stewart ☎212/586-2477, ⓦwww.thedailyshow.com /tickets.jhtml. Book online or send an email to ⓔrequesttickets@thedailyshow .com. Email your full name, telephone number, and dates of interest. There's no point in showing up for standby tickets; as a last resort call ☎212/586-2477 to find out if there are any cancellations.

David Letterman ☎212/247-6497. Fill out a form at ⓦwww.cbs.com/latenight /lateshow/show_info/tickets/form, or request tickets in person at 1697 Broadway, between W 53rd and W 54th streets (Mon–Fri 9.30am–12.30pm, Sat & Sun 10am–6pm). Standby tickets are available by calling ☎212/247-6497 from 11am on the day you wish to attend. Shoots Monday through Thursday at 5.30pm, with an additional show Thursday at 8pm.

Late Night with Conan O'Brien ☎212/664-3056. Call NBC ticket office at ☎212/664-3056. For standby tickets go to the NBC Studios marquee on the 49th street side of 30 Rockefeller Plaza before 9am. Only one ticket will be issued per person.

Saturday Night Live ☎212/664-4000. It's tough to get tickets in advance; for each upcoming season (usually Oct–May), you must send an email, in August only, to ⓔsnltickets@nbcuni.com – include all contact information. If selected, you'll get two tickets assigned randomly (you cannot fix the date). Alternatively, standby tickets are distributed at 7am on the 49th St side of 30 Rockefeller Plaza on Saturday morning (some weeks are reruns; call ahead). You can opt for either the 8pm dress rehearsal or the 11.30pm live taping.

offend. The listings are quite good; look for its "Best of Manhattan" special edition, published each September.

Other leading weeklies include *New York* magazine ($3.99; ⓦwww.newyorkmetro .com), which has reasonably good listings and is more of a society and entertainment journal, and *Time Out New York* ($3.99; ⓦwww.timeoutny.com) – a clone of its London original, combining the city's most comprehensive "what's on" listings with New York–slanted stories and features. The venerable *New Yorker* ($4.50; @www.newyorker.com) has good highbrow listings, and features poetry and short fiction alongside its much-loved cartoons. The wackiest, and perhaps best, alternative to the *Voice* is *PaperMag* ($4; @www.papermag.com), a monthly that carries witty and well-written rundowns on city nightlife and restaurants as well as current news and gossip. If you want a weekly with more of a political edge, there's the ironic *New York Observer* ($2; @www.observer.com) and the *Forward* ($1; @www.forward.com), a century-plus-old Jewish publication that's also published in Russian and Yiddish editions.

Many neighborhoods and ethnic communities have their own weeklies, led by the politically oriented African-American *Amsterdam News* (75¢; @www.amsterdamnews.org), and the *Brooklyn Papers* (free; @www.brooklynpapers.com).

International publications

British, European, Latin American, and Asian newspapers are widely available, usually a day after publication – except for the *Financial Times*, which is printed (via satellite) in the US and sold on most newsstands. If you want a specific paper or magazine, try any Universal News or Hudson News, sprinkled throughout the city. Barnes & Noble superstores (see p.387) stock magazines and international newspapers, which you can peruse for **free** over coffee (not free).

Television

Any American will find on TV in New York mostly what they find at home, plus several multilingual stations and some wacky public access channels. Channels 13 and 21 are given over to **PBS** (Public Broadcasting Service), which has earned the nickname "Purely British Station" for its fondness of British drama series, although it excels at documentaries and educational children's shows. The 70-plus stations available on **cable** in most hotel rooms may be a bit more fascinating for foreign travelers; most cable channels are no better than the major networks (**ABC**, **CBS**, **NBC**, and **Fox**), although a few of the specialized channels can be fairly interesting. **NY1** is the city's 24-hour local news channel, available exclusively on cable.

Radio

The FM dial is crammed with local stations of varying quality and content. The *New York Times* lists highlights daily; explore on your own, and you're sure to come across something interesting.

Incidentally, it's possible to tune in to the BBC World Service on the 49-meter shortwave band, or just the World Service news, broadcast on a number of the public radio stations. **BBC** (@www.bbc.co.uk/worldservice), **Radio Canada** (@www.rcinet.ca), and **Voice of America** (@www.voa.gov) list all the World Service frequencies around the globe.

Tourist information

There is a veritable torrent of information available for visitors to New York City. Chances are, the answers to any questions you may have are readily accessible on a website or in a brochure.

General information

The best place for **information** is **NYC & Company** (the official visitors bureau), 810

Seventh Ave at 53rd St (Mon–Fri 8.30am–6pm, weekends and holidays 9am–5pm; ☎212/484-1222, @www.nycvisit.com). They have bus and subway maps,

Information centers and kiosks

Bloomingdale's International Visitors' Center Lexington Ave at 59th St ☎212/705-2098.

Brooklyn Tourism and Visitors Center Brooklyn Borough Hall, 209 Joralemon St ☎718/802-3846, Ⓦwww.visitbrooklyn.org. Open Mon–Fri 10am–6pm.

Chinatown Visitor Information Kiosk Junction of Canal, Walker, and Baxter sts. Open weekends only 10am–6pm.

Dairy Visitor Center & Gift Shop Central Park (mid-park at 65th St) ☎212/794-6564, Ⓦwww.centralparknyc.org. Open Tues–Sun 10am–5pm. Check also Ⓦwww.nycparks.org, the official word on all of the obscure, famous, and thrilling events in the city's parks.

Federal Hall Information Center Federal Hall National Memorial, 26 Wall St. Open Mon–Fri 9am–5pm.

Lower East Side Visitor Center 261 Broome ☎866/224-0206, Ⓦwww.lowereastsideny.com.

NYC Heritage Tourism Center Southern end of City Hall Park, Broadway at Park Row.

Times Square Visitor Information Center 1560 Broadway ☎212/869-1890, Ⓦwww.timessquarenyc.org.

information on hotels and accommodation (including discounts), and up-to-date leaflets on what's going on in the arts and elsewhere. Their quarterly *Official NYC Guide* is good too, though the kind of information it gives – on restaurants, hotels, shopping, and sights – is also available in the various free tourist magazines and brochures in hotels and elsewhere. You'll find other small **tourist information centers** and kiosks all over the city, starting with the airports, Grand Central and Penn stations, and Port Authority Bus Terminal. For a list of kiosks in other areas see the box above.

Maps

Other than our maps, the best **maps** of New York City are the free **bus maps** (ask any subway teller or librarian for one), as well as the huge, minutely detailed **neighborhood maps** found fixed to the wall near the teller booth of subway stations. **Professional maps**, like *The Rough Guide Map of New York City*, which is rip-proof and waterproof, fill in the gaps. A great selection of New York City maps is available at Ⓦwww.randmcnally.com. Street atlases of all five boroughs cost around $10–15; if you're after a map of one of the individual outer boroughs, try those produced by Geographia or Hagstrom, on sale online and in bookstores for $5–15.

Tours

There are many different ways to take in the city. First-time visitors may be interested in taking a tour – they come in all kinds of lengths, themes, and modes of transportation.

Bus tours

Bus tours provide a good way to orient yourself with the city. Gray Line New York, Port Authority Terminal at 42nd St and Eighth Ave (☎800/669-0051 or 212/445-0848, Ⓦwww.graylinenewyork.com), runs a large number of popular bus tours that range from two hours to two days. Discounts are available for children under 12. Call or look at the website for complete information and to book a tour.

Helicopter tours

A more exciting option is to look at the city by **helicopter**. This is expensive, but you won't easily forget the experience. **Liberty Helicopter Tours** (☎212/967-6464, Ⓦwww.libertyhelicopters.com), at the VIP Heliport (W 30th St and 12th Ave) and the Downtown Heliport at Pier 6 (near the Staten Island Ferry), offers flights ranging from $110 per person (for six to eight minutes) to $204

(16–20min). Reservations are required; times and locations vary on Sundays and holidays. **New York Helicopter** offers similar rates (ⓦwww.newyorkhelicopter.com).

Boat tours

A great way to see the island of Manhattan is to take one of many harbor cruises on offer. The **Circle Line** (☎212/563-3200, ⓦwww.circleline42.com) sails from Pier 83 at W 42nd St and Twelfth Ave, circumnavigating Manhattan and taking in everything from the Statue of Liberty to Harlem, complete with a live commentary; the three-hour tour runs year-round ($31, seniors $26, under-12s $18). The evening two-hour Harbor Lights Cruise (March–Nov; $27, seniors $23, under-12s $16) offers dramatic views of the skyline. Thrill-seekers should try *The Beast* (May–Oct $19, 12 and under $13), a speedboat painted to look like a shark that will throw you around for thirty minutes at a wave-pounding 45 miles per hour.

Circle Line Downtown (☎1-866/925-4631, ⓦwww.circlelinedowntown.com) runs harbor cruises in Downtown Manhattan from South Street Seaport; March to December on *Zephyr* (1hr; adults $25, seniors $23, children $15), and speedboat rides on the *Shark* May to September (30min; adults $21, seniors $19, children $15).

Alternatively, check out tours offered by **NY Waterway** (☎800/533-3779, ⓦwww.nywaterway.com). Its 90-minute Harbor Cruises ($23, seniors $19, under-12s $13) leave the west end of Pier 78 at W 38th St several times daily, year-round – check the website for a range of specialty cruises. You can also cruise the harbor in style aboard

one of the historic yachts based at the South Street Seaport (p.61), or Chelsea Piers (see Sports and outdoor activities p.412).

Walking tours

Options for walking tours of Manhattan or the outer boroughs are many and varied. You'll find fliers for some of them at the various visitor centers; for what's happening in the current week, check the weekly print edition of *Time Out New York*, or the weekly *Village Voice* (ⓦwww.villagevoice.com). **Columbia and NYU** run very frequent tours of their campuses, free of charge. Not all tour operators are open year-round, with the more esoteric running only a few outings annually. Phone ahead or check websites for the full schedules.

Tour companies

Art Entrée ☎718/391-0011, ⓦwww.artentree .com. Runs a range of art tours throughout the city, focusing on different art scenes, museums, galleries, neighborhoods, and genres like glass art and portraits.

Big Onion Walking Tours ☎212/439-1090, ⓦwww.bigonion.com. Guided by history grad students from local universities, venerable Big Onion specializes in tours with an ethnic and historical focus: pick one, or take the "Immigrant New York" tour and learn about everyone. Cost is $15, $12 for seniors and students; the food-included "Multi-Ethnic Eating Tour" costs $20. These last about two hours.

Brooklyn Center for the Urban Environment ☎718/788-8500, ⓦwww.bcue.org. This organization runs neighborhood and park tours on summer weekends, most of them in Brooklyn. All walking tours, such as "Bats in Brooklyn!", "Rust and Remembrance," and "Walt Whitman's Brooklyn," cost $13, students and seniors $8. Ask about the $50

Big Apple Greeter

If you're nervous about exploring New York, look into **Big Apple Greeter**, 1 Centre St, Suite 2035 (☎212/669-8159, ⓦwww.bigapplegreeter.org), one of the best – and certainly cheapest – ways to see the city. This not-for-profit organization matches visitors with their active corps of trained volunteer "greeters." Specify the part of the city you'd like to see, indicate an aspect of New York life you'd like to explore, or plead for general orientation – whatever your interests, chances are they will find someone to take you around. Visits have a friendly, informal feel, and generally last a few hours. The service is free. You can call once you're in New York, but it's better to contact the organization as far in advance as possible.

($40 for members, students, and seniors) ecology boat tours along the Gowanus Canal.

City Hunt ☎877/HUNT-FUN, ⓦwww.cityhunt.org. Innovative scavenger hunts and urban "safaris" like the "Da Vinci Hunt," which begins at the Met, and private pub crawls. Prices range from $20 to $30.

Greenwich Village Literary Pub Crawl ☎212/613-5796. Actors from the New Ensemble Theater Company lead you to several of the most prominent bars in literary history and read from associated works. Tours meet at the White Horse Tavern, 567 Hudson St (see p.346). Reservations are required: $15, students and seniors $12.

Harlem Heritage Tours ☎212/280-7888, ⓦwww.harlemheritage.com. Thorough cultural tours of the historic neighborhood, ranging from "Spanish Harlem Salsa Walking Tour" to "Malcolm X Walking Tour." The tours sometimes include food, a cultural performance, film clips, and/or bus service. Prices range from $25 to $40.

Harlem Spirituals Gospel and Jazz Tours ☎212/391-0900, ⓦwww.harlemspirituals.com /gospel.php. Professionally run, excellent-value tours ranging from Sunday-morning church services to soul food and jazz affairs taking in dinner and a club. $55–125 per person (discounts for children). Reservations required.

Municipal Arts Society ☎212/935-3960, ⓦwww.mas.org/calendar.php. Opinionated, incredibly detailed historical and architectural tours in Manhattan, Brooklyn, Queens, and the Bronx. Free ($10 donation suggested) tours of Grand Central Terminal start Wednesdays at 12.30pm from the information booth. Walking tours cost $15.

NoshWalks ☎212/222-2243, ⓦwww.noshwalks .com. Weekend ethnic culinary tours of neighborhoods in Manhattan, Queens, Brooklyn, and the Bronx, incorporating local history and culture, by the author of two NYC food guidebooks. $35, plus food. Reservations recommended.

Travel essentials

Costs

On a **moderate budget**, expect to spend at least $200 per night on accommodation in a mid-range, centrally located hotel in high season, plus $20–30 per person for a moderate sit-down dinner each night and about $15–20 more per person per day for takeout and grocery meals. Getting around will cost $25 per person per week for unlimited public transportation, plus $10 each for the occasional cab ride. Sightseeing, drinking, clubbing, eating haute cuisine, and going to the theater have the potential to add exponentially to these costs. The New York City sales tax is 8.375 percent. Hotels are subject to a separate 13.38 percent hotel tax, and a $3.50 per night "occupancy tax."

You're expected to **tip** in restaurants, bars, taxicabs, hotels (both the bellboy and the cleaning staff), and even some posh restrooms. In restaurants in particular, it's unthinkable not to leave the minimum (15 percent of the bill) – even if you hated the service.

Crime and personal safety

In two words: don't worry. New York has come a long way in recent years. While the city can sometimes feel dangerous, the reality is somewhat different. As far as per capita crime rates go, New York is America's safest city with a population over one million. Take the **normal precautions** and you should be fine; carry bags closed and across your body, don't let cameras dangle, keep wallets in front – not back – pockets, and don't flash money around. Mugging can and does happen, but rarely during the day. Avoid wandering empty streets or the subway late at night (especially alone). If you are unlucky enough to be mugged, try to stay calm and hand over the money. When the mugger has run off, hail a cab and ask to be taken to the nearest police station. You'll get sympathy and little else; file the theft and take the incident report to claim your insurance back home.

Note that possession of any "controlled substance" is absolutely illegal. Should you be found in possession of a very small amount of marijuana, you probably won't go to jail – but you can expect a hefty fine and, for foreigners, the possibility of deportation.

Each area of New York has its own **police** precinct; to find the nearest station, call ☎646/610-5000 (during business hours only) or ☎311, or check the phone book. In emergencies, phone ☎911 or use one of the outdoor posts that give you a direct line to the emergency services. This information, plus crime stats, is available at ☎www.nyc.gov/nypd.

Electricity

US electricity is 110V AC, and most plugs are two-pronged. Unless they're dual-voltage, most foreign-bought appliances will need a voltage converter as well as a plug adapter. Be warned, some converters may not be able to handle certain high-wattage items, especially those with heated elements.

Entry requirements

Under the **Visa Waiver Program**, citizens of Australia, Ireland, New Zealand, and the UK do not require visas for visits to the US of ninety days or less. You will, however, need to present a machine-readable passport and a completed visa waiver form to Immigration upon arrival; the latter will be provided by your travel agent or by the airline. Canadians now require a passport to cross the border, but can travel in the US for an unlimited amount of time without a visa. For visa information, visit ☎www.travel.state.gov. For customs information, visit ☎www.customs.treas.gov.

Consulates in New York City

Australia 34/F, 150 E 42nd St ☎212/351-6500, ☎www.australianyc.org.
Canada 1251 Sixth Ave, at 50th St ☎212/596-1628, ☎www.canada-ny.org.

Ireland 17/F, 345 Park Ave, between 51st and 52nd sts ☎212/319-2555, ✉congenny@aol.com.
New Zealand 222 E 41st St, Suite 2510, between Second and Third aves ☎212/832-4038.
South Africa 333 E 38th St, between First and Second aves ☎212/213-4880, ☎www.southafrica-newyork.net/consulate.
UK 845 Third Ave, between 51st and 52nd sts ☎212/745-0200, ☎www.britainusa.com/ny.

Health

There are few health issues specific to New York City, short of the common cold. Minor ailments can be remedied at **drugstores**, which can more or less be found every few blocks. **Duane Reade** is the city's major chain. Foreign visitors should bear in mind that many pills available over the counter in other countries (for example, codeine-based painkillers) are only available by prescription here. If you need advice, ask at the **pharmacy**, where prescription drugs are dispensed.

Should you find yourself requiring a **doctor**, look in the *Yellow Pages* under "Clinics" or "Physicians and Surgeons." Should you be in an **accident**, a medical service will pick you up and charge later. For minor accidents, **emergency rooms** are open 24 hours at these and other Manhattan hospitals (though be aware that even a short visit can cost around $1000): **St Vincent's**, Seventh Ave and W 11th St (☎212/604-7996); **New York Presbyterian (Cornell)**, E 70th St at York Ave (☎212/746-5050); and **Mount Sinai**, Madison Ave at 100th St (☎212/241-7171). Call ☎911 for an ambulance.

Insurance

You will want to invest in **travel insurance**. A typical travel-insurance policy usually provides cover for the loss of baggage, tickets, and – up to a certain limit – cash or checks, as well as cancellation or curtailment of your journey. Many policies can be chopped and changed to exclude coverage you don't need – for example, sickness and accident benefits can often be excluded or included at will. Before you take out a new policy, however, it's worth checking whether you are already covered: some all-risks home-insurance policies may cover your possessions when overseas, and many private medical schemes include cover when abroad.

Rough Guides has teamed up with Columbus Direct to offer you travel insurance that can be tailored to suit your needs. Products include a low-cost backpacker option for long stays; a short break option for city getaways; a typical holiday package option; and others. There are also annual multi-trip policies for those who travel regularly. Different sports and activities (trekking, skiing, etc) can usually be covered if required.

See our website (Ⓦwww.roughguides.com /website/shop) for eligibility and purchasing options. Alternatively, UK residents should call Ⓣ0870/033 9988; Australians should call Ⓣ1300/669 999 and New Zealanders should call Ⓣ0800/55 9911. All other nationalities should call Ⓣ+44 870/890 2843.

Internet

Wireless Internet (wi-fi) is widespread throughout New York City. Cafés like *Starbucks* have free "hotspots," as do a good number of motels and hotels. If you're traveling without your own computer, there are any number of places to access the Internet. Try the *cybercafe*, 250 W 49th St (Ⓣ212/333-4109, Ⓦwww.cyber-cafe.com) or web2zone at 54 Cooper Square in the East Village (Ⓣ212/614-7300, Ⓦwww .web2zone.com) to name but. A great, free alternative is to stop by a branch of the **New York City Public Library**, where limited Internet access and printing are available. Each branch has its own rules; ask a librarian how to get online. Another option is **Bryant Park**, where free wi-fi Internet access is also available.

Laundry

Hotels do it but charge a lot. You're much better off going to an ordinary laundromat or dry cleaner, of which you'll find plenty listed in the *Yellow Pages* under "Laundries." Most laundromats also offer a very affordable drop service, where, for about $1 per pound or less, you can have your laundry washed, dried, and tidily folded – often the same day. Some budget hotels, YMCAs, and hostels also have coin-operated washers and dryers.

Living and working in New York

It's not easy to live and work in New York, even for US residents. For anyone looking for short-term work, the typical urban employment options are available – temporary office work, waiting tables, babysitting, etc – as well as some quirkier opportunities, like artist's modeling in Soho or Tribeca. For ideas and positions, check the employment ads in the *New York Times*, *New York Press*, *Village Voice*, and the free neighborhood tabloids available throughout the city.

If you're a foreigner, you start at a disadvantage. Unless you already have family in the US (in which case special rules may apply), you need a **work visa**, and these can be extremely difficult to get. The US visa system is one of the world's most complex, with a bewildering range of visa types to suit every circumstance – most people hire a lawyer to do the paperwork ($2000 and up). Essentially, you'll need a firm offer of work from a US company; unless you have a special skill, few companies will want to go through the hassle of sponsoring you however, and since tourists are not supposed to seek work, legally you'll have to apply for jobs from overseas. Plenty of foreigners do manage to work for short periods illegally in New York (typically cash-in-hand jobs, bar work or freelancing); be warned however that the penalties for doing so can be harsh (deportation and being barred from the US for up to ten years), and that if you repeatedly enter the country on a visa-waiver, you are likely to be severely questioned at immigration. For further visa information, go to Ⓦwww.unitedstatesvisas.gov.

Finding a place to stay is tricky for everyone. A **studio apartment** – a single room with bathroom and kitchen – in a popular neighborhood in Manhattan can rent for upwards of $1800 per month. Many newcomers share studios and one-bedrooms among far too many people; it makes more sense to look in the outer boroughs or the nearby New Jersey towns of Jersey City and Hoboken. However, some of these neighborhoods are becoming expensive, and to find a real deal you must hunt hard and check out even the most unlikely possibilities. It frequently takes up to a month or two to find a place.

The best source for finding an apartment or room is **word of mouth**. Watch the **ads** in the *Village Voice*, the *New York Times*, and on ⓦwww.newyork.craigslist.org (actually a great resource for all kinds of classified listings in New York). Try commercial and campus bulletin boards too, where you might secure a temporary apartment or sublet while the regular tenant is away.

Lost property

For things **lost** on buses or the subway, contact the NYC Transit Authority, at the 34th St/Eighth Ave Station (#A, #C, and #E), on the lower-level subway mezzanine (Mon, Tues & Fri 8am–4pm, Wed & Thurs 11am–7pm; ☎212/712-4500). For anything lost on Amtrak, contact Penn Station upper level, near tracks 5 and 6 East (Mon–Fri 7.30am–4pm; ☎212/630-7389). For items lost on Metro North, go to Grand Central Terminal lower level (Mon–Fri 7am–6pm, Sat 9am–5pm; ☎212/340-2555). For property left in a cab: Taxi & Limousine Commission Lost Property Dept (Mon–Fri 9am–5pm except national holidays; ☎212/227-0700); you can file a report online (ⓦwww.nyc.gov /taxi) if you have the cab's medallion number (printed on your receipt).

Mail

Post offices in New York City are generally open Monday to Friday 9am to 5pm (though some open earlier), and Saturday from 9am to noon or later. The main post office in Midtown, 421 Eighth Ave, at W 33rd St (☎212/967-8585), is open 24 hours, seven days a week. There are many post offices in the city; for the nearest one, search at ⓦwww.usps.gov. You can buy **stamps** at post offices, as well as in some shops, supermarkets, and delis, although these may cost more than the face value. **Ordinary mail** within the US costs 42¢ for letters weighing up to an ounce, and 27¢ for postcards; addresses must include a **zip code** (postal code) and a return address in the upper left corner of the envelope. **Air mail** to anywhere else in the world costs 94¢ for a letter or postcards.

You can have mail sent to you c/o **General Delivery** (known elsewhere as **poste restante**), New York City, NY 10116. Letters will end up at the aforementioned main post office in Midtown and will be held there for thirty days before being returned to sender, so make sure the envelope has a return address.

Money

US currency comes in **bills** of $1, $5, $10, $20, $50, and $100, plus various larger (and rarer) denominations. The dollar is made up of 100 cents (¢) in coins of 1 cent (usually called a penny), 5 cents (a nickel), 10 cents (a dime), 25 cents (a quarter), 50 cents (a half-dollar), and one dollar. The $2 bill and the half-dollar and dollar coins are seldom seen. Change – especially quarters – is needed for buses, vending machines, and telephones, so always carry plenty.

Most people on vacation in New York withdraw **cash** as needed from **automatic teller machines (ATMs)**, which can be found at any bank branch and at many convenience stores and delis in the city, though these can charge fees of up to $2 for the service (in addition to bank charges). If you're visiting from abroad, make sure you have a personal identification number (PIN) that's designed to work overseas. A **credit card** is a must; American Express, Master-Card, and Visa are widely accepted, and are almost always required for deposits at hotels. If you bring **traveler's checks**, it's best to have them in US dollar denominations, as they can be changed in any bank and used as cash in many stores.

Banking hours are usually Monday–Friday 9am–4pm; some banks stay open later on Thursdays or Fridays, and have limited Saturday hours. Major banks – such as Citibank and Chase – will exchange traveler's checks and currency at a standard rate.

The value of the US dollar tends to vary considerably against other currencies, but has remained relatively weak for a number of years, helping to mitigate New York's high prices for most foreign visitors. At press time, one dollar was worth 0.51 British pounds (£), 0.64 euros, 1 Canadian dollar (Can$), 1.06 Australian dollars (Aus$), and 1.31 New Zealand dollars (NZ$). For current exchange rates check ⓦwww.xe.com.

Opening hours

The opening hours of specific attractions are given throughout the Guide. As a general rule, most **museums** are open Tuesday through Sunday, 10am to 5 or 6pm, though most have one night per week where they stay open at least a few hours later. Government **offices** are open during regular business hours, usually 9am to 5pm. Store hours vary widely, depending on the kind of store and what part of town you're in, though you can generally count on them being open Monday to Saturday from around 10am to 6pm, with limited Sunday hours. Many of the larger chain or department stores will stay open to 9pm or later, and you generally don't have to walk more than a few blocks anywhere in Manhattan to find a 24-hour deli. On national **public holidays** (see box opposite), banks and offices are likely to be closed all day, and most shops will be closed or have reduced hours.

Phones

Public telephones are becoming hard to find. The cost of a local call is 50¢. Long-distance rates are pricier, and you're better off using a **prepaid calling card** ($5, $10 and $20), which you can buy at most grocery stores and newsstands. If your payphone won't accept your quarter, the change box is full.

If you want to use your **mobile phone** in New York, you'll need to check with your phone provider to make sure it will work, and what the call charges will be. Unless you have a tri-band phone, it is unlikely that a mobile bought for use outside the US will work inside the States. You can rent mobile phones via Phonerental (US ☏1-800-335-3705,

Public holidays

New Year's Day Jan 1
Martin Luther King, Jr's Birthday Third Mon in Jan
Presidents' Day Third Mon in Feb
Memorial Day Last Mon in May
Independence Day July 4
Labor Day First Mon in Sept
Columbus Day Second Mon in Oct
Veterans' Day Nov 11
Thanksgiving Day Fourth Thurs in Nov
Christmas Day Dec 25

international ☏+1-619-446-6980, ⊛www .phonerentalusa.com); rental is free for the first week (though you need to make a minimum $25 in calls) and $3 per day thereafter. You get charged $0.69 per minute for incoming and all local and national outgoing calls. Arrange the rental in advance and the company will deliver your phone to the airport or your hotel for pick-up. Triptel (☏877-874-7835, ⊛www .triptel.com) offers a similar service with GSM phones ($15/week rental).

There are five **area codes** in use in New York: ☏212 and ☏646 for Manhattan, ☏718 and ☏347 for the outer boroughs and ☏917 for (mostly) cell phones. You must dial the area code, even if you're calling a number from a phone within the same area. For directory assistance, call ☏411.

Time

New York City is on **Eastern Standard Time** (EST), which is five hours behind Greenwich Mean Time (GMT).

Calling home from the US

Note that the initial zero is omitted from the area code when dialing the UK, Ireland, Australia, and New Zealand from abroad. The US country code (which it shares with Canada) is 1.
Australia 011 + 61 + city code + local number.
Canada city code + local number.
New Zealand 011 + 64 + city code + local number.
UK 011 + 44 + city code + local number.
Republic of Ireland 011 + 353 + city code + local number.

Travelers with disabilities

New York City has had **disabled access** regulations imposed on an aggressively disabled-unfriendly system. There are wide variations in accessibility, making navigation a tricky business. At the same time, you'll find New Yorkers surprisingly willing to go out of their way to help you. If you're having trouble and you feel that passers-by are ignoring you, it's most likely out of respect for your privacy – never hesitate to ask for assistance.

For wheelchair users, getting around on the **subway** is next to impossible without someone to help you, and even then is extremely difficult at most stations. Several, but not all, lines are equipped with elevators, but this doesn't make much of a difference. The Transit Authority is working to make stations accessible, but at the rate they're going it won't happen soon. **Buses** are another story, and are the first choice of many disabled New Yorkers. All MTA buses are equipped with wheelchair lifts and locks. To get on a bus, wait at the bus stop to signal the driver you need to board; when he or she has seen you, move to the back door, where he or she will assist you. For travelers with other mobility difficulties, the driver will "kneel" the bus to allow you easier access. For a Braille subway map, call ☎718/694-4903; for more information about accessibility, call ☎718/596-8585.

Taxis are a viable option for visitors with visual and hearing impairments and minor mobility difficulties. For wheelchair users, taxis are less of a possibility unless you have a collapsible chair, in which case drivers are required to store it and assist you; the unfortunate reality is that most drivers won't stop if they see you waiting. If you're refused, try to get the cab's medallion number and report the driver to the Taxi and Limousine Commission at ⓦwww.nyc.gov/html/tlc/html/passenger/file_complaint.shtml.

Women travelers

Women traveling alone or with other women in New York City should attract no more attention than in any other urban destination in the US. As always, the usual precautions should suffice; a big part of visiting New York is to look as if you know what you're doing and where you're going. If someone's bugging you, either turn away, leave, or let him know your feelings loudly and firmly. Avoid getting noticeably intoxicated unless you are with a trusted friend. If you are being followed, turn around and look at the person following you, and step off the sidewalk and into the street; attackers hate the open. If you're unsure about the area where you're staying, ask other women's advice. However, don't avoid parts of the city just through hearsay – you might miss out on what's most of interest – and learn to expect New Yorkers (Manhattanites in particular, many of whom feel incorrectly that anywhere outside of the borough shouldn't be risked) to sound alarmist; it's part of the culture.

Services for disabled travelers

Big Apple Greeter 1 Centre St ☎212/669-3602, ⓦwww.bigapplegreeter.org. Accepted by many as the main authority on New York accessibility. This free service matches you with a volunteer who spends a few hours showing you the city. Big Apple Greeter has also compiled a resource list for travelers with disabilities, which they will supply on request.

FEGS 315 Hudson St ☎212/366-8400, ⓦwww.fegs.org. Formerly the New York Society for the Deaf, this is a good source of information on interpreter services, plus services for deaf individuals ranging from HIV-test counseling to kosher lunches.

The Lighthouse 111 E 59th St ☎212/821-9200, ⓦwww.lighthouse.org. General services for the visually impaired.

The Mayor's Office for People with Disabilities 100 Gold St, 2nd floor ☎212/788-2830, TTY 788-2838, ⓦwww.nyc.gov/html/mopd. General information and resources.

The City

The City

The Harbor Islands

T he southern tip of the island of Manhattan, together with the shores of
neighboring New Jersey, Staten Island, and Brooklyn, encloses the broad
expanse of **New York Harbor**. One of the finest natural harbors in the
world when the Dutch arrived in 1624 it was teeming with fish, seals,
whales, and half of the world's oysters, a veritable marine Eden. With the water
heavily polluted, the last oyster bed was closed in 1927, and though things are
much improved (the harbor is officially clean enough to swim and fish), it will
take many generations to recover its former glory.

For now, the main attractions lie above water, where ferries provide a proper
sense of New York's uniqueness and the best views of the celebrated skyline. You
can experience this by taking a boat ride out to **Liberty**, **Ellis**, or **Governors
islands** – three highly compelling destinations – or, if you're feeling less
purposeful, by catching the Staten Island Ferry, which traverses the harbor.

Visiting Ellis and Liberty islands: ferry logistics

The only way to get to any of the Harbor Islands is by **ferry**. Take the #1 train to
South Ferry or the #4 or #5 trains to Bowling Green, then walk to the boat pier in
Battery Park. From the pier, **Statue Cruises** go to Liberty, then on to Ellis Island
(daily, every 30–45min, 9.30am–3.30pm; round-trip $12, seniors $10, children 3–12
$5). Note that you must be at security 30min before departure. You can buy tickets
at Castle Clinton (see p.58), in the park, or **buy them in advance** (highly recommended) with a credit card at ☎877/523-9849 or ⓦwww.statuecruises.com. If you
want to visit the museum inside the Statue of Liberty, you need to buy a ticket with
"monument access" (no extra charge). Lines can be extremely long at any time of
year, but they're especially bad in the summer; you must line up to buy tickets, and
then join another line to clear security before boarding the ferry. The best way to
avoid the long wait is to buy tickets in advance, preferably reserving the 9am slot,
and have the tickets emailed to you; assuming you can print them out, you can go
straight to the security line.

Give yourself at least half a day to see both Liberty and Ellis islands, and more time
if you don't want to be rushed. Liberty Island needs at least one hour (that's only if
you're walking around the island, and not going inside the statue – there is another
long line to clear security for the interior), and Ellis requires at least two hours to do
its museum justice. Start out as early as possible: keep in mind that if you take the
last ferry of the day to Liberty Island, you won't be able to get over to Ellis.

Alternatively, the **Staten Island Ferry** (free; ⓦwww.siferry.com) departs every half
an hour and shuttles between Manhattan and its namesake island. While it provides
a beautiful panorama of the harbor and downtown skyline, it doesn't actually stop at
any of the Harbor Islands (see p.58).

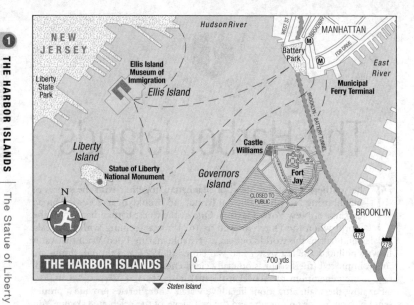

NEW JERSEY

Hudson River

MANHATTAN

Battery Park

East River

Liberty State Park

Ellis Island Museum of Immigration

Ellis Island

Municipal Ferry Terminal

Castle Williams

Liberty Island

Fort Jay

Statue of Liberty National Monument

Governors Island

N

CLOSED TO PUBLIC

BROOKLYN

THE HARBOR ISLANDS

0   700 yds

▼ *Staten Island*

The Statue of Liberty

Of all America's symbols, none has proved more enduring than the **Statue of Liberty** (daily 9.30am–5pm; free; ☎212/363-3200, ⓦwww.nps.gov/stli), looming over the harbor from its pedestal on tiny Liberty Island. Indeed, there is probably no more immediately recognizable profile in existence than that of Lady Liberty, who stands with torch in hand, clutching a stone tablet. Measuring some 305ft from the pedestal base, she has acted as the figurehead of the American Dream for more than a century. For Americans, the statue is a potent reminder of their country's heritage as a land of immigrants. When the first waves of European refugees arrived in the mid-nineteenth century, it was she who greeted them – the symbolic beginning of a new life.

These days an immigrant's first view of the US is more likely to be the customs check at JFK Airport, but the statue nevertheless remains a stirring sight. **Emma Lazarus**'s poem *The New Colossus*, inspired by the new immigrant experience and inscribed on a tablet on the bronze pedestal, is no less quotable now than when it was written in 1883:

"Give me your tired, your poor,
Your huddled masses yearning to breathe free,
The wretched refuse of your teeming shore.
Send these, the homeless, tempest-tost to me,
I lift my lamp beside the golden door!"

Some history

Native American shell middens found on Liberty Island date back hundreds of years, and in the early colonial period the abundance of shellfish nearby earned it the name Great Oyster Island. Sold by the British to Dutch merchant Issac Bedloo in 1668, it was known as Bedloe's Island until 1956. Fort Wood was built here in 1812 as a defensive measure, and the War Department controlled much of the island well into the 1930s – the landscaped grounds you see today were created after the National Park Service assumed full ownership in 1937.

The **statue** itself, which depicts Liberty throwing off her shackles and holding a beacon to light the world, is the creation of French sculptor **Frédéric Auguste Bartholdi**, who crafted it a hundred years after the American Revolution, supposedly to commemorate the solidarity between France and America. (Actually, he originally intended the statue for Alexandria, Egypt.) Bartholdi built Liberty in Paris between 1874 and 1884, starting with a terra-cotta model and enlarging it through four successive versions to its present size of 151ft. The final product is a construction of thin copper sheets bolted together and supported by an iron framework designed by **Gustave Eiffel**. The arm carrying the torch was exhibited in Madison Square Park for seven years, but the rest of the statue remained in France until it was officially accepted on behalf of the American people in 1884.

Liberty had to be taken apart into hundreds of pieces in order to ship the statue to New York, where it was finally reassembled, although it was another two years before the figure could be properly unveiled. Only through the efforts of newspaper magnate Joseph Pulitzer, a keen supporter of the statue, were the necessary funds raised. **Richard Morris Hunt** built a pedestal around star-shaped Fort Wood, and Liberty was formally dedicated by President Cleveland on October 28, 1886, amid a patriotic outpouring that has never really stopped. Indeed, fifteen million people descended on Manhattan for the statue's centennial celebrations, and some three million people make the pilgrimage here each year.

The museum and statue interior

In order to get inside the statue – the museum gallery and pedestal observation levels – you must get a "Monument Access" ticket (no extra cost) when you purchase your ferry ticket (preferably in advance, see box, p.43). Note that you must go through another security screening before entry, and that access above the pedestal observation level remains closed. From Memorial Day weekend through Columbus Day weekend, final entry is at 4.30 pm, and 3.30pm at other times.

The museum is definitely worth a look, the downstairs lobby containing the original torch and flame (completed first and used to raise funds for the rest of the statue), and the small exhibition upstairs telling the story of the figure with prints, photographs, posters, and replicas. There are images of the statue from all kinds of sources – indicative of just how iconic an image it is. At the top of the pedestal you can look up into the center of the statue's skirts – make sure you get a glance of her riveted and bolted interior, and her fire-hazard staircase. After you've perused the statue's interior offerings, take a turn around the balcony outside – the views are predictably superb. Informative and usually entertaining **ranger-guided tours** of the island's grounds are offered free of charge throughout the day (program listings are posted at the island's information building).

Ellis Island

Just across the water from Liberty Island, and fifteen minutes farther from Manhattan by ferry, sits **Ellis Island**, once the first stop for over twelve million immigrants to the US. It remained open until 1954, when it was abandoned and left to fall into atmospheric ruin. After $162 million was donated for its restoration, the main complex reopened in 1990 as the impressive, free **Ellis Island Museum of Immigration**.

Some history

The Dutch purchased the island from the Lenape Indians in 1630 (who had called it Kioshk or "Gull Island"), naming it Little Oyster Island after its famed beds of fist-sized shellfish. The English used it for hanging captured pirates and knew it as Gibbet Island, but the current name derives from Samuel Ellis, a New York merchant who bought the whole thing in the 1770s. Sold to the Federal government in 1808, Ellis Island was fortified during the War of 1812 but played a largely uneventful role in the history of the city for the next eighty years.

Up until the 1850s, there was no official **immigration process** in New York. It was at this point that a surge of Irish, German, and Scandinavian immigrants forced authorities to open an immigration center at Castle Clinton in Battery Park. By the 1880s, millions of desperate immigrants (mostly southern and eastern Europeans) were leaving their homelands in search of a new life in America. The Battery Park facilities proved totally inadequate, and in 1892 Ellis Island became the new **immigration station**.

The main building was constructed in 1903 (its predecessor had burned down in 1897), and various additions were built in the ensuing years – hospitals, outhouses, and the like, usually on bits of landfill. The immigrants who arrived here were all steerage-class passengers; richer immigrants were processed at their leisure on-board ship. The scenes on the island were horribly confused: though the processing center had been designed to accommodate 500,000 immigrants per year, double that number arrived during the early part of the twentieth century. As many as 11,747 immigrants passed through the center on a single day in 1907.

Once inside, each family was split up – men sent to one area, women and children to another – while a series of checks weeded out the undesirables and the infirm. The latter were taken to the second floor, where doctors would check for "loathsome and contagious diseases" as well as signs of insanity. Those who failed medical tests were marked with a white cross on their backs and either sent to the hospital or put back on the boat. Steamship carriers had an obligation to return any immigrants not accepted into America to their original port, though according to official records, only two percent of all immigrants were ever rejected, and of those, many jumped into the sea and tried to swim to Manhattan, or committed suicide. On average, eighty percent of immigrants were processed in less than eight hours, after which they headed either to New Jersey and trains to the West, or into New York City, where they settled in one of the rapidly expanding ethnic neighborhoods, such as the Lower East Side.

After 1924, Ellis Island became primarily a detention facility (during World War II some seven thousand German, Italian, and Japanese people were detained here), before finally closing in 1954.

Ellis Island Museum of Immigration

Today, the four-turreted main building serves as the **Ellis Island Museum of Immigration** (daily 9.30am–5.15pm; free; ☎212/363-3200, ⓦ www.nps.gov /elis, ⓦ www.ellisisland.com). This is an ambitious museum that eloquently recaptures the spirit of the place with artifacts, photographs, maps, and personal accounts that tell the story of the immigrants who passed through Ellis Island on their way to a new life in America. Some 100 million Americans can trace

▲ Ellis Island Museum of Immigration

their roots back through Ellis Island, and, for them especially, the museum is an engaging display. On the first floor, located in the old railroad ticket office, the excellent permanent exhibit "Peopling of America" chronicles four centuries of immigration, offering a statistical portrait of those who arrived at Ellis Island – who they were, where they came from, and why they came. The huge, vaulted **Registry Room** on the second floor, scene of so much immigrant trepidation, elation, and despair, has been left imposingly bare, with just a couple of inspectors' desks and American flags. In the side halls, a series of interview rooms recreates the process that immigrants went through on their way to naturalization; the white-tiled chambers are soberingly bureaucratic. Each room is augmented by recorded voices of those who passed through Ellis Island, recalling their experiences, along with photographs, thoughtful and informative explanatory text, and small artifacts – train timetables, toiletries, and toys from home. Descriptions of arrival and subsequent interviews are presented, as well as examples of questions asked and medical tests given. One of the dormitories, used by those kept overnight for further examination, has been left almost intact. On the top floor, you'll find evocative photographs of the building before it was restored, along with items rescued from the building and rooms devoted to the peak years of immigration.

Among the additional features of the museum are thirty-minute long re-enactments of immigrant experiences, based on oral histories from the museum's archives (April–Oct, usually around 7 times daily in the museum's theatre; $6; call ☎212/561-4500 for advance tickets). A short documentary film, *Island of Hope, Island of Tears*, is shown throughout the day; it also lasts thirty minutes, and is free. If you turn up early enough to get a place, you can get a free, 45-minute **ranger-guided tour** (every hr) of the museum (they can't be booked in advance).

The museum's **American Family Immigration History Center** (timings same as the museum; Ⓦwww.ellisisland.org) offers an interactive research database that contains information from ship manifests and passenger lists concerning over 22 million immigrants who passed through the entire Port of New York between 1892 and 1924. Outside, the names of over 600,000 immigrants who passed through the building over the years are engraved in copper; while the "Wall of Honor" (Ⓦwww.wallofhonor.com) is always accepting new submissions, it controversially requires families to pay $150 to be included on the list.

Governors Island

"Nowhere in New York is more pastoral," wrote travel writer Jan Morris of **Governors Island**, a 172-acre tract of land across from Brooklyn with unobstructed views of lower Manhattan and New York Harbor. Until the mid-1990s, this was the largest and most expensively run Coast Guard installation in the world, housing some 1600 service personnel and their families. Today the island is being developed into a leafy historical park, its village greens and colonial architecture reminiscent of a New England college campus, making a dramatic contrast with the skyscrapers across the water.

Some history

The Lenape people referred to the island as Pagganck ("Nut Island") after the island's abundant chestnut, hickory, and oak trees. When the Dutch arrived in 1624, they actually made camp here first, before cautiously occupying Manhattan. In a pattern that was becoming ominously familiar, the Dutch "purchased" what they called Noten Island from the Native Americans in 1637, only to lose it to the British in the 1660s. Set aside for the "benefit and accommodation of His Majesty's Governors," Governors Island formally received its current name in 1784. Between 1794 and 1966 the US Army occupied the island, and for the following thirty years it was the US Coast Guard's largest and most extensive installation.

In 2003, 22 acres were sold to the National Park Service as the **Governors Island National Monument** (Ⓣ212/825-3045, Ⓦwww.nps.gov/gois), while the remaining 150 acres was purchased by the Governors Island Preservation and Education Corporation (GIPEC), jointly owned by the state and city of New York (Ⓦwww.govisland.com). In December 2007, GIPEC selected a design team to further develop the island's public spaces and historic district, an incredibly ambitious project that will take several years to complete.

Visiting Governors Island

The only way to reach Governors Island is via **ferry** (free) from the Battery Maritime Building at Slip 7 just northeast of the Staten Island Ferry Terminal (see p.58). The island is expected to **open** from at least May 31 to October 5 in 2009 and 2010. You can visit, by way of free, two-hour **tours** on Wednesday or Thursday (ferries depart at 10am & 1pm). On Friday (ferries every hour 10am–3pm; last ferry back 5pm), and Saturday and Sunday (ferries every hour 10am–5pm; last ferry back 7pm) you can tour the island independently. Access to the ferries is on a first-come, first-served basis, and limited to 400 people per trip (the weekday tours are limited to 60 people). Call ahead or check the websites for the schedule. Entry to the island is **free**. Note that **food** options on the island comprise a couple of hot-dog stalls and vending machines – bring a picnic.

The island

A visit to Governors Island makes for an intriguingly offbeat and bucolic day trip, just minutes from Downtown Manhattan. Until the larger southern section starts to open in 2009, visits are confined to the Historic Landmark District at the northern end, which includes the portion managed by the National Park Service. Ferries arrive at Soissons Dock, where you'll find the small visitors' center (with maps and information about the Island) and a gift shop. From here it's a short stroll up to Fort Jay, completed in 1794. Reinforced in 1808, its dense stone walls, stacked with over 100 cannons, helped to deter the British from attacking the city in 1812. Nearby you can wander the shady lanes of Nolan Park, home to some beautifully preserved Neoclassical and Federal-style mansions (occupied by officers during the army period), notably the Governor's House and Admiral's Mansion, site of the Reagan-Gorbachev Summit in 1988. Other highlights include Colonels Row, another collection of historic housing, some of which dates from 1810, and Castle Williams, a circular fort completed in 1811 to complement the near-identical Castle Clinton in Battery Park (see p.58). Used as a prison until 1966, the tiny cells inside held as many as 1000 Confederate soldiers during the Civil War. The island also has plenty of green spaces in which to lounge in the sun, as well as a breezy promenade with stellar views of Manhattan. Free ranger-guided tours are offered every hour on open days.

The Financial District

With its incredible assemblage of skyscrapers, the **Financial District** in Lower Manhattan has long been synonymous with the New York of popular imagination. What the celebrated skyline doesn't show, though, is the area's layers of dense development – from the prime vantage point of the Brooklyn waterfront or a harbor ferry you would never know that buildings of all vintages, styles, and sizes are packed in along narrow, canyon-like streets. This is where New York began in the 1620s, and today the heart of the world's financial markets is still home to some of the city's most historic streets and sights, as well as some of its most modern corporate headquarters.

Over time, the area has seen more than its fair share of destruction and renewal. Many of the early colonial buildings that once lined these blocks burned down in either the Revolutionary War or the Great Fire of 1835. In September 2001, the character of the Financial District was altered radically once again when the attacks on the World Trade Center destroyed the Twin Towers and killed thousands (see box, p.55). Yet the regeneration of lower Manhattan is startling: work has begun not just on the new World Trade Center, but on a spate of ambitious projects from parks and office towers to transportation hubs and new hotels, and at times it can seem half of the district is smothered in scaffolding. Though numerous banks and businesses still maintain corporate headquarters here, the most dramatic change is in the increase of residential development, as new condos and luxury conversions (many from former bank buildings) prove that the Financial District is once again in the process of integrating its present and future into its past.

Begin your tour of the Financial District at Wall Street, accessible by the #2, #3, #4, and #5 trains. If you don't care for crowds and want to stroll here in relative peace, head to the narrow streets on the weekend, when the whole district is eerily vacant. The illuminating **Wall Street Walking Tour** (Thurs & Sat noon; free; ☎212/606-4064) begins on the steps of the Museum of the American Indian and takes around 90min, running year-round, rain or shine, apart from major public holidays.

Along Wall Street

It was the Dutch who provided **Wall Street** with its name when they built a wooden stockade at the edge of New Amsterdam in 1653, in an effort to protect themselves from the British colonies further north. The street has been associated with money for hundreds of years, and despite the onset of electronic

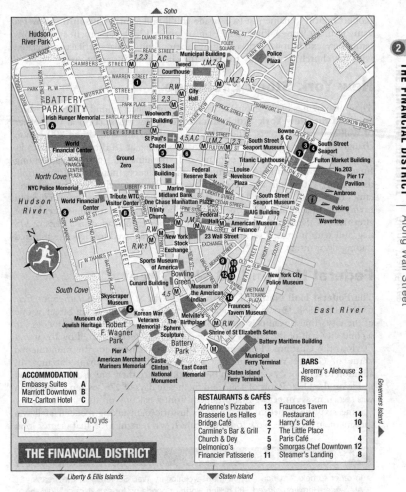

ACCOMMODATION

Embassy Suites	A
Marriott Downtown	B
Ritz-Carlton Hotel	C

0 — 400 yds

THE FINANCIAL DISTRICT

BARS

| Jeremy's Alehouse | 3 |
| Rise | C |

RESTAURANTS & CAFÉS

Adrienne's Pizzabar	13	Fraunces Tavern	
Brasserie Les Halles	6	Restaurant	14
Bridge Café	2	Harry's Café	10
Carmine's Bar & Grill	7	The Little Place	1
Church & Dey	5	Paris Café	4
Delmonico's	9	Smorgas Chef Downtown	12
Financier Patisserie	11	Steamer's Landing	8

▼ Liberty & Ellis Islands   ▼ Staten Island

trading, remains the apex of the global financial system. Though it can be hard
to appreciate from street level, Wall Street boasts some exceptional architecture
and many of the tallest buildings in the city.

Trinity Church

Perched at Wall Street's western end on Broadway is **Trinity Church** (Mon–
Fri 7am–6pm, Sat 8am–4pm, Sun 7am–4pm; free; ☏212/602-0800, ⓦwww
.trinitywallstreet.org), a stoic onlooker of the street's dealings. The church was
established in 1697, but this knobby neo-Gothic structure – the third model –
only went up in 1846. It was the city's tallest building for fifty years – a reminder
of just how relatively recently high-rise Manhattan has sprung up. Trinity has
the air of an English country church (hardly surprising, given its architect,
Richard Upjohn, was English), especially in the sheltered **graveyard**, the resting
place of many early Manhattanites: Alexander Hamilton and steamboat king

Robert Fulton to name just two. Inside you'll find a small **museum** (Mon–Fri 9am–5pm, Sat 9am–3.45pm, Sun 10am–11am & 12.30–3.45pm; free) that hosts temporary exhibitions with a religious theme, and displays artifacts associated with the church's past. Daily **tours** of the church (free) start at 2pm.

New York Stock Exchange

The purse strings of the capitalist world are controlled behind the Neoclassical facade of the **New York Stock Exchange** (Ⓦ www.nyse.com) at the corner of Wall and Broad streets, where 2.5 billion shares are traded and $90 billion changes hands on an average day. The main building at 18 Broad Street, with its six mammoth Corinthian columns and monumental statues representing Integrity surrounded by Agriculture, Mining, Science, Industry, and Invention, dates from 1903, and was designed by famed turn-of-the-century architect James B. Post. In 1922, the 11 Wall Street building, designed by Trowbridge and Livingston in a similar style, opened next door to expand trading space. In the aftermath of September 11 the main facade has been draped in a massive US flag, and with increased security, the public is not allowed to view the frenzied trading floor inside.

Federal Hall and 23 Wall Street

The **Federal Hall National Memorial**, 26 Wall St (Mon–Fri 9am–5pm; free; Ⓣ 212/825-6888, Ⓦ www.nps.gov/feha), on the corner of Nassau Street, is one of the city's finest examples of Greek Revival architecture. Built in 1699 as the second city hall of the colony of New York, it was reconstructed by Town and Davis as the Customs House in 1842 and is best known for the monumental statue of George Washington that stands guard over its main entrance. In addition to temporary exhibits on New York history, there are also small displays inside on the Draft Riots of 1863 and the heady days of 1789 when Washington was sworn in as America's first president from a balcony on this site.

Some sixty years before Washington's historic oath-taking, Federal Hall was the site of an ominous blow to British rule. It was here in 1735 that printer John

---

The early days of stocks and bonds

In order to help America finance the Revolutionary War, Secretary of the Treasury Alexander Hamilton offered $80 million worth of bonds up for sale. Not only did the public snap them up, but merchants also started trading the bonds, along with bills of exchange, promissory notes, and other commercial paper. Trading became so popular that in 1792 a group of 22 stockbrokers and merchants gathered beneath a buttonwood tree on Wall Street, signing the "Buttonwood Agreement" and forming the initial trading group that would go on to be renamed the **New York Stock Exchange** in 1817.

In the 1840s, a more individualistic group of stockbrokers forged a similar bond on the curbs of Broad Street. These "curb brokers," who specialized in risky stocks, were unable to meet the requirements of the New York Stock Exchange, but survived nonetheless, with phone clerks in the windows of buildings several stories above the street using hand signals to relay customers' orders. In 1921, the New York Curb Market moved indoors at 86 Trinity Place and in 1953 became the **American Stock Exchange** (Ⓦ www.amex.com). After remaining independent for more than 100 years, AMEX was acquired by the parent company of the New York Stock Exchange, NYSE Euronext, for $260 million in 2008.

The trial of John Peter Zenger

German immigrant **John Peter Zenger** (1697–1746) rapidly established a reputation as a printer and journalist for the *New York Weekly Journal*, which took an anti-British stance and published inflammatory writings in an age when British law maintained that truth was no defense in cases of libel. The *Journal*'s views made him unpopular with the royal authorities in New York, and in 1734 Zenger was arrested for articles considered libelous against the Crown, and spent eight months in prison. Philadelphia attorney **Andrew Hamilton** took Zenger's case *pro bono*, ensuring that his libel trial became a fight for freedom of the press. Urging the jury to find in Zenger's favor, the fiery Hamilton declaimed that "The laws of our country have given us a right: the liberty of both exposing and opposing arbitrary power by speaking and writing the truth." It took only minutes before the jury reached a verdict of not guilty. After he was acquitted, Zenger was appointed public printer of New York and New Jersey.

Peter Zenger was tried and acquitted of libel charges, thereby setting an important precedent for freedom of the press in America (see box above). The documents and models inside are worth a look, as is the hall itself, with its elegant rotunda, and Cretan maidens worked into the decorative railings. Ranger-led **tours** take place at 10am, noon, and 2pm.

Just across Wall Street at **no. 23** is the unassuming building that once lay at the heart of the global financial system. In 1912 financier **J.P. Morgan** had his marble-clad headquarters built here (though he died before its completion in 1914); the extravagant use of what was the most expensive real estate in the world at the time (the building is only four stories tall) epitomized the patrician aloofness of the period – the bank didn't even bother adding its name to the facade. J.P. Morgan had been based on this spot since 1873, taking his father's words to heart – "always be a bull on America" – and engineering a wave of massive corporate mergers, as well as famously managing the financial panic of 1907. In 1920, a horse-drawn cart blew up out front, killing 38 and wounding over a hundred (including Joseph P. Kennedy, JFK's father). The bombing has never been explained, though the most popular theory holds that the blast was planned by Italian anarchists taking revenge for the executions of Sacco and Vanzetti. The marks on the building's wall will have never been repaired, out of respect for the victims. In 2003 JP Morgan sold the building for $100 million, with part of the structure to be absorbed by the conversion of 15 Broad Street into luxury condos by Philippe Starck.

Museum of American Finance and around

Further along Wall Street, the former **Bank of Manhattan Trust building** at no. 40 was briefly the world's tallest building in 1930, before being topped by the Chrysler Building (whose designers secretly increased the height of their skyscraper after no. 40 was completed). Today it's known as the Trump Building after the flamboyant tycoon who bought it for just $8m in 1995 (it's worth at least $400m now). Across William Street, the former Bank of New York building at 48 Wall St houses the **Museum of American Finance** (Tues–Sat 10am–4pm; adults $8, students & seniors $5; ☎212/908-4110, ⓦwww .financialhistory.org). The fittingly grand former main banking hall holds the largest public archive of financial documents and artifacts in the world, featuring such objects as the bond signed by Washington bearing the first dollar sign ever used on a Federal document, and a stretch of ticker tape from the opening moments of 1929's Great Crash. Fortunately, this isn't just a self-congratulatory temple to big business; it also features genuinely educational exhibits, as well as giant screens showing videos of stock, bond, and futures trading. Financial pioneer **Alexander Hamilton** is commemorated with his own room, while documentaries on Wall Street are shown throughout the day.

One block south of Wall Street, *Delmonico's*, 56 Beaver St, at William Street, is technically the oldest restaurant in the country, although it's been closed for prolonged periods and has exchanged owners several times over the years. The original was built here in 1837, the Swiss-born Delmonico brothers, Giovanni and Pietro, opening their doors to much acclaim and instantly attracting the city's wealthiest denizens. At the time, eating options in New York were generally restricted to British-style taverns, and this was the first French-style restaurant; Charles Dickens, French exile Louis-Napoléon and generals Grant and Sherman all dined here. The building is a bastion of opulence, with its grand portico supported by columns brought from the ruins of Pompeii and a menu that features many of the restaurant's culinary inventions, including baked Alaska and the Delmonico steak (see p.308 for review). Just to the south, **Hanover Square** is home to the majestic **India House**, built in 1853 and now an exclusive club for august financial types, the more accessible *Harry's Café* (see p.308), and the **British Memorial Garden**, dedicated in 2008 as a gift to the US and memorial to the 67 British citizens killed on September 11. From here you can grab some food at historic Stone Street (see p.61) or return to Wall Street to continue your tour.

Federal Reserve Bank

Three blocks north of Wall Street lies the **Federal Reserve Bank**, where Liberty Street meets Nassau Street. Completed in 1924, there's good reason for the **building**'s iron-barred exterior: stashed 80ft below the somber neo-Gothic interior are most of the "free" world's gold reserves – 5000 tons of them, occasionally shifted from vault to vault as wars break out or international debts are settled. Free **tours** (1hr) of the stacks of gleaming gold bricks are given Monday to Friday (9.30am, 10.30am, 11.30am, 1.30pm, & 2.30pm), but you must reserve in advance. Contact the Public Information Department, Federal Reserve Bank, 33 Liberty St, NY 10045 (☎212/720-6130, ⓦwww.ny.frb.org), preferably one month ahead, as tickets have to be mailed. The tour includes visits to the gold vault, as well as coin and interactive exhibits. Upstairs, in the bank, dirty money and counterfeit currency are weeded out of circulation by automated checkers that shuffle dollar bills like endless packs of cards.

Ground Zero and around

The former location of the Twin Towers, **Ground Zero** remains a vast construction site, with hundreds of workers laboring away at the new **World Trade Center**. Seven buildings in total were destroyed as a result of the 2001 terrorist attacks, but today the area is booming, invigorated by the huge surge of investment as part of the regeneration of Lower Manhattan.

At 8.46am on September 11, 2001, a hijacked airliner slammed into the north tower of the **World Trade Center**; seventeen minutes later another hijacked plane struck the south tower. As thousands looked on in horror – in addition to hundreds of millions more viewing on TV – the south tower collapsed at 9.50am, its twin at 10.30am. All seven buildings of the World Trade Center complex eventually collapsed, and the center was reduced to a mountain of steel, concrete, and glass rubble. As black clouds billowed above, the whole area was covered in a blanket of concrete dust many inches thick; debris reached several hundred feet into the air. The devastation was staggering. While most of the 50,000 civilians working in the towers had been evacuated before the towers fell, many never made it out of the building; hundreds of firemen, policemen, and rescue workers who arrived on the scene when the planes struck were crushed when the buildings collapsed. In all, **2996 people perished** at the WTC and the simultaneous attack on the Pentagon in Washington DC, in what was, in terms of casualties, the largest foreign attack on American soil in history. Radical Muslim Osama bin Laden's terrorist network, al-Qaeda, claimed responsibility for the attacks.

Dominating Lower Manhattan's landscape from nearly any angle, the 110-story Twin Towers always loomed over their surroundings. The first tower went up in 1972 and the second one year later, and while becoming integral parts of the New York skyline, they also evolved into emblems of American power in the eyes of Islamic extremists.

In the days after the attack, downtown was basically shut down, and the seven-square-block area immediately around the WTC was the focus of an intense rescue effort. New Yorkers lined up to give blood and volunteered to help the rescue workers; vigils were held throughout the city, most notably in Union Square, which was peppered with candles and makeshift shrines. Then-Mayor **Rudy Giuliani** cut a highly composed and reassuring figure as New Yorkers struggled to come to terms with the assault on their city.

Moving forward

In 2003, Polish-born architect **Daniel Libeskind** was named the winner of a competition held to determine the overall design for the new World Trade Center, though his plans were initially plagued with controversy and he's had little subsequent involvement with the project. In 2006, a modified design, still incorporating Libeskind's original 1776ft-high **Tower of Freedom**, was finally accepted and construction is now well under way supervised by architect **David Childs**. The whole $12bn scheme, which also involves a Santiago Calatrava-designed transportation hub and four subsidiary towers conceived by Norman Foster, Richard Rogers, Fumihike Maki and the firm Kohn Pedersen Fox, should be complete by 2012. In addition, the project includes the **National September 11 Memorial and Museum**, designed by Michael Arad and Peter Walker. The memorial, *Reflecting Absence*, will comprise two voids representing the footprints of the original towers, surrounded by oak trees and rings of water falling into illuminated pools. The underground museum will use artifacts and exhibits to tell the story of September 11 and also the attack of 1993. Since the memorial will be on ground level, Libeskind's original plan called for the northeast corner of the site to remain open; dubbed the **Wedge of Light**, sunlight is supposed to flood onto the memorial around September 11 each year, though there is considerable doubt whether this will actually happen.

Many continue to make the pilgrimage to Ground Zero, though there's precious little to see. The best **viewing points** lie on the temporary covered walkways to the north (Vesey St) and south (Liberty St) of the site, though you also get a decent view from the World Financial Center on the west side. Work on the new site is slated for completion in 2012, but the **Freedom Tower** (see box, p.55) should start to emerge from street level by early 2009. To get oriented, visit the excellent **Tribute WTC Visitor Center** (Mon & Wed–Sat 10am–6pm, Tues noon–6pm, Sun noon–5pm; $10, children under 12 free; ☎212/393-9160, ⓦwww.tributewtc.org), 120 Liberty St (between Greenwich and Church sts), which also arranges daily walking **tours** of the site's perimeter (Mon–Fri 11am, 1pm, & 3pm, Sat & Sun noon, 1pm, 2pm, and 3pm; $10; ☎212/422-3520), and self-guided audio tours for the same price. The center houses five small galleries which commemorate the attacks of September 11, beginning with a model of the Twin Towers and a moving section about the day itself, embellished with video and taped accounts of real-life survivors. A handful of items found on the site – a pair of singed high-heel shoes, pieces of twisted metal – make heart-rending symbols of the tragedy. Note that you can also learn more about September 11 at St Paul's Chapel (see below) and the New York City Fire Museum (p.74), and can view the temporary memorial in Battery Park (p.58). Almost every firehouse in Manhattan holds a memorial to firefighters lost on that day; **Ladder Co 10, Engine Co 10** next to the Tribute Center is a good example.

St Paul's Chapel

Both the oldest church and the oldest building in continuous use in Manhattan, **St Paul's Chapel** (Mon–Sat 10am–6pm, Sun 9am–4pm; free; ☎212/233-4164, ⓦwww.saintpaulschapel.org), at Fulton Street and Broadway, dates from 1766, making it almost prehistoric by New York standards. The main attraction inside is **Unwavering Spirit**, a poignant exhibition on September 11. For eight months after the September 11 attacks, St Paul's Chapel served as a sanctuary for the rescue workers at Ground Zero, providing food, a place to nap, and spiritual support. The exhibit effectively chronicles the church's role in these recovery efforts, with a moving ensemble of photos, artifacts and testimonies from those involved. The church itself was based on London's St Martin-in-the-Fields, with a handsome interior of narrow Corinthian columns and ornate chandeliers, though even **George Washington's pew**, preserved shrine-like from 1789–1790 (when New York was the US capital), forms part of the September 11 exhibition (it served as a foot treatment chair for firefighters). Outside, the historic cemetery is worth a wander, sprinkled with colonial headstones and the recently added **Bell of Hope**, a gift from London; the bell is rung every September 11 but also March 11 and July 7 to commemorate terrorist attacks in Madrid (2004) and London (2005) respectively.

South along Broadway

Heading south on Broadway from St Paul's, you'll see the **US Steel Building** at 1 Liberty Plaza, between Liberty and Cortlandt streets, a black mass that has justly been called a "gloomy, cadaverous hulk." To make way for it, the famed Singer Building, one of the most delicate features of the Manhattan skyline, was demolished in 1968. Today the NASDAQ Stock Market has its corporate offices in the building, which looks out over **Zuccotti Park**, a pleasant gap between the skyscrapers containing Mark di Suvero's 70ft steel sculpture Joie de Vivre (1998).

Stroll beyond Trinity Church (p.51) and you'll reach the **Sports Museum of America** (Mon–Fri 9am–7pm, Sat & Sun 9am–9pm; adults $27; seniors and students $24, children 4–14 $20; ⓦ www.sportsmuseum.com), which opened in 2008 inside the former headquarters of John D. Rockefeller's Standard Oil Company at 26 Broadway (entrance on Beaver St). The museum showcases every major American sport through a combination of video, information boards, and rare memorabilia, primarily jerseys and equipment donated by star athletes, and as such is expected to prove one of the city's most popular attractions, despite the high entry fees. You'll need to be familiar with US sporting history – the 1980 "Miracle on Ice" for example – to get the most out of this; items include bricks from Ebbet's Field, Billie Jean King's tennis racket and the now infamous sports bra revealed by Brandi Chastain after scoring her Soccer World Cup goal in 1999. Overall, the nineteen interactive, multimedia galleries inside contain six hundred artifacts, 1100 photos, and twenty original films, including sections dedicated to the Heisman Trophy, great American Olympians like Jesse Owens, baseball, basketball, and Nascar racing.

In front of the museum on the street partition is a sculpture of a **Charging Bull** – not originally envisioned as a symbol of a "bull market" for Wall Street stocks, though that's how it is perceived by New Yorkers today. As the story goes, on December 15, 1989, Arturo Di Modica installed his sculpture in the middle of Broad Street. The city removed the sculpture the next day, but was forced to put it back when public support of the statue was surprisingly vocal.

Bowling Green

Broadway ends at the city's oldest public park, **Bowling Green**. The green is supposedly the location of the most famous real estate deal in history, when Peter Minuit, the newly arrived director general of the Dutch colony of New Amsterdam, in 1626 bought the whole island from the Native Americans for a bucket of trade goods worth sixty guilders (the figure of $24 was calculated in the 1840s). Though we don't know for sure who "sold" the island to Minuit (it was probably a northern branch of the Lenni Lenape), the other side of the story (and the part you never hear) was that the concept of owning land was utterly alien to Native Americans – they had merely agreed to support Dutch claims to *use* the land, as they did. Later, the park became the site of the city's meat market, but in 1733 it was transformed into an oval of turf used for lawn bowling by colonial Brits, on a lease of "one peppercorn per year." The encircling iron fence is an original from 1771, though the crowns that once topped the stakes were removed during the Revolutionary War, as was a statue of George III. The statue was melted into musket balls – little bits of the monarch that were then fired at his troops.

National Museum of the American Indian

The Bowling Green sees plenty of office folk picnicking in the shadow of Cass Gilbert's **US Customs House**, home of the **National Museum of the American Indian** (daily 10am–5pm, Thurs 10am–8pm; free; ☎212/514-3700, ⓦ www.americanindian.si.edu). This excellent collection of artifacts from almost every Native American tribe was largely assembled by one man, George Gustav Heye (1874–1957), who traveled through the Americas picking up such works for over fifty years. Only a small portion of the collection is actually on display here – the majority of it lives in a sister museum on the Mall in Washington DC. Items include intricate basketry and woodcarvings, feathered bonnets, and objects of ceremonial significance. A rather extraordinary facet of the museum is its repatriation policy, adopted in 1991, which mandates that it give back to Indian tribes, upon request, any human remains, funerary objects, and ceremonial and religious items it may have illegally acquired.

Built in 1907, the Customs House was intended to pay homage to the booming maritime market and is adorned with ornate statuary representing the major continents and world's great commercial centers. Ironically, it stands on what was once **Fort Amsterdam**, the site of the first formal European presence on the island, but now the only place in Manhattan dedicated to Native American culture.

Battery Park

Due west of the Customs House, lower Manhattan lets out its breath in **Battery Park**, a breezy, spruced-up space with tall trees, green grass, lots of flowers, and views overlooking the panorama of the Statue of Liberty, Ellis Island, and America's largest harbor. Various monuments and statues, honoring everyone from Jewish immigrants to Celtic settlers to the city's first wireless telegraph operators, adorn the park.

Before a landfill closed the gap, **Castle Clinton** (daily 8.30am–5pm), the 1811 fort on the west side of the park, was on an island, one of several forts positioned to defend New York Harbor with its battery of cannons. In 1823 it was ceded to the city, which leased it to a group that recreated it as the Castle Garden resort. For a time, it found new life as a prestigious concert venue before doing service (pre-Ellis Island) as the drop-off point for arriving immigrants; from 1855 to 1890 eight million immigrants passed through the walls. The squat castle is now the place to buy tickets for and board ferries to the Statue of Liberty and Ellis Island (see p.43). South of Castle Clinton stands the **East Coast Memorial**, a series of granite slabs inscribed with the names of all the American seamen who were killed in World War II. To the castle's north, perched 10ft out in the harbor, is the **American Merchant Mariners Memorial**, an eerie depiction

Crossing the harbor

The **Staten Island ferry** (☎718/727-2508, ⊛www.siferry.com) sails from a modern terminal on the east side of Battery Park, built directly above the South Ferry subway station (at the end of the #1 line – you must be in the first five cars of the train to disembark here). The #R or #W trains to Whitehall Street and the #4 and #5 to Bowling Green also let you off within easy walking distance. Weekday departures are scheduled every 15–20 minutes during rush hours (7–9am and 5–7pm), every half-hour through the rest of the day and evenings, and every 60 minutes late at night (the ferry runs 24hrs). On weekends, boats run every half-hour from Manhattan, but slightly less frequently on the return trip.

The 25-minute ride is truly New York's best bargain: it's absolutely free, with wide-angle views of the city and the Statue of Liberty becoming more spectacular as you retreat. You also pass very close to Governors Island (near Manhattan, east of the boat) and the 1883 Robbins Reef Lighthouse (closer to Staten Island, off to the west). By the time you arrive on **Staten Island** (see p.266), the Manhattan skyline stands mirage-like: the city of a thousand and one posters, its skyscrapers almost bristling straight out of the water.

of a marine futilely reaching for the hand of a man sinking underneath the waves. At the bottom of Broadway, the park entrance holds the city's first official memorial to the victims of **September 11**; its focal point is the cracked fifteen-foot steel-and-bronze sculpture *The Sphere* – designed by Fritz Koenig to represent world peace. The sculpture once stood in the WTC Plaza and survived the collapse of the towers, the only artwork on the premises not to be destroyed in the attack.

The Skyscraper Museum and the Museum of Jewish Heritage

Incorporated into the ground floor at the back of the *Ritz-Carlton Hotel*, 39 Battery Place facing Battery Park, is the **Skyscraper Museum** (Wed–Sun noon–6pm; adults $5, students & seniors $2.50; ☏212/968-1961, ⓦwww .skyscraper.org). The core display area is usually taken up with temporary exhibits, but always with a New York skyscraper focus. Smaller exhibits are dedicated to the history of building technology, from the steel cages of the 1880s to the concrete and composite giants of the twenty-first century. You'll also find sections on Burj Dubai (easily the world's tallest building), the new World Trade Center, and the Sears Tower in Chicago.

Just opposite at 36 Battery Place, the **Museum of Jewish Heritage** (Sun–Tues & Thurs 10am–5.45pm, Wed 10am–8pm, Fri 10am–5pm; closed Jewish holidays; $10, seniors $7, students $5, children free; ☏646/437-4200, ⓦwww .mjhnyc.org) was designed in 1997 by Kevin Roche as a memorial to the Holocaust; its six sides represent both the six million dead and the Star of David. The moving and informative collection, which covers three floors of exhibits, begins with practical accouterments of everyday Eastern European Jewish life, before moving on to the horrors of the Holocaust and ending, more optimistically, with the establishment of Israel and subsequent Jewish achievements. Some of the more notable items include Himmler's personal annotated copy of *Mein Kampf* and a notebook filled by the inhabitants of the "barrack for prominent people" (slightly more comfortable quarters for famous or influential members of the Jewish community) in the Terezín Ghetto. Admission is free on Wednesday 4–8pm.

Battery Park City and the Irish Hunger Memorial

The hole dug for the foundations of the former World Trade Center threw up a million cubic yards of earth and rock, which was then dumped into the Hudson River to the west to form the 23-acre base of **Battery Park City**. This self-sufficient island of office blocks, apartments, chain boutiques, and landscaped esplanade feels a far cry from the rest of Manhattan indeed.

Battery Park City's southern end is anchored by **Robert F. Wagner Jr Park**. Zen-like in its peacefulness, the park is a refuge from the ferry crowds – you can follow the **Esplanade** up the Hudson from here as far as Chelsea. The center-piece of the Battery Park development is the **World Financial Center** (☏212/945-2600, ⓦwww.worldfinancialcenter.com), a rather grand and imposing fourteen-acre business, shopping, and dining complex that looks down onto Ground Zero from just across West Street. At its center is the **Winter Garden**, a huge, glass-ceilinged public plaza that brings light and life into a mall full of shops and restaurants. Decorated by sixteen palm trees – forty-foot

Washingtonia palms from Florida – the plaza is a veritable oasis. Just north of the World Financial Center, facing the Hudson at the end of Vesey Street, the **Irish Hunger Memorial** is a sobering monument to the more than one million Irish that starved to death during the Great Famine of 1845–1852. The tragedy sparked a flood of Irish immigration to the US, mostly through New York. An authentic famine-era stone cottage, one of many abandoned in the west of Ireland, was transported from County Mayo by artist Brian Tolle and set on a raised embankment overlooking the water. The passageway underneath echoes with haunting Irish folk songs, and you can follow the meandering path through the grassy garden and stones 25ft to the top.

State Street

State Street curves along Battery Park's east side. A rounded, dark, red-brick Georgian facade identifies the **Shrine of St Elizabeth Ann Seton**, 7 State St (daily 7am–5pm; ☎212/269-6865, ⓦ www.setonshrine.com), honoring the first native-born American to be canonized. The shrine is part of a working Catholic chapel, the Church of Our Lady of Rosary, with a small room at the front containing a statue of the saint and rather pious illustrations of her life. Before moving to Maryland to found a religious community, St Elizabeth lived here briefly (1801–03) in a small house adjacent to the church, one of a few old buildings in the area that has survived the modern onslaught. Seton was canonized in 1975, principally in recognition of her work establishing charities and schools for poor women and children.

Cut through the buildings to Pearl Street from here and you'll see the small memorial marking the site of **Herman Melville's birthplace**. The author of *Moby Dick* was born in a small townhouse on this spot in 1819, now long gone.

Water and Pearl streets

For a perspective of Manhattan's eighteenth-century heart, check out the **Fraunces Tavern Museum**, 54 Pearl St at Broad St (Tues–Sat noon–5pm; $4, children under 18 and seniors $3; ☎212/425-1778, ⓦ www.frauncestavern museum.org), which escaped the 1835 fire. The ochre-and-red-brick Fraunces Tavern claims to be a colonial inn (the restaurant inside is a great place for lunch, see p.308), although in truth it is more of an expert fake. Having survived extensive modifications, several fires, and a brief stint as a hotel in the nineteenth century, the three-story Georgian house was almost totally reconstructed by the Sons of the Revolution in the early part of the twentieth century to mimic how it appeared on December 4, 1783 – complete with period interiors and furnishings. It was then, after the British had been conclusively beaten, that a weeping George Washington took leave of his assembled officers, intent on returning to rural life in Virginia: "I am not only retiring from all public employments," he wrote, "but am retiring within myself." With hindsight, it was a hasty statement – six years later he was to return as the new nation's president. The Long Room where the speech was made has been faithfully decked out in the style of the time, and the tavern's second floor contains a mix of permanent and temporary exhibits tracing the site's history. The museum's expansive collection of Revolutionary War artifacts includes over two hundred flags, and a lock of Washington's hair, preserved like a holy relic.

Around the corner at 85 Broad St are a few more remnants of colonial New York. This was the site of the city's first tavern, transformed into City Hall in 1653 when New Amsterdam was officially incorporated – the city government still dates its foundation from this year. Nothing remains from that period, but archeologists have uncovered the foundations of **Governor Lovelace's Tavern**, a British pub dating from the 1670s, preserved under glass panels just off the street. At Coenties Slip you can turn left to reach historic **Stone Street**, a narrow lane of post-1835 rowhouses packed with restaurants (see p.308), or turn right to **Vietnam Veterans Plaza** facing the river. The **Vietnam Veterans Memorial**, dedicated in 2001, is an unattractive assembly of glass blocks etched with troops' letters home. The mementos are sad and often haunting, but the place is a peaceful spot for contemplation.

Walk up South Street to Old Slip, where you'll find the small but ornate building that once housed the **First Precinct Police Station**, now home to the **New York City Police Museum** (Mon–Sat 10am–5pm; adults $7, students and seniors $5; ☏212/480-3100, ⊛www.nycpolicemuseum.org). Very simply, it showcases the history of New York's Finest by displaying the tools of their trade: night sticks, guns, uniforms, photos, and the like – over 10,000 items in all. There's a copper badge from 1845 of the kind worn by the sergeants of the day, earning them the nickname of "coppers," and a pristine-looking Tommy gun – in its original gangster-issue violin case – that was used to rub out Al Capone's gang leader, Frankie Yale. A special multimedia exhibit commemorates the NYPD's role in September 11.

South Street Seaport

The **South Street Seaport**, located on the east side of Manhattan's southern tip between the Battery and Fulton Street, dates back to the 1600s and was the center of New York City's port district from 1815 to 1860, favored by sea captains for providing shelter from the westerly winds and the ice that floated down the Hudson River during the winter. **Robert Fulton** started a ferry service from here to Brooklyn in 1814, leaving his name for the street and then its market, New York's largest – the fish market finally closed in 2006. When FDR Drive was constructed in the 1950s, the Seaport's decline was rapid, but beginning in 1966, a private initiative rescued the remaining warehouses and saved the historical seaport just in time. Today, the Seaport is a mix of attractively restored buildings and ships with fairly standard main-street stores and cafés: a fair slice of commercial gentrification was necessary to woo developers and tourists.

The Seaport Museum and Paris Café

Housed in a series of painstakingly restored 1830s warehouses, the **South Street Seaport Museum**, 12 Fulton St (April–Oct Tues–Sun 10am–6pm, Nov–March Fri–Sun 10am–5pm all galleries; Mon 10am–5pm Schermerhorn Row Galleries only; $10; seniors and students $8; $5 children 5–12;

▲ South Street Seaport

☎212/748-8600, ⊛www.southstseaport.org), offers a spread of refitted ships and chubby tugboats (the largest collection of sailing vessels – by tonnage – in the US), plus a handful of revolving maritime art and trades exhibits, a museum store, and info about the now-gone Fulton Fish Market. The main gallery on Fulton Street is housed in **Schermerhorn Row**, a unique ensemble of Georgian Federal-style early warehouses dating to about 1811, but your ticket also includes a look around the *Ambrose* (a 1908 lightship) and *Peking* (a huge 1911 barque), moored at nearby Pier 16. The *Wavertree*, a graceful tall ship built in 1885, is still being restored. The second gallery is around the corner at 209 Water St, next door to **Bowne & Co., Stationers** (Wed–Sun 10am–5pm; ☎212/748-8651), a gas-lit nineteenth-century shop producing wonderfully authentic letterpress printing.

The museum also offers daytime, sunset, and night-time cruises around New York Harbor on the *Pioneer*, an 1885 schooner that accommodates up to forty people (May–Sept; $25, students and seniors $20, children under 12 $15; reservations on ☎212/748-8786). Cruises normally last two hours and depart on both weekdays (3–5pm, 7–9pm & 9.30–11.30pm) and weekends (1–3pm, 4–6pm, 7–9pm & 9.30–11.30pm), though you'll pay an extra $10 at peak times (4–6pm & 7–9pm). Call in advance for the latest information. More leisurely excursions up the Hudson are available on the 1893 fishing schooner *Lettie G. Howard* (☎212/748-8757; $100 day-trips, $500 for the weekend) and the tug *W.O. Decker*, which coasts around the harbor (☎212/748-8786; $100); check the website for the schedule.

Paris Café, at 119 South St, located in *Meyer's Hotel* at the end of Peck Slip, played host to a panoply of luminaries in the late nineteenth and early twentieth centuries. Thomas Edison used the café as a second office while designing the first electric power station in the world on Pearl Street; the opening of the Brooklyn Bridge was celebrated on the roof with Annie Oakley and Buffalo Bill Cody as guests; Teddy Roosevelt broke bread here; and journalist John Reed and other members of the Communist Labor Party of America met secretly here in the early 1920s. These days, even without presidents or communists, the elegant square bar, tempting seafood specials, and outdoor seating still pull in a lively crowd (see p.308), despite the location being marred somewhat by the FDR overpass.

Pier 17 and the rest of the Seaport

As far as tourism is concerned, **Pier 17** is the focal point of the district, created from the old fish-market pier that was demolished and then restored in 1982. A three-story glass-and-steel pavilion houses all kinds of restaurants and shops; a bit more interesting is the outdoor promenade, where you'll find the museum ships and booths selling cruise and water-taxi tickets. Circle Line Downtown (℡1-866/925-4631, Ⓦwww.circlelinedowntown.com) runs harbor cruises March to December on *Zephyr* (1hr; adults $25, seniors $23, children $15), and speedboat rides on the *Shark* May to September (30min; adults $21, seniors $19, children $15). The views of the Brooklyn and Manhattan bridges from the promenade are fantastic (and free) at any time of year.

Just across South Street, there's an assemblage of up-market chain shops like Ann Taylor, Abercrombie & Fitch, and the Body Shop that line Fulton and Front streets, as well as the official Yankees baseball team store and Met Museum gift shop. Keep your eyes peeled for some unusual buildings preserved here, like **203 Front St**; this giant J. Crew store was an 1880s hotel that catered to unmarried laborers on the dock. Opposite, the old Fulton Market Building contains the ever-popular **Bodies** exhibition (daily 9am–10pm adult $26.50, seniors $22.50, children 4–12 $20.50; ℡1-888/926-3437), with its presentation of 20 real human bodies and 260 organs, polymer-preserved in fascinating but slightly disturbing detail. Opening in 2005, the exhibition has been extended indefinitely, though a 2007 *New York Times* article claimed that such displays have created "a ghastly new underground mini-industry" in China, the origin of the preserved cadavers.

City Hall Park and the Brooklyn Bridge

Since New York's earliest days as an English-run city, **City Hall Park** has been the seat of its municipal government. Though many of the original civic buildings are no longer standing, you can still find some fine architecture here: within the park's borders is stately **City Hall**, with **Tweed Courthouse** just to the north; the towers of **Park Row** and the **Woolworth Building** stand nearby; the **Municipal Building** watches over Police Plaza and the city's courthouses; and the **Brooklyn Bridge**, a magnificent feat of engineering, soars over the East River. In stark contrast, the **African Burial Ground National Monument** is a poignant and powerful reminder of the city's early African population. Coming to the park by subway, take the #2 or #3 trains to Park Place; the #4, #5, or #6 trains to Brooklyn Bridge–City Hall; or the #R or #W trains to City Hall.

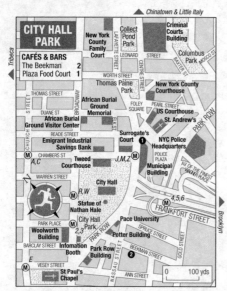

City Hall Park

First landscaped in 1730, **City Hall Park** is bounded by Chambers Street to the north and the intersection of Broadway and Park Row to the south. Facing City Hall is a bronze statue of the shackled figure of **Nathan Hale**, who was captured in 1776 by the British and hanged for spying, but not before he'd spat out his famous last words: "I only regret that I have but one life to lose for my country."

City Hall

Towards the northern end of the park sits **City Hall**, which was completed in 1812 and is the oldest in the US to maintain its original government function. The **mayor's office** and the chambers of the New York City Council are inside, while official receptions and press conferences are also held here. Its front and sides are gleaming white marble, but the back of the building, which faces north, is dull red sandstone – allegedly because the architects couldn't imagine anyone peering around behind the structure, which was built when this area was at the farthest north fringe of the city. The building's first moment of fame came in 1865 when Abraham Lincoln's body lay in state here for 120,000 sorrowful New Yorkers to file past. In 1927, the city feted aviator Charles Lindbergh, lately returned from Paris, and the building became the traditional finishing point for tickertape parades down Broadway, over time honoring everyone from astronauts to returned hostages to championship-winning teams. An elegant meeting of arrogance and authority, the building, with its sweeping interior spiral staircase and fine collections of nineteenth-century American art and furnishings, has unfortunately been closed to individual visitors since the July 2003 shooting of City Councilman James E. Davis here by a political rival. Increased security means the building is fenced off from the rest of the park, and the only way you can see the attractive interior is to arrange a **free guided tour** offered by the Art Commission, well worth your time (Mon–Fri; ☏ 212/788-2656, ⓦ www.nyc.gov/html/artcom). You must call and reserve tours in advance. Alternatively, you can sign up for a public tour (Wed noon; max 20 people) at the **NYC Heritage Tourism Center** (Mon–Fri 9am–6pm, Sat & Sun 10am–5pm) opposite the Woolworth Building, a small booth with local maps and brochures.

Park Row and the Woolworth Building

The southern tip of City Hall Park is flanked on either side by impressive early twentieth-century skyscrapers. **Park Row**, the eastern edge of the park, was once known as "Newspaper Row," and the intersection with Spruce and Nassau streets was Printing House Square. From the 1830s to the 1920s, the city's most influential publishers, news services, trade publications, and foreign-language presses all had their offices on this street or surrounding blocks. The *New York Times* operated from no. 41, a Romanesque structure that grew from five stories to sixteen to accommodate the booming paper until it relocated uptown in 1904 (Pace University moved here in 1952). The wildly ornamented Potter Building at no. 38 dates from 1886, when it was a pioneer in fireproofing, thanks to its ironclad lower floors and durable terracotta trim. Today, as with much of downtown, it's being converted into high-end apartments (with a *Starbucks* on the first floor).

The **Park Row Building**, at no. 15, was completed in 1899; at 391 feet, it was the tallest in the world. Behind the elaborate limestone-and-brick facade were the offices of the Associated Press as well as the headquarters of the IRT subway (investor and gambler August Belmont financed both this tower and the transit system). The Park Row Building towered over its surroundings until 1908, when the Singer Building, at 165 Broadway (now demolished), surpassed it.

By 1913, the tallest building was on the opposite side of City Hall Park: the **Woolworth Building**, at 233 Broadway, held the title until the Chrysler Building topped it in 1929. Cass Gilbert's "Cathedral of Commerce" oozes money and prestige. The soaring, graceful lines are covered in white terracotta tiles and fringed with Gothic-style gargoyles and decorations that are more whimsical than portentous. Frank Woolworth made his fortune from his "five and dime" stores – everything cost either 5¢ or 10¢, strictly no credit. True to his philosophy, he paid cash for the construction of his skyscraper, and reliefs at each corner of the lobby show him doing just that: counting out the money in nickels and dimes. Unfortunately, the lobby is closed to sightseers, but if you feel like risking the wrath of the security guards, do walk in the front doors to bask in the honey-gold glow of the mosaics that cover the vaulted ceilings (and the gaze of Teddy Roosevelt, complete with monocle, staring down from the left). Look quickly – you'll probably only have a few seconds before you get shooed back outside.

Tweed Courthouse

If City Hall is the acceptable face of New York's municipal bureaucracy, the genteel Victorian-style **Tweed Courthouse**, just to the north with its entrance at 52 Chambers St, is a reminder of the city government's infamous corruption in the nineteenth century. The man behind the gray-marble county courthouse, William Marcy "Boss" Tweed, worked his way up from nowhere to become chairman of the Democratic Central Committee at Tammany Hall (see p.119) in 1856. Tweed manipulated the city's revenues into his pockets and the pockets of his supporters, for a while strangling all dissent (even over the courthouse's budget, which rolled up from $3 million to $12 million during its construction between 1861 and 1881), until political cartoonist Thomas Nast and the editor of the *New York Times* (who'd refused a $500,000 bribe to keep quiet) turned public opinion against him in the late 1860s. Fittingly, Tweed was finally tried in an unfinished courtroom in his own building in 1873, and died in 1878 in Ludlow Street Jail – a prison he'd had built while he was Commissioner of Public Works.

Tweed's monument to greed, which now houses the Department of Education, looks more like a mansion than a municipal building: its long windows and sparse ornamentation are, ironically, far less ostentatious than those of many of its peers. Its interior, however, is flashier, with a grand octagonal rotunda soaring upward in a series of red-and-white arches. Extensive renovations removed eighteen layers of paint and unearthed architectural details long hidden; in the process, the building was simultaneously returned to its former glory and stripped of its unsavory reputation. To see the inside, contact the Art Commission (Mon–Fri; ☎212/788-2656, ⓦwww.nyc.gov/html /artcom) and arrange a **free guided tour** in advance.

The Municipal Building and around

At the east end of Chambers Street, across Centre Street, stands the 25-story **Municipal Building**, looking like an oversized chest of drawers. Built between 1908 and 1913, it was the first skyscraper constructed by the well-known architectural firm McKim, Mead, and White, although it was actually designed by one of the firm's younger partners, William Mitchell Kendall. At its top, an extravagant "wedding cake" tower of columns and pinnacles, including the frivolous eighteen-foot gilt sculpture *Civic Fame*, attempts to dress up the no-nonsense home of public records and much of the city government's offices (it's also the destination for civil wedding ceremonies). The shields decorating the molding above the colonnade represent the various phases of New York as colony, city, and state: the triple-X insignia is the Amsterdam city seal, and the combination of windmill, beavers, and flour barrels represents New Amsterdam and its first trading products, images used on the city seal today.

Walk north and you'll pass the neo-Georgian Catholic Church of **St Andrew's** (rebuilt in 1938), dwarfed by the surrounding structures, and the side of the grandiose **United States Courthouse**, now dedicated to Thurgood Marshall and used as a court of appeals. Designed by Cass Gilbert and completed in 1933, the building is undergoing a massive restoration that should be complete by the end of 2010. Its columned facade looks onto **Foley Square**, named for the sheriff and saloonkeeper Thomas "Big Tom" Foley, one of the few admirable figures in the Tammany Hall era. The focal point of the wide concrete plaza is Lorenzo Pace's 300-ton black granite sculpture, *The Triumph of*

▲ Municipal Building

The Notorious Five Points

East of Foley Square is the area once known as **Five Points**, named for the intersection of Mulberry, Worth, Park, Baxter, and Little Water streets, the last of which no longer exists. A former pond known as the Collect, it was filled in as part of a public-works project around 1812, but the fetid, damp location soon became a massive slum as a relentless influx of immigrants, sailors, and criminals sought refuge here, and toxic industries were shunted to this unlovely side of town. In 1829 the local press started using the Five Points moniker, and by 1855, when immigrants formed 72 percent of the population, its muddy streets – called Bone Alley, Ragpickers' Row, and other similarly inviting names – were lined with flimsy tenements. Diseases like cholera skipped easily from room to overcrowded room.

The neighborhood was further marred by vicious pitched battles among the district's numerous Irish gangs, including the Roach Guards, the Plug Uglies, and the Dead Rabbits (depicted with flair in Martin Scorsese's *The Gangs of New York*). After the Civil War, when the area's Irish majority gave way to the new waves of Italian and Chinese immigrants, the gangs consolidated to form the Five Pointers. The group acted as a strong arm for Tammany Hall, effectively training the top names of organized crime, including Al Capone.

Upper-class sightseers like Charles Dickens (who came here in 1842), both fascinated and repelled by Five Points, invented the concept of "slumming" in their tours of the neighborhood. They made lurid note of the crime, filth, and other markers of obvious moral depravity, but most New Yorkers were not gravely concerned until 1890, when police reporter and photographer Jacob A. Riis published *How the Other Half Lives*, a report on the city's slums. In particular, his gripping images, which retained his subjects' dignity while graphically showing the squalor all around them, helped convince readers that these people were not poor simply due to moral laxity. The book was remarkably successful in its mission to evoke sympathy for the plight of this troubled community, and it's in large part thanks to Riis that Five Points has been relegated to colorful history, replaced by a park and a towering courthouse.

the Human Spirit, a tribute to the many thousands of enslaved Africans who died on American soil – particularly those whose bodies were discovered in the African burial ground just off the west side of the square (see below). The grassy section at the northern end of the square was dubbed **Thomas Paine Park** in 1977, after the influential thinker and writer (see p.109), while the northeast edge is dominated by the **New York County Courthouse**, one of the state's supreme courts. A massive hexagonal building built in 1927, it merits a quick peek into the lobby to see its rotunda, decorated with storybook murals illustrating the history of justice. The 1950s courtroom drama *Twelve Angry Men* was filmed here.

African Burial Ground National Monument

In 1991, construction of a federal office building at 290 Broadway uncovered one of the most important US archeological finds of the twentieth century, the remains of 419 skeletons in what was once a vast African burial ground. Today, the **African Burial Ground National Monument** (daily 9am–5pm; free; Ⓦ www.africanburialground.gov) on Duane Street occupies a tiny portion of a cemetery that covered five blocks (between Broadway and Lafayette, and down to Chambers) during the 1700s. Then outside the city boundary, this was the only place Africans could be buried. After being examined at Howard University, the skeletons, along with artifacts (such as beads) buried with them, were re-interred at this site in 2003, marked by seven grassy mounds and a highly polished black granite monument. The soaring Ancestral Chamber in the center is a symbolic counterpoint to the infamous "gate of no return" on Gorée Island in Senegal, through which slaves would leave Africa for the New World. Instead of captivity and departure, this gateway represents spiritual freedom and return, facing east towards Africa. The spiral path into the Ancestral Libation Court, four feet below street level, is engraved with signs and symbols of the African Diaspora, inspired by the discovery of one symbol, the *sankofa*, on the coffin of a former slave – heart-rending evidence that despite their situation, slaves maintained spiritual links with their homeland (the *sankofa* symbolized "returning to your roots"). The court itself is where the skeletons were originally found, and commemorates the ritual of libation, a traditional African ceremony which affirms the link between past, present, and future generations. Despite its relatively small size, the curving walls and mystical symbols create a meditative, temple-like atmosphere, in utter contrast to its skyscraper-bound surroundings.

To learn more about the burial ground, walk around the corner to 290 Broadway and the small **visitor center** inside (Mon–Fri 9am–5pm; free; ℡212/637-2019), which spills out into the lobby (you'll have to go through security to enter the building). Videos (played on demand), panels, displays, and replicas of the artifacts found here are used to recount the history of the site, where experts believe as many as 20,000 free and enslaved blacks were buried, and shed light on the often brutal life of the city's black population – examination of the bones revealed a cycle of back-breaking toil that began in childhood. One of the reasons the site is considered so significant is that even today, slavery (and the cruelty that went with it) is something most Americans associate with the Deep South. In reality, New York had the second largest enslaved population outside of South Carolina in 1776, and slave labor built much of the colonial city. Maya Angelou alluded to this misconception at the emotional re-interment ceremony: "You may bury me in the bottom of Manhattan. I will rise. My people will get me. I will rise out of the huts of history's shame". Slavery was abolished in New York State in 1827.

From here, if you retrace your steps to Foley Square and down Centre Street, you can catch the footpath that runs over the Brooklyn Bridge.

The Brooklyn Bridge

One of several spans across the East River, today the **Brooklyn Bridge** is dwarfed by lower Manhattan's skyscrapers, but in its day, the bridge was a technological quantum leap, its elegant gateways towering over the brick structures around it. For twenty years after its opening in 1883, it was the world's largest and longest suspension bridge, the first to use steel cables, and – for many more years – the longest single-span structure. To New Yorkers, it was an object of awe, the concrete symbol of the Great American Dream. Italian immigrant painter Joseph Stella called it "a shrine containing all the efforts of the new civilization of America." Indeed, the bridge's meeting of art and function, of romantic Gothic and daring practicality, became a sort of spiritual model for the next generation's skyscrapers. On a practical level, it expanded the scope of New York City, paving the way for the incorporation of the outer boroughs and the creation of a true metropolis.

The bridge didn't go up without difficulties. Early in the project, in 1869, architect and engineer John Augustus Roebling crushed his foot taking measurements for the piers and died of tetanus less than three weeks later. His son Washington took over, only to be crippled by the bends after working in an insecure underwater caisson; he subsequently directed the work from his sickbed overlooking the site. Some twenty workers died during the construction, and a week after the opening day, twelve people were crushed to death in a panicked rush on the bridge's footpath. Despite this tragic toll (as well as innumerable suicides over the years), New Yorkers still look to the bridge with affection, celebrating its milestone anniversaries with parades and respecting it as a civic symbol on a par with the Empire State Building.

The **view** from below (especially on the Brooklyn side) as well as the top is undeniably spectacular. You can **walk across** its wooden planks from Centre Street, but resist the urge to look back till you're at the midpoint, when the Financial District's giants stand shoulder to shoulder behind the spidery latticework of the cables. You can follow the pedestrian path straight to its end, at the corner of Adams and Tillary streets in **Downtown Brooklyn** (see p.220), behind the main post office. More convenient for sightseeing, however, is to exit the bridge at the first set of stairs: walk down and bear right to follow the path through the park at Cadman Plaza. If you cross onto Middagh Street, you'll be in the core of **Brooklyn Heights** (see p.223); or follow Cadman Plaza West down the hill to Old Fulton Street and the **Fulton Ferry District** (see p.220).

If you're not up to walking over the bridge (though it really is the most interesting way), a taxi from the City Hall area to Brooklyn Heights will be about $6–7.

Tribeca and Soho

T he adjoining neighborhoods of **Tribeca** and **Soho** encompass the area from Ground Zero north to Houston Street (pronounced HOW-ston) and east from the Hudson River to Broadway. Acting as a sort of segue between the businesslike formality of the Financial District and the relaxed artiness of the West Village, the district is home to wealthy New Yorkers with a taste for retro-industrial cool and the stores that cater to them. Nineteenth-century warehouses have been converted into vast lofts overlooking cobblestone streets, and the area's cast-iron buildings (and their enormous ground-floor windows) make it a perfect spot for purveyors of fine art, antiques, and luxury goods.

The art scenes that flourished here in the 1970s and 1980s have, for the most part, moved on to Chelsea and the outer boroughs, but there are still plenty of reasons to visit the area. Tribeca feels more residential, its sidewalks populated by stylish moms and their hip tots, as well as the occasional celebrity. Soho is also the haunt of young and fashionable Hollywood types, with rents that have now eclipsed the West Village, though the focus here is on dining and especially shopping.

Tribeca

Tribeca (try-BECK-a), the Triangle below Canal Street, is a former wholesale-food district that has become an enclave of urban style; its old industrial buildings house the spacious loft apartments of the area's gentry. Most who trek to Tribeca do so for its **restaurants**, the best of which can be found along Hudson and Greenwich streets (see "Restaurants," p.309). Less a triangle than a crumpled rectangle, the neighborhood is bounded by Canal and Murray streets to the north and south, and Broadway and the Hudson River to the east and west. It is accessible via the #1 train to Canal Street (for the north edge), Franklin Street (center), and Chambers Street (south side; the #2 and #3 also stop here).

Some history

The name "Tribeca" is a semiotic construct, a mid-1970s invention of entrepreneurial real-estate brokers who thought the name better suited to the neighborhood's increasing trendiness than its former moniker, **Washington Market**. The namesake market was a massive hall near the river, south of Chambers Street. In 1968, the market building was torn down as part of the scheme for the World Trade Center – though by that time many of the wholesalers had already moved out of the area's cramped streets to the modern Hunts Point complex in the Bronx.

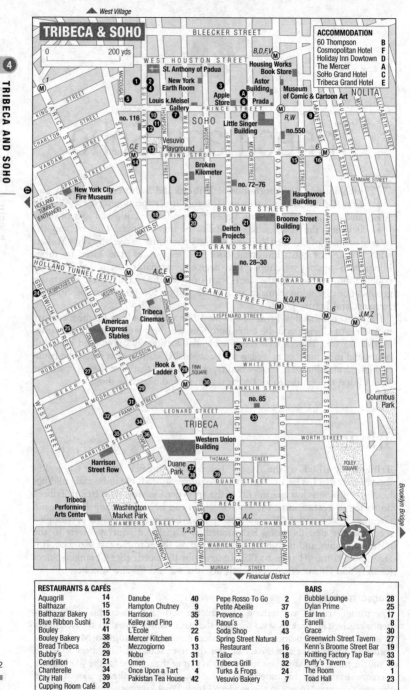

TRIBECA & SOHO

West Village ▲

BLEECKER STREET

0   200 yds

WEST HOUSTON STREET

St. Anthony of Padua

New York Earth Room

Louis k.Meisel Gallery

no. 116

Housing Works Book Store

Apple Store

Astor Building

Prada

Museum of Comic & Cartoon Art

NOLITA

SOHO

Little Singer Building

no.550

R,W

Vesuvio Playground

SPRING STREET

Broken Kilometer

no. 72–76

Haughwout Building

New York City Fire Museum

HOLLAND TUNNEL (ENTRANCE)

BROOME STREET

Broome Street Building

Deitch Projects

WATTS ST

GRAND STREET

no. 28–30

HOLLAND TUNNEL (EXIT)

HOWARD STREET

CANAL STREET

N,Q,R,W

Tribeca Cinemas

LISPENARD STREET

American Express Stables

WALKER STREET

J,M,Z

WHITE STREET

Hook & Ladder 8

FINN SQUARE

FRANKLIN STREET

Columbus Park

no. 85

LEONARD STREET

TRIBECA

Western Union Building

WORTH STREET

Harrison Street Row

THOMAS STREET

FOLEY SQUARE

Duane Park

DUANE STREET

Tribeca Performing Arts Center

Washington Market Park

READE STREET

Brooklyn Bridge ▶

CHAMBERS STREET

CHAMBERS STREET

1,2,3

WARREN STREET

MURRAY STREET

▼ Financial District

Meanwhile, the blocks around Broadway were the headquarters of the country's largest **textile industry**. Like the food wholesalers, the cloth dealers also slowly dispersed in the 1960s, when many of their workshops on Worth Street were razed. A few smaller fabric stores are the only trace of the industry today.

The area was a ghost town for more than a decade, until artists such as Richard Serra began using the abandoned warehouses as studios in which to work on large-scale sculptures and canvases. When nearby Soho rapidly turned chic during the art-market boom of the late 1980s, buyers scrambled for more affordable warehouses in Tribeca. Since then, living space in the neighborhood has reached Soho's in status and price, and an influx of high-profile residents has lent the area a certain cachet; Kirsten Dunst, Mariah Carey, Gwyneth Paltrow and novelist Patrick McGrath own apartments here. One big name in the neighborhood is Robert De Niro, who helped found both the **TriBeCa Film Center**, a state-of-the-art building catering to producers, directors, and editors, and the Tribeca Film Festival. Started in 2002 to aid in the recovery of Lower Manhattan after the September 11 attacks, the event has grown increasingly star-studded and attractive to distributors each April.

Chambers Street to Duane Park

Heading west along Chambers Street from City Hall Park, you'll get a taster of Tribeca's historic roots at the triangular intersection with West Broadway. The Bogardus Triangle Garden – more of a large median – is dedicated to **James Bogardus**, an ironmonger who put up the city's first cast-iron building in 1849. You can see one his few remaining creations at 85 Leonard St between Church and Broadway, a graceful building completed in 1868.

Keeping walking west and you'll reach **Washington Market Park**, a compact green space that pays tribute, in name at least, to the neighborhood's old function; it's mainly a playground for Tribeca's stroller set. Next door, the **Tribeca Performing Arts Center** (see p.363 for details) is the largest arts complex in Lower Manhattan.

From here you can wander up Greenwich Street to the thoroughly incongruous **Harrison Street Row**, such a contrast to the surrounding concrete that its nine Federal-style houses seem like reproductions. Though three of these late eighteenth-century homes were moved here in the 1970s, all are original, rare reminders of the area's pre-industrial past. Immediately to the west lies the traffic-choked West Side Highway and the eminently more appealing **Hudson River Park** beyond, a riverside promenade that links Chelsea with the Battery City Esplanade, just to the south.

To continue exploring Tribeca, stroll over to **Duane Park**, a sliver of green between Duane, Hudson, and Greenwich streets. The second-oldest park in New York City (after Bowling Green), it was also once the site of the city's egg, butter, and cheese markets – the original depots, alternating with new residential buildings, form a picturesque perimeter around the little triangle.

Varick Street and around

Just north of Leonard Street, **Varick Street** splits off from **West Broadway**, one of Tribeca's main thoroughfares, lined with boutiques and restaurants, and angles northwest, becoming Seventh Avenue once it crosses Houston Street. The New York City Fire Department's **Hook and Ladder Company #8**, 14 N Moore St, at Varick, operates from an 1865 brick-and-stone firehouse dotted with white stars. Movie buffs may recognize the building from the *Ghostbusters* films of the 1980s; more recently, it played a role in the rescue efforts of September 11. As it is a working firehouse, you can't do more than admire it from the outside. Two blocks north, **Tribeca Cinemas**, 54 Varick St just south of Canal (☏212/941-2000, ⓦwww.tribecacinemas.com), is an art theater managed by De Niro and partners, also hosting numerous special screenings.

If you cross the pedestrian bridge to the west, over the tangle of traffic headed into the Holland Tunnel, you'll be at the intersection of Laight Street and Hudson, on Tribeca's barely renovated fringes. At Laight and Collister stand the elegant **American Express Stables**, currently being converted into luxury loft apartments. Built in 1867, the building is a relic from the company's first incarnation as a delivery service; so too is the high-relief seal with a dog's head. (You can see another, not quite identical, head on the south face of the building – squeeze down narrow Collister to Hubert St.) Keeping walking north to Spring Street and the **New York City Fire Museum** (Tues–Sat 10am–5pm, Sun 10am–4pm; $5, seniors & students $2, under 12 $1; ☏212/691-1303 ⓦwww.nycfiremuseum.org) at no. 278. Housed in a 1904 Beaux-Arts firehouse, the museum displays old fire trucks dating back to the 1840s and plenty of art and NYFD memorabilia, but also acts as a touching memorial to the 343 firefighters that died on September 11. The NYFD lost 778 men in the line of duty between 1865 and September 10, but the devastating losses of the following day drew worldwide sympathy. Photos, videos, and artifacts found at the site record the disaster, and tiles commemorate those lost. Walking east along Spring Street from here brings you right into central Soho.

Soho

Like Tribeca to the south, **Soho** (short for *S*outh of *Ho*uston) has also undergone a series of transformations in the past few decades. In the 1980s, Soho was the center of New York's art scene. The latest victims of the city's ever-climbing rents, the most forward-looking galleries have relocated to cheaper spaces in West Chelsea and the outer boroughs, and a mostly nonresident crowd uses the area between Houston and Canal streets and Sixth Avenue and Lafayette Street as an enormous outdoor shopping mall. By day a place to buy khakis or trendy trousers, at night the neighborhood becomes a playground for gangs of well-groomed bistro- and bar-goers.

Despite the commercialism, Soho's artistic legacy hasn't been completely eradicated. If anything, it has been incorporated into the neighborhood's new character. You can still visit a couple of permanent installations tucked away on upper floors, or just cruise the visionary **Prada boutique**, designed by Dutch architect Rem Koolhaas. The store, at Prince Street and Broadway, acts as a sort of gatekeeper to the area's myriad shopfronts, which showcase everything from avant-garde home décor to conceptual fashion. The #R or #W train to Prince drops you at Prada's front door; the #D, #F, or #V to Broadway–Lafayette deposits you a block north at Houston. For access to the west side of the neighborhood, take the #C or #E to Spring Street.

Broadway

Any exploration of Soho's streets entails crisscrossing and doubling back, but an easy enough starting point is the intersection of Houston Street and **Broadway**.

▲ Shopping in Soho

Broadway reigns supreme as downtown's busiest drag. Numerous storefronts, most of them jazzed-up chain shops trying to compete with Soho's pricey designer boutiques, make it easy to get swept up in the commercial frenzy. For more visual stimulation, pop upstairs to the **Museum of Comic and Cartoon Art**, on the fourth floor at 594 Broadway (Fri–Mon noon–5pm; $5, under 12 free; ☏212/254-3511, ⊛www.moccany.org), where you may catch a themed exhibit on anything from World War II propaganda to contemporary *anime*.

Broadway is also the place to start a tour of Soho's distinctive **cast-iron architecture**. The stately **Astor Building**, 583 Broadway, was built in 1896 on the site of the house where John Jacob Astor, America's original tycoon, died in 1848. One of the later examples of the form is the **Little Singer Building**, 561 Broadway, which is actually an L-shape building with a second front on Prince Street. The twelve-story terracotta-tiled office and warehouse of the sewing-machine company was erected in 1904 by architect Ernest Flagg, who went on to build the record-breaking Singer Tower in the Financial District in 1908, thus rendering this earlier creation "little" in comparison. Here, Flagg used wide plate-glass windows set in delicate iron frames – a technique that pointed the way to the glass curtain wall of the 1950s. Across the street at 550 Broadway is the original location of legendary jewelers **Tiffany & Co.**; the 1854 structure's cast-iron facade was added in 1901, and today it serves as a Banana Republic store. A block and a half south, on the northeast corner of Broome and Broadway, stands the magnificent 1857 **Haughwout Building**, the oldest cast-iron structure in the city, as well as the first building of any kind to boast a passenger elevator – the lift, designed by Elisha Otis, was steam-powered. The facade of

Soho's cast-iron architecture

In vogue from around 1860 to the turn of the twentieth century, the **cast-iron archi-tecture** that is visible all over Soho initiated the age of prefabricated buildings. With mix-and-match components molded from iron, which was cheaper than brick or stone, a building of four stories could go up in as many months. The heavy iron cross-beams could carry the weight of the floors, allowing greater space for windows.

The remarkably decorative facades could be molded on the cheap, so that almost any style or whim could be cast in iron and pinned to the front of an otherwise dreary building: instant face-lifts for Soho's existing structures, and the birth of a whole new generation of beauties. Glorifying Soho's sweatshops, architects indulged themselves in Baroque balustrades and forests of Renaissance columns. But as quickly as the trend took off, it fell out of favor. Stricter building codes were passed in 1899, when it was discovered that iron beams, initially thought to be fireproof, could easily buckle at high temperatures. At the same time, steel proved an even cheaper building material.

With nearly 150 structures still standing, Soho contains one of the largest collec-tions of cast-iron buildings in the world, and the **Soho Cast-Iron Historic District**, from Houston Street south to Spring Street and from West Broadway to Crosby Street on the east, helps preserve the finest examples.

the former housewares emporium, which provided Abraham Lincoln's White House with its china, is mesmerizing; 92 colonnaded arches are framed behind taller columns. The whole building was painted off-white to mimic marble, but it looks more like an elaborate sculpture in buttercream frosting. Diagonally opposite and equally impossible to ignore, the ostentatious wedding-cake exterior of the **Broome Street Building**, 487 Broadway, was completed in 1896. By the turn of the century this was known as the Silk Exchange, but the building is mostly residential today.

Despite the shops, traffic, and hordes of people, the growing number of luxury apartments in this part of town has attracted plenty of celebrities. A block east from Broadway, just beyond Crosby Street, 421 Broome St is where actor Heath Ledger was found dead in January 2008. Flowers and tributes piled up at the building in the days after the tragedy, but in New York time really is money – within a few weeks his $22,000-per-month rental apartment was back on the market.

Greene Street and the Cast-Iron Historic District

If you continue down Broadway to Grand Street and turn right (west), you'll be in a prime position to appreciate a couple of architectural gems on **Greene Street**. First dip south to **no. 28–30**, the building known as the "Queen of Greene Street." Architect Isaac Duckworth's five-story French Second Empire extravagance dates from 1873.

Head back north to Grand, where, if you're into installation art, you can detour west to **Deitch Projects**, 76 Grand St (Tues–Sat noon–6pm; ☎212/343-7300, ⒲www.deitch.com), a singularly edgy gallery in now-staid Soho. Its exhibitions, which range from bead-covered landscapes to the newest graffiti, often call for a complete rebuilding of the interior space, and the opening parties are the stuff of legend in the art world.

Continuing north on Greene, you'll see more of Duckworth's artistry at **no. 72–76**. Thanks to its mass of columns and peaked cornice, this creation, completed just prior to no. 28–30, has naturally been given the title "King of Greene Street." (Alas, its existence came at the expense of one of the neighborhood's finest bordellos.) Farther on along Greene Street, past Spring, you officially enter the **Cast-Iron Historic District**, where you'll see similarly vivacious facades, as well as curlicue bishop's-crook cast-iron lampposts. None is quite as splendid as Duckworth's, but all are beautifully preserved and make excellent display cases for the dazzling retail offerings inside. The busiest store is one of the few not devoted to fashion, cosmetics or high-end art: the landmark **Apple Store** occupying the former post office on the corner of Greene and Prince streets. This stretch of Prince is also lined with high-quality art, craft, and jewelry stalls.

Head west on Prince Street, then north to **The New York Earth Room**, 141 Wooster St (Wed–Sun noon–3pm & 3.30–6pm; free; Ⓦ www.earthroom .org), a permanent installation by land artist Walter de Maria. Since 1980, this second-floor loft has been some of the most squandered real estate in NYC, as it is covered in almost two feet of moist brown earth, all of which weighs some 280,000 pounds. Commissioned and maintained by the Dia Art Foundation, the dirt is periodically aerated and cleaned, to keep mushrooms and bugs from flourishing. The entrance is easy to miss; press the buzzer and walk up to the second floor. Note that the installation is usually closed in July and August.

West Broadway and around

The north–south avenue of **West Broadway**, lined on either side with stately buildings, is the edge of the cast-iron district and was once the traditional boundary of Soho, though these days the blocks to the west are usually considered part of the area. Smaller and more residential, this section was once known as the South Village, its primarily Italian residents an extension of the Greenwich Village community until Robert Moses' brutal widening of Houston Street in 1940 effectively split them in two. The change in architecture is obvious, as the high-rise cast-iron warehouses give way to older Federal and Greek Revival rowhouses, cafés, and small Italian bakeries. One of the most famous is the *Vesuvio Bakery*, 160 Prince St, established in 1920, while further up Sullivan Street, **St Anthony of Padua Church** was built in 1888 by the oldest Italian congregation in the US. The church hosted the 2005 funeral of local resident and mafioso Vincent Gigante, better known as "the Oddfather" because he feigned mental illness for years to avoid prison. Walk back down to 116 Sullivan St to find one of the oldest homes in the neighborhood, an elegant Federal-style townhouse completed in 1832 and particularly noted for its carved wooden doorway.

Back on West Broadway, **no. 420** was the home of the most influential art galleries in the city between the 1970s and 1990s. In 1971, art dealers Leo Castelli, André Emmerich, and John Weber, along with Castelli's ex-wife Ileana Sonnabend, moved here from their offices uptown. Perhaps the most over-the-top exhibition occurred in 1991 in Sonnabend's gallery, when Jeff Koons debuted his *Made in Heaven* collection, a series of graphic photos and sculptures featuring his porn-star wife, La Cicciolina. The art-market bubble burst a year later, and Castelli died in 1999, at the age of 91; Sonnabend now operates from West Chelsea and today the building is occupied by a DKNY store and residential apartments.

At 393 West Broadway, about a block south, you can find **Broken Kilometer**, another installation by Walter de Maria (Wed–Sun noon–3pm & 3.30–6pm; free; Ⓦ www.brokenkilometer.org). This collection of five hundred carefully arranged brass rods is a slightly disorienting study in scale and perspective, as well as a testament to the sturdiness of cast-iron buildings – the collected rods weigh more than eighteen tons.

Chinatown, Little Italy, and Nolita

With some 200,000 residents (more than half of them of Chinese descent and the rest of other Asian heritage), seven Chinese newspapers, a dozen Buddhist temples, around 500 restaurants, and hundreds of garment factories, **Chinatown** is Manhattan's most densely populated ethnic neighborhood. For generations bounded by Canal Street to the north, over the last twenty years it has pushed across its traditional border into the smaller enclave of **Little Italy**, and today it has begun to sprawl east across Division Street and East Broadway into the periphery of the Lower East Side. On the northern fringes of Little Italy, the hip quarter known as **Nolita** is known for a number of chic restaurants, bars, and boutiques. Together, these three bustling neighborhoods can make for a diverting side-trip away from Manhattan's more ordered districts.

Chinatown and Little Italy are best reached by taking the #6, #J, #M, #N, #Q, #R, #W, or #Z trains to Canal Street. The Spring Street stop on the #6 is the most direct to Nolita.

Chinatown

On the surface, **Chinatown** is prosperous – a "model slum," some have called it – with the highest employment and least juvenile delinquency of any city district. Walk through its crowded streets at any time of day and you will find every shop doing a brisk trade. Restaurants are packed full; storefronts display heaps of shiny squid, clawing crabs, and fresh lobsters; and street markets offer overflowing piles of exotic green vegetables, garlic, and ginger root.

Beneath the neighborhood's prosperous facade, however, is a darker legacy. In recent years, some of the most regrettable institutions associated with the area – namely non-union sweatshops – have closed, or at least moved (rising rents in Manhattan have forced these factories out to satellite Chinatowns in Queens and Brooklyn), but other sharp practices continue to flourish. Organized crime is prevalent, illegal immigrants are commonly exploited, and living conditions can be abysmal for poorer Chinese.

Outsiders, however, won't see anything sinister, nor will they miss the Chinatown of yore in all the commercial hubbub. The neighborhood is a melange of vintage

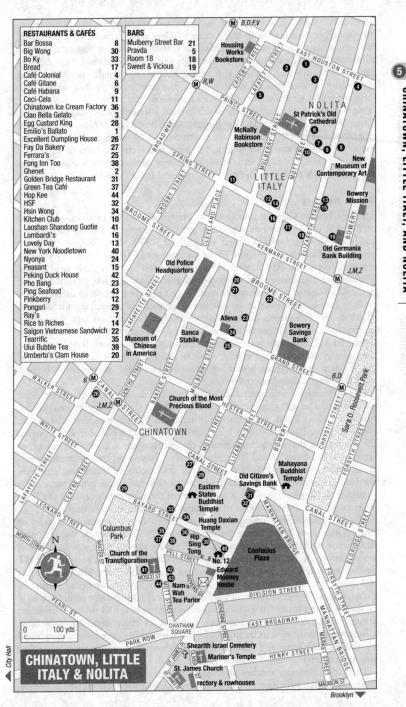

storefronts, modern Chinese graffiti, and tourist-oriented kitsch, like pagoda roofs on phone booths. Lined with tacky shops and frequently a pedestrian traffic jam, the unappealing east–west thoroughfare of **Canal Street** is unfortunately often all visitors ever see of Chinatown – perhaps along with the inside of a *dim sum* palace on Mott Street. Explore the narrow sidestreets, though, and you will be rewarded with a taste of a Chinatown that functions more for its residents than for tourists and retains many of its older traditions.

Mott Street is the main north–south avenue, although the streets around it – Canal, Pell, Bayard, Doyers, and the Bowery – also host a glut of restaurants, tea and rice shops, and grocery stores that are fun to browse. Nowhere in this city can you **eat** so well, and so much, for so little. For restaurant recommendations see p.312.

You can pick up additional maps, brochures, and coupon booklets at the **visitors' kiosk** (daily 10am–6pm) at Canal and Baxter streets.

Some history

The first known Chinese immigrant to New York arrived in 1858, and settled on Mott Street. He was not joined by significant numbers of his countrymen – and they were virtually all men – until the 1870s. By 1880, the Chinese population had risen from just 75 to an estimated 700, and the 1890 census recorded about 12,000 Chinese. Most of these men had previously worked out West on the transcontinental railroad or in gold mines, and few intended to stay in the US. Their idea was simply to make a nest egg, then return to their families and the easy life in China; as a result, the neighborhood around the intersection of Mott and Pell streets became known as the "bachelor society." Inevitably, money took rather longer to accumulate than expected, and though some men did go back, Chinatown soon became a permanent settlement. Residents made their livings as cooks, cigar vendors, sailors, and operators of *fan-tan* parlors and opium dens (upper-class bohemian New Yorkers were particularly obsessed with the latter cultural contribution).

The authorities did not particularly welcome the development of a permanent Chinatown. The growing neighborhood, built on the swampy ground of the filled-in Collect Pond, was a warren of tenements, flophouses, and saloons; the notorious Five Points slum (see box, p.68) stood where Columbus Park is today. By the end of the nineteenth century, the quarter was notoriously violent, in large part due to its Triad-like "tongs." These Chinese organized-crime operations, which originated in the California gold fields as secret brotherhoods, doubled as municipal-aid societies and thrived on prostitution, gambling, and the opium trade. Beginning in the waning years of the nineteenth century, the Tong Wars raged well into the 1930s in the form of intermittent assassinations.

The US government attempted to curtail such crime by passing a series of immigration laws. The Chinese Exclusion Act of 1882 completely forbade entry to Chinese workers for ten years, and in the early twentieth century, additional immigration quotas, particularly the 1924 National Origins Provision (NOP), further restricted the flow of Asians to America. In 1965, the Immigration Act did away with the NOP, and some 20,000 new Chinese immigrants, many of them women, began to arrive in Chinatown. Local businessmen took advantage of the declining midtown garment business and made use of the new, unskilled female workforce to open garment factories of their own. In little time, Chinatown overflowed its traditional boundaries, taking over blocks abandoned by Italians and Jews, and had an internal economy stronger than any other immigrant neighborhood in New York.

The early 1990s saw another major shift, as large numbers of illegal immigrants from the Fujian province of China arrived. Unlike the established Cantonese,

Before Chinatown was Chinatown

As is true for many of the neighborhoods in New York City, the area that is now known as Chinatown has undergone several transformations over time. Different immigrant groups have come and gone; the pan-Asian mini-metropolis is only the most recent development here. As you tour Chinatown's streets, you'll catch the occasional glimpse of the neighborhood as it was prior to the Chinese influx around 1870.

The first trace of another culture is the **cemetery of Congregation Shearith Israel**, just south of Chatham Square on St James Place. The oldest Jewish congregation in North America, Shearith Israel was established in New York in 1654 by a small group of Sephardim from Brazil, descendants of Jews who had fled the Spanish Inquisition. This small graveyard was in use from 1683 to 1833, but all that remains today is a collection of seventeenth- and eighteenth-century headstones. The cemetery is opened every year around Memorial Day, when a special ceremony pays tribute to those Jews interred here who died in the Revolutionary War, but at other times you can just peer through the iron railings.

Just around the corner on James Street, the **St James Church** marks the presence of the Irish in the mid-nineteenth century. A big Greek-Revival brownstone, the church was the gathering place of the first American division of the Irish-Catholic brotherhood, the Ancient Order of Hibernians in 1836. True to the cultural mixing that is characteristic of Manhattan's slums, St James Church was founded with the help of a Cuban priest, Félix Varela, who was also instrumental in the early Catholic period of the Church of the Transfiguration on Mott Street. If you walk around the corner from St James Church to Oliver Street, you'll see the former church rectory in a row of tenement-style homes, as well as the much-worse-for-wear **Mariner's Temple**, established in 1845 and the oldest Baptist church in Manhattan.

Perhaps the most overlooked anachronism is the **Edward Mooney House**, a tiny Georgian-style brick building at the corner of the Bowery and Pell Street that looks very out of step with its plastic-facade neighbors. Built in 1785, it's the oldest surviving rowhouse in New York City, erected by a merchant who saw this neighborhood's future as a center for commerce.

who had dominated Chinatown's politics for a century or so, the Fujianese were largely uneducated laborers who spoke their own dialects and Mandarin. Cultural and linguistic differences made it difficult for them to find work in Chinatown, and a large number turned to more desperate means. By 1994, Fujianese-on-Fujianese violence comprised the majority of Chinatown's crime, prompting local leaders to break the neighborhood's traditional bond of silence and call in city officials for help. Despite the fact that Mandarin-speaking "mainlanders" (immigrants from mainland China) and in particular the Fujianese are now the majority here, Cantonese is still the *lingua franca* of Chinatown; though many well-off Cantonese have moved to the outer boroughs, they remain the district's most important customers, and businesses remain largely Cantonese-owned.

Columbus Park

The southern limits of Chinatown begin just a few blocks north of City Hall Park at the intersection of Worth and Baxter streets. From here, **Columbus Park** stretches north, a green sward away from Chinatown's hectic consumerism. It's favored by the neighborhood's elderly, who congregate for morning *t'ai chi* and marathon games of *xiangqi* (Chinese chess). The park was laid out by Calvert Vaux, of Central Park fame, but little of his original plan remains today – ball fields take up one end, while craggy rock-gardens are the backdrop on the north side. Facing Bayard Street, an open-air concert pavilion is a relic of the late nineteenth century.

East to Chatham Square

Head east from the park along narrow Mosco Street, and you'll be in the oldest section of Chinatown, where the streets are lined with barely renovated tenements. At the corner of Mott Street, the green-domed **Church of the Transfiguration**, an elegant Georgian building with Gothic details, is known as the "church of immigrants" for good reason. It opened in 1801 as a Lutheran parish, then was sold to Irish Catholics fifty years later; the plaque honoring those killed in World War I lists primarily Italian names, while today, Mass is said daily in Cantonese, English, and Mandarin. The pretty interior makes a tranquil contrast to the frenetic activity outside, and is usually open throughout the day.

The next block over (head north on Mott, then east one block on Pell) is crooked **Doyers Street**. Once known as the "Bloody Angle" for its role as a battleground during the Tong Wars, there's little more malicious than barber shops operating here now. In the late nineteenth century, the building opposite the post office was the neighborhood's largest Chinese opera house. In 1905, the Hip Sing Tong confronted the On Leong Tong here in a shootout in front of several hundred people. When the police arrived, however, there was scant evidence of the battle, as the gangs had dragged the bodies away through an adjacent tunnel. The underground passage, which had been dug to provide cold storage in the pre-refrigerator era, is now just a warren of employment agencies. Also keep an eye out for *Nam Wah Tea Parlor*, 13 Doyers St, which was established in 1920 and has changed little since.

Doyers Street dead-ends at the Bowery and **Chatham Square**, really a tiny triangle, where Fujianese civic organizations have erected a statue of **Lin Zexu**, a Qing-dynasty official who is revered in China for cracking down on the opium trade. Lin arrested thousands of Chinese opium dealers, destroyed 2.6 million pounds of the drug and kicked out the British opium merchants in 1839, thereby precipitating the Opium Wars. The Fujianese, often stereotyped as Chinatown's drug lords, have cast their hero as a "pioneer in the war against drugs," according to the inscription. Also in Chatham Square is a small arch that pays tribute to Chinese-Americans killed in World War II. Just to the north looms **Confucius Plaza**, a 1970s housing complex that's still considered some of the best living quarters in Chinatown. A statue of the Chinese philosopher was erected outside in 1976.

East from Chatham Square is the "new" Chinatown – the district expanded by the Fujianese and other mainland immigrants in the past few decades. **East Broadway**, often called Little Fuzhou, is the main commercial avenue, but has little appeal unless you're heading for the Lower East Side (see p.88).

North along Mott Street

To continue your tour of Chinatown's historical center, return from Chatham Square to **Mott Street** via Pell Street. On the corner of Pell Street and the Bowery you'll find the **Huang Daxian Temple** (daily 9–6pm), one of Chinatown's few Taoist temples and, like all of them, a converted shopfront. This one is dedicated to Huang Daxian, a quasi-historical figure who is said to have lived in China in the fourth century, worshipped today for his supposed powers of healing. Better known as Wong Tai Sin in Cantonese, he remains one of the most popular Taoist deities in Hong Kong.

Around the corner on Pell Street, **no. 12** is now a hair salon but was once the Chinatown Music Hall and later the *Pelham*, the saloon where Irving Berlin first worked as a singing waiter in 1906. **No. 16** is the headquarters of the United in Victory Association, aka the Hip Sing Tong, where some seventy people were killed when the rival On Leong group raided the place in 1924.

At first glance, Mott Street, the "dragon's spine" of Chinatown, is a strip of tacky gift shops and countless modern tea shops. Look past the kitsch, though, and you'll also find retailers, like herbal-medicine vendors and furniture dealers, catering to the neighborhood's residents. The **Eastern States Buddhist Temple**, 64 Mott St (daily 8am–6pm), is the oldest temple on the East Coast. Established in 1962 as a social club for unassimilated elderly Chinese men, the room's linoleum floors and dropped ceiling make it more functional than fancy. The main deity here is Sakyamuni Buddha, but note also the glass-encased gold statue of the "four-faced Buddha," a replica of the revered image in Bangkok's Erawan Shrine (actually an incarnation of Hindu god Brahma).

North of Canal, Mott Street is home to a wide variety of produce stands, seafood shops, and butchers. This is where visitors will feel most strongly the Chinese culture of today: snow peas, bean curd, assorted fungi, numerous varieties of bok choi, and dried sea cucumbers spill out onto the sidewalks, while racks of ribs, whole chickens, and lacquered Peking ducks glisten in store windows. Perhaps even more fascinating than the assortment of foodstuffs are the herbalists, in whose shops you will find myriad drawers and jars, all filled with roots and powders that are centuries-old remedies for nearly every human ailment.

Canal and Grand streets

Say "Canal Street" to most New Yorkers, and they'll think not of a real canal (which this busy thoroughfare was until 1820), but of counterfeit handbags, which you'll see on sale in nearly every shop you pass. A casual stroll here is impossible; the sidewalks are lined with food vendors, souvenir stalls, and hawkers talking up their knock-off bargains – foot traffic often grinds to a halt.

Toward the east end of Canal, at the junction with the Bowery, the former **Citizen's Savings Bank** is something of a local landmark, its neo-Byzantine bronze dome looming majestically above the chaotic streets. Completed in 1924, it now functions as a branch of HSBC. Chinese influence is more obvious at the gilded **Mahayana Buddhist Temple**, opposite at 133 Canal St (daily 8am–6pm; ☎ 212/925-8787), much more lavish than its counterpart on Mott Street. Drop a dollar in the donation box for good fortune, then proceed to the main hall. Candlelight and blue neon glow around the giant gold Buddha on the main altar, while along the walls are 32 plaques that tell the story of Buddha's life. Despite the assault of red and gold, it's a surprisingly peaceful place. The entrance hall contains a smaller shrine to Buddhist bodhisattva Guanyin (known as the "Goddess of Mercy"), and the small shop upstairs sells books and statues.

Canal Street channels its eastbound traffic onto the **Manhattan Bridge**, which crosses the East River to Brooklyn. The grand Beaux-Arts arch over the center lanes looks a bit out of place compared to the neon signs and abandoned Chinese cinemas gathered around the piers below, but it's in good company with the regal **Bowery Savings Bank**, two blocks north of Canal on the Bowery, at the corner of Grand Street (the city's main east–west avenue in the 1800s). Designed by Stanford White in 1894, the building is a shrine to the virtue of saving money. Today the building is a posh location for private dinners and functions, known as Capitale.

▲ Canal Street, Chinatown

From here you could head east one block to Chrystie Street, which forms the nominal border between Chinatown and the Lower East Side, or you could go west along Grand Street, through a few more blocks of Chinatown hubbub, and end up at the **Museum of Chinese in America**.

Museum of Chinese in America

By early 2009 the fascinating Museum of Chinese in America (Tues–Sat noon–6pm; $2, students and seniors $1; ⊤212/619-4785, ⓦwww.moca-nyc.org) should have moved into brand-new premises at 215 Centre St (just south of Grand St). Designed by Maya Lin (best-known for her Vietnam Veterans Memorial in Washington, D.C.), the new space will be five times bigger than the museum's old digs in the heart of Chinatown. Dubbed the "Chinese American Experience," the core exhibition will provide an historical overview of the Chinese in the US through an evocative blend of multimedia displays, artifacts, and filmed interviews of real people. The whole thing will be arranged around a sun-lit courtyard, reminiscent of a traditional Chinese house, and divided into six themed sections. Some of the issues tackled will include the Chinese Exclusion Act of 1882, the "Red Scare" during China's Communist Revolution, and the identity of second-generation Chinese Americans since the 1960s. From here it's a short stroll into the heart of Little Italy, once the center of the city's considerable Italian community.

Little Italy

Bounded roughly by Canal Street to the south, Houston Street to the north, Mulberry Street to the east, and Broadway to the west, **Little Italy** is light years away from the solid ethnic enclave of old, but it's still fun for a stroll, a schmaltzy kick, and a decent cappuccino on the hoof. The area was settled in the latter half of the nineteenth century by a huge influx of Italian immigrants, who supplanted the district's earlier Irish inhabitants and, like their Chinese and Jewish counterparts, clannishly cut themselves off to recreate the Old Country. The neighborhood is smaller and more commercial than it once was, with Chinatown encroaching on three sides – Mulberry Street is the only Italian territory south of Broome Street.

If you walk north on Mulberry from Chinatown to get here, the transition from the throngs south of Canal to Little Italy's somewhat forced Big Tomato hoopla can be a little difficult to stomach. The red, green, and white tinsel decorations along Mulberry Street and the suited hosts who aggressively lure out-of-town visitors to their restaurants are undeniable signs that the neighborhood is little more than a tourist trap. Few Italians still live here, though a number still visit for a dose of nostalgia, some Frank Sinatra, and a plate of fully *Americano* spaghetti with red sauce. For a more vibrant, if workaday, Italian-American experience, you'll want to head to Belmont in the Bronx (see p.259).

This is not to advise missing out on Little Italy altogether. Some original bakeries and *salumerias* (Italian specialty food stores) do survive, and there, amid the imported cheeses, sausages, and salamis hanging from the ceiling, you can buy sandwiches made with slabs of mozzarella or eat slices of fresh focaccia. In addition, you'll still find plenty of places to indulge with a cappuccino and a pastry, not least of which is *Ferrara's*, 195 Grand St, the oldest and most popular café. Another establishment of note is the belt-defying *Lombardi's*, 32 Spring St, which is not only the city's oldest pizzeria, but is also one of its finest. (For more on Little Italy's comestibles, see p.292 & p.313.)

Along Mulberry Street

Little Italy's main strip, **Mulberry Street** is an almost solid row of restaurants and cafés – and is therefore filled with tourists. The street is particularly lively, if a bit like a theme park, at night, when the lights come on and the sidewalks fill with restaurant hosts who shout menu specials at passers-by. If you're here in mid-September, the ten-day **Festa di San Gennaro** (see p.421) is a wild and tacky celebration of the patron saint of Naples. Italians from all over the city converge on Mulberry Street, and the area is filled with street stalls and numerous Italian fast-food and snack vendors. The festivities center on the 1892 **Church of the Most Precious Blood**, 109 Mulberry St (main entrance on Baxter St), providing visitors with a chance to see the inside of this small church, which is normally closed.

None of the eating places around here really stands out, but the northwest corner of Mulberry and Hester streets, the former site of *Umberto's Clam House* (now relocated two blocks north), was quite notorious in its time: in 1972 it was the scene of a vicious gangland murder when "Crazy Joey" Gallo was shot dead while celebrating his birthday with his wife and daughter. Gallo, a big talker and ruthless businessman, was keen to protect his interests in Brooklyn; he was alleged to have offended a rival family and so paid the price. For a more tangible Mafia vibe, you can't beat the 1908 *Mulberry Street Bar*, at no. 176 1/2, where the back room, all fogged mirrors and tile floors, has been the setting for numerous Mob movies and episodes of *The Sopranos*.

Take a peek through the window of the former **Banca Stabile**, 189 Grand St at Mulberry. It opened in 1885, and offered services to immigrants, including translation, letter writing, wire transfers, and travel booking. Though the bank has been shut for decades, the gilt windows and elaborate interior are still preserved by the building's owner. On the opposite corner, **Alleva** (Ⓦwww.allevadairy.com), established in 1892, claims to be the oldest cheese-maker in the US – perhaps true if the definition of cheese is limited to mozzarella and ricotta.

Jog west of Mulberry on Broome Street to see the grandeur of the **Old Police Headquarters**, a palatial 1909 Neoclassical construction at the corner of Centre Street. Meant to cow would-be criminals into obedience with its high-rise copper dome and lavish ornamentation, it was more or less a complete failure: the blocks immediately surrounding the edifice were some of the most corrupt in the city in the early twentieth century. Police headquarters moved to a bland modern building near City Hall in 1973, and the overbearing palace was converted in 1987 into up-market condominiums. Residents have included Calvin Klein, Winona Ryder, and Christy Turlington; one-bedroom apartments were selling for over $1.8 million in 2008.

Nolita

The blocks surrounding St Patrick's Old Cathedral, particularly north to Houston and east to the Bowery, were rechristened **Nolita** ("North of Little Italy") by savvy real estate developers in the late 1990s. Stylish shop-owners are the newest variety of immigrant here, as numerous tiny boutiques have taken over former Italian haunts. Most are above Spring Street, but the trendiness has spread south, too. Although this district is not cheap by any means, it is a bit more personal and less status-mad than much of neighboring Soho. The shops showcase handmade shoes, custom swimwear, and items with vintage flair, often sold by the designers themselves, or at least by obsessive buyers who have strong affection for the goodies they've collected from elsewhere.

If you're not interested in shopping, you should definitely check out the **New Museum of Contemporary Art** on the Bowery, a stylish showcase for the latest trends in multimedia art. Nolita is also an appealing place to put up your feet after a long walking tour. Choose from any of the numerous cafés – the tea shops inside the McNally Robinson bookstore (50 Prince St; Mon–Sat 10am–10pm, Sun 10am–8pm) and Housing Works Used Book Café (126 Crosby St; Mon–Fri 10am–9pm, Sat & Sun noon–7pm) are ideal spots to chill out. From Nolita, you can walk west past Lafayette to the cast-iron grandeur of Soho, north across Houston to the East Village, or east to the Lower East Side.

St Patrick's Old Cathedral

St Patrick's Old Cathedral, on Mott and Prince streets, is the spiritual heart of Little Italy and the oldest Catholic cathedral in the city. When it was conse-crated in 1815, it served the Irish immigrant community and hosted the Roman Catholic archdiocese in New York. Catholic leadership has moved uptown to a newer St Patrick's Cathedral on Fifth Avenue at 50th Street, relegating "old St Pat's" to the status of a parish church. It now serves English-, Spanish-, and Chinese-speaking worshippers. Designed by Joseph-François Mangin, the architect behind City Hall, the building is grand Gothic Revival, with an 85-foot vault, a gleaming gilt altar, and a massive pipe organ that was installed in 1868, when the church was restored following a terrible fire. The church is usually open throughout the day.

Equally notable is the **cemetery** behind the church, which is ringed with a brick wall that the Ancient Order of Hibernians used as a defense in 1835, when anti-Irish rioters threatened to burn down the church. The cemetery is almost always locked, but try to peek through one of the gates – you may recognize the view from a scene in Martin Scorsese's *Mean Streets* (one of the few parts of the movie actually shot here, even though the film was allegedly set in Little Italy).

The Bowery

Forming the boundary between Nolita and the Lower East Side, **the Bowery** was until relatively recently a byword for poverty and destitution, America's original **skid row**. At its peak in 1949, around 14,000 homeless people could be found here, most dossing down in hostels known as flophouses. Today only eight flophouses remain, and these mostly cater to Chinese laborers at the southern end of the Bowery. The street runs north from Chatham Square in Chinatown to Cooper Square in the East Village, where it is increasingly lined with smart, contemporary buildings (see p.97).

Yet the current gentrification of this wide thoroughfare is just the latest of many changes over the years: the street takes its name from *bouwerie*, the Dutch word for farm, when it was the city's main agricultural supplier. In the nineteenth century it was flanked by music halls, opera houses, vaudeville theaters, hotels, and middle-market restaurants, drawing people from all parts of Manhattan – including opera lover **Walt Whitman** (see box, p.223). The good times did not last, and by the early twentieth century the street was becoming associated with crime and poverty, attracting religious and social welfare institutions like the **Bowery Mission**, which opened in 1880. The Bowery's notoriety immortalized it in literature, with many writers making use of its less than stellar reputation. Theodore Dreiser closed his 1900 tragedy *Sister Carrie* with a suicide in a Bowery flophouse, while fifty years later William S. Burroughs alluded to the area in a story that complained of bums waiting to "waylay one in the Bowery." The Great Depression signaled a low-point in the Bowery's fortunes, and between the 1940s and 1980s the whole strip was synonymous with bums, alcoholics, and the homeless. Those days are largely gone, and though pockets of the old Bowery remain (check out the graffiti-smothered walls of the **old Germania Bank Building**, on the corner of Spring St), wine stores, galleries and high-end apartments are becoming far more prevalent.

New Museum of Contemporary Art

Two blocks east from St Patrick's Old Cathedral, the **New Museum of Contemporary Art** (Wed, Sat & Sun noon–6pm, Thurs & Fri noon–10pm; ⊤212/219-1222, ⓦwww.newmuseum.org; $12, seniors $8, students $6) is a powerful symbol of the Bowery's rebirth. The building itself, at 235 Bowery opposite Prince Street, is as much the attraction as the avant-garde work inside, a stack of seven shimmering aluminum boxes designed by Tokyo-based architects Kazuyo Sejima and Ryue Nishizawa.

An industrial elevator glides between the four main floors, each holding one exhibition space. The warehouse-like galleries, all brilliant white with shiny concrete floors, are spacious but still small enough to digest without overdosing on the often thought-provoking and diverse range of temporary exhibits inside. The shop in the lobby has a fabulous book section and café, while the Sky Room on the 7th floor opens at weekends for rare views across the Lower East Side and Nolita. The 5th floor is an educational centre dedicated to sister art galleries all over the world. Excellent guided tours (free) take place at 2pm and 4pm Wednesday to Sunday, and also 7pm on Friday. Museum entry is free on Thursdays after 7pm.

The Lower East Side

istorically the epitome of the American ethnic melting pot, the
Lower East Side – bordered to the north by Houston Street, the
south by East Broadway, the east by the East River, and the west by
the Bowery – is one of Manhattan's most enthralling downtown
neighborhoods. A fair proportion of its inhabitants are working-class
Dominicans and Chinese, but among them you're also likely to find small
Jewish communities, students, moneyed artsy types, and hipster refugees from
the more gentrified areas of Soho and the East Village. With the possible
exception of the still somewhat seedy southeastern reaches around East
Broadway and Grand Street, the Lower East Side has been considerably
maintained in recent years, bringing in all sorts of visitors. Many come for
the shopping; most of the city's best vintage-clothing and furniture stores are
here, which has in turn attracted a number of emerging designers as well.
The plethora of drinking, dancing, and food options also draws large crowds
every night of the week.

To begin your tour of the Lower East Side, take the #F train to Lower East
Side–Second Avenue or Delancey Street. For information about local events
and tours, visit the **Lower East Side Visitor Center** at 261 Broome St
(Mon–Fri 9am–5pm, Sat & Sun 10am–4pm; ℡866/224-0206, ⓦwww
.lowereastsideny.com).

Some history

Some of the first people to live in this area were freed slaves, who farmed small
plots of land in the seventeenth century, most of which were confiscated and
sold after the American Revolution.

The first tenement buildings in the city, which housed Irish immigrants, were
constructed on the Lower East Side in 1833, and the development of *Kleindeut-
schland* (Little Germany) along the Bowery followed closely behind in 1840.
The neighborhood attracted international humanitarian attention toward the
end of the nineteenth century, when it became an insular slum for over half a
million Jewish immigrants and the most densely populated spot in the world.
Mainly from Eastern Europe, these refugees came to America in search of a
better life, but instead found themselves scratching out a living in a free-for-all
of textile sweatshops and pushcarts. In the 1880s the area became America's
garment capital, and by 1900, 70 percent of the nation's women's clothing
was manufactured here – today, there are still around 180 garment factories in
the Lower East Side.

The area's lank brick tenements were a bleak destiny for those who crossed
the Atlantic. Low standards of hygiene and abysmal housing made disease rife

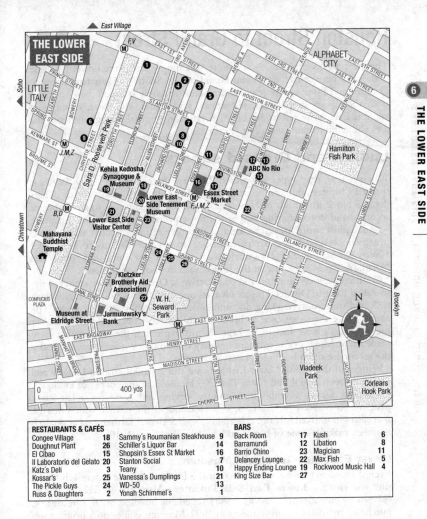

THE LOWER EAST SIDE

East Village

Soho

LITTLE ITALY

Chinatown

Brooklyn

ALPHABET CITY

Hamilton Fish Park

Kehila Kedosha Synagogue & Museum

ABC No Rio

Essex Street Market

Lower East Side Tenement Museum

Lower East Side Visitor Center

Mahayana Buddhist Temple

Kletzker Brotherly Aid Association

W. H. Seward Park

Museum at Eldridge Street

Jarmulowsky's Bank

Confucius Plaza

Vladeck Park

Corlears Hook Park

N

0   400 yds

RESTAURANTS & CAFÉS			
Congee Village	18	Sammy's Roumanian Steakhouse	9
Doughnut Plant	26	Schiller's Liquor Bar	14
El Cibao	15	Shopsin's Essex St Market	16
Il Laboratorio del Gelato	20	Stanton Social	7
Katz's Deli	3	Teany	10
Kossar's	25	Vanessa's Dumplings	21
The Pickle Guys	24	WD-50	13
Russ & Daughters	2	Yonah Schimmel's	1

BARS			
Back Room	17	Kush	6
Barramundi	12	Libation	8
Barrio Chino	23	Magician	11
Delancey Lounge	22	Max Fish	5
Happy Ending Lounge	19	Rockwood Music Hall	4
King Size Bar	27		

and life expectancy low: in 1875, the infant mortality rate was forty percent, mainly due to cholera. It was conditions like these that spurred reformers like Jacob Riis and Stephen Crane to record the plight of the city's immigrants in writing and photographs, thereby spawning not only a whole school of journalism but also some notable changes in urban planning.

The Chinese and Dominicans moved into the area in the 1980s, but it wasn't until the 1990s that the Lower East Side saw high-end development when Retro clubs, chic bars, gourmet restaurants, and unique boutiques sprouted up all over. Things have mellowed a bit since then, with the more bleeding-edge cool-seekers having decamped for less well-trammeled parts of Brooklyn. Despite the changes, the Lower East Side clings on to its immigrant roots; about 40 percent of the people living here were born in another country, with a quarter of residents Spanish-speaking, and around 20 percent from China and other parts of east Asia.

Houston Street to Grand Street

The most readily explorable – and most rewarding – part of the Lower East Side is the area between Houston and Grand streets. South of **Houston**, between Orchard and Essex streets, Jewish immigrants indelibly stamped their character with their own shops, delis, restaurants, synagogues, and, later, community centers. Even now, with Chinatown overflowing into the neighborhood, the area still exhibits remnants of its Jewish past.

Ludlow and Orchard streets

When a few artsy types discovered **Ludlow Street** in the early 1990s, it sparked a hipster migration south from the East Village. A half-dozen or so bars dot the block just south of Houston. The street is also home to a number of second-hand stores offering kitschy items – especially gorgeous retro furniture – and slightly worn treasures. Around the intersection of Allen and Stanton streets are several more bar/performance spaces like the no-cover *Arlene's Grocery*, 95 Stanton St (Ⓦ www.arlenesgrocery.net). For a pre-show tipple, see "Drinking," p.342, for one of the funky watering holes in this area.

Continue west on Houston and you'll arrive at **Orchard Street**, center of the so-called Bargain District. This area is at its best on Sundays, when it's filled with stalls and storefronts hawking discounted designer clothes and accessories. The rooms above the stores used to house sweatshops, so-named because whatever the weather, a stove had to be kept warm for pressing the clothes that were made there. Much of the garment industry moved uptown ages ago, and today the rooms are often home to pricey apartments.

Vestiges of the Jewish Lower East Side are still apparent around Ludlow and Orchard streets. You'll find *Katz's Deli*, 205 Houston, at the corner of Ludlow – it's famous for its assembly-line counter service and good for a late-night pastrami binge. *Russ & Daughters*, 179 Houston, at the corner with Orchard, specializes in smoked fish and caviar, and *Yonah Schimmel*, farther west at no. 137, has been making some of New York's best knishes since 1910.

Lower East Side Tenement Museum

Even if you don't have the time to tour the Lower East Side extensively, make sure you visit the **Lower East Side Tenement Museum** (Ⓣ 212/431-0233, Ⓦ www.tenement.org), a restored 1863 tenement building at 97 Orchard St, purchased by the museum founders in 1992. Museum guides do a brilliant job bringing to life the building's (and the neighborhood's) past and present, aided by documents, photographs, and artifacts found on site, concentrating on the area's multiple ethnic heritages. This will probably be your only chance to see the claustrophobic interior of a tenement (the first ever to be designated as a landmark), with its deceptively elegant entry hall and two toilets for every four families. Various apartments inside have been renovated with period furnishings to reflect the lives of its tenants, from the mid-nineteenth century when there was no plumbing, electricity, or heat, to the mid-twentieth century when many families ran cottage industries out of their apartments. The whole affair is an earnest and sympathetic attempt to document the immigrant experience.

The tenement is accessible only by various themed **guided tours** ($17, students and seniors $13) which run throughout the day. For tickets, go to the museum's **visitor center** at 108 Orchard St (Mon 11am–5.30pm, Tues–Fri 11am–6pm, Sat & Sun 10.45am–6pm). Tours (1hr; no tours Mon) include

▲ Lower East Side Tenement Museum

"Getting By: Weathering the Great Depressions of 1873 and 1929" (Tues–Fri every 40min 1–4.45pm; Sat & Sun every 30min 11am–4.30pm) and the kid-friendly "Confino Living History Tour" (Sat & Sun 1 & 3pm). The museum also offers a 1hr 30min walking tour of the area's ethnic neighborhoods for the same price (April–Dec Sat & Sun 1 & 3pm); come early or book in advance.

Delancey and Essex streets

Orchard Street bisects **Delancey Street**, once the horizontal axis of the old Jewish Lower East Side, now a tacky boulevard leading to the **Williamsburg Bridge** and Brooklyn. The construction of the bridge in 1903 greatly altered the social demographic of both the Lower East Side and Williamsburg. When it opened, an influx of Jewish settlers crossed the "Jews' Bridge" to Williamsburg, inducing its longtime Irish and German residents to migrate to Queens. In a historical twist, in recent years it's the hipsters who've made the migration to the Lower East Side, and from there to Williamsburg, following in the footsteps of the Jewish immigrants.

Two blocks east, at Delancey and Essex, sprawls the **Essex Street Market** (Mon–Sat 8am–6pm, Ⓦ www.essexstreetmarket.com), erected under the aegis of Mayor LaGuardia in 1939, when pushcarts were made illegal (ostensibly because they clogged the streets, but mainly because they competed with established businesses). Here you'll find all sorts of fresh produce and fish, along with random clothing bargains and the occasional trinket or piece of tat. Two blocks south of Delancey on Essex you'll find *The Pickle Guys*, 35 Essex St, where people line up outside the store to buy fresh home-made pickles, olives, and other yummy picnic staples from huge barrels of garlicky brine.

East of Essex Street, the historical Jewish Lower East Side gives way to a contemporary, sometimes incongruous mix of Puerto Ricans and Dominicans hanging out at homey Spanish diners and hipster foodies trolling the high-end eateries that line **Clinton Street**. North on Clinton from Delancey, a welded gate composed of old gears and scrap metal identifies **ABC No Rio**, 156 Rivington St (℡212/254-3697, ⓦwww.abcnorio.org), a long-downtrodden but still vibrant community arts center that has hosted gallery shows, raucous concerts, a 'zine library, art installations, and the like. Despite an extensive and ongoing renovation, the center still runs Hardcore/Punk Matinees every Saturday at 3.30pm, and the Sunday Open Series of poetry readings at 3pm each week, featuring new works by local neighborhood poets and writers.

Canal Street and East Broadway

Though the southern half of **East Broadway** is now almost exclusively Chinese, the street used to be the hub of the Jewish Lower East Side. To get a feel for the old quarter, start on Canal Street at Eldridge Street, two blocks west of Orchard, and wind your way east. Just south of Canal, at 12 Eldridge St, you'll find the thoroughly absorbing **Museum at Eldridge Street** (Sun–Thurs 10am–4pm; $10, students and seniors $8; ℡212/219-0888, ⓦwww.eldridgestreet.org). Built in 1887 as the first synagogue constructed by Eastern European Orthodox Jews in the city, the wonderfully restored site opened as a museum in 2007. In its day it was one of the neighborhood jewels: a brick and terracotta hybrid of Moorish and Gothic influences, it was known for its rich woodwork and stained-glass windows, including the west-wing rose window – a spectacular Star of David roundel. The synagogue is still a functioning house of worship, but half-hourly guided tours (1hr) take you upstairs to the main sanctuary, the Family History Center (focusing on the experience of immigrant families), and the Limud Discovery Center, providing a thorough introduction to the history of the building and the area through displays of nineteenth-century artifacts and interactive exhibits. The museum also hosts concerts, lectures, art installations, and festivals (check the website for details).

East on Canal Street at nos. 54–58, above the row of food and electrical stores, is the ornate facade of **Sender Jarmulowsky's Bank**, dwarfing the buildings around it. Founded in 1873 by a peddler who made his fortune reselling ship tickets, the bank catered to the financial needs of the area's non-English-speaking immigrants. As the threat of war in Europe grew, the bank was plagued by runs and riots when panicked patrons tried to withdraw their money to send to relatives back in Europe. In 1914, the bank collapsed; on its closure, thousands lost what little savings they had accumulated.

At the corner of Canal and Ludlow streets, the **Kletzker Brotherly Aid Association** building at 41 Canal St is a relic of a time when Jewish towns set up their own lodges (in this case, the town was Kletzk, in modern-day Belarus) to provide community health care and Jewish burials, assistance for widows, and other similar services. Today it's a Chinese funeral home, though if you walk around the corner, the second entrance at 5 Ludlow Street still displays the Kletzker name and establishment date of 1892. The once-prominent Star of David here has been removed by the new owners, but look closely and you can still see its faded outline.

The East Village

L ike the Lower East Side to the south, the **East Village**, which extends
east from Broadway to Avenue D and north from Houston Street to
14th Street, was once a solidly working-class refuge for immigrants. In
the early part of the twentieth century, rents began to rise in the city's
traditional bohemia in Greenwich Village, sending New York's nonconformist
intelligentsia scurrying here. By the 1990s, the rents here had begun their own
upward climb, and the East Village is now no longer the hotbed of dissidence
and creativity that it once was. The last fifteen years have seen it become
downright mainstream – you're likely to walk by a pretty standard cross-
section of boutiques, thrift stores, and record shops patronized by more tourists,
students, and uptowners than authentic bohemians. The area's high standard of
living and panoply of restaurants and bars, never mind its proximity to NYU,
ensure that rents here are almost – although not quite – as insane as those in
the neighboring West Village. Nevertheless, despite the vaudevillian circuses of
St Mark's Place and Cooper Square, and creeping invasion of *Starbucks* (note

The East Village's cultural heritage

Over the years, the East Village has been home to its share of **famous artists**,
politicos, and **literati**. In the mid-seventeenth century, Peter Stuyvesant, Director-
General of New Amsterdam, developed the land between what are now 6th and 16th
streets, and from Third Avenue to the East River, for his country estate.

Fast-forward to the twentieth century: W.H. Auden lived at 77 St Mark's Place
between 1953 and 1972; years earlier the Communist journal *Novy Mir* operated from
the basement, numbering among its contributors Leon Trotsky, who lived for a brief
time in New York. In the 1950s, the East Village became one of the main New York
haunts of the Beat poets – Kerouac, Burroughs, Ginsberg – who, when not riding
trains across the country, would get together at Ginsberg's house on East 7th Street
for declamatory readings. Later, Andy Warhol debuted the Velvet Underground at the
Fillmore East, which played host to just about every band you've ever heard of – and
forgotten about – before becoming *The Saint* (also now defunct), a gay disco famous
for its three-day parties.

By the 1980s, the East Village was best known for its **radical visual artists**,
including Keith Haring, Jeff Koons, and Jean-Michel Basquiat. Toward the end of
the decade, the neighborhood was the center of a different kind of attention: the
city evicted the homeless from Tompkins Square Park, and the neighborhood's
many dead-broke squatter artists were forced out, a story memorialized in the hit
Broadway musical *Rent*. With suitable irony, the show has made millions of dollars
since its debut in 1996, and was successfully adapted for the big screen in 2005 – its
Broadway run finally ended in 2008.

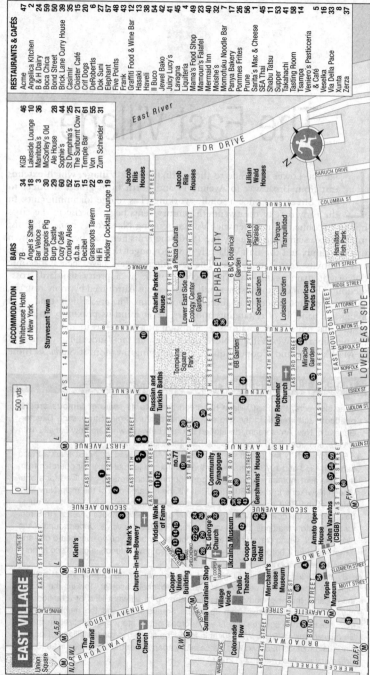

EAST VILLAGE

ACCOMMODATION

Whitehouse Hotel of New York	A
Stuyvesant Town	

RESTAURANTS & CAFÉS

Acme	47
Angelica Kitchen	2
B & H Dairy	24
Boca Chica	59
Bond Street	50
Brick Lane Curry House	39
Casimir	35
Cloister Café	15
Crif Dogs	20
DeRobertis	6
Dok Suni	27
Elephant	57
Five Points	48
Frank	43
Graffiti Food & Wine Bar	12
Hasaki	13
Haveli	38
Il Buco	54
Juicy Lucy's	42
Jewel Bako	41
Lavagna	45
Liquiteria	4
Mama's Food Shop	49
Mamoun's Falafel	23
Mermaid Inn	40
Moishe's	32
Momofuku Noodle Bar	7
Panya Bakery	17
Pommes Frites	26
Prune	1
Sarita's Mac & Cheese	56
SEA Thai	45
Shabu Tatsu	11
Supper	53
Takahachi	41
Tasting Room	58
Tsampa	14
Veniero's Pasticceria & Café	5
Veselka	16
Via Della Pace	33
Xunta	8
Zerza	37

BARS

7B	34
Angel's Share	18
Bar Veloce	3
Bourgeois Pig	30
Burp Castle	29
Cozy Café	60
Croxley Ales	52
d.b.a.	25
Decibel	51
Grassroots Tavern	22
Hi Fi	9
Holiday Cocktail Lounge	19
KGB	46
Lakeside Lounge	10
Manitoba's	36
McSorley's Old Ale House	28
Sophie's	44
St Dymphna's	25
The Sunburnt Cow	21
Temple Bar	61
Von	55
Zum Schneider	31

the two across from each other at Astor Place), thoughtful resistance to the status quo can still be found, and further east **Alphabet City** retains a strong Latino identity.

The East Village can best be reached by taking the #6 train to Astor Place, or the #N or #R trains to the 8th Street station.

Astor Place and around

At Third Avenue and East 8th Street, on the western fringes of the East Village, lies **Astor Place**, named for real-estate tycoon John Jacob Astor. In the 1830s, Lafayette Street, which is a block east of Broadway and runs south from Astor Place, was home to the city's wealthiest residents, not least of whom was Astor himself. Infamous for his greed (supposedly he was still dispatching servants to collect rents even when he was so old and sick he couldn't leave his bed), Astor made his initial fortune in the fur trade and was the wealthiest person in the US at the time of his death in 1848 (worth $115 billion in modern terms) – he remains the fourth richest person in American history. One year earlier, Astor Place Opera House was erected on the corner of Astor Place and East 8th Street, infamous as the site of the **Astor Place Riot** in 1849. Ostensibly the result of a dispute between English Shakespearean actor William Macready and local stage-star Edwin Forrest, the riot exposed the bitter class divisions of the time; Macready was supported by Anglophile, upper-class theatre lovers, while Forrest was backed by the predominantly Irish working class in the area, who were fervently anti-British. Protestors tried to stop Macready's performance, and in the resulting clashes 22 people died. Today the old-fashioned kiosk of the Astor Place subway station, a replica, is bang in the middle of the nearby junction, along with the *Alamo*, a giant black cube installed in 1966 by Tony Rosenthal.

Noho

Squashed between Astor Place, the Bowery, Broadway, and Houston Street, **Noho** was considered part of the East Village until the name was invented by a group of local activists in the 1970s. Hard to believe, but in the nineteenth century this was one of the city's most desirable neighborhoods; these days **Lafayette Street** cuts a grimy trail down into Soho. All that's left to hint that this might once have been more than a down-at-heel gathering of industrial buildings is **Colonnade Row**, a strip of four 1833 Greek-Revival houses with twelve Corinthian columns, just south of Astor Place. Originally over twice as long, the row was constructed as residences for the likes of Cornelius Vanderbilt; it now holds the Astor Place Theater (longtime home to The Blue Man Group; see p.361). The stocky brownstone-and-brick building across Lafayette was once the **Astor Library**. Built with a bequest from John Jacob Astor between 1853 and 1881 (in a belated gesture of *noblesse oblige*), it was the first public library in New York. It became the **Public Theater** in 1967, under the direction of Joseph Papp, founder of Shakespeare in the Park (see p.159).

A quick detour east onto East 4th Street takes you to the **Merchant's House Museum** at no. 29 (Mon & Thurs–Sun noon–5pm; $8, students and seniors $5; ☎212/777-1089, ⓦwww.merchantshouse.com). Constructed in 1832, this elegant Federal-style rowhouse offers a rare and intimate glimpse of domestic life in New York during the 1850s. The house was purchased by Seabury Tredwell in 1835, a successful metal merchant. Remarkably, much of the mid-nineteenth century interior remains in pristine condition, largely

▲ Alamo, Astor Place

thanks to Seabury's daughter Gertrude, who lived here until 1933 – it was preserved as a museum three years later. Folders loaded with information provide ample material for a self-guided tour of the house, providing fascinating background, anecdotes and quotes from the family, their servants and neighbors. Highlights include furniture fashioned by New York's best cabinetmakers, the mahogany four-poster beds upstairs (where both Gertrude and Seabury passed away) and the tiny brass bells in the basement, used to summon the servants.

From here, the site of the legendary underground music club **CBGB** is just a few blocks south, at 315 Bowery. The New York **punk-rock** scene began here in the 1970s, famously hosting bands such as the **Ramones**, **Blondie**, **Patti Smith**, and the **Talking Heads**. In 2003, the city renamed the corner of East 2nd Street and the Bowery "Joey Ramone Place," in honor of the late punk legend. The club finally closed in 2006, and in a sign of the times has become a John Varvatos fashion boutique; designer clothes and vinyl records are displayed in the original, dimly lit interior, with walls plastered with punk memorabilia. Another vestige of the East Village's radical past lies across the Bowery at 9 Bleecker St, where the **Yippie Museum and Café** (T212/677-5918, Wwwwyippiemuseum.org) hosts informal concerts and readings. Although the museum moniker might be slightly misleading at the moment, the place eventually aims to display old Yippie newspapers and protest fliers. The counterculture/antiwar group, led by Abbie Hoffman (who died in 1989), has been based here since 1973, despite being regularly faced with eviction.

Cooper Square and St Mark's Place

East of Astor Place is **Cooper Square**, a busy crossroads formed by the intersection of the Bowery, Third and Fourth avenues, and St Mark's Place/ East 8th Street, where countless teenagers and out-of-town hipsters mill around, wolfing pizza, drinking cheap beer, or skateboarding. Despite the construction of several glitzy contemporary buildings nearby, the focus of the square remains the seven-story brownstone mass of **Cooper Union for the Advancement of Science and Art**, erected in 1859 as a college for the poor by the wealthy industrialist Peter Cooper. Historically, Cooper Union is known as the place where, in 1860, Abraham Lincoln wowed an audience of New Yorkers with his so-called "right makes might" speech, criticizing the pro-slavery policies of the Southern states – before going to *McSorley's* on East 7th St (see p.344) to quench his thirst. It was also the site of Clara Lemlich's rousing speech (in Yiddish) in support of the landmark shirtwaist strike of 1909, also known as the **Uprising of the 20,000**. The strike resulted in higher wages and shorter hours for most workers, though many factories (such as the Triangle factory, see p.106) paid lip-service to the strikers' demands, with tragic results. Today, Cooper Union remains a prestigious art and architecture school, whose nineteenth-century glory is evoked with a statue of the benevolent Cooper just in front.

St Mark's Place extends east from Cooper Square. Between Second and Third avenues its independent book and discount record stores compete for space with hippie-chic clothiers and newly installed chain restaurants, signaling the end of the gritty atmosphere that had dominated this thoroughfare for years. To the north and south of St Mark's Place, East 7th and 9th streets boast used-clothing stores as well as several original boutiques, while 6th Street between First and Second avenues is known as "Indian" or "Curry" Row after the preponderance of restaurants here from the subcontinent, most with a Bengali slant.

Cooper Square to Second Avenue

Just behind Cooper Square is an area long-inhabited by New York's Ukrainian community, most evidenced by the beautifully adorned exterior of St George's Catholic Church on East 7th Street, and the **Ukrainian Museum**, 222 E 6th St (Wed–Sun 11.30am–5pm; $8, students and seniors $6;

212/228-0110, www.ukrainianmuseum.org), primarily a collection of Ukrainian folk costumes, modern art, and examples of the country's famous painted eggs, known as *pysanky*. You can buy them at the **Surma Ukrainian Shop** at 11 E 7th Street (Mon–Fri 11am–6pm, Sat 11am–4pm), along with Ukrainian music, newspapers, cards, and icons.

Across on Second Avenue, between East 5th and 6th streets, the apartment on the second floor of no. 91 was the childhood home of the **Gershwin** brothers, one of the greatest musical partnerships in history. George and Ira grew up in the heart of the **Yiddish Theater district**, centered on Second Avenue, which by World War I rivaled Broadway in scale and quality. The Immigration Act of 1924 signaled the end, however, and today all that remains of this once exuberant art form is the **Yiddish Walk of Fame** at the corner of East 10th Street.

A few blocks north along Second Avenue at East 10th Street is **St Mark's Church-in-the-Bowery**, the second oldest church building in the city. In 1660, **Peter Stuyvesant** built a small chapel here close to his farm, and was buried inside in 1672. Stuyvesant was the last Dutch Director-General of the New Netherlands, arriving in what was then New Amsterdam in 1647 and surrendering the city to the English in 1664 (see p.434). The box-like Episcopalian house of worship that currently occupies this space was completed in 1799 over his tomb, and sports a Neoclassical portico that was added fifty years later. The church is usually locked (services Sun 11am, Wed 6.30pm, Fri noon, Sat 5.30pm), but Stuyvesant's tombstone is now set into the outer walls. Nearby is a bust of the Director-General donated by the Dutch in 1915, looking far nobler than the crude early English caricatures of "Peg-leg Pete" suggest.

W.H. Auden and Allen Ginsberg read poetry inside (Ginsberg's memorial service was held at the church in 1997), and the St Mark's Poetry Project (212/674-0910, www.urbanwordnyc.org) was founded in 1966 to ignite artistic and social change. It remains an important literary rendezvous, with regular readings, dance performances, and music recitals most Monday, Wednesday, and Friday evenings at 8pm ($8).

Tompkins Square Park

Fringed by avenues A and B and East 7th and 10th streets, **Tompkins Square Park**, once part of the estate of President James Monroe, has long been a focus for the Lower East Side/East Village community as well as one of New York's great centers for political protest. The late Yippie leader Abbie Hoffman lived nearby, and residents like him, along with the many incidents in the square, are what have given the East Village its maverick reputation. The first annual **Wigstock**, a celebration of high kitsch and cross-dressing, was held here in 1985. In 2003, Wigstock was folded into the first **Howl Annual Festival of East Village Arts**, a week-long event in August or September named for Allen Ginsberg's famous poem and founded to channel the neighborhood's creative spirits.

In recent years, Tompkins Square Park has evolved from its former identity as a place of protests, squatters, and riots (see box opposite) to a desirable outdoor space that appeals to both local families and drag queens. The cleaned-up park features handball courts and a dog run. There's even a farmers' greenmarket on Sundays, as well as free concerts, a regular summer pastime for locals.

One of the few things to see in the area is a small marble monument showing two children gazing forlornly out to sea, which you can find just inside the brick enclosure on the north side of the park. In 1904, the local community,

The Tompkins Square riots

Until the early 1990s, Tompkins Square Park was more or less a shantytown (known locally as "Tent City"). Hundreds of homeless people slept on benches or under makeshift shelters between the paths. In the winter, only the really hardy or truly desperate lived here, but when the weather got warmer the numbers swelled, as activists, anarchists, and all manner of statement-makers descended upon the former army barracks, hoping to rekindle the spirit of 1988. That was the year of the **Tompkins Square Riots**, when massive demonstrations against a 1am curfew for the previously 24-hour park led the police, badges covered and nightsticks drawn, to attempt to clear the square of people. In the ensuing battle, 44 demonstrators and bystanders were hurt. The investigation that followed heavily criticized the police for the violence. In the summer of 1995 another riot erupted as police tried to evict a group of squatters from an empty apartment building nearby. This time, protesters were armed with video cameras, but, though heated, the riot never reached the proportions of 1988. Despite resistance, the park was eventually overhauled, its winding pathways and playground restored; the changes are enforced by an 11pm lock-up and police surveillance.

then mostly made up of German immigrants, was devastated by the burning and sinking of a cruise ship, the *General Slocum*, in Long Island Sound. In the aftermath, most of the traumatized German-Americans in the neighborhood moved away, many to Yorkville (see p.184). The monument commemorates the 1021 lives lost, mostly women and children, with a moving quote from Shelley's poem *Revolt of Islam*. Near the center of the park is the **Prabhupada elm tree**. Planted in 1965, it was the site of the Hare Krishna movement's first ceremony outside of India, held in 1966.

At 151 Avenue B, on the east side of the park, is the famous saxophonist and composer **Charlie Parker's house** (Ⓦ www.charlieparkerresidence.net), a simple whitewashed structure with a Gothic doorway. Bird, as he was know to colleagues, friends and fans, lived here from 1950 until his death of a pneumonia-related hemorrhage in 1954. The house is privately owned (and closed to the public) by jazz photographer Judy Rhodes, who led the campaign to have the house listed as an historic landmark in the 1990s.

Alphabet City

East of Tompkins Square Park and north of Houston Street is **Alphabet City**, one of the most dramatically revitalized areas of Manhattan. Deriving its name from the grid of avenues lettered A–D, where the island bulges out beyond the city's grid structure below 14th Street, Alphabet City is also known to its remaining Puerto Rican residents as **Loisaida** (a Spanglish rendering of "Lower East Side"). Like Tompkins Square Park, this used to be a notoriously unsafe corner of town run by drug pushers and gangsters; most of this was brought to a halt in 1983 with "Operation Pressure Point," a massive police campaign to make the neighborhood livable again. This aim has certainly been achieved: the crime rate is way down, many of the old buildings have been renovated, and the streets are increasingly the haunt of twenty-somethings and edgier tourist youth. Only Avenue D might still give you some pause, in terms of safety, at night; avenues A, B, and C have some of the coolest bars, cafés, and stores in the city. Comestibles aside, it's worth wandering around this part of town just to see some of the murals and **public art**, as well as the numerous community gardens (see box, p.100).

Community gardens

In the 1970s, huge parts of the East Village burned to the ground after cuts in the city's fire-fighting budget closed many of the local firehouses. Since then, East Village residents have reclaimed these neglected and empty lots, turning the rubble-filled messes into some of the prettiest and most verdant spaces in lower Manhattan. Unable to leave them alone, the city decided that these spaces could be used for something much more valuable than grass – more real estate. Despite a 1999 agreement which ensured the safety of around 100 of the neighborhood's over 600 gardens, the battle reached fever pitch in February 2000, when El Jardin de la Esperanza (Hope Garden) on East 7th Street between avenues B and C was bulldozed to make way for market-priced housing. Around thirty local residents were arrested while protesting the action; the city began to bulldoze the garden while the last resister was being removed – a mere forty minutes before an injunction was issued to prevent the city from destroying any community gardens.

The fight seems to have been well worth it. There is no nicer way to spend a summer evening or a Sunday afternoon than by grabbing some picnic ingredients and relaxing among the lush trees and carefully planted foliage of these spaces. Of particular note is the East 6th Street and Avenue B affair, overgrown with wildflowers, vegetables, trees, and roses, and home to the spectacular 65-foot **"Tower of Toys"** maintained by local character Eddie Boros until his death in 2007. The garden also provides a space for yoga classes in the morning and performance art in the evening during the summer, as well as a forum for bake sales, sing-alongs, and other community events. Other gardens include the very serene 6 B/C Botanical Garden on East 6th Street between B and C; Miracle Garden on East 3rd Street between A and B; Loisaida Garden on East 4th Street between B and C; the Parque de Tranquilidad on East 4th Street between C and D; and the Lower East Side Ecology Center Garden on East 7th Street between B and C.

8

The West Village

When the *Village Voice*, the venerable listings/comment/investigative magazine, began chronicling Greenwich Village nightlife in 1955, "the Village" had a dissident, artistic, vibrant voice. And though it's still one of the more progressive neighborhoods in the city, Greenwich Village (now commonly called the **West Village**) has attained a moneyed status over the last four decades and is definitely the place for those who have Arrived. (Perhaps not coincidentally, the *Voice* moved its offices to Cooper Square in the East Village in 1991.) Celebrities seem to snap up properties right and left, and the historic enclave is booming with development. These famous residents – the likes of Nicole Kidman, Philip Seymour Hoffman, Ethan Hawke, and Cameron Diaz, for example – have come for the same reasons that the intelligentsia did a century ago: quaint sidestreets, charming brownstones, and brick townhouses unrivaled elsewhere in Manhattan. It's quiet and residential, but with a busy streetlife that keeps humming later into the night than in many other parts of the city. Restaurants, cafés, bars, and boutiques clutter most every corner, and Washington Square is a hub of superbly aimless activity throughout the year.

Bounded by 14th Street to the north, Houston Street to the south, the Hudson River to the west, and Broadway to the east, the West Village is easily reached by the #1 train to Christopher Street or the #A, #C, #E, #F, or #V to West 4th Street.

Some history

Greenwich Village was originally designed as a rural retreat away from the frenetic nucleus of early New York City. During the yellow fever epidemic of 1822 it became highly sought-after as a refuge from infected downtown streets, and there was even talk of moving the entire city center here when the fever was at its height. Thankfully, the Village was spared that dubious honor, and was instead left in peace to grow into a wealthy residential neighborhood. Before long it had sprouted elegant Federal and Greek-Revival terraces and lured some of the city's highest society names.

At the close of the nineteenth century, German, Irish, and Italian immigrants swarmed to jobs in breweries, warehouses, and coal yards along the Hudson River, causing the once-genteel veneer of New York City's refined "American Ward" to disappear. As the immigrants moved in, rents plummeted and the neighborhood took on a much more working-class atmosphere. Left behind when the rich migrated farther and farther uptown, the area's large houses proved a fertile hunting ground for struggling artists and intellectuals on the lookout for cheap rents and a community of

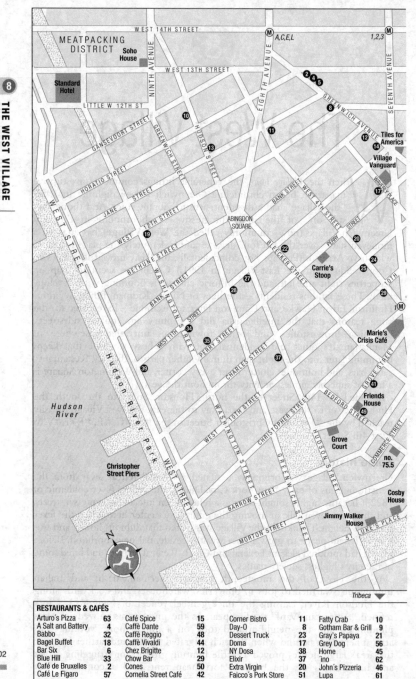

RESTAURANTS & CAFÉS

Arturo's Pizza	63	Café Spice	15	Corner Bistro	11	Fatty Crab	10
A Salt and Battery	4	Caffè Dante	59	Day-O	8	Gotham Bar & Grill	9
Babbo	32	Caffè Reggio	48	Dessert Truck	23	Gray's Papaya	21
Bagel Buffet	18	Caffè Vivaldi	44	Doma	17	Grey Dog	56
Bar Six	6	Chez Brigitte	12	NY Dosa	38	Home	45
Blue Hill	33	Chow Bar	29	Elixir	37	´ino	62
Café de Bruxelles	2	Cones	50	Extra Virgin	20	John's Pizzeria	46
Café Le Figaro	57	Cornelia Street Café	42	Faicco's Pork Store	51	Lupa	61

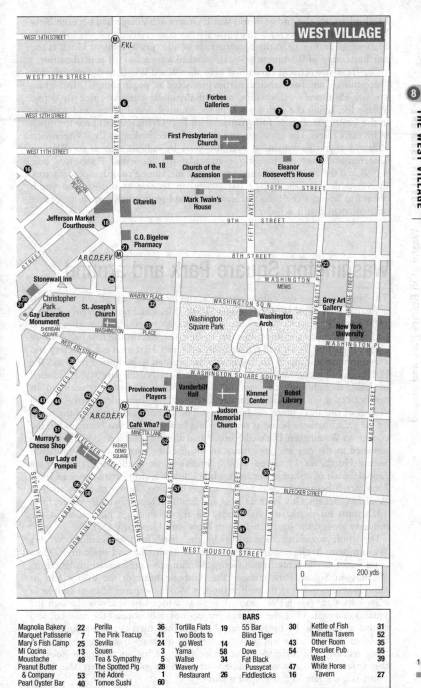

WEST 14TH STREET   Ⓜ F,V,L

WEST 13TH STREET

WEST 12TH STREET

WEST 11TH STREET

SIXTH AVENUE

Forbes Galleries

First Presbyterian Church

no. 18   Church of the Ascension

Eleanor Roosevelt's House

10TH STREET

Citarella   Mark Twain's House

Jefferson Market Courthouse

9TH STREET

C.O. Bigelow Pharmacy

FIFTH AVENUE

8TH STREET

A,B,C,D,E,F,V   Ⓜ

Stonewall Inn

WASHINGTON MEWS

Grey Art Gallery

UNIVERSITY PLACE

GREENE STREET

Christopher Park

Gay Liberation Monument

SHERIDAN SQUARE

St. Joseph's Church

WAVERLY PLACE

WASHINGTON SQ N

Washington Square Park

Washington Arch

New York University

WASHINGTON PL

WEST 4TH STREET

WASHINGTON PLACE

WASHINGTON SQUARE SOUTH

Provincetown Players

Vanderbilt Hall

Kimmel Center

Bobst Library

MERCER STREET

JONES ST.

CORNELIA ST.

A,B,C,D,E,F,V   Ⓜ

Café Wha?

W. 3RD ST.

Judson Memorial Church

Murray's Cheese Shop

BLEECKER STREET

FATHER DEMO SQUARE

MINETTA LANE

Our Lady of Pompeii

SEVENTH AVENUE

CARMINE STREET

MINETTA STREET

MACDOUGAL STREET

SULLIVAN STREET

THOMPSON STREET

LAGUARDIA PLACE

BLEECKER STREET

SIXTH AVENUE

DOWNING STREET

WEST HOUSTON STREET

0   200 yds

Magnolia Bakery	22	Perilla	36	Tortilla Flats	19	**BARS**
Marquet Patisserie	7	The Pink Teacup	41	Two Boots to		55 Bar	30
Mary's Fish Camp	25	Sevilla	24	go West	14	Blind Tiger
Mi Cocina	13	Souen	3	Yama		Ale	43
Moustache	49	Tea & Sympathy	5	Wallse	34	Dove	54
Peanut Butter		The Spotted Pig	28	Waverly		Fat Black
& Company	53	Thé Adoré	1	Restaurant	26	Pussycat	47
Pearl Oyster Bar	40	Tomoe Sushi	60			Fiddlesticks	16

Kettle of Fish	31
Minetta Tavern	52
Other Room	35
Peculier Pub	55
West	39
White Horse	
Tavern	27

Yama 58

freethinkers. By the end of World War I, Greenwich Village had become New York's Left Bank. Decrepit rowhouses were converted into bohemian-style apartments, and in 1926 the construction of a luxury apartment block at the northern edge of Washington Square marked a turn toward gentrification.

The **Beat movement** flourished here after World War II, as did unorthodox "happenings," and bacchanalian parties promoted as "pagan romps." Meanwhile, the neighborhood's cafés, clubs, and off-Broadway theaters came to define Village life, laying the path for rebellious, countercultural groups and activities in the 1960s, particularly **folk music**, with Bob Dylan resident here for much of his early career. The mystique and allure of a freethinking activist Greenwich Village was further enhanced over the years by radicals such as the Weather Underground, history-changing events like the Stonewall Riots (see box, p.109), and the area's invigorating intellectual life, among countless other factors. In recent decades, the Village has grown up, leaving its impassioned youth behind to become the fashionable, historic, and increasingly expensive corner of Manhattan that it is today.

Washington Square Park and around

The best way to see the Village is to walk, and by far the best place to start is its natural center, **Washington Square Park**. Memorialized in Henry James's 1880 novel *Washington Square*, the city began an extensive renovation of the park in 2007, with the first phase due to be completed in the first half of 2009 – until then, much of it will remain sadly off limits. First used as a cemetery and execution ground (up to 10,000 bodies are reputed to be buried here and the Hangman's Elm continues to grow in the park today), the park was established in 1827, though only the row of elegant Greek Revival mansions on its northern edge – the "solid, honorable dwellings" that James described – remind visitors of the area's more illustrious past. The author based much of the novel on his grandmother's house at no. 19, while James himself was born around the corner on Washington Place (the house had already been torn down when he returned to the city in 1906, much to his disgust). Further along Washington Square North, no. 11 served as Will Smith's home in the 2007 movie *I am Legend* (much of it shot in the area), while Edith Wharton lived at no. 7 in 1882. Later, no. 3 became known as the "studio building," home to artists such as William Glackens, Guy Pène du Bois, and Edward Hopper, who lived here from 1913 until his death in 1967. Today, all these buildings, like much of the property around the square, belong to New York University (NYU).

The most imposing monument in the park itself is Stanford White's **Washington Arch**, inspired by the Arc de Triomphe and built in 1892 to commemorate the centenary of George Washington's presidential inauguration. Washington Square Park remains the symbolic heart of the Village and its radicalism – so much so that when Robert Moses, the paver of great chunks of New York City (see p.154), wanted to plow a four-lane roadway through the square's center in 1952, the ensuing protests not only stopped the road but also caused all traffic to be banned from the park, then used as a turnaround point by buses. For years the square was something of an open-air drug bazaar, but more recently a heavy undercover police presence has put an end to most of that activity. Not that you should be worried about your safety here; these days, crime is quite rare in this part of town.

▲ Chess tournament, Washington Square Park

During the spring and summer months, the square becomes a combination running track, performance venue, giant chess tournament, and social club, boiling over with life as skateboards flip, dogs run, and guitar notes crash through the urgent cries of performers calling for the crowd's attention.

NYU and south of the square

The south and east sides of the square are lined with bulky New York University buildings, although even nonstudents will be interested in the university's innovative **Grey Art Gallery**, 100 Washington Square E (Tues, Thurs & Fri

The Triangle Shirtwaist Fire

One of New York's most infamous tragedies occurred on March 25, 1911, at the corner of Washington Place and Greene Street, when a fire started on the eighth floor of the **Triangle Shirtwaist garment factory**, one of the city's most notorious sweatshops. A terrible combination of flammable fabrics, locked doors, collapsing fire escapes, and the inability of fire-truck ladders to reach higher than the sixth floor, resulted in the deaths of 146 workers – almost entirely women, primarily immigrants, and some only 13 years old – in less than fifteen minutes. The fire led to legislation requiring improved safety standards, and helped spur the growth of the International Ladies' Garment Workers' Union. The site is now known as the Brown Building and forms part of NYU, with flowers left in front of the plaque commemorating the disaster on March 25 each year.

11am–6pm, Wed 11am–8pm, Sat 11am–5pm; suggested donation $3; ☏ 212/998-6780, ⓦ www.nyu.edu/greyart/). The space hosts top-notch traveling exhibitions, which rotate every three months and feature a wide range of media, including sculpture, painting, photography, and provocative video shows. On the south side of the square only the elaborate **Judson Memorial Church** (☏ 212/477-0351, ⓦ www.judson.org) stands out amid a messy blend of modern architecture, one of Stanford White's most elegant Italianate creations. Built as a Baptist church in 1892, with seventeen gorgeous stained-glass windows by John La Farge, the church is a hub of local activism today, particularly in the areas of immigration, Fair Trade, and anti-war protest.

Over the years, many notable authors have called Washington Square South home. A penniless **Edgar Allan Poe** lived nearby at 85 W 3rd Street while writing *The Raven* in the 1840s, and playwright **Eugene O'Neill**, one of the Village's most acclaimed residents, lived (and in 1939, completed *The Iceman Cometh*) at **38 Washington Square South**, now the site of NYU's Vanderbilt Hall. O'Neill consumed vast quantities of ale at *The Golden Swan Bar*, which once stood on the corner of Sixth Avenue and West 4th Street and is now a garden. *The Golden Swan* (variously called *The Hell Hole*, *Bucket of Blood*, and other such inviting names) was best known in O'Neill's day for the dubious morals of its clientele – a gang of Irish hoodlums known as the Hudson Dusters – and for the pig in the basement that ate the customers' trash. O'Neill was great pals with this crowd and drew many of his characters from the bar's personalities.

South along MacDougal Street

From the southwest corner of the park, follow MacDougal Street south to no. 133, home of the **Provincetown Players**, who, on the advice of Village resident John Reed (author of *Ten Days that Shook the World*, a firsthand account of the Russian Revolution), moved here from Massachusetts in 1915 and opened this theater in 1918. Continue to 115 MacDougal, home of the famous **Café Wha?**, where "soul food for the ear, mind, and, body" was offered in the 1960s. Jimi Hendrix and Bill Cosby began their careers here, and Allen Ginsberg and Abbie Hoffman were regular customers. Continue south until you reach Bleecker Street, with its touristy concentration of boutiques, delis, restaurants, and European-style sidewalk cafés.

North of Washington Square

This is college country, so throngs of students are a permanent part of the scenery in the area. Running between University Place and Fifth Avenue just north of the square, **Washington Mews** stands out from the legions of coffee shops and quick-fix bodegas. The pin-neat prettiness of the small cobblestone street and old pastel buildings seems out of place amid the grand brownstones that abut the square. This alley was used to stable horses until it was redesigned in 1916 to stable humans, and most recently NYU professors.

If you head north up Fifth Avenue, off which the neighborhood's low-slung residential streets lead to some eminently desirable apartment buildings, you'll pass a couple of imposing churches. On the corner of West 10th Street stands the Episcopal **Church of the Ascension** (Mon–Sat noon–1pm; Ⓦwww .ascensionnyc.org), built in 1841 by Richard Upjohn (the Trinity Church architect), where a vast but gracefully toned La Farge altar painting and some fine stained glass are on view.

Continuing the Gothic theme, Joseph Wells's bulky, chocolate-brown **First Presbyterian Church** (Mon–Fri noon–12.30pm; services Sun 11am; Ⓦwww .fpcnyc.org), just across 11th Street, was completed in 1845 with a crenellated tower modeled on the one at Magdalen College in Oxford, England. Inside you'll find carved black-walnut pews, a soaring altarpiece and a fabulous Tiffany Rose Window.

One block north you'll see one of the city's quirkiest small museums, the **Forbes Galleries**, 62 Fifth Ave, at 12th St (Tues–Sat 10am–4pm; free; Ⓣ212/206-5548, Ⓦwww.forbesgalleries.com), which contain a rather whimsical collection of treasures assembled by the Forbes family, owners of the publishing empire. The 10,000-strong host of tin soldiers, over 500 model boats, and early Monopoly boards, will appeal primarily to aficionados and kids, though the galleries also hold temporary exhibitions of a diverse range of art work, from cartoons to rare Art Deco gems.

Walk west on West 10th and 11th streets and you'll find some of the best-preserved early nineteenth-century townhouses in the Village, with the exception of the rebuilt facade of **18 W 11th St** (see box below).

The Weathermen

In 1969, disillusioned by the failure of peaceful protest to stop the Vietnam War, a militant faction of pressure group Students for a Democratic Society set up a bomb factory in the basement of the Henry Brevoort–designed house at 18 W 11th St. Known as the **Weathermen**, the group aimed to bomb a military ball to be held at Fort Dix, New Jersey, but the plan backfired disastrously. On March 6, 1970, the house's arsenal exploded, killing three of the group (two escaped). The organization went into hiding soon after, becoming the **Weather Underground** and evading capture by the FBI, despite being on their Most Wanted List. The group was responsible for several bombings in the 1970s, though the loss of life was studiously avoided – though buildings in New York and Washington, D.C, were damaged, the group's most notorious exploit was busting counterculture guru Timothy Leary out of prison in 1970. By 1980 most of the group had surrendered to the authorities, though few were ever charged; the FBI had broken so many laws trying to catch them, most evidence was inadmissible.

Incidentally, the Weathermen's neighbor at the time of the 11th Street bomb was actor Dustin Hoffman, whose home at no. 16 suffered extensive damage from the blast.

Mark Twain lived at 14 W 10th St between 1900 and 1902 (the celebrated author died in New York in 1910), while poet **Emma Lazarus** lived at no. 18. **Eleanor Roosevelt** resided at 20 E 11th St between 1933 and 1942, but since this period coincided with her husband's presidency, it's probable that she spent more time talking domestic and foreign policies than playing bridge with her West Village neighbors.

Sixth Avenue and west

Although **Sixth Avenue** is for the most part lined with mediocre stores, restaurants, and modern buildings, there are some exceptions, like the unmistakable clocktower of the nineteenth-century **Jefferson Market Courthouse** at West 10th St. Erected in 1876, this imposing High Victorian–style edifice, complete with gargoyles, first served as an indoor market but went on to be a firehouse, a jail, and, since 1967, a public library. Across the street from the courthouse and opening onto West 10th Street, **Patchin Place** is a tiny mews constructed in 1848. The rowhouses were home to the reclusive author Djuna Barnes for more than forty years. Supposedly, Barnes's long-time neighbor e e cummings used to call her "just to see if she was still alive." Patchin Place has also been home to Marlon Brando, Ezra Pound, and Eugene O'Neill. Heading south, look out for **C.O. Bigelow Pharmacy**, at 414 Sixth Ave, just north of West 8th Street, founded in 1838 and probably the city's oldest drugstore.

Off Sixth Avenue's west side are some of the Village's prettiest residential streets, where you can easily spend a couple hours strolling and soaking up the neighborhood's charms. To start exploring, cross Father Demo Square and walk up **Bleecker Street** past the Italian-Renaissance style **Our Lady of Pompeii Church**, built in 1929. Until the 1970s there was an Italian open marketplace on this stretch, and it's still lined by a few Italian stores and cafés, notably *Faicco's* (see p.296) and **Rocco's** (best-known for its nut-sprinkled *cannoli*), as well as celebrated deli **Murray's Cheese** (see p.399). If folk music is your thing, **Bob Dylan** lived for a time at 161 W 4th St, and the cover of his 1963 *Freewheelin'* album was shot a few paces away on Jones Street, just off Bleecker, a scene faithfully recreated in the Cameron Crowe movie *Vanilla Sky*.

If you turn down Leroy Street, and continue west across Seventh Avenue, you'll come to St. Luke's Place, a tranquil block favored by TV and movie directors; no. 10 was used as the exterior of the **Cosby house**. No. 6 (recognizable by the two gas lamps at the bottom of the steps) is the ex-residence of **Jimmy Walker**, mayor of New York in the 1920s. Walker was for a time the most popular of mayors, a big-spending wisecracker who gave up working as a songwriter for politics and lived an extravagant lifestyle that rarely kept him out of the gossip columns – he resigned in 1932, accused of corruption.

Bedford and Grove streets

Just north of St Luke's Place, **Bedford Street** runs west off Seventh Avenue to become one of the quietest and most desirable Village addresses. Edna St Vincent Millay, the young poet and playwright who did a lot of work with the Provincetown Players, lived at no. 751/2. At only 9ft wide, it is one of the narrowest houses in the city. The brick and clapboard structure next door at no. 77 is the **Isaacs–Hendricks House**, built in 1799 and the oldest house in the Village.

On the corner with Barrow Street, the former speakeasy *Chumley's*, 86 Bedford St, was once recognizable only by the metal grille on its door – a low profile useful in Prohibition years that makes it hard to find today. Closed in 2007 after a wall collapsed, the bar was expected to reopen in late 2008, though its future remains uncertain.

The building at no. 90, right on the corner of **Grove Street** (above the *Little Owl*), served as the exterior for Monica's apartment in *Friends*, though the TV series was shot entirely in L.A. studios. Opposite is **17 Grove St**, built in 1822 and one of the most complete wood-frame houses in the city. Turn left here down Grove Street and you'll find **Grove Court** just off the road, one of the neighborhood's most attractive and exclusive little mews.

Heading back to Seventh Avenue on Grove Street, keep an eye out for *Marie's Crisis Café* at no. 59. Now a gay piano bar, this was the site of the rented rooms where English revolutionary writer and philosopher **Thomas Paine** died in 1809. Paine, who was reviled in England for his support of both the American and French revolutions, was the author of the eighteenth century's three best-selling pamphlets, his *Common Sense* of 1776 generally credited for turning public opinion in favor of US independence. Cantankerous and conceited to the end, Paine made plenty of enemies, and after the publication of the *Age of Reason*, many Americans assumed he was an atheist (he was actually a deist). By the time he died here, he was poverty-stricken and abandoned by his former friends, including Thomas Jefferson. The current building dates from 1839, the café named in part after Paine's masterful essay *The American Crisis*.

Christopher Street and around

Christopher Street, the main artery of the West Village, runs west from Jefferson Market Courthouse and past Christopher Park – the traditional center of the city's gay community. Confusingly, the park holds a pompous-looking statue of Civil War cavalry commander General Sheridan, though Sheridan Square is actually the next space down, where West 4th Street meets Washington Place. Historically, the area is better known, however, as the scene of one of the worst ... New York's [riots for a the Gay] (p.435), when a marauding ... of the black community, ... here in 1969, when the ... (see box below). The riots ... **liberation Monument**

[handwritten note: The Cosby House?]

... and started arresting its ... est occurrence in a long ... other bars in the area, and ... angry protestors, resulting ... d with several arrests and ... or their rights, it was the ... persecution and, as such, ... is honored by the Annual ... st referred to as the **Gay** ... e is one of the city's most

in the park, four life-size white-painted figures (two males, two females), unveiled in 1992.

Nowadays, however, the gay community is fairly synonymous with Greenwich Village life; for complete listings of gay bars and clubs, see p.375 and p.377.

The area **north of Christopher Street** contains some of the most appealing and expensive residential streets in the city, with a bevy of unique stores, coffee bars, and restaurants catering to its upwardly mobile and moneyed residential community. The *Village Vanguard* (see p.356), at 178 Seventh Ave, has been a jazz mecca since 1935, a live venue which has played host to every major jazz star and where Sonny Rollins and John Coltrane made classic album recordings in the 1950s and 1960s. Further west, you'll probably see small groups of excited fans taking photos at 66 Perry St, between Bleecker and West 4th Street, used as the exterior of Carrie's apartment in *Sex and the City* ("Carrie's Stoop"), while almost constant lines form outside lauded **Magnolia Bakery** at Bleecker and West 11th St (see p.295). The historic *White Horse Tavern*, over at West 11th St and Hudson, was frequented by Norman Mailer and Hunter S. Thompson among others, and is where legend claims Dylan Thomas had his last drink (see p.346); Jack Kerouac rented an apartment opposite. Between 1971 and 1973, John Lennon and Yoko Ono lived in relative obscurity at 105 Bank St, a block from the White Horse at Greenwich Street, before moving uptown (see p.193).

Chelsea

A squat grid of renovated tenements, rowhouses, and warehouses, **Chelsea** lies west of Broadway between 14th and 30th streets, though most consider the area between 14th and 23rd streets to be the heart of the neighborhood. For years, these dreary, overlooked buildings and bare streets gave Chelsea an atmosphere of neglect and did not encourage visitors to linger. Over the past few decades, however, Chelsea has become quite commercial, influenced greatly by the arrival of a large gay community in the late 1980s and early 1990s. Today, its districts are filled with affluent townhouses whose inhabitants relish the luxury of extra living space. Stores and restaurants pepper the scene, along with excellent cutting-edge art **galleries** and increasingly up-market real estate.

RESTAURANTS & CAFÉS				BARS	
Amy's Bread	25	Empire Diner	9	The Old Homestead	27	Elmo	15
Billy's Bakery	12	F + B	7	Paradou	30	Half King	5
Bottino	3	Hill Country	2	Park	20	Hiro Ballroom	22
Cafetiera	21	La Lunchonette	19	Rafaella on Ninth	13	Hogs & Heifers	29
Chelsea Ristorante	26	La Taza de Oro	28	Red Cat	4	Marquee	1
Cookshop	14	Maroon's	23	Rocking Horse	16	Peter McManus Café	18
Eleni's Cookie's	24	Monster Sushi	11	Royal Siam	10	Trailer Park Lounge	6
El Quijote	8	Moran's	17				

To begin your visit to Chelsea, take the #1, #2, or #3 train to 14th Street and Seventh Avenue, or take the #C or #E to 14th and Eighth.

Some history

The neighborhood, developed on former farmland, began to take shape in 1830 thanks to **Clement Clarke Moore**, famous as the author of the surprise poetic hit *A Visit from St Nick* (popularly known as *'Twas the Night Before Christmas*), whose estate comprised most of what is now Chelsea. That year, Moore, anticipating Manhattan's movement uptown, laid out his land for sale in broad lots. However, stuck as it was between the ritziness of Fifth Avenue, the hipness of Greenwich Village, and the poverty of Hell's Kitchen, the area never quite made it onto the shortlist of desirable places to live. Manhattan's chic residential focus leapfrogged over Chelsea to the East 40s and 50s, and the arrival of the slaughterhouses, an elevated railroad, and working-class poor sealed Chelsea's reputation as a rough-and-tumble no-go area for decades.

The last few decades have seen a totally new Chelsea emerge. New York's drifting art scene has been extremely influential in the neighborhood's transformation. In the early 1990s, a number of respected **galleries** began making use of the large spaces available in the low-rise warehouses of Chelsea's western reaches, securing the area's cultural edge. This influx has been counterbalanced by the steadily expanding presence of retail superstores, especially along **Sixth Avenue**, and the building of the **Chelsea Piers** mega-sized sports complex. For years now, the neighborhood has been crowded with shoppers, restaurant-goers, and the like, and it shows no signs of quieting down.

Meatpacking District

Creating a buffer between the West Village and Chelsea proper, the **Meatpacking District** between Gansevoort Street and West 15th Street, west of Ninth Avenue, has seen the majority of its working slaughterhouses converted to French bistros, after-hours clubs, wine bars, and fancy galleries. Though a few wholesale meat companies remain, the area is now very much designer territory, with Stella McCartney and Alexander McQueen among the fashion boutiques

The High Line

One of New York's most ambitious urban regeneration projects, the High Line (Ⓦ www.thehighline.org) should be open by 2009 as a unique city park, slicing through the high-rises on a former elevated rail line. Constructed between 1929 and 1934, the line was effectively abandoned in 1980, and has been a rusting eyesore ever since. In 1999, a group of local business-owners joined together to press for the High Line's preservation, and with the city finally on board, construction began in 2006. The first section will run from Gansevoort Street to West 20th Street, with phase two eventually extending 1.5 miles up to West 33rd Street in midtown. Access points will rise from street level about every two blocks. The park's innovative design includes pathways made of smooth concrete planks, tapered at the ends to allow plants to push up through the gaps, the reintroduction of steel rail tracks to symbolize links with the past, and cutting-edge landscaping conceived by Dutch designer Piet Oudolf, combining trees, flowers and liberal use of the local wild plants that first colonized the ruined tracks. The Whitney Museum of American Art is planning a new museum at the southern entrance, to be designed by Renzo Piano (most famous for the Pompidou Center in Paris), while the plush *Standard Hotel* will straddle the park at Little West 12th Street.

lining the cobblestone streets. In a telling confirmation of the district's dramatic transformation (or deterioration into an "urban theme park," according to some critics), the writers of TV series *Sex and the City* had Kim Catrall's character move into a fictional apartment on Gansevoort Street in Season 3 (2000). The opening of the **High Line** (see box opposite) should only add to the area's appeal, providing a tranquil greenway right into the heart of Chelsea.

Ninth and Tenth avenues

As you head north up **Ninth Avenue**, the red-brick **Chelsea Market** fills an entire block between 15th and 16th streets. This high-class food temple is housed in the old National Biscuit Company (aka "Nabisco") factory, where legend has it the Oreo cookie was created. Many of the factory's features remain, including pieces of rail track used to transport provisions. The handpicked retailers inside sell fresh fruit, fish, bread, wine, brownies, and flowers (for more details, see Shopping, p.399).

Farther north, on West 20th, 21st, and 22nd streets between Ninth and Tenth avenues, is the **Chelsea Historic District**, which boasts a picturesque variety of predominantly Italianate and Greek-Revival rowhouses. Dating from the 1830s to the 1890s, they demonstrate the faith some early developers had in Chelsea as an up-and-coming New York neighborhood. The **oldest house** in the area, at 404 W 20th St (just off Ninth Ave), stands out with its 1829 wood siding, predating as it does the all-brick constructions of James Wells, Chelsea's first real-estate developer. The ornate iron fencing heading west along this block, known as **Cushman Row**, is original and quite impressive. Closer to Tenth Avenue, Jack Kerouac lived at 454 20th St with his wife Joan Haverty in 1951 while he wrote *On the Road* (mostly at the Hotel Chelsea, see p.115).

Across the road, the block bounded by 20th and 21st streets between Ninth and Tenth avenues contains one of Chelsea's secrets, the 1817 **General**

▲ Chelsea Market

Theological Seminary (@ www.gts.edu). Clement Clarke Moore donated this island of land to the institute, and today the harmonious assembly of ivy-clad Gothic structures surrounding a green feels like part of a college campus. Though the buildings still house a working Episcopal seminary – the oldest in the United States – it's possible to explore the site Monday to Saturday 11am to 3pm, as long as you sign in and keep quiet. The entrance is temporarily located on West 21st St while parts of the site undergo an extensive renovation.

London Terrace Gardens

Just north of the historic district at 435 W 23rd St is one of New York's premier residences for those who believe in understated opulence. **London Terrace Gardens**, two rows of apartment buildings a full city block long, sit between Ninth and Tenth avenues and surround a private interior garden. The building had the misfortune of being completed in 1930 at the height of the Great Depression, and despite a swimming pool and other posh amenities, many of the 1670 apartments stood empty for several years. The first management, wanting to evoke thoughts of Britain, made the doormen wear London-style police uniforms, thereby giving the building its name. The apartments were later nicknamed "The Fashion Projects" because of their designer, photographer, and model residents (including Isaac Mizrahi, Annie Leibovitz, and Debbie Harry). Novelist and political activist Susan Sontag also lived here until her death in 2004. Though Sontag and Leibovitz began a romantic relationship in the 1980s, the two kept close but separate apartments in the building (Sontag's was worth around $3.75m).

West of Tenth Avenue

Tenth Avenue serves as a dividing line between Chelsea's more historic and quainter side to the east and its industrial past to the west. For years there was not much to see or do along this stretch – that is, until the galleries started swarming in. Along 22nd Street between Tenth and Eleventh avenues, as well as farther north up to West 29th, lie the **galleries** and **warehouse spaces** that house one of New York's most vibrant art scenes. (See "Commercial galleries," p.380, for more details on Chelsea's 150-odd galleries.) Even the ovular entryway to Comme des Garçons – the store is just west of Tenth Avenue at 520 W 22nd St – masquerades as art in this part of town. The buildings used by Chelsea's galleries are especially imposing above West 23rd Street, and in some cases even stretch for a whole block. Visit @ chelseaartgalleries.com to get the latest information on artists, shows, and events.

At West 23rd Street and the West Side Highway, you'll find **Chelsea Piers** (@ www.chelseapiers.com), a glitzy, family-friendly, and somewhat incongruous entertainment development stretching from piers 59 to 62. First opened in 1910, this was where passengers would disembark from the great transatlantic liners (it was en route to the Chelsea Piers that the *Titanic* sank in 1912). By the 1960s, however, the piers had fallen into decay through disuse, and as late as the mid-1980s an official report condemned them as "shabby, pathetic reminders of a glorious past." Since then, money and effort have been poured into the revival of this once illustrious area. Reopened in 1995, the new Chelsea Piers, whose commercial aura begs comparison with South Street Seaport (see p.61), is primarily a huge sports complex, with ice rinks and open-air roller rinks, as well as a skate park, bowling alley, and a landscaped golf driving range (for more details, see "Sports and outdoor activities," p.412).

Across from Chelsea Piers, at the end of 19th Street, warehouses and parking lots have given way to the billowing, fluid walls of Frank Gehry's **IAC Building**, one of New York's newest and most fanciful examples of contemporary architecture. By 2010 this strip will be jammed with condos, designed in a similarly eye-catching style.

Eighth Avenue

Double back east along 23rd Street to Chelsea's main drag, **Eighth Avenue**, where the more laid-back vibe of the West Village, below 14th Street, segues into a stretch of vibrant retail energy. Along here, dozens of trendy bars, restaurants, health-food stores, gyms, bookstores, and clothes shops cater to Chelsea's large, out, and proud gay population.

Just beyond Eighth Avenue, at 222 E 23rd St, is one of the neighborhood's major claims to fame – the **Hotel Chelsea** (see p.279 for accommodation details). Originally built as a luxury cooperative apartment building in 1883 and converted to a hotel in 1905, the building has been the undisputed residence of the city's harder-up literati. Mark Twain, Tennessee Williams, Dylan Thomas and Thomas Wolfe all spent time here, and in 1951 Jack Kerouac, armed with a specially adapted typewriter (and a lot of Benzedrine), typed the first draft of *On the Road* nonstop onto a 120-foot roll of paper. William Burroughs (in a presumably more relaxed state) completed *Naked Lunch* at the Chelsea, and Arthur C. Clarke wrote *2001: A Space Odyssey* while in residence.

In the 1960s, the *Chelsea* entered a wilder phase. Andy Warhol and his doomed protégées Edie Sedgwick and Candy Darling holed up here and made the film *Chelsea Girls*. In probably the hotel's most infamous moment, **Sid Vicious** stabbed Nancy Spungen to death in 1978 in their suite, a few months before he fatally overdosed on heroin. The photographer Robert Mapplethorpe and Patti Smith also lived here in the late 1960s and early 1970s, and the hotel inspired Joni Mitchell's song *Chelsea Morning* and Leonard Cohen's *Chelsea Hotel No.2*.

With a pedigree like this it's easy to forget the hotel itself, which has a down-at-the-heel Edwardian grandeur all of its own. The lobby, with its famously phallic wall-mounted sculpture *Chelsea Dogs*, and plastered with more respectable work by Larry Rivers, is worth a gander.

East Chelsea

Sandwiched between infinitely more interesting blocks, the eastern edge of Chelsea has become a buzzing strip of commerce, concentrated mostly along **Sixth Avenue** between West 17th and 23rd streets. In the last few years, a crush of discount emporiums like Best Buy, and mediocre national chain restaurants have mostly driven out the mom-and-pop businesses, and the trend only seems to be accelerating. On weekends especially, Sixth Avenue teems with bargain hunters lugging oversized bags from places like Bed, Bath and Beyond, the Container Store, and the Sports Authority.

For a brief escape from the commercialism, visit the **Rubin Museum of Art** (Mon & Thurs 11am–5pm, Wed 11am–7pm, Fri 11am–10pm, Sat & Sun 11am–6pm; $10, students and seniors $7; ⊤212/620-5000; ⊛www.rmanyc .org) at 150 W 17th Street, between Sixth and Seventh avenues. The museum is one of the city's less visited gems, a collection of two thousand paintings, sculptures, and textiles from the Himalayas and surrounding regions, spanning the period from the second to the twentieth century. Each piece is clearly labeled and explained, making this an especially enlightening experience for anyone new to Asian art.

Nearby, at the corner of Sixth Avenue and 17th Street, the weekend-only **Chelsea Outdoor Flea Market** occupies one of the few remaining open spaces in this part of town. The recent construction of soaring condos has chased away many stall-owners (mostly to Hell's Kitchen, see p.149), though the **Garage Antiques Market** at 112 W 25th St (between Sixth and Seventh aves) and the **West 25th Street Market** (between Sixth and Fifth aves) still take place at the weekend (see "Shopping," p.398).

The area around West 28th Street is Manhattan's **Flower Market** – not really a market as such, more the warehouses and storefronts where potted plants and cut flowers are stored before brightening offices and atriums across the city. There are no signs to mark the strip, and you come across it by chance: the greenery bursting out of drab blocks provides a welcome touch of life in a decidedly industrial neighborhood.

West 28th Street's historical background couldn't be more at odds with its present incarnation: from the mid-1880s until the 1950s, the short block between Sixth Avenue and Broadway was the original **Tin Pan Alley**, where music publishers would peddle songs by the likes of Irving Berlin and George Gershwin to artists and producers from vaudeville and Broadway. The name came from the piano-playing racket coming out of the publishing houses here at any time of the day, a sound that one journalist compared to banging on tin pans. Sadly, competition from rock'n'roll and folk in the 1950s and 1960s proved too much, and business on the tiny strip dried up at around that time. However, some of the best-known songs produced here – such as Fats Waller's *Ain't Misbehavin'* and *Do Nothin' Till You Hear from Me* by Duke Ellington – continue to inspire.

Union Square, Gramercy Park, and the Flatiron District

S andwiched between the bohemian chic of the East Village and the opulence of midtown, the knot of close-knit neighborhoods east of Fifth Avenue might seem rather bland in comparison. Yet while it sees far less tourists, this part of town is equally dynamic, with a spate of new construction projects, some of the city's best restaurants and stores, and several of New York's most historically significant buildings and landmarks. Chief among the latter is **Union Square** between 14th and 17th streets, a bustling open space that breaks up Broadway's pell-mell dash north. To the northeast is the posh neighborhood of **Gramercy Park**, with its private clubs and members-only park. Straddling Broadway northwest of Union Square and running up to 23rd Street, the **Flatiron District** was once the center of Manhattan's fine shopping and still retains a certain elegance and energy, while foodies should make the pilgrimage to revitalized **Madison Square Park** to sample the celebrated burgers at *Shake Shack*. It is here, as you head north in the blocks between Third, Park, and Fifth avenues, that midtown Manhattan's skyscrapers begin to rise from downtown's generally low-lying buildings.

Union Square and around

Located at the confluence of Broadway, Fourth, and Park avenues between 14th and 17th streets, **Union Square** is an inviting public space. Among the statues here are George Washington as equestrian; Gandhi; a Lafayette by Bartholdi (more famous for the Statue of Liberty); and, at the center of the green, a massive flagstaff base whose bas-reliefs symbolize the forces of Good and Evil in the American Revolution. Opened as a park in 1839, the square is still surrounded by a crush of commerce and serves as a welcome respite from crazed taxi-drivers and rushed pedestrians on 14th Street. Mostly, however, Union Square is beloved

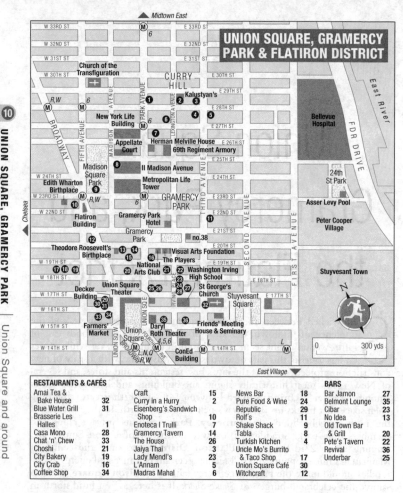

▲ Midtown East

UNION SQUARE, GRAMERCY PARK & FLATIRON DISTRICT

East Village ▼

0   300 yds

RESTAURANTS & CAFÉS				BARS	
Amai Tea &		Craft	15	News Bar	18
Bake House	32	Curry in a Hurry	2	Pure Food & Wine	24
Blue Water Grill	31	Eisenberg's Sandwich		Republic	29
Brasserie Les		Shop	10	Rolf's	11
Halles	1	Enoteca I Trulli	7	Shake Shack	9
Casa Mono	28	Gramercy Tavern	14	Tabla	8
Chat 'n' Chew	33	The House	26	Turkish Kitchen	4
Choshi	21	Jaiya Thai	3	Uncle Mo's Burrito	
City Bakery	19	Lady Mendl's	23	& Taco Shop	17
City Crab	16	L'Annam	5	Union Square Café	30
Coffee Shop	34	Madras Mahal	6	Witchcraft	12

BARS	
Bar Jamon	27
Belmont Lounge	35
Cibar	23
No Idea	13
Old Town Bar	
& Grill	20
Pete's Tavern	22
Revival	36
Underbar	25

for its **Greenmarket** – the largest in Manhattan (see p.399) – which sells all sorts of seasonal goods and non-edible products, like hand-spun wools and flowers.

Like the generally more rambunctious Washington Square in the West Village, Union Square Park is also often the site of civil demonstrations. After September 11, hundreds of vigils were held here, and the entire square became a makeshift memorial to the victims until it was finally ordered dismantled by then-Mayor Rudy Giuliani. The park's southern boundary serves as the informal center of Manhattan protest against miscellaneous causes, everything from the war in Iraq to legalized marijuana, with raggedly dressed protesters brandishing megaphones at passers-by day and night.

The square is flanked by a range of excellent restaurants, as well as by buildings in a mismatched hodgepodge of architectural styles, not least of which is the old **American Savings Bank** at 20 Union Square East – now the **Daryl Roth Theatre** – of which only the grandiose columned exterior survives, completed in 1923. The pedimented Union Square Theater just north of here at 17th St

▲ Union Square Greenmarket

became the second **Tammany Hall in 1929**, once headquarters of the Democratic Party and a fine example of Colonial-Revival architecture. The **Consolidated Edison** (or ConEd) building, one block east on 14th Street, is home to the company responsible for providing the city with both energy and steaming manholes. The majestic Warren & Wetmore-designed tower, completed in 1929, is topped by a 38-foot-high bronze lantern, a memorial to employees killed in World War I. The narrow **Decker Building** on the other side of the park at 33 Union Square West was where Andy Warhol moved his **Factory** in 1968, occupying the sixth floor until 1973; the artist was shot by Valerie Solanas here shortly after the move. The building itself, completed in 1893, is a lavish, Moorish-inspired skyscraper.

Irving Place

East of Union Square, walk the six graceful blocks of **Irving Place** north toward Gramercy Park. Irving Place was named for Washington Irving, the early nineteenth-century writer best known for his creepy tale of the Headless Horseman, *The Legend of Sleepy Hollow*, and also for supposedly being the first American to earn a living from his writing. Although he only lived for a short time at no. 56 (he did make frequent visits to his nephew's house on East 21st St), this strip nevertheless bears his name. A bust of Irving stands in front of the early nineteenth-century Washington Irving High School at East 17th St. Another celebrated author, Pulitzer Prize-winning short-story writer O. Henry, lived at no. 55 (opposite *Cibar*) between 1902 and 1910. Landmark **Pete's Tavern**, at 18th St and Irving Place, is one of New York's oldest bars, in business since 1864. The tavern promotes itself as the place where O. Henry dreamed up and wrote *The Gift of the Magi* and, although this is disputed, the legend serves the place and its atmosphere well.

Stuyvesant Square

The area between Irving Place and the East River is somewhat of a no-man's-land, with a clutch of nondescript apartment buildings and businesses. It is, however, a good place for a stroll, even if only to hop off the beaten path and to check out the neighborhood's few historical points of interest. The land that makes up **Stuyvesant Square**, between East 15th and 17th streets, was gifted to the city in 1836 by **Peter Gerard Stuyvesant**, a descendant of the last Director-General of New Amsterdam (see Contexts, p.434). The park contains Gertrude Vanderbilt Whitney's bronze statue of the Director-General (replete with peg-leg), unveiled in 1941, and a sculpture of Czech composer **Antonín Dvořák** who lived nearby on East 17th Street in the 1890s. Though framed by the buildings of Beth Israel Medical Center and bisected by bustling Second Avenue, the park still retains something of its secluded quality, especially on the western side. Here you'll find the **Friends' Meeting Houses and Seminary** (1860), whose austere Greek-Revival facade contrasts with the grand Romanesque brownstone of **St George's Episcopal Church** next door, completed in 1856. The most famous member of the congregation was J.P. Morgan, who lived just up the road (see p.131). Remembered as the most powerful and ruthless banker of the Gilded Age, Pierpont, as he was commonly known, was also a devout Episcopalian; in St George's, says Morgan biographer Ron Chernow, "he seemed mesmerized by ritual and lapsed into reveries of mystic depth". His funeral, held here in 1913, was more akin to that of a head of state, and was conducted by an unprecedented three bishops (the tycoon is buried in Hartford, Connecticut). The church is normally open for services only (Sun 11am), but is worth a quick peek for its soaring wood-beam roof, monument to Henry Bacon (designer of the Lincoln Memorial in Washington, D.C.) and the carved pulpit, dedicated to J.P.

Gramercy Park and around

Irving Place comes to an end at the ordered open space of **Gramercy Park**. This former "little crooked swamp" (which is what the Dutch called it before the name was Anglicized) between East 20th and 21st streets is one of the city's prettiest squares. It is beautifully manicured and, most noticeably, completely empty for much of the day – principally because it is the city's last private park and the only people who can gain access are those rich or fortunate enough to live here. Famous past key-holders have included Mark Twain, Uma Thurman, and Julia Roberts, as well as a host of Kennedys and Roosevelts. Despite the park's exclusivity, it's well worth a walk around the edge for a glimpse of the trim, historic area that was once the city's main theater district.

Inside the park gates stands a statue of the actor **Edwin Booth** (brother of Lincoln's assassin, John Wilkes Booth) in the guise of Hamlet, one of his most famous roles. (Ironically, Edwin rescued Lincoln's son, Robert, from a train accident years before John's fatal action.) In 1887, aided by architect (and Gramercy Park resident) Stanford White, Booth turned his home at 16 Gramercy Park South into the private club **The Players**. The porch railings on this rather forbidding building are decorated with distinctive figures representing Comedy and Tragedy. In the nineteenth century, actors and theater types were not accepted in general society, so Booth created the club for play and socializing – neglecting, however, to admit women, who were not allowed in until 1989. Later members included the Barrymores, Frank Sinatra, and (oddly) Sir Winston Churchill, while more recent inductees are Morgan Freeman and Liv Ullmann. These days it seems to be the club that is trying to keep regular society out – rather than vice versa. The club does, however, host a year-round program of lunch-hour theater called

Food for Thought, featuring one-act plays by writers as diverse as Anton Chekhov and Tony Kushner and supplemented by a light buffet lunch. The program often feels more like an exclusive salon featuring marquee-name actors, making advance booking highly recommended (shows twice per week on Mon, Wed, Thurs, or Fri; lunch 12.30pm, show 1.30pm; $75; ☎212/362-2560, ⓦwww.foodforthought productions.com).

Next door at no. 15 is the equally patrician **National Arts Club** (☎212/475-3424, ⓦwww.nationalartsclub.org), fittingly located in the rather grand Tilden Mansion. Built in 1840, the mansion was Victorianized in the 1870s by Central Park co-designer Calvert Vaux at the request of owner Governor Samuel Tilden, and is studded with terracotta busts of Shakespeare, Milton, and Franklin, among others. The National Arts Club was founded in 1898 by Charles de Kay, a *New York Times* art critic, who wanted to create a meeting place for artists, patrons, and audiences of all the arts; it moved here in 1906. Non-members are permitted to visit the temporary art exhibitions inside, usually open Monday to Friday 10am to 5pm, but call or check the website to confirm. On the other side of The Players is the **Visual Arts Foundation** at no. 17, occupying the former home of Joseph Pulitzer, while at no. 38 on the northeast corner of the square is the mock-Tudor building in which John Steinbeck, then a struggling reporter for the now defunct *New York World*, lived from 1925 to 1926 (it took getting fired from that job to plunge him into fiction). At 2 Lexington Ave and Gramercy Park North is the imposing 1920s bulk of the **Gramercy Park Hotel** (see "Accommodation," p.278), whose elite early residents included Mary McCarthy, a very young John F. Kennedy, and Humphrey Bogart. Once a fairly stodgy, old-fashioned affair, it was renovated by entrepreneur Ian Schrager in 2006 and turned into a minimalist interior-design masterpiece; hotel guests also get access to Gramercy Park. Lastly, lining Gramercy Park West is a splendid row of brick Greek Revival townhouses from the 1840s with ornate wrought-iron work; James Harper, of the publishing house Harper & Row, lived at no. 4 until his death in 1869.

The Flatiron District

The small district north and northwest of Union Square, between Fifth and Park avenues up to 23rd Street, is generally known as the **Flatiron District**, taking its name from the distinctive early skyscraper on the southwest corner of Madison Square Park. This area is a nice enough place to stroll around in, though there's little to see. This stretch of Broadway was once the heart of the so-called "**Ladies' Mile**," which during the mid-nineteenth century was lined with fancy stores and boutiques. The area started losing its luster around the turn of the twentieth century, and by World War I, Ladies' Mile had all but disintegrated due to the department stores' uptown migration. However, a few sculpted facades and curvy lintels remain as mementos of that gilded age, including Lord & Taylor's Victorian wedding-cake of a building at 901 Broadway at 20th St (the store is now at 424 Fifth Ave, at 38th St).

Standing apart from its rather commercial surroundings at 28 E 20th St is **Theodore Roosevelt's Birthplace** (Tues–Sat 9am–5pm; $3; ☎212/260-1616), or at least a reconstruction of it, viewable on an obligatory guided tour (every hour, on the hour). In 1923, the house was rebuilt as it would have been when Roosevelt was born there in 1858, the rooms restored to reflect their appearance between 1865 and 1872. Teddy remains the only US president from New York City, and this rather somber mansion also contains a small gallery documenting the president's life.

The lofty, elegant, and decidedly anorexic **Flatiron Building** (originally the Fuller Construction Company, later renamed in honor of its distinctive shape) is set on a narrow, triangular plot of land at the manic intersection of Broadway, Fifth Avenue, and 23rd Street. It is one of the city's most famous buildings, evoking images of Edwardian New York. Though it's hard to believe today, the Flatiron was the city's first true skyscraper (a fact hotly debated by architectural-history buffs), hung on a steel frame in 1902 with its full twenty stories dwarfing all the other buildings around. Its uncommonly thin, tapered structure creates unusual wind currents at ground level, and years ago policemen were posted to prevent men gathering to watch the wind raise the skirts of women passing on 23rd Street. The cry they gave to warn off voyeurs – "23 Skidoo!" – has passed into the language. Such behavior would presumably have horrified **Edith Wharton**, who was born in 1862 at 14 W 23rd St, just around the corner. Her parent's brownstone has been altered many times since then, and is currently occupied by a *Starbucks*.

Madison Square Park and around

Just northeast of the Flatiron Building, between Park and Fifth avenues, lies **Madison Square Park**. Though enveloped by a maelstrom of cars, cabs, buses, and dodging pedestrians, because of the stateliness of the surrounding buildings and its peaceful green spaces, it possesses a grandiosity and neat seclusion that Union Square has long since lost – be sure to grab a burger at *Shake Shack* in the middle (see p.298).

On the park's east side, at no. 5 Madison Avenue, stands the tiered, stately **Metropolitan Life Tower**, which at 700ft was the world's tallest building between 1909 and 1913 (when it was surpassed by the Woolworth Building, see p.65). The tower was sold to a developer in 2007 for $200 million, and, like much of the area, is expected to be converted into either residential apartments or a hotel.

Met Life also once owned **11 Madison Ave**, across East 24th Street (it now houses Credit Suisse), connected to the tower building by a sky-bridge. Completed in 1929, the onset of the Great Depression quashed Met Life's plans to make this section a mind-blowing hundred stories high – viewed from the park, you can see how it was designed to be the base for something much bigger. On the other side of 25th Street, at 27 Madison Ave, the **Appellate Division** of the **New York State Supreme Court** boasts a Corinthian-columned marble facade, resolutely righteous with its statues of Justice, Wisdom, and Peace. The grand structure opposite is the **New York Life Building**, the work of Cass Gilbert, creator of the Woolworth Building downtown. It went up in 1928 on the site of the original **Madison Square Garden**, renowned scene of drunken and debauched revels of high and Broadway society. Some believe that the junction nearby, at Madison and West 27th Street, is the birthplace of baseball, as the members of the country's first ball club, the New York Knicker-bockers, started playing in a vacant sandlot here in 1842.

Nothing remains of this semi-legendary past, but there is one reminder of the time when the area was New York's theaterland: the **Church of the Transfiguration**, just off Fifth Avenue at 1 E 29th St (chapel open daily 8am–6pm). Built in 1849, this dinky, rusticated church, made of brown brick, topped with copper roofs, and set back from the street, has long been a traditional place of worship for showbiz people and other social outcasts. It was not until 1870, though, that members of the theater profession started coming here to pray. That year, the place was tagged with the name "The Little Church Around the Corner" after a devout priest from a larger, stuffier church had refused to officiate at the funeral of an actor named George Holland, sending the bereaved here instead. Since then, the church has been a haven for actors, and there is even an Episcopal Actors' Guild. The chapel itself is an intimate little building in a gloriously leafy garden, providing comfort and solace away from the skyscrapers on Fifth Avenue. Its interior is furnished in warm wood and lit with soft candlelight. The figures of famous actors (most notably Edwin Booth as Hamlet) are memorialized in the stained glass.

Lexington Avenue

Two blocks east of Madison, **Lexington Avenue**, which begins its long journey north at Gramercy Park, passes the lumbering **69th Regiment Armory** at 26th Street. The site of the famous Armory Show of 1913, which brought modern art to New York, it retains its original function as the headquarters of the National Guard's "Fighting Sixth-Ninth," though its drill hall is still used for exhibitions.

Just west of the Armory, on the corner of Park Avenue, 104 E 26th St was once the brownstone home of **Herman Melville**, long since replaced with a modern office building. The author moved here in 1863, working on the unfinished *Billy Budd* before dying in the house in 1891. The nearby intersection is named Herman Melville Square in his honor.

Return to the Armory and continue north into what is sometimes dubbed **Curry Hill**, a collection of Indian restaurants and stores along Lexington Avenue between East 27th and 30th streets – blink, and you might miss it altogether. Most of New York's Indian population lives in Queens, but since the late 1980s the cluster of businesses here (many of them Tamil) has just about warranted the moniker. *Kalustyan's*, 123 Lexington Ave between East 28th and 29th streets, is a heavenly scented store that has been selling Indian food products, spices, and hard-to-find ingredients since 1944; it also has a selection of foods from around the globe.

Madison Square Garden and the murder of Stanford White

Stanford White, a partner in the illustrious architectural team of McKim, Mead, and White, which designed many of the city's great Beaux-Arts buildings, including the General Post Office, the old Penn Station, and Columbia University, was something of a rake by all accounts. His dalliance with millionaire Harry Thaw's future wife, Evelyn Nesbit, a Broadway showgirl (who was unattached at the time), had been well publicized – even to the extent that the naked statue of the goddess Diana on the top of the Madison Square Garden building was said to have been modeled on her. Violent and possessive, Thaw could never accept his wife's past, and one night in 1906 he burst into the roof garden of White's tower apartment in Madison Square Garden, found the architect surrounded, as usual, by doting women and admirers, and shot him through the head. Thaw was carted away to spend half of his life in mental institutions, and his wife's show-business career took a tumble: she resorted to drugs and prostitution, dying in 1966 in Los Angeles. Madison Square Garden has moved twice since then, first to a site on Eighth Avenue and 50th Street in 1925, and finally in 1968 to its present location in a hideous drum-shaped eyesore on the corner of 32nd Street and Seventh Avenue (see p.145).

11

Midtown East

L argely corporate and commercial, and anchored by **Grand Central Terminal**, Cornelius Vanderbilt's Beaux-Arts transportation hub, the area known as **Midtown East** rolls north from the 30s through the 50s, and east from Fifth Avenue. Some of the city's most determinedly modish boutiques, richest Art Deco facades, and most sophisticated Modernist skyscrapers are in this district, primarily scattered along **Fifth**, **Madison**, and **Park avenues**. This is where you'll find the **Empire State Building**, the soaring symbol of New York City; the **Seagram Building**; the Art Deco, automobile-inspired **Chrysler Building**; the rambling, geometric bulk of the **United Nations** complex; and the renovated **Museum of Modern Art** (see Chapter 12).

Fifth Avenue

For the last two centuries, an address on **Fifth Avenue** has signified prosperity, respectability, and high social standing. Whether around Washington Square or far uptown around the Harlem River, the boulevard has traditionally been the home to Manhattan's finest mansions, hotels, churches, and stores. Thanks to its show of wealth and opulence, Fifth Avenue has always drawn crowds, nowhere more than on the stretch between 34th and 59th streets, home to grand institutions like **Rockefeller Center** and the **New York Public Library**. It's also home to most of the city's many processions (see Chapter 33, "Parades and festivals," for more details).

The Empire State Building

The city's tallest skyscraper, the **Empire State Building**, 350 Fifth Ave, between 33rd and 34th streets, has easily been the most potent and evocative symbol of New York since its completion in 1931. The building occupies what has always been a prime piece of real estate, originally the site of the first *Waldorf-Astoria Hotel*, built by William Waldorf Astor and opened in 1893 (its current Art Deco home lies on Park Avenue; see p.134).

Wall Street visionary John Jacob Raskob and his partner Alfred E. Smith, a former governor, began compiling funds in October 1929, just three weeks before the stock market crash. Despite the ensuing Depression, the Empire State Building proceeded full steam ahead and came in well under budget after just fourteen months. Since the opening, the building has seen its share of celebrity:

MIDTOWN EAST

Upper East Side

E 64TH ST
E 63RD ST
E 62ND ST
E 61ST ST
E 60TH ST
E 59TH ST
E 58TH ST
E 57TH ST
E 56TH ST
E 55TH ST
E 54TH ST
E 53RD ST
E 52ND ST
E 51ST ST
E 50TH ST
E 49TH ST
E 48TH ST
E 47TH ST
E 46TH ST
E 45TH ST
E 44TH ST
E 43RD ST
E 42ND ST
E 40TH ST
E 39TH ST
E 38TH ST
E 37TH ST
E 36TH ST
E 35TH ST
E 34TH ST
E 33RD ST
E 32ND ST
E 31ST ST
E 30TH ST
E 29TH ST
E 28TH ST

W 47TH ST
W 46TH ST
W 45TH ST
W 43RD ST
W 42ND ST
W 38TH ST
W 37TH ST
W 36TH ST
W 32ND ST
W 31ST ST
W 30TH ST
W 29TH ST

Zoo
Central Park
Museum of American Illustration
Bloomingdale's
Roosevelt Island Tram
Queensboro Bridge
Plaza Hotel
Bergdorf Goodman
General Motors Building
Fuller Building
Trump Tower
IBM Building
Sony Building
Museum of Modern Art
Museum of American Folk Art
Citicorp Center
Paley Center for Media
'21' Club
Seagram Building
St Bartholomew's Church
Radio City Music Hall
St Patrick's Cathedral
General Electric Building
Rockefeller Center
Saks Fifth Avenue
Waldorf-Astoria Hotel
United Nations Headquarters
Met-Life (Pan Am) Building
Algonquin Hotel
ICP Midtown
Trump World Tower
Grand Central Terminal
Chrysler Building
Bryant Park
Mobil Building
Daily News Building
New York Public Library
MURRAY HILL
Morgan Library & Museum
Macy's
Empire State Building
Gramercy Park

East River
East River Drive
Queens-Midtown Tunnel

Times Square
Garment District

0   400 yds

125

RESTAURANTS & CAFÉS

2nd Avenue Deli	25
Aquavit	3
Buttercup Bake Shop	14
Comfort Diner	22
El Rio Grande	24
Ess-a-Bagel	15
Four Seasons	13
Fresco by Scotto on the Go	12
Hatsuhana	20
La Grenouille	11
Le Colonial	2
Luna Piena	9
Montparnasse	16
Naples 45	21
Oyster Bar	23
Smith & Wollensky	19
Solera	10
The Mordern	7
Tea Box Takashimaya	5
Viand	1
Vong	6
Zarela	17

BARS

Campbell Apartment	23
Le Colonial	2
FUBAR	18
Lever House	8
P.J.Clarke's	4

King Kong clung to it while grabbing at passing aircraft; in 1945, an actual B-25 bomber negotiating its way through heavy fog crashed into the building's 79th story, killing fourteen people; and in 1979, two Englishmen parachuted from its summit to the ground, only to be carted off by the NYPD for disturbing the peace. The darkest moment in the building's history came in February 1997, when a man opened fire on the observation deck, killing one tourist and injuring seven others; as a result there is tighter security upon entrance, with metal detectors, package scanners, and the like. This vigilance has only increased since the attacks on the World Trade Center in 2001.

From toe to TV mast, the building is 102 stories and 1454 feet tall, but its height is deceptive, rising in stately tiers with steady panache. Inside, the basement, finished with delicate Art Deco touches, is an underground shopping mall, featuring newsstands, beauty parlors, cafés, and even a post office. On the second floor is the **New York Skyride**, a pricey, eight-minute simulated flight over the city's landmarks (daily 8am–10pm; for tickets bought online, $25.50, youths and seniors $18.50; $4 more at box office; ⊤212/279-9777 or 1-866/SKY-RIDE, Ⓦwww.skyride.com). Few people come for either the shopping or the Skyride; neither is as interesting as a trip to the top of the building.

Getting to the top

A first set of elevators takes you to the **86th floor**. The views from the outdoor walkways here are as stunning as you'd expect; on a clear day visibility can be up to eighty miles, but, given the city's air pollution, on most it's more likely to be between ten and twenty. For an additional $15, a second set of elevators will take you to the **102nd-floor observatory**, the base of the radio and TV antennas. (Daily 8am–2am, last trip 1.15am; $21, seniors and youths 12–17 $19, children ages 5–11 $15, children under 5 and military personnel free; combined tickets for New York Skyride and the Observatory $43; audio tour $8; bring photo ID; ⊤212/736-3100, Ⓦwww.esbnyc.com.)

The New York Public Library and around

Several unexceptional blocks north of the Empire State Building on Fifth Avenue is one of midtown Manhattan's most striking buildings: the **New York Public Library** (Tues & Wed 11am–7.30pm, Mon & Thurs–Sat 11am–6pm, Sun 1–5pm; ⊤212/930-0800, Ⓦwww.nypl.org), which stretches between 40th and 42nd streets. Beaux Arts in style and faced with white marble, it is the headquarters of the largest public-library system in the world. To explore the library, either walk around yourself or take one of the **free tours** (Mon–Sat 11am and 2pm, Sun 2pm), which last an hour and give a good all-round picture of the building, including the **Map Room**, which reopened to the public in December 2005 after a $5m renovation project. Tours start at the information desk in Astor Hall (the main lobby). The highlight of the library is the large, coffered 636-seat **Reading Room** on the third floor. Authors Norman Mailer and E.L. Doctorow worked here, as did Leon Trotsky during his brief sojourn in New York just prior to the 1917 Russian Revolution. It was also here that Chester Carlson came up with the idea for the Xerox copier and Norbert Pearlroth searched for strange facts for his "Ripley's Believe It or Not!" cartoon strip in the famed research library – the largest with a circulating stock in the world. Its 88 miles of books are stored beneath the reading room on eight levels of stacks, which run the half-acre length of Bryant Park (behind the library; see opposite).

Bryant Park

The restoration of **Bryant Park**, just behind the library to the west between 40th and 42nd streets, is one of the city's resounding success stories. An eyesore until 1992, it is now a beautiful, grassy block filled with trees, flowerbeds, and inviting chairs (the fact that they aren't chained to the ground is proof enough of revitalization).

You can grab a slice of pizza or an ice-cream cone at one of the park's small, reasonably priced eateries. There's also a rather aggressive singles' scene at the outdoor *Bryant Park Café* (which becomes the indoor *Bryant Park Grill* during colder months). Summertime brings life to the park – there are free dance and yoga classes, as well as various performances throughout the week, free wireless Internet service and free outdoor movies on Monday evenings. Games, lectures, and rallies also take place in the park, and you can even rent a portion of it for your own event (☎212/768-4242, ⊛www.bryantpark.org).

North to Rockefeller Center

The **Chase Bank**, on the southwest corner of West 43rd Street and Fifth Avenue, is an eye-catcher. An early glass'n'gloss box, it teasingly displays its vault (no longer in use) to passers-by. Around the next corner, West 44th Street contains several old-guard New York institutions. The Georgian-style **Harvard Club**, no. 35 (☎212/840-6600, ⊛www.hcny.com), has an interior so lavish that lesser mortals aren't even allowed to enter (you must be a Harvard alumnus/a). Built in 1894, the Harvard Club was the first of several elite associations in the neighborhood.

The **New York Yacht Club**, 37 W 44th St (☎212/382-1000, ⊛www.nyyc .org), chartered in 1844, is just next door. In its current location since 1901, this playfully eccentric exterior of bay windows is molded as ships' sterns; waves and dolphins complete the effect of tipsy Beaux-Arts fun. For years this has been the home of the America's Cup, a yachting trophy first won by the schooner *America* in 1851.

"Dammit, it was the twenties and we had to be smarty," said Dorothy Parker of the sharp-tongued wits known as the Round Table (see box below), whose members lunched and drank regularly at the **Algonquin Hotel**, 59 W 44th St (☎212/840-6800). The bar, the *Oak Room*, is still one of the most civilized in town and hosts an acclaimed cabaret series.

The Round Table

All across the globe, the period between World War I and World War II saw an incredible outpouring of creative energy. In America, one of the groups involved in this burst of productivity was the so-called **Round Table**, which originated at the **Algonquin Hotel**. Several writers, many of whom had worked together for the Army newspaper *Stars and Stripes*, met in June 1919 at the hotel to roast *New York Times* drama critic Alexander Woollcott. They had so much fun that they decided to return the following afternoon; it wasn't long before their meeting became a ritual. At the heart of the group were Dorothy Parker, Robert Benchley, Robert Sherwood, Irving Berlin, Harold Ross (founder of *New Yorker* magazine), George Bernard Shaw, and George S. Kaufman, among others. Outspoken and unafraid to comment on the state of the postwar world, they wielded an increasing influence on social issues through the 1920s; when the Round Table spoke, the country listened. Then the Great Depression arrived, and a decade after its inception, it finally faded from the scene.

▲ Diamond Row

West 47th Street, or **Diamond Row** (marked by the diamond-shaped lamps mounted on pylons at the Fifth- and Sixth-avenue ends of the st), is a diverting (though pricey) side-trip from Fifth Avenue, a strip of wholesale and retail shops chock-full of gems and jewelry first established in the 1920s. These shops are largely managed by Hasidic Jews, who impart much of the street's workaday vibe, making the Row feel less like something just off ritzy Fifth Avenue and more like the Garment District, by way of the Middle East. Come here to get jewelry fixed at reasonable prices; see p.391 in Chapter 31, "Shopping," for more.

Before heading down there, it's worth ducking into the **Fred F. French Building** at 551 Fifth Ave. The colorful mosaics near the top of the building's exterior are a mere prelude to the combination of Art Deco and Near Eastern imagery on the vaulted ceiling and bronze doors of the lobby.

Rockefeller Center

Taking up the entire block between Fifth and Sixth avenues and 49th and 50th streets, **Rockefeller Center** (℡212/332-6868, ⓦwww.rockefellercenter.com) is one of the finest examples of urban planning in New York. Built between 1930 and 1939 by John D. Rockefeller, Jr, son of the oil magnate, its offices, cafés, theater, underground concourse, and rooftop gardens work together with an intelligence and grace rarely seen. Just adjacent on the Sixth Avenue side stands the similarly Art Deco–style **Radio City Music Hall**, arguably the most famous theater in the United States (see p.150).

You're lured into the Center from Fifth Avenue down the gentle slope of the **Channel Gardens** to the focus of the Center – the **GE Building** (formerly the RCA Building), nicknamed "30 Rock" by entertainment insiders aware of the television studios in its towers. Rising 850ft, its monumental lines echo the scale of Manhattan, though they are softened by symmetrical setbacks to prevent an overpowering expanse of wall. At the foot

New York architecture

New York is a true architectural display-case –
all of the significant and influential movements
of the last two centuries are represented in
the city's magnificent structural landmarks.
For an up-close look, take a stroll around the
concrete jungle – it will leave you with a crick
in the neck, but also with a palpable sense of
New York's remarkably dynamic and enduring
urban landscape.

The nineteenth and early-twentieth century

It was the advent of cast-iron constructions in the mid-nineteenth century that really thrust New York to the forefront of architectural sophistication (see box, p.76), and several buildings in Soho retain their cast-iron embellishments – notably the 1859 **Haughwout Building**.

The **Flatiron Building** on Madison Square (1902) is regarded as the city's first real skyscraper; though the **Park Row Building** by City Hall Park is in fact older and taller, it was considered a greater feat to make the triangular, iron-frame Flatiron stand up. The **Woolworth Building** (1913), with its decorative Gothic spires and gargoyles, continued the sky-touching trend, rising several stories higher than the Flatiron, while other contemporary buildings, like the **US Customs House** (1907), stuck firmly to traditional Neoclassical forms. The **Grand Central Terminal** (1919) is a crowning example from this era.

Flatiron Building ▲

Chrysler Building ▼

The glory years

Architects began to experiment in the 1920s, and the artistic liveliness of the Jazz Age permeates many buildings from this period. Ironically, two of the most impressive structures in the city – the **Chrysler Building** (1930) and the **Empire State Building** (1931) – went up just after the 1929 Wall Street Crash. The **Rockefeller Center** complex, which was worked on throughout the 1930s, is perhaps the apogee of this self-contained urban planning. Looming over the center, the **GE Tower** marks the zenith of Art Deco style in New York.

The 1950s and 1960s saw the Modernist style further refined with the arrival of European architectural movements like Bauhaus and Le Corbusier, whose mantra of form following function influenced the glass-curtain-wall buildings of Mies van der Rohe: the **United Nations Complex** (1950), **Lever House** (1952), and the **Seagram Building** (1958), all in Midtown East. This style culminated, most famously, in the now-destroyed twin towers of the **World Trade Center** (1973).

▲ Midtown East skyline

▼ Rowhouses in the Chelsea Historic District

Five architectural days out in New York

Financial District Where it all began. Come here to see some of the city's oldest buildings, St Paul's and Trinity churches, as well as some of its newest.

Greenwich Village, Chelsea Historic District and around Still home to the city's best domestic architecture, with quiet mews, handsome rowhouses, and elegant apartment blocks.

Midtown Manhattan A smorgasbord of architectural styles, including some of the city's greatest skyscrapers (the Empire State and GE buildings), Neoclassical beauties (the New York Public Library and Grand Central Terminal), and Modernist masterpieces (the Seagram Building and Lever House).

Brooklyn Heights This peaceful, low-rise district has a wide selection of domestic styles, from early Federal rowhouses to large neo-Romanesque and neo-Gothic villas.

Harlem Some of the most beautiful residential architecture in the city, exemplified by blocks of brownstones and other styles south of 125th Street, and developments farther north like Strivers' Row and Hamilton Heights.

▼ Empire State Building

The modern day

Postmodernism afforded late twentieth-century architects a renewed playfulness – witness the Chippendale pediment on the 1983 **Sony Building** on Madison Avenue - though these kinds of conceits are toned down a bit on the **Citicorp Center** (1978). More recently, the twin towers of the **Time Warner Center** (2003) at Columbus Circle stand out mainly for their (gargantuan) size, while the **Condé Nast Building** (2000) on Times Square has been a major trendsetter in the move to "green" architecture. Frank Gehry's **IAC Building** (2007) in Chelsea is one of New York's most exuberant examples of contemporary architecture, and the "**Tower of Freedom**" at Ground Zero will be the city's tallest building by 2012 (see box, p.55).

Citicorp Center ▲

Street sign, midtown Manhattan ▼

Manhattan skyline ▼

Skyscrapers

New York is one of the best places in the world to see **skyscrapers**. Manhattan's iconic, almost medieval skyline traces over 40 buildings higher than 200 meters–there are more skyscrapers here than in any other urban center.

The city's skyscrapers peak at two points on the island: in the Financial District, where the tall structures loom over narrow streets, and midtown, with its larger, more bombastic buildings. This is no accident: Manhattan's bedrock lies closest to the surface in these two areas, meaning that early engineers found it easiest to build high-rises there. At first skyscrapers were sheer vertical monsters, with no regard to how neighboring buildings were affected. City authorities later invented the concept of "air rights," limiting how high a building could be before it had to be set back from its base – a law most elegantly adhered to by the **Empire State Building**.

of the building, the **Lower Plaza** holds a sunken restaurant in the summer months – a great place for afternoon cocktails – linked visually to the downward flow of the building by **Paul Manship**'s sparkling sculpture *Prometheus*. In winter this sunken area becomes an **ice rink**, and following a New York tradition that dates to 1931, a huge tree is displayed at Christmas time, drawing hordes of locals and tourists alike.

Inside, the GE Building is no less impressive. **José Maria Sert**'s lobby murals, *American Progress* and *Time*, are faded but still in tune with the 1930s ambience – presumably more so than the original paintings by Diego Rivera, which were removed by John D.'s son Nelson Rockefeller when the artist refused to scrap a panel glorifying Lenin. A leaflet available from the lobby desk details a self-guided tour of the Center (also available online).

Among the GE Building's many offices is **NBC Studios** (70min behind-the-scenes tours Mon–Sat 8.30am–5.30pm, Sun 9.30am–4.30pm; reservations at the NBC Experience Tour Desk; $18.50, children $15.50; call ☎212/664-7174 to reserve or buy a combination ticket with Rockefeller Center tour, $23.50) on 49th Street between Fifth and Sixth avenues, which produces, among other things, the long-running sketch-comedy hit *Saturday Night Live* and the popular morning program the *Today Show*. To become part of the throng that appears (and waves frantically) when the anchors step outside, all one has to do is show up – the earlier the better. This is especially true on summer Fridays when the *Today Show* hosts concerts (for information on other show tapings visit ⓦwww.nbc.com/Footer/Tickets or call the ticket line at ☎212/664-3056. See also p.31 in Basics).

The observation deck on the top of Rockefeller Center, first opened in 1933, fell into disuse and was closed in the 1980s. The owners returned to John D.'s original vision by restoring the platform on the structure's 70th floor in November 2005. And in contrast to the Empire State Building, **Top of the Rock** (daily 8am–midnight, last elevator at 11pm; $20, children $13; ☎212/698-2000, ⓦwww.topoftherocknyc.com) offers completely unobstructed views, and the timed-entry scheme and decent square footage of the deck makes a visit seem less like a cattle call. A "Sunrise Sunset" ticket option ($30) allows particularly dedicated visitors to scale the building twice in one day, to experience 30 Rock, and midtown laid out beneath it, in two different veils of sunlight.

North to Central Park

Return to Fifth Avenue and you'll see another sumptuous Art Deco component of Rockefeller Center, the **International Building**. The lobby looks out on **Lee Lawrie**'s bronze *Atlas* which rules the space – a thorough cleaning in the summer of 2008 has returned its luster – and the muscle man gazes toward **St Patrick's Cathedral** across the avenue. Designed by James Renwick and completed in 1888, St Patrick's sits on the corner of 50th Street amid the glitz like a misplaced bit of moral imperative, painstakingly detailed yet – notwithstanding the mysticism of **Lady Chapel** to the rear – spiritually lifeless. Despite its shortcomings, St Patrick's is still an essential part of the midtown landscape, a foil for Rockefeller Center and one of the most important Catholic churches in America.

Across the street from St Patrick's are the striped awnings of **Saks Fifth Avenue** at no. 611, one of the last of New York's premier department stores to relocate to midtown from Herald Square. With its columns on the ground floor and yellow-brick-road pathways through fashion collections, Saks is every bit as glamorous today as it was when it opened in 1924.

Paley Center for Media

If your body needs the kind of rejuvenation only an hour in front of a television can offer, visit the **Paley Center for Media**, 25 W 52nd St between Fifth and Sixth avenues (Tues, Wed & Fri–Sun noon–6pm, Thurs noon–8pm; $10, seniors and students $8; ⊕212/621-6800, ⓦ www.paleycenter.org). Formerly known as the Museum of Television & Radio, the space was renamed in 2007 with a nod to the eventual inclusion of digital media. In a building designed by Philip Johnson, the organization preserves an archive of 140,000 mostly American TV shows, radio broadcasts, and commercials, accessible via an excellent computerized reference system.

The '21' Club and the Museum of American Folk Art

Right next door to the Paley Center is the **'21' Club**, 21 W 52nd St (⊕212/582-7200), which has been providing food (and drink) since the early days of Prohibition, and remains an Old Boys institution. Founded by Jack Kriendler and Charlie Berns, the club quickly became one of the most exclusive establishments in town, a place where the young socialites of the Roaring Twenties could spend wild nights dancing the Charleston and enjoying wines and spirits of the finest quality. Although '21' was raided more than once, federal agents were never able to pin anything on Jack and Charlie. At the first sign of a raid, they would activate an ingenious system of pulleys and levers, which would sweep bottles from the bar shelves and hurl the smashed remains down a chute into the New York sewer system.

The next block up, and steps away from the **Museum of Modern Art** (p.139), is the excellent **Museum of American Folk Art**, 45 W 53rd St (Tues–Thurs, Sat & Sun 10.30am–5.30pm, Fri 10.30am–7.30pm; $9, students/seniors $7; ⊕212/265-1040, ⓦ www.folkartmuseum.org), which exhibits multicultural folk art from all over America, with a permanent collection that includes over 3500 works from the seventeenth to twentieth centuries. The affiliated Folk Art Institute runs courses, lectures, and workshops.

53rd Street to Grand Army Plaza

After a stint at the art museums, take a break in the authentic tearoom at the New York branch of Japan's largest department store chain, **Takashimaya**, no. 693, at the northeast corner of Fifth Avenue and 54th Street. Northward from here, the avenue's ground floors shift from mundane offices to an elegant stretch of exclusive shops and art galleries. Taking ostentatious wealth to the extreme is **Trump Tower**, no. 725 at 56th St. Perfumed air, polished marble paneling, and a five-story waterfall are calculated to knock you senseless with expensive "good taste." The building itself is clever: a neat little outdoor garden is squeezed high in a corner, and each of the 230 apartments above the atrium provides views in three directions.

The stores on these blocks are more sights than shops, with **Cartier**, **Gucci**, and **Tiffany & Co** among the many gilt-edged names. Farther north at no. 754 is the famed rich people's department store **Bergdorf Goodman**, offering a wedding-cake interior of glossy pastels, chandeliers, and pink curtains. Just next door are the glittering (and virtually priceless) window displays of **Harry Winston Jewelers**, beloved by countless celebrities (see "Shopping," Chapter 31, for more on this area's stores).

At 59th Street, Fifth Avenue reaches **Grand Army Plaza** and the fringes of Central Park, where a golden statue of William Tecumseh Sherman stands guard amid all the highbrow shopping, and the copper-edged 1907 **Plaza Hotel** looms impressively on the plaza's western border. The *Plaza* was sold for $675 million in August 2004 to the El-Ad Group, which announced that the space would be converted to high-end condominiums. This prompted outrage among New York City's traditionalists, replaced by a heavy sense of nostalgia (and consumerism) as the new owners sold off the Plaza's fixtures and kitchenware to the public. Meanwhile, the New York Hotel Trades Council established a "Save the Plaza" movement that was more concerned with the 900 union jobs that would be lost in such a conversion. El-Ad scaled back its plans and reintroduced hotel rooms into the mix, and Mayor Bloomberg hammered out a deal between the two sides that allowed for a third of the workers to keep their jobs, with the rest getting an enhanced severance on early retirement.

After a $400 million update, the hotel started its official reopening in the fall of 2007. Preservationists had nothing to be afraid of; everything was in its right place, it only looked less tired. The rooms still whisper "elegance" – as do the bathrooms, covered in mosaic tile and featuring 24-carat gold fixtures. But in a concession to today's digital life, they now also include some technological updates. The famed *Oak Bar* and *Palm Court* have returned as well, but aside from those establishments, due to the hotel's new mixed-use status, access is a bit limited for casual gawkers. In its heyday, the hotel's reputation was built not just on looks, but on lore: it boasts its own historian, keeper of such tidbits as when legendary tenor Enrico Caruso, enraged by the loud ticking of the hotel's clocks, stopped them all by throwing a shoe at one (they were calibrated to function together). The management apologized with a magnum of champagne.

Madison Avenue

Madison Avenue parallels Fifth with some of the grandeur but less of the excitement. In the East 30s, the avenue runs through the heart of the mundane and residential **Murray Hill** neighborhood, an area distinguished mostly by the presence of the historical **Morgan Library**. Heading north to the East 40s and the Upper East Side, you encounter the Madison Avenue of legend, the center of the international advertising industry in the 1960s and 1970s. Today, this section of town is a major upscale shopping boulevard.

Murray Hill and the Morgan Library

Madison Avenue is the main artery of **Murray Hill**, a tenuously tagged residential area (no commercial building was allowed until the 1920s) of statuesque, canopy-fronted buildings bounded by East 34th and 40th streets, and lacking any real centre or sense of community. Indeed, you're likely to pass through without even realizing it.

When Madison Avenue was on a par with Fifth as the place to live, Murray Hill was dominated by the Morgan family, including the crusty old financier J.P. and his offspring, who at one time owned a clutch of properties here. Morgan Junior lived in the brownstone on the corner of 37th Street and Madison (now headquarters of the American Lutheran Church), his father in a house that was later pulled down to make way for an extension to his library next door. The **Morgan Library & Museum**, 225 Madison Ave at E 36th St (Tues–Thurs 10.30am–5pm, Fri 10.30am–9pm, Sat 10am–6pm,

Sun 11am–6pm; $12, students/seniors $8, free Fri 7–9pm; ☎212/685-0008, Ⓦwww.morganlibrary.org), housed in a mock-Roman villa, still stands here though. Morgan would often come to his library to luxuriate among the art treasures he had acquired on his trips to Europe: manuscripts, paintings, prints, and furniture. The library recently underwent a three-year, $106 million renovation, reopening in April 2006. The changes, designed by Pritzker Prize-winner Renzo Piano, have doubled the exhibition space and added several new features to the building, including an entrance on Madison Avenue, a four-story piazza-style gathering space, a performance hall, and a naturally lit reading room. The library's collection is priceless, including nearly 10,000 drawings and prints by such greats as Da Vinci, Degas, and Dürer; manuscripts by Dickens, Austen, and Thoreau; and a copy of the 1455 Gutenberg Bible (the museum owns three out of the eleven that survive; another rests in the New York Public Library, p.126).

North of Murray Hill

Leaving behind the relative quiet of Murray Hill, Madison Avenue becomes progressively more commercial the farther north one goes. Several good stores – notably several specializing in men's haberdashery, shoes, and cigars – still cater to the needs of the more aristocratic consumer. Brooks Brothers, traditional clothiers of the Ivy League and inventors of the button-down collar, occupies a corner of East 44th Street. Between 50th and 51st streets the **Villard Houses**, a replica collection of Italian palazzos (ones that didn't quite make it to Fifth Ave) by McKim, Mead, and White, merit more than a passing glance. The houses have been surgically incorporated into the *Helmsley Palace Hotel*, and the interiors polished up to their original splendor.

Madison's most interesting sites come in a four-block strip above 53rd Street. The tiny, vest-pocket-sized **Paley Park** is on the north side of East 53rd between Madison and Fifth avenues. Its soothing mini-waterfall and transparent water tunnel are juxtaposed with a haunting five-panel section of the former Berlin Wall. Around the corner, the **Continental Illinois Center** looks like a cross between a space rocket and a grain silo, but the **Sony Building** (formerly the AT&T Building), at no. 550 between 55th and 56th streets, has grabbed more headlines. A Johnson–Burgee collaboration, it follows the postmodernist theory of borrowing from historical styles: a Modernist skyscraper is sandwiched between a Chippendale top and a Renaissance base. The **IBM Building**, no. 580–590, between 56th and 57th streets, has a far more user-friendly plaza than the Sony Building. In the calm, glass-enclosed atrium, tinkling music, tropical foliage, yet another coffee bar, and comfortable seating make for a livelier experience. The first three floors were formerly occupied by the **Dahesh Museum of Art** (Ⓦwww.daheshmuseum.org), a small repository of 3000 nineteenth- and early twentieth-century European artworks. The museum is currently searching for a new home in New York City, while pieces of its collection float around the globe to join temporary exhibits in other city's museums.

Across East 57th Street at no. 41–45 is the eye-catching **Fuller Building**. Black-and-white Art Deco, it has a fine entrance and tiled floor. Cut east on 57th Street to no. 57 to find the **Four Seasons Hotel**, notable for sweeping marble and limestone design by I.M. Pei.

Park Avenue

In 1929, author Collinson Owen wrote that **Park Avenue** is "where wealth is so swollen that it almost bursts." Things have changed little since. The focal point of the avenue is the hulking **Grand Central Terminal**, at 42nd Street. South of Grand Central, Park Avenue narrows in both width and interest, but to the north of the building it becomes an impressively broad boulevard. Built to accommodate elevated rail tracks, the area quickly became a battleground, as corporate headquarters and refined residences jostled for prominence. Whatever your feelings about conspicuous wealth, from the 40s north, Park Avenue is one of the city's most awesome sights. Its sweeping expanse, genteel facades, and sculpture-studded medians capture both the gracious and grand sides of New York in one fell swoop.

Grand Central Terminal

Park Avenue hits 42nd Street at Pershing Square, where it lifts off the ground to make room for the massive **Grand Central Terminal** (Ⓦwww .grandcentralterminal.com). More than just a train station, the terminal is a full-blown destination unto itself. When it was constructed in 1913 at the order of railroad magnate Cornelius Vanderbilt, the terminal was a masterly piece of urban planning. After the electrification of the railways made it possible to reroute trains underground, the rail lines behind the existing station were sold off to developers and the profits went toward the building of a new terminal – built around a basic iron frame but clothed with a Beaux-Arts skin. While Grand Central soon took on an almost mythical significance, today its traffic consists mainly of commuters speeding out to Connecticut, Westchester County, and upstate New York, and any claim to being a gateway to an undiscovered continent is purely symbolic.

The most spectacular aspect of the building is its **size**, though in height it is dwarfed by the Met Life building (see p.134). The station's main concourse is one of the world's finest and most imposing open spaces, 470ft long and 150ft high. The **barrel-vaulted ceiling** is speckled like a Baroque church with a painted representation of the winter night sky, its 2500 stars shown back to front – "as God would have seen them," the French painter Paul Helleu reputedly remarked. Stand in the middle and you realize that Grand Central represents a time when stations were seen as miniature cities. Walking around the marble corridors is an elegant experience. You can explore Grand Central on your own or take the excellent **tour** run by the Municipal Arts Society (every Wed 12.30pm; $10 suggested donation; Ⓦwww.mas.org).

In addition to its architectural and historical offerings, there are fifty shops here, including the tantalizing Grand Central Market, which sells every gourmet food imaginable, and over 30 restaurants, many of which are on the terminal's lower concourse. Chief among the restaurants is the *Grand Central Oyster Bar* (Ⓣ212/490-6650), which is located in the vaulted bowels of the station and is one of the city's most celebrated seafood eateries; it serves a dozen varieties of oyster and is packed at lunchtime. Just outside of the restaurant is something that explains why the *Oyster Bar*'s babble is not solely the result of the people eating there: two people can stand on opposite sides of any of the vaulted spaces and hold a conversation just by whispering, an acoustic fluke that makes this the loudest eatery in town.

For a civilized cocktail, stop into the *Campbell Apartment* (see p.347). The grand one-time home of the terminal's architect, it is found near the terminal's west-side taxi stand.

Around Grand Central

Across East 42nd Street to the south, the former **Bowery Savings Bank**, now one of Harry Cipriani's upscale eateries, echoes Grand Central's grandeur. **The Grand Hyatt Hotel**, meanwhile, next to Grand Central Terminal on the south side of 42nd Street, is another notable instance of excess, and perhaps the best (or worst) example in the city of all that is truly vulgar about contemporary American interior design. The thundering waterfalls, lurking palms, and gliding escalators represent plush-carpeted bad taste at its most meretricious.

Just north of Grand Central, impressive more for its size than grandeur, stands the Bauhaus bulk of the **Met Life Building**, 200 Park Ave, which was built in 1963 as the Pan Am Building. Bauhaus guru Walter Gropius had a hand in designing the structure, and the critical consensus is that he could have done better. As the headquarters of the now-defunct international airline, the building, in profile, was meant to suggest an airplane wing. The blue-gray mass certainly adds drama to the cityscape, although it robs Park Avenue of its southern views, sealing off 44th Street and sapping much of the vigor of the surrounding buildings.

The Helmsley Building, the Waldorf–Astoria, and north

Standing astride the avenue at 46th Street at no. 230 is the high altar of the New York Central Building (built in 1928 and years later rechristened the **Helmsley Building**). A delicate construction with a lewdly excessive Rococo lobby, it rises up directly in the middle of the avenue; twin tunnels allow traffic to pass beneath it. In its mid-twentieth century heyday it formed a punctuation mark to the avenue, but its thunder was stolen in 1963 by the completion of the Met Life Building, which looms above and behind it.

Wherever you placed the solid mass of the **Waldorf-Astoria Hotel**, no. 301 (see p.281), a resplendent statement of Art Deco elegance between 49th and 50th streets, it would more than hold its own. Duck inside to stroll through a block of vintage grandeur, sweeping marble, and hushed plushness where such well-knowns as Herbert Hoover, Cole Porter, and Princess Grace of Monaco have bunked.

Crouching just across 50th Street, **St Bartholomew's Church** is a low-slung Byzantine hybrid that adds an immeasurable amount of character to the area, lending the lumbering skyscrapers a much-needed sense of scale. The church fought against developers for years, and ultimately became a test case for New York City's landmark preservation law. Today, its congregation thrives and its members sponsor many community-outreach programs. Directly behind St Bartholomew's, the spiky-topped **General Electric Building** seems like a wild extension of the church, its slender shaft rising to a meshed crown of abstract sparks and lightning strokes that symbolizes the radio waves used by its original owner, RCA. A New York-designated landmark, the building is another Art Deco delight, with nickel-silver ornamentation, carved red marble, and a lobby with a vaulted ceiling (entrance at 570 Lexington Ave).

Among all this architectural ostentation it's difficult at first to see the originality of the **Seagram Building**, 375 Park Ave between 52nd and 53rd streets.

Designed by Mies van der Rohe and Philip Johnson, and built in 1958, this was the seminal curtain-wall skyscraper: deceptively simple and cleverly detailed, with floors supported internally rather than by the building's walls, allowing a skin of smoky glass and whiskey-bronze metal. Although the facade has now weathered to a dull black, it remains the supreme example of Modernist reason. The **plaza**, an open forecourt designed to set the building apart from its neighbors and display it to advantage, was such a success as a public space that the city revised the zoning laws to encourage other high-rise builders to supply similar plazas.

Across Park Avenue between 53rd and 54th streets is **Lever House**, no. 390, the building that set the Modernist ball rolling on Park Avenue when it was constructed in 1952. Back then, the two right-angled slabs that form a steel and glass bookend seemed revolutionary when compared with the surrounding buildings. Its vintage appeal helps to make the restaurant of the same name one of the hottest places in town to eat, tipple, and be seen. The restaurant-bar interior was conceived by internationally acclaimed designer Marc Newson and opened in August 2003, and features all sorts of Modernist elements from the 1950s.

Lexington Avenue

One block east of Park Avenue, **Lexington Avenue** marks a sort of border between East Side elegance and the everyday avenues closer to the East River. It roars into life around 42nd Street and the Chrysler Building, and especially through the mid-40s, where commuters swarm around Grand Central Terminal. From there, Lexington lurches northward past 53rd Street and the towering aluminum and glass **Citicorp Center**, to the bulk of **Bloomingdale's** department store at 59th Street, which marks the end of the avenue's midtown stretch of highlights.

The Chrysler Building and around

The Chrysler Building, 405 Lexington Ave, dates from 1930, a time when architects married prestige with grace and style. For a fleeting moment, this was the world's tallest building; it was surpassed by the Empire State Building in 1931, and is (reportedly) currently tied with the new Times building (p.148) for no. 3. However, since the rediscovery of Art Deco, it has become one of Manhattan's best-loved structures. The golden age of motoring is evoked by the building's car-motif friezes, hood-ornament gargoyles, radiator-grill spire, and the fact that the entire building is almost completely fashioned from stainless steel. Its designer, William Van Alen, indulged in a feud with an erstwhile partner, H. Craig Severance, who was designing a building at 40 Wall St at the same time. Each was determined to have the higher skyscraper. Van Alen secretly built the stainless-steel spire inside the Chrysler's crown, and when 40 Wall St finally topped out a few feet higher than the Chrysler, Van Alen popped the 185-foot spire out through the top of the building and won the day.

The Chrysler Corporation moved out decades ago, and for a while the building was allowed to decline by a company that didn't wholly appreciate its spirit. The current owner has pledged to keep it lovingly intact, and it was renovated in 2000 by Philip Johnson. The lobby, once a car showroom, is all you can see for the time being (there's no observation deck), but that's enough in itself. The opulent walls are covered in African marble and the ceiling shows a realistic, if rather faded, study of airplanes, machines, and brawny builders who worked on the tower.

On the south side of 42nd Street flanking Lexington Avenue are two more noteworthy buildings. The **Chanin Building**, 122 E 42nd St, on the right, is another Art Deco monument, cut with terracotta carvings of leaves, tendrils, and sea creatures. Also interesting is the design of the weighty **Mobil Building** across the street at no. 150. Built in 1956, it was the first metal-clad office building in the world at the time. Made with 7,000 panels of chromium-nickel stainless steel, it was designed to enable the wind to keep it clean.

Citicorp Center and around

Just as the Chrysler Building dominates the lower stretches of Lexington Avenue, the chisel-topped **Citicorp Center**, 153 E 53rd St, between 53rd and 54th streets, towers above northern midtown. Opened in 1978, the building, now one of New York's most conspicuous landmarks, looks as if it is sheathed in shiny graph paper. Its slanted roof was designed to house solar panels and provide power, but the idea was ahead of the technology and Citicorp had to satisfy itself by adopting the distinctive top as a corporate logo.

Hiding under the Center's skirts at 619 Lexington Ave is **St Peter's Lutheran Church**, known as "the Jazz Church" for being the venue of many a jazz musician's funeral and host to a long-running jazz-tinged vespers service. The tiny church was built to replace the one demolished to make way for Citicorp, and part of the deal was that the church had to stand out from the Center – which explains the granite material. Explore the thoroughly modern interior, including sculptor **Louise Nevelson**'s **Erol Beaker Chapel**, the venue for Wednesday lunchtime jazz performances (and evening concerts as well). Another Nevelson sculpture (*Night Presence IV*) can be seen at East 92nd St, on the median running down Park Avenue.

One block north on Lexington Ave, and in direct contrast to the simple, contemporary St Peter's, stands the reform **Central Synagogue**, 652 Lexington Ave, at East 55th St. Striking because of its Moorish appearance, this landmark structure was built in 1870–72 by German immigrant Henry Fernbach. The oldest continually used Jewish house of worship in the city, it was heavily damaged in a blaze in 1998, and although repairs were unable to fully restore all the site's features, services are still held as they always have been.

Third, Second, and First avenues

While the construction of the Citicorp Center spurred the development of **Third Avenue** in the late 1970s, most life, especially at night, seems to have shifted east to **Second Avenue**, with most of the area's architectural attractions lying on or around 42nd Street. The stone facade of the somber yet elegant former **Daily News Building**, 220 E 42nd St, fronts a surprising Art Deco interior. The most impressive remnant of the original 1929 décor is a large globe encased in a lighted circular frame (with updated geography), made famous by Superman movies when the Daily News Building appropriately housed the *Daily Planet*. The tabloid after which the building is named has since moved to 450 W 33rd St, and the building is not open on weekends.

Just north and around the corner from the Daily News, at 320 E 43rd St, between First and Second avenues, is one of the city's most peaceful (if surreal) spaces – the **Ford Foundation Building**. Built in 1967, the building featured the first of the atria that are now commonplace across Manhattan. Structurally, the atrium is a giant greenhouse, gracefully supported by soaring granite columns and edged with two walls of offices visible through the windows. This subtropical garden, which changes with the seasons, was one of the first attempts to create a "natural" environment inside a building, and it's astonishingly quiet. Forty-second Street is no more than a murmur outside, and all you can hear is the burble of water, the echo of voices, and the clipped crack of feet on the brick walkways. The indoor/outdoor experience here is one of New York City's great architectural coups.

At the east end of 42nd Street, steps lead up to the 1925 **Tudor City**, which rises behind a tiny tree-filled park. With coats of arms, leaded glass, and neat neighborhood shops, this area is the very picture of self-contained residential respectability. It's an official historic district to boot. Head down the steps here and you'll be plum opposite the **United Nations**.

The United Nations

Some see the **United Nations complex** – built after World War II, when John D. Rockefeller, Jr donated $8.5 million to buy the eighteen-acre East River site – as one of the major sights of New York. Others, usually those who've been there, are not so complimentary. Despite the symbolism of the UN, few buildings are quite so dull to walk around. What's more, as if to rationalize the years of UN impotence in international war and hunger zones, the (obligatory) guided tours emphasize that the UN's main purpose is to promote dialogue and

▲ UN Headquarters

awareness rather than enforcement. The organization itself moves at a snail's pace – bogged down by regulations and a lack of funds – which is the general feel of the tour as well.

For the determined, the complex consists of three main buildings – the thin, glass-curtained slab of the **Secretariat**; the sweeping curve of the **General Assembly Building**, whose chambers can accommodate more than 191 national delegations; and the low-rise **Conference Wing**, which connects the other two structures. Construction on the complex began in 1949 and finished in 1963, the product of a suitably international team of architects that included Le Corbusier – though he pulled out before the construction was completed. Guided tours (Mon–Fri 9.30am–4.45pm; tours last 45min; $13.50, seniors and students $9, children $7.50; bring ID; ☎212/963-8687, ⓦwww.un.org) take in the UN conference chambers and its constituent parts. Even more revealing than the stately chambers are its thoughtful exhibition spaces and artful country gifts on view, including a painting by Picasso and a huge (12ft by 15ft) stained- glass window by artist Marc Chagall, commissioned in 1964 as a memorial to Dag Hammarskjold, the second Secretary-General of the United Nations. Council chambers visited on the tour include the **Security Council**, the **Economic and Social Council**, and the **Trusteeship Council** – all of which are similarly retro (note the clunky machinery of the journalists' areas) and sport some intriguing Marxist murals. Once you've been whisked around all these sites and have seen examples of the many artifacts that have been donated to the UN by its various member states, the tour is more or less over and will leave you in the basement of the General Assembly Building. A **restaurant** serves a daily lunch buffet with dishes from different UN member countries, but the food, like the tour, is fairly taste-free. Where the UN has real class is in its beautiful **gardens**, with their modern sculpture and views of the East River.

Beekman Place and Sutton Place

Outwith the environs of the UN, **First Avenue** has a certain rangy looseness that's a relief after the concrete claustrophobia of midtown. **Beekman Place** (49th to 51st sts between First Ave and the East River) is quieter still, a beguiling enclave of garbled styles. Similar, though not quite as intimate, is **Sutton Place**, which stretches from 53rd to 59th streets between First Avenue and the river. Originally built for the lordly Morgans and Vanderbilts in 1875, Sutton Place increases in elegance as you move north and, for today's *crème de la crème*, **Riverview Terrace** (off 58th St at the river) is a (very) private enclave of five brownstones. The UN Secretary-General has an official residence on Sutton Place, and the locals are choosy about who they let in: disgraced ex-president Richard Nixon was refused on the grounds he would be a security risk.

The Museum of Modern Art

New York City's **Museum of Modern Art** – **MoMA** to its friends – offers the finest and most complete collection of late nineteenth- and twentieth-century art anywhere, with a permanent collection of more than 150,000 paintings, sculptures, drawings, prints, and photographs, as well as a world-class film archive. Despite its high admission price, it's an essential stop for anyone even remotely interested in the world of modern art.

Founded in 1929 by three wealthy women, including Abby Aldrich Rockefeller (wife of John D., Jr), as the very first museum dedicated entirely to modern art, MoMA moved to its present home ten years later. Philip Johnson designed expansions in the 1950s and 1960s, and in 1984 a steel-pipe and glass renovation by Cesar Pelli doubled gallery space. The latest renovation was completed in 2004 by Japanese architect Yoshio Taniguchi, doubling the exhibition space yet again and creating new and vibrant public areas.

The building is quite clever: it's easy to navigate, but it also constantly and deliberately gives glimpses of other levels, like the sculpture garden, the lobby, and the spacious second-floor landing where large canvases or installations are often displayed. The core collection – at least in the Painting and Sculpture galleries – is arranged more or less in chronological order, with substantial

MoMA practicalities

The Museum of Modern Art (☏ 212/708-9400, ⓦ www.moma.org) is located at 11 W 53rd St, just off Fifth Avenue. Take the #E or #V train to 5th Ave–53rd St, or the #B, #D, or #F train to 47–50th Sts/Rockefeller Center. **Hours** are Monday and Wednesday through Sunday 10.30am to 5.30pm, Friday until 8pm; it is **closed Tuesdays** throughout the year, as well as Thanksgiving Day and Christmas Day. **Admission** is $20, seniors $16, students $12, children 16 and under are free. Thanks to corporate sponsorship, the **museum is free** for everyone on Fridays from 4 to 8pm – predictably, the lines are extremely long at this time, so get there by 3.30pm at the latest, or after 6.30pm, when the initial rush has (usually) died down. At other times, you can avoid waiting in line by **booking tickets in advance** on the website. Note also that you must check large shopping bags and backpacks of any size – don't bring them if you want to avoid another wait for the cloakroom.

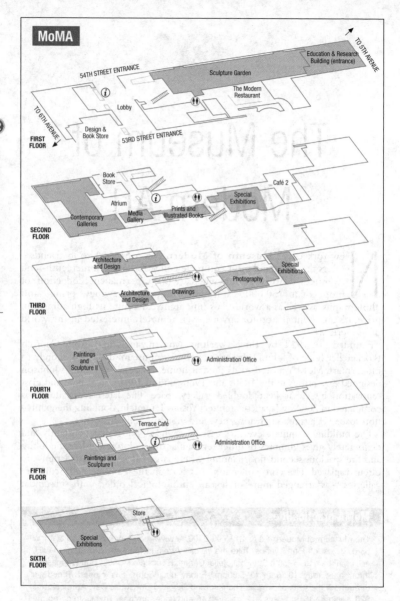

collections of photography, drawings, architectural design, and contemporary art each having their own galleries on the third and second floors, and temporary exhibitions also afforded their own dedicated areas. Despite all this space, the main galleries in MoMA can still feel very crowded, especially during weekends and holidays, and lines can be long at the entrance, cloakroom, and cafés. Buy tickets in advance, and get here early or late in the afternoon, to avoid the worst of it.

Painting and Sculpture I

The core of the collection is the Painting and Sculpture galleries, numbered from 1 to 25. Most visitors head directly for the fifth floor – to **Painting and Sculpture I**, which covers 1880 to 1940. Gallery 1 opens with the **Post-Impressionists** of the late nineteenth century, with works by **Cézanne**, **Seurat**, **Van Gogh**, and **Gauguin** mixed in with vivid early paintings by **Derain**, **Braque**, and **James Ensor** that already hint at a more Modernist perspective. This is developed in the next gallery by **Picasso**, most notably with his seminal *Demoiselles d'Avignon*, as well as by some of his later, more Cubist pieces. More works by Picasso and **Leger** follow in Gallery 3, and, beyond them, the big swirling colors of **Boccioni** and the Italian Futurists. Gallery 5 is an explosion of color, with paintings by **Chagall**, **Kandinsky**, and **Kirchner**, while Gallery 6 is entirely devoted to **Matisse**. Featured are his *Red Studio*, *Piano Lesson*, and other paintings, as well as his lumpy series of sculpted heads of *Jeanette*. After Matisse is a so-called **"Crossroads" gallery (7)**, which houses some of the most recognizable works of the modern age – Picasso's *Three Women at the Spring*, the same artist's *Three Musicians*, and Leger's *Three Women*, all painted the same year (1921), as well as some haunting works by **de Chirico**. The adjoining galleries are devoted to the paintings of the Dutch *De Stijl* movement. **Duchamp** and **Malevich** are featured in Gallery 8, and you can trace the development of the movement's leading light, **Mondrian,** in Gallery 10, from his tentative early work to the pure color abstract of *Broadway Boogie Woogie*, painted in New York in 1943. **Monet**'s vast canvas *Reflections of Clouds on the Water Lily Pond* takes up half of Gallery 9, which it shares with **Bonnard**'s soft studies, while Gallery 11 features artists of the German *Neue Sachlichkeit* school, **Otto Dix** and **Max Beckmann**. Gallery 12 is devoted to the Surrealists, and many of the works here will be familiar from popular

▲ Museum of Modern Art

reproductions: the vivid creations of **Miró**, **Magritte**'s *The Menaced Assassin*, and the famously drooping clocks of **Dalí**'s *Persistence of Memory*, though the latter is often on loan to other galleries. Finally, tiny Gallery 13 has a few paintings by American artists: **Wyeth**'s *Christina's World*, and some of **Charles Sheeler**'s American industrial landscapes.

Painting and Sculpture II

Painting and Sculpture II, the next floor down, displays work from the 1940s to 1960s and inevitably has a more American feel, starting with works by **Rothko** and **de Kooning** in Gallery 15. In Gallery 16, **Dubuffet**'s challenging paintings sit with **Giacometti**'s stick-like figures and paintings by **Bacon** – *Study of a Baboon* – and **Picasso**, while Gallery 17 is devoted to **Pollock**. Beyond here the **Abstract Expressionists** hold sway, with vast canvases by **Barnett Newman** (18) and Rothko (19) – all at the height of their influence in the 1950s, when these paintings were done. Later galleries contain lots of work familiar from the modern canon – **Jasper Johns**' *Flag*, **Robert Rauschenberg**'s mixed-media paintings, **Warhol**'s soup cans and *Marilyn Monroe*, **Lichtenstein**'s cartoons, and **Oldenburg**'s soft sculptures.

Photography, Architecture and Design, Drawings

The other sections of the museum's collection are just as impressive and shouldn't be missed. On the third floor, the **Photography** galleries are devoted to a rotating selection of exceptional work from visiting artists and the Museum's permanent collection, such as the candid street photos of Paris by **Cartier-Bresson** and **Robert Capa**'s stunning pictures of the modern-day US.

Architecture and Design, on the same floor, hosts revolving exhibits showcasing every aspect of design from the mid-nineteenth century to the present; illustrations of buildings, interior design, lots of glass and ceramics, and a series of neat large-scale objects like vintage cars, bikes, and even helicopters.

The **Drawing** galleries, also on the third floor, show revolving exhibitions by a glittering array of twentieth-century artists, including **Pollock**, **Rauschenberg**, **de Kooning**, **Warhol**, **Jasper Johns**, and **Roy Lichtenstein**. Finally, the second-floor galleries give MoMA the chance to show its **Contemporary art** in all media, and basically show works from the 1970s onward, including pieces by **Bruce Nauman**, **Jeff Koons**, and other stellar names from the world of contemporary art.

Midtown West

B etween West 30th and 59th streets and west of Sixth Avenue, much of midtown Manhattan is enthralling, noisy, and garish, packed with attractions meant to entertain the legions of tourists staying in the area's many hotels. The heart of **Midtown West** is **Times Square**, where jostling crowds and huge neon signs assault the senses at all times of the day. It's here that the east side's more sedate approach to capitalism finally overflows its bounds and New York City reaches its commercial zenith. South of Times Square is the bustling, business-oriented **Garment District**, home to Madison Square Garden and Macy's department store, while just north of the once "naughty, bawdy 42nd Street" is the **Theater District**, which offers the most impressive concentration of live theater in the world.

For glimpses of vintage seediness, head west beyond Eighth Avenue to **Hell's Kitchen** – though keep in mind that the buzzing forces of gentrification are hard at work in this part of town, and shiny open-air eateries are far more common than peep-show pavilions these days. There aren't many tourist attractions per se in this direction, though if you hike all the way over to the Hudson River, you'll come upon the massive **Intrepid Sea, Air & Space Museum**, which is housed in a retired aircraft carrier. Back over in the center of the island, **Sixth Avenue**, its architecture melding cultural and corporate New York, is good for a stroll, while **57th Street** has some of the city's most distinctive shops and steadfast clusters of galleries, many of which display some of the world's greatest works of art.

The Garment District

Squeezing in between Sixth and Eighth avenues from West 30th to 42nd streets, the **Garment District**, home to the twin modern monsters of Penn Station and Madison Square Garden, offers little of interest to the casual tourist.

It is in this tiny district that three-quarters of all the women's and children's clothes made in America are put together, though you'd never believe it from walking around. Outlets are almost entirely wholesale, and don't bother to woo customers; the only visible evidence of the industry is the racks of clothes shunted around on the street and occasional bins of off-cuts that give the area the look of an open-air rummage sale.

One of the benefits of walking through this part of town, though, is taking advantage of the designers' **sample sales**, where floor samples and models' castoffs are sold to the public at cheap prices (see p.397 for more on sample sales).

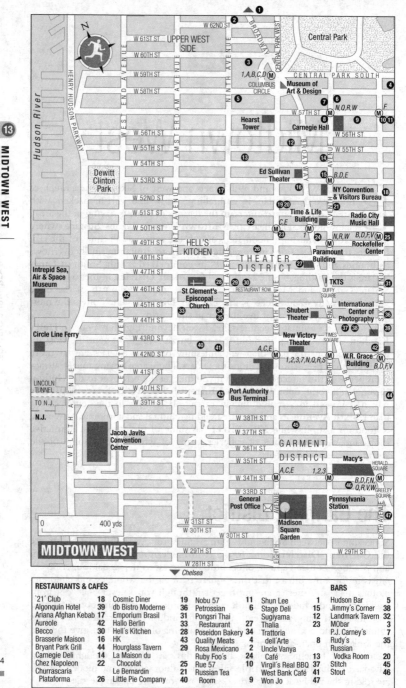

MIDTOWN WEST

RESTAURANTS & CAFÉS

`21` Club	18	Cosmic Diner	19	Nobu 57	11	Shun Lee	1
Algonquin Hotel	39	db Bistro Moderne	36	Petrossian	6	Stage Deli	15
Ariana Afghan Kebab	17	Emporium Brasil	31	Pongsri Thai		Sugiyama	12
Aureole	42	Hallo Berlin	33	Restaurant	27	Thalia	23
Becco	30	Hell´s Kitchen	28	Poseidon Bakery	34	Trattoria	
Brasserie Maison	16	HK	43	Quality Meats	4	dell´Arte	8
Bryant Park Grill	44	Hourglass Tavern	29	Rosa Mexicano	2	Uncle Vanya	
Carnegie Deli	14	La Maison du		Ruby Foo´s	24	Café	13
Chez Napoleon	22	Chocolat	25	Rue 57	10	Virgil´s Real BBQ	37
Churrascaria		Le Bernardin	21	Russian Tea		West Bank Café	41
Plataforma	26	Little Pie Company	40	Room	9	Won Jo	47

BARS

Hudson Bar	5	P.J. Carney´s	7
Jimmy´s Corner	38	Rudy´s	35
Landmark Tavern	32	Russian	
MObar	3	Vodka Room	20
		Stitch	45
		Stout	46

Greeley and Herald squares

Sixth Avenue collides with Broadway at West 34th Street at an unremarkable triangle given the somewhat overblown title **Greeley Square**, in honor of Horace Greeley, founder of the *New York Tribune* newspaper. One could make the case that Greeley deserves better: known for his rallying call to the youth of the nineteenth century ("Go West, young man!"), he also supported the rights of women and trade unions, denounced slavery and capital punishment, and commissioned a weekly column from Karl Marx.

The somewhat more interesting **Herald Square** faces Greeley Square in a continuation of the battle between the *New York Herald* newspaper and its arch rival, Horace Greeley's *Tribune*. (The two papers merged in 1924 to form the *New York Herald Tribune*, which was published until 1967.) During the 1890s this was the Tenderloin area, with dance halls, brothels, and rough bars like *Satan's Circus* and the *Burnt Rag* thriving beside the elevated railway that ran up Sixth Avenue. These days its sidewalks are congested with consumers, many heading for the massive Macy's department store adjacent to the square.

Macy's

Macy's, 151 W 34th St (℡212/695-4400, Ⓦwww.macys.com), bills itself as "the world's largest store," which is not overly hyperbolic, considering the building takes up an entire city block and offers about two million square feet of selling space. Founded in 1858, the store moved to its current location in 1902 although it wasn't until the 1980s that Macy's went fashionably up-market, with designers – such as Tommy Hilfiger – building their own shops in-store. Macy's fortunes declined dramatically, however, when the economy went into a tailspin in 1990, burdened as it was by overexpansion and debt. The store scrambled out of its 1992 bankruptcy in the nick of time, complete with a debt-restructuring plan that allowed it to continue financing its famed annual Thanksgiving Day Parade. One of the best-attended Manhattan processions, it is known for its giant cartoon-character balloons and the arrival of Santa (see Chapter 33, "Parades and festivals").

Madison Square Garden and Penn Station

The most prominent landmark in the Garment District, the **Pennsylvania Station and Madison Square Garden complex** takes up the whole block between Seventh and Eighth avenues and 32nd and 33rd streets. It's a combined box-and-drum structure: at the same time its train-station belly swallows up millions of commuters, its above-ground facilities house Knicks basketball and Rangers hockey games, as well as professional wrestling and boxing matches (for ticket details, see p.410).

There's nothing memorable about the train station; its grimy subterranean levels are an example of just about everything that's wrong with the subway. The original 1910 Penn Station, which brought an air of dignity to the neighborhood and set the stage for the ornate General Post Office and other elaborate *belle époque* structures, was demolished in 1963 to make way for this monstrous structure. One of McKim, Mead, and White's greatest designs, the station's original edifice reworked the ideas of the Roman Baths of Caracalla to awesome effect: the floors of the grand arcade were pink marble, the walls pink granite. Glass floor tiles in the main waiting room allowed light from the glass roof to flow through to the trains and platforms below. Architectural historian

Old Penn Station and the Landmarks Preservation Law

When the old **Penn Station** was demolished in 1963 in order to expand the Madison Square Garden sports complex, the notion of conservation was only a gleam in the eye of its middle-class supporters, at the time few and far between but ten years later a broad-based power group. Despite the vocal opposition of a few, "modernization" was the theme of the day – so much so that almost nothing of the original building was saved. A number of the carefully crafted statues and decorations actually became landfill for New Jersey's Meadowlands complex just across the Hudson River.

At around the same time, the Singer Building, an early, graceful skyscraper in the Financial District, was demolished to make way for the hulking US Steel Building. In the end, it was public disgust with the wanton destruction of these two buildings that brought about the passing of the **Landmarks Preservation Law**. This act ensures that buildings granted landmark status – a designation based on aesthetic value or historical importance – cannot be destroyed or even altered. The law goes beyond protecting buildings, and also applies to districts, such as Fort Greene and Soho, as well as "scenic" landmarks, including Verdi Square at Broadway and West 73rd Street.

Vincent Scully lamented the differences in the two structures in the 1960s, saying, "Through it one entered the city like a god... One scuttles in now like a rat." Some of Penn Station's lost luster may be restored when – or rather, if – an expanded station opens in the General Post Office building; with costs (pledged by developers and city and state agencies) having ballooned from $900m in 2005 to $3bn through 2008, the project's future looks uncertain. Madison Square Garden's decision in March 2008 to refurbish its present home (instead of moving adjacent to the post office site) only complicated matters further, as the whole scheme had hinged on the demolition of MSG as the first step in producing the new transportation hub.

Glimpses of the original structure are visible in photos hanging in the Amtrak waiting area of today's Penn Station, as well as in the four-faced clock on display in the Long Island Railroad (LIRR) ticket area on 34th Street and Seventh Avenue. Andrew Leicester's 1994 *Ghost Series* lines the walls, including terracotta wall murals saluting the Corinthian and Ionic columns of the old Penn Station. Also look for a rendering of Adolph A. Weinman's sculpture *Day & Night*, an ornate statue surrounding a clock that welcomed passengers at the old station's entrance. Be sure to look above your head in the LIRR ticket area for Maya Lin's *Eclipsed Time*, a sculpture of glass, aluminum, and fiber optics that alludes to the immeasurability of time with random number patterns.

The General Post Office

Immediately behind Penn Station at 421 Eighth Ave, the **General Post Office** (aka the James A. Farley Post Office) is a 1913 McKim, Mead, and White structure that survived the push for modernization, and stands as a relic from an era when municipal pride was all about making statements. There's still a working post-office branch here, although the main sorting stations have moved into more modern spaces farther west. That said, the building is no architectural dinosaur: a new Penn Station for Amtrak was to be built inside, keeping the original exterior preserved, but it's uncertain if that will ever come to pass (see the section on Madison Square Garden, above). Originally set to open in 2011, the redevelopment was to be named Moynihan Station, after the late New York State Senator Daniel Patrick Moynihan. Ironically, in his later years, Moynihan lamented the city's ability to make good on its many planned public-works projects.

Port Authority Bus Terminal
One of midtown's more reviled landmarks, the **Port Authority Terminal Building** crouches on Eighth Avenue between West 40th and 42nd streets (for practical details see p.23). Not long ago, the Port Authority served as a magnet for down-and-outs, but it is spruced up and remarkably safe now. Greyhound buses leave from here, as do several other regional services.

Times Square and around

Forty-second Street meets Broadway at the southern outskirts of **Times Square**, the center of the Theater District (see box below), where the constantly pulsating neon conjures up the notion of a beating heart for Manhattan. The area is certainly always alive with activity. Traditionally a melting pot of debauchery, depravity, and fun, for decades the quarter was a place where out-of-towners provided easy pickings for petty criminals, drug dealers, and prostitutes. Most of Times Square's legendary pornography and crime are long gone, replaced by sanitized superstores, high-rise office buildings, and boutique hotels that have killed off the square's historically greasy appeal. This doesn't mean, though, that the area is without charm, and hundreds of thousands of people stil mass here every New Year's Eve, when a giant sparkling ball drops from the top of Times Tower on the stroke of midnight. If you have never seen Times Square, plan your first visit for after dark. Without passing through the square, take a taxi to 57th and Broadway and

The Theater District

Though many of the **theaters** hosting big-budget musicals and dramas considered to be "Broadway shows" are not technically on that avenue, they are, for the most part, located within a couple blocks of it in the West 40s. Sadly, the majority of New York's great theaters have been destroyed to make way for office buildings. However, some of the old grandeur still survives. The **New Amsterdam**, 214 W 42nd St, and the family-oriented **New Victory**, 209 W 42nd St, both between Seventh and Eighth avenues, were refurbished by Disney some years ago, two of the truly welcome results of the massive changes here. The **Lyceum**, 149 W 45th St, retains its original facade, while the **Shubert Theater**, 225 W 44th St, still occupies its own small space. At 432 W 44th St is **The Actors Studio**, where Lee Strasberg taught the principles of "method-acting," a technique invented by Russian actor Constantin Stanislavski to help actors "live the part."

The famous **neon**, so much a signature of Times Square, was initially confined to the theaters and spawned the term "the Great White Way." Today the illumination is not limited to theaters. Myriad ads, forming one of the world's most garish nocturnal displays, promote hundreds of products and services. Businesses that rent offices here are actually required to allow signage on their walls – the city's attempt to retain the square's traditional feel, paradoxically enough, with the most advanced technology possible.

▲ Times Square

start walking south. The spectacle will open out before your eyes, slowly at first, and then with a rush of energy and animation.

Like nearby Greeley and Herald squares, Times Square took its name from a newspaper – the *New York Times* built its offices here in 1904. While the *Herald* and *Tribune* fought each other in ever more vicious circulation battles, the *Times* stood on more restrained ground under the banner "All the news that's fit to print," a policy that has enabled both its survival and its current status as most powerful newspaper in the country. The newspaper's old headquarters, **Times Tower**, is at the southernmost end of the square on a small block between 42nd and 43rd streets. Originally an elegant building modeled on Giotto's Campanile in Florence, the famous zipper sign displaying the news of the world was added in 1928. In 1965, the building was "skinned" and covered with the lifeless marble slabs visible today. The paper's offices have long since moved, most recently to a newly constructed 52-story Renzo Piano tower across from the Port Authority, and most of the printing is done in New Jersey.

Not actually a square at all, Times Square is formed by the intersection between arrow-straight Seventh Avenue and left-leaning Broadway; the latter more or less follows true north through much of the island, which tilts to the northeast. So narrow is the angle between these two thoroughfares that Broadway, which meets Seventh Avenue at 43rd Street, does not begin to strike off on its own again until 48th Street, just above the traffic island of **Duffy Square**. Not much to look at itself, Duffy Square offers an excellent view of Times Square's lights, megahotels, theme stores, and restaurants. A glass "stairway to nowhere," modest in comparison, is balanced on the renovated **TKTS booth**, which sells half-price, same-day tickets for Broadway shows (whose exorbitant prices these days make a visit to TKTS a necessity; see p.360 for details). A lifelike statue of Broadway's doyen **George M. Cohan** looks on, while at eye level you can find enough gifts in the souvenir shops for your five hundred closest friends.

One block east and an easy walk from Times Square is the **International Center of Photography**, 1133 Sixth Ave at 43rd St (Tues–Thurs, Sat & Sun 10am–6pm, Fri 10am–8pm; $12, students and seniors $8; ☎212/857-0000, ⓦwww.icp.org). Founded in 1974 by Cornell Capa (brother of war photographer Robert Capa), this exceptional museum and school sponsors twenty exhibits a year dedicated to "concerned photography," avant-garde works, and retrospectives of modern masters.

Hell's Kitchen

Sprawling across the blocks west of Times Square to the Hudson River between 30th and 59th streets lies **Clinton** (named for nineteenth-century Governor Dewitt Clinton, not president Bill), more famously known as **Hell's Kitchen**, an area centered on the restaurants, bars, and ethnic delis of **Ninth Avenue**.

Head to Hell's Kitchen from Eighth Avenue by walking west on 46th Street along so-called **Restaurant Row** – the area's preferred haunt for pre- and post-theater dining, even though most of the strip's eateries are mediocre at best. Check out the decidedly unstuffy **St Clement's Episcopal Church**, 423 W 46th St: it doubles as a community theater and its foyer features a picture of Elvis Presley and Jesus with the caption, "There seems to be a little confusion as to which one of them actually rose from the dead."

Among New York's most violent and lurid neighborhoods at one time, Hell's Kitchen was rumored to be named for a tenement at 54th Street and Tenth Avenue. More commonly, the name has been attributed to a veteran policeman who went by the sobriquet "Dutch Fred the Cop." In response to his young partner's comment – while watching a riot – that the place was hell, Fred reportedly replied, "Hell's a mild climate. This is Hell's kitchen." The area originally contained slaughterhouses and factories that made soap and glue, with sections named "Misery Lane" and "Poverty Row." Irish immigrants were the first inhabitants; they were soon joined by Greeks, Puerto Ricans, and African-Americans. Amid the overcrowding, tensions rapidly developed between (and within) ethnic groups – the rough-and-tumble neighborhood was popularized in the musical *West Side Story* (1957). A violent Irish gang, the Westies, claimed the streets in the 1970s and early 1980s, but the area has since been cleaned up and is far less dangerous than it ever has been (although you should still keep your wits about you), attracting a new population of musicians, Broadway types, and a growing number of professionals.

The Intrepid Sea, Air & Space Museum and around

If you continue west to the river from Times Square, you will reach the **Intrepid Sea, Air & Space Museum**, 46th St and Twelfth Ave at Pier 86 (☎212/245-0072, ⓦwww.intrepidmuseum.org). This huge (900-foot-long) old aircraft carrier has a distinguished history: it picked up capsules from the Mercury and Gemini space missions and made several trips to Vietnam. It holds an array of modern and vintage air- and sea-craft, including the A-12 Blackbird, the world's fastest spy plane, and the USS *Growler*, the only guided-missile submarine open to the public. The museum also has recently revamped interactive exhibits and simulators, an on-board restaurant, and the recently retired

Concorde, formerly operated by British Airways. If you're visiting at the end of May, **Fleet Week** (the week leading up to Memorial Day) is a big deal here, and deservedly so, with ships visiting from all corners of the globe, as well as military demonstrations and competitions.

Sixth Avenue

Sixth Avenue is officially named **Avenue of the Americas** but no New Yorker ever calls it that. While there's little of the ground-floor glitter of Fifth or the razzmatazz of Broadway, there is **Diamond Row**, a jewelry lovers' Shangri-la since the 1920s (see p.128 for description).

There's also the **Rockefeller Center Extension**, defining the stretch from 47th to 51st streets. Following the **Time & Life Building** at 50th Street, three near-identical buildings went up in the 1970s. Though they don't have the romance of their predecessor, they at least possess some of its monumentality. Backing onto Rockefeller Center proper, the repeated statement of each building comes over with some power, giving Sixth Avenue much of its visual excitement. (For the full account on all that Rockefeller Center holds, see p.128.)

Radio City Music Hall and north

On the corner of Sixth Avenue and 50th Street is **Radio City Music Hall**, a sweeping and dramatic Art Deco jewel box that represents the last word in 1930s luxury. The staircase is positively regal, the chandeliers are the world's largest, and the auditorium looks like an extravagant scalloped shell: "Art Deco's true shrine," as critic Paul Goldberger rightly called it. To explore, take a tour from the lobby (daily 11am–3pm; hour-long "Stage Door" behind-the-scenes walking tours include a meeting with a Rockette; $17, children under 12 years $10; for tickets, call ☏212/307-7171, tour info ☏247-4777, ⊛www.radiocity.com).

Farther north, at no. 1290, is the **AXA Financial Center**, which hosts Thomas Hart Benton's *America Today* murals. This creation (1931) was celebrated for its representation of ordinary pre-Depression-era Americans from a variety of classes, shown both at work and at leisure. It spurred an interest in murals as public art, and lent momentum to the Federal Arts Project (which provided both employment for artists suffering through the decade, and a morale boost for the rest of the public) in the 1930s.

Keep an eye open for the **CBS Building** on the corner at 51 W 52nd St. Dark and inscrutable, this has been compared to the monolith from the film *2001: A Space Odyssey*. While Sixth Avenue proceeds grandly and placidly north for several blocks before reaching the green expanse of Central Park, it's the **Ed Sullivan Theater**, a block north and west on 1697 Broadway between 53rd and 54th streets, that attracts the most people in this neighborhood. Lines wrap around 53rd Street for stand-by tickets to see the *Late Show* with David Letterman, just as they might have 50 years ago for the wildly popular Ed Sullivan variety show shot on the same stage. Situated nearby, between 56th and 57th streets on Eighth Avenue, is the **Hearst World Headquarters**, which had its 597-foot tower completed in June 2006. The tower, designed by Lord Norman Foster, is incongruously attached atop a multi-style six-story base of precast limestone. It is certified as one of the most environmentally friendly high-rise buildings ever constructed, employing technologies to reduce pollution and energy consumption, while fully utilizing renewable energy resources.

57th Street

The area just around 57th Street between Fifth and Sixth avenues competes with Soho and Chelsea as a center for **up-market art sales**. Galleries here are noticeably snootier than their downtown relations, and often require appointments for viewings. Two that usually don't include the **Kennedy Galleries**, 730 Fifth Ave (℡212/541-9600), which deal in nineteenth- and twentieth-century American painting, and show a wide variety of styles, and the venerable **Tibor de Nagy Gallery**, 724 Fifth Ave, 12th floor (Tues–Sat 10am–5.30pm; closed Aug; ℡212/262-5050), which was established in 1950 but still shows exciting works. Also noteworthy is the **Art Students League**, 215 W 57th, built in 1892 by Henry J. Hardenbergh (who later built the *Plaza Hotel*) to mimic Francis the First's hunting lodge at Fontainebleau. Today this art school provides inexpensive art classes to the public. (For more on galleries in this area, see Chapter 30, "Commercial galleries.")

At 154 W 57th St is stately **Carnegie Hall**, one of the world's greatest concert venues, revered by musicians and audiences alike. The Renaissance-inspired structure was built in the 1890s by steel magnate and self-styled "improver of mankind" Andrew Carnegie, and the still-superb acoustics ensure full houses most of the year. Tchaikovsky conducted the program on opening night and Mahler, Rachmaninov, Toscanini, Frank Sinatra, and Judy Garland have all performed here (not to mention Duke Ellington, Billie Holiday, the Beatles, Spinal Tap, and Missy Elliott). Tours are available September through June only (Mon–Fri 11.30am, 2pm & 3pm; $10, students and seniors $7, children under 12 $3; tours ℡212/903-9765, tickets ℡247-7800, ⓦwww.carnegiehall.org). It's just a couple blocks north of here at the southwestern corner of Central Park that Eighth Avenue and Broadway empty into the swirling maelstrom of traffic and construction that is Columbus Circle, gateway to the Upper West Side and Central Park. Nearby is the **Gainsborough Studios** building, 222 Central Park South, between Broadway and Seventh Avenue. Built in 1905, it became an official city landmark in 1988 and is notable for the Moravian tiles that dominate the top two floors, as well as the double-story windows that peer onto Central Park. Note the bust of the building's namesake, English artist Thomas Gainsborough, which hovers above the entrance on the facade.

Central Park

"**A**ll radiant in the magic atmosphere of art and taste," raved *Harper's* magazine on the occasion of the opening of **Central Park** in 1876. A slight overstatement, perhaps, although today few people could imagine New York City without the park. Devotedly used by locals and visited by travelers, it serves purposes as varied as the individuals who take advantage of it: it's an environmental haven, a theater for all things cultural, a beach, a playground, and a running track. Over the years, the park has occasionally fallen on hard times, experiencing everything from official neglect to some truly horrible crime waves. Recently, though, it has benefited from a series of major renovations, and is now cleaner, safer, and more user-friendly than ever.

Park practicalities

General park information can be obtained by calling ☎212/310-6600 or 212/360-1311, or by going to ⊛www.centralparknyc.org, which contains a slew of information, including flower blooming schedules and Central Park's starring and co-starring roles in the movies.

The **Central Park Conservancy**, founded in 1980, is a nonprofit organization dedicated to preserving and managing the park. It runs four **Visitor Centers**, which have free maps and other helpful literature, as well as feature special events. All are open year-round Tuesday through Sunday 10am to 5pm: The **Dairy** (65th St at mid-park; ☎212/794-6564); **Belvedere Castle** (79th St at mid-park; ☎212/772-0210); the **North Meadow Recreation Center** (mid-park at 97th St; ☎212/348-4867); and the **Charles A. Dana Discovery Center** (110th St off Fifth Ave; ☎212/860-1370).

Restrooms are available at Hecksher Playground, the Boat Pond (Conservatory Water), Mineral Springs House (northwest end of Sheep's Meadow), Bethesda Terrace, Loeb Boathouse, the Delacorte Theater, the East 85th St Playground, the Tennis House (94th St mid-park), the North Meadow Recreation Center, the Conservatory Garden, the Robert Bendheim Playground (E 100th St at Fifth Ave), and the Charles A. Dana Discovery Center.

Manhattan Urban Park Rangers (activities info line ☎212/628-2345, ⊛www.nyc.gov/parks) are in the park to help; they lead walking tours, give directions, and provide necessary first aid.

In case of emergency, use the **emergency call boxes** located throughout the park and along the park drives (they provide a direct connection to the Central Park Precinct), or dial ☎911 at any payphone.

Some history

Poet and newspaper editor **William Cullen Bryant** is credited with first publicizing the idea for an open public space in Manhattan in 1844; seven years later, City Hall finally agreed to carry out his plan, paying $5 million for 840 acres north of the (then) city limits at 38th Street, a desolate swampy area occupied at the time by scattered shantytowns whose residents were evicted as planning began to pick up speed.

In 1857, after a fierce design contest, **Frederick Law Olmsted** and **Calvert Vaux** were chosen to create the rural paradise they called "Greensward," an illusion of the countryside smack in the heart of Manhattan. The sparseness of the existing terrain didn't just attract builders; it also provided Olmsted and Vaux with the perfect opportunity to plan the park according to the precepts of classical English landscape gardening. They designed 36 elegant bridges, each unique, and planned an ingenious system of four sunken transverse roads to segregate different kinds of traffic.

It took sixteen years and $14 million ($260 million in today's money) to construct the entire park, though the sapling trees planted here didn't reach their full height for five decades. Central Park opened to the public in 1876. So great was the acclaim for Olmsted and Vaux that they were soon in demand as park architects all over the United States. Locally, they went on to design Riverside and Morningside parks in Manhattan, as well as Prospect Park in Brooklyn.

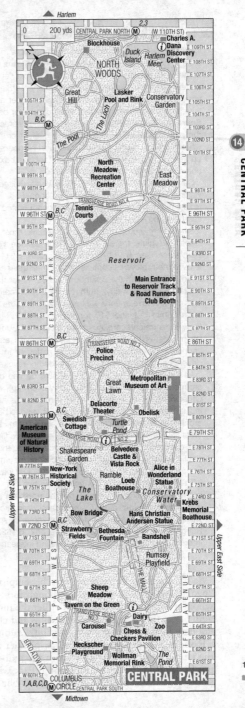

Central Park is so enormous that it's impossible to miss entirely and nearly as impossible to cover in one visit. The intricate **footpaths** that meander through the park are some of its greatest successes. If you've lost your way among them, though, there are several tricks to finding it again. Every feature has a name in order that rendezvous can be precise. Even the bodies of water are differentiated (a loch, a pool, a lake, and even a meer) so that there can never be confusion. But if you do need **to figure out exactly where you are**, find the nearest **lamppost**. The first two digits on the post indicate the number of the nearest cross street, while the last two show whether you're nearer the east side (odd numbers) or west side (even). You can pick up free maps at any of the Visitor Centers (see box, p.152) or two dozen freestanding unmanned kiosks throughout the park.

Car access to the park's drives is severely limited outside rush hours. Even if you're visiting during a car-free period, you should still keep a watchful eye: crossing the road amid the hordes of goggled and headphoned rollerbladers, cyclists, and joggers can be trying – just be patient.

Since there are no bus routes in the park, most people either walk or don rollerblades and glide there. Other options include **renting a bicycle** from the Loeb Boathouse (see p.156) or Metro Bicycles (1311 Lexington Ave ☎212/427-4450, ⓦwww.metrobicycles.com; ask about their other shops, since another may be closer to you). Bikes from the Boathouse are $9–15 for the first hour, and from Metro $7 an hour (or $35 for the day); both require a credit card or refundable cash deposit.

All of the above options are better deals than the famed **romantic buggy rides** ($40 for a 20min trot and $10 for every additional 15min after that; ☎212/736-0680, ⓦwww.centralparkcarriages.com). Incidentally, don't worry about the horses: a 1994 law mandates that they must get fifteen-minute rest breaks every two hours, and they cannot work more than nine hours a day or in temperatures above 90ºF. Buggy drivers can get their licenses suspended or revoked for non-compliance.

As for **safety** in the park, you should be fine during the day everywhere except around the Blockhouse on the northwestern tip, which is best visited only on a tour. Otherwise, just stay alert to your surroundings and try to avoid being alone in an isolated area; after dark, it's safer than it used to be, but it's still not advisable to walk around, especially not by yourself. If you want to look at the buildings of Central Park West lit up, as they were in Woody Allen's iconic film *Manhattan*, the best option is to fork out for a buggy ride. The one exception to the after-dark rule is in the case of a public evening event such as a concert or a summertime Shakespeare in the Park performance; these events are very safe – just leave when the crowds do.

The **Reservoir** divides Central Park in two. The larger **southern park** holds most of the attractions (and people), but the **northern park** (above 86th St) is well worth a visit for its wilder natural setting and dramatically quieter ambience. Organized walking tours are available from a number of sources, including the Urban Park Rangers and the Visitor Centers (see box, p.152), but almost any stroll, formal or informal, will invariably lead to something interesting.

At its opening, the powers that be emphasized that Central Park was a "people's park," available to all – though most of the impoverished masses for whom it was allegedly built had neither the time nor the carfare to come up to 59th Street from their downtown slums and enjoy it, people eventually started flooding in as the city grew in size and wealth.

Robert Moses, a relentless urban planner and the power behind some of the city's largest building projects in the mid-twentieth century, tried hard to put his imprint (concrete) on Central Park while he served as parks commissioner from 1935 to 1960. Thankfully, public opinion kept damage from his developments to a minimum; he only managed to pave over a small portion of the park, mostly in the form of unnecessary parking lots (since reconverted to green space). When he tried to tear down a park playground in 1956 to build a parking lot for *Tavern on the Green*, Moses was thwarted by outraged citizens – mothers and their young children stood in the way of the bulldozers, and the city sheepishly backed down.

The park hit rock bottom in 1973, by which point it had degenerated into a vandalized, crime-infested eyesore on which the bankrupt city had no money to spare (see p.438). It was only the threat that the park would be turned over to the National Park Service that mobilized both politicians and local citizens to find funds to refit it. That ongoing effort is now overseen by a feisty nonprofit group called the Central Park Conservancy, which works in conjunction with the city government to maintain the park, increase its policing, and restore areas like Bethesda Terrace (see p.156).

Despite the advent of motorized traffic, the idea of nature-as-disorder intended by Olmsted and Vaux largely survives. (About two-thirds of the park is either identical or quite similar to the original design.) Cars and buses cut through the park in the sheltered, sunken transverses originally intended for horse-drawn carriages, and remain mostly unseen from the park itself. The skyline, of course, has drastically changed, but the buildings that menacingly thrust their way into view are kept at bay by a fortress of trees, adding to the feeling that you're on a green island in the center of a magnificent city.

The southern park

Most visitors enter the park at Grand Army Plaza (Fifth Ave and 59th St; see p.130). From here, **The Pond** lies to the left, and a little farther north is the **Wollman Memorial Rink** (63rd St at mid-park; Nov–March ice skating Mon & Tues 10am–2.30pm, Wed & Thurs 10am–10pm, $9.50; Fri & Sat 10am–11pm, Sun 10am–9pm, $12; ☎212/439-6900, ⊛www.wollmanskatingrink.com). As well as ice skates, you can rent rollerblades, the most versatile and popular mode of park transportation (skate rental $5, locker rental $4 plus $6.25 refundable deposit; no credit cards).

East of the skating rink, at 64th Street and Fifth Avenue, lies the small **Central Park Zoo** (Nov–March daily 10am–4.30pm; April–Oct Mon–Fri 10am–5pm, Sat, Sun & holidays 10am–5.30pm; $8, children ages 3–12 $3, children under 3 free; ☎212/439-6500, ⊛www.centralparkzoo.com). This welcoming wildlife center has over a hundred species on view in mostly natural-looking homes. The animals are as close to the viewer as possible: the penguins, for example, swim around at eye level in Plexiglas pools. Other top attractions include the polar bears, the monkeys, a nocturnal exhibit, and the sea lions, which cavort in a pool right by the zoo entrance. This complex also boasts the **Tisch Children's Zoo**: there's a petting area, interactive displays, and a musical clock just outside the entrance that draws rapt children at the top of each hour. The zoo is a charming stop-off for an hour or two, but if you're a dedicated animal-lover, or have older children, you're better off heading to the Bronx Zoo (see p.260).

Close by stands the **Dairy** (65th St at mid-park), a cutesy yellow neo-Gothic chalet built in 1870 as a café. Despite local lore, there were never any cows here, though it did sell milk for children. It's now one of the park's Visitor Centers

(see p.152). Weekend walking tours often leave from here – check ⓦwww
.centralparknyc.org for times and routes. You can also pick up pieces here for
the **Chess and Checkers Pavilion** near the zoo.

Just west of the Dairy, you will see the octagonal brick building that houses the
Carousel (64th St at mid-park; April–Oct Mon–Fri 10am–6pm, Sat & Sun
10am–7pm; Nov–Dec daily 10am–dusk, Jan–March Sat & Sun 10am–dusk,
weather permitting; $2; ☎212/879-0244). Built in 1903 and moved to the park
from Coney Island in 1951, this is one of the park's little gems. There are fewer
than 150 such carousels left in the country (one of the others is still at Coney
Island – see p.238). A ride on it is a magical experience: its hand-carved, colorfully
painted jumping horses are accompanied by the music of a military-band organ.

Heading north from the Dairy, you'll pass through the avenue of trees known
as **The Mall**. The trees, whose branches tangle together to form a "roof"
(hence its nickname, "The Cathedral"), are elms, a rarity in America. The statues
that line the avenue are all literary and artistic greats: Shakespeare arrived first,
and others from across the world soon followed, often privately funded by the
appropriate immigrant groups – hence Italy's Mazzini and Germany's
Beethoven. At the base of the Mall is one of only two acknowledgments to
either park architect: a small memorial garden in Frederick Law Olmsted's
name. Poor Calvert Vaux wasn't commemorated anywhere until April 2008,
when the 72nd Street transverse was rechristened "Olmsted & Vaux Way."

To the west lies the **Sheep Meadow** (between 66th and 69th sts), fifteen acres
of commons where sheep grazed until 1934, when they were banished to
Brooklyn's Prospect Park. In the summer, the meadow is crowded with
picnickers, sunbathers, and Frisbee players. Two grass bowling and croquet lawns
are maintained on a hill near the Sheep Meadow's northwest corner; to the
southeast are a number of very popular volleyball courts (call ☎212/360-8133
for information on lawn bowling; call ☎212/408-0226 for volleyball and other
ball-field permit information). On warm weekends, an area between the Sheep
Meadow and the north end of the mall is usually filled with rollerbladers
dancing to funk, disco, and hip-hop – one of the best free shows in town. Just
west of the Sheep Meadow is the once exclusive, still expensive, but now tacky,
landmark restaurant, **Tavern on the Green** (see p.331). The original 1870
building housed a fold for the animals who grazed the nearby meadow. Take a
look at the exterior of the eatery, a colorful and intricate design done in the
Victorian Gothic style, with street lamps which originally lined the Champs
Elysées in Paris.

East of the restaurant, at the northernmost point of the Mall, lie the **Bandshell**
and **Rumsey Playfield**, the sites of the free SummerStage performance series
(see box, p.159). There's also the **Bethesda Terrace and Fountain** (72nd St
at mid-park), one of the few formal elements planned by Olmsted and Vaux.
The crowning centerpiece of the fountain is the nineteenth-century *Angel of
the Waters* sculpture, the only statue included in the original park design. Its
earnest puritanical angels were recently made famous again by Tony Kushner's
Pulitzer Prize-winning play *Angels in America*, of which the last scene is set here.
The subterranean arcade is the subject of a series of major renovations aimed at
restoring the intricate Minton tiling that once covered the ceiling. The fountain
overlooks **The Lake**, where you can go for a Venetian-style gondola ride or
rent a rowboat from the Loeb Boathouse on the eastern bank (April–Oct daily
10am–5.30pm, weather permitting; rowboats $12 for the first hour, $3 each
15min thereafter; $30 refundable cash deposit; gondola rides available 5–10pm,
$30 per 30min per group, requires reservations; ☎212/517-2233, ⓦwww
.thecentralparkboathouse.com).

The narrowest point on the lake is crossed by the elegant cast-iron and wood **Bow Bridge**. Take this bridge if you want to amble to **The Ramble** on the lake's northern banks, a 37-acre area of unruly woodland, filled with narrow winding paths, rocky outcroppings, streams, and an array of native plant life. Once a favorite spot for drug dealers and anonymous sex, it is now a great place to watch for one of the park's 54 species of birds or take a quiet daytime stroll. Clean-up notwithstanding, steer clear of this area at night.

To the west of Bethesda Terrace, along the 72nd St Drive, is the **Cherry Hill Fountain**. Originally a turnaround point for carriages, it was designed to have excellent views of the Lake, the Mall, and the Ramble. One of the pretty areas paved by Moses in the 1930s for use as a parking lot, it was restored to its natural state in the early 1980s.

West of here, across the Park Drive, is **Strawberry Fields** (72nd St and Central Park W), a peaceful area dedicated to John Lennon, who was murdered in 1980 in front of his home at the Dakota Building, across the street on Central Park West. (See box, p.193 for more on the death of John Lennon.) Strawberry Fields is always crowded with those here to remember Lennon, at no time more so than December 8, the anniversary of his murder. Near the West 72nd Street entrance to the park is a round Italianate mosaic with the word "Imagine" at its center, donated by Lennon's widow, Yoko Ono. This is also a favorite spot for picnickers and resting seniors.

Back to the east of Bethesda Terrace is the **Boat Pond** (72nd St and Fifth Ave), where model-boat races are held every Saturday in the summer; you can participate by renting a craft from Central Park Sailboats (☎917/796-1382). The fanciful *Alice in Wonderland* statue at the northern end of the pond was donated by publisher George Delacorte and is a favorite climbing spot for kids. During the summer the New York Public Library sponsors Wednesday-morning (11am) storytelling sessions for children at the *Hans Christian Andersen* statue on the west side of the pond (☎212/340-0906 for more

▲ Boat Pond, Central Park

Picnicking in the park

Central Park has ample **picnicking opportunities**, the most obvious of which is the hectic, perpetually crowded expanse of the Sheep Meadow. For (a very) little more peace and quiet, you might try one of these other fine locations: the western shore of the Lake, near Hernshead; the lawn in front of Turtle Pond, which has a nice view of Belvedere Castle; the Conservatory Garden; the lawn immediately north of the Ramble; Strawberry Fields; the Arthur Ross Pinetum; and the areas around the Delacorte Theater.

information). A storyteller from the Central Park Conservancy also appears here at 11am on Saturdays throughout the summer.

Continue north to reach the backyard of the **Metropolitan Museum of Art** to the east at 81st Street (see p.161). Behind the museum to the west stands the **Obelisk**, the oldest structure in the park, which dates from 1450 BC. It was a gift to the city from Egypt in 1881, and, like its twin on the Thames River in London, is nicknamed "Cleopatra's Needle." Immediately west of the needle is the **Great Lawn** (81st St at mid-park). It was the site of the park's original reservoir from 1842 until 1931, when the water was drained to create a playing field. Years later, the lawn became a popular site for free concerts and rallies (Simon and Garfunkel, Elton John, Garth Brooks, Sting, and the Pope, who celebrated mass here in 1995, have all attracted crowds numbering over half a million), but it was badly overused and had serious drainage problems. Reopened in 1998 after a massive two-year, \$18.2-million reconstruction, the lawn's engineering and sandy soil now mean that even if there's a heavy downpour at lunchtime, the grass will be dry by evening. Rebuilt, reseeded, and renewed, it will hopefully stay that way by only hosting the more sedate free New York Philharmonic and Metropolitan Opera concerts (see box opposite). The lawn features eight softball fields and, at its northern end, new basketball and volleyball courts and an eighth-mile running track.

The refurbished **Turtle Pond** is at the southern end of the Lawn, with a new wooden dock and nature blind designed for better views of the aquatic wildlife (yes, there actually is wildlife here, including ducks, fish, and frogs). Note the massive statue of fourteenth-century Polish king **Wladyslaw Jagiello** on the southeast corner of the pond, donated by the Polish governmen, as a Holocaust memorial.

Southwest of the Lawn is the **Delacorte Theater**, the venue of the annual free Shakespeare in the Park festivals (see box opposite). In another of the park's Shakespearean touches, the theater features Milton Hebald's sculptures of Romeo and Juliet and *The Tempest*'s Prospero, while the tranquil **Shakespeare Garden** next door claims to hold every species of plant or flower mentioned in the Bard's plays. East of the garden is **Belvedere Castle**, a mock medieval citadel first erected on top of Vista Rock in 1869 as a lookout on the highest point in the park. It's still a splendid viewpoint, and houses the New York Meteorological Observatory's weather center; there's also a handy Visitor Center here (see p.152). For more plays of the puppet kind, check out the **Swedish Cottage Marionette Theater** (79th St at mid-park) at the base of Vista Rock, which holds shows for kids like *The True Story of Rumpelstiltskin* or *Pippi Longstocking* (July–May Tues–Fri 10.30am & noon, Sat & Sun 1pm; \$8, kids \$5; ⊕212/988-9093 for reservation).

The northern park

There are fewer attractions, but more open spaces, above the Great Lawn. Much of the northern park is taken up by the **Reservoir** (86th–97th streets at mid-park, main entrance at 90th St and Fifth Ave), a 107-acre, billion-gallon reservoir originally designed in 1862 and no longer active. It's a favorite place for active uptown residents: the raised 1.58-mile track is a great place to get breathtaking 360-degree views of the skyline. North of the reservoir are a tennis-court complex and the soccer fields of the **North Meadow Recreation Center** (97th St at mid-park; ☎212/348-4867; for tennis permits and info, call ☎212/316-0800). The landscape north of here, in the aptly named North Woods, feels more like upstate New York than Manhattan: the 90-acre area contains man-made but natural-looking stone arches plus the **Loch**, which is now more of a stream, and the **Ravine**, which conceals five small waterfalls.

If you see nothing else in the park above 86th Street, don't miss the **Conservatory Garden** (daily 8am–dusk; E 104th–106th sts along Fifth Ave with entrance at 105th). Filled with flowering trees and shrubs, planted flower-beds, fanciful fountains, and shaded benches, the space actually houses three gardens, each landscaped in a distinct style. You'll first walk through the Italian

Seasonal events and activities

SummerStage and **Shakespeare in the Park** are two of the most popular cultural summer programs in Manhattan. Both activities are free and help to take the sting out of New York's infamous hazy, hot, and humid summers. In 1986, **SummerStage** presented its inaugural Central Park concert with Sun Ra performing to an audience of fifty people. When he returned with Sonic Youth six years later, the audience numbered ten thousand. The musical acts are of consistently good quality, and cover pretty much every genre during the festival's mid-June through mid-August run. Located at the Rumsey Playfield near 72nd Street and Fifth Avenue, concerts here are crowded and sticky, but unbeatable. Dance performances, DJ sets, and (paid admission) benefit shows also share the stage. More information: ☎212/360-2777 or ⊛www.summerstage.org, **Shakespeare in the Park** takes place at the open-air Delacorte Theater, located near the West 81st Street entrance to the park. Pairs of free tickets are distributed daily at 1pm for that evening's performance, but you'll have to get in line well beforehand, as a crowd often starts to gather by 7am. You can also pick them up at the Public Theater (425 Lafayette St at Astor Place in the East Village) from 1pm on the day of the performance, though again, expect to wait. Alternatively, you can try for a ticket via their online draw-register on the website below. Performances are Tues–Sun at 8pm, mid-June through early Sept. More information: ☎212/539-8750 or ⊛www.publictheater.org.

New York Philharmonic in the Park (☎212/875-5709, ⊛www.newyork philharmonic.org) and **Metropolitan Opera in the Park** (☎212/362-6000, ⊛www .metopera.org) hold several evenings of classical music in the summer, often with a booming fireworks display to usher the crowds home.

Horseback-riding is available by special arrangement with the Riverdale Equestrian Center (☎718/548-4848, ⊛www.riverdaleriding.com). Rides are $100 per person per hour, and are conducted from spring through Thanksgiving.

The Harlem Meer Festival (110th St between Fifth and Lenox aves; ☎212/860-1370) offers fairly intimate and enjoyable free performances of jazz and salsa music outside the Charles A. Dana Discovery Center on Sundays from Memorial Day through Labor Day from 2 to 4pm.

garden, a reserved oasis with neat lawns and trimmed hedges. To the south is the English area, enhanced by the Burnett Fountain, which depicts the two children from F.H. Burnett's classic book *The Secret Garden*. The French garden, the northernmost of the three, hosts sculptor Walter Schott's *Three Dancing Maidens*. Visit the French garden for the flowers – 20,000 tulips in spring and 2000 Korean chrysanthemums in fall. North of this green space is the stand-alone **Robert Bendleim Playground** for disabled children, at 108th Street near Fifth Avenue, where physically challenged youngsters can play in "accessible" sandboxes and swings, or work out their upper bodies on balance beams.

At the top of the park is the **Charles A. Dana Discovery Center**, an environmental education center and Visitor Center (see box, p.152). Crowds of locals fish in the adjacent **Harlem Meer**, an eleven-acre pond stocked with more than 50,000 fish. The Discovery Center provides free bamboo fishing poles and bait.

In the extreme northeast corner of the park, at 110th Street and Fifth Avenue, is a 1997 monument to **Duke Ellington**, the esteemed musician and composer of such classics as *Mood Indigo*. On top of the three columns that summon the nine muses, the Duke stands before his grand piano, symbolically looking toward Harlem for the next generation of musical vanguards. In the park's northwestern corner stands the **Blockhouse**, one of the few landmarks still to be awaiting renovation: one of several such houses built as a lookout over pancake-flat Harlem during the War of 1812, it's the only one which remains. Now a ruin, it's a picturesque but iffy place to visit even during the daytime – stick to seeing it from one of the park's scheduled tours.

The Metropolitan Museum of Art

The **Metropolitan Museum of Art**, or the **Met**, as it's usually called, is the foremost art museum in America. It started in 1870 in a brownstone downtown before decamping to its present site in Central Park, a Gothic-Revival building designed by Jacob Wrey Mould and Calvert Vaux in 1880. Over time various additions to the site have completely surrounded the original structure; the museum's familiar multi-columned, wide-stepped facade on Fifth Avenue was conceived by Richard Morris Hunt and completed in 1902, while the north and south wings were added by McKim, Mead, and White between 1911 and 1913.

The museum's collection includes over two million works of art from the Americas, Europe, Africa, and the Far East, as well as the classical and ancient worlds. There's also plenty to see in some of the **less famous collections**, which range from Islamic Art to the Arms and Armor Galleries, the largest and most important in the western hemisphere.

There is one **main entrance** to the museum; it leads to the **Great Hall**, a deftly lit Neoclassical cavern where you can consult floor plans, check tour times, and pick up info on the Met's excellent lecture listings. Straight across from the entrance is the Grand Staircase, which leads to, for many visitors, the museum's single greatest attraction – the European Painting galleries. Make sure

Met practicalities

The Met (☎212/535-7710, ⊛www.metmuseum.org) is on Fifth Avenue at 82nd Street, set into Central Park. Take subway #4, #5, or #6 to 86th St–Lexington Ave.

The museum is **open** Tuesday through Thursday and Sunday 9.30am to 5.30pm, Friday and Saturday 9.30am to 9pm. There is **no set admission price**, but the suggested donation is $20, $15 for senior citizens and $10 for students (includes admission to the Cloisters on the same day; see p.215). These suggested amounts are exactly that – suggestions. Whether you pay 12¢ or $12, the cashier won't flinch, so if you can, spread out your exploration over several days. Recorded audio tours of the major collections are $7. The museum staff also offer free guided tours daily. Call or check the website for schedules. Be aware that the collection is regularly reorganized and galleries can be **closed**, so call ahead to confirm if there are particular pieces you want to see.

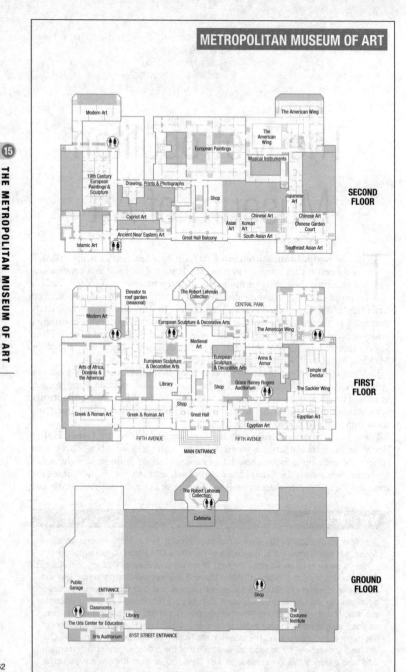

METROPOLITAN MUSEUM OF ART

SECOND FLOOR

Modern Art

The American Wing

The American Wing

European Paintings

Musical Instruments

19th Century European Paintings & Sculpture

Drawing, Prints & Photographs

Shop

Japanese Art

Cypriot Art

Chinese Art

Chinese Art

Ancient Near Eastern Art

Asian Art

Korean Art

Chinese Garden Court

Great Hall Balcony

South Asian Art

Islamic Art

Southeast Asian Art

FIRST FLOOR

Elevator to roof garden (seasonal)

The Robert Lehman Collection

CENTRAL PARK

Modern Art

European Sculpture & Decorative Arts

The American Wing

Medieval Art

Arts of Africa, Oceania & the Americas

European Sculpture & Decorative Arts

European Sculpture & Decorative Arts

Arms & Armor

Temple of Dendur

Library

Shop

Grace Rainey Rogers Auditorium

The Sackler Wing

Greek & Roman Art

Greek & Roman Art

Shop

Great Hall

Egyptian Art

Egyptian Art

FIFTH AVENUE

FIFTH AVENUE

MAIN ENTRANCE

GROUND FLOOR

The Robert Lehman Collection

Cafeteria

Public Garage

ENTRANCE

Shop

The Costume Institute

Classrooms

Library

The Uris Center for Education

Uris Auditorium

81ST STREET ENTRANCE

you pick up the detailed room-by-room gallery **maps** for the European Painting and Nineteenth-Century Painting collections, available at the **main information desk** in the Great Hall.

The Met is so big that at least some sections are likely to be closed for renovation when you visit. Much of the American Wing will be closed until 2010, and the layout of the European Paintings galleries is likely to be changed during the life of this guide edition.

European Art

The Met's **European Art** galleries, located on the second floor at the top of the Grand Staircase, are divided in two parts: the European Painting section – which traces several centuries' worth of work – and the more narrowly focused Nineteenth-Century European Paintings and Sculpture section. The **European Painting galleries** begin with huge works by **Tiepolo** and a room full of eighteenth-century French portraits by the likes of Elizabeth Vigée-Lebrun, Marie-Denise Villers and Jacques-Louis David. In the current layout, turning right here brings you to the **Spanish** galleries; highlights include **Goya**'s widely reproduced portrait of a toddler in a red jumpsuit, *Don Manuel Osorio Manrique de Zuniga*, **Velázquez**'s piercing and somber *Portrait of Juan de Pareja*, and a room of freaky, dazzling canvases by **El Greco**, each of which underscores the jarring modernism of his approach. In solitary contrast is his wraith-like *View of Toledo*, one of the best of his works displayed anywhere in the world, though this painting often spends long periods on loan at other galleries. The next series of galleries contains **Italian Painting**, with **Duccio**'s sublime *Madonna and Child* currently holding court in room 3. Described by the Met as "one of the great single acquisitions of the last half century," the delicately crafted painting is an extremely rare example of early Renaissance art, acquired by the Met in 2004 for around $45m. The collection continues with the Sienese school before moving into the High Renaissance, with **Botticelli**'s *Last Communion of St Jerome* one of the few high points; other standouts include works by **Mantegna** and **Carlo Crivelli**, as well as an outstandingly preserved chunk of **Ghirlandaio fresco**. As for later pictures, there's Mannerist master **Bronzino**'s dapper but haughty *Portrait of a Young Man* and a showy **Raphael**, *Madonna and Child Enthroned with Saints*, which features his signature, pin-up-pretty Virgin Mary. There are also rooms filled with massive works by **Titian** and **Tintoretto**, though it's **Veronese**'s raunchy and artfully composed *Mars and Venus United by Love* that's especially appealing among the Venetians.

Northern European Painting

Galleries dedicated to **Rembrandt**, **Vermeer**, and **Hals** follow the Italian rooms, with **Vermeer** particularly well represented. Most haunting of all is the great *Portrait of a Young Woman*: she's an odd-looking creature with huge doleful eyes and twinkly earrings, her enigmatic expression making her Vermeer's own Mona Lisa.

While Vermeer's paintings focused on stillness and light, the portraits of **Hals** and **Rembrandt** burst with life. At first, these galleries simply seem full of men in jaunty hats and ruffles, but the personalities of the sitters emerge on closer inspection, from the heavy-lidded world-weariness of Rembrandt's *Portrait of a Man* to his deeply reflective *Aristotle with a Bust of Homer*.

Other highlights include Flemish Painting from the fifteenth and sixteenth centuries. Particularly prominent are the paintings of **Jan Van Eyck**, who is usually credited with beginning the tradition of North European realism. The freestanding panels of *The Crucifixion* and *The Last Judgment* were painted early in his career and are full of scurrying, startled figures, tightly composed with expressive and even horrific detail. Another great Northern Gothic painter, **Gerard David**, used local settings for his religious scenes; the background of his exquisite *Virgin and Child with Four Angels* is medieval Bruges and *The Rest on the Flight to Egypt* features a forest glade, again with the turrets of Bruges visible down below. Head across to **Pieter Bruegel the Elder**'s *Harvesters* to see how these innovations were assimilated. Made charming by its snapshot ordinariness (check the sprawling figure napping under a tree), this is one of the Met's most reproduced pictures.

The Met's elegant collection of **English pictures**, usually in room 15, is also worth seeking out. **Sir Thomas Lawrence**'s study of actress *Elizabeth Farren*, which he painted at the precocious age of 21, is impressive, as much for how well it conveys her spirited personality as for its technical mastery. Look out also for **Thomas Gainsborough**'s *Wood Gatherers*, one of his most famous paintings.

Impressionist Painting

Most visitors head directly to the **Nineteenth–Century European Paintings and Sculpture gallery**, following the left-hand corridor at the top of the Grand Staircase. This passage leads to another hall, which is littered with stunning **Rodin** sculptures in white marble and bronze. Twenty rooms branch off from here, leading to an array of Impressionist and Post-Impressionist paintings and nineteenth-century European sculpture.

To the far left, you'll find the precursors of the **Impressionists** such as **Delacroix** and **Ingres**. The latter is well represented by *Mme Jacques-Louis Leblanc*, a matron with a glancing smile on her lips. The central section is devoted to **Degas**, where fans will find studies in just about every medium, from pastels to sculpture. Many examine one of his favorite themes: dancers.

To the right, the Annenberg Collection houses galleries dedicated to all the big names; several works by **Manet**, the Impressionist movement's most influential predecessor, whose early style of contrasting light and shadow with modulated shades of black can be firmly linked to the traditions of Hals, Velázquez, and Goya. *Boating* evokes a vividly fresh, spring morning, while the striking *Young Lady in 1866* is a realistic portrayal of a girl in her peignoir.

Monet was one of the Impressionist movement's most prolific painters, returning again and again to a single subject in order to produce a series of images capturing different nuances of light and atmosphere. The Met's hoard runs like Monet's Greatest Hits: the museum has a canvas from almost every major sequence by the artist, including *Waterlilies*, *Rouen Cathedral (The Portal in Sun)*, *The Houses of Parliament (Effect of Fog)*, and *Haystacks (Effect of Snow and Sun)*.

Cézanne's technique was very different. He labored long to achieve a painstaking analysis of form and color, an effect clear in the *Landscape of Marseilles*. Of his few portraits, the jarring, almost Cubist angles and spaces of the rather plain *Mme Cézanne in a Red Dress* seem years ahead of their time: she looks clearly pained, as if she'd rather be anywhere than under her husband's gaze. Take a look, too, at *The Card Players*, whose dynamic triangular structure thrusts out, yet retains the quiet concentration of the moment. Though there's also work here by every Impressionist name from **Berthe Morisot** to **Pissarro**, it's **Renoir** who's perhaps the best represented. Sadly, most of his works are from after 1878, when he began to move away from the techniques he'd learned while working with Monet and toward the chocolate-boxy soft focus that plagued his later work. Of these, *Mme Charpentier and Her Children* is a likeable enough piece, one whose affectionate tone manages to sidestep the sentimentality of Renoir's later work.

Post-Impressionist Painting

Paintings of the **Post-Impressionists**, logically enough, lie behind these first galleries. One of the highlights of the collection is **Gauguin**'s masterly *La Orana Maria*. This Annunciation-derived scene, a Renaissance staple, has been transferred to a different culture in an attempt to unfold the symbolism, and perhaps voice the artist's feeling for the native South Sea islanders. *Two Tahitian Women* hangs adjacent – an example of skillful, studied simplicity.

All of this scratches little more than the surface of the galleries – for example, there are also more than a half-dozen canvases by **Van Gogh**. Many of them are fine works, especially his *Self Portrait with Straw Hat*, famed *Irises*, and the twisty, thrashing trees of *Cypresses*. Otherwise, make sure to stop by one of the two Pointillist pictures by the master of the technique, **Georges-Pierre Seurat**, who only finished a handful of works before his early death at age 32. The sparkling night-time scene *Circus Sideshow* was the first attempt to replicate artificial light using multicolored dots; there's also a small canvas that was the final study for Seurat's masterpiece *Sunday Afternoon on the Island of La Grande Jatte*.

Asian Art

Also on the second floor are the **Asian Art** galleries, an impressive, schizophrenic collection that includes works in various media from most major civilizations; China, India, Japan, and Korea. First up is **Chinese Sculpture**, a collection of stone works arranged around a serene, twenty-foot-high Buddha and equally large Bodhisattva. The focal point, however, is the enormous (and exquisite) fourteenth-century mural, *The Pure Land of Bhaishajyaguru*. This piece was carefully reconstructed after being severely damaged in an earthquake and is a study in calm reflection.

Take the right fork from this gallery to arrive at **South Asian Art**. There's a vast, if rather monotonous, range of **statues** of Hindu and Buddhist deities here, alongside numerous pieces of friezes, many of which still possess exceptional detail despite years of exposure. *The Great Departure and the Temptation of the Buddha*, carved in the third century, is particularly lively: Siddhartha sets out on his spiritual journey, chased by a harem of dancing girls and grasping cherubs.

Beyond a pristine reproduction of a Jain Meeting Hall lies **Chinese Art**, yet the real highlight in this area is the **Chinese Garden Court**, a serene, minimalist retreat enclosed by the galleries, and the adjacent **Ming Room**, a typical salon decorated in period style with wooden lattice doors. Assembled by experts from China, the naturally lit garden is representative of one found in wealthy Chinese homes of the Ming Dynasty: a pagoda, small waterfall, and stocked goldfish pond landscaped with limestone rocks, trees, and shrubs conjure up a sense of peace.

The Sackler Wing

After meditating in the garden, head into the **Sackler Wing**, part of a cluster of rooms dedicated to **Japanese Art**. This collection has been organized very differently from much of the rest of the Met's holdings. It contains objects from the prehistoric to the present, ordered not chronologically but thematically, with rotating exhibits divided by medium; ceramics, textiles, paintings, and prints. Some of the oldest pieces in the collection are the *dogu*, female figurines dating from between 10,500 BC and 400 BC, but the undeniable showstoppers here are the seventeenth- and eighteenth-century hand-painted **Kano screens**. These range from the elegantly mundane (books on a shelf) to elaborate scenes of historical allusion and divine fervor. Since all the exhibited paintings, calligraphy, and scrolls of Asian art are rotated every six months or so, the scenes change, but their beauty remains constant.

The American Wing

Close to being a museum in its own right, the **American Wing** is a thorough introduction to the development of fine art in America, with a vast collection of paintings, period furniture, glass, silverware, and ceramics. Unfortunately, much of this will be closed for renovation until 2010; many pieces remain on view on the mezzanine level, crammed into glass cases, and you'll find some of the furniture on the first floor. Sadly, *Washington Crossing the Delaware* by **Emanuel Leutzes**, the celebrated image of Washington escaping across the river in the winter of 1776, is unlikely to be on show until the renovation is complete.

American Painting

Much of the **American Painting** collection is worth seeking out, though the mezzanine display areas – in use until the renovation is complete – are hardly ideal; ask one of the guards if you are looking for a specific piece. There are several works by **Benjamin West**, who worked in London and taught or influenced many of the American painters of his day – *The Triumph of Love* is typical of his Neoclassical, allegorical works. Look out also for work of the nineteenth century, when American painters embraced landscape painting and

> ### The Cantor Roof Garden
>
> From May through October, you can ascend to the **Cantor Roof Garden**, located on top of the Lila Acheson Wallace Wing (see Modern Art, p.170). The leafy garden is an outdoor gallery, and each summer it's used to showcase contemporary sculpture (Jeff Koons has been a recent subject); it's also nominally a bar, though the mediocre drinks and pricey snacks aren't the reason to come here. The views are what draw most visitors – from this height, you can grasp how vast Central Park truly is; you're also within close view of Cleopatra's Needle. By far the best time to come for a cocktail is October, when the weather's cooler and the foliage has begun to turn.
>
> To reach the garden, head for the southwest elevators on the first floor, just outside the Modern Art gallery – you'll find them if you head left of the main marble stairs in the entrance hall.

nature. The painters of the **Hudson Valley School** glorified the landscape in their vast lyrical canvases; **Thomas Cole**, the school's doyen, is represented by *The Oxbow*, while his pupil **Frederic Church** has the immense *Heart of the Andes*, which combines the grand sweep of the mountains with minutely depicted flora. **Albert Bierstadt** and **S.R. Gifford** concentrated on the American West – their respective works *The Rocky Mountains*, *Lander's Peak*, and *Kauterskill Falls* have a near-visionary idealism, bound to a belief that the westward development of the country was a manifestation of divine will.

Winslow Homer is also well represented, from his early illustrations of the Civil War to his late, quasi-Impressionistic seascapes, of which *Northeaster* is one of the finest. Highlights of American art of the **late nineteenth and early twentieth centuries** include **J.W. Alexander**'s *Repose*, **Thomas Eakin**'s subdued, almost ghostly *Max Schmitt in a Single Scull*, and **William Merritt Chase**'s *For the Little One*, an Impressionist study of his wife sewing. The collection is crowned with a selection of works by the best-known American artist of the era: **James Abbott McNeill Whistler**. The standout is *Arrangement in Flesh Color and Black: Portrait of Theodore Duret*, a realist portrait of one of the Impressionists' most supportive patrons – it's a tribute to Whistler's mastery of his technique that despite laboring on the painting for a long time, it retains the spontaneity of a sketch.

Medieval Art

Although you could move straight to the **Medieval Art** from the American Wing, you'd miss out on the museum's carefully planned approach. Instead, enter these galleries via the corridor from the western end (or rear) of the Great Hall on the left of the main staircase. There you'll see displays of the sumptuous Byzantine metalwork and jewelry that financier **J.P. Morgan** donated to the museum in its early days. At the end of the corridor is the **main sculpture hall**, piled high with religious statuary and carvings; it's divided by a 52-foot-high *reja* – a decorative open-work, iron altar screen – from Valladolid Cathedral. If you're here in December, you'll see a highlight of New York's Christmas season: a beautifully decorated, twenty-foot-high Christmas tree lit up in the center of the sculpture hall. The **medieval treasury** to the right of the hall has an all-encompassing display of objects religious, liturgical, and secular. Beyond this are the **Jack and Belle Linski Galleries**, containing Flemish, Florentine, and Venetian painting, porcelain, and bronzes.

The Egyptian collection

The Met hogs a collection of more than 35,000 objects from Ancient Egypt, most of which are displayed to their full potential. Brightly efficient corridors steer you through the treasures of the museum's own digs during the 1920s and 1930s, as well as other art and artifacts from 3000 BC to the Byzantine period of Egyptian culture.

Prepare to be awed as you enter from the Great Hall on the first floor: the large **statuary**, **tombs**, and **sarcophagi** in the first few rooms are immediately striking. As you move into the interior galleries, arranged chronologically, the smaller, quieter sculptural pieces are also quite eye-catching. Don't miss the finely crafted models of ships, a brewery and a cattle stable in gallery four, offerings found in the **Tomb of Meketre**. Incredibly well preserved, they look as if they were made yesterday, not four thousand years ago, and offer a rare insight into everyday Egyptian life. Look, too, for the chipped dark-brown bust, *Face of Senwosret III*, in gallery eight; with his realistically hollow cheeks and bug eyes, he stands out amid the idealized portraits of other rulers. Nearby is the dazzling collection of **Princess Sit-Hathor-yunet jewelry**, a pinnacle in Egyptian decorative art from around 1830 BC.

The Temple of Dendur

At the end of the collection sits the **Temple of Dendur**, housed in a vast airy gallery lined with photographs and placards about the temple's history and its original site on the banks of the Nile. Built by the Emperor Augustus in 15 BC for the Goddess Isis of Philae, the temple was moved here as a gift from the Egyptian government during the construction of the Aswan High Dam in 1965 – otherwise it would have drowned. Though you can't walk all the way inside, you can go in just far enough to get a glimpse of the interior rooms, their walls chock-full of hieroglyphs. The temple itself is on a raised platform and surrounded by a narrow moat, which in the front widens to become a rather pretty reflecting pool, no doubt designed to make visitors think of the Nile – it doesn't, but is a nice touch anyway. The entire gallery is glassed-in on one side, and looks out onto Central Park; the most magical time to view the temple is when it's illuminated at night and the gallery seems to glow, lending it an air of mystery that's missing during the day.

Greek and Roman Art

Thanks to a magnificent renovation completed in 2007, one of the largest collections of ancient art in the world occupies some of the most attractive wings of the museum. Enter from the southern end of the Great Hall, and you'll find yourself in the wonderfully bright **Greek Sculpture Court**, a fittingly elegant setting for sixth- to fourth-century BC marble sculptures. The adjacent galleries display Greek art from the prehistoric era through to the fourth century BC. Lookout for the fanciful **Minoan vase** in the shape of a bull's head from around 1450 BC (first gallery on the right), and the **New York Kouros** (second gallery on the left) – one of the earliest examples of a *kouros*, or funerary statue, to have survived intact. Dating from 580 BC and originally from Attica, it marked the grave of the son of a wealthy family, created according to tradition as a memorial to ensure he would be remembered.

Beyond here, the vast **Sardis Column** from the Temple of Artemis marks the entrance into the spectacular **Leon Levy and Shelby White Court**, a soaring two-story atrium of **Roman sculpture** from the first century BC to the second century AD, with mosaic floors, Doric columns, and a glass ceiling – take a moment to soak up your surroundings at the fountain in the center. Highlights include the incredibly detailed *Badminton Sarcophagus* towards the back, and the enigmatic bust of the emperor Caracalla from the third century.

▲ Metropolitan Museum of Art

Art of Africa, Oceania, and the Americas

Michael C. Rockefeller, son of Governor Nelson Rockefeller, disappeared during a trip to West New Guinea in 1961. In 1969, Nelson donated the entire contents of his missing son's **Museum of Primitive Art** – over 3300 works, plus library and photographic material, much of it collected by his son – to the Met. This wing, on the first floor past the Greek and Roman galleries, stands as a memorial to Michael. It includes many Asmat objects, such as carved *mbis* (memorial poles), figures, and a canoe from Irian Jaya, alongside the Met's comprehensive collection of art from **Africa**, **Oceania**, and **the Americas**.

It's a superb set of galleries, the muted, understated décor throwing the exhibits into sharp and often dramatic focus. The **African exhibit** offers an overview of the major geographic regions and their cultures, though West Africa is better represented than the rest of the continent. Particularly awe-inspiring is the display of art from the Court of Benin (in present-day Nigeria) – tiny carved ivory figures, created with astonishing detail.

The **Pacific collection** covers the islands of Melanesia, Micronesia, Polynesia, and Australia, and contains a wide array of objects, including wild, somewhat frightening, wooden masks with all-too-realistic eyes. Sadly, **Mexico**, **Central**, and **South America** get somewhat short shrift, though there is a respectable collection of pre-Columbian jade, Mayan and Aztec pottery, and Mexican ceramic sculpture. But the best part by far is the **Jan Mitchell Treasury**, an entire room filled with South American gold jewelry and ornaments –

particularly the exquisite hammered-gold nose ornaments and earrings from Peru and the richly carved, jeweled ornaments from Colombia.

Modern Art

Many people bypass the Met's **Modern Art** collection – housed over two floors in the Lila Acheson Wallace Wing (named in honor of the founder of *Reader's Digest*), directly to the rear of the Rockefeller Wing – in favor of its headline-grabbing Old Masters. That's a shame, since this is a fine hoard that includes several stunning individual works, from mid-century experimental and abstract canvases to contemporary sculpture.

1905 to 1940

Work on the first floor is arranged roughly by school and period, covering **American and European art from 1905 to 1945**. The first galleries on the right side are dedicated to American art, beginning with the mural-like images of Broadway and Wall Street by **Florine Stettheimer**, and including the paintings of **Arthur Dove**, **Charles Sheeler**, and **Georgia O'Keeffe**, whose moody *From the Faraway, Nearby* resembles a progressive rock album cover.

Beyond here the European galleries begin with the Surrealists, with work from **Miró** and **Dalí** giving way to **Picasso**, **Bonnard**, **Braque**, and **Modigliani**. Picasso is particularly well represented, his work sprinkled throughout the first floor, from his Blue Period, through his Cubist Period, to more familiar skewed-perspective portraits; his somber *Girl Asleep at a Table*, *Woman in an Armchair*, and *Still Life with Pipes* are considered Cubist masterpieces. Following small rooms dedicated to **Matisse** and **Paul Klee**, the galleries end with the Fauvism of **Derain** and **Soutine** and more Cubism from Picasso, Braque, and **Gris**. Note that some of the most famous pieces in the collection – **Modigliani**'s firm-breasted *Reclining Nude* for example – are often moved around or on loan elsewhere.

1945 to the present

The mezzanine and second floor contain **European and American art from 1945 to the present**, from installations to vast abstracts. The mezzanine level displays the work of **Chuck Close**, whose *Lucas* has the characteristic intense stare of his giant portraits, as well as **Andy Warhol**'s camouflage-patterned *Last Self-Portrait* from 1986. The second floor is filled with giant, abstract canvases, with an entire room devoted to grumpy Abstract Expressionist **Clyfford Still** who once "repossessed" a picture by knifing it from its frame when he fell out with the owner. Another Abstract Expressionist, **Mark Rothko**, is represented by several creations, including *Number 13; White, Red, on Yellow* filled with bright, sketchy boxes of color. Don't miss Jasper Johns' *White Flag* either – a monochrome collage of the Stars and Stripes, built up piecemeal using scraps of newsprint, fabric, and charcoal. You'll also find **Jackson Pollock**'s swirling *Autumn Rhythm (No. 30)* here, and in the room leading to the Nineteenth-Century galleries (p.164), **Damien Hirst**'s provocative tiger shark in formaldehyde, *The Physical Impossibility of Death in the Mind of Someone Living*, on display at the Met until 2010.

European Sculpture and Decorative Arts

Most people pass right through the **European Sculpture and Decorative Arts** section on their way between Modern Art and the Medieval galleries, but there are a couple of reasons to pause. The recently renovated **European Sculpture Court** is a gorgeous sun-lit courtyard studded with grand marble statues, notably *Andromeda and the Sea Monster* (1694) by **Domenico Guidi** and the agonizing *Ugolino and his Sons* (1867) by **Carpeaux**, depicting the Pisan traitor from Dante's *Inferno*. There's also a copy of **Rodin**'s *Burghers of Calais*, an impressive bronze ensemble recalling the Hundred Years' War. The decorative arts section – furniture, ceramics, glassware, and the like – is less appealing, but displayed in some opulent Baroque and Rococo-style rooms reminiscent of a French palace.

The Lehman Pavilion

Another of the Met's many gems, the two-floor **Lehman Pavilion** was tacked on to the rear of the Met in 1975 to house the holdings of Robert Lehman, a relentless collector and scion of the Lehman Brothers banking family. Lehman bequeathed his entire collection with the stipulation that the galleries retain the appearance of a private home, and parts of this extension – an octagonal building centered on a brilliantly lit atrium – do resemble rooms in his former mansion. The overall impression is of a charmingly cluttered grand old house.

Italian Renaissance art

Lehman's artistic interests fill important gaps in the Met's collection, notably the **Italian Renaissance**. This period was his passion, and his personal hoard includes some standout works like the tiny, easily missed *Annunciation* by **Botticelli**; it's stashed in a glass cabinet in the first room. More impressive are the Venetian works, including a glassy *Madonna and Child* by **Bellini** in which Mary looks like a 1920s screen goddess, and cartoonish wooden icons by **Carlo Crivelli** featuring a grumpy St Peter.

Other Old Master paintings

As for **non-Italian art**, Lehman evidently liked **Ingres**, whose languid, sculptural portrait of the *Princesse de Broglie* in her bright-blue dress sparkles on the wall; similarly impressive is **Goya**'s *Countess of Altamira and Her Daughter*, the soft pink of her outfit contrasting sharply with her plain features. One picture stands out from them all, though: **Rembrandt**'s unflinching *Portrait of Gerard de Lairesse*, his bug eyes and snout-like nose evidence of the ravages of congenital syphilis.

The final galleries at the rear of the building house **Northern European works**, from **Hans Holbein the Younger**, **Petrus Christus** and mostly uninteresting **Impressionist** works from **Derain** and **Cézanne**, two late **Renoirs**, and several canvases by **Edouard Vuillard**; one work worth looking for in the atrium display, however, is **Balthus**'s creamy and disturbing *Nude with a Mirror*.

16

The Upper East Side

T he defining characteristic of Manhattan's **Upper East Side** – a two-square-mile grid that runs from 59th to 96th streets and includes **Fifth**, **Madison**, and **Park avenues** – is wealth. While other neighborhoods have been affected by influxes of immigrant groups and changing artistic trends, this area has remained an enclave of the well-off since they migrated here from downtown in the late nineteenth century. Largely residential, the buildings are all well preserved and the streets clean and relatively safe; scattered between the luxurious apartments are some of the city's finest museums and upscale shops. Recent squeezes in the housing market have produced waves of high-rise construction and brownstone restoration on the avenues and streets east of **Lexington Avenue**, while farther east, in the middle of the East River, sits **Roosevelt Island**, an area distinctly different from the rest of the city, and one that many Manhattanites frequently forget is there.

Fifth Avenue

Fifth Avenue has been the haughty patrician face of Manhattan since Central Park opened in 1876. Wealthy families like the Carnegies, Astors, Vanderbilts, and Whitneys were lured north from lower Fifth Avenue and Gramercy Park by the green space, and they built their fashionable residences alongside the park. To this day Fifth Avenue addresses remain so prestigious that buildings which front the thoroughfare but lack proper entrances onto it go by their would-be Fifth Avenue addresses rather than their more accurate sidestreet numbers. The park-side buildings on Fifth Avenue went up when Neoclassicism was the rage, so the surviving originals are cluttered with columns and classical statues. A great deal of what you see, though, is third- or fourth-generation construction.

Upper Fifth Avenue is nicknamed "**Museum Mile**" – it is home to New York's greatest concentration of art museums and other exhibitions, several of which are housed in the area's few remaining mansions. Henry Clay Frick's House at East 70th Street, marginally less ostentatious than its neighbors, is now the intimate and tranquil home of the **Frick Collection**, one of the city's must-see spots, while the controversial, modern structure of the **Guggenheim** is farther north at 89th Street.

RESTAURANTS & CAFÉS

Alice's Tea Cup	34
Atlantic Grill	23
Barking Dog Luncheonette	2
Beyoglu	17
Café Boulud	22
Café Sabarsky in the Neue Galerie	10
Caffè Buon Gusto	24
Candle Café	26
Carino	6
Daniel	32
Dawat	39
Donguri	13
E.A.T.	16
Ecco-La	3
Etats-Unis	18
Fred's at Barney's	35
Heidelberg	12
King's Carriage House	15
Le Refuge	14
Mariella Pizza	37
Maya	33
Mitchell London	31
Payard Patisserie & Bistro	29
Persepolis	27
Pig Heaven	19
Rao's	1
Rectangles	28
Rohrs, M.	11
Saigon Grill	8
Serendipity	38
Sushi of Gari	21
Taco Taco	4
Tal Bagels	9
Wildgreen Café	7

BARS

American Trash	25
Auction House	5
Bar Coastal	20
Stir	30
Subway Inn	36

ACCOMMODATION

Franklin	B
Mark	C
Pierre	D
Sherry Netherland	E
Wales	A

UPPER EAST SIDE

0 ——— 500 yds

16

THE UPPER EAST SIDE

Queens & Roosevelt Island

173

Grand Army Plaza to the Frick

Grand Army Plaza marks the shift between Fifth Avenue's fancy shopping (in the blocks to the south) and its fancy living (in the grand mansions to the north). This oval, where Fifth Avenue hits Central Park South (as 59th St is known while it runs along the park's southern edge), is one of the city's most dramatic public spaces, with a dazzling gold statue of Civil War General William Tecumseh Sherman on horseback. To the southwest stands the extended copper-lined chateau of the **Plaza Hotel** – now partly converted to condominiums – with the dark, swooping facade of the **Solow Building** behind it. Across the plaza to the east, you'll see the imposing **General Motors Building**, home to one of the last surviving branches of the fabled toy store F.A.O. Schwarz; the chain declared bankruptcy in 2003, though a white-knight investor snapped up two locations (here and Las Vegas) and relaunched them the next year. Continuing north, Fifth Avenue and its sidestreets are dotted with **private clubs** that served, and still cater to, the city's wealthy (see box below).

America's largest reform synagogue, the **Temple Emanu-El**, stands on the corner of 65th Street and Fifth Avenue (Mon–Thurs 10.30am–4.45pm; free; ☎212/744-1400). The brooding Romanesque-Byzantine cavern – a dark, moody, and contemplative place – manages to feel bigger inside than it looks from outside. There's also a smallish on-site museum on the second floor, accessible via the 65th Street entrance (same hours; free); its three rooms hold both temporary exhibits on religious themes like the Kabbalah as well as an artifact-heavy history of the temple itself.

The streets off Fifth Avenue are a trim mix of apartment houses and elegant townhouses while E 65th St holds a decidedly presidential air: the **Sarah Delano Roosevelt Memorial House** at no. 47, at Madison Ave, was commissioned by Mrs Roosevelt as a townhouse for her son Franklin in 1908, and Richard Nixon lived for a few years at no. 142.

Members only

When industrialists like **J.P. Morgan** and **William and Cornelius Vanderbilt** arrived on the New York social scene in the 1890s, established society still looked askance at bankers and financiers – the city's new money. Downtown social clubs were kept closed to Morgan and anyone else considered less than up to snuff. Not one to be slighted, Morgan commissioned Stanford White to design a club for him – one that would be bigger, better, and grander than all the rest. Such was the birth of the **Metropolitan Club**, 1 E 60th St at Fifth Ave, an exuberant construction with a marvelously outrageous gateway: just the thing to greet its affluent members (both then and now).

Another group of New Yorkers unwelcome in the downtown clubs, prosperous Jews, founded the elegant **Harmonie Club** in the 1850s, building its home at 4 E 60th St (across the road from the Metropolitan) around the same time. The perceived effrontery of so many **parvenus** led to a mushrooming of private societies, including the **Knickerbocker Club**, a handsome Federal-style structure on the corner of Fifth Avenue and 62nd Street, which was founded in 1913 in response to the "relaxed standards" of the **Union Club**, 101 E 69th St at Park Ave, which had finally admitted several friends of Morgan and the Vanderbilts.

All the clubs, both restrictive and lax, refused to open their doors to women. In 1903, with the opening of the **Colony Club**, 564 Park Ave at 62nd St, the ladies fought back, founding the first social club for members of their sex. The **Cosmopolitan Club**, 122 E 66th St at Park Ave, also opened as a women's institution.

The Frick Collection

A spectacular feat of acquisitive good taste, the **Frick Collection**, 1 E 70th St at Fifth Ave, is one of New York's finest sights (Tues–Sat 10am–6pm, Sun 11–5pm; $15; ☎212/288-0700, ⓦwww.frick.org). Housed in his former mansion, the collection consists of the art treasures amassed by **Henry Clay Frick**, one of New York's most ruthless robber-barons. Uncompromising and anti-union, Frick broke strikes at his coal and steel plants with state troopers and was hated enough to provoke a number of attempts on his life. The legacy of his ill-gotten gains – he spent millions on the best of Europe's art – is a superb assembly of works, and as good a glimpse as you'll find of the sumptuous life enjoyed by New York's early industrialists.

Opened in the mid-1930s, for the most part the museum has been kept as it looked when the Fricks lived there at the beginning of the twentieth century. What sets it apart from most galleries – and the reason many rate the Frick so highly – is that it strives hard to be as unlike a museum as possible. There is no wall text describing the pictures, though you can dial up info on each piece using the handheld guides available in the lobby (included with the price of admission). There are few ropes, fresh flowers on every table, and chairs provided for weary visitors, even in the most sumptuously decorated rooms. Make sure you pay a visit to the enclosed central courtyard, where marble floors, fountains, and greenery, all simply arranged, exude serenity.

A gallery one short flight up from the ground level shows temporary exhibits from the permanent collection, as well as pieces on loan from other institutions (other temporary groupings may be shown in the Oval Room or the Garden Court). It's a more modern space; the pale walls and carpets are designed not to compete with whatever is on display. Accessible only by a steep spiral staircase just to the left outside the entry hall, it's easy to miss unless you're looking for it.

The collection

With its magnificent array of Old Master works, the collection rivals to a certain extent the much larger holdings of the Met, especially in the quality of Italian Renaissance pieces, an area in which the Met is comparatively weak.

Keep an open mind as you start your visit in the Boucher Room. With its flowery walls, overdone furniture, and Boucher's Rococo representations of the arts and sciences in gilded frames, it is not to modern tastes. More reserved English pictures pack the **Dining Room**: look for Reynolds' bug-eyed but determined *General Burgoyne* as well as lighter portraits by Romney and Gainsborough, whose *St James's Park* is a study in social mores – there isn't a woman walking under the trees who isn't assessing the competition. The other irresistible painting here is Hogarth's *Miss Mary Edwards*, a portrait of a feisty heiress that just about hums with personality. Outside in the **hall** there's more of Boucher's work, including the cutesy *Four Seasons* canvases, starring his signature doll-eyed women, while in the **Fragonard Room** is the painter's *Progress of Love* series, painted for Louis XV's mistress Madame du Barry but discarded by her soon afterwards.

The **Living Hall** houses one of the most impressive Renaissance pictures anywhere in America: Bellini's sublime *St Francis in the Desert*. Stunningly well preserved, the picture suggests Francis's vision of Christ. This canvas unfairly overshadows the rest of the pieces in the room, although also notable are a couple of knockout portraits by Hans Holbein the Younger, including the masterpiece *Sir Thomas More*, whose world-weariness is graphically evidenced by the bags under his eyes and his five-o'clock shadow, as well as El Greco's restrained *St Jerome*. Move into the **Library** to see more British pictures, such as Reynolds' *Lady Taylor*, who's dwarfed by her huge blue ribbon and feather hat, and one of Constable's *Salisbury Cathedral* series; there's also a portrait of Frick himself here, as a white-bearded old man. Across in the **North Hall**, look for a beguiling portrait by Ingres, *Comtesse d'Haussonville*.

The **West Gallery** is another important space: the long, elegant room is decorated with dark-green walls and carpet, a concave glass ceiling, and ornately carved wood trim. There's a clutch of snazzy Dutch pictures here, including a set of piercing self-portraits by Rembrandt and a couple of uncharacteristically informal portraits of Frans Snyders and his wife by Van Dyck, Frick's favorite artist. This gallery is also the location of the last picture Frick himself bought before his death in 1919: Vermeer's seemingly unfinished *Mistress and Maid*, a snapshot of an intimate moment.

At the far end of the West Gallery is the tiny **Enamel Room**, named for the exquisite set of mostly sixteenth-century Limoges enamels on display. There's also a collection of small altarpieces by Piero della Francesca; it's another sign of Frick's good taste that he snapped up work by this artist, who is now one of the acknowledged Italian masters but was little regarded in the nineteenth century. The **Oval Room** at the other end of the West Gallery is jarringly modern, filled with a quartet of pretty portraits by Whistler, while the **East Gallery** displays a mishmash of styles and periods.

Neue Galerie

On the corner of 86th Street stands the former Vanderbilt mansion, which in 2001 was transformed into the **Neue Galerie**, 1048 Fifth Ave (Mon, Thurs, Sat & Sun 11am–6pm, Fri 11am–9pm; $15; ☎212/628-6200, ⓦwww.neuegalerie .org). The museum is dedicated to the arts, furniture, and crafts of Germany and Austria from the nineteenth and twentieth centuries, a distinct group of works. The most impressive part of the collection is on the second floor, where a host of turn-of-the-twentieth-century Viennese works focus on the likes of **Egon Schiele** and **Oskar Kokoschka**, examining their impact on architecture and design in Austria. Temporary exhibitions are housed upstairs; otherwise, expect twentieth-century works from all the major art movements in Germany, from Bauhaus to the Brücke group. At the Neue's *Café Sabarsky* (see p.299), you can pause for exquisite Viennese pastries before heading back to Museum Mile.

The Guggenheim Museum

Multistory parking garage or upturned beehive? Whatever you may think of the collection, it's the **Guggenheim Museum** building (at 1071 Fifth Ave at 89th St) that steals the show (Mon–Wed, Sat & Sun 10am–5.45pm, Fri 10am–7.45pm (pay what you wish from 5.45pm); $18; ☎212/423-3500, ⓦwww.guggenheim.org). The structure, designed by **Frank Lloyd Wright** specifically for the museum, caused a storm of controversy when it was unveiled in 1959, bearing, as it did, little relation to the statuesque apartment buildings of this most genteel part of Fifth Avenue. Reactions ranged from disgusted disbelief to critical acclaim – "one of the greatest rooms erected in the twentieth century," wrote Philip Johnson, himself no slouch in the architectural genius stakes. Ornery Wright missed much of the criticism, though, since he died six months before construction was completed. Time has been kinder than his contemporaries were – nearly half a century later, the museum is now a beloved New York landmark.

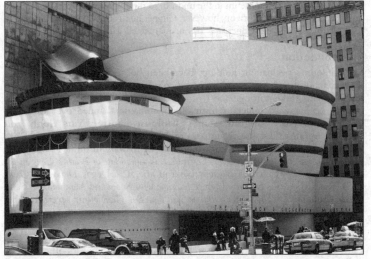
▲ Guggenheim Museum

The institution's namesake, **Solomon R. Guggenheim** (1861–1949), was one of America's richest men, thanks to his silver and copper mines. Although abstract art was considered little more than a fad at the time, Guggenheim, always a man with an eye for a sound investment, began collecting modern paintings with fervor. He bought wholesale the canvases of **Kandinsky**, then added works by **Chagall**, **Klee**, and **Léger**, among others, and exhibited them to a bemused American public in his suite of rooms in the *Plaza Hotel*. The Guggenheim Foundation was created in 1937; after exhibiting the collection in various rented spaces, it commissioned Wright to design a permanent home. The Foundation now includes museums in Berlin, Bilbao, and Venice (which is named for Solomon's niece Peggy, another art-collecting magpie).

The building

Collection of art aside, it's the structure that dominates – it's not hard to theorize that the egomaniacal Wright engineered it that way. Most visitors find it difficult to not be impressed (or sidetracked) by the tiers of cream concrete overhead. The circular galleries rise upward at a not-so-gentle slope, so you may prefer to start at the top of the museum and work your way down; most of the temporary exhibits are designed to be seen that way.

Proposed changes to the Guggenheim have historically caused an uproar, as proved by the debate in the early 1990s over the museum's extension. The building was closed for two years, during which the original Wright structure underwent a $60-million face-lift. When it was reopened, offices, storage rooms, and bits of chicken wire were all removed to expose the uplifting interior spaces so that the public could experience the spiral of the central rotunda from top to bottom. At the same time, a clever extension added the sort of tall, straight-walled, flat-floored galleries that the Guggenheim needed to adapt to its distinct shape.

More recently, the museum was caught in a fresh storm of controversy after the media-savvy director, **Thomas Krens**, tried to duplicate the museum with failed outposts in Vegas and Rio, the latter scrapped after a local outcry over the incongruity of a $33m museum in the midst of so much poverty. Far more unlikely outposts are still on the horizon, however; Guggenheims in Guadalajara (Mexico), Abu Dhabi (U.A.E.), and Bucharest (Romania) are all slated to debut by 2011.

The collection

The museum's permanent holdings have been bolstered since Guggenheim's day via acquisitions and donations – the collection has broadened in scope to span the late 1800s through most of the twentieth century. A significant gift came in 1976 when collector Justin K. Thannhauser handed over works by **Cézanne**, **Degas**, **Gauguin**, **Manet**, **Toulouse-Lautrec**, **Van Gogh**, and **Picasso**, among others, greatly enhancing the museum's Impressionist and Post-Impressionist holdings. It's almost overwhelming to walk into the Thannhauser Collection and immediately see Cézanne's *Still Life: Plate of Peaches*, *Bend in the Road Through the Forest*, and *Bibémus*. Next in line are a Degas, *Dancers in Green and Yellow*; two works by Van Gogh, *Landscape with Snow* and *Mountains at Saint Remy*; Monet, with *The Palazzo Ducale Seen from San Giorgio*; and several notable pieces by Picasso, including *Le Moulin de la Galatte*, the bizarre *Accordionist*, and the recognizable *Woman with Yellow Hair*.

Though you'll be able to see the entire museum in an afternoon, two galleries offer a representative sample of the Guggenheim's **permanent collection**: a quick but comprehensive survey of the **Cubists** on the second floor of the tower and, in the restored small rotunda, a collection of **Impressionist**, **Post-Impressionist**, and early modern masterpieces, like Picasso's scratchy *Woman Ironing*.

Ironically, given Guggenheim's eminent position in the twentieth-century art world, it's not its permanent collection that usually makes the news: it's the magnificent **temporary exhibitions** in the main rotunda. (Most temporary shows are linked, albeit tenuously, to pieces in the permanent collection.) During his tenure as museum director, Krens has overseen shows on the likes of the motorbike and Giorgio Armani as well as the modern-art surveys the museum was once best known for. Although some find Krens' headline-chasing grating, he knows how to put on a good show, both literally and figuratively; for that reason, he'll be missed (Krens stepped down late in 2008).

The National Academy of Design

A group of artists, including Samuel Morse, founded the little-known **National Academy of Design**, 1083 Fifth Ave at 89th St, in 1825 (Wed & Thurs noon–5pm, Fri–Sun 11am–6pm; $10; ☏212/369-4880, Ⓦwww .nationalacademy.org). It was intended to ape London's prestigious Royal Academy, and is housed in the Huntington Mansion, a bow-fronted, Beaux-Arts townhouse owned by Archer Huntington, whose father made a fortune in San Francisco overseeing early American railways.

The member list of the National Academy has included big names like **Richard Diebenkorn**, **Chuck Close**, **Robert Rauschenberg**, and **Jasper Johns**. Each artist – famous, notorious, or neither – is required to donate a picture to the place when they join.

The Cooper-Hewitt National Design Museum

The **Cooper-Hewitt National Design Museum**, 2 E 91st St at Fifth Ave, is part of the Smithsonian network, and offers impressive shows, so it's a shame that it's rarely on visitors' itineraries (Mon–Thurs 10am–5pm, Fri 10am–9pm,

Sat 10am–6pm, Sun noon–6pm; $15; ☎212/849-8400, ⓦwww.cooperhewitt .org). The displays are housed in a mansion commissioned by millionaire industrialist Andrew Carnegie, a beautiful, spacious mansion with dark wood-paneled walls, carved ceilings, and parquet floors – too decorative to be plain, too large to be modest. The frilly green copper portico above the main entrance is especially enchanting. Inside, two floors of temporary exhibits focus on the history, nature, and evolution of design and decorative arts – commercial, utilitarian, and high art.

Very little of the large permanent collection is on view at any one time, except when pieces are involved in the museum's temporary exhibitions. These shows are almost always worth checking out: recent standouts included a thematic show exploring the evolution of dining utensils and table decorations. Design-aholics can also access (by appointment only) the museum's Doris and Henry Dreyfuss Study Center Library and Archive and its four curatorial departments. The collection is expansive, holding 40,000 objects in applied arts and industrial design, 160,000 drawings and prints, and 40,000 examples of wallcoverings and textiles, some dating from the first century AD.

The Jewish Museum

Given how Jewish culture has flourished in New York, it is fitting that the **Jewish Museum**, 1109 Fifth Ave at 92nd St, is the largest museum of Judaica outside Israel (Sun–Wed & Sat 11am–5.45pm, Thurs 11am–8pm; $12, Sat admission is free; ☎212/423-3200, ⓦwww.jewishmuseum.org). The museum's centerpiece is a permanent presentation of Jewish culture as it has developed over four thousand years. A collection of Hanukkah lamps, on view throughout the year, is a highlight, as are two drawings from the 1640s by Dutch artist Rembrandt Harmensz van Rijn.

The Museum of the City of New York

The sweet, if rather dainty, **Museum of the City of New York**, 1220 Fifth Ave at 103rd St, is housed in another repurposed mansion, this time a smaller and later neo-Georgian example (Tues–Sun 10am–5pm; $9; ☎212/534-1672, ⓦwww.mcny.org). The permanent collection provides a history of the city from Dutch times to the present, displaying prints, photographs, costumes, and furniture across four floors. There's also a film narrated by Stanley Tucci – a quick and painless must-see that puts the museum (and city) into perspective. It runs on a loop and glosses over New York's 400-year history in 25 minutes, so put your seatbelt on. The most engaging of the permanent exhibits is "New York Toy Stories," that consists of all manner of motion toys, board games, sports equipment, and doll houses (look for the one with original artwork by **Duchamp** and **Lachaise**) dating from the late 1800s to today.

Madison Avenue

Immediately east of Fifth Avenue is **Madison Avenue**, the swankiest shopping street in the city. This strip was entirely residential until the 1920s, though you'd never know it now, lined as it is with the offerings of high-end jewelers and designers. It's also where you'll find the establishment-baiting **Whitney**

Museum of American Art, as well as the tiny **Margo Feiden Galleries**, 699 Madison Ave at 63rd St, which display the work of the great New York carica-turist Al Hirschfeld, famous for his line drawings of Broadway stars. The other notable exception to the glitz is the stately and elaborate neo-Gothic facade of **St James' Church**, 865 Madison Ave at 71st St (☎212/288-4100), with its graceful, gilded Byzantine-inspired altar; it's best known as the place where the funeral service for Jacqueline Kennedy Onassis was held.

The Whitney Museum of American Art

In a gray, arsenal-like building designed in 1966 by Marcel Breuer, the **Whitney Museum of American Art**, 945 Madison Ave at 75th St, has – from the outside at least – a suspiciously institutional air (Wed, Thurs, Sat & Sun 11am–6pm, Fri 1–9pm) pay what you wish 6–9pm; $15; ☎1-800/WHITNEY, ⓦwww.whitney.org). Once inside the exhibition space, though, first impressions prove wildly off-base: not only does the Whitney incorporate some of the best-designed exhibition space in the city, but the intelligent, challenging shows, designed from its eminent collection of twentieth-century American art, are outstanding.

Gertrude Vanderbilt Whitney, a sculptor and champion of American art, established the Whitney Studio in 1914 to exhibit the work of living American artists who could not find support in established art circles – she was the first to exhibit Edward Hopper in 1920. By 1929 she had collected more than 500 works by various artists, all of which she offered, with a generous endowment, to the Met. When her offer was refused, she set up her own museum in Greenwich Village in 1930, with her collection as its core exhibit, relocating to its current spot in 1966. The Brutalist building was initially a controversial addition to the neat townhouses of the Upper East Side, but it's a sign of how beloved the structure has become that plans to wreck its integrity with a Neoclassical addition were shouted down in the late 1990s. Forced to find more space, the Whitney kicked its administrative offices off-site and transformed the fifth floor into additional galleries.

Like many of the other institutions in this neighborhood, the Whitney is best known for its superb **temporary exhibitions**, to which it devotes most of its time and space (even stairwells). Many of these exhibitions are retrospectives of established artists or debuts of their lesser-known counter-parts: Jasper Johns, Cy Twombly, and Cindy Sherman were all given their first retrospectives here, and hipster photographer Ryan McGinley also had a solo show. But the most thought-provoking exhibitions push the boundaries of art as a concept – strong showings of late have been in the realms of video installations (incorporating names such as Bill Viola and Nam June Paik) and computer and digital technology.

Without a doubt, though, the Whitney is most famous for its **Biennial**, which was first held in 1932 and continues to occur between March and June in even-numbered years. Designed to give a provocative overview of what's happening in contemporary American art, it's often panned by critics, sometimes for good reason. Nonetheless, the Biennial is always packed with visitors, so catch it if you can.

The collection

The museum owns more than 12,000 paintings, sculptures, photographs, and films by almost 2000 artists as diverse as Calder, Nevelson, O'Keeffe, de Kooning, Rauschenberg, and LeWitt. For an overview of its holdings, see the

The streets that zigzag between the main drags of Madison and Park avenues have attractions of their own: rather than museums, though, these gawp-worthy spots are mostly the houses of the rich and (in)famous. Take the mansion-cum-gallery of the Wildenstein family, on East 64th Street between Madison and Park. This intensely private and fabulously wealthy clan first came under attack for handling art stolen by the Nazis, and plastic-surgery fanatic Jocelyn Wildenstein later became embroiled in a tawdry divorce battle in 1999. At least one former neighbor would have relished Jocelyn's tabloid-powered fifteen minutes of fame: **Andy Warhol** lived here in a surprisingly conservative brick house at 57 East 66th Street and Madison Avenue from 1974 to his death in 1987. It's easy to understand why Warhol would not allow friends inside: it was here that his eccentricities were given free rein – when he died he left behind a raft of oddities, including a massive collection of cookie jars.

Highlights of the Permanent Collection, a somewhat arbitrary pick of the Whitney's best: the fifth floor takes you from Hopper to the mid-century, while the second floor brings you from Jackson Pollock to today. The works form a superb introduction to twentieth-century American art, best evaluated with the help of the free gallery talks designed to explain the paintings and sculptures, and their place within various movements.

Included in the Highlights is **Gaston Lachaise**'s *Standing Woman*, which greets visitors at the entrance to the fifth floor. The bronze statue is modeled after Isabel Dutaud Nagle, Lachaise's muse. Just over *Standing Woman*'s left shoulder, **George Bellows**' painting, *Dempsey and Firpo*, captures what many sports photographers today try for: the moment of the fallen champion. **Robert Henri**'s 1916 painting *Gertrude Vanderbilt Whitney*, also grouped with the Highlights, is an ode to the woman who defied the rules that defined her generation. She appears in pants, a *faux pas* at the time. Consequently, the painting was never shown in her Fifth Avenue mansion.

In deference to its origins, the rest of the permanent collection is particularly strong on **Edward Hopper** (2000 of his works were bequeathed to the museum in 1970), and several of his best paintings are here. *Early Sunday Morning* is typical of many of his works: it focuses on light and shadow, a bleak urban landscape, uneasily tense in its lighting and rejection of topical detail. The street could be anywhere (in fact it's Seventh Ave); for Hopper, it becomes universal. Additional major bequests include a significant number of works by **Milton Avery**, **Charles Demuth**, and **Reginald Marsh**.

As if to balance the figurative works that formed the nucleus of the original collection, more recent purchases have included an emphasis on abstract art. **Marsden Hartley**'s *Painting Number 5* is a strident work painted in memory of a German officer friend killed in the early days of World War I. **Georgia O'Keeffe**'s *Abstraction* is gentler, though with its own darkness: it was suggested by the noises of cattle being driven to slaughter.

The **Abstract Expressionists** are also a strong presence, with great works by masters **Pollock** and **de Kooning**. **Mark Rothko** and the **Color Field** painters are also well represented – though you need a sharp eye to discern any color in **Ad Reinhardt**'s *Black Painting*. In a different direction, **Warhol, Johns**, and **Oldenburg** each subvert the meaning of their images. Warhol's silk-screened *Coke Bottles* fade into motif; Johns' celebrated *Three Flags* erases the emblem of patriotism and replaces it with ambiguity; and Oldenburg's lighthearted *Soft Sculptures*, with its toilets and motors, falls into line with his declaration, "I'm into art that doesn't sit on its ass in a museum."

Park Avenue

Park Avenue, one block east of Madison, is stolidly comfortable and often elegant. Aside from glimpses of Manhattan's elite, it's worth wandering down Park for the sweeping view south, where it coasts down to the hulking Grand Central Terminal and Met Life Buildings (see p.134). Its twin arteries sandwich a lush green median, which is often accented with a changing series of public artworks. Just above 96th Street, at the point where the subway line emerges from underground, the neighborhood rather joltingly transitions from blocks of quiet, moneyed apartment buildings to **El Barrio**, or **Spanish Harlem**.

The Park Avenue Armory

The **Park Avenue Armory** (℡212/616-3930, ⓦwww.armoryonpark.org) dominates the block between East 66th and 67th streets. Built in the 1870s, the exterior features pseudo-medieval crenellations, and the interior a grand double staircase and spidery wrought-iron chandeliers. It's noteworthy as the only surviving building from the era before New York's railroad tracks were roofed over; without that innovation, Park Avenue would have remained a clattering, noisy mess. While the building is generally only accessible by special arrangement, tours are given occasionally, depending on interest (call for info). The most reliable way to get a peek is to try to attend one of the frequent art and antique shows staged here, which also showcase the enormous drill hall inside. January's Winter Antiques Show is especially large. (The website is the best place to find out about upcoming exhibits.)

The Asia Society

A prominent educational resource founded by John D. Rockefeller III, the **Asia Society**, 725 Park Ave at 70th St (Tues–Thurs, Sat & Sun 11am–6pm, Fri until 9pm except July and Aug; $10; ℡212/517-ASIA or ℡212/288-6400, ⓦwww.asiasociety.org), offers a small but nevertheless enthralling exhibition space dedicated to both traditional and contemporary art from all over Asia. In addition to the usually worthwhile temporary exhibits, ranging from Japanese lacquerware to ancient Buddhist sculpture, a variety of intriguing performances, political roundtables, lectures, films, and free events are frequently held here.

Lexington Avenue and east

Lexington Avenue is Madison Avenue's upstart sibling; it was only gentrified in the 1960s, as the western stretches of the neighborhood increased in value, and money-savvy property developers rushed in to snap up real estate farther east. Only forty years later, the signs of its hip economic heyday are already long gone, and this is now one of the cheaper residential areas in the city. The proliferation of small apartments (as well as a generous number of hip restaurants and sports bars) means that the East 60s and 70s are home to a number of young, unattached, and upwardly mobile professionals – for some years now it has been one of the more popular areas with just-out-of-college types looking to make their start in the business world.

Dozens of **foreign consulates** to the United Nations are scattered on Upper East Side blocks in this area: many countries – including the poorer ones, spending more than they can afford – have purchased handsome homes. The Russians occupy an entire apartment building on East 67th St between Lexington and Third avenues. Here and there you will notice a small kiosk occupied by a police officer, likely as not placed near a consulate of a country whose politics may tend to provoke street protests or unwelcome callers.

The southern stretches

At the southern end of Lexington Avenue's Upper East Side stretch is department store legend **Bloomingdale's**, which takes up the block between 59th and 60th streets; note its Art Deco facade (see p.389).

A few blocks east of here is the **Mount Vernon Hotel Museum and Garden**, 421 E 61st St at York Ave (Tues–Sat & Sun 11am–4pm, except June & July Tues 11am–9pm; $8; ☏212/838-6878, ⓦwww.mvhm.org). Formerly the Abigail Adams Smith Museum, this wasn't the actual home of the daughter of President John Adams; rather, this building served as the stables, and it has since been restored with Federal-period propriety by the Colonial Dames of America (a ragtag association of patriotic history buffs). The house is hemmed in by decidedly non-historic buildings and overlooked by the **Queensboro Bridge**, which may stir memories as the 59th Street Bridge of Simon and Garfunkel's *Feelin' Groovy* or from the title credits of TV's *Taxi*. This glut of clanging steel links Manhattan to Long Island City in Queens, but is utterly unlike the suspension bridges that elsewhere lace Manhattan to the boroughs.

If you'd rather spend time dawdling over cartoons than dodging cars, head to the **Museum of American Illustration**, 128 E 63rd St at Lexington Ave (Tues 10am–8pm, Wed–Fri 10am–5pm, Sat noon–4pm; free; ☏212/838-2560, ⓦwww.societyillustrators.org). Rotating selections from the museum's permanent collection of more than 2000 illustrations include everything from

▲ Queensboro Bridge

wartime propaganda to political and other cartoons and drawings, to contemporary ads. Exhibitions are based on a theme or illustrator; designed primarily for aficionados, they are nonetheless accessible, well presented, and topical.

On East 67th Street, east of Lexington and beyond the rear of the Park Avenue Armory, look for a remarkable ensemble of fanciful **Victorian buildings** that resemble a movie set, including the blue-trimmed local Police Precinct, the Fire Station with its red garage doors, and the whimsical ochre Park East Synagogue, with Moorish arches, stained glass, and campanile.

There's not much north of here until you hit the New York auction gallery of London-based **Sotheby's**, 1334 York Ave at 72nd St (℡212/606-7000, 🖰 www .sothebys.com), the oldest fine-arts auctioneer in the world. It's weathered a price-fixing scandal in recent years, though the cost was high: the company had to sell this stunning, purpose-built New York headquarters and then lease it back to pay off the fines incurred. If you want to look inside, there's normally a viewing of some kind going on most days, though admission to most of the auctions is by invitation only.

Yorkville and around

It's only in **Yorkville** that the Upper East Side displays minute traces of New York's European immigrant history: this was originally a German–Hungarian neighborhood that spilled out from East 77th to 96th streets between Lexington and the East River. Three near-simultaneous events around 1900 drove the center of German life uptown to Yorkville: the influx of Italian and Slavic immigrants to the Lower East Side; the opening of the island-long Elevated Railway, which ran along Second Avenue; and the tragic sinking of an excursion steamer carrying Tompkins Square residents, killing 1021 and decimating that neighborhood's German community. Other immigrant groups followed not long after, and some splendid little townhouses were built for these newcomers, such as **The Cottages** on Third Avenue between East 77th and 78th streets, whose stylish English Regency facades and courtyard gardens remain intact.

You do have to search hard to detect a German flavor to the area; the prospect of cheap rent with an Upper East Side address has lured many fresh-out-of-college folks, who now blend amicably with the few elderly German-speaking residents who still reside here. Amid all the video stores and fast-food joints, there are a few hints of the old neighborhood, notably the traditional German delicatessens: look for the septuagenarian **Schaller and Weber**, 1654 Second Ave at 86th St (℡212/879-3047). Even older is **Orwasher's Handmade Bread**, 308 E 78th St near Second Ave (℡212/288-6569).

Fronting the park between 77th and 78th streets are the **Cherokee Apartments**, originally the Shively Sanitarium Apartments, an understatedly elegant row with a splendid courtyard. Up the block at 81st Street is **John Finley Walk**, where a concrete promenade named for **Carl Schurz**, a nineteenth-century German immigrant who rose to fame as Secretary of the Interior under President Rutherford B. Hayes and as editor of *Harper's Weekly* and the *New York Evening Post*, runs north into the park. Winding pathways lead through this small, model park – a breathing space for elderly German-speakers and East Siders alike. FDR Drive cuts beneath the green, and there are views of Queens and of the confluence of dangerous currents where the Harlem River, Long Island Sound, and the Harbor meet – not for nothing known as Hell Gate. It's a few blocks west to the **Church of the Holy Trinity**, 316 E 88th St at Second Ave (℡212/289-4100), a picturesque and discreet Victorian building with an enchanting little garden.

Gracie Mansion and Henderson Place

One of the reasons Schurz Park is so exceptionally well manicured and maintained is the high-profile security that surrounds **Gracie Mansion** (East End Ave at 88th St; telephone reservations required for tours, Wed 10am, 11am, 1pm, 2pm; $7; ⓣ212/570-4751). Built in 1799 on the site of a Revolutionary fort, it is one of the best-preserved colonial buildings in the city. Constructed the same year as the Mount Vernon Hotel Museum, Gracie Mansion has been the official residence of the mayor of New York City since 1942, when Fiorello LaGuardia set up house; the name's a misnomer, since it's more a cramped cottage than a grand residence. The mansion itself isn't particularly compelling, and the tours are perfunctory – frankly, it's most interesting for the stories associated with past mayors than any architectural features.

Small wonder, then, that billionaire mayor Michael Bloomberg opted not to live there full-time – dropping Gracie Mansion from the headlines. It's a far cry from the Rudy Giuliani era when, thanks to an acrimonious split, he and his wife continued to live in the same home even when his new companion was visiting.

Across from the park and just below Gracie Mansion, at East 86th Street and East End Avenue, is **Henderson Place**, a set of old servants' quarters now transformed into a "historic district" of luxury cottages. Built in 1882 by John Henderson, a fur importer and real-estate developer, the small and sprightly Queen Anne-style dwellings were intended to provide close and convenient housing for servants working in the palatial old East End Avenue mansions, most of which have now been torn down. Ironically, these servants' quarters now represent some of the most sought-after real estate in the city, offering the space, quiet, and privacy that most of the city lacks.

Roosevelt Island

An aerial tramway near the Queensboro Bridge connects Manhattan with **Roosevelt Island**, in the middle of the East River. Though the island was hooked up to the subway system in the 1990s, the tram has long been the more popular way to arrive (trams run every 15min Sun–Thurs 6am–3am, Fri & Sat 6am–3.30am; every 7½min during rush hours; $2 one way; ⓣ212/832-4555, ⓦwww.rioc.com); from there, take the 25¢ bus to the northern part of the island.

Roosevelt Island's a thorough oddity, perhaps because the place has passed through so many hands and names over the years. Only two miles long and no more than 800ft wide, **Blackwell Island** was first owned, inhabited, and farmed by the family of the same name from 1676 to 1828. At that time, the city of New York snapped up the land and assigned it for use as a **quarantine site** for criminals, lunatics, and smallpox victims; by 1921, it was officially known as **Welfare Island**. There are still several reminders of those days: the Octagon Tower at the north end, now off-limits, was once an insane asylum and briefly housed Emma Goldman and even Mae West after a particularly bawdy performance in 1927. On the opposite tip of the island, look for the stabilized ruins of what was once the island's **Smallpox Hospital**, now a ghostly Gothic shell, as well as the Strecker Laboratory, the city's premier laboratory for bacteriological research when it opened in 1892. These derelict buildings are an example of what the whole island looked like by the 1960s: deserted, forgotten, and unloved. Forward-thinking city mayor John Lindsay enlisted architects John Burgee and Philip Johnson to demolish most of the old buildings and create a master plan for new residential living areas in the late 1960s. Duly rechristened Roosevelt Island in 1973, the island received its first new inhabitants two years later. The narrow streets, bold signage, and modular buildings are considered a triumph of **urban planning**, though some may find it reminiscent of the village in the TV series *The Prisoner*.

Paranoid impressions aside, it is nonetheless somewhat cultish. Locals are fiercely protective of their hidden enclave: to snag one of the cheap apartments here, you'll have to join the years-long official waiting list. The island has a small-town feel, notably along the narrow, brick-paved Main Street, though if that's too much and you want to look back at the city, head for the Meditation Steps and the River Walk, a walking and rollerblading path on the west side of the island. The other fine vantage point is the northern tip, which affords excellent views of the upper reaches of the East River and the surging waters of Hell Gate, and Lighthouse Park is a romantic retreat of grassy knolls and weeping willows. This tip is also home to the Roosevelt Island **Lighthouse**, which dates back to 1872.

17

The Upper West Side and Morningside Heights

W hile the Upper East Side has always been a patrician stronghold, the Upper West Side, only minutes away on the other side of the park, has grown into its position as a somewhat younger, somewhat hipper, but nonetheless affluent counterpart. Later to develop, it has seen its share of struggling actors, writers, and opera singers come and go over the years. In the 1990s, the Upper West Side was the neighborhood of choice for upwardly mobile dot-commers, and though the frenzy has calmed down, young professionals and their stroller-bound children still make up a sizable part of the population.

This isn't to say it lacks glamour; the lower stretches of **Central Park West** and **Riverside Drive** are quite fashionable, while the network of performing spaces at **Lincoln Center** makes the neighborhood New York's de facto palace of culture. As you move north, though, the neighborhood diversifies and loses some of its luster, culminating in **Morningside Heights**, home to **Columbia University** at the edge of Harlem, as well as the monolithic **Cathedral of St John the Divine**.

The Upper West Side

North of 59th Street, the somewhat tawdry Midtown West becomes decidedly less commercial and garish, and then morphs into the largely residential **Upper West Side**. The neighborhood stretches along Central Park, running west from the park to the Hudson River, and north from Columbus Circle at 59th Street to 110th Street and the beginning of Morningside Heights. Its main artery is **Broadway** and its twin pinnacles of prosperity are the historic apartment houses of **Central Park West** and **Riverside Drive**. In between is a checkerboard of modern high-rise buildings, old brownstones, gourmet markets, and

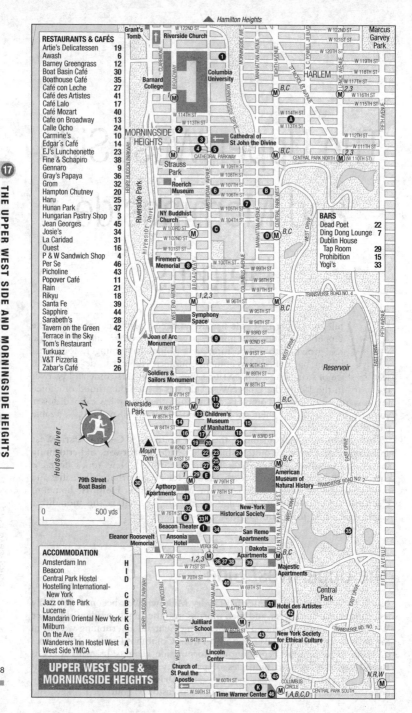

Like practically every other neighborhood in the city, the Upper West Side was once fecund farmland. That began to change in 1879, when the opening of the Ninth Avenue elevated train made the open space west of Central Park more accessible to city residents, who mainly still lived downtown. Cheap tenements began to pop up, and the New York Central Railroad line, which transported livestock to the 60th Street stockyards, went in about a year later, adding the smell of farm animals to what was already a sensory overload. Between 59th and 65th streets, the neighborhood became home to more warehouses than anything else, and the district had the early makings of a soulless slum.

One diamond in the rough, though, was the Dakota Building on 72nd Street, built in 1884. Slowly, other townhouses and high-class living quarters rose around it, displacing some of the hulking warehouses. Ten years later, as Manhattan began to grow north in earnest, the confluence of Eighth Avenue, Broadway, and 59th Street became a hot bed of excitement. Concerts were held at the Majestic Playhouse on Broadway and 60th Street, area theaters showcased popular vaudeville acts, and quality watering holes multiplied. By the 1920s, theaters for all types of entertainment (some more risqué than others) lined the Ninth Avenue train circuit. By 1929, shopping had taken over as the neighborhood's main attraction, and the area has hardly looked back since.

upscale boutiques and restaurants. Even the downbeat northern reaches above 90th Street have begun to gentrify, as middle-class families have moved into areas that they previously would have shunned.

Columbus Circle and around

Columbus Circle, located at the intersection of Broadway, Central Park West, and 59th Street, is a roundabout, a rarity in Manhattan. It's also a pedestrian's worst navigation nightmare – be careful crossing the street. Amid the hum of traffic it's easy to overlook Columbus himself, who stands uncomfortably atop a lone column in the center island. Recently, the city's attention has turned to this long-ignored intersection for two reasons. Firstly, the glitzy **Time Warner Center**, a massive, multi-million-dollar home for companies like CNN and Warner Books, finally opened here in February 2004 after a highly publicized and problematic construction that included worker deaths and an on-site fire. The business part of the complex squats on top of a multistory mall where, aside from over three dozen shops, you'll find five of the city's priciest restaurants, including *Per Se*, run by Thomas Keller (see p.331). If your budget doesn't allow for $100 per head for dinner, kill some time at the massive, and usually crowded, *Whole Foods* store in the basement.

Columbus Circle's other point of interest is also architectural, though its provenance is somewhat contentious. The oddball, vaguely Venetian building of white marble capped by lollipop columns and portholes that once loomed over the roundabout's southern side (at no. 2) was originally constructed as a museum showplace for Huntington Hartford's private art collection, opening its doors to the public in 1964. As a misjudged counter to his contemporaries' funding of expressionist art, however, the museum lasted only five years, while the building itself was considered by some New York residents to be one of the city's grand follies, a sentiment that resonated for years afterwards. Despite this, and after years of vacancy and disrepair, preservationists were furious when the **Museum of Arts & Design** (Wed, Fri–Sun 11am–6pm, Thurs 11am–8pm;

$15, students and seniors $12; ☎212/299-7777, ⓦwww.madmuseum.org) chose the place for the relocation of its collection. The battle was fought over whether or not the museum's practical needs should take precedence over the building's architectural importance to the city. In the end, with lawsuits flying all around, the museum won out. The Museum of Arts & Design moved in after $90 million worth of renovations had converted the former gallery into a sleek tower with random cutaways that allow light to penetrate the building and which tripled the exhibition space. The eclectic collection, featuring everything from blown-glass *objets d'art* to contemporary jewelry, is now displayed to full effect on the buildings' twelve floors, which also contain a small theater and artist-in-residence studios. Changing exhibits cover a wide array of media (from paper to porcelain to metal to glass), and are often accompanied by lectures and workshops.

Opposite Columbus Circle, on the park side, stands the **Maine Monument**, a large stone column with the prow of a ship jutting out from its base, erected in 1913 and dedicated to the 260 seamen who died when the battleship *Maine* inexplicably exploded in Havana Harbor in 1898, propelling forward the Spanish-American War. Across the street, at the junction of Broadway and Central Park West, are the glittering **Trump International Hotel** and condos.

For aesthetic relief, go west a few blocks and contemplate the **Church of St Paul the Apostle**, Columbus Ave and 60th St (☎212/265-3495), a beautiful Old Gothic structure housing Byzantine basilica features, including a high altar by Stanford White. A few steps north is the **New York Society for Ethical Culture**, 2 W 64th St at Central Park W (☎212/874-5210, ⓦwww.nysec.org), "a haven for those who want to share the high adventure of integrating ethical ideals into daily life." Founded in 1876 (though the building itself wasn't built until 1902), this distinguished organization also helped to found the NAACP (National Association for the Advancement of Colored People) and the ACLU (American Civil Liberties Union). It holds regular Sunday meetings, and organizes occasional recitals and lectures on social responsibility, politics, and other related topics.

Lincoln Center

One of the boulevards that lead out from Columbus Circle, Broadway, continues north to the **Lincoln Center for the Performing Arts**, an imposing group of six marble-and-glass buildings arranged around a large plaza between 63rd and 66th streets. It's not, as most assume, named for President Abraham Lincoln; rather, it honors the name of the surrounding area in Manhattan's early times, likely named Lincoln for a tenant farmer who tilled the land here. Robert Moses came up with the idea of creating a cultural center here in the 1950s as a way of "encouraging" the area's gentrification, one of his rare exercises in urban renewal that has been extremely successful. A number of architects worked on the plans, and the complex was finally built in the mid-1960s on a site that formerly held some of the city's poorest slums. In a case of life imitating art imitating life, once the slums were emptied and their residents moved to ghettos farther uptown, the deserted area became a movie set: before construction began in 1960, the run-down buildings served as the open-air location for *West Side Story*, which was based on the stage musical set here.

Home to the world-class **Metropolitan Opera**, the **New York City Ballet**, and the **New York Philharmonic**, as well as a host of other smaller companies, Lincoln Center is worth seeing even if you're not catching a performance; the best way is on an **organized tour** – otherwise you'll only be allowed to peek into the ornate lobbies of the buildings. Hour-long tours leave from the booth on the concourse level, and take in the main part of the Center (daily beginning at 10.30am, appx. every two hours until 4.30pm; $15, students $12; ☎212/875-5350). Be warned that tours can get booked up and times vary, since the schedule is made up a week in advance; it's best to phone ahead to be sure of a place. Backstage tours of the Met are also available; see p.192 for more information.

If your budget's tight, you may want to stop by here for the **free entertainment** that is often offered: there's the Autumn Crafts Fair in early September, folk and jazz bands at lunchtime, and dazzling fountain and light displays every evening in the summer. In addition, Lincoln Center hosts a variety of affordable summertime events, including Midsummer Night Swing, a dance series that allows you to swing, salsa, hustle, and ballroom dance on an outdoor bandstand at the Lincoln Center Plaza Fountain. Contact **Lincoln Center Information** (☎212/875-5000, ⓦ www.lincolncenter.org) for specifics.

Visitors to Lincoln Center these days will find it somewhat revitalized. Alice Tully Hall (see p.363), virtually unchanged since its opening in 1969, is the beneficiary of a recent makeover that brings the theater up to date with new seats and furnishings, enhanced staging capabilities, and a stunning three-story glass-enclosed foyer. To be unveiled in early 2009, it's just one of a number of initiatives (this most recent one under the umbrella title of the West 65th St Development Project) which will serve to aesthetically unify Lincoln Center's varied components; The Juilliard School, the Film Society, Lincoln Center Theater, the Chamber Music Society, and the School of American Ballet will each get a "dramatic street-level identity." Another piece of the $650m renovation (which will also submerge its driveway, and, as a result, improve pedestrian access to the complex) is scheduled to be completed by the end of 2009.

The New York State Theater and Avery Fisher Hall

Philip Johnson's spare and elegant **New York State Theater**, on the south side of the plaza, is home to both the New York City Ballet (including its famed annual Dec performances of the *Nutcracker*) and the New York City Opera. Its foyer is ringed with balconies embellished with delicate bronze grilles and boasts an imposing, four-story ceiling finished in gold leaf. The ballet season runs from late November through February and early April through June; the opera season starts in July and runs through mid-November. Call ☎212/870-5570 for ticket information.

Johnson also had a hand in **Avery Fisher Hall**, opposite the theater on the north side of the plaza, where the New York Philharmonic plays; he was called in to refashion the interior after its acoustics were found to be below par. The Philharmonic performs here from September through May, while Mostly Mozart, the country's first and most popular indoor summer chamber-music series, takes place in July and August. Call ☎212/875-5030 for performance information.

The Metropolitan Opera House

In contrast to the surrounding Modernist starkness, the plaza's focal point, the **Metropolitan Opera House** (aka "the Met"), is gushingly ornate and oozes opulence, with enormous crystal chandeliers and red-carpeted staircases, designed for grand entrances in evening wear. Behind two of the high arched windows hang **murals by Marc Chagall**. The artist wanted stained glass, but at the time it was felt that glass wouldn't last long in an area still less than reverential toward the arts, so paintings were hung behind square-paned glass to give a similar effect. These days, they're covered for part of the day to protect them from the sun; the rest of the time they're best viewed from the plaza outside. The mural on the left, *Le Triomphe de la Musique*, is cast with a variety of well-known performers, while *Les Sources de la Musique* is reminiscent of Chagall's renowned scenery for the Met production of *The Magic Flute*: the god of music strums a lyre while a Tree of Life, Verdi, and Wagner all float down the Hudson River. You can learn more about the Opera House on one of the **backstage tours** of the building (Sept–June Mon–Fri 3.30pm, Sun 10.30am; reservations required; $15, students $8; ⊕212/769-7020). For performance information, see p.363.

The rest of Lincoln Center

Two piazzas flank the Met. To the south there is **Damrosch Park**, a large space facing the Guggenheim Bandshell, where chairs are set up in the summer so you can catch free lunchtime concerts and various performances. To the north you will find a lovely, smaller plaza facing the **Vivian Beaumont Theater**, designed by Eero Saarinen in 1965 and home to the smaller **Mitzi E. Newhouse Theater**. The **New York Public Library for the Performing Arts** (Tues, Wed, Fri & Sat noon–6pm, Mon & Thurs noon–8pm; free; ⊕212/870-1630, ⊚www.nypl.org/lpa) is located behind the Vivian Beaumont and holds over eight million items (everything from performing-arts ephemera to scores and manuscripts), plus a museum that exhibits costumes, set designs, and music scores. At the corner of Broadway and 65th Street is **Alice Tully Hall**, a recital hall that houses the Chamber Music Society of Lincoln Center, and the **Walter E. Reade Theater**, which features foreign films and retrospectives and, together with the Avery Fisher and Alice Tully halls, hosts the annual New York Film Festival in September (see p.421). The celebrated **Juilliard School of Music** is in an adjacent building (the best way to check it out is via one of the regular concerts by its students; see p.363 for details).

The smallish **Dante Park**, an island on Broadway across from the main Lincoln Center Plaza, features a statue of its namesake; the American branch of the Dante Alighieri Society put it up in 1921 to commemorate the 600th anniversary of the writer's death. But the park's *pièce de résistance* is a piece of art dating from 1999: *Time Sculpture*, a bronze and stone masterwork featuring a series of large clocks, was designed by Philip Johnson and dedicated to the patrons of Lincoln Center.

Central Park West

Central Park West stretches north from Columbus Circle to 110th Street along the western edge of the park. Home to some of the city's most architecturally distinguished apartment buildings, like the **Dakota** and **Majestic**, as well as the enormous **American Museum of Natural History**, Central Park West bustles with taxis and tour buses. In contrast, the sidestreets between Central Park West and Columbus Avenue in the upper 60s and 70s are quiet, tree-lined, and filled with beautifully renovated brownstones, many of which are single-family homes.

Most of the monolithic, mansion-inspired apartment complexes in this area date from the early twentieth century and rim the edge of the park, hogging the best views. The southernmost of these is the Hotel des Artistes, 1 W 67th St at Central Park West. It was built in 1917 especially for artists (hence the name), and was once the Manhattan address for the likes of Noel Coward, Norman

▲ Imagine, Strawberry Fields

Rockwell, Isadora Duncan, and Alexander Woollcott. Though the building is now expensive co-op apartments, you can still see the original interior on the ground floor, via the similarly pricey and famous *Café des Artistes* (see p.332).

The death of John Lennon

The Dakota Building, 1 W 72nd St, is most famous as the former home of **John Lennon** – and present home of his widow, **Yoko Ono**, who owns a number of the building's apartments. It was outside the Dakota, on the night of December 8, 1980, that the ex-Beatle was murdered – shot by a man who professed to be one of his greatest admirers.

His murderer, **Mark David Chapman**, had hung around outside the building all day, clutching a copy of his hero's latest album, **Double Fantasy**, and accosting Lennon for his autograph, which he received. This was nothing unusual: fans loitered outside the building and hustled for a glimpse of the singer. But when the couple returned from a late-night recording session, Chapman was still there, and he pumped five .38 bullets into Lennon as he walked through the Dakota's 72nd Street entrance. Lennon was picked up by the doorman and rushed to the hospital in a taxi, but he died on the way from blood loss. A distraught Yoko issued a statement immediately: "John loved and prayed for the human race. Please do the same for him." No one really knows the reasons behind Chapman's actions. Suffice it to say his obsession with Lennon had obviously unhinged him. Chapman was given a sentence of twenty years to life in prison; he has since been denied parole on three separate occasions – Ono told the parole board she wouldn't feel safe with Chapman walking the streets. He's expected to remain behind bars for the foreseeable future.

Fans of Lennon may want to light a stick of incense across the road in **Strawberry Fields** (see p.157), a section of Central Park that has been restored and maintained in his memory through an endowment by Ono. Its trees and shrubs were donated by a number of countries as a gesture toward world peace. The gardens are pretty enough, if unspectacular, though it would take a hard-bitten cynic not to be a little bit moved by the **Imagine** mosaic on the pathway.

Four blocks north, between 71st and 72nd streets, you'll find the fittingly named **Majestic**. This gigantic, pale yellow, Art Deco landmark was thrown up in 1930 and is best known for its twin towers and avant-garde brickwork. The next block north houses one of New York's more illustrious residences: the **Dakota Building**, 1 W 72nd St. The rather hoary story of its name is that when construction finished in 1884, its uptown location was considered as remote as the Dakota territory by Manhattanites. Whatever the origin of its name, this grandiose hulk of German Renaissance masonry is undoubtedly impressive. Its turrets, gables, and other odd details were all included for one reason: to persuade wealthy New Yorkers that life in an apartment could be just as luxurious as in a private house. For the large part, the developers succeeded: over the years, few of the residents here haven't had some sort of public renown, from Lauren Bacall and Judy Garland to Leonard Bernstein; of course, it's best known as the home of the late John Lennon (see box, p.193).

Continue north to the **San Remo**, 145–146 Central Park West at 74th St. Another apartment complex, this one dates from 1930 and is one of the most significant components of the skyline here: its ornate twin towers, topped by columned, mock-Roman temples, are visible from most points in Central Park. Architecture aside, the residents' board here is known for its snooty exclusiveness: they rejected Madonna as a buyer of a multi-million-dollar co-op, though her former boyfriend Warren Beatty did live here with Diane Keaton. A block farther north is the **Central Park Historic District**, from 75th to 77th streets on Central Park West, and on 76th Street toward Columbus Avenue, home to a number of small, turn-of-the-nineteenth-century rowhouses, as well as the **Kenilworth Apartments**, 151 Central Park West at 75th St, notable for its mansard roof and carved limestone exterior.

The New-York Historical Society

The oft-overlooked **New-York Historical Society**, 170 Central Park West (Tues–Sat 10am–6pm, Fri until 8pm, free 6–8pm, Sun 11am–5.45pm; $10; ☎212/873-3400, ⓦwww.nyhistory.org), houses a permanent collection of books, prints, and portraits, as well as a research library. One room focuses on the work of **James Audubon**, the Harlem artist and naturalist who specialized in lovingly detailed paintings of birds: astonishingly, the Historical Society holds all 432 original watercolors of Audubon's landmark *Birds of America*. Other galleries hold a broad cross-section of **nineteenth-century American painting**, principally portraiture and Hudson River School landscapes, among them Thomas Cole's famed and pompous *Course of Empire* series. Another highlight is the permanent children's area called **Kid City**, which offers interactive exhibitions, such as a child-size recreation of a block on Broadway in 1901. More a museum of American than New York history, the society also features various temporary exhibitions that mix high and low culture with intelligence and flair. Don't miss the museum **library** either: among its massive holdings – more than two million manuscripts and maps, as well as almost 650,000 books – are the original Louisiana Purchase document and the correspondence between Aaron Burr and Alexander Hamilton that led up to their deadly duel (see p.213).

The American Museum of Natural History

The **American Museum of Natural History**, Central Park W at 79th St, is one of the best museums of its kind in the world, an enormous complex of buildings full of fossils, gems, taxidermy, and other natural specimens (daily 10am–5.45pm, Rose Center open until 8.45pm on first Fri of month; $15 with additional cost for IMAX films, certain special exhibits, and Hayden Planetarium; ☎212/769-5100, ⓦwww.amnh.org). This elegant giant fills four blocks with a strange architectural mélange of heavy Neoclassical and rustic Romanesque styles – it was built in several stages, the first of which was overseen by Central Park designer Calvert Vaux. Founded in 1869, it is one of the oldest natural-history museums in the world, with four floors of exhibition halls and 32 million items on display.

The collection

The museum's vast marble front steps on Central Park West are a great place to read or soak up the sun. An appropriately haughty statue of museum co-founder Theodore Roosevelt looks out toward the park from his perch on horseback, flanked by a pair of Native Americans marching gamely alongside. This entrance (which opens onto the second floor) leaves you well positioned for a loop of the more interesting halls on that level: principally the **Hall of Asian People** and **Hall of African People**, both of which are filled with fascinating, often beautiful, art and artifacts, and backed up with informal commentary and indigenous music. The Hall of Asian People begins with artifacts from Russia and Central Asia, moves on to pieces from Tibet – including a gorgeous recreation of an ornate, gilded Tibetan Buddhist shrine – and then on to China and Japan, with displays of some fantastic textiles, rugs, brass, and jade ornaments. The Hall of African People displays ceremonial costumes, musical instruments, and masks from all over the continent. Another highlight of this floor is the lower half of the **Hall of African Mammals**, a double-height room whose exhibits continue on to the third-floor balcony: don't miss the life-size family of

▲ Dinosaur Exhibit, American Museum of Natural History

elephants in the center of the room (it's fairly difficult to do so). Once you're on the third floor, stop by the mildly creepy **Reptiles and Amphibians Hall**, filled with samples of almost any species in the category. A little less interesting is the **Eastern Woodlands and Plains Indians** exhibit, a rather pedestrian display of artifacts, clothing, and the like.

The fourth floor is almost entirely taken up by the wildly popular **Dinosaur Exhibit**; spreading across five spacious, well-lit, and well-designed halls, the museum houses the largest dinosaur collection in the world, with more than 120 specimens on display. Here, you can touch fossils, watch robotic dinosaurs, and walk on a transparent bridge over a fifty-foot-long Barosaurus spine. The multi-level exhibits are also supplemented by interactive computer programs and claymation videos, which add a nice hands-on appeal to the exhibit.

Downstairs on the first floor is the **Hall of Gems and Minerals**, which includes some strikingly beautiful crystals – not least the Star of India, the largest blue sapphire ever found. The enormous, double-height gallery dedicated to **Ocean Life** includes a 94-foot-long (life-size) Blue Whale disconcertingly suspended from the ceiling. The exhibit of **North American Mammals** hasn't changed in ages – the dark halls, marble floors, and illuminated diorama cases filled with stuffed specimens have seen over fifty years' worth of children on school trips. The greatest draw on this floor, however, is the **Hall of Biodiversity**. It focuses on both the ecological and evolutionary aspects of biodiversity, with multimedia displays on everything from the changes humans have wrought on the environment (with examples of solutions brought about by local activists and community groups in all parts of the world) to videos about endangered species. The **NatureMax Theater**, also located on this floor, presents some interesting nature-oriented IMAX films (there is an additional charge).

The Rose Center for Earth and Space

Across from the Hall of Biodiversity is the **Rose Center for Earth and Space**, including the **Hall of Planet Earth**, a multimedia exploration of how the earth works, with displays on a wide variety of subjects such as the formation of planets, underwater rock formation, plate tectonics, and carbon dating. Items on display include a 2.7-billion-year-old specimen of a banded iron formation and volcanic ash from Mount Vesuvius. One of the newer displays is an earthquake monitoring system; a three-drum seismograph and color screen work together to show real-time seismic activity from around the globe. The centerpiece of the room is the Dynamic Earth Globe, where visitors are able to watch the earth go through its full rotation via satellite, getting as close as possible to the views astronauts see from outer space.

The Hall of Planet Earth links visitors to the rest of the Rose Center, which is made up of the **Hall of the Universe** and the **Hayden Planetarium**. The center boasts an enormous sphere, 87ft in diameter, which appears to be floating inside a huge cube above the main entrance to the center. The sphere actually houses the planetarium, which includes two theaters, as well as research facilities and classrooms, and is illuminated rather eerily at night. Inside, the state-of-the-art **Space Theater** uses a Zeiss projector to create sky shows with sources like the Hubble telescope and NASA laboratories.

On the planetarium's second floor, the **Big Bang Theater** offers a multisensory recreation of the "birth" of the universe, while the **Cosmic Pathway** is a sloping spiral walkway that takes you through thirteen billion years of cosmic evolution via an interactive computerized timeline. It leads to the Hall of the Universe, which offers exhibits and interactive displays on the formation and evolution of the universe, the galaxy, stars, and planets, including a mini-theater where visitors can journey inside a black hole through computerized effects. There is even a display here entitled The Search for Life, which examines the planetary systems on which life could exist – in case you hadn't questioned the meaning of existence enough by this point.

North on Broadway

Back on Broadway, at 72nd Street, tiny, triangular **Verdi Square** makes a fine place to take a break from the marvels of Lincoln Center. From the square, featuring a craggy statue in the likeness of the composer, you can fully appreciate the ornate balconies, round towers, and cupolas of the **Ansonia Hotel** across the street at 2109 Broadway (at W 73rd St). Never actually a hotel (it was planned as upscale apartments), the Ansonia was completed in 1904 and the dramatic Beaux-Arts building is still the *grande dame* of the Upper West Side. It's been home to luminaries like Enrico Caruso, Arturo Toscanini, Lily Pons, Florenz Ziegfeld, Theodore Dreiser, Igor Stravinsky, and even Babe Ruth.

The enormous limestone **Apthorp Apartments**, 2211 Broadway between 78th and 79th streets, occupy an entire block from Broadway to West End Avenue. Built in 1908 by William Waldorf Astor, the ornate iron gates of the former carriage entrance lead into a central courtyard with a large fountain visible from Broadway, though you won't be allowed to stroll in. The building's in a fair enough state now, though its fortunes have hiccuped over the years – it was used as the location for the crack factory in the 1991 movie *New Jack City*. The Upper West Side past 79th Street has seen a lot of changes in the last decade as the forces of gentrification have surged northward. One of the older establishments in the area is gourmet hub **Zabar's**, 2245 Broadway at 80th St, which has been selling baked goods, cheese, caviar, gourmet coffee and tea, and an exhaustive collection of cooking gadgets since 1934. For more on the store, see p.400.

Nearby, the **Children's Museum of Manhattan**, 212 W 83rd St near Broadway (Tues–Sun 10am–5pm; $9; ☎212/721-1223, ⓦwww.cmom.org), fills a delightful five-story space. It offers interactive exhibits that stimulate learning, in a fun, relaxed environment for kids (and babies) of all ages; the storytelling room, filled with books kids can choose from, will keep everyone amused and quiet for at least an hour.

Weaving your way north through Broadway's invariably crowded sidewalks, you will reach **Symphony Space**, 2537 Broadway at 95th St (☎212/864-5400, ⓦwww.symphonyspace.org), one of New York's premier performing-arts centers, with short-story readings, classical and world music performances, screenings of revival and foreign films, and an annual free marathon reading of James Joyce's *Ulysses* every Bloomsday (June 16).

Riverside Park and Riverside Drive

At the western edge of 72nd Street begins the four-mile stretch of **Riverside Park** (ⓦwww.nycgovparks.org). The entrance is marked by Penelope Jencks' pensive *Eleanor Roosevelt Monument* on the corner of 72nd Street and Riverside Drive, dedicated in 1996 by then-First Lady Hillary Rodham Clinton. A less appealing local landmark is the new forest of skyscrapers overlooking the park from what used to be derelict shipping yards south of 72nd Street. Although officially named the Penn Yards Project, this cluster of luxury condos is colloquially known as **Trump City** (for who else but the billionaire developer).

Riverside Park was conceived in the mid-nineteenth century as a way of attracting the middle class to the remote Upper West Side and covering the unappealing Hudson River Railway tracks that had been built along the Hudson in 1846. Though not as imposing or as spacious as Central Park, Riverside was designed by the same team: Frederick Law Olmsted and Calvert Vaux. Begun in 1873, the park took 25 years to finish; rock outcroppings and informally arranged trees, shrubs, and flowers surround its tree-lined main boulevards, and the overall effect is much the same today as it was then. The biggest changes to the park came in the 1960s, when Robert Moses widened it and added some of his usual concrete touches, including the rotunda at the 79th Street Boat Basin. The basin is a delightful place for a break, with paths leading down to it located on either side of 79th Street at Riverside Drive (you'll hit Moses' rotunda first – keep going until you see water). Not on many visitors' itineraries, this is a small harbor and one of the city's most peaceful locations; a few hundred Manhattanites live on the water in houseboats, while others just moor their motorboats and sailboats.

The main artery of this neighborhood is **Riverside Drive**: starting at West 72nd Street, it winds north, flanked by palatial townhouses and multistory apartment buildings, mostly thrown up in the early part of the twentieth century. In the 70s, especially, there is a concentration of lovely turn-of-the-twentieth-century townhouses, many with copper-trimmed mansard roofs and private terraces or roof gardens. Between 80th and 81st streets you will find a row of historic **landmark townhouses**: classic brownstones, they have bowed exteriors, bay windows, and gabled roofs. You'll also find a number of other architectural surprises in this area, as many of the residences in the 80s between Riverside and West End have stained-glass windows as well as stone gargoyle faces leering from their facades.

Riverside Drive is also dotted with notable monuments: at West 89th Street, look for the **Soldiers and Sailors Monument** (1902), a marble memorial to the Civil War dead. Then there's the **Joan of Arc Monument** at West 93rd Street, which sits on top of a 1.6-acre cobblestone-and-grass park named Joan of Arc Island and located in the middle of the Drive. Finally, you'll hit the **Firemen's Memorial** at West 100th Street, a stately frieze designed in 1913 with the statues of *Courage* and *Duty* on its ends.

There are more historic apartment buildings on Riverside Drive as you head north between 105th and 106th streets. What is now the Riverside Study Center (used by the shadowy Catholic sect Opus Dei) at 330 Riverside is a glorious five-story Beaux-Arts house built in 1900 – note the copper mansard roof, stone balconies, and delicate iron scrollwork. The current headquarters of the **New York Buddhist Church** is at 331 Riverside Drive, though it was formerly the home of Marion "Rosebud" Davies, a 1930s actress most famous for her role as William Randolph Hearst's mistress.

The odd little building next door to no. 331 is also part of the church; it showcases a larger-than-life bronze statue of Shinran Shonin (1173–1262), the Japanese founder of the Jodo-Shinsu sect of Buddhism. The statue originally stood in Hiroshima and somehow survived the atomic explosion of August 1945. In 1955 it was brought to New York as a symbol of "lasting hope for world peace" and has been in this spot ever since. When it arrived, local lore had it that the statue was still radioactive, so in the 1950s and 1960s children were told to hold their breath as they went by. The River Mansion, as 337 Riverside Drive is called, was home to **Duke Ellington** – and the stretch of West 106th Street between here and Central Park has been tagged Duke Ellington Boulevard in his honor.

Nearby, in a manicured brownstone at 319 W 107th St, is the overlooked but appealing **Roerich Museum** (Tues–Sun 2–5pm; suggested donation $5; ℡212/864-7752, ⓦwww.roerich.org). It contains a small, weird, and virtually unknown collection of original paintings by Nicholas Roerich, a Russian artist who lived in India and was influenced by religious mysticism. Also on West 107th Street, at the terminus of West End Avenue – itself running more or less parallel to Riverside Drive - is the small, triangular **Strauss Park**. The statue by Augustus Lukeman of a reclining woman gazing over a water basin was dedicated by Macy's founder Nathan Strauss to his brother and business partner, Isidor, and Isidor's wife, Ida, both of whom went down with the *Titanic* in 1912.

Morningside Heights

North of the Upper West Side, **Morningside Heights** stretches from 110th Street to 123rd Street, west to the Hudson River, and east to Morningside Park, a small and rather unspectacular green space. The neighborhood has a somewhat funky, college-town aura, a diverse mix of academics, professionals, and working-class families, who have banded together in the name of community preservation. Excepting the massive **Cathedral of St John the Divine** and **Columbia University**, there are few sights here per se, but it's worth ambling up here to get a sense of a close-knit neighborhood, a feeling that the Upper West Side lost some time ago.

The Cathedral Church of St John the Divine

The Cathedral Church of St John the Divine, 1047 Amsterdam Ave at 112th St (Mon–Sat 7am–6pm, Sun 7am–7pm except July & Aug 7am–6pm; free; ℡212/316-7540, ⓦwww.stjohndivine.org), rises out of its surroundings with a solid majesty – hardly surprising, since it is the largest Gothic-style cathedral in the world, a title it holds even though it remains incomplete.

This Episcopal church was conceived, in 1892, as a Romanesque monolith. When the architect in charge was replaced in 1911, the building's style shifted: it has ended up French neo-Gothic. Work progressed well until the outbreak of war in 1939, and it wasn't until the mid-1980s that it resumed. The church's problems aren't limited to timely construction, though: it declared bankruptcy in 1994, fraught with funding difficulties and cast under suspicion by people who think the money might be better spent directly on the local community. Church members launched a massive international fundraising drive, which helped clear them from bankruptcy, but in 2001 church finances again became precarious following a fire that did significant damage to the cathedral. Water and smoke damage created the need for an all-out restoration, and even now it is unclear when the repairs will be completed. Don't let the building's raw state put you off visiting – the church is one of New York's most impressive sights.

Though the structure appears finished at first glance, take a look up into one of its huge, incomplete towers, and you'll see how much there is left to do. In reality, only two-thirds of the church is finished, and given the problems with funding, it's impossible to estimate when it'll be done – the earliest date is 2050. The one activity that continues is small-scale carving, much of it undertaken by locals who are trained by English stonemasons in the church's own sculpture/ stone workshops. Regardless of when, or if, it is finished, its floor space – 600ft long by 320ft wide at the transepts – is big enough to swallow both the cathedrals of Notre Dame and Chartres whole, or more prosaically, two full-size football fields. For some idea of how the completed cathedral will look, stop in at the gift shop, where there's a scale model of the projected design, as well as an interesting array of books and souvenirs.

The **Portal of Paradise** at the cathedral's main entrance was completed in 1997, and is dazzlingly carved from limestone and painted with metallic oxide. Keep an eye out for the 32 biblical figures depicted (both male and female) and such startling images as a mushroom cloud rising apocalyptically over Manhattan. The portal is evidence of just how slow progress here really is: the carving took ten years. Only after entering the church does its staggering size become clear; the space is awe-inspiring, and definitely adds to the building's spiritual power. The interior shows the melding of the two architectural styles, particularly in the choir, where a heavy arcade of Romanesque columns rises to a high, Gothic vaulting; it is hoped the temporary dome will someday be replaced by a tall, delicate Gothic spire.

Construction aside, St John's is very much a **community church**. It houses a soup kitchen and shelter for the homeless; sponsors AIDS awareness and health outreach initiatives, and other social programs; and has a gymnasium, as well as plans for an amphitheater. The open-minded, progressive nature of the church is readily visible throughout the cathedral building: note the intricately carved wood **Altar for Peace**, the **Poets Corner** (with the names of American poets carved into its stone-block floor), and an altar honoring AIDS victims. The amazing stained-glass windows include scenes from both the Bible and American history. All kinds of art, both religious and secular, grace the interior, from teak Siamese prayer chests, to seventeenth-century tapestries, to a rare religious work by the late graffiti artist Keith Haring.

Outdoors, the cathedral's south side features the **Bestiary Gates**, their grills adorned with animal imagery (celebrating the annual blessing of the animals ceremony held here on the Feast of St Francis), and a **Children's Sculpture Garden**, showcasing small bronze animal sculptures created by local schoolchildren. Afterwards, take a stroll through the cathedral yard and workshop where, if work has begun again, you can watch Harlem's apprentice masons tapping away at the stone blocks of the future cathedral.

Public **tours** are given Tuesday through Saturday at 11am and 1pm, and Sunday at 1pm ($5) – meet at the Info Center, the blue booth right inside the main door. Access to the top of the cathedral was restricted for years due to the 2001 fire, but "vertical tours" have resumed. To clamber up spiral stone staircases to the roof, and be rewarded with a super view, call ⓣ212/932-7347 to make a reservation (Sat noon & 2pm; $15).

Columbia University and around

The **Columbia University** campus fills seven blocks between Broadway and Morningside Drive from 114th to 121st streets, with its main entrance at Broadway and 116th Street. It is one of the most prestigious academic institutions in the country and a member of the Ivy League. Established in 1754, Columbia has a long and venerable history – it is the country's fifth-oldest institution of higher learning, it awarded the first MD degree in America, and the university sponsored ground-breaking atomic research in the 1940s. The Morningside Heights campus, modeled after the Athenian *agora* (or town square), was laid out by McKim, Mead, and White after the university moved here from midtown in 1897.

Amid the campus's Italian Renaissance-style structures, the domed and colonnaded **Low Memorial Library**, 116th Street at Broadway, is most noteworthy. Built in 1902, it's on the New York City Register of Historic Places and is a commanding sight. Tours of the campus leave from the Visitor Center here (Mon–Fri 11am and 3pm; free; ☎212/854-4900, ⓦwww.columbia.edu). Across Broadway sits **Barnard College**. Now part of Columbia University, it was a women's college until Columbia finally went coeducational in the mid-1980s. Many women still choose to study here, and Barnard retains its status as one of America's elite "Seven Sisters" colleges.

Running alongside the campus, Broadway is characterized by a lively bustle, with numerous inexpensive restaurants, bars, and cafés, and a few bookstores. The space at 2911 Broadway at 113th St, formerly the West End tavern, was the hangout of Jack Kerouac, Allen Ginsberg, and the Beats in the 1950s; it still serves a student crowd, although it's now a Cuban eatery.

Riverside Church and Grant's Tomb

Several blocks north and west of the university, **Riverside Church**, 490 Riverside Drive at 120th St (daily 9am–4.30pm, Sun service 10.45am; ☎212/870-6700), has a graceful French Gothic Revival tower, loosely modeled on the cathedral at Chartres. Like St John the Divine, it has become a community center for the surrounding parish. Take the elevator to the tower's twentieth floor and ascend the steps around the **carillon** (the largest in the world, with 74 bells) for some great views of Manhattan's skyline, New Jersey, and beyond. Make sure to root around inside the body of the church, too: its open interior stands in stark contrast to the mystery of St John the Divine.

Up the block from the church is **Grant's Tomb**, at Riverside Drive and 122nd Street (daily 9am–5pm; free; ☎212/666-1640, ⓦwww.nps.gov/gegr). This Greek-style memorial is the nation's largest mausoleum, home to the bodies of conquering Civil War hero (and blundering eighteenth US president) Ulysses S. Grant and his wife, in two black-marble Napoleonic sarcophagi.

Harlem and north

T he most famous African-American community in America (and, arguably, the birthplace of modern black culture), **Harlem** languished as a low-rent, high-crime neighborhood for much of the mid-twentieth century, justly earning a reputation as a place of racial tension and urban decay. Over the past couple of decades, though, things have begun to look up, and it is far less dangerous than it once was – indeed, some pockets are among the more up-and-coming areas in Manhattan. Many local observers worry, however, that the influx of investment may come at too high a price in the long run, diluting or wiping out the district's unique Afro-American spirit and history.

Harlem's main thoroughfares – **125th Street**, **Adam Clayton Powell, Jr Boulevard**, and **Lenox Avenue** – should be well traveled, and you should have few worries about running into trouble. Farther uptown is **Hamilton Heights**, a largely residential spot pepped up by an old Federal-style historic mansion and the campus of the City College of New York. Continuing north from there, you'll hit the Dominican stronghold of **Washington Heights**, a patchy place with few visitor attractions and one area where it pays to take care at night. The northernmost tip of the island, known as **Inwood**, is home to **The Cloisters**, a museum as mock medieval monastery that holds the Metropolitan Museum's superlative collection of medieval art. It's easily the most visited site in the city north of Central Park.

Harlem

Practically speaking, **Harlem**'s sights are too spread apart to amble between: they stretch out over seventy blocks. You'll do best to make several trips if you want to see them all. It can be helpful to take a **guided tour** to get acquainted with the area and to get you thinking about what you want to come back and see on your own. If you intend to see Harlem without a tour guide, it will serve you well to familiarize yourself with the areas you plan to visit before you go, and to stick to well-trodden streets and act relaxed once you get there.

Some history

Although the Dutch founded the settlement of **Nieuw Haarlem** in 1658, naming it for a town in Holland, the area remained primarily farmland up until the mid-nineteenth century, when the New York and Harlem Railroad linked

HARLEM

0   500 yds

HAMILTON
HEIGHTS

Hamilton
Grange

Strivers Row

Renaissance
Ballroom

St.
Nicholas
Park

Smalls
Paradise

Abyssinian
Baptist Church

Schomburg
Center

THE
BRONX

Harlem River

HARLEM

City
College

Grant's
Tomb

Apollo
Theater

Sylvia's

Theresa Towers

Studio
Museum

Riverside Church

Morningside
Park

Marcus
Garvey
Park

St Martin's Church

Mount Olivet
Church

Columbia
University

Mintons
Playhouse

EL BARRIO

Cathedral of
St John
the Divine

Central
Park

Duck
Island

Harlem
Meer

Charles A. Dana
Discovery Center

Great
Hill

Lasker
Pool & Rink

Art for
Change

Taller
Boricua

Museo
del Barrio

18

HARLEM AND NORTH | Harlem

RESTAURANTS & CAFÉS				BARS		Striver's Lounge	1
Amy Ruth's	10	Londel's Supper Club	1	Sisters	8	The Den	2
Café Amrita	11	M & G Diner	7	Sylvia's		MoBay Uptown	6
Dinosaur Bar-B-Que	3	Patsy's Pizza	9	Restaurant	5	Showmans	4

ACCOMMODATION

Uptown Hostel A

Wanderers Inn Hostel West B

the area with Lower Manhattan. The new rail line and the steadily developing suburb's new, fashionable brownstones attracted better-off immigrant families, mainly German Jews from the Lower East Side. Although good-quality homes sprang up alongside the IRT-Lenox line (now the #1, #2, and #3 subway) later in the century, they failed to tempt the wealthy northwards. Black real-estate agents saw their chance: over the next fifteen years they snapped up the empty houses for next to nothing, then rented them to the city's growing community of displaced blacks.

The Harlem Renaissance

The **Harlem Renaissance**, during which the talents of such icons as Billie Holiday, Paul Robeson, and James Weldon Johnson took root and flowered, served as inspiration for generations of African-American musicians, writers, and performers. In the 1920s, Manhattan's white residents began to notice Harlem's cultural offerings: after downtown went to bed, the sophisticated set drove north, where **jazz musicians** like Duke Ellington, Count Basie, and Cab Calloway played in packed nightspots like the Cotton Club, Savoy Ballroom, Apollo Theater, and Smalls Paradise, and the liquor flowed freely, despite Prohibition. But the Harlem Renaissance wasn't just about music. It was also characterized by the rich body of **literature** produced by Johnson, Langston Hughes, Jean Toomer, and Zora Neale Hurston, among many others.

Yet even before the Great Depression it was hard to scrape out a living here, and the economic downturn of the 1930s drove out the middle class. It may be because evening revelers never stayed longer than the last drink that neither they, nor many histories of the period, recall the rampant poverty that went hand-in-hand with Harlem's raunchy, anything-goes nightlife.

One of the lasting legacies of this period, however, has been the neighborhood's sense of racial consciousness. First evidenced during the 1920s and 1930s in the writings and speeches of men like Marcus Garvey, W.E.B. DuBois, and Charles S. Johnson, the same spirit is still alive today in such larger-than-life Harlem firebrands as Al Sharpton and the Reverend Calvin Butts.

Once this real-estate boom began, the Jewish, German, and Italian populations of Harlem relocated farther north, and the area became predominantly black by the 1920s. The first signs of Harlem's explosion of black culture quickly appeared, and the musical and literary movement known as the **Harlem Renaissance** (see box above) made the streets north of Central Park a necessary destination for anyone interested in the artistic cutting-edge. The Depression and post war years were not kind to the area, however, and the Renaissance was followed by several decades of worsening economic conditions.

In the early 1970s, and then again in the late 1990s, things began to turn around, and the beginnings of redevelopment became evident. Years of disgraceful living conditions brought residents to a boiling point, and slumlords and absentee landlords were held accountable for their roles in the area's ruin. A plethora of urban and community grants were put into effect for commercial and retail development, housing, and general urban renewal. Some years later, that initial investment is paying off: Harlem's historic areas are well maintained and there seems to be construction everywhere you turn. Savvy locals have purchased many of the district's nineteenth-century brownstones, which are some of the most beautiful in the city.

The federally established Upper Manhattan Empowerment Zone, encompassing Harlem and part of the South Bronx, is pumping millions into various area projects – many of them retail-driven. The program has helped usher in neighborhood branches of chains like Pathmark and *Starbucks*, as well as a Magic Johnson multiplex cinema and several chic retailers. In fact, in May 2008, Mayor Bloomberg and the city's planning commission approved a broad re-zoning of 125th Street, which could bring stately office towers, thousands of condos (at market rates), hotels, galleries, and retail establishments to the storied street in the next decade.

As for community-led changes, an organization involving ninety local churches and spearheaded by the Abyssinian Development Corporation (the development arm of the Abyssinian Baptist Church – see p.211) has become the owner of a number of business sites. The questions facing the community now are not about how to drive interest or investment here, but rather how to manage and control the area's evolution, as well as how to reconcile it with the poverty and unemployment still very much in evidence.

Along 125th Street

To begin exploring Harlem, take the #2 or #3 train to 125th Street; you'll exit the station at 125th Street and Lenox Avenue. The stretch of **125th Street** between Broadway and Fifth Avenue is Harlem's main commercial drag. It's here that recent investment in the area is most obvious – note the presence of fashion retailer H&M. This was Malcolm X's beat in the 1950s and 1960s – he strolled and preached on 125th Street, and photos of him and his followers have passed into legend. If you need a landmark, look for the **Adam Clayton Powell, Jr State Office Building** looming on the corner of Adam Clayton Powell, Jr Boulevard. Commissioned in 1972, it replaced a constellation of businesses that included Elder Louis Michaux's bookstore, one of Malcolm X's main rallying points. When construction began, the protests of squatters were so vehement that the city made several concessions: the bookstore was relocated one avenue eastward, and the building was named in honor of Adam Clayton Powell, Jr, Harlem's first black congressman (see box, p.210).

Apollo Theater and around

Walk a little west from the Powell Building and you reach the legendary **Apollo Theater**, 253 W 125th St at Frederick Douglass Blvd (☎212/531-5300, ⓦwww.apollotheater.com). Although it's not much to look at from the outside, from the 1930s to the 1970s this venue was the center of black entertainment in New York City and the northeast US. Almost all the great figures of jazz and blues played here, along with singers, comedians, and dancers; past winners of its famous Amateur Night have included Ella Fitzgerald, Billie Holiday, Luther Vandross, The Jackson Five, Sarah Vaughan, Marvin Gaye, and James Brown. Since its heyday, the Apollo has served as a warehouse, a movie theater, and a radio station; in its latest incarnation it is the venue for a weekly TV show, *Showtime at the Apollo*. Renovations have been ongoing since 2002: the interior has been overhauled, as have the old sign and marquee. Officially a landmark building, the Apollo offers daily 60-minute tours, but only to groups of twenty or more (call to arrange at ☎212/531-5337).

Across the way, the tall, narrow **Theresa Towers** office building, 2090 Adam Clayton Powell, Jr Blvd at 125th St, was until the 1960s the *Theresa Hotel*. Designed by George and Edward Blum in 1913, it still stands out from the rest of the street, thanks to its gleaming white terracotta patterns topped with sunbursts. Not desegregated until 1940, the hotel became known as the "Waldorf of Harlem." Fidel Castro was a guest here in 1960 while on a visit to the United Nations, when he shunned midtown luxury in a popular political gesture. Look, too, for the former **Blumstein's** store, 230 W 125th St at Eighth Ave, which now operates as the Touro College Medical School. Founded by a German-Jewish immigrant in 1898, this was once the largest department store in the area. Like many white-owned local businesses, for many years Blumstein's refused to hire black workers except as menial laborers. In 1934 it became the focal point of a community-wide boycott led by Adam Clayton Powell, Jr – pointedly called "Don't Buy Where You Can't Work." The campaign was effective: the

▲ Apollo Theater

department store not only began hiring blacks, but it also became the first shop in the area to use black mannequins and feature a black Santa at Christmas.

Studio Museum in Harlem

Founded in 1968, the **Studio Museum in Harlem**, 144 W 125th St at Lenox Ave (Wed–Fri & Sun noon–6pm, Sat 10am–6pm; suggested donation $7; ☎212/864-4500, ⓦwww.studiomuseum.org), has over 60,000 square feet of exhibition space dedicated to showcasing contemporary African-American painting, photography, and sculpture. The permanent collection is displayed on a rotating basis and includes works by Harlem Renaissance-era photographer James Van Der Zee, as well as paintings and sculptures by postwar artists. A neighborhood-oriented perspective, skillful curatorial work, and supplementary lectures, author readings, and music performances combine to create an atmosphere more like a community center than a museum.

Lenox Avenue and around

North of Central Park, Sixth Avenue becomes **Lenox Avenue**, one of Harlem's main north–south arteries. It was officially rechristened **Malcolm X Boulevard** in the late 1980s, but is still known to most by its old name.

Mount Morris Park Historic District

The area around Lenox Avenue between West 118th and 124th streets is known as the **Mount Morris Park Historic District**. It was one of the first districts north of Central Park to attract residential development after the elevated railroads were constructed. Initially inhabited by White Anglo Saxon Prostestant-y (WASPy) commuters, the area then became home to the city's second-largest neighborhood of Eastern European Jewish immigrants (after the Lower East Side), and finally shifted to a primarily black neighborhood in the 1920s. This series of complex demographic shifts has created a profusion of diverse religious structures, and has helped place the neighborhood on the National Register of Historic Places. The district has an active community-improvement association, which runs a historic-home tour (call for details ☎212/369-4241, ⓦwww.mmpcia.com).

One of the district's most interesting buildings is **Mount Olivet Church**, 201 Lenox Ave at 120th St, a Greco-Roman–style temple that was once a synagogue. Compare its design with the somber, bulky, Gothic **St Martin's**, at the southeast corner of Lenox Avenue and 122nd Street; both these institutions have been fortunate in avoiding the decay that has afflicted much of the area. Elsewhere, the Mount Morris district includes some lovely rowhouses that were constructed during the speculation boom of the 1890s: most outstanding of all are **133–143 W 122nd St** at Lenox Ave. Arguably the finest row of Queen Anne-style homes in the city, they were designed by leading architect Francis H. Kimball in 1885–87. The orange-brick houses have gables, dormers, and some lovely stained glass. Double back west and pause in front of **Hale House**, 152 W 122nd St (☎212/663-0700, ⓦwww.halehouse.org). It was established in 1969 by "Mother" Clara Hale, whose program for substance-addicted (and now HIV-infected) infants and mothers was one of the first in the country; a plaque in front of the house is decorated with bronze renderings of children's faces and encircles a statue of Hale herself.

From Hale House, head east to **Marcus Garvey Park**, formerly Mount Morris Park; it takes its new name from the black leader of the 1920s. The park is situated between East 120th and 124th streets, between Mount Morris Park West and Madison Avenue, its most notable feature being an elegant octagonal fire tower built in 1857 on a peak in the middle of the space, a unique example of the early-warning devices once found throughout the city.

Schomburg Center for Research in Black Culture

If you're more interested in learning about Harlem's past than pondering its uncertain future, it's worth taking a walk up to the **Schomburg Center for Research in Black Culture**, 515 Lenox Ave at 135th St (Mon–Wed noon–8pm,

Harlem was once home to any number of nightspots, many of which attracted hordes of white patrons from downtown as well as middle-class blacks. Several of these, especially the once-famous **jazz venues**, have survived decades of disuse. Although their current boarded-up state is sobering, many of these beautiful buildings are slated for restoration and refurbishment.

The Abyssinian Development Corporation, the development arm of the Abyssinian Baptist Church, acquired the **Renaissance Ballroom**, Adam Clayton Powell, Jr Blvd at 138th St, as a likely future home for the Classical Theater of Harlem, though plans are moving ahead very slowly. This tile-trimmed, square-and-diamond-shaped dance club hosted Duke Ellington and Chick Webb in the 1920s. Nicknamed the "Rennie," it was a haven for middle-class blacks – look for the original light-up "Chop Suey" sign (once considered an exotic dish) that's now rusting away on the exterior. The same corporation, in partnership with the city, has transformed another former club, **Small's Paradise** on the southwest corner of Adam Clayton Powell, Jr Blvd and 135th St, into a public school. This finial-topped brick building was built in 1925 and hosted a mixed black and white crowd from the beginning, when the club was known as "The Hottest Spot in Harlem." Across 135th Street at 2300 Adam Clayton Powell, Jr Blvd was the Big Apple Restaurant and Jazz Club, which is rumoured to be the birthplace of New York City's nickname. It's said that when jazzmen met on the road in the 1930s, they would call to each other, "See you at the Big Apple" as a sort of shorthand reference to the city. The term duly entered the vernacular after local journalists started using it. The ground floor of the **Cecil Hotel**, 206–210 W 118th St at St Nicholas Ave, still displays the light-up sign advertising **Mintons Playhouse**, supposedly the birthplace of bebop. In the 1940s, after finishing their sets at Harlem's clubs, Thelonious Monk, Dizzy Gillespie, Charlie Parker, John Coltrane, and other greats would gather at Mintons for late-night jam sessions that gave rise to the improvised jazz style. As for the **Cotton Club**, it was originally at 142nd St and Lenox Ave, and was a segregated establishment – though most of the performers here were black, as was the staff, only whites were allowed to attend as guests. That building was demolished in 1958, but the club reopened in Harlem in 1978 at 666 W 125th St, where it continues to put on a good jazz show at night as well as a Sunday gospel brunch. For more on Harlem's nightlife today, see "The performing arts & film," p.359, and "Nightlife," p.352.

Thurs & Fri 11am–6pm, Sat 10am–5pm; free; ☎212/491-2200, ⓦwww.nypl .org/research/sc), a member of the New York Public Library system. Originally a lending branch, the Division of Negro Literature, History and Prints was created in 1925 after the community began rallying for a library of its own. The collection grew dramatically, thanks to Arthur Schomburg, a black Puerto Rican nicknamed "The Sherlock Holmes of Black History" for his obsessive efforts to document black culture. Schomburg had acquired over 10,000 manuscripts, photos, and artifacts, and he sold them all to the NYPL for $10,000; he then worked as curator for the collection, sometimes using his own funds for upkeep, from 1932 until his death six years later. Since that time, the amassing of over five million items has made the center the world's top research facility for the study of black history and culture. Aside from its letters archive and book collections, the center is also the site of the ashes of renowned poet Langston Hughes, best known for penning *The Negro Speaks of Rivers*. That poem inspired Houston Conwill's terrazzo and brass "cosmogram" in the atrium beyond the main entrance; it's a mosaic built over a tributary of the Harlem River. Seven of Hughes' lines radiate out from a circle, and the last line, "My soul has grown deep like the rivers," located in a fish at the center, marks where he is interred.

The Schomburg Center also features community-heritage displays, book readings, and art and music events in its halls, gallery, and two auditoriums – call for information on special events.

Along 116th Street

Moving east from campus, it's along **116th Street** that the spirit of the late Malcolm X, founder of a movement that emphasized austerity and African-American self-reliance, is perhaps the most palpable. Look for the green onion-dome of the **Masjid Malcolm Shabazz mosque**, 102 W 116th St at Lenox Ave; it's named for him. Between Lenox and Fifth avenues on 116th Street, at no. 52, you'll pass the bazaar-like **Malcolm Shabazz Harlem Market** (daily 10am–8pm; ☎212/987-8131), its entrance marked by colorful fake minarets. The market's offerings include cloth, T-shirts, jewelry, clothing, and more, all with a distinctly Afro-centric flavor – it's worth stopping by, mostly since what's on sale here differs so much from the usual flea-market staples. Ironically, the vendors, who used to run from police and clash with other local merchants, now pay taxes, accept credit cards, and take accounting courses at the mosque.

The stretch of 116th Street between Lenox and Manhattan avenues has recently become a hub for recent West African immigrants and is unofficially known as **Little Senegal** – listen for snatches of French on the street. It's estimated that at least 25,000 Senegalese have settled in New York in the last few years. They've opened up shops, beauty parlors, and restaurants here to create a thriving neighborhood.

There are also some much older African-influenced buildings nearby, including the fanciful blue-and-white Moorish-style First **Corinthian Baptist Church**, 1912 Adam Clayton Powell, Jr Blvd at 116th St (☎212/864-5976). Originally built as the Regent Theater in 1912, this was one of America's earliest movie palaces before being transformed into a church in 1929. If you want to see one of the few churches built by a black architect, head up to 134th Street between Frederick Douglass and Powell boulevards: that's the site of **St Philip's Church**, an elegant brick-and-granite building constructed by Vertner Tandy in 1910–11.

El Barrio

South and east of here, **Spanish Harlem** extends from the affluence of the Upper East Side, and encompasses everything from the Harlem River to as far west as Park Avenue and its end at East 132nd Street. The area's name is misleading, though, as it has little in common with Harlem proper other than its uptown location. This neighborhood is one of the centers of Manhattan's large Puerto Rican community, and is better known by locals as **El Barrio** – a term that can sometimes imply a slum, but to its residents simply means "the neighborhood."

What's immediately evident as you walk around here is the quality of the buildings or, rather, the lack thereof. There are no swathes of old brownstones waiting to be remodeled and restored. Instead, there are blocks of low-rise, low-income housing that give the area an intimidating atmosphere. Although El Barrio was originally a working-class Italian area, it's been predominantly Puerto Rican since the early 1950s and while it has yet to see any significant gentrification, changes are coming. The area's ethnic focus is shifting, as more Mexicans arrive, and its cultural and creative strengths are being explored by second-generation immigrants, often known as NuYoricans (the word's a blend of New York and Boricua, the original name for the island of Puerto Rico).

The hub of the neighborhood has long been **La Marqueta**, on Park Avenue between 111th and 116th streets, though it's in a sorry state. Originally a five-block street market of Hispanic products, it's now largely vacant. The remaining occupied storefronts sell everything from tropical fruits and vegetables, jewelry, religious figurines, and clothing to dried herbs and snake oils. Mayor Bloomberg has assigned a task force to look at ways to improve and upgrade La Marqueta and, with it, the entire area.

If you're looking for insight into New York's Latin culture, you're better off heading to the **Museo del Barrio** (see below) or even **La Casa de la Herencia Cultural Puertorriqueña**, a Puerto Rican heritage library in the Heckscher Building at 1230 Fifth Ave (℡212/722-2600, ⓦwww.lacasapr .org). To check out the contemporary-art scene here, stop by two notable galleries, **Taller Boricua**, 1680 Lexington Ave (℡212/831-4333), and **Art for Change**, 1699 Lexington Ave at 107th St (℡212/348-7044, ⓦwww .artforchange.org), both of which are alternative spaces for local artists of Latin and African-American origin.

Museo del Barrio

Literally translated as "the neighborhood museum," the **Museo del Barrio**, 1230 Fifth Ave at 104th St, was founded in 1969 by a group of local Puerto Rican parents, educators, and artists who wanted to teach their children about their heritage (Wed–Sat & Sun 11am–5pm; $6; ℡212/831-7272, ⓦwww .elmuseo.org). In keeping with its "homegrown" vibe, the museum was started in a school classroom and still feels more like a community center than a stuffy cultural institution. In 2004, the museum undertook a major renovation project designed to broaden its focus beyond strictly Puerto Rican subjects, including the expansion of its one permanent exhibit on **the Taino**, a highly developed people from the Caribbean (1200–1500 AD).

There are temporary exhibits as well as a theater on site – the **Teatro Heckscher** hosts Latin-influenced plays and movies (call for schedules; tickets $10–20). However, the best time to visit is for one of the summertime concerts, held one night during the week when the museum stays open late (usually Thurs).

Adam Clayton Powell, Jr Boulevard

Above 110th Street, Seventh Avenue becomes **Adam Clayton Powell, Jr Boulevard**, a broad sweep that pushes north between low-built houses – perhaps the only strip in Manhattan on which the sky can break through. Since its conception, Powell Boulevard has vied with 125th Street as Harlem's main commercial

---

Reverend Adam Clayton Powell, Jr

In the 1930s, the **Reverend Adam Clayton Powell, Jr** was instrumental in forcing Harlem's stores, most of which were white-owned and retained a white workforce, to begin employing the blacks whose patronage ensured the stores' survival. Later, he became the first black on the city council, then New York's first black congressional representative, during which time he sponsored the country's first minimum-wage law. His distinguished career came to an embittered end in 1967, when amid strong rumors of the misuse of public funds, he was excluded from Congress by majority vote. This failed to diminish his standing in Harlem, where voters re-elected him: he sat until the year before his death (1972), and there's a fitting memorial on the boulevard that today bears his name.

concourse, but while big-name retailers are returning to the latter, this boulevard remains forlorn. Years of decline show in its graffiti-splattered walls and storefronts and empty lots; there isn't much to see until you reach 138th Street.

Abyssinian Baptist Church

At 132 W 138th St, at Adam Clayton Powell, Jr Blvd, stands the **Abyssinian Baptist Church** (T212/862-7474, W www.abyssinian.org), first incorporated in 1808 in what is now Tribeca. Its founders included a group of African-Americans living in New York, as well as some Ethiopian merchants, who were tired of segregated seating at Baptist churches in New York (the church's name comes from the traditional name for Ethiopia). The Abyssinian started becoming the religious and political powerhouse that it is today in 1908, when the **Reverend Adam Clayton Powell, Jr** was appointed pastor (see box opposite). Construction on the current Gothic and Tudor building was completed in 1923. It's worth a trip here just to see and hear the gut-busting **choir** – see the box below for details.

Strivers' Row

Just west of Powell Boulevard along 138th and 139th streets stands **Strivers' Row**, some of the finest blocks of rowhouses in Manhattan. A dignified Renaissance-derived strip that's an amalgam of simplicity and elegance, it was conceived during the 1890s housing boom by McKim, Mead, and White amongst others. Note the unusual rear service alleys of the houses, reached via iron-gated cross streets. At the turn of the nineteenth century, this came to be the desirable place for ambitious professionals within Harlem's burgeoning black community (starting with rail porters) to reside – hence its nickname.

Hamilton Heights

Much of Harlem's western edge, between 135th and 145th streets, is taken up by the area known as **Hamilton Heights**; like Morningside Heights to the south, there's a blend of campus buildings (in this case, belonging to the City College of New York) and residences here, lightened by a sprinkle of slender parks on a bluff above Harlem. However, one stretch, the **Hamilton Heights**

Sunday gospel

Harlem's incredible **gospel music** has long enticed visitors, and for good reason: both it and the entire revival-style Baptist experience can be amazing and invigorating. Gospel tours are big business, and churches seem to be jockeying among themselves to see who can attract the most tourists. Many of the arranged tours are pricey, but they usually offer transportation uptown and brunch after the service. If you don't feel like shelling out the cash, or if you're looking for a more authentic experience, you can also easily go it alone. The choir at the **Abyssinian Baptist Church** is arguably the best in the city, but long lines of tourists make the experience, well, touristy. Another fairly popular option is the **Metropolitan Baptist Church**, 151 W 128th St at Adam Clayton Powell, Jr Blvd (T212/663-8990). **Mount Nebo Baptist Church**, 1883 Adam Clayton Powell, Jr Blvd at W 114th St (T212/866-7880), is much less of a circus; worship here is taken seriously and services are not designed as tourist attractions, but the congregation is very welcoming to nonmembers. Wherever you go, dress accordingly: jackets for men and skirts or dresses for women.

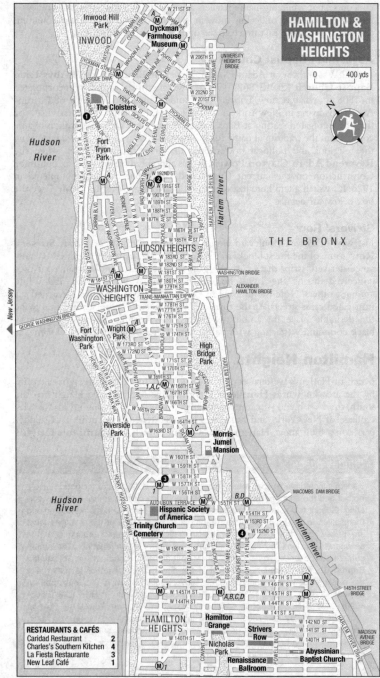

HAMILTON & WASHINGTON HEIGHTS

0   400 yds

N

Hudson River

New Jersey

George Washington Bridge

Inwood Hill Park

INWOOD

Dyckman Farmhouse Museum

W 211TH ST

W 206TH ST

UNIVERSITY HEIGHTS BRIDGE

W 202ND ST

W 201ST ST

The Cloisters

Fort Tryon Park

W 192ND ST
W 191ST ST
W 190TH ST
W 189TH ST
W 188TH ST
W 187TH ST

HUDSON HEIGHTS

W 186TH ST
W 185TH ST

W 183RD ST
W 182ND ST
W 181ST ST
W 180TH ST
W 179TH ST

WASHINGTON HEIGHTS

WASHINGTON BRIDGE

ALEXANDER HAMILTON BRIDGE

Trans-Manhattan Expwy

W 178TH ST
W 177TH ST
W 176TH ST

Fort Washington Park

Wright Park

W 175TH ST
W 174TH ST
W 173RD ST
W 172ND ST
W 171ST ST
W 170TH ST

THE BRONX

Harlem River

High Bridge Park

W 169TH ST
W 168TH ST
W 167TH ST
W 166TH ST

W 165TH ST

W 164TH ST

W 163RD ST

Morris-Jumel Mansion

Riverside Park

W 160TH ST
W 159TH ST
W 158TH ST
W 157TH ST
W 156TH ST

MACOMBS DAM BRIDGE

Hudson River

Audubon Terrace

Hispanic Society of America

Trinity Church Cemetery

W 155TH ST
W 154TH ST
W 153RD ST
W 152ND ST

W 150TH

W 147TH ST
W 146TH ST
W 145TH ST
W 144TH ST
W 141ST ST

HAMILTON HEIGHTS

Hamilton Grange

Nicholas Park

Strivers Row

W 142ND ST
W 141 ST ST
W 140TH ST

145TH STREET BRIDGE

MADISON AVENUE BRIDGE

Renaissance Ballroom

Abyssinian Baptist Church

RESTAURANTS & CAFÉS

Caridad Restaurant	2
Charles's Southern Kitchen	4
La Fiesta Restaurante	3
New Leaf Café	1

▼ Upper West Side   ▼ Harlem

Alexander Hamilton

Alexander Hamilton's life is much more fascinating than his house. Born in the West Indies, he came to America as a young man. He was an early supporter of the Revolution, and his intelligence and enthusiasm quickly brought him to the attention of George Washington. Hamilton became the general's aide-de-camp, and rose quickly through military ranks. When Washington was elected President, he named Hamilton as the first Secretary of the Treasury. Hamilton, quick in both understanding and temper, tended to tackle problems head-on, a propensity that made him enemies as well as friends. He alienated both John Adams and Thomas Jefferson, and when Jefferson won the presidency in 1801, Hamilton was left out in the political cold. Temporarily abandoning politics, he moved away from the city to his grange (or farm) to tend his plantation and conduct a memorably sustained and vicious feud with **Aaron Burr**, who had beaten Hamilton's father-in-law in a Senate election.

Following a short tenure as Vice President under Jefferson, Burr ran for governor of New York; Hamilton strenuously opposed his candidacy and, after an exchange of extraordinarily bitter letters, the two men fought a duel in Weehawken, New Jersey (roughly where the Lincoln Tunnel now emerges), on July 11, 1804. When pistols were drawn, Hamilton honourably discharged his into the air, a happening possibly explained by the fact that his eldest son had been killed in a duel on the same field a few years earlier. Burr, evidently made of lesser stuff, aimed carefully and fatally wounded Hamilton. He remains one of two non-presidents to find his way onto US money (Benjamin Franklin's the other): you'll find his portrait on the $10 bill.

Historic District, bounded by Amsterdam and St Nicholas avenues from 140th to 145th streets, pulls Hamilton Heights well up from the ranks of middle class, with rowhouses in a variety of architectural styles, including Beaux Arts and Romanesque Revival.

Visitors wandering up from Harlem or exiting the 135th Street and St Nicholas Avenue #B or #C subway station will likewise be pleasantly surprised by **Convent Avenue**. From here to 140th street, its secluded, blossom-lined streets have a garden-suburb prettiness that's spangled with Gothic, French, and Italian Renaissance influences in happily eclectic 1890s houses. The feathery span of the Shepard Archway at 140th Street announces **City College**, a rustic-feeling campus of Collegiate-Gothic halls mantled with white terracotta fripperies. Founded in 1905, City College didn't charge tuition, and thus became the seat of higher learning for many of New York's poor, including polio-vaccine pioneer Jonas Salk and soldier-turned-statesman Colin Powell. Even though free education here came to an end in the 1970s, three-quarters of the students still come from minority backgrounds.

Hamilton Grange

Until recently, Convent Avenue also contained Hamilton Heights' single historical lure – the 1798 house of founding father Alexander Hamilton, **Hamilton Grange National Memorial** (Ⓦ www.nps.gov/hagr/). The Grange has bounced around the island a couple of times: it stood at its original site on 143rd Street until 1889, and is now scheduled to reopen in its new location in the northwest corner of St Nicholas Park in 2009. The National Parks Service, which runs the home, had been trying to relocate it for years, and finally received the funds needed to renovate it, restoring the top floor for visitors, and repairing unstable porches and sagging floors that have deteriorated over the years. There was still the matter, however, of how to transplant the house out of its cramped quarters at 287 Convent Ave, in the shadow of the fiercely Romanesque St Luke's Church to which it was originally donated. In early June 2008 the 298-ton structure was lifted (in one piece, no less) up and over the church's entryway to begin the journey to its new home.

For more on Alexander Hamilton, see box, p.213.

Washington Heights

Washington Heights is the name given to most of the northern tip of Manhattan; it encompasses the majority of ground between 145th and 200th streets. From Hamilton Heights, walk along Convent Avenue until it joins St Nicolas Avenue, which – once past Sylvan Terrace – becomes Broadway a few blocks north. This is the main drag of a once elegant, now mostly raggedy neighborhood. Demographically, it's largely Dominican, a vibrant and lively place by day, but somewhere to exercise caution come nightfall.

Audubon Terrace and around

One of the few sights worth at least a quick look in Washington Heights is **Audubon Terrace**, at 155th St and Broadway (easily reached by the #1 train to 157th and Broadway). This Acropolis of folly is what's left of a weird, clumsy, nineteenth-century attempt to glorify 155th Street, when museums were dolled up as Beaux-Arts temples.

There is only one museum left here, the **Hispanic Society of America** (Tues–Sat 10am–4.30pm, Sun 1–4pm, library closed Aug; free; ☎212/926-2234, Ⓦwww.hispanicsociety.org), but it makes the trip worthwhile. The Hispanic Society owns one of the largest collections of Hispanic art outside Spain, including over 3000 paintings by masters such as Goya, El Greco, and Velázquez, as well as more than 6000 decorative works of art. The collection ranges from an intricately carved ivory box dating from 965 AD, to fifteenth-century textiles, to Joaquín Sorolla y Bastida's joyful mural series *Provinces of Spain* (commissioned specifically for the society in 1911). Displays of the permanent collection rarely change, so you can be fairly certain you'll see the highlights. The 200,000-book library, which includes over 16,000 works printed before the eighteenth century, is a major reference site for scholars studying Spanish and Portuguese art, history, and literature.

One avenue east, at 155th Street and Amsterdam, lies the **Trinity Church Cemetery** (☎212/368-1600, Ⓦwww.trinitywallstreet.org), its large, placid grounds dotted with some fanciful mausolea. Robber-baron John Jacob Astor is buried up here, as are naturalist James Audubon and Chelsea developer Clement Clark Moore. It hasn't always been so tranquil: two large bronze slabs on the grounds mark the particularly bloody Battle of Washington Heights during the Revolutionary War.

The Morris–Jumel Mansion and around

Within easy walking distance of Audubon Terrace and the cemetery is the **Morris–Jumel Mansion**, 65 Jumel Terrace at 160th St and Edgecombe Ave (Wed–Sun 10am–4pm; $4; ☎212/923-8008, Ⓦwww.morrisjumel.org). Another uptown surprise, the mansion somehow survived the urban renewal (or better, destruction) that occurred all around it, and is now one of the city's more successful house museums, its proud Georgian outlines faced with a later Federal portico. Built as a rural retreat in 1765 by Colonel Roger Morris, the house served briefly as Washington's headquarters before falling into the hands of the British. Wealthy wine merchant Stephen Jumel bought the derelict mansion in 1810 and refurbished it for his wife (and ex-mistress) Eliza, formerly a prostitute. New York society didn't take to such a past, but when Jumel died in 1832, Eliza married ex-Vice President Aaron Burr, twenty years her senior: the marriage lasted for six months before old Burr left, having gone through her inheritance, only to die on the day of their divorce. Eliza battled on to the age of 91, and on the top floor of the house you'll find her obituary, a magnificently fictionalized account of a "scandalous" life (for more on Burr, see the Alexander Hamilton box on p.213).

Just opposite the entrance to the mansion's grounds is the quaint block of **Sylvan Terrace**, a tiny cobblestone mews lined with yellow and green wooden houses built in the 1880s – and seeming impossibly out of place just barely off the wide-open intersection of Amsterdam and St Nicholas avenues. North of here at 165th and Broadway is the **Audubon Ballroom**, scene of Malcolm X's assassination in 1965 and now, after some controversy, a part of the Columbia-Presbyterian Hospital complex.

George Washington Bridge

From most western parts of Washington Heights you can get a glimpse of the **George Washington Bridge**, which links Manhattan to New Jersey. It's arguable that the feeder road to the bridge has created two distinct areas: below is bleakly run-down, one of the biggest areas of illegal drug activity in the city; above, the streets relax in smaller, more diverse, ethnic old-time neighborhoods of Jews, Greeks, Central Europeans, and especially Irish immigrants, though a major Hispanic community has been growing since the 1970s. A skillful, dazzling sketch high above the Hudson, the bridge skims almost a mile across the channel in massive metalwork and graceful lines, a natural successor to the Brooklyn Bridge. "Here, finally, steel architecture seems to laugh," said Le Corbusier of the 1931 construction.

The Cloisters Museum and around

The only reason most visitors come this far uptown is to see **The Cloisters Museum** in Fort Tryon Park (Tues–Sun: March–Oct 9.30am–5.15pm; Nov–Feb 9.30am–4.45pm; suggested donation $20, $15 seniors, $10 students, includes same-day admission to the Metropolitan Museum; ☎212/923-3700, ⓦ www.metmuseum.org). It stands above the Hudson like some misplaced Renaissance palazzo-cum-monastery, and is home to the Metropolitan Museum of Art's collection of medieval tapestries, metalwork, paintings, and sculpture. Impressive artwork aside, you'll find an additional reward in the park itself, cleverly landscaped by Frederick Law Olmsted, Jr (son of the Central Park planner). The promenade overlooking the river and the English-style garden make for a stunningly romantic spot. Inside the museum, the central cloister, with pink marble arcades and a fountain purchased from the French monastery of Saint-Michel-de-Cuxa, might trick you into believing that you're in south-western France. Portions of five medieval cloisters (basically, covered walkways and their enclosed courtyards) are incorporated into the structure, the folly of collectors **George Grey Barnard** and **John D. Rockefeller, Jr.** To get here, take the #A train to 190th Street–Fort Washington Avenue.

Some history

Barnard started a museum on this spot in 1914 to house his personal collection of medieval works, mostly sculpture and architectural fragments acquired in France. Later, Rockefeller donated funds to the Met, enabling the museum to purchase the site and its collection, as well as the 66 acres of land around it – now Fort Tryon Park. With commendable foresight, Rockefeller himself purchased 700 acres of land across the way in New Jersey to ensure perpetually good views. Barnard and Rockefeller each shipped over the best of medieval Europe for the museum: **Romanesque chapels** and **Gothic halls**, dismantled and transplanted brick by brick, along with tapestries, paintings, and sculptures. The completed museum opened in 1938, and is still the only museum in the US specializing in medieval art (though, technically, it's not a stand-alone institution, but rather a branch of the Metropolitan Museum of Art).

The collection

The best approach if you're coming from the 190th Street subway is directly across the park: the views are tremendous. Once at the museum, start from the entrance hall and work counterclockwise: the collection is laid out in roughly chronological order. First off is the simplicity of the **Romanesque Hall**, featuring French remnants such as an arched, limestone doorway dating to 1150 and a thirteenth-century portal from a monastery in Burgundy. The frescoed Spanish **Fuentidueña Chapel** is dominated by a huge, domed twelfth-century apse from Segovia that immediately induces a reverential hush. The hall and chapel form a corner on one of the prettiest of the five cloisters here, **St Guilhelm**, which is ringed by Corinthian-style columns topped by carved capitals from thirteenth-century southern France. The nearby **Langon Chapel** is enhanced by a twelfth-century ciborium (a permanent altar canopy) that manages to be formal and graceful in just the right proportions.

At the center of the museum is the **Cuxa Cloister**, from the twelfth-century Benedictine monastery of Saint-Michel-de-Cuxa near Prades in the French Pyrenees; its Romanesque capitals are brilliantly carved, with monkeys, eagles, and lions whose open mouths reveal half-eaten human legs. Central to the scene is the garden, planted with fragrant, almost overpowering, herbs and flowers and offering (bizarrely) piped-in birdsong.

The museum's smaller **sculpture** collection is equally impressive. In the **Early Gothic Hall** are a number of carved figures, including one memorably tender Virgin and Child, carved in France in the thirteenth and fourteenth centuries, probably for veneration at a private altar. The next room holds a collection of tapestries, including a rare surviving Gothic work showing the Nine Heroes, popular figures of the ballads of the Middle Ages.

The **Unicorn Tapestries** (c.1500, Netherlands) in the following room are even more spectacular – brilliantly alive with color, observation, and Christian symbolism. The entire series is on display to the public: the most famous is the seventh and last, where the slain unicorn has miraculously returned to life and is trapped in a circular pen. It isn't just the creature's resurrection that's mysterious – the entire sequence is shrouded in mystery: aside from the fact that they were designed in France and made in Brussels, little else is known for certain, even who the intended original recipients were (the most plausible claim is

Anne of Brittany, wife of King Louis XII). As for the tapestries' allegorical meaning, the unicorn is said to represent both a husband captured in marriage and Christ risen again.

Most of the Met's medieval paintings are to be found downtown, but one important exception is **Campin**'s *Altarpiece*. This fifteenth-century triptych depicts the Annunciation scene in a typical bourgeois Flemish home of the day, and is housed in its own antechamber, outfitted with a desk, chair, cupboard, and other household articles from that period (though from different countries of origin). On the left of the altarpiece, the artist's patron and his wife gaze timidly on through an open door; to the right, St Joseph works in his carpenter's shop. St Joseph was mocked in the literature of the day, which might account for his rather ridiculous appearance – making a mousetrap, a symbol of the way the Devil traps souls.

The **Late Gothic Hall** next door is filled with expressively detailed, large sculptural **altarpieces** depicting biblical scenes. Especially noteworthy is the rarely depicted *Death (Dormition) of the Virgin* in dark wood, whose right side displays the girdle of the Virgin being dropped to St Thomas by an angel, conveying her assumption into heaven.

On the first floor, a large Gothic chapel boasts a high vaulted ceiling and mid- to late fourteenth-century Austrian stained-glass windows, along with the monumental **sarcophagus of Ermengol VII**, with its whole phalanx of (now sadly decapitated) family members and clerics carved in stone to send him off. Also on the first floor are two further cloisters to explore (one with a small café), along with an amazing **Treasury**. As you amble round this part of the collection, try not to miss the *Belles Heures de Jean, Duc de Berry*, perhaps the greatest of all medieval Books of Hours; it was executed by the Limburg Brothers with dazzling miniatures of seasonal life and extensive border-work in gold leaf. Other highlights are the *Reliquary Shrine of Elizabeth of Hungary* and the twelfth-century walrus tusk **altar cross** from Bury St Edmunds in England, containing a mass of 92 tiny expressive characters from biblical stories. Finally, hunt out a golf-ball-sized **rosary bead** from sixteenth-century Flanders: with a representation of the Passion inside, it barely seems possible that it could have been carved by hand (it's made of separate tiny pieces of boxwood painstakingly fitted together with the aid of a magnifying glass).

Inwood

Back at the Cloisters, Fort Tryon Park joins **Inwood Hill Park** by the Hudson River; it's possible to walk across Dyckman Street and into the park. The path up the side of the river gives a beautiful view of New Jersey, surprisingly hilly and wooded this far upstream. Keep walking and you'll reach the very tip of Manhattan, an area referred to as *Spuyten Duyvil* ("the spitting devil" in Dutch) after the turbu-lence of the identically named creek nearby; nowadays, though, it's better known as the site of Columbia University's athletic stadium. Inwood Hill Park itself is fairly wild, once the stomping ground for Indian cave-dwellers, although the site of their original settlement is now buried under the Henry Hudson Parkway.

Inwood, a largely Dominican residential enclave boasting some Art Deco apartment buildings, warrants a mention as the childhood home of basketball's Kareem Abdul-Jabbar. Today, however, its main tourist attraction is the **Dyckman Farmhouse Museum**, 4881 Broadway at 204th St (Wed–Sat 11am–4pm, Sun noon–4pm; $1; ⊤212/304-9422, ⓦwww.dyckmanfarmhouse .org). A pleasant enough period home (an eighteenth-century Dutch farmhouse), it's really only worth visiting if you're already up here for the Cloisters.

Brooklyn

"The Great Mistake." So ran local newspaper headlines when **Brooklyn** became a borough of New York in 1898. Then the fourth-largest city in the US, it has since labored in the shadow of its taller but smaller brother across the East River, drawing hordes to famous Coney Island beach – the closest white-sand beach to Manhattan – but generally not offering much in the way of high culture. Over the past few years, though, Brooklyn has come into its own, its signature brownstone townhouses and tree-lined streets complemented by top-rated restaurants, trendy bars, world-class museums, and galleries and performance spaces that present more daring work than you'll generally find in Manhattan.

The most accessible district in the borough is pretty, elite **Brooklyn Heights**, a clutch of old mansions and townhouses abutting the East River directly opposite Lower Manhattan. A little north of here, the once-derelict warehouses of the area known as **DUMBO** have been converted to expensive condos, art galleries, and theaters overlooking two popular waterfront parks. Due south of the Heights lie **Boerum Hill**, **Cobble Hill**, and **Carroll Gardens**, or "**BoCoCa**," a trio of upscale neighborhoods with no real attractions but block after block of historic brownstones and some of the borough's best restaurants, including a few old-school Italian spots. West of the Brooklyn-Queens Expressway, Carroll Gardens shades into **Red Hook**, whose half-exposed stone-block streets are lined with an oddball mix of hulking warehouses (some transformed into galleries and artists' studios), vacant lots, garden centers, and detached three-story houses – as well as a vast new Ikea store.

A mile or so southeast of BoCoCa, **Prospect Park**, designed by Central Park creators Frederick Law Olmsted and Calvert Vaux, contains the usual ballfields and trails, along with the first-rate Brooklyn Botanic Garden and Brooklyn Museum, while to the west is the leafy and brownstone-laden, cultured and kid-saturated neighborhood of **Park Slope**. North of the park, increasingly trendy **Prospect Heights** leads into **Fort Greene**, where you'll find some of the most pristine residential blocks in the city along with the famous Brooklyn Academy of Music performance complex. Fort Greene adjoins **Bedford–Stuyvesant**, the largest African-American community in New York, which in turn links to **Crown Heights**, home to the newly expanded Brooklyn Children's Museum and a large Hasidic Jewish population.

Then there's coastal Brooklyn: start in polyglot **Bay Ridge** for a scenic bike ride along the water, then visit **Coney Island**, the venerable seaside amusement district known for its rattletrap roller-coaster, the Cyclone, and the New York Aquarium. Grab some borscht at nearby **Brighton Beach**, where the Russian-born population tops 320,000.

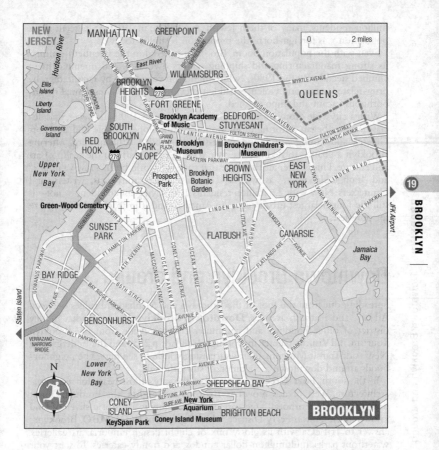

Finally, anyone visiting New York for contemporary art should head to gallery-dotted **Williamsburg**, just one stop on the #L train from Manhattan's East Village and also a top choice for eating and drinking among the young and trendy. **Greenpoint**, just north of Williamsburg on the border of Long Island City, Queens (see p.247), houses the artsy overflow from Williamsburg but maintains a quieter feel, thanks to the Polish old guard that still dominates the area.

Some history

In 1636, **Dutch colonists**, who had already settled New Amsterdam on Manhattan Island under the auspices of the Dutch West India Company, bought farmland from the **Lenape Indians** amid the flat marshes in the southwestern corner of Long Island. The **Village of Breuckelen** received a charter from the company in 1646. The town only began to take on its present form in 1814 when Robert Fulton's steamship service linked Long Island with Manhattan and Brooklyn Heights was established as a leafy retreat for wealthier Manhattanites.

Brooklyn's **incorporation** into the city of New York in 1898, ostensibly so that Manhattan's tax wealth would aid Brooklyn's poor, was a bitterly fought political battle. In the end it was decided by just 277 votes – a tiny percentage of the total 129,000 cast. By the early 1900s, Brooklyn had more than one million residents, many of them Jewish and Italian; in 1910, 35 percent of its population was foreign-born (the proportion is similar today).

Even with the population boom, Brooklyn suffered in the twentieth century: its strong manufacturing and shipping sectors dwindled, and unemployment climbed steadily. By the 1980s, "white flight," provoked first by racism, then by drug-related crime and violence, had left previously desirable residential neighborhoods vacant and impoverished.

With a citywide drop in crime beginning in the mid-1990s, however, middle-class families began restoring brownstones in Park Slope, Cobble Hill, and Fort Greene, and young artists and professionals flooded Williamsburg, offering Brooklyn a chance to rekindle its civic dignity, particularly in the realm of art and culture. This is, after all, the place that gave the world both "How ya doin'?" and "Fuhgeddaboudit," as well as countless artists, musicians, writers, and filmmakers. Now with 2.6 million residents, Brooklyn – independent or not – is still the fourth-largest urban center in America, and it probably takes the prize for proudest.

Downtown Brooklyn and around

Spreading out from the foot of the Brooklyn and Manhattan bridges between Atlantic and Flatbush avenues, **Downtown Brooklyn** is a somewhat motley district of office buildings and commuter colleges. Aside from the Brooklyn Tourism and Visitors Center in Borough Hall (see p.225) and the underground New York Transit Museum, there's surprisingly little to see here. The neighborhoods around downtown are a different story, though.

To the south, **Fort Greene** has some of the city's most beautiful residential architecture. West of downtown is **Brooklyn Heights**, the borough's most prestigious neighborhood. Due east of the Heights is a historic sliver of land known as the Fulton Ferry District, which is adjacent to **DUMBO**, Brooklyn's answer to TriBeCa with its glossy mix of chichi design emporia, art galleries, waterfront parks, multimillion-dollar condos, and trendy eateries. To start your trip in grand style, walk or bicycle here from Lower Manhattan over the Brooklyn Bridge (see p.69), and try to be on the DUMBO waterfront or the Brooklyn Heights promenade at sunset – the light is magical.

Fulton Ferry District

Though you'd hardly guess it today, this small historic district, bounded by the East River, Old Fulton Street, Front Street, and Main Street, was at one time the busiest spot on the Brooklyn waterfront. If you do arrive **on foot** from the Brooklyn Bridge, take the first set of stairs off the bridge and follow Cadman Plaza West down the hill to Old Fulton Street on the west edge of the district. The #A and #C **subway** trains to High Street will also let you off at Cadman Plaza West. The **ferry** is a pleasant alternative in the summer months – it runs between Wall Street, Midtown Manhattan, Long Island City, Queens, and Williamsburg, Brooklyn (hop-on/hop-off day pass $20; $15 children; $3–5.50 per one-way trip; schedule at ☏212/742-1969, ⊛www.nywatertaxi.com).

Named for **Robert Fulton**, the area area was the hub of steamship traffic until the 1883 opening of the Brooklyn Bridge precipitated an economic slump only recently remedied by the booming residential real estate market. Check

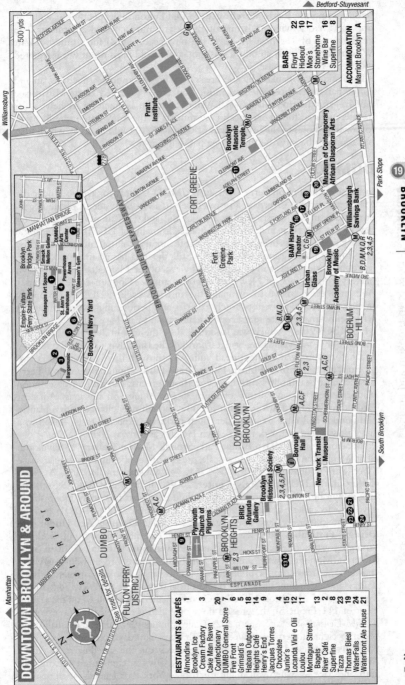

DOWNTOWN BROOKLYN & AROUND

500 yds

0

▲ Bedford-Stuyvesant

▲ Williamsburg

▲ Manhattan

BARS
Floyd	22
Hideout	10
Moe's	17
Stonehome Wine Bar	16
Superfine	8

ACCOMMODATION
Marriott Brooklyn A

Pratt Institute

Brooklyn Masonic Temple

FORT GREENE

Fort Greene Park

Brooklyn Navy Yard

MANHATTAN BRIDGE

Brooklyn Bridge Park
Empire-Fulton Ferry State Park

DUMBO
Smack Mellon Gallery
Galapagos Art Space
St. Ann's Warehouse
Powerhouse Arena
Gleason's Gym
DUMBO Arts Center

Bargemusic

BROOKLYN BRIDGE

See inset for details

East River

BROOKLYN-QUEENS EXPRESSWAY

278

278

DUMBO

FULTON FERRY DISTRICT

Plymouth Church of Pilgrims

BROOKLYN HEIGHTS

BRIC Rotunda Gallery

Brooklyn Historical Society

DOWNTOWN BROOKLYN

Borough Hall

New York Transit Museum

Urban Glass

BAM Harvey Theater

Brooklyn Academy of Music

Museum of Contemporary African Diasporan Arts

Williamsburgh Savings Bank

BOERUM HILL

Park Slope ▼

South Brooklyn ▼

RESTAURANTS & CAFÉS
Almondine	1
Brooklyn Ice Cream Factory	3
Cake Man Raven Confectionary	20
DUMBO General Store	7
Five Front	6
Grimaldi's	5
Habana Outpost	18
Heights Café	14
Henry's End	9
Jacques Torres Chocolate	4
Junior's	15
Locanda Vini e Olii	12
Loulou	11
Montague Street Bagels	13
River Café	2
Superfine	8
Tazza	23
Thomas Biesl	19
WaterFalls	24
Waterfront Ale House	21

19

BROOKLYN

221

out the imposing **Eagle Warehouse**, 28 Old Fulton St; its penthouse, with the huge glass clock-window, is one of Brooklyn's most coveted apartments. The headquarters of *The Brooklyn Eagle*, the newspaper edited for a time by **Walt Whitman**, previously stood on this spot, and its old press room was integrated into the 1893 warehouse.

The landing is flanked by the area's two biggest tourist attractions, an old coffee barge that hosts classical music concerts – so-called **BargeMusic** (see p.364) – and the ritzy *River Café*, 1 Water St, known as much for its views as for its fare. As far as food goes, locals (and tourists in the know) are more likely to follow their noses to the brick ovens of *Grimaldi's*, 19 Old Fulton St, which turn out some of the city's best pizza (see p.334 for review).

DUMBO

Just east of the Fulton Ferry District, **DUMBO** is short for Down Under the Manhattan Bridge Overpass, a term coined in 1978 by residents of the neighborhood – mostly artists – who thought the awkward moniker would deter developers. No such luck: in the past decade many of DUMBO's handsome brick factories have been transformed into luxury condominiums, joined by glass towers housing more of the same. Still, the area has an undeniable allure, its cobblestone streets and jaw-dropping views of the Manhattan and Brooklyn bridges forming one of New York's most dramatic, Gotham-esque cityscapes. And in a canny move to maintain the district's cachet, DUMBO property owners have lured some top-notch galleries and performing-arts organizations with below-market-rate rents; cool restaurants and bars have followed.

DUMBO's core – which was landmarked by the city in 2007 – lies between the Brooklyn and Manhattan bridges, north of the Brooklyn-Queens Expressway. But before you head inland, thread your way through the neighborhood's two glorious parks. **Empire–Fulton Ferry State Park**, adjoining the Fulton Ferry District, is a beautifully landscaped waterfront greenspace with an observation platform, benches, and plenty of room to just lounge on the grass. Adjacent **Brooklyn Bridge Park** is similar for now, though may change with a plan to add condos and retail to its border. Both parks are expected to be linked to a huge new waterfront park in Brooklyn Heights as early as 2009.

Just across from Brooklyn Bridge Park, **Smack Mellon Gallery**, 92 Plymouth St at Washington St, mounts large-scale, site-specific works in a spectacular space (Wed–Sun noon–6pm; ☎718/834-8761, ⓦwww.smackmellon.org). A block farther in, the **DUMBO Arts Center**, 30 Washington St at Water St, was the first nonprofit arts group in the neighborhood. Its hosts five or six group shows a year in its gallery space (Thurs–Mon 10am–6pm; ☎718/694-0831, ⓦwww .dumboartscenter.org) and also organizes the huge **Dumbo Art Under the Bridge Festival**, a three-day affair in late September showcasing work by emerging artists (see p.421). Newcomer **Powerhouse Arena**, 37 Main St at Water St (Mon–Fri 10am–7pm, Sat & Sun 11am–7pm; ☎718-666-3049, ⓦwww .powerhousearena.com), a publisher of photography books, maintains a huge gallery and eminently browsable bookstore and sponsors the New York Photo Festival in mid-May. Most of DUMBO's other galleries are housed on the second floor of **111 Front St**, the ground floor of which is occupied by the excellent *Dumbo General Store* café (see p.302). Gallery hours vary, but you'll usually find seven or eight of them open Wednesday through Saturday afternoons.

If you're interested in live performance, check out the schedule at **St Ann's Warehouse**, 38 Water St (☎718/834-8794, ⓦwww.stannswarehouse.org), an intimate space in which you might catch New York rock legends or all manner

Though he was only sporadically celebrated during his lifetime, poet **Walt Whitman** (1819–1892) has since been elevated to the pantheon of Great American Writers. And of all the places that he lived – and they were many – none was as influential as Brooklyn.

Born in Huntington, Long Island, Whitman moved to the borough at the age of four, moving from place to place thanks to his family's precarious financial situation. His formal schooling ended at age 11, after which he began working as a typesetter's apprentice in what is now downtown Brooklyn. Whitman went on to found his own paper, the *Long-Islander*, which he sold after only nine months, but it was enough experience to get him hired as editor of the *Brooklyn Eagle*, a post he held for two years – a record for the peripatetic young writer.

During his tenure at the *Eagle* – still published in Brooklyn Heights – he argued for the establishment of Fort Greene Park and fought for recognition of local artists. But most important, he gathered ideas for his magnum opus, *Leaves of Grass*, which he would begin to write in 1850. Whitman himself paid for the publication of the first edition in 1855, even helping with the typesetting at a Scottish-owned press on Fulton Street to help keep costs down. Predictably, he couldn't even sell the first run of 795 copies, and when newspapers did get around to reviewing it, many denounced it as obscene.

Undeterred, Whitman revised *Leaves* for the rest of his life, expanding the original 12-poem booklet to a 400-page tome. These first lines of the penultimate poem, "Crossing Brooklyn Ferry," capture the theme that runs throughout the book – Whitman's wide embrace of all humanity – and display the repetitive cadences that would be so influential to later poets, from Gertrude Stein to Allen Ginsberg of the Beats:

Crowds of men and women attired in the usual costumes, how curious you are to me.

On the ferry-boats the hundreds and hundreds that cross, returning home, are more curious to me than you suppose,

And you that shall cross from shore to shore years hence are more to me, and more in my meditations, than you might suppose.

of experimental music, opera, theater, and even puppetry. **Galapagos Art Space** (16 Main St; ☎718/782-5188, ⓦwww.galapagosartspace.com) is another strong bet: a longtime fixture on Williamsburg's performance scene, Galapagos moved to DUMBO in summer 2008, turning an old stable into the city's first "green" cultural venue, complete with an indoor lake. Programming includes performance art and rock music as well as literary events and experimental film.

To savor what's left of DUMBO's old-fashioned grit, head to **Gleason's Gym** (77 Front St, 2nd floor; ☎718/797-2872, ⓦwww.gleasonsgym.net), where tomorrow's prizefighters train. Gleason's, first established in Manhattan in 1937, has coached everyone from Jake LaMotta to Muhammad Ali; drop by on a Saturday before 2pm or on a weekday after 5pm for the best chance of catching a practice bout (for a $10 entrance fee). Once-a-month fights cost $20 (call for schedule).

Brooklyn Heights

Brooklyn Heights is one of New York City's most beautiful and historical neighborhoods and still the borough's most coveted zip code. The best trains are the #A or #C to High Street, the #2 or #3 to Clark Street, or the #N or #R to Court Street. If you're already in the Fulton Ferry District, walk up the hill on Everit or Henry streets. The Brooklyn Historical Society (see p.224) provides a very useful walking-tour map, also available at the Brooklyn Tourism and Visitors Center (see p.33).

Downtown bankers and financiers began building brownstones here in the early nineteenth century, while writers flocked to the Heights after the subway opened in 1908; W.H. Auden, Carson McCullers, Truman Capote, Tennessee Williams, Norman Mailer, and Paul and Jane Bowles (pre-Morocco) all lived in the neighborhood. Although many single-family brownstones were divided into apartments during the 1960s and 1970s and the streets now feel fairly cosmopolitan – if a bit frumpier than you'd expect given what it costs to live here – Brooklyn Heights today is in many ways not much different from how it was a hundred years ago.

The north edge, along Henry Street and Columbia Heights, is the oldest part of the neighborhood, where blocks are lined with Federal-style brick buildings. However, it's actually the unassuming wooden structure at **24 Middagh St** (at the corner of Willow), erected in 1824, that is the area's longest-standing house. Two streets south, on Orange between Hicks and Henry, the simple **Plymouth Church of the Pilgrims** went up in the mid-nineteenth century and became famous as the preaching base of **Henry Ward Beecher**, abolitionist and campaigner for women's rights. His fiery orations drew men like Horace Greeley and Abraham Lincoln, and Mark Twain based *Innocents Abroad* on travels with the church's social group. The building was also a stop on the Underground Railroad, where slaves were hidden on their way to freedom. Fitting then, that in 1963, Martin Luther King Jr delivered an early version of his "I Have a Dream" speech here. These days, you can see the interior only when a service is in progress.

Continuing south on Henry, you soon reach **Pierrepont Street**, which is studded with fine brownstones. One block east of Henry, at the corner of Pierrepoint and Monroe Place, look in if you can on the **First Unitarian Church**, notable for its exquisite neo-Gothic interior, built in 1844. Across the street at no. 128, the **Brooklyn Historical Society** (Wed–Sun noon–5pm; $6, students and seniors $4, under 12 free; T718/222-4111, Wwww.brooklyn history.org) investigates the borough's neighborhoods, architecture, ecology, and subcultures with changing exhibits. Just down the street, **BRIC Rotunda Gallery**, 33 Clinton St, presents multimedia work by Brooklyn-based artists (Tues–Sat noon–6pm; T718/875-4047, Wwww.rotundagallery.org).

Walk back west on any street between Clark and Remsen to reach the **Promenade** (more formally known as the Esplanade), a pedestrian path with terrific views of the Statue of Liberty, downtown Manhattan's skyscrapers, and the Brooklyn Bridge.

Downtown Brooklyn

The core of **downtown Brooklyn** – an area bordered by (clockwise from north) Sands and Middagh streets, Flatbush Avenue, Atlantic Avenue, and Court Street – reflects the borough's split personality. While it still has touches of metropolitan grandeur and civic pride, for the most part it lacks Manhattan's sophistication, and in the past two decades much of the area has been transformed into an ill-planned assortment of ungainly office and academic buildings – the so-called **MetroTech Center** – linked by pedestrian streets devoid of life after the nine-to-five grind.

The situation is rapidly changing, though – since 2004 real estate interests have invested more than $9 billion. If everything that has been proposed is actually constructed, downtown Brooklyn will have 15,000 more residents, a huge shopping and entertainment complex, and a new greenspace by 2012. "If" is the operative word: though New York has so far escaped the real-estate slump that has engulfed the rest of the country, some investors are already scaling back their plans (see "The New Battle of Brooklyn," p.226).

The eastern edge of residential Brooklyn Heights is defined by **Cadman Plaza**, created after World War II when the city decided to move Brooklyn's elevated streetcars underground. Nowadays it hosts a farmers' market (Tues & Sat year-round, plus Thurs from April to mid-Dec). Just south of the plaza, at Court and Montague streets, stands the lovely, massive **State Supreme Court** (not actually the highest court in the state – that's the Court of Appeals in Albany), designed by the same architects who made the Empire State Building. Further south, the Greek-style **Borough Hall**, 209 Joralemon St, looks tiny in comparison; it was erected in 1849, then topped with its odd cupolated belfry near the end of the century. Step inside to snag some local papers, maps, and brochures from the **Brooklyn Tourism and Visitors Center** (Mon–Fri 10am–6pm; ☎718/802-3846, ⓦwww.visitbrooklyn.org).

New York Transit Museum

Two blocks south of Borough Hall, on the corner of Boerum Place and Schermerhorn Street, the **New York Transit Museum** (Tues–Fri 10am–4pm, Sat & Sun noon–5pm; $5, children and seniors $3; ☎718/694-1600, ⓦwww.mta .info/mta/museum) is housed underground in the refurbished Court Street shuttle station from the 1930s. Exhibits include antique turnstiles, restored subway and "el" (elevated) train cars, maps, models, and photographs.

Fort Greene

Cross over chaotic Flatbush Avenue, and Fulton Street will bring you into the heart of **Fort Greene**, a historically African-American neighborhood that withstood the dark days of the 1970s and 80s better than most places in Brooklyn and is now quite prosperous, thanks in part to director Spike Lee, who gave the place a vote of confidence when he set up his production company here 22 years ago. The area is very easy to reach by subway: take any train to Atlantic Avenue or the #C to Lafayette Avenue.

If you are arriving on foot from the Fulton Mall, the first place you'll reach is **UrbanGlass**, 647 Fulton St (entrance at 57 Rockwell Place; ☎718/625-3685, ⓦwww.urbanglass.org), the East Coast's oldest and largest open glassworking studio. The studio hosts five-yearly open houses, during which you can tour the facility, watch glass-blowing demonstrations, and try your hand at glassworking (call for schedule and reservations). If you can't make an open house, drop by the **gallery** (daily 10am–6pm) to see works of art in glass.

Right next door is the BAM Harvey Theater, where the **Brooklyn Academy of Music** stages most of its plays, many with top-tier actors. Ian McKellan, Patrick Stewart, and Cate Blanchett have all performed here in the past few years. The interior has been preserved in a state of glamorous pseudo-decay. Turn south on Ashland Place to reach BAM's main building – the 1908 opera house, 30 Lafayette Ave, with its colorful terra-cotta cornice and undulating glass canopy (☎718/636-4100, ⓦwww.bam.org). Brooklyn's most acclaimed cultural center, BAM hosts (in addition to theater) opera, dance, classical music, and film of both the independent and art-house varieties. The swanky, glittering *BAMcafé*, on the second floor of the opera house, offers free live music – jazz, blues, R&B – every Friday and Saturday night from 9.30pm until around midnight.

Sharing the block with BAM is the **Williamsburgh Savings Bank Tower**, Brooklyn's tallest building (for now; see box, p.226) and its most iconic. Built in

1927 but only recently turned into luxury condos, it stands 512feet (34 stories) tall and sports one of the biggest four-sided clocks in the world, each face measuring 27feet in diameter.

Walk east on Hanson Place to the intersection with South Portland Avenue, where the **Museum of Contemporary African Diasporan Arts**, 80 Hanson Place, has made its new home (Wed–Sun 11am–6pm; $4; ☎718/230-0492, ⓦ www.mocada.org). The gallery space is small, but the three multimedia exhibits mounted there every year are provocative, taking on issues like race, class, and police violence. There's also a fine gift shop. Continue north on South Portland and you'll soon come to one of the prettiest blocks in all of New York City – South Portland Avenue between Lafayette and DeKalb avenues, which is lined with stately brownstones and brick townhouses with high stoops under a lush canopy of trees. The annual Fort Greene House Tour in early May allows you to peek inside several residences, gardens, and artists' studios (☎718/875-1855, ⓦ www.historicfortgreene.org).

South Portland Avenue dead-ends at **Fort Greene Park**, designed by Frederick Law Olmsted and Calvert Vaux in 1867, and named after Revolutionary War general Nathaniel Greene. Seventy years later, Walt Whitman, as editor of the *Brooklyn Eagle*, urged that the space be turned into parkland, a "lung" for the growing borough. At the park's summit, the 148-foot **Prison Ship Martyrs Monument** (1908) commemorates the estimated 11,500 Americans who died in the floating prison camps maintained by the British during the Revolutionary War. Sixteen squalid ships, rife with smallpox, were moored in old Wallabout Bay (just offshore from what's now the Brooklyn Navy Yard). The bones of the dead, collected as they washed ashore for decades after, are housed in a small crypt at the base of the tower.

Continue east on Dekalb until you get to Clermont Street, then turn right and continue one block to Lafayette, where the 1909 **Brooklyn Masonic Temple** (317 Clermont St, ☎718/638-1256, ⓦ www.masonicboom.com) rises up like a fortress. Masons no longer meet here, but hipsters do, with indie bands and DJs plying the renovated theater. The schoolyard across the street from the temple hosts the **Brooklyn Flea** (ⓦ www.brownstoner.com /brooklynflea) on Sundays from 10am to 5pm rain or shine, with about two hundred vendors selling all manner of vintage goods. A growing army of

The new Battle of Brooklyn: Atlantic Yards

In a borough rampant with real estate development, no single project is as huge or as controversial as the one known as **Atlantic Yards**. First proposed by Cleveland developer Forest City Ratner in December 2003, the development initially called for the building of sixteen skyscrapers and a Frank Gehry–designed arena for the New Jersey Nets basketball team, all crammed onto a parcel only one and a half times the size of the World Trade Center site. Few disputed that the railyards that separated Fort Greene and Prospect Heights (p.235) needed *some* sort of makeover, but Atlantic Yards was deemed way over the top – upon completion, it would form the densest Census tract in America.

Residents of the surrounding neighborhoods rebelled with an ongoing series of protests and lawsuits disputing, among other things, the environmental impact of the project (thousands more cars and people, but no additional schools or hospitals), but the slowing economy was what finally tripped up Ratner. In spring 2008 he was forced to admit that it was too risky to build anything but the stadium and three stubby glass towers around it on the eastern corner of the site (near the intersection of Flatbush and Atlantic avenues) until market conditions improve.

food carts serve *pupusas*, Belgian waffles, organic ice cream, and other treats. From January to March a smaller version of the Flea continues indoors; visit the website for location.

South Brooklyn

The neighborhoods of **Cobble Hill**, **Boerum Hill**, and **Carroll Gardens**, along with the former industrial zone along the **Gowanus Canal** and the wharves of **Red Hook**, make up the area traditionally known as **South Brooklyn** – confusing, because geographically, much of the borough is actually south of this area. Until 1894, however, this was the southern border of the city of Brooklyn, so the term has stuck. The most popular areas to visit here are Court and Smith streets, which run north–south through Cobble Hill and Carroll Gardens. They're lined with some of Brooklyn's best boutiques and – on Smith Street in particular – places to dine (see Chapter 25, "Restaurants," for reviews). If industrial decay is more your style, don't miss the Gowanus Canal and Red Hook, both of which have active art scenes.

The #F or #G to Bergen Street deposits you on the border between Cobble Hill and Carroll Gardens; the Carroll Street stop on the same lines leaves you at the southern end of Carroll Gardens, closest to Gowanus and a bus ride (or long walk) to Red Hook. If you're walking here from Brooklyn Heights, simply continue on Court Street; this artery runs from downtown through South Brooklyn and all the way to Red Hook.

Cobble Hill and Boerum Hill

Just south of Atlantic Avenue, the main east–west streets through **Cobble Hill** – Amity, Congress, and Warren – are a mix of brownstones and red-brick rowhouses built between the 1840s and the 1880s. **Court Street** is the neighborhood's main commercial artery, with lots of cute shops and a few cafés. Restaurants and bars are more abundant on slightly grittier **Smith Street**, which caters to a younger crowd.

South on Clinton Street, which runs parallel to Court Street one block west, sits the idyllic little **Cobble Hill Park**. Along the park's southern border is a cobblestone alleyway – **Verandah Place**, a renovated mews built in the 1850s. Writer Thomas Wolfe lived in the basement at no. 40 in the 1930s and described the apartment in his novel *You Can't Go Home Again*: "Here, in winter, the walls …sweat continuously with clammy drops of water. Here, in summer, it is he who does the sweating."

Living conditions weren't nearly so dismal in the nearby **Home Buildings**, a tidy row of red-brick cottages lining a pedestrian mews, Warren Place. Built in 1878 as utopian workers' housing, the 44 homes are each only eleven feet wide.

East of Cobble Hill, **Boerum Hill** is less architecturally impressive than its neighbor, though it has its share of sober Greek Revival and Italianate buildings, developed around the same period, as well as some lovely gardens and trees.

Carroll Gardens and Gowanus

As you walk south along Court Street, Cobble Hill blends into **Carroll Gardens** around DeGraw Street. Built as a middle and upper-class community

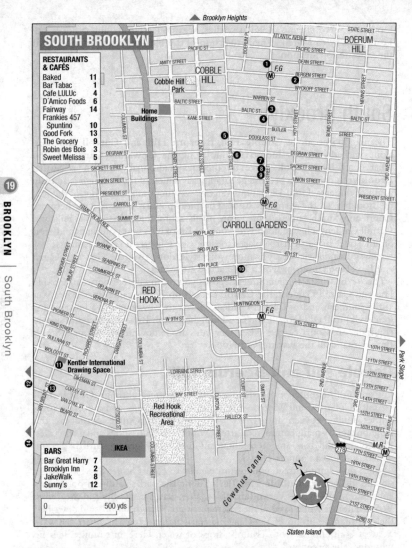

SOUTH BROOKLYN

RESTAURANTS & CAFÉS

Baked	**11**
Bar Tabac	**1**
Cafe LULUc	**4**
D'Amico Foods	**6**
Fairway	**14**
Frankies 457 Spuntino	**10**
Good Fork	**13**
The Grocery	**9**
Robin des Bois	**3**
Sweet Melissa	**5**

BARS

Bar Great Harry	**7**
Brooklyn Inn	**2**
JakeWalk	**8**
Sunny's	**12**

0   500 yds

between 1869 and 1884, this part of South Brooklyn has been an Italian enclave since dockworkers arrived here in the early 1900s; **Al Capone** is said to have been married in 1918 at the Saint Mary Star of the Sea Church on Court Street. The area was later named for Charles Carroll, the only Roman Catholic to sign the Declaration of Independence.

Many of the neighborhood's older Italian residents have moved out to Staten Island and New Jersey, but you'll still find a few classic pizza parlors, pastry shops, and red-sauce joints alongside the hipper new places on Court Street and on Union Street between Henry and Columbia streets. This section of Union is the main commercial drag of the **Columbia Street Waterfront District**, a perpetually up-and-coming district of shops and restaurants that forms the gateway to grittier Red Hook further south. Don't expect Brooklyn Heights esplanade, however; the waterfront here is still an active loading and unloading area for deep-sea container ships and, since 2006, cruise ships, with very limited public access.

Gowanus

The southeast edge of Carroll Gardens is defined by the **Gowanus Canal**, a name that inspires a bit of a shudder in older Brooklynites. Originally a wetlands area famous for its oysters, it became a fetid stillwater around 1870, thanks to sewers from Park Slope that drained here and oil refineries that sat along its banks. In 1999, however, city engineers finally repaired the drain pump so water could flow freely through the canal and into Gowanus Bay, and the canal now supports a surprising amount of marine life, including shrimp and oysters, as well as a burgeoning art and nightlife scene.

The **Gowanus Dredgers Canoe Club** (℡718/243-0849, ⓦwww .waterfrontmuseum.org/dredgers) runs free canoe tours of the canal from March through October, starting at Second Street at Bond; walking and bike trips along the banks are an option for anyone still leery of the water. The tongue-and-cheek *Gowanus Yacht Club*, 323 Smith St at President, has long been the Dredgers' go-to spot for an outdoor brew and hot dog after a weekend paddle, but it's actually in Carroll Gardens, not Gowanus proper. Over toward Third Avenue, panini specialist *Bar Tano*, 457 3rd Ave at 9th St, is a welcoming outpost in a rather-grim area – or the first wave of gentrification, depending on how you look at it (℡718/499-3400, ⓦwww.bartano.com).

Red Hook

Though only a half-mile from the Columbia Street Waterfront District, **Red Hook** feels oddly like the outskirts of a city in the Deep South, a place where hulking red-brick warehouses crumble along the waterfront while, inland, two- and three-story apartment buildings share cobblestoned blocks with garden centers and car-repair shops. Along the main strip, **Van Brunt Street**, is a handful of quirky boutiques, restaurants, and cafés where the service is almost universally relaxed and friendly.

No subway line goes out to Red Hook, but it's easy enough to reach by bus. Take the #B61 bus from Columbia Street in Cobble Hill or the #B77 bus from Smith and 9th streets in Carroll Gardens. **New York Water Taxi** (℡212/742-1969, ⓦwww.nywatertaxi.com) also runs a free weekend ferry service from Pier 11 in Manhattan to **Ikea**, at the southern tip of Red Hook; boats leave and arrive every 40min.

Settled by the Dutch in 1636, Red Hook got its name from the color of the soil and the shape of the land, which forms a corner, or *hoek*, where the Upper New York Bay meets the Gowanus Bay. It eventually became one of the busiest and toughest shipping centers in the US, inspiring Elia Kazan's film *On the Waterfront* and Arthur Miller's play *A View from the Bridge*. Some say that urban planner **Robert Moses** deliberately severed the notoriously crime-ridden neighborhood from the rest of Brooklyn when he routed the Brooklyn-Queens Expressway down Hicks Street in 1954. In any case, by the 1960s, the increasing automation of the docking industry left longshoremen out of work and sent most of the freighters from Red Hook to bigger ports in New Jersey.

Red Hook's waterfront is now a curious assemblage of abandoned and repurposed warehouses and parkland. Head down Van Dyke Street to Pier 41, where at *Steve's Authentic Key Lime Pies*, 204 Van Dyke St, you can pick up a four-inch tart made with fresh-squeezed juice ($4) and eat it with a spoon as you wander

▲ Red Hook

the area (☎718/858-5333, ⓦwww.stevesauthentic.com). From the end of the
pier Governors Island appears almost within wading distance and Lady Liberty
seems to raise her torch just for you. Nearby, the **Waterfront Museum and
Showboat Barge** (Thurs 4–8pm; donation requested; ☎718/624-4719, ⓦwww
.waterfrontmuseum.org) presents historical exhibits and occasional children's
shows in a restored railroad barge moored off a small park at the end of Conover
Street. Adjacent **Fairway**, 480–500 Van Brunt St, is Brooklyn's best supermarket,
with a staggering selection of produce and gourmet goodies like olives, cheese,
and smoked fish. Thread your way to the back, where there's a reasonably priced
café with waterfront seating (see review p.303). In the warehouse across the street
from Fairway, the **Brooklyn Waterfront Artists Coalition (BWAC)**, 499 Van
Brunt St, holds three group shows per year, on weekends from mid-May to
mid-June, from late July to mid-August, and from late September to late October
(☎718/596-2507, ⓦwww.bwac.org). The other gallery of note in the area is
Kentler International Drawing Space, 353 Van Brunt St, which as its name

suggests displays fine works on paper by artists worldwide (Thurs–Sun noon–5pm; ☎718/875-2098, Ⓦwww.kentlergallery.org).

There are a couple of good cafés and restaurants in the neighborhood (see Listings), but if you're in Red Hook on a summer weekend it's a tradition to eat at the **Red Hook Recreational Area** (aka the Red Hook ballfields), where Latinos gather for ultra-competitive soccer in the shadow of a long string of linked grain silos and a dozen or so food-stands dole out delicious tacos, tamales, ceviche, *pupusas*, *huaraches*, and more. To reach the fields, head east on Van Dyke Street.

Prospect Park and around

Where Brooklyn really surpasses itself is on Flatbush Avenue in the vicinity of **Grand Army Plaza**, an elegant, if congested, traffic circle around a stately memorial arch. The plaza faces the **Brooklyn Public Library** and the entrance to **Prospect Park**, and immediately east of it on Eastern Parkway, the **Brooklyn Museum** houses, among other things, an excellent ancient Egyptian trove and the **Brooklyn Botanic Garden** teems with greenery. The plaza also

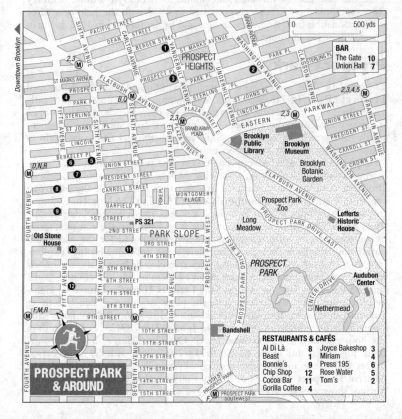

RESTAURANTS & CAFÉS
Al Di Là	8	Joyce Bakeshop	3
Beast	1	Miriam	4
Bonnie's	9	Press 195	6
Chip Shop	12	Rose Water	5
Cocoa Bar	11	Tom's	2
Gorilla Coffee	4		

BAR
| The Gate | 10 |
| Union Hall | 7 |

acts as a border to several very different neighborhoods, including up-and-coming **Prospect Heights** and the serene liberal bastion of **Park Slope**. The Grand Army Plaza stop on the #2 and #3 subway line is the most central for the arch, while the museum has its own stop just a few blocks farther down the line. The #B and #Q trains to Prospect Park get you closest to the park's main attractions, while Park Slope's chief subway stops are the #F to 7th Avenue/9th Street and the #R to 4th Avenue/Union Street.

Grand Army Plaza

Central Park architects Frederick Law Olmsted and Calvert Vaux designed **Grand Army Plaza** in the 1860s and 1870s as an approach to Prospect Park, but it didn't take on its current grandeur until the end of that century. The 80ft-tall triumphal **Soldiers' and Sailors' Memorial Arch**, modeled on Paris's Arc de Triomphe, a tribute to the Union victory in the Civil War, was unveiled in 1892.

Saturday is by far the best day to visit the plaza, when dozens of farmers from New York and New Jersey set up stalls here at the city's second-largest **Green-market** (year-round 8am–4pm). At the height of summer, expect to find bounteous fresh produce, meats, flowers, jams, pickles, and syrups, along with occasional cooking demonstrations. The wintertime selection can be a bit thin, but you can always get a crunchy apple, a doughnut, and a steaming cup of cider.

On the east side of the plaza, the immense **Brooklyn Public Library** (Ⓦ www.brooklynpubliclibrary.org), started in 1912 with the help of a $1.6-million donation from Andrew Carnegie and finally finished in 1941, is just as grand, although a bit more serene.

Prospect Park

Energized by their success with Central Park, Olmsted and Vaux landscaped **Prospect Park** (Ⓣ 718/965-8951, Ⓦ www.prospectpark.org) in the early 1860s. Its 585 acres include a 60-acre lake on the east side, a 90-acre open meadow on the west, and a circular 3.35-mile park drive around the periphery, primarily reserved for runners, cyclists, and rollerbladers (vehicular traffic is allowed during weekday rush hours only).

Despite attractions that have sprung up over the years – an Audubon Center, a tennis center, an ice-skating rink (Nov–March), and the popular Celebrate Brooklyn outdoor music festival – Prospect Park remains for the most part remarkably bucolic. The **Audubon Center** (April to late Nov Thurs–Sun & holidays noon–5pm, rest of the year weekends and school holidays noon–4pm, Ⓣ 718/287-3400), in the Boathouse at mid-park on the east side, serves as the park's main visitor center as well as the trailhead for the park's four nature trails; there's also a pleasant café here, some well-done ecology exhibits, free wi-fi, and the dock for the *Independence*, an electric boat that spins around the lake on 25-minute tours from April to October ($6, $3 children 3–12, under 3 free). Nearby, tour guides at the **Lefferts Historic House**, an eighteenth-century Dutch farmhouse, use the place as a prop to talk (mostly to children) about what Brooklyn was like in the 1820s (April–Nov Thurs–Sun noon–5pm, Dec–March Sat–Sun noon–4pm; Ⓣ 718/789-2822). Just south of the house stands a 1912 **carousel** (April–Oct Thurs–Sun & holidays noon–5pm, July–Aug until 6pm; $1.50; Ⓣ 718/282-7789) with 51 hand-carved horses and other animals; it was originally installed at Coney Island. The adjacent **Prospect Park Zoo**, run by the venerable Wildlife Conservation Society, showcases sea lions, kangaroos, red pandas, poisonous frogs, baboons,

▲ Prospect Park

and sundry other fauna in natural-looking habitats (April–Oct daily 10am–5pm; Nov–March 10am–4.30pm; $6, children 3–12 $2; ⊤718/399-7339, ⓦwww.prospectparkzoo.org).

For less-structured fun, head to the **Drummers' Grove** near the Parkside and Ocean Avenue entrance on the southeast corner of the park; the crowd that gathers on Sunday afternoons is no amateur circle – some very accomplished musicians have been jamming here for decades. The **Celebrate Brooklyn** concert series likewise draws top-notch musical and dance talent to its summer series of outdoor concerts, held at the **Bandshell**, just off Prospect Park West at 10th St ($3 donation requested; ⊤718/855-7882, ⓦwww.celebratebrooklyn.org).

The Brooklyn Museum

East of Grand Army Plaza and the Public Library stands the imposing **Brooklyn Museum**, 200 Eastern Parkway (Wed–Fri 10am–5pm, Sat & Sun 11am–6pm, first Sat of every month until 11pm; suggested donation $8, students and seniors $4; ⊤718/638-5000, ⓦwww.brooklynmuseum.org). If you're coming by subway, take the #2 or #3 train to Eastern Parkway.

Designed by McKim, Mead, and White, it's second only to the Metropolitan Museum of Art in terms of exhibit space in New York City, with five floors of galleries. The museum is best known for its distinguished store of Egyptian relics but has recently won acclaim for adding a feminist art wing that includes Judy Chicago's ground-breaking 1970s installation, *The Dinner Party*, and hosting blockbuster shows such as a 2008 retrospective of work by Japanese pop artist Takashi Murakami. The museum's regular schedule of talks, arts-and-crafts demonstrations, and performances are best experienced via the free **First Saturdays** program, held on the first Saturday evening of each month. On these nights, the museum stays open until 11pm (admission is free after 5pm), transforming itself into a vast all-ages party with live music and often raucous dancing.

The collection

Just inside the front entrance stands a changing selection of a dozen bronze sculptures by Auguste Rodin. But the highlight of the first floor is the museum's collection of 5000 works of **African Art**, representing fifty cultures over a 2500-year span; particularly splendid is a sixteenth-century ivory gong from Benin.

The second floor is dedicated to the **Asian and Islamic galleries**, with pieces from China, Korea, India, and Japan, as well as Ottoman Turkish and Qajar Persian textiles, mosaics, manuscripts, and jewelry. Don't miss the ferocious *Head of a Guardian* from thirteenth-century Japan.

The delicately carved stone "Brooklyn Black Head" of the Ptolemaic period, arguably the museum's crown jewel, is one of 1200 objects in the authoritative **Ancient Egyptian Art** collection – one of the largest outside of Egypt – on the third floor. Sarcophagi and sculptures are nicely complemented by small galleries of Assyrian, Sumerian, and other ancient Middle Eastern art. On the same floor, "About Time: 700 Years of European Painting" presents a non-chronological array of **European work** from *The Adoration of the Magi* (c.1480) by Milanese artist Bernardo Butanone to Monet's *Houses of Parliament*.

One floor up, most of the **Decorative Arts collection** is in six evocative **period rooms**, including a nineteenth-century Moorish smoking room from John D. Rockefeller's estate.

On the fifth floor, Georgia O'Keeffe's sensual 1948 paean to the borough, *Brooklyn Bridge*, opens the somewhat uneven "American Identities" permanent exhibition, which draws thematic connections among works in the museum's extremely varied **Painting and Sculpture** collection. Also on the fifth floor is the **Elizabeth A. Sackler Center for Feminist Art**, inaugurated in March 2007. It contains changing exhibits of contemporary art by women as well as **The Dinner Party**, a massive triangular dinner table with custom-made China place settings for 39 famous women. Constructed in 1974–79 by artist Judy Chicago and hundreds of volunteers, it's an impressive and moving display, even if the explanatory timeline – or "herstory" – in the adjoining gallery feels a bit dated.

The Brooklyn Botanic Garden

Located just behind the museum, the **Brooklyn Botanic Garden**, 900 Washington Ave, is one of the most enticing park spaces in the city (March–Oct Tues–Fri 8am–6pm, Sat, Sun & holidays 10am–6pm; Nov–Feb Tues–Fri 8am–4.30pm, Sat, Sun & holidays 10am–4.30pm; $8, students and seniors $4, free Tues, Sat before noon, Nov–Feb weekdays, seniors free Fri; T718/623-7200, W www.bbg.org). Plants from around the world occupy 22 gardens and exhibits spread over 52 acres, all sumptuous but not overmanicured. What you'll see depends largely on the season. March brings color to Daffodil Hill, while April sees the cherry trees bloom in the Japanese Garden, designed in 1914 and the oldest garden of its kind outside of Japan. The Rose Garden starts to flourish in the early summer, the elaborate water-lily ponds are at their best in late summer and early autumn, and the fall colors in the Rock Garden are striking. A winter visit lets you enjoy the warmth of the Steinhardt Conservatory, filled with orchids, tropical plants, palms, the largest collection of bonsai trees in the West, and a lovely lower-level gallery for art inspired by nature. A gift shop stocks a wide array of exotic plants, bulbs, and seeds, and there is a pleasant outdoor café.

Park Slope

The western exits of Prospect Park leave you in **Park Slope**, a district of stately nineteenth-century brownstones inhabited since the 1970s by a notoriously liberal crew of urban pioneers; it's also in an eternal baby boom, and strollers jam the sidewalks, especially on weekends. The most central subway station is the Seventh Avenue stop on the #F line (the cross street is 9th St), but you can also walk down Fifth or Sixth avenues from the Bergen Street stop on the #2 and #3 trains.

The tree-lined blocks between Prospect Park West and Eighth Avenue from Union to 15th Street contain some of the finest Romanesque and Queen Anne residences in the US, helping this area earn the nickname "The Gold Coast of Brooklyn." Almost all the buildings were constructed in the 1880s and 1890s, but they're hardly uniform, displaying a fine array of building materials (brick, brownstone, and granite in various combinations) and details, from original gaslights to turrets and bay windows. **Seventh Avenue** is the Slope's traditional main drag, lined with all the essentials, from florists and wine shops to cafés and boutiques, but it can feel a bit frumpy. These days you'll find a younger crowd, along with trendier shops, bars, and restaurants, on **Fifth Avenue**.

Though they are now far outnumbered by straight couples, lesbians have flocked to Park Slope since the 1970s, and there are still a couple of lesbian bars in the neighborhood (see Chapter 29, "Gay and lesbian New York," for hangouts). The **Brooklyn Pride Festival & Parade**, a community-oriented, relatively noncommercial event, takes place every June. Older festival-goers say it resembles New York Pride in its early days.

You can learn about the Slope's history at the **Old Stone House** in J.J. Byrne Park, Fifth Ave at 3rd St (Sat–Sun noon–4pm; $3; ℡718/768-3195, ⓦwww .historichousetrust.org), famous as the site of one of the most dramatic skirmishes of the Battle of Brooklyn and the first headquarters of the Brooklyn Dodgers baseball team. It now contains changing exhibits and a diorama of the house as it looked in its early days.

Prospect Heights

Just north of Grand Army Plaza, **Prospect Heights** has seen a major wave of gentrification since 2000, with its handsome and varied late nineteenth-century residences now fetching prices rivaling those of nearby Park Slope. You could spend a pleasant hour or so walking up and down its lovely side streets, but its main appeal will likely be its **food and drink** options, which are within easy walking distance of the Brooklyn Museum and the Brooklyn Botanic Garden. See the listings on p.303 and p.336 or just head down **Vanderbilt Avenue**, where a new wine bar seems to open every other week.

Green-Wood Cemetery

Southwest of Prospect Park is the famed **Green-Wood Cemetery** (8am–4pm; ⓦwww.green-wood.com). You can walk here from Park Slope or take the #R train to 25th Street; the cemetery's main entrance is about a block away from the subway stop at Fifth Avenue.

Founded in 1838 and almost as large as Prospect Park at 478 acres, Green-Wood was very much the place to be buried in the nineteenth century. Interred here are politician and crusading newspaper editor Horace Greeley; famed preacher Henry Ward Beecher; William Marcy "Boss" Tweed, Democratic chief and scoundrel; and the entire Steinway clan of piano fame, at peace in a 119-room mausoleum.

Central Brooklyn

The neighborhoods within **Central Brooklyn** – most notably **Bedford-Stuyvesant** and **Crown Heights**, to the northeast and east of Prospect Park – are far rougher than those in South Brooklyn, but they are worth a look for their architecture and street culture. Predominantly African-American, Bed-Stuy, as it's called, is experiencing a real-estate rush on its brownstones, and Crown Heights, with its Hasidic Jewish and West Indian populations, may not be far behind. Keep in mind that while the area is generally safe during the daytime, there's still some street crime, so remain alert.

Bedford-Stuyvesant

Immediately east of Clinton Hill, **Bedford-Stuyvesant** is the nation's largest black community after Chicago's South Side, with more than 400,000 residents. It stretches north–south from Flushing to Atlantic avenues, and east as far as Saratoga; its main arteries include Bedford and Nostrand avenues and Fulton Street. The **Nostrand Avenue** stop on the #C train lies closest to the center of the neighborhood.

Originally two separate areas, the adjacent districts of Bedford and Stuyvesant were populated by both blacks and whites in the nineteenth century. During the Great Migration between 1910 and 1920, large numbers of southern African Americans moved north and settled in this area. In the 1940s the white population began to leave, taking funding for many important community services with it. Economic decline continued for several decades, reaching an all-time low in the 1980s.

Weeksville

In the shadow of a housing project on the eastern reaches of Bed-Stuy, stands one of the most fascinating historical sights in Brooklyn – the remnants of the once-thriving town of **Weeksville**. Founded by African-American James Weeks in 1838 just eleven years after New York abolished slavery, Weeksville soon became a refuge for both escaped slaves from the South and free blacks fleeing racial violence in the North. By the 1860s it had its own schools and businesses, and had begun turning out some of the city's first black professionals. Weeksville existed until the 1930s, but an influx of Eastern European immigrants and a flurry of construction brought it to its end, and by the 1950s all but four wood-frame cottages from the town had been destroyed. Fortunately, in the 1960s local activists petitioned the city to preserve these, the so-called **Hunterfly Road Houses**, 1698 Bergen St between Buffalo and Rochester, and eventually open three of them to the public. Tour guides do an admirable job filling in atmosphere with stories about Weeksville, gleaned from ongoing research, oral histories, and archeological digs (Tues–Fri at 1, 2, and 3pm; Sat 11am–3pm; $4; ☎718/623-0600, ⓦwww.weeksvillesociety.org). To get to Weeksville, take the #A or #C train to Utica Avenue, walk four blocks south on Utica to Bergen, and turn left.

The poverty and neglect had an unintended upside: because few of its brown-stones were razed in the name of economic development, the neighborhood has the densest collection of pre-1900 homes in New York, attracting a fervent crowd of young fixer-uppers – both white and black – since around 2003.

Gothic, Victorian, and other classic brownstones abound, especially inside the **Stuyvesant Heights Historic District**, which includes parts of MacDonough, Macon, Decatur, Bainbridge, and Chauncey streets primarily between Tompkins and Stuyvesant avenues; an annual five-hour house tour is conducted in October (ⓦ www.brownstonersofbedstuy.org). Just a couple of blocks away from the district, the café *Common Grounds*, 376 Tompkins at Putnam, serves espresso drinks and tasty Belgian waffles (ⓣ 718/484-4368).

Crown Heights

South of Bedford-Stuyvesant and east of Prospect Heights is thrumming **Crown Heights**, bounded by Atlantic Avenue and Empire Boulevard to the north and south, and Ralph and Washington avenues to the east and west. This community is home to the largest **West Indian** community in New York as well as an active, established population of about ten thousand **Hasidic Jews**, most of them belonging to the Russian Lubavitcher sect.

Eastern Parkway, the large throughway that runs past the Brooklyn Museum, is the main traffic artery of Crown Heights, and landscaped walkways on either side of the path provide much-needed green space. The Hasidic community has a strong presence with the glitzy **Jewish Children's Museum**, on Eastern Parkway at Kingston Ave (Mon–Thurs 10am–4pm, Sun 10am–6pm; $10; ⓣ 718/907-8833, ⓦ www.jcmonline.org), which presents Jewish traditions with every bell and whistle possible, including an educational mini-golf course. North of Eastern Parkway, the **Brooklyn Children's Museum**, 145 Brooklyn Ave at St Mark's Ave, is slated to reopen in September 2008 after a major "green" renovation and expansion by Uruguayan architect Rafael Viñoly (ⓣ 718/735-4400, ⓦ www.brooklynkids.org). Founded in 1899, it was the city's first museum of its kind; galleries hold state-of-the-art hands-on exhibits concentrating on science, the arts, and the environment. The closest subway is the #3 to Kingston Avenue.

Over Labor Day weekend, Crown Heights hosts the annual **West Indian–American Day Parade and Carnival**, during which almost two million revelers dance, eat, and applaud colorful floats and steel-drum outfits. The parade, which organizers claim is the biggest in the nation, runs west along Eastern Parkway from Rochester Avenue in Crown Heights to Grand Army Plaza (see Chapter 33, "Parades and festivals," for more information). To get a taste of West Indian culture and cuisine year-round, take the #3 train to Nostrand Avenue, where there's a string of dirt-cheap Caribbean snack joints. Of these, *Imhotep Health and Vegan*, 734 Nostrand Ave at Park Place, and *Gloria's*, 745 Nostrand Ave at St John's Place, are both reliably good.

Coney Island and around

It's possible, in theory, to walk, rollerblade, or bike almost the entire southern **coast** of Brooklyn. On occasion, paths disappear, and you must share the service road off the highway with cars, but you'll never be on the highway itself. Even those of less sturdy stock will find this area – which stretches east from **Bay Ridge** through **Coney Island**, **Brighton Beach**, and several smaller neighborhoods all the way to maritime Sheepshead Bay – worth visiting for the breathtaking views, carnival amusements, and varied cuisine. If you're not on a bike or similarly speedy transport, though, you'll do best to focus on Brighton Beach and adjacent Coney Island, which make an easy afternoon trip by subway.

Bay Ridge

The last few stops of the #R train are in Bay Ridge, in the farthest corner of southwest Brooklyn. This large, quiet neighborhood is known for its ethnic mix (Chinese, Irish, Italians, Scandinavians, and Lebanese) and good schools; senior citizens, many of them longtime residents, make up a large chunk of the population.

The main reason to visit Bay Ridge is to ride the **Shore Road Bike Path**, which offers a glorious ride along the bay, including views of the shimmering **Verrazano Narrows Bridge** (1964), which flashes its minimalist message across the entrance to New York Bay. At 4260ft, this slender, beautiful span was, until Britain's Humber Bridge opened in 1981, the world's longest. The bridge, which connects Brooklyn to Staten Island (p.266), is named for the first European explorer of New York Harbor, Giovanni da Verrazano. You can't pedal across it, unfortunately: urban planner Robert Moses vetoed the pedestrian/ bicycle pathways that flanked the roadway in the original design for fear they'd lead to a rash of suicides.

To reach the bike path, get off the #R train at Bay Ridge Avenue (locals know it as 69th St) and ride west toward the water (if you are on foot, the #B1 and #B9 buses can take you this way). At the pier, a path leads south right along the water's edge, but to see some of Bay Ridge's nicest homes, turn left before the water on Shore Road. Wind through Shore, Narrows, and River roads between 75th and 83rd streets, where you'll see some Greek and Gothic Revival houses. Most distinctive is the **Gingerbread House** (8220 Narrows Ave at 83rd St); the 1916 structure, done in a rare style known as Black Forest Art Nouveau, looks like a witch's backwoods lair, all piled-up stones and drooping eaves.

A bit less pastoral but still worth a visit, the **US Army Garrison Fort Hamilton** is a historic military base at 101st Street and Fort Hamilton Parkway. The **Harbor Defense Museum** of Fort Hamilton (Mon–Fri 10am–4pm, Sat 10am–2pm; free; ☎718/630-4349, ⓦ www.harbordefensemuseum.com) is in an 1840 stone structure once used to protect the fort from any possible rear attack. Artifacts and weapons – guns, mines, missiles, cannons – tell the official history of the defense of New York Harbor.

Coney Island

Accessible to anyone for the price of a subway ride (take the #D, #F, #N, or #Q train to the last stop at Stillwell Avenue), beachfront **Coney Island** has given working-class New Yorkers a holiday ever since a kerosene-lit carousel opened here in 1867. A series of fabulous amusement parks drew huge crowds on hot summer days over the years until the 1960s, when the area fell into slow decline, only to be adopted and re-popularized by a hip crowd of historians and artists drawn to its retro charm in the 1990s.

While Coney's down-at-the-heel days may be numbered (see box opposite), it remains, as of summer 2008, a delightfully seedy place to spend an afternoon

A Corporate Coney Island?

Since the cleanup in Times Square in the 1990s, Coney Island has stood as the city's last great outpost of borderline-seedy, honky-tonk commercialism. But whether its ramshackle charm will remain intact in coming years is unclear: a local developer, Thor Equities, bought up big swathes of the district in 2006 and wants to build a billion-dollar **Vegas-style resort** on the boardwalk, complete with luxury condos and "entertainment retail." Community leaders raised a predictable fuss, arguing that a national treasure would be lost in the corporate makeover, and the city agreed (sort of), finally presenting, in April 2008, a proposal to buy about nine acres of the historic amusement zone and "**bling it up**" with year-round attractions like a glass-enclosed water park, bowling alley, movie theaters, and a House of Blues club – measures ultimately deemed less offensive than Thor's. While the plan was being reviewed, Thor declared the 2008 season the "Summer of Hope," mounting a Coney Island-style sideshow with a hundred-pound rat and the world's smallest woman, hoping to curry favor with locals (who protested the show on its opening day). However the development shapes up, Coney Island's most iconic features – its wooden boardwalk, roller-coaster, Ferris wheel, hot dog stand, baseball park, and museum – will remain intact.

or evening. Most rides and attractions are open daily only from late May to early September, with weekend hours in the spring and fall, though "Captain Bob," a former Belize jungle guide, conducts **historical walking tours** of the area every weekend year-round starting at *Nathan's* hot dog stand at the corner of Stillwell and Surf Avenues (noon & 2pm; $12 per person; ☏718/907-0315; Ⓦwww.captainbob.8k.com). If you can, visit Coney Island on a Friday night during the season, when the beach is lit up by an impressive **fireworks** display. The raucous annual **Mermaid Parade** (Ⓦwww.coneyislandusa.com) in mid-to late June ranks as one of the oddest, glitziest small-town festivals in the country, where participants dress (barely) as mermaids, King Neptunes, and other sea-dwellers.

Upon arrival, head straight for the aforementioned **Nathan's**, on the corner of Surf Avenue, when you get off the subway. This is the home of the "famous Coney Island hot dog," and even if you'd otherwise skip this all-American delicacy, only vegetarians have an excuse for missing it here. *Nathan's* holds a well-attended annual **Hot Dog Eating Contest** on July 4; in a surprise upset, Californian Joey Chestnut trounced slender repeat-champion Takeru "Tsunami" Kobayashi of Japan in 2007 by eating 66 hot dogs in just twelve minutes – twelve more than the previous world record. One block from *Nathan's* is the famous **boardwalk**, where hip-hop blares from boom boxes and loudspeakers, and the language of choice is Spanish or Russian as often as English.

Though the amusement park area, inland of the boardwalk, is in flux, its two best rides – **the Wonder Wheel and the Cyclone** – aren't going anywhere. Of these, the **Wonder Wheel** ($6; ☏718/372-2592, Ⓦwww.wonderwheel.com) is a must. An official New York City landmark, the 1920 ride is the world's tallest Ferris wheel aside from the London Eye. From the top you get panoramic views of Coney Island and the ocean. Far scarier, the **Cyclone** roller coaster ($5; ☏718/265-2100, Ⓦwww.astroland.com), a creaky wooden contraption more than 80 years old, is not for the faint of heart – as you wait in the snaking line, you can actually see the cars lose contact with the metal rails at one point. Sit in front for the most terrifying view, in back for an extra-strong sense of vertigo.

Another great summer attraction is **KeySpan Park**, on Surf Avenue between West 17th and 19th streets, the scenic oceanside baseball-stadium that has

▲ The Cyclone, Coney Island

helped lend a more prosperous air to the neighborhood. The park is home to the **Brooklyn Cyclones** (see p.404), a New York Mets-affiliated minor-league team that draws a dedicated crowd. Seating is intimate, beer flows freely, and tickets start at just $7.

Coney Island Museum and New York Aquarium

East of Stillwell Avenue, the nonprofit **Coney Island Museum**, 1208 Surf Ave (Fri & Sat noon–5pm; 99¢; ☎718/372-5159, Ⓦwww.coneyislandusa.com), is one indoor destination you don't want to miss. You can tour relics of Coney Island past, hear a lecture on the beach's history, or catch a night-time burlesque performance or film screening. **Sideshows by the Seashore**, on W 12th St at Surf Ave, is a 45-minute show featuring sword-swallowers, contortionists, fire-eaters, glass walkers, and other skillful masochists (late May to early Sept Fri 2–8pm, Sat–Sun & holidays 1–9pm; weekends only from Easter to Memorial Day and Sept; $7.50 adults, $5 children; no reservations).

Continue east on the boardwalk, halfway to Brighton Beach, to reach the seashell-shaped **New York Aquarium**, Surf Ave and W 8th St (June–Aug Mon–Fri 10am–6pm; weekends until 7pm; rest of the year closing times vary from 4.30pm to 5.30pm; $12, seniors $10, children 3–12 $9; ☎718/265-FISH, ⓦwww.nyaquarium.com), a top-of-the-line operation run by the Wildlife Conservation Society, which also administers New York's four excellent zoos. More than 8000 eye-grabbing creatures from all over the world live here in an array of indoor and outdoor tanks and pools. Especially worth seeing are the otherworldly jellies, corals, and anemones in the Alien Stingers Exhibit.

Brighton Beach

East along the boardwalk from Coney Island, at Brooklyn's southernmost end, **Brighton Beach** was once an affluent seaside resort of its own. Often called Little Odessa, it is now home to the country's largest community of immigrants from Russia and the former Soviet states, who started relocating here in the 1970s. The eldest of them pack the boardwalk benches to soak up the sun and gossip. Reach the neighborhood by riding the #B or #Q train to the Brighton Beach stop, or just walk down the boardwalk from Coney Island.

Brighton Beach Avenue runs parallel to the boardwalk; the street is a bustling mixture of Russian souvenir shops and **food emporiums**. Pick up picnic fixings at **M & I International**, 249 Brighton Beach Ave (☎718/615-1011), which has a staggering selection of smoked fish, sausages, cheeses, pickles (many soaked in vodka rather than vinegar), and breads. Sit-down food is also readily available at restaurants on the boardwalk, though you might want to wait until evening, when the **supper clubs** open up. These cavernous places offer a near-parody of a rowdy Russian night out, complete with lots of food, loud music, surreal floor shows, and plenty of vodka (see Restaurant listings, p.336, for reviews).

Northern Brooklyn

Northeast of downtown and past Fort Greene are the neighborhoods of **Williamsburg**, which is divided among artsy refugees from Manhattan and sections that are strongly Hasidic or Latino, and **Greenpoint**, a Polish stronghold that's being inundated by artsy refugees from Williamsburg. While short on typical tourist attractions, these districts are long on atmosphere, whether you want to ogle tattooed twenty-somethings or immerse yourself in the sounds of Spanish, Yiddish, or Polish.

Williamsburg

Step off the #L train at the **Bedford Avenue** stop and you'll be in the heart of hip Williamsburg, one of the youngest, freshest, coolest vibes in New York where the sidewalks teem with a particular breed of self-consciously down-market bohemian, decked out in vintage clothes and hopping from coffee shop to record store to nifty boutique. According to one local curator, Williamsburg boasts more than 100,000 resident artists – the largest such geographical cluster in the world.

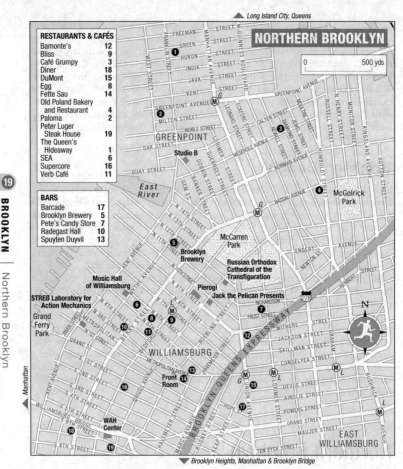

NORTHERN BROOKLYN

RESTAURANTS & CAFÉS

Bamonte's	12
Bliss	9
Café Grumpy	3
Diner	18
DuMont	15
Egg	8
Fette Sau	14
Old Poland Bakery and Restaurant	4
Paloma	2
Peter Luger Steak House	19
The Queen's Hideaway	1
SEA	6
Supercore	16
Verb Café	11

BARS

Barcade	17
Brooklyn Brewery	5
Pete's Candy Store	7
Radegast Hall	10
Spuyten Duyvil	13

0   500 yds

GREENPOINT

McGolrick Park

East River

McCarren Park

Russian Orthodox Cathedral of the Transfiguration

Studio B

Brooklyn Brewery

Music Hall of Williamsburg

STREB Laboratory for Action Mechanics

Grand Ferry Park

Pierogi

Jack the Pelican Presents

WILLIAMSBURG

Front Room

WAH Center

EAST WILLIAMSBURG

BROOKLYN-QUEENS EXPRESSWAY

N

19 | BROOKLYN | Northern Brooklyn

◄ Manhattan

The densest concentration of activity in Williamsburg is on Bedford itself, but many of the more interesting spots are found elsewhere, having gravitated towards cheaper rents. **Grand Street**, for one, is lined with some fine galleries and shops, and some of the formerly industrial spaces on **North Sixth Street** between Bedford and Wythe avenues are now filled with bars and design stores. **Metropolitan Avenue** also has some good bars and restaurants.

Of the forty or so galleries in the neighborhood, perhaps the most influential is **Pierogi**, 177 N 9th St between Bedford and Driggs (Thurs–Mon noon–6pm; ☎718/599-2144, ⓦwww.pierogi2000.com), which shows consistently amusing and challenging work and invites visitors to peruse (with white gloves) its flat file of original works by more than eight hundred artists. Just around the corner, **Jack the Pelican Presents**, 487 Driggs Ave (Thurs–Mon noon–6pm; ☎718/782-0183, ⓦwww.jackthepelicanpresents.com), complements issue-driven mixed-media installations with a "salon" full of more traditional painting and sculpture. The city's best secondhand clothing store, **Buffalo Exchange**, 504 Driggs Ave (☎718/384-6901, ⓦwww.buffaloexchange.com), stands opposite Jack the Pelican, offering a huge and well-priced selection of designer and

Brooklyn beer

In 1900 nearly fifty breweries operated in Brooklyn, but the last of these, Schaefer and Rheingold, closed in 1976. For years after its founding in 1976, the **Brooklyn Brewery**, 79 N 11th St (T718/486-7422, Wwww.brooklynbrewery.com), was "Brooklyn" in name only – the founders had their beer produced upstate. But in 1996 the operation moved into its Williamsburg headquarters, reviving Brooklyn's brewing tradition and making Brooklyn Lager a very popular beverage citywide.

The community-oriented Brooklyn Brewery hosts events throughout the year; hang out in its cafeteria-style beer hall 6–11pm Fridays or take a free tour on Saturdays (1, 2, 3, & 4pm, no reservations necessary). Tours are perfunctory – they're just a hurdle on the way to the free beer at the end, when you can sample a half-glass each of the two best drafts – Brooklynator Dobbelbock and Brooklyn Extra Brune – or the special seasonal brews.

vintage items for both men and women. On the other end of the neighborhood, next to the Williamsburg Bridge, the **Williamsburg Art and Historical Center**, 135 Broadway at Bedford (Sat & Sun noon–6pm or by appointment; T718/486-7372, Wwww.wahcenter.net), displays local painting and sculpture in a vast gallery on the second floor of the imposing Kings County Savings Bank.

If you're interested in doing serious gallery-hopping in the neighborhood, pick up the free monthly booklet *Wagmag*, which includes a Williamsburg gallery map and a list of special events, at any bookstore or gallery (Pierogi always has a good supply), or visit on the second Friday night of the month for **Williamsburg Every Second**, when many galleries stay open until 9 or 10pm and host performances and parties.

As befits a place with vast warehouses to be used and culture-hungry twenty-somethings to be fed, Williamsburg hosts a thriving music and performance scene, with venues like the **Music Hall of Williamsburg**, 66 N 6th St at Wythe (T718/486-5400, Wwww.musichallofwilliamsburg.com), sponsoring some of the best indie-rock shows in the city. Nearby at the **STREB Laboratory for Action Mechanics**, 51 N 1st St at Kent (T718/384-6491, Wwww.strebusa.org), a troupe of gymnastic athletes puts on a stripped-down version of Cirque du Soleil – flying through the air in harnesses, dodging spinning iron beams, springing off trampolines, and doing flips off the wall – during its fall and spring SLAM shows.

But the cutting-edge feel of Williamsburg is already changing: ultra-sleek waterfront high-rises are sprouting up at an alarming rate, capitalizing on views like the one from tiny **Grand Ferry Park**, where Grand Street dead-ends and the Williamsburg Bridge soars over the river. And at least one major cultural fixture – **Galapagos Art Space**, now in DUMBO (p.223) – has been pushed out by the stratospheric rent increases. Artists themselves have been forced further down the #L line to gritty Bushwick to find affordable housing and studio space.

South-side Williamsburg, by contrast, seems frozen in time, especially in the vicinity of **Lee Avenue** or Bedford Avenue, which run parallel between Division Avenue and the Brooklyn–Queens Expressway. Here, kosher delicatessens line the streets and signs are written in Yiddish and Hebrew thanks to the large population of **Hasidic Jews** in the area. The community has been here since 1903, when the Williamsburg Bridge brought over many Jews from the cramped Lower East Side. At the end of World War II a further settlement of Yiddish-speaking Hasidic Jews, mainly from Romania, became the majority.

Greenpoint

Quiet **Greenpoint**, which hugs the northern border of the borough, has the distinction of being the childhood home of Mae West, the birthplace of the oft-ridiculed Brooklynese accent, and home to the largest Polish community in New York City; there's also a substantial Puerto Rican contingent. Reachable by the #G train to Greenpoint Avenue, the homely, low-rise area has absorbed some of the artsy feel of Williamsburg to the south, but the younger residents haven't diluted the Polish character of the businesses along its tidy main strip, **Manhattan Avenue** (partly because they're establishing their own strip on **Franklin St**).

While Greenpoint and neighboring areas were originally known as Boswijck (later Bushwick), meaning "wooded district", the Industrial Revolution took the "green" out of Greenpoint, as the area became home to the "Black Arts" – printing, pottery, gas, glass, and iron. In 1950, refineries caused a 17- to 30-million-gallon underground oil spill, larger than the *Exxon Valdez* disaster in Alaska, which spilled "only" 11 million gallons. It's not immediately visible except as an occasional slick on the surface of Newtown Creek, which separates Greenpoint from Queens, but it's very much on the minds of residents who fear the toxic effects of the residue. Finally, in 2007, the city sued ExxonMobil and other companies to clean it up, if that is even possible at this point.

These things aside, Greenpoint bears a quick visit for its blend of Polish and hipster cultures and their respective cuisines. If you're coming from Williamsburg, take Driggs Avenue north past the **Russian Orthodox Cathedral of the Transfiguration**, N 12th St at Driggs, a New York City landmark whose five green-copper onion domes hover above the trees of **McCarren Park**. The park itself forms the unofficial line between Greenpoint and Williamsburg, and is set to undergo a major renovation in 2009 to 2012 – when the pool will be restored and reopened – though many locals have enjoyed the empty pool's status (since 2005) as a **summer rock venue** hosting the likes of Cat Power and the Beastie Boys. It's unclear whether concerts will continue during and after the construction.

Turn left on Manhattan Avenue and continue straight to get to the heart of Greenpoint. Along the way you'll find an assortment of Polish delis and bakeries, which spill over onto Nassau, where **Steve's Meat Market**, 104 Nassau Ave between Leonard and Eckford (℡718/383-1780), claims to make the best *kielbasa* (spicy Polish sausage) in the US. Wander down the narrow side-streets and you'll get a feel for the tightknit local community – and how it is changing. *Café Grumpy*, 193 Meserole Ave at Diamond, is a magnet for newcomers, with top-of-the-line espresso and a consistently cool soundtrack, while further toward the water, an assortment of bars and restaurants has sprouted up along Franklin Street and around Greenpoint Avenue.

20

Queens

O f New York City's four outer boroughs, **Queens** was for many years probably the least visited – not counting when outsiders passed through Queens' airports, JFK and LaGuardia. If Brooklyn, with its strong neighborhood identities and elegant architecture, represents the old, historic city, then Queens, with its ever-shifting ethnic composition and frankly utilitarian housing stock, represents the "new" New York – the city as an international crossroads, the melting pot on full boil.

Queens is, in fact, the most diverse county in the US, with nearly half of the borough's 2.2 million residents foreign-born, and these hailing from 150 different countries. Not surprisingly, the borough is something of a culinary hotspot. Take the elevated #7 train to **Woodside**, **Jackson Heights**, and **Flushing** and you can eat Thai drunken noodles, Indian vindaloo, and Colombian *arepas*, respectively. In **Astoria** (#N, #R, and #W lines) you'll find Bosnian *burek* and Greek *spanikopita*, Brazilian *feijoada* (black bean stew), and Egyptian braised lamb cheeks.

Culturally, the richest spot in Queens is **Long Island City**, where a cluster of galleries has cropped up around the contemporary art center PS 1, a MoMA affiliate. Farther out, **Flushing Meadows–Corona Park** draws sports fans and families – the former to the **New York Mets'** new stadium, Citi Field (which replaced Shea), and the USTA Billie Jean King National Tennis Center, home of the **US Open Tennis Championships** each fall, and the latter to the Queens Museum, Queens Zoo, and New York Hall of Science. At the southeast end of the borough (accessible via the #A train), in **Jamaica Bay** and the **Rockaways**, lie pristine parks and beaches that feel miles from the city.

For information on the borough and discounts at local merchants, contact Discover Queens (℡718/263-0546, Ⓦwww.discoverqueens.info).

Navigating Queens

One reason many New Yorkers have no love for Queens is the deeply unsettling street-number system, which can leave you baffled on the corner of 30th Road and 30th Street. But the so-called "Philadelphia method" of addressing, applied borough-wide in the 1920s, does have an underlying logic.

Basically, **streets** run north–south, while **avenues**, **roads**, **and drives** run east–west. Avenue numbers get higher as you head south, while street numbers get higher as you head east (First Street is on the East River, and 180th is in Jamaica). And in Queens, addresses let you know right where you are: the digits before the hyphen indicate the cross street: 20-78 33rd Street, for instance, is between 20th and 21st avenues.

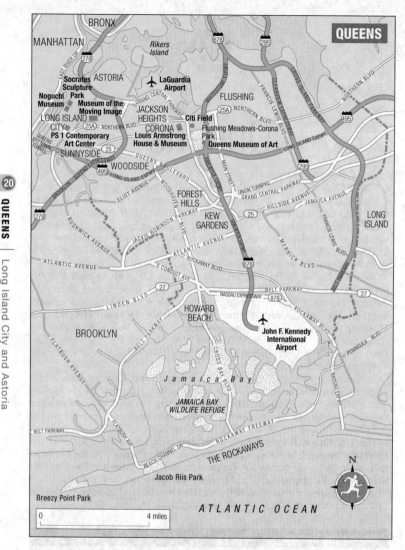

BRONX

MANHATTAN

Rikers
Island

Socrates ASTORIA
Sculpture
Park
Noguchi
Museum
Museum of the
Moving Image
LONG ISLAND
CITY
PS 1 Contemporary
Art Center
SUNNYSIDE

LaGuardia
Airport

JACKSON
HEIGHTS
CORONA
Louis Armstrong
House & Museum

FLUSHING

Citi Field
Flushing Meadows-Corona
Park
Queens Museum of Art

WOODSIDE

FOREST
HILLS

KEW
GARDENS

LONG
ISLAND

BUSHWICK AVENUE

ATLANTIC AVENUE

BROOKLYN

HOWARD
BEACH

John F. Kennedy
International
Airport

Jamaica Bay

JAMAICA BAY
WILDLIFE REFUGE

THE ROCKAWAYS

Jacob Riis Park

Breezy Point Park

ATLANTIC OCEAN

N

0   4 miles

Long Island City and Astoria

Long Island City and **Astoria**, only a few minutes by subway from midtown
Manhattan, rank as the hippest neighborhoods in Queens by far. It can be a little
unclear which is which on account of the fact that the whole area is technically
Long Island City, with Astoria a self-designated neighborhood within it. Practi-
cally speaking, though, most people think of Astoria as the part of Long Island
City north of 36th Avenue, and Long Island City as the area south of the
Queensboro Bridge and north of the Long Island Expressway.

Edging the East River right across from the United Nations, Long Island City thus defined is a mixed residential-industrial area best known as the home of MoMA-affiliated PS 1, which anchors a small but lively visual arts scene. Long Island City's other famous purveyor of culture, **Silvercup Studios**, the largest film and television production studio on the East Coast, stretches out along 21st Street next to the Queensboro Bridge. *The Sopranos* and *Sex and the City* were both shot here.

By contrast, Astoria is overwhelmingly residential, with a diverse population – young professionals and every immigrant group you can imagine – occupying sturdy 1930s brick apartment blocks and vinyl-sided rowhouses along tree-lined streets. Astoria's main claims to fame are its Greek food (though many other fine cuisines are also in abundance), its movie studio and museum, and waterfront Astoria Park, with its mammoth public pool. The serene Noguchi Museum, established on the site of the late sculptor Isamu Noguchi's studio, is also located here.

Long Island City

Only a five-minute ride on the #7 train from Grand Central Terminal, **Long Island City** is well worth the trip if you're interested in cutting-edge art, particularly if you've been to MoMA, since your ticket stub from that institution gets you into **PS 1** free. **SculptureCenter** and the **Fisher Landau Center for Art** also put on first-rate shows, as do a number of small galleries. Despite the recent construction of some massive high-rise condo buildings on the waterfront, there's a keen sense of community here, which you can feel in the eating and drinking establishments in the **Hunters Point** neighborhood along **Vernon Boulevard** between 46th and 51st avenues. Stroll two blocks west to get some eye-grabbing views of the United Nations and the east side of Manhattan from sylvan **Gantry Plaza State Park** or **Water Taxi Beach**, a swatch of white sand with an outdoor bar and grill, picnic tables, volleyball courts, and live bands in the summer.

In the warmer months, the **New York Water Taxi** (Ⓦ www.nywatertaxi.com) docks at the beach, providing a scenic alternative to the subway; you can catch it from East 34th Street in Manhattan, four minutes away, or at a handful of other docks (see the website for schedule and map). The #Q103 bus, which runs along Vernon Boulevard, connects Long Island City with the Noguchi Museum and Socrates Sculpture Park in Astoria.

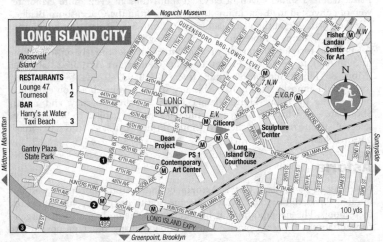

PS 1 Contemporary Art Center and around

Just steps from the 45th Road–Court Square stop on the #7 (as well as the #E, #V, and #G trains at 23rd St–Ely Ave) or a ten-minute walk from Hunters Point, the renowned **PS 1 Contemporary Art Center**, 22-25 Jackson Ave at 46th Ave (Mon & Thurs–Sun noon–6pm; $5 suggested donation; ⓣ718/784-2084, ⓦwww.ps1.org), occupies a hundred-room nineteenth-century brick schoolhouse. Founded in 1971, it became affiliated with the **Museum of Modern Art** in 2000. Aside from a few long-term installations, PS 1 has no permanent collection of its own, instead using its substantial space to mount sprawling thematic shows and retrospectives such as the recent "Wack! Art and the Feminist Revolution," which filled three floors with manifestos, photographs, paintings, films, and sculptures including a fortress of mattresses. *Le Rosie's Café* on the ground floor (museum admission not required) is a pleasant, airy spot to rest your feet while grabbing a bite (soups, salads, sandwiches), glass of wine, or coffee.

There are a few art galleries in the vicinity of PS 1 that are worth popping into if you have the time, including **Dean Project**, 45-43 21st St (Thurs–Sun noon–7pm & Mon by appointment; ⓣ718/706-1462; ⓦwww.deanproject.com), which displays painting and photography by international artists in a small, whitewashed space, and **Dorsky Gallery**, 11-03 45th Ave (Mon & Thurs–Sun 11am–6pm; ⓣ718/937-6317, ⓦwww.dorsky.org), which puts on intelligently curated exhibitions with an eye toward increasing public understanding of contemporary art. Across Jackson Avenue from PS 1, the warehouse called **5 Pointz** (not open to the public) is covered with graffiti art contributed by some six hundred artists over the course of a decade.

A few blocks north along Jackson Avenue, past the Neoclassical **Long Island City Courthouse** and the Citicorp building (at 48 stories, the tallest building in the city outside of Manhattan), SculptureCenter, 44-19 Purves St (Mon & Thurs–Sun 11am–6pm; $5 suggested donation; ⓣ718/361-1750, ⓦwww.sculpture-center.org), displays innovative work in a former trolley-repair shop that was cleverly renovated by architect Maya Lin.

Fisher Landau Center for Art

Continuing along Jackson Avenue, you'll soon reach dank, chaotic Queens Plaza, where a spider's web of elevated trains tops an even more elaborate web of congested roads, including those to and from the Queensboro Bridge. On the north side of the plaza, Jackson turns into 31st Street, over which the #N and #W trains rumble into Astoria. Follow the path of the train to 39th Avenue and turn left, then right on 30th Street (or take the #N or #W trains to 39th Ave), to get to the **Fisher Landau Center for Art**, 38-27 30th St (Mon & Thurs–Sun noon–5pm; free; ⓣ718/937-0727, ⓦwww.flcart.org). You'll almost certainly have this airy space to yourself as you contemplate works by Jenny Holzer, Jasper Johns, Matthew Barney, and Yinka Shonibare – or whatever other contemporary masters happen to be currently selected from real-estate heiress Emily Fisher Landau's thousand-item personal stash.

Astoria

Northeast of Long Island City is **Astoria**, bounded on the north and west by the East River, to the south by 36th Avenue, and to the east by 46th Street or thereabouts. The neighborhood is best known for being home to the largest concentration of Greeks outside Greece though many other groups are in

ASTORIA

N

East River

Roosevelt Island

Socrates Sculpture Park

Rainey Park

Noguchi Museum

Long Island City

BARS

| Bohemian Beer Hall & Garden | 2 |
| Café-Bar | 9 |

RESTAURANTS & CAFÉS

Agnanti Meze	1
Athens Café	4
Djerdan	6
Kabab Café	5
Malagueta	10
Omonia Café	8
Taverna Kyclades	3
Uncle George's	7

Kaufman Astoria Studios

Museum of the Moving Image

0   300 yds

---

abundance as well, including Moroccans and Egyptians, Bangladeshis, Bosnians, and Brazilians. The #N and #W trains from Manhattan run north through the middle of the neighborhood, stopping at all of the major avenues, each of which forms its own community: 30th Avenue and Broadway are liveliest, with Greek coffee joints and nightclubs, discount department stores, butchers, fishmongers, and ethnic restaurants of every stripe; a few cafés and restaurants on 34th and 35th Avenues cater to **Kaufman Astoria Studios'** workers and visitors. The **Astoria Boulevard** stop will get you closest to New York's biggest and best beer garden, *Bohemian Hall* (see p.351). Quieter Ditmars Boulevard is home to some of Astoria's oldest residents – the Italians predate the Greeks – and is near **Astoria Park**, which has beautiful views of Manhattan and a huge public pool.

Alternatively, you can take the #R to Steinway Street, which accesses the east side of the neighborhood; between 28th Avenue and Astoria Boulevard, Steinway is a strip of Egyptian- and Moroccan-run businesses, including a glut of **hookah cafés** where you can watch Arabic TV, sip tea, and savor sweet apple tobacco.

Museum of the Moving Image

Between 1920 and 1928, Astoria was the capital of America's **silent film industry**, and Paramount Pictures got its start at the present site of Kaufman Astoria Studios, 35th Ave at 36th St, drawing stars such as Rudolph Valentino

Steinway piano factory

Astoria has a reputation as an international crossroads, but it boasts few international exports, with one notable exception: **Steinway pianos**. Founded in 1853 in Manhattan by German immigrant Henry Steinway, the company moved its factory to Astoria in the late nineteenth century and has been turning out the finest pianos in the world ever since (though only 3 percent of pianos are Steinways, 98 percent of recording artists use them). About 2000 Steinway grand pianos are built in New York every year, retailing from $40,000 to well over $100,000. They are said to be the most complex object on earth that's put together by hand, with 12,000 parts assembled over the course of nine months. See this fascinating process yourself on a free guided tour (dates are limited; call well ahead for reservations: ☎718/721-26000). Take the #N or #W to Ditmars Boulevard, walk seven blocks east to 38th Street and then go three blocks north to 19th Ave.

and the Marx Brothers. Business dried up in the 1930s, when moviemakers were lured to Los Angeles by more reliable weather, but was rekindled in the 1977 with the shooting of Sidney Lumet's **The Wiz**, and the studios are now extremely busy with everything from commercials to Woody Allen films to blockbusters.

Part of the Kaufman Astoria complex is dedicated to the **Museum of the Moving Image** (☎718/784-0077, ⓦwww.movingimage.us), which is undergoing a major expansion and renovation and will be closed until winter 2009–10. The museum's growing collection contains more than 125,000 objects, including posters, fan magazines, film stills, costumes, special-effects equipment, video games, and the complete diner set from *Seinfeld*. When it reopens, the museum will display some of these objects in interactive exhibits and will also resume its excellent weekend repertory-film program.

Noguchi Museum and Socrates Sculpture Park

Off the beaten track but definitely worth the detour, the **Noguchi Museum**, 9-01 33rd Ave (Wed–Fri 10am–5pm, Sat & Sun 11am–6pm; $10, students and seniors $5; ☎718/204-7088, ⓦwww.noguchi.org), is devoted to the works of Japanese-American abstract sculptor Isamu Noguchi (1904–88), who worked in Long Island City for many years and designed this museum shortly before his death. At its center is a garden filled with his stone sculptures, while the surrounding galleries include a special section on his design work. To get to the museum, take the #N or #W train to the Broadway (Queens) station; head west to Vernon Boulevard, then south two blocks to 33rd Avenue – about a fifteen-minute walk or a five-minute ride on the #Q104 bus. You can also take the #Q103 bus from Hunters Point or, on Sundays, take a shuttle bus from the Asia Society (p.182); departures are at 12.30pm, 1.30pm, 2.30pm, and 3.30pm, with return trips on the hour between 1 and 5pm. The cost is $5 each way.

While you're out this way, stop in at **Socrates Sculpture Park**, one block north of the Noguchi Museum, on Broadway at Vernon Boulevard (daily 10am–sunset; ☎718/956-1819, ⓦwww.socratessculpturepark.org). The park was an abandoned landfill until 1986, when sculptor Mark di Suvero transformed it into an outdoor studio, with space for artists to build on a massive scale. The resulting works range from ingenious kinetic installations to bizarre structures that appear to be growing out of the lawn.

Sunnyside, Woodside, and Jackson Heights

After Astoria, the #E, #R, and #V trains run north of **Sunnyside** and **Woodside**, historically Irish enclaves now also home to many Asian and Latino immigrants. You're not missing too much if you skip these neighborhoods on your way to the more interesting **Jackson Heights**, though planning enthusiasts may want to see the **Sunnyside Gardens** development, a utopian working-class "garden city" built in 1924 with encouragement from Eleanor Roosevelt and Lewis Mumford; take the #7 train (which runs straight through Sunnyside and Woodside) to the 46th Street stop and walk north on 46th (the opposite direction from the Art Deco "Sunnyside" sign on Queens Boulevard).

Jackson Heights

East of Sunnyside, the #7 train swings away from Queens Boulevard and heads up narrower Roosevelt Avenue. Get off at 74th Street or 82nd Street (or take the #E, #F, #R, or #V to Roosevelt Ave), and you'll find yourself in central **Jackson Heights**, where English is rarely the tongue of choice.

Developed just after the construction of the elevated train in 1917, the area was laid out as a unified district of tidy brick homes and apartment blocks with attractive garden courtyards (the term "**garden apartment**" was coined here), lending the area a cohesiveness that's rare in Queens. Walking tours of the **historic district** – including its private gardens – are offered during Historic Jackson Heights Weekend each June (Ⓦ www.jhbg.org). If you're on your own,

▲ Roosevelt Avenue, Jackson Heights

take a stroll down 35th and 37th avenues between 78th and 88th streets to get a feel for the architecture.

The neighborhood is the most diverse in the city, with especially large concentrations of Latin American immigrants. Amble up **Roosevelt Avenue** and you'll find Argentine steakhouses, Colombian street vendors selling treats such as *arepas* (savory corn cakes), and Mexican bakeries displaying stacks of bread and pastries.

Little India, along 74th Street between Roosevelt and 37th Avenue, is something of a contrast. This is the largest Indian community in New York, and South Asians from all over come here to find colorful saris, elaborate gold jewelry for weddings, groceries, music, and perhaps a pungent betel leaf from a street cart. The restaurants here far surpass the more quotidian fare on better-known East 6th Street in Manhattan: *Jackson Diner*, 37-47 74th St, is one of the best – see p.338 for a review. Just a block away, the **Eagle Theater**, 73-07 37th Rd (☎718/205-2800), screens Bollywood movies in Hindi with English subtitles.

Corona and Flushing Meadows

East of Jackson Heights is gritty **Corona**, immortalized in Queens native Paul Simon's song *Me and Julio Down by the Schoolyard*. Once entirely Italian (*corona* is Italian for "crown"), the neighborhood is now mostly first-generation immigrants from the Dominican Republic, Mexico, Ecuador, and Colombia, and about a fifth of households live below the poverty line. It's also home to **Louis Armstrong House** and **Flushing Meadows–Corona Park**, home to the Mets' Citi Field (which replaces Shea Stadium in April 2009) and the USTA National Tennis Center.

To get to the **Louis Armstrong House**, 34-56 107th St, between 34th and 37th avenues (Tues–Fri 10am–5pm, Sat & Sun noon–5pm; $8, under 12, students and seniors $6; ☎718/478-8274, ⓦwww.satchmo.net), take the #7 train to 103rd Street–Corona Plaza, walk north on 104th Street, turn right on 37th Avenue, and then left on 107th Street. Opened as a museum in 2003, the great jazz artist's home has been preserved just as he and his wife, Lucille, left it. Armstrong, who lived here from 1943 until his death in 1971, made audio recordings of the day-to-day goings-on in the house, and these play inside, creating a ghostly atmosphere. Guided tours, which show off Armstrong's trumpets and various other artifacts, start every hour on the hour. If you'd like to learn more about Queens' substantial jazz history, you can also see the house as part of the **Queens Jazz Trail Tour**, which runs from Flushing Town Hall (see p.254) on the first Saturday of every month and visits the neighborhoods where Ella Fitzgerald, Count Basie, and others lived.

Flushing Meadows–Corona Park

About seven blocks east of the Armstrong House, **Flushing Meadows–Corona Park** is an enormous (1200-acre) swathe of green first laid out in the 1930s, and its few key attractions – a couple of interesting museums, a zoo, and some relics of the two World's Fairs held here (see box opposite) – make for a good afternoon out, especially if you have children who need space to run around. Take the #7 train to the Shea Stadium/Citi Field stop and walk south past the tennis complex to the park; or head directly to the museums by getting off at the 111th Street station and walking south on 111th Street until you hit the park's northwest corner.

Citi Field replaces decrepit Shea Stadium as the home field of the **New York Mets** baseball team in April 2009. The new stadium seats 45,000 (10,000 fewer than Shea) and has an old-fashioned facade of brick, granite, and cast-stone, mimicking that of old Ebbets Field in Brooklyn, former home of the Brooklyn Dodgers, New York's previous National League franchise. The Mets have a loyal fan base, if for no other reason than that many Queens and Brooklyn residents can't stand the Yankees, though the team's erratic late-season performances have alienated many. Due south of the stadium stands the US Tennis Association's **Billie Jean King National Tennis Center**, the largest public tennis facility in the world, with more than twenty indoor and outdoor courts. The main event, the US Open Tennis Championships, takes place at the end of each summer. Tickets to the early matches are easy enough to come by; closer to the finals, you may have to buy from scalpers. For more details on seeing the Mets and the US Open, see p.405 and p.409.

A concrete and stained-glass structure retained from the 1964 World's Fair, the **New York Hall of Science**, 111th St at 46th Ave, dazzles imaginative kids with interactive science exhibits (July & Aug Mon–Fri 9.30am–5pm, Sat & Sun 10am–6pm; Sept–June Tues–Thurs 9.30am–2pm, Fri 9.30am–5pm, Sat & Sun 10am–5pm; $11, students and children $8, free Sept–June Fri 2–5pm & Sun 10–11am; T718/699-0005, W www.nyhallsci.org). Parking ($10) is not available during the US Open.

The adjacent **Queens Zoo**, 53-51 111th St (April–Oct Mon–Fri 10am–5pm, Sat & Sun 10am–5.30pm; Nov–March daily 10am–4.30pm; $6, ages 3–12 $2, seniors $2.25; T718/271-1500, W www.queenszoo.org), is not nearly as spectacular as those in Central Park and the Bronx, although it has transformed Buckminster Fuller's 1964 geodesic dome into a dizzying aviary, and some beautiful big animals, including bison, Shetland cattle, and elk, roam the grounds.

East of the zoo, the **Unisphere** is a 140-foot-high, stainless-steel globe that weighs 380 tons – probably the main reason why it was never moved after the 1964 fair. Robert Moses intended this park to be the "Versailles of America," but the severe, perfectly symmetrical pathways radiating out from the sphere,

The world comes to Queens

In late April 1939, as the US emerged from the Great Depression and war loomed, 1200 acres of the new Flushing Meadows–Corona Park became the stage for America's love affair with modernity. Drawing visitors from across the nation (and delegates in 62 others), the **1939–40 World's Fair** featured displays of technologies yet to be realized, including robotics and fluorescent lights. General Motors sponsored a "Futurama" ride through a utopian modern city, and New Yorkers saw broadcast television for the first time. The fair was a great success, and brought attention to this little-known borough. In part due to the reputation established by the expo, the United Nations briefly operated from here following World War II.

The **1964–65 World's Fair**, held in the same location, in many ways bookended the era of jubilant optimism that the 1939 fair had opened. While technological and engineering advances such as lasers and computers thrilled 52 million fair-goers, the fair's tone – in the wake of President Kennedy's assassination – was markedly different. Many of the temporary structures stand around the park, either appropriated for other uses or left to decay.

the anachronistic and often bizarrely ugly architecture, and the roaring Grand Central Parkway all feel more Eastern Bloc than French – particularly when you look south and see the rusting towers of Philip Johnson's 1964 **New York Pavilion**, now home to Queens Theatre in the Park (T718/760-0064, W www.queenstheatre.org). Fortunately, the whole picture is softened a bit on sunny days, when the park swarms with kids on bikes and skateboards.

The park's finest attraction is the **Queens Museum of Art**, housed right next to the Unisphere in a building from the 1939 fair that served briefly as the first home of the United Nations (Wed–Fri 10am–5pm, Sat & Sun noon–5pm; suggested donation $5; T718/592-9700, W www.queensmuseum.org). Plans are afoot to double the size of the museum by incorporating half of the adjacent building currently occupied by the World's Fair Skating Rink by 2010. The one must-see item in the museum – which should be open throughout the renovation – is the **Panorama of the City of New York**, a product of the 1964 fair. With a scale of one inch to one hundred feet, the 9300-square-foot panorama is the world's largest architectural model, incorporating 895,000 buildings, each hand-carved out of wood, as well as rivers, harbors, bridges, and even tiny planes drifting in and out of the airports. Guided tours are held on weekends at 4pm. The only other permanent exhibit of note in the museum is the collection of glassworks by **Louis Comfort Tiffany**, who established his design studios in Corona in the 1890s.

For refreshment after seeing the park, visit the *Lemon Ice King of Corona*, 52-08 108th St, which has been dishing out refreshing handmade fruit ices since shortly after the 1939 fair.

Flushing

Beyond the eastern edge of the park, at the end of the #7 line, lies **Flushing**, originally an early Quaker community but now most notable as New York's second Chinatown: 55 percent of its population claiming Asian ancestry. While it's not as architecturally quaint as Manhattan's Chinatown, it feels more authentic, its bustling **restaurants** and shops catering almost exclusively to locals, not tourists. Chowhounds say they can taste the difference. (See p.305 & p.338 for recommendations.)

Head north on **Main Street** from the subway station and you'll pass a couple of old Quaker landmarks, as well as a few other historical buildings. On the west side of Main Street between 39th and 38th avenues is **St George's Church**, an elegant 1854 Gothic landmark with a tall central tower. Just around the corner from Main Street a few blocks north, Romanesque Revival **Flushing Town Hall**, 137-35 Northern Blvd (daily noon–5pm; T718/463-7700, W www.flushingtownhall.com), is now a cultural center with a sophisticated calendar of musical performances; there's also an art gallery inside. Just across the street is a shingle cottage, the **Friends Meeting House**, which dates from 1694, making it the oldest surviving house of worship in the city and the second-oldest Quaker institution in the country. It is open Sundays at 11am for services and noon for tours, on which you can also see the centuries-old cemetery (sans headstones, per Quaker tradition).

Flesh out the Quaker story with a quick visit to the **Kingsland Homestead**, 145-35 37th Ave (Tues, Sat & Sun 2.30–4.30pm; $3; T718/939-0647, W www.queenshistoricalsociety.org), a small wooden farmhouse maintained by the

Queens Historical Society. You can see the house from Bowne Street (which runs south from Northern Boulevard), where it is set back in **Weeping Beech Park**. South of the park on Bowne Street, the 1661 Quaker-style **Bowne House** was the home of John Bowne, who helped Flushing acquire the tag "birthplace of religious freedom in America" by resisting discrimination at a time when the Dutch persecuted anyone who wasn't Calvinist; the house is currently being restored.

Alternatively, you might head south from the Main Street subway station; at the first intersection, with 40th Road, a sidewalk counter, *Corner Restaurant and Caterers*, serves succulent Peking duck to go, either on the bone or in a bun. Veer off on Kissena Boulevard and you'll pass the stately **Free Synagogue of Flushing**, no. 41-60 (℡718/961-0030, Ⓦwww .freesynagogue.org), on your right. The oldest surviving Reform Jewish synagogue in the US, it looks like a small-town courthouse, but with brick additions and blue stained-glass windows.

The #Q65 bus runs south from the synagogue into an Indian community, passing the impressive **Sri Mahã Vallabha Ganapati Devasthãnam**, 45-59 Bowne St (Mon–Fri 8am–9pm, Sat & Sun 7.30am–9pm; ℡718/460-8484, Ⓦwww.nyganeshtemple.org). Also known as the **Ganesh Temple**, this building honors the elephant-headed Hindu god. *Dosa Hutt*, next door on Bowne Street, provides tasty south Indian snacks while you're down this way.

Jamaica Bay and the Rockaways

The southern edge of Queens is the place to take a break from urban life. **Jamaica Bay Wildlife Refuge** (℡718/338-3338, Ⓦwww.nps.gov/gate) is named for the Jameco Indians, whose territory this once was. Near Broad Channel on the largest of these islands (take the #A train to Broad Channel and walk a half-mile north; the #Q53 bus from Rockaway Park or Jackson Heights also stops here), you can hike trails through the diverse habitats of more than 325 varieties of migrating **birds**, including several endangered species. A unit of the 26,607-acre Gateway National Recreation Area, which extends through coastal areas of Queens, Brooklyn, Staten Island, and New Jersey, this is one of the most important urban wildlife areas in the United States.

Partly enclosing the bay, the spit of **Rockaway** stretches for ten miles southwest of Brooklyn, and is the only place to surf in New York City – take the #A or the #S Rockaway Shuttle, depending on the time of day, to Rockaway Park–Beach 116th Street. The lovely beach of **Jacob Riis Park** (℡718/318-4300) on the western end of the spit is quieter and more pristine, because it's part of the Gateway NRA. The subway doesn't go there – instead, take the #Q22 bus from Beach 116th or the #Q35 from Flatbush Avenue in Brooklyn; the latter is by far the faster option from Manhattan. This is widely considered to be New York City's best beach, and it features a brick bathhouse and an outdoor clock that have been New York City landmarks since the 1930s. At the westernmost tip of the peninsula, beyond the reach of public transit but an easy bicycle ride from the end of the train line, the heavily Irish cooperative community of **Breezy Point** feels like a beach town imported from another state – come here to truly escape New York.

21

The Bronx

"The **Bronx**?" wrote poet Ogden Nash in 1931. "No thonx!" Nash eventually recanted his two-line barb, but most New Yorkers still harbor similar feelings due to the borough's reputation for being tough and crime-ridden. Still, what is true in the **South Bronx** – still one of the city's poorest areas – hardly applies to the whole of the Bronx, which harbors beautiful parks, posh neighborhoods, a world-class botanic garden and zoo, and, of course, **Yankee Stadium**.

With a unique landscape that ranges from greenery to high-rises, the Bronx is New York's only mainland borough. As might be expected, its hilly geography is more like neighboring Westchester County than Long Island and Manhattan.

First settled in the seventeenth century by a Swedish landowner named **Jonas Bronck**, it became part of New York City in the late nineteenth century. For half a century, it was solidly working-class and middle-class, only taking a turn into serious poverty in the 1950s, when urban planner Robert Moses sliced the borough in half with the **Cross Bronx Expressway**, severing the South Bronx from its wealthier neighbors to the north. The South Bronx was literally left to burn in the 1970s, taking the reputation of the whole borough down with it, but it has been making a slow recovery in the years since, with substantial residential development in the 2000s.

With a few exceptions, such as the **Little Italy** section of Belmont, which is within walking distance of the **Bronx Zoo** and the **New York Botanical Garden,** the Bronx doesn't lend itself to extensive wandering, mainly because sights are spread so far apart. Smart use of public transportation, though, can make getting around pretty painless, especially if you use the **bus** and **commuter train** in addition to the subway. The #Bx12 bus winds a useful west–east route, connecting many of the Central Bronx sights and linking the north–south subway lines. (Pick up a Bronx bus map in any subway station.) Special **express buses** run up Madison Avenue, headed straight to the zoo and botanical garden. And the Metro North train will get you to the spectacular **Wave Hill** estate from Grand Central Terminal in less than half an hour.

Find out more about the borough from the **Bronx Tourism Council** (Ⓦwww.ilovethebronx.com) or the **Bronx Council on the Arts** (Ⓣ718/931-9500, Ⓦwww.bronxarts.org). BCA sponsors the free **Bronx Cultural Card**, which provides ten- to fifty-percent discounts on a couple dozen of the Bronx's best attractions, shops, and restaurants. Pick up a card at any public library in the Bronx or at the BCA office, 1738 Hone Ave.

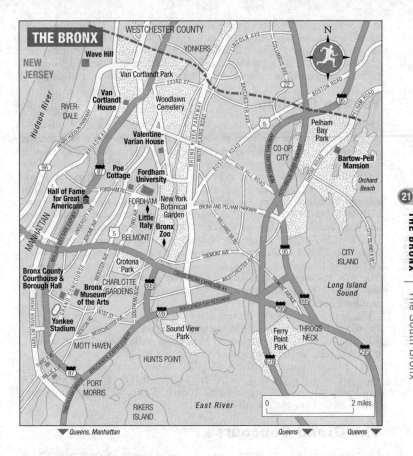

The South Bronx

When most people hear the words "the Bronx," they think of the **South Bronx**, the mostly residential, mostly impoverished area south of the Cross-Bronx Expressway. It was here, on the streets of Hunts Point and other tough neighborhoods of "the Boogie Down" – hip-hop's name for the borough – that rap, break-dancing, and graffiti art were born in the late 1970s. Anyone interested in street culture should do a lot of random strolling, preferably by day, or take **A Hip Hop Bus Tour Led by Pioneers of Rap** (℡212/209-3370, Ⓦwww.hushtours.com; $75, students $50), led by scene insiders.

The main reason most people visit the South Bronx, though, is to see the New York **Yankees** play on their home field, **Yankee Stadium**. Although the original stadium will be demolished in 2009, the adjacent new stadium will feature many of the old one's best attributes, including Monument Park.

The area around the stadium – along the southern section of the **Grand Concourse**, the borough's main thoroughfare, and in the neighborhoods of Hunts Point and Mott Haven – is also a locus of culture for the Bronx, with the **Bronx Museum of the Arts**, a handful of community-oriented art galleries and boutiques, and some small performance spaces. Every first Wednesday of the month (except in Sept and Jan), from 5.30 to 7.30pm, the Bronx Council on the Arts sponsors a free **culture trolley** touring some of these sights (☎718/931-9500, ext 33; ⓦwww.bronxarts.org), starting at the Longwood Art Gallery at Hostos Community College, 450 Grand Concourse at 149th St.

Yankee Stadium

Off the 161st Street–Yankee Stadium stop on the #B, #D, and #4 trains, the new **Yankee Stadium** is home to the legendary **New York Yankees** baseball team (see box below) and – appropriately, perhaps, given the team's gigantic payroll – is the most expensive stadium ever built in the US. The design of the 53,000-capacity, open-air park, to be inaugurated in April 2009, revives aspects of the 1923 stadium – "the house that (Babe) Ruth built" – that were lost in subsequent renovations, such as the limestone and granite exterior facade, and includes a spot for Monument Park, where fans can find retired jersey numbers and plaques honoring famous Yankees. There'll also be a million-square-foot retail and food hall. As of summer 2008, only one major scandal had rocked the project: in 2007 a construction worker buried a rival Boston Red Sox jersey underneath the new visitors' dugout in an effort to place a hex on the Yankees. The shirt was later exhumed and sold on eBay for $175,000 to benefit one of the Yankees' charities, but the worker warned that other bad-luck items remained undiscovered.

The best way to see the stadium is, of course, to catch a game (see p.410 for ticket information), though diehards may want to take an hour-long guided tour, which offers access to Monument Park, the field, the dugouts, the press box, and club house when available (schedules vary; $20 adults, under 14 and seniors $15; ☎718/579-4531, ⓦwww.yankees.com). If you do snag tickets to a game, consider taking the **ferry** (☎1-800/533-3779, ⓦwww.nywaterway.com) or **Metro North Railroad** (ⓦwww.mta.info) instead of the jam-packed subway.

The Grand Concourse

From the stadium, walk east up to the aptly named **Grand Concourse**, which is a rather low-income area, though you wouldn't guess it from the street's

---

The Bronx Bombers

The **Yankees**, who inspire love and loathing in New York (and mostly the latter outside the city), moved from north Manhattan to the Bronx in 1923. Leading the way was **George Herman "Babe" Ruth**, who had joined the team in 1920 (from the Boston Red Sox, still the team's archrivals). The original "Bronx Bomber," Ruth hit the stadium's first home run – soon enough, Yankee Stadium was known as "**The House That Ruth Built.**"

Playing alongside Ruth, **Lou Gehrig** earned the nickname "The Iron Horse" by playing in 2130 consecutive games. **Joe DiMaggio**, "**Yogi**" **Berra**, **Mickey Mantle**, and **Reggie Jackson** also all wore the famous Yankee pinstripes.

The Yankees won the World Series an amazing nineteen times between 1927 and 1962 and finished the twentieth century with three straight titles, but despite the largest payroll in baseball (nearly twice that of the team with the next highest), the Yankees haven't won the World Series since 2000. For their devoted fans (and devoted enemies), though, they remain the team to beat.

architecture. In its southern reaches, the concourse is a magnificent wide boulevard marked by tree-lined medians and opulent Art Deco buildings that now house apartments, social-service organizations, and retirement homes. Across from the stadium at 161st Street is the massive **Bronx County Courthouse and Borough Hall**, a 1933 construction that combines Neoclassical columns with Art Deco friezes and statuary. North of here stretches **Joyce Kilmer Park**, named for the man who penned the lines "I think that I shall never see / A poem lovely as a tree..." A monument to Louis J. Heintz, who first proposed the Grand Concourse, and the white Lorelei Fountain form a gracious backdrop for residents, who come here to take in the sun on benches and stroll at sunset.

At Grand Concourse and East 165th Street, the **Bronx Museum of the Arts** (Mon, Thurs, Sat, & Sun noon–6pm, Fri noon–8pm; suggested donation $5, students and seniors $3, under 12 free, ☎718/681-6000, ⓦwww .bronxmuseum.org) occupies a converted synagogue that was expanded and modernized by the renowned firm Arquitectonica in 2006; look for the jagged glass facade. Exhibits of contemporary art by Asian, Latino, and African-American artists lie within, and eclectic performances are held on the **first Friday** evening of each month, when admission is free.

The Central Bronx

The **Central Bronx**, north of the Cross-Bronx Expressway and south of Gun Hill Road, has neither the intense grit of the South Bronx nor the quiet ritz of the borough's extreme north. As in much of the Bronx, its inhabitants are working-class African-Americans, Puerto Ricans, and Dominicans, though its historical center is prestigious (and predominantly white) **Fordham University**, founded by Jesuits in 1841 and set on lush green lawns. Other points of interest include **Belmont**, better known as the Bronx's Little Italy, and verdant **Bronx Park**, home to the city's prized **Bronx Zoo** and **New York Botanical Garden**. Serious sightseers can seek out the **Poe Cottage** and the **Hall of Fame for Great Americans**.

Belmont

Smack in the middle of the Bronx, and within easy walking distance of the Fordham University campus, the New York Botanical Garden, and the Bronx Zoo, **Belmont** is home to one of New York's largest Italian-American communities, with its main thoroughfare, **Arthur Avenue**, offering a more authentic and low-key alternative to Little Italy in Manhattan. To get here, take the #4 or #D train to Fordham Road, then transfer to the eastbound #Bx12 for the short ride to Arthur Avenue, or take the #2 train to Pelham and transfer to the #Bx12 bus headed west. Almost everything you'll want to see (and taste) lies on Arthur between Crescent Avenue and East 187th Street.

The neighborhood dates to the late nineteenth century, when Italian craftsmen building the Bronx Zoo settled here, and although Haitians, Mexicans, and Albanians also operate businesses on Arthur Avenue, the Italian community still dominates, with daily mass at **Our Lady of Mount Carmel Church**, E 187th St at Belmont Ave, still held in Italian. Try to come during the Ferragosto di Belmont, on the second Sunday in September, when residents turn out in their festive best to dance, eat, perform commedia dell'arte and compete in the annual cheese-carving contest.

There is no better part of the Bronx to visit if you want to **eat**. For a snack, opt for clams or oysters on the half-shell from *Cosenza's Fish Market*, 2354 Arthur Ave, which runs a sidewalk stand outside the shop in warm weather, or stop in to the **Arthur Avenue Retail Market**, no. 2344, a small maze of hanging salami and mozzarella; try *Mike's Deli* near the back for an enormous focaccia sandwich. If you'd rather build your own sandwich, pick up some cheese, meat, and antipasto in the market, then head down the block to what is arguably the best Italian bakery in the city, *Madonia Brothers Bakery*, no. 2348 – the olive bread, thick and chewy and studded with whole salty olives, is a knockout. For pastries and Italian ice, drop by the *DeLillo Bakery*, 606 E 187th St at Arthur, once owned by author and native son Don DeLillo's parents. *Roberto*, 603 Crescent Ave at Arthur, is your best bet for dinner in the area, with elegantly prepared fresh pasta served family style. See p.339 for full reviews.

Bronx Zoo

One of the Bronx's main attractions, the **Bronx Zoo** is the largest urban wildlife park in the country (April–Oct Mon–Fri 10am–5pm, Sat, Sun & holidays 10am–5.30pm; Nov–March daily 10am–4.30pm; $15, seniors $13, kids ages 3–12 $11; Wed by donation, parking $10, additional charges for some rides and exhibits; ℡718/367-1010, ⓦwww.bronxzoo.org). If you're walking from Arthur Avenue, follow 187th Street seven blocks east to reach the main entrance, at Southern Boulevard. The closest subway stop is West Farms Square–East Tremont Avenue on the #2 or #5, three blocks south of the Asia Gate at the southeast corner of the zoo. Another option is the #BxM11 express bus ($5, exact change), which runs from Madison Avenue in midtown Manhattan, dropping visitors near the Bronx River Gate, on the northeast corner. Plan

▲ Bronx Zoo

ahead and bring a picnic lunch; there are tables throughout the park where you can spread your feast. And come on a weekday to avoid large crowds.

Opened in 1899, the zoo has significantly expanded from its small cluster of original buildings to reach 265 wooded acres harboring nearly 18,000 creatures in natural-looking habitats. The forty-acre **Wild Asia** exhibit (May–Oct; $4), where tigers, elephants, and gaur (big cows) roam relatively freely, is one of the zoo's highlights, though don't expect to linger; the only way to see it is on a narrated twenty-minute, all-inclusive ride on the Bengali Express Monorail train. Also open only in warm weather are the **Children's Zoo** ($3), which allows kids to climb with lemurs, learn camouflage skills from tortoises, and feed farm animals, and the **Skyfari gondola** ($3), which provides some of the most memorable views of the park.

The innovative **Congo Gorilla Forest** ($3) houses more than 400 African animals representing 55 species, including tiny colobus monkeys, mandrill baboons, and the largest population of western gorillas in the country. **Madagascar!**, unveiled in June 2008, showcases lemurs, crocodiles, parrots, and other rare animals. Look also at the **World of Darkness** (a collection of nocturnal species), the **Sea Bird Colony**, and the **Himalayan Highlands**, home to endangered species like the red panda and the snow leopard.

In winter, many animals are kept in indoor enclosures without viewing areas, but the endangered Siberian tigers love a snowy day, and if you visit the three-acre **Tiger Mountain** habitat then, it may just be you and these enormous cats, separated by a thin plate of glass. In the month and a half before Christmas, **holiday lights** transform the zoo into a winter wonderland.

New York Botanical Garden

Adjacent to the zoo, just north of Fordham Road, is a quieter but equally worthwhile attraction: the lush, 250-acre **New York Botanical Garden** (Tues–Sun, Mon & holidays 10am–6pm; $20, students and seniors $18, under 12 $7, parking $12; ☎718/817-8700, ⓦwww.nybg.org). Prices listed above are for all-access tickets, including the conservatory, children's garden, rock and native plant garden, and tram tour. For a short visit, grounds-only tickets ($6, students and seniors $3) offer a lot of bang for the buck, especially in warm weather. The main entrance, on Kazimiroff Boulevard opposite Fordham University, is a short walk north from the zoo along Southern Boulevard, which changes to Kazimiroff Boulevard; the gates will be on your left. The nearest subway stop is Bedford Park on the #B or #D lines (about a twenty-minute walk), but the quickest way to get here from Manhattan is on the Metro North Railroad's Harlem Line, a twenty-minute ride from Grand Central. Get off at the Botanical Garden station and walk across Kazimiroff Boulevard to the Mosholu Gate.

The glittering glass **Enid A. Haupt Conservatory**, built when the park opened in 1891, acts as a dramatic entrance, magnificently showcasing rainforest, aquatic, and desert ecosystems. It also houses a palm court with towering old trees and a fern forest, and hosts special exhibits like the popular orchid show in March and the **Holiday Train Show**, a twinkling winter wonderland of miniature structures and model trains, which opens the day after Thanksgiving and runs through mid-January. Elsewhere at the garden, cherry, lilac, maple, conifer, crab apple, and rock gardens edge a 50-acre core of native **forest**, and three thousand rose plants make up the recently restored **Peggy Rockefeller Rose Garden**, in bloom in late May and early September.

Kids can head to the **Everett Children's Adventure Garden**, twelve acres of plant and science exhibits and some nifty mazes. Programs let kids cook, taste, and draw popular plants such as peppermint, chocolate, and vanilla.

Poe Cottage and the Valentine-Varian House

West of Fordham University, just off the Kingsbridge Road stop on the #B and #D trains, is the **Edgar Allan Poe Cottage**, Grand Concourse and East Kingsbridge Rd (Sat 10am–4pm, Sun 1–5pm; $5; ☎718/881-8900, ⓦwww.bronxhistoricalsociety.org), built in 1812. This white-clapboard anachronism on a twenty-first-century working-class Latino block was Edgar Allan Poe's rural home from 1846 to 1849, just before he died in Baltimore. It originally sat on East Kingsbridge Road near East 192nd Street, but was moved here when threatened with demolition. Never a particularly stable character and dogged by financial problems, Poe also had to contend with the death of his wife, Virginia, shortly after they moved in. In his gloom, he did manage to write the short, touching poem *Annabel Lee* (a homage to his wife) and other famous works during his stay. The cottage displays several rooms as they were in Poe's time, as well as a small gallery of 1840s artwork.

The Bronx Historical Society also runs the **Valentine-Varian House**, 3266 Bainbridge Ave (Sat 10am–4pm, Sun 1–5pm; $5; ☎718/881-8900, ⓦwww .bronxhistoricalsociety.org), an eighteenth-century Georgian stone farmhouse that was occupied by the British during the American Revolution. Only recommended for serious history buffs (it requires an extra jaunt north two stops on the #D to Norwood–205th St), the museum stands in a small park and contains numerous old photographs that show just how rapidly the Bronx shifted from an agrarian landscape to an urban one.

Hall of Fame for Great Americans

On the picturesque campus of the Bronx Community College – formerly New York University's Bronx campus – stands the **Hall of Fame for Great Americans** (daily 7am–dusk; tours ☎718/289-5161), a 630ft-long open-air hilltop colonnade designed by the renowned architect Stanford White in 1900 and studded with bronze busts of the 98 honorees. Together they form a peculiar cast of characters, with world-famous figures like George Washington and Henry David Thoreau rubbing shoulders with virtual unknowns like steamboat builder James Buchanan Eads and dentist William Thomas Green Morton. To get here, take the #4 to Burnside Avenue and walk four blocks west to University Avenue, two blocks north to Hall of Fame Terrace, then west again two blocks to the entrance.

The North Bronx

The **North Bronx**, shorthand for the area above 225th Street in the west and Gun Hill Road in the east, is the northernmost area of the city; anyone who makes it up here usually wants to see the stately **Riverdale** neighborhood and its incredible riverfront estate **Wave Hill**, the rolling hills of **Woodlawn Cemetery** and **Van Cortlandt Park**, or the ocean views of **City Island** and **Orchard Beach**. Getting up this way by public transport is not impossible –

the Metro North Railroad is particularly useful in getting to Riverdale – but if you have access to a car, this is a good time to use it.

Woodlawn Cemetery

With entrances at Jerome Avenue at Bainbridge (last stop, Woodlawn, on the #4) and at Webster Avenue and East 233rd Street (#2 or #5 to 233rd St or Metro North Harlem Line railroad to Woodlawn), venerable **Woodlawn Cemetery** (daily 8.30am–5pm; T718/920-0500, Wwww.thewoodlawn cemetery.org) is a huge place. Like Green-Wood in Brooklyn, it boasts a number of tombs and mausolea that are memorable mainly for their gaudiness, although a few monuments stand out: Oliver Belmont, financier and horse dealer, rests in a Gothic fantasy modeled on the resting place of Leonardo da Vinci in Amboise, France; F.W. Woolworth built himself an Egyptian palace guarded by sphinxes; and sculptor Patricia Cronin's 2002 marble *Memorial to a Marriage* depicts the artist and her partner, Deborah Kass, locked in a sleepy embrace. Walking tours run on Sundays at 2pm ($10, $5 students and seniors; call for availability and reservations T718/920-1470), or you can pick up a self-guided walking tour map at the main gates and security booths to locate the many famous individuals buried here, including **Herman Melville**, Irving Berlin, Elizabeth Cady Stanton, Fiorello LaGuardia, Robert Moses, Celia Cruz, **Miles Davis**, and **Duke Ellington**.

Van Cortlandt Park

Immediately west of the cemetery across Jerome Avenue (you can also take the #1 train to the end of the line at 242nd St and Broadway) lies vast **Van Cortlandt Park**, a forested and hilly all-purpose recreation space. Apart from the pleasure of hiking and running through its woods, the best thing here is the **Van Cortlandt House Museum** (Tues–Fri 10am–3pm, Sat & Sun 11am–4pm; $5, students and seniors $3, Wed free; T718/543-3344, Wwww .vancortlandthouse.org), nestled in the park's southwest corner not far from the #1 subway station. This is the Bronx's oldest building, an authentically restored Georgian structure built in 1748, complete with a historically accurate herb garden. New York City's archives were buried for safekeeping on the hills above, and it was in this house that George Washington slept before marching to victory in Manhattan in 1783.

Riverdale and Wave Hill

The lovely, moneyed heights of **Riverdale** – one of the most desirable neighborhoods in the city – rise above Van Cortlandt Park. The simplest way to get here is to take the Metro North Hudson Line train to Riverdale, a twenty-minute ride from Grand Central; the spectacular country estate of **Wave Hill**, 249th St at Independence Ave, is only a short walk from the station and offers one of the city's best escapes from the urban grind, with lush exotic gardens, greenhouses, an art gallery, several easy but varied nature trails, and rolling lawns dotted with Adirondack chairs overlooking the Hudson River and dramatic Palisades (mid-April to mid-Oct Tues–Sun 9am–5.30pm, July & Aug Wed until 9pm; mid-Oct to mid-April Tues–Sun 9am–4.30pm; $6, seniors and students $3, Sat 9am–noon & all day Tues free; T718/549-3200, Wwww.wavehill.org). From the Metro North Station, walk up 254th Street three steep blocks, turn right on Independence Avenue, and proceed two blocks to Wave Hill gate.

At various times home to Teddy Roosevelt (as a child), Arturo Toscanini, and Mark Twain, the Wave Hill house was built in 1843 by jurist William Lewis Morris, but credit for the site's astounding beauty goes to George W. Perkins, a partner at J.P. Morgan, who linked the house's property with that of the adjacent villa (now called the Glyndor House) in the early twentieth century and landscaped the grounds with an artistry rivaling that of Central Park creator Frederick Law Olmsted. The Perkins family donated the estate to the city in 1960. Free garden and greenhouse tours begin at the Perkins Visitor Center every Sunday at 2.15pm; you can pick up a map there anytime. The busy events calendar includes everything from classical music concerts to family art classes to beekeeping workshops. Check the website for details.

City Island

On the east side of the Bronx, 230-acre **City Island** juts into Long Island Sound and has the feel of a seaside New England town (the population is around 5000), albeit one with a bit of urban grit. To get here, take the #6 train to the end of the line (Pelham Bay Park) and transfer to the #Bx29 bus, which runs over a short causeway to and from the mainland, or visit on the first Friday of the month, from 5.30 to 9.30pm, when a **free trolley** runs from the subway station to the Bartow-Pell Mansion Museum, around the island, and back (☎718/885-9100, ⓦwww.cityislandchamber.org).

There are a few quirky shops here, like Exotiqa International Arts, 280 City Island Ave, as well as a small museum, the **City Island Nautical Museum**, 190 Fordham St (Sun 1–5pm or by appointment; donation; ☎718/885-0507, ⓦwww.cityislandmuseum.org), which touts all of the island's claims to fame – the yachts that won the America's Cup from 1958 through 1987 were built here, for instance – and often hosts interesting lectures by local historians.

Most people come for the waterfront **restaurants**, though: the food may not be particularly creative, but waterfront dining is a treat. To avoid crowds, come on a weekday, when the fish is also fresher. Try the venerable *Lobster Box*, 34 City Island Ave (☎718/885-1952, ⓦwww.lobsterbox.com), for old-school seafood, or romantic *Le Refuge Inn*, 586 City Island Ave (☎718/885-2478, ⓦwww.lerefugeinn.com), for French country fare and accommodations; a few of the fishing piers sell fried clams and beer – *Johnny's* at the end of the road is a good bet.

If you'd like to catch your own dinner, rent a boat and pick up some bait at Jack's Bait and Tackle, 551 City Island Ave (four-person boats $49.99 per day Mon–Fri, $59.99 Sat & Sun, including gear; ☎718/885-2042, ⓦwww.jacksbaitandtackle.com), or charter a boat with a captain who knows the waters (inquire at Jack's for rates and availability).

Pelham Bay Park and Orchard Beach

From City Island, it's an easy walk to **Orchard Beach**, the easternmost part of expansive **Pelham Bay Park** and one of the few really pleasant additions the "master builder" Robert Moses made to the city. Just make a right after the causeway, then follow the path along the water. Beach and boardwalk pulse constantly with a salsa beat, and **free concerts** are common in summer.

At the northern end of the boardwalk, a sign for the **Kazimiroff Nature Trail** points the way into a wildlife preserve named for Theodore Kazimiroff, co-founder of the Bronx County Historical Society and an amateur naturalist who helped stop these wetlands from being turned into a landfill. The network

The Bronx's phantom theme-park

Pelham Bay Park looks to the west over **Co-op City**, a seemingly endless tract of middle-class housing that is one of the Bronx's bleaker icons. Few residents know that their homes stand on New York's great, lost amusement park: **Freedomland**.

Built in the shape of the United States, the 205-acre park opened in 1960 with entertainments based on American history: the great fire of 1871 raged in Chicago, gunfights blazed in the Old Southwest, and earthquakes rocked San Francisco. Reporters loved Freedomland because it inspired such headlines as "Stagecoach Wreck Injures 10 in the Bronx." But the public was not so enthralled. Park developers blamed competition from the 1964 World's Fair in Flushing, though the expo had barely begun when Freedomland declared bankruptcy late in the year. By 1965, Co-op City was in progress: Freedomland had vanished without a trace.

of trails, which winds through 189 acres of meadow, forest, and marsh, is serene and peaceful – a stark contrast with the rest of Pelham Bay Park, now crisscrossed by highways.

The Greek Revival **Bartow–Pell Mansion Museum** (Wed, Sat & Sun noon–4pm; $5, students and seniors $3, under 6 free; ☎718/885-1461, ⓦwww .bartowpellmansionmuseum.org) is a national landmark worth seeing for its beautifully furnished interior, which gives a glimpse of how the other half lived in the 1800s (Mayor LaGuardia wisely commandeered the place for his summer office in 1936); the lavish gardens overlook Long Island Sound. To get there, go back to the Pelham Bay Park subway #6 station and take Westchester Bee-Line bus #45 (☎914/813-7777, ⓦbeelinebus.westchestergov.com).

Staten Island

L ike the rest of New York City, Staten Island was first settled by the Dutch, who finally defeated the Lenape natives in 1661. Three years later, the island and the rest of New York City were in British hands, and in 1783, it saw the last shot of the American Revolution.

Roughly triangular, Staten Island is almost 14 miles long and 7.5 miles wide, making it more than twice the size of Manhattan. It was annexed by New York

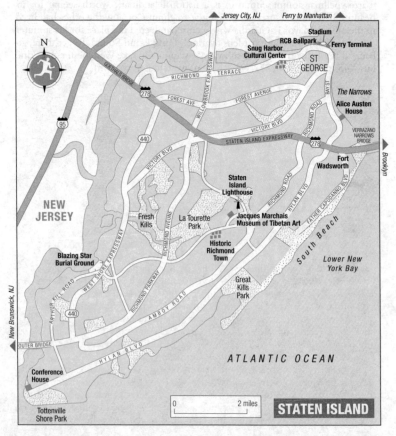

Jersey City, NJ   Ferry to Manhattan

N

Stadium
RCB Ballpark   Ferry Terminal
Snug Harbor
Cultural Center   ST
GEORGE

GOETHALS BRIDGE

RICHMOND TERRACE

278

FOREST AVE   FOREST AVENUE

WILLOWBROOK EXPRESSWAY

The Narrows
Alice Austen
House

95

VICTORY BLVD

RICHMOND ROAD

BAY ST

440

STATEN ISLAND EXPRESSWAY

VICTORY BLVD

278

VERRAZANO
NARROWS
BRIDGE

Brooklyn

NEW
JERSEY

Staten
Island
Lighthouse

Fort
Wadsworth

Fresh
Kills

La Tourette
Park

Jacques Marchais
Museum of Tibetan Art

RICHMOND ROAD

HYLAN BLVD

FATHER CAPODANNO BLVD

South Beach

Blazing Star
Burial Ground

Historic
Richmond
Town

RICHMOND AVENUE

Lower New
York Bay

New Brunswick, NJ

ARTHUR KILL ROAD

WEST SHORE EXPRESSWAY

RICHMOND PARKWAY

Great
Kills
Park

440

AMBOY ROAD

OUTER BRIDGE

HYLAN BLVD

ATLANTIC OCEAN

Conference
House

0   2 miles

Tottenville
Shore Park

STATEN ISLAND

▲ Staten Island Ferry Terminal

City in 1898 but could be reached only by ferry or a long drive through New Jersey (to which it's physically closer) until 1964, when the **Verrazano Narrows Bridge** opened, connecting it with Brooklyn. The resulting influx of land-hungry New Yorkers promptly turned the island's rural landscape into a full-fledged suburbia densely packed with tidy, bland middle-class homes. Large pockets of nature remain – its hilly topography includes marshes, hardwood forests, and beaches – but culturally Staten Island has more in common with New Jersey than with the other four boroughs.

The majority of tourists take the **Staten Island ferry** (see box, p.58) for the views it provides of Manhattan and the Statue of Liberty, then promptly hop the next boat back to the big city. There are a handful of interesting museums and parks here, though, a few of which are within walking distance of the ferry terminal. For the rest, you'll need to take a bus or the single-line Staten Island

Railway (SIR); you can use your MetroCard on both modes of transport. Bus maps are available at the ferry terminals.

For more information on Staten Island events and attractions, or to download free maps, visit ⓦwww.statenislandarts.org or ⓦwww.statenislandusa.com.

St George and around

Passengers disembark the ferry on the northeast corner of the island, in the village of **St George**, which stretches from Westervelt Avenue in the west to Bay Street on the hill above the ferry terminal and is bordered on the south by Victory Boulevard. While it's no waterfront paradise, with views blocked by high-rises and the town cut off from the harbor by large roads, it does house a small **historic district** that includes portions of St Mark's Place, Carroll Place, Westervelt Avenue, Hamilton Avenue, and stretches of Richmond Terrace. The 1906 Beaux-Arts **Borough Hall** (Mon–Fri 9am–5pm; ☎718-816-2000), straight ahead as you walk out of the ferry terminal, has a lobby adorned with WPA murals illustrating the island's history. Two blocks farther, the small **Staten Island Museum**, 75 Stuyvesant Place (Sun–Fri noon–5pm & Sat 10am–5pm; $2; ☎718/727-1135, ⓦwww.statenislandmuseum.org), has exhibits on the history of the ferry, the island's geology, and the Lenape Indians, as well as local fine art. Plans are afoot to move the museum to the Snug Harbor Cultural Center complex, pending a major renovation of two buildings there; check the website for details.

Just northeast of the ferry terminal, the **Richmond County Bank Ballpark**, home of the Staten Island Yankees, is about as beautiful as a ballpark can get, with a view from the bleachers straight out to the open harbor (see p.404 for more information).

Snug Harbor Cultural Center

In contrast to the more urban area around the ferry terminal, the atmosphere of the **Snug Harbor Cultural Center**, 1000 Richmond Terrace (☎718/448-2500, ⓦwww.snug-harbor.org), in nearby New Brighton, is one of bucolic calm, with museums, gardens, performance spaces, artists' studios, and galleries spread over 83 rolling acres. To get there, take the #S40 bus from the terminal, a five-minute ride east along the waterfront; buses run every 15–30min.

The campus functioned as a retirement community for "aged, decrepit, and worn-out sailors" from 1833 to 1976, before being renovated for public use, with its 28 remaining buildings ranging in style from grand Greek-Revival halls to cozy cottages. The oldest building functions as the **visitor center** (Tues–Sun 10am–5pm), where you can get a free map. In one of the other Greek-Revival halls, the **Noble Maritime Collection** (Thurs–Sun 1–5pm; $5; ☎718/447-6490, ⓦwww.noblemaritime.org) displays the work of nautical painter John Noble, as well as his restored houseboat studio and one of the original sailors' dorm rooms. South of the museum buildings, the **Staten Island Children's Museum** (June–Aug Tues–Sun 10am–5pm, Sept–May Tues–Sun noon–5pm; $5, grandparents free Wed; ☎718/273-2060, ⓦwww.statenislandkids.org) offers exhibits such as "Bugs and Other Insects," animal feedings, and arts-and-crafts programs – enough to divert kids, if not utterly enthrall them. A snack bar here serves sandwich wraps, salad, and other snacks.

The rest of the Snug Harbor grounds are given over to the **Staten Island Botanical Garden** (daily dawn to dusk; free; ☎718/273-8200, ⓦwww.sibg.org). This 86-acre sanctuary, built in 1977, includes a section of all-white blooms, flowers catering to butterflies, an antique rose garden, and a children's maze entered through a medieval-look castle ($2 admission). The best attraction, though, is the **New York Chinese Scholar's Garden** (April–Oct Tues–Sun 10am–5pm; Nov–March Wed–Sun 10am–4pm; $5, students, under 12, and seniors $4, free Tues 10am–1pm), a complex of pagoda-roofed halls, including a traditional tea-house, linked by artfully planted courtyards and pools; the admission price also includes entrance to the maze.

The Alice Austen House

Southeast of St George, the **Alice Austen House**, 2 Hylan Blvd (March–Dec Thurs–Sun noon–5pm; suggested donation $2; ☏718/816-4506, ⓦwww.aliceausten.org), is a Victorian cottage facing the Verrazano Narrows, and the spectacular view from the front lawn takes in the Verrazano Bridge as well as the Brooklyn shore. Reach the house by taking the #S51 bus from the ferry dock to Hylan Boulevard, then walking one block east down the hill toward the waterfront.

Austen (1866–1952) was a pioneering amateur photographer whose work comprises one of the finest records of American daily life in the early twentieth century. At a time when photography was both difficult and expensive, she developed her talent and passion for the art expertly, yet never considered going professional. Austen's work was rediscovered only shortly before her death in 1952. The dignified house exhibits only a small selection of her photos (the Staten Island Historical Society owns the whole collection of more than 3000 negatives), but they're fascinating, and the home's beautiful location is a sight in and of itself.

Along the east coast and inland

At the base of the Verrazano Narrows Bridge, a critical position for the defense of the New York Harbor, the vast complex called **Fort Wadsworth** (Wed–Sun 10am–5pm; free; ☏718/354-4500, ⓦwww.nps.gov/gate) marks the north end of Staten Island's eastern coast; take the #S51 bus, or walk fifteen to twenty minutes from the Alice Austen House. The fort, which housed a missile-defense system during the Cold War and was in use until 1996, is attractively ruined and overgrown and provides fantastic views (it's also the staging ground for the annual New York Marathon, which starts on the bridge); ranger-led tours leave the visitor center Wed–Sun at 2.30pm.

South of here – the same bus continues along Father Capodanno Blvd – are several public beaches, not as nice as the Rockaways in Queens, but often less crowded. You first reach **South Beach**, a once thriving resort for New York's wealthy that's known for the two-and-a-half-mile **FDR Boardwalk**, a great place to jog or rollerblade. Farther down the coast, wilder-feeling **Great Kills Park** is, along with Fort Wadsworth, part of the Gateway National Recreation Area. In addition to the beach, which is on a long spit, you'll find nature trails amid scrubby coastal forest. This part of the coast is more easily accessible via the Bay Terrace stop on the SIR.

The Jacques Marchais Museum of Tibetan Art and around

In the middle of Staten Island's residential heartland, the **Jacques Marchais Museum of Tibetan Art**, 338 Lighthouse Ave (Wed–Sun 1–5pm; $5, seniors and students $3, kids $2; ☏718/987-3500, ⓦwww.tibetanmuseum.com), is an unlikely find. Take the #S74 bus and ask to be let off at Lighthouse Avenue (the bus driver may not know of the museum), then hike about ten minutes up the steep hill. A cab from the ferry terminal will cost you $12–14.

Despite being christened Jacques, Marchais was, unusually for a New York art dealer in the 1940s, actually female. She was also successful, and used her income to indulge a passion for Tibetan art. Eventually she assembled about 1200 pieces, and between 1943 and 1947 she built this small fieldstone complex, which clutches onto the steep hillside much as monasteries in Tibet do. One building houses the museum gift shop and a small gallery, and the other, designed to resemble a *gompa*, or temple, displays changing exhibits and a small fraction of the collection, including religious sculptures, *thangka* paintings, a rare Bhutanese sand mandala, and a 250-year-old carved-wood *stupa*. In October, monks in maroon robes perform ritual ceremonies, and food and crafts are sold, at the annual Tibetan Festival.

While you're on this small hill, you'll get a glimpse of the 91-foot-tall **Staten Island Lighthouse**, owned by the Coast Guard but not open to the public; it's a strange thing to see so far inland, but at 231 feet above sea level it has been in near-constant use since it was erected in 1912.

Historic Richmond Town

On the main Richmond Road at St Patrick's Place, a short walk west and south from the Tibetan museum (or a ride on the #S74 bus from the ferry terminal) brings you to **Historic Richmond Town**, 441 Clarke Ave (July & Aug Wed–Sat 10am–5pm, Sun 1–5pm; Sept–June Wed–Sun 1–5pm; $5, seniors $4, children $3.50; ☏718/351-1611, ⓦwww.historicrichmondtown.org). Home to the Staten Island Historical Society, it's a "reinvention" of the village of Richmond, a frontier outpost and center of the island's government from the seventeenth to the late nineteenth century. The 25 original houses are often staffed by costumed volunteers who use traditional techniques to make wooden water buckets and weld tin – it's all carried off to surprisingly picturesque and un-gimmicky effect. You can either explore the dirt roads and buildings on your own, or join the free guided tour that runs weekdays at 2.30pm and on weekends at 2pm and 3.30pm, visiting such gems as the 1695 Dutch-style **Voorlezer's House**, the nation's oldest existing school building.

Conference House

At the far southern end of the island, in the quiet seaside neighborhood known as **Tottenville**, the **Conference House**, 7455 Hylan Blvd (SIR to Tottenville; tours April to mid-Dec Fri–Sun 1–4pm; $3, seniors and children $2; ☏718/984-0415, ⓦwww.theconferencehouse.org), is a stately seventeenth-century stone manor. Its claim to fame is acting as host to failed peace talks, led by Benjamin Franklin and John Adams, during the American Revolution. Step inside for a peek at period furnishings, the original kitchen, which has been restored to working order, and the occasional art show or colonial music concert. The surrounding grounds are occupied by the lovely 267-acre **Conference House Park**.

The west coast

For the intrepid only: Staten Island's west coast is home to the **Arthur Kill boat graveyard**, a stretch of shoreline dotted with rotting hulls of tugboats, barges, ferries, and other once-graceful ocean-going craft. To add to the spooky effect, the **Blazing Star Burial Ground**, named for the ferry that used to run from here to New Jersey, is nearby. Some gravestones date from the 1700s, and many of Staten Island's best families are interred here. Take the #S74 bus from St George to just past Huguenot Avenue – look for the cemetery sign.

Listings

Listings

Accommodation

Accommodation in New York definitely eats up the lion's share of most travelers' budgets. Many **hotels** in the city charge in the neighborhood of $200 a night, and most go well beyond that price (these are pre-**tax** rates – see p.276). It is possible to get a safe, clean room for less than that, but it's almost always easier to find a place to splurge on than it is to find a bargain.

Anywhere you're going to want to stay is going to require **reservations**; make them as far in advance as possible, especially for visits during the high season (May to Sept and Nov to early January) – you're likely to find everything chock-full if you wait until the last minute. Most hotels in New York only hold reservations until 5 or 6pm unless you've warned them that you'll be arriving late.

There are three ways to book a room: directly through the hotel (either by phone or through its website), on a travel website, or through a travel agent. If you're going to do it yourself, try to use the local phone number, as it can be much more expedient than going through the national service at the "800" number. In either case, inquire about discounts; prices are often reduced on weekends (especially downtown choices, as they tend to be devoid of their usual business travelers then), in the low season (Feb to April and Oct), and via corporate promotions. Travel websites list all-inclusive flight and hotel package vacations and occasionally offer special deals; Ⓦ www.nycvisit.com has a good selection of specials for American Express cardholders (which come with a list of restrictions). Travel agents provide more or less the same services. If you're looking for lodging in a particular area, refer to the Accommodation map, pp.274–275, for help.

There are plenty of **hostels** with dormitory accommodation for the young or budget-minded. Other moderately priced options include **bed and breakfasts**, which basically entail staying in somebody's spare room with all the amenities of a private apartment. These rooms go for approximately $80 and up for a double and can be booked through an agency listed in the appropriate section below.

Wherever you stay, you'll be expected to **pay in advance**, or at least provide a deposit for the first night. If you're booking over the phone or on the Internet, be prepared to give a credit-card number. Most places will run the credit card through when you arrive as a preliminary (you won't be charged until you leave), but they'll also accept cash, and occasionally travelers' checks.

Keep in mind that even though there are thousands of guest rooms in New York City, there are still not enough to go around. Most properties have a steady parade of occupants, and as a result show some wear and tear. Unless you're checking into a luxury hotel – and sometimes even then – don't be surprised

Le Parker Meridien	9
Library	45
Mansfield	41
Marriot Marquis	32
Mayfair	24
Metro	51
Michelangelo	19
Milford Plaza	36
Millennium Broadway	37
Morgans	50
Murray Hill Inn	59
Muse	31
Novotel	17
Paramount	30
Park Savoy	8
Pierre	2
Plaza	5
Pod	20
Radisson	25
Roger Smith	28
Roger Williams	56
Salisbury	7
Sanctuary	27
Seventeen	72
Shelburne Murray Hill	49
Sherry Netherland	3
Shoreham	13
Stanford	54
Thirty-One	58
Thirty Thirty	60
The Time	23
Vanderbilt YMCA	29
W Union Square	71
Waldorf-Astoria	21
Warwick	14
Washington Square	75
Wellington	12
Westin New York at Times Square	75
West Side YMCA	42

to occasionally see chipped furniture and scuffs on the wall. That said, there is a difference between continuous use and unsanitary conditions; if you feel your room is dirty or unsafe, don't hesitate to talk to the management.

Hotels

Most of New York's **hotels** are in midtown Manhattan, in close proximity to many of the main tourist sights, though there are also a growing number of options downtown. The Upper West or Upper East sides should do if your taste runs more to Central Park and the high culture of museums and Lincoln Center. As for New York hotel design and marketing, the most recent concept is the "boutique" hotel. These establishments are typically fairly intimate (100 or fewer rooms), with less square footage per room but more in the way of guest amenities.

Most hotels do not offer free **breakfast**, though complimentary continental breakfasts have become increasingly popular. If you have to pay for breakfast, you'll do better at a nearby diner. Tipping is expected at upmarket hotels: unless you firmly refuse, a bellhop will grab your bags when you check in and expect a few dollars to carry them to your room. The cleaning staff will really appreciate your tip when you leave (figure $2 minimum per day for cheaper hotels, $5 a day for the nicer establishments). Minibars, stocked with booze and chocolate goodies at astronomical prices, are formulated to appeal to your sense of laziness; these and the hotel shops that sell basic necessities at three times the street price should be avoided.

Taxes are added to your hotel bill, and hotels will nearly always quote you the price of a room before tax. Taxes will add 13.375 percent to your bill (state tax 8.375 percent, city tax 5 percent), and there is also a $3.50 per night "occupancy tax." All told, this will add about $35 to a $200 room.

The following selection of hotels runs the gamut from the city's cheapest to most luxurious and/or hippest. Unless noted, the prices quoted at the end of each listing represent the price of the hotel's cheapest double room, excluding all taxes, during the high season when rates are at a premium. Regardless, prices change daily, so it's best to check early and often. Hotels are listed alphabetically within each geographical region below. For a visual overview of where to find a listed hotel, see the main Accommodation map on pp.274–275, or the neighborhood maps.

Downtown: south of 14th Street

60 Thompson 60 Thompson St, between Spring and Broome sts ☏1-877/431-0400, ⓦwww.60thompson.com. Designed by Thomas O'Brien's Aero Studio, rooms at this boutique property ooze sophistication and tempt guests with countless amenities – including gourmet minibars stocked with goodies from Dean & Deluca (p.399) – and a 24hr concierge. In summer there's a rooftop lounge with views of Soho. $649
Cosmopolitan 95 W Broadway, at Chambers St ☏1-888/895-9400 or 212/566-1900, ⓦwww.cosmohotel.com. A great Tribeca location, smart, well-maintained rooms, and incredibly low prices make the *Cosmopolitan* a steal. $219
Embassy Suites 102 North End Ave, at Vesey St ☏1-800/EMBASSY or 212/945-0100, ⓦwww.embassysuites.com. Near the quiet Battery Park City esplanade, the *Embassy Suites* is a little out of the way, but the roomy bedroom and living areas have tons of amenities, and a cook-to-order breakfast is included (virtually unheard of elsewhere). Weekend stays are discounted. $449
Gansevoort 18 Ninth Ave, at W 13th St ☏1-877/426-7368 or 212/206-6700, ⓦwww.hotelgansevoort.com. When cobblestone streets in the Meatpacking District were torn up to make room for this sleek

Hotel booking services

Central Reservation Service ☏1-800/555-7555 or 407/740-6442, ⓦ www.crshotels.com

Hotel Discounts ☏1-800/715-7666, ⓦ www.hoteldiscount.com

Meegan's Services ☏1-800/441-1115 or 718/995-9292

Quikbook ☏1-800/789-9887, ⓦ www.quikbook.com

hotel, preservationists were horrified, but the neighborhood seems to have benefitted. Rooms, in muted tones, are spiffy, with top-notch electronics, but you're really paying for the 360-degree views, the full spa, the heated rooftop pool (one of very few in the city), and the scene. $385

Holiday Inn Downtown 138 Lafayette St, at Howard St ☏1-800/HOLIDAY or 212/966-8898, ⓦ www.holiday-inn.com. Just north of busy Canal St, this member of the well-known chain is also a stone's throw from Soho and Tribeca. Though the rooms are small for the price, the rates fluctuate so booking early should get you a better deal. $269

Larchmont 27 W 11th St, between Fifth and Sixth aves ☏212/989-9333, ⓦ www .larchmonthotel.com. A budget hotel, in a terrific location on a tree-lined street in Greenwich Village. Rooms are small but homey and clean. A robe and slippers are thoughtfully provided so you can traipse down the hall to the shared bath. Includes continental breakfast. $119

Marriott Downtown 85 West St, between Carlisle and Albany sts ☏212/385-4900, ⓦ www.marriott.com. This civilized business hotel boasts excellent service as well as superb views of the Hudson River and New York Harbor. It's situated near the relaxing Battery Park City esplanade, but you've got to cross the West Side Highway to get there. $359

Mercer 147 Mercer St, at Prince St ☏212/966-6060, ⓦ www.mercerhotel.com. Housed in a Romanesque Revival building in Soho, the *Mercer* is one of the top accommodation choices of visiting celebs. Suites top out at $3100 (and 1400sq-ft) but even the 250-sq-ft courtyard rooms are fairly pricey. It's all worth it for the amenities, though: the concierge can arrange private training or massage virtually around the clock, there's free access to local gyms, and the excellent *Mercer Kitchen* restaurant (see p.310) provides 24hr room service. $595

▲ Mercer Kitchen, at the Mercer Hotel

Ritz-Carlton 2 West St, Battery Park City ☏212/344-0800, ⓦ www.ritzcarlton.com. The views of New York Harbor and the Statue of Liberty don't get much better than from the rooms here. The hotel features a bar that serves some of the city's best margaritas, boasts 425-square-foot rooms with soothing, muted tones (the harbor rooms even come with telescopes), and has "bath butlers" draw baths and deliver warm towels. $495

SoHo Grand 310 W Broadway, between Canal and Grand sts ☏212/965-3000, ⓦ www.sohogrand.com. In a great location at the edge of Soho, this place draws guests of the model/actor variety. The stylish, chocolate-hued rooms have personality to match, while cast-iron staircases with vault lights, a glass elevator shaft and 20-foot ceilings lend the common areas an industrial yet inviting feel. There's also a sharp-looking bar, restaurant, and hidden outdoor terrace. $349

Tribeca Grand 2 Ave of the Americas, between White and Walker sts ☎212/519-6600, Ⓦwww .tribecagrand.com. Craving anonymity, the *Tribeca Grand* is unlabeled and tucked behind a brick facade. Inside, the striking *Church Lounge* beckons with a warm glow (it's a great space in which to hang out). Rooms are fashionably understated, though bathrooms boast phones and TVs, and the staff is extra attentive. Off-season weekends can be several hundred dollars cheaper. $369

Washington Square 103 Waverly Place, at Washington Square Park ☎212/777-9515, Ⓦwww.washingtonsquarehotel.com. In the heart of Greenwich Village, this hotel is quite close to the area's many nightlife options. Don't be deceived by the posh-looking lobby – the rooms are surprisingly plain for the price (though the Art Deco "Deluxe" rooms have a bit more character). Continental breakfast is included. $225

The East Side: E 14th to 36th streets

Carlton 88 Madison Ave ☎1-800/601-8500 or 212/532-4100, Ⓦwww.carltonhotelny.com. A smartly located, Beaux-Arts building entered by a stylish if unflashy portal, the *Carlton* offers roomy quarters outfitted in cream-and-tan-striped wallpaper and mahogany furnishings. Beds are all fluffiness and Frette linens, while the clubby restaurant/lounge offers superb service. $369

Giraffe 365 Park Ave S, at 26th St ☎1-877/296-0009 or 212/685-7700, Ⓦwww.hotelgiraffe.com. The tall and slender *Giraffe* is similar in tone and amenities to sister hotels *Library* (see p.280) and *Casablanca* (see p.281), but these rooms invoke the sleek Art Moderne style of the 1920s and 1930s. Prices

include complimentary breakfast, afternoon wine and cheese, and a 24hr espresso bar. $459

Gramercy Park 2 Lexington Ave, at E 21st St ☎1-877/898-3200 or 212/920-3300, Ⓦwww .gramercyparkhotel .com. The Ian Schrager Group renovated the staid *Gramercy Park* and opened it in 2006 as a totally unique property done in a style the hotel calls "Surreal Contemporary" or "Haute Bohemian." That means the grand entrance gets a red carpet and a chandelier, but also reclaimed lumber, modern artworks, strange light fixtures, and a toreador's jacket. Rooms are similarly eclectic, bold and luxurious. It's also in a lovely location – guests get a key to the adjacent private park. $495

Murray Hill Inn 143 E 30th St, between Lexington and Third aves ☎212/683-6900, Ⓦwww.murrayhillinn.com. It's easy to see why young travelers and backpackers line the *Inn*'s narrow halls. Although the inexpensive rooms can be tiny, they all have a telephone, a/c, and cable TV; some also have private bathrooms. $139

Roger Williams 131 Madison Ave, at E 31st St ☎1-888/448-7788 or 212/448-7000, Ⓦwww.hotelrogerwilliams.com. The first thing you'll notice at the *Roger* is the use of color; the Scandinavian/Japanese fusion rooms utilize both mellow and vibrant tones (even the business card dons bright stripes). There's a hot lounge and an up-to-date fitness room. $400

Seventeen 225 E 17th St, between Second and Third aves ☎212/475-2845, Ⓦwww.hotel17ny .com. *Seventeen*'s rooms come with basic amenities; many share baths. The hotel itself is neat and nicely situated on a pleasant tree-lined street just minutes from Union Square and the East Village. $150

Thirty-One 120 E 31st St, between Park and Lexington aves ☎212/685-3060, ⓦwww .hotel31.com. An affordable Murray Hill option run by the folks who own *Seventeen*. The 60 rooms are clean and the location is quiet; some rooms share a bath. $140

🏃 **Thirty Thirty** 30 E 30th St, between Park and Madison aves ☎1-800/804-4480 or 212/689-1900, ⓦwww.thirtythirty-nyc.com. Small, welcoming hotel, with a few minor but welcome design touches, including CD players, dataports, and framed black-and-white scenes of old New York in all the rooms. $269

W Union Square 201 Park Ave S at E 17th St ☎212/253-9119, ⓦwww.whotels.com. This stylish chain of luxury hotels – there are four other locations in Manhattan – offers top-to-bottom comfort; rooms (Wonderful, Spectacular and Mega) are outfitted with all the amenities a traveler could ever need. Also houses a branch of celebrity chef Todd English's *Olives* restaurant. $479

The West Side: W 14th to 36th streets

Affinia Manhattan 371 Seventh Ave, at W 31st St ☎1-866/233-4642 or 212/563-1800, ⓦwww .affinia.com. This all-suite hotel is housed in a 1929 building opposite Penn Station and Madison Square Garden. Though it's a bustling address, the friendly staff foster relaxation by way of an in-room spa service and a 6-option pillow menu. $329

Chelsea Lodge 318 W 20th St, between Eighth and Ninth aves ☎212/243-4499, ⓦwww .chelsealodge.com. The *Lodge* is a gem of a place: upon entrance, you'll be greeted by Early American/Sportsman décor. As a former boarding house, normal rooms, which offer in-room showers and sinks (there's a shared toilet down the hall), are a little snug for two, but the few deluxe

rooms are great value and have full bathrooms. A three-day cancellation policy applies. $129

Chelsea Savoy Hotel 204 W 23rd St, at Seventh Ave ☎212/929-9353, ⓦwww.chelseasavoynyc .com. A few doors away from the *Chelsea Hotel*, the *Savoy* has none of its neighbor's funky charm. The rooms, decent-sized, are clean and nicely decorated and the staff is reasonably helpful. Try to avoid rooms facing the main drags outside though; they can be noisy. $250

Comfort Inn Chelsea 18 W 25th St, between Sixth Ave and Broadway ☎212/645-3990, ⓦwww.comfortinn.com. The *Comfort Inn Chelsea* is a solid hotel with very good prices and clean, albeit smallish, rooms. Near Madison Square Park, it's equidistant from downtown and midtown. Off-season rates drop significantly. $259

Comfort Inn Manhattan 42 W 35th St, between Fifth and Sixth aves ☎212/947-0200, ⓦwww .comfortinnmanhattan.com. The best things about this hotel are the free, deluxe continental breakfast and cheery, good-value rooms. The management, though, can be less than helpful; it's not always possible to see a room before you decide to bunk down. $199

Herald Square 19 W 31st St, between Fifth Ave and Broadway ☎1-800/727-1888 or 212/279-4017, ⓦwww.heraldsquarehotel.com. The original home of *Life* magazine, *Herald Square* still features Philip Martiny's sculpted cherub *Winged Life* over its Beaux-Arts doorway. The inside is clean but somewhat soulless and without much in the way of extras. $239

🏃 **Hotel Chelsea** 222 W 23rd St, between Seventh and Eighth aves ☎212/243-3700, ⓦwww.hotelchelsea.com. One of New York's most notorious landmarks, this aging neo-Gothic building boasts a fabulously

Expense-account hotels

Make sure the bill goes to someone else so you can enjoy these lavish locations without worrying about your wallet:

Bryant Park Hotel 40 W 40th St, between Fifth and Sixth aves; p.281
Mercer 147 Mercer, at Prince St; p.277
The Plaza Fifth Ave at Central Park South p.283
Sherry Netherland 781 Fifth Ave, at E 59th St; p.285
SoHo Grand Hotel 310 W Broadway, between Canal and Grand sts; p.277

seedy and artistic past (see p.115). Most of the spacious rooms and suites have been renovated, but not so that they've given up their history: they still come with wood floors, log-burning fireplaces, and kitchenettes. $99

Hotel Pennsylvania 401 Seventh Ave, between W 32nd and 33rd sts ☏212/736-5000 or 1-800/223-8585, ⊛www.hotelpenn.com. Boasting the same telephone number since 1917 (the "Pennsylvania six five thousand" of the Glenn Miller song), this hotel across from Madison Square Garden offers a range of amenities in its 1705 rooms, though you can't help thinking things looked better back in Glenn's day. $279

🏃 **The Metro 45 W 35th St, between Fifth and Sixth aves ☏212/947-2500, ⊛www .hotelmetronyc.com.** A very stylish hotel, with old b&w Hollywood posters on the walls and understated, inviting rooms. There's also a fitness room and a restaurant, while freebies (wi-fi throughout the hotel, expanded continental breakfast) and a delightful seasonal rooftop terrace make it more than decent value. $375

Stanford 43 W 32nd St, between Broadway and Fifth Ave ☏1-800/365-1114 or 212/563-1500, ⊛www.hotelstanford.com. A clean, moderately priced hotel on the block known as Little Korea. The rooms are a tad small, but attractive and very quiet. Free continental breakfast, jazz Sat nights in the *Maxim* lounge, and an efficient, friendly staff. $199

Midtown East: E 36th to 59th streets

🏃 **Alex Hotel 205 E 45th St, off Third Ave ☏212/867-5100, ⊛www.thealexhotel .com.** This sleek, beige-toned spot is a serene midtown oasis. Rooms are bright and airy, with modern Scandinavian touches and a handful of fun eccentricities (a tiny TV in the bathroom, hideaway cabinets and compartments). The award-winning chef from *Aquavit* (see p.324) heads the restaurant-bar Riingo which provides 24hr room service. $469

Beekman Tower 3 Mitchell Place, at E 49th St and First Ave ☏1-866/298-4506 or 212/355-7300, ⊛www.thebeekmanhotel.com. Populated with 174 traditional-looking rooms (actually, suites with fully equipped kitchens) on 26 floors, the hotel is one of the more stylish in the area, with great views from the Top of the top-floor *Tower* bar/lounge. It's also quiet, if a bit out of the way. $349

Dylan 52 E 41st St, between Park and Madison aves ☏1-866/55-DYLAN or 212/338-0500, ⊛www.dylanhotel.com. Classy and clever, *Dylan*'s rooms have been attentively designed (the 11ft ceilings make them look quite large) and bathrooms are clad in Italian marble. If you're looking to splurge, book the Alchemy Suite, a one-of-a-kind Gothic bedchamber with a vaulted ceiling and stained-glass windows. $399

Fitzpatrick Manhattan 687 Lexington Ave, between E 56th and 57th sts ☏212/355-0100 or 1-800/367-7701, ⊛www.fitzpatrickhotels .com. This handsome Irish-themed hotel is perfectly situated for visits to midtown stores, Upper East Side museums, and Central Park. A hearty Irish breakfast ($15) is served all day. $429

Jolly Madison Towers 22 E 38th St, at Madison Ave ☏212/802-0600, ⊛www .jollymadison.com. This NYC outpost of the leading Italian chain offers restful, fairly spacious rooms outfitted with handcrafted furnishings and Venetian glass. Check the website for specials. $269

Library 299 Madison Ave (entry on E 41st St) ☏1-877/793-READ or 212/983-4500, ⊛www .libraryhotel.com. The *Library*'s concept, one of New York hostelry's more unusual, has each floor devoted to one of the ten major categories of the Dewey Decimal System. Colored in shades of brown and cream, the rooms are average in size but nicely appointed with big bathrooms. The hotel's quirky, sumptuous appeal is worth spending a few extra dollars on. $369

Morgans 237 Madison Ave, between E 37th and E 38th sts ☏1-800/334-3408 or 212/686-0300, ⊛www.morganshotel.com. Still one of the chicest hotels in town, and still frequented by the stars. Rooms, with maple paneling and neutral tones are soothing, with specially-commissioned black-and-white photos by the late Robert Mapplethorpe. Continental breakfast included. $499

🏃 **Pod 230 E 51st St, between Second and Third aves ☏212/355-0300, ⊛www .thepodhotel.com.** This pleasant hotel (the former *Pickwick Arms*) is one of the best deals in midtown. All 370 pods (solo, double, bunk, or queen, all reminiscent of a colorful ship's quarters) come with a/c, iPod docks, free wi-fi and LCD TVs, although some are shared bath. The open-air roof-deck bar is a bonus, with stunning views. $249

Radisson 511 Lexington Ave, at E 48th St ☎212/755-4400, 🖥www.radisson.com. Nicer than one would expect, with recently refreshed and airy rooms, fully furnished fitness center, and capable concierge. $329

Roger Smith 501 Lexington Ave, at E 47th St ☎212/755-1400, 🖥www.rogersmith.com. Stylish and helpful, with inviting rooms individually decorated in contemporary, whimsical American style, and bold, colorful artwork on display in the public spaces. In sum, lots of personality. Breakfast is included. $349

Shelburne Murray Hill 303 Lexington Ave, between E 37th and 38th sts ☎212/689-5200, 🖥www.affinia.com. Luxurious hotel (totally renovated as of 2009) in the most elegant part of Murray Hill. All the rooms have kitchenettes, and there's a separate restaurant downstairs that specializes in gourmet burgers (and provides room service). There's also a buzzing bar scene on the roof terrace in season. $419

Waldorf-Astoria 301 Park Ave, at E 50th St ☎1-800/WALDORF or 212/355-3000, 🖥www .waldorf.com. One of the city's first grand hotels (see p.134), the *Waldorf* has been restored to its 1930s glory and is a wonderful place to stay, if you can afford it. It's no wonder this is a favorite pick for presidents and visiting heads of state – the spacious accommodations feature the latest electronic gadgets, triple sheeting, and marble baths. At least drop by for a drink at the legendary mahogany bar, a peek at one of the opulent banquet halls, or a treatment at the full-service spa. $459

Midtown West: W 36th to 59th streets

Algonquin 59 W 44th St, between Fifth and Sixth aves ☎1-888/304-2047 or 212/840-6800, 🖥www.algonquinhotel.com. New York's oldest continuously-operated hotel and one of the city's famed literary hangouts (see p.127) also employs the warmest staff in hoteldom. The *Algonquin* has retained its old-club atmosphere and décor from the days of the Round Table, though the rooms have been refurbished to handsome effect (large flat-screens,

▲ The Algonquin

refreshed carpets and bedding) and the lobby has had a mini-facelift. Ask about summer and weekend specials. $549

Ameritania Hotel 54 230 W 54th St, at Broadway ☎1-888/66-HOTEL or 212/247-5000, 🖥www.nychotels.com. With sleek, angular furnishings, soaring columns and a bold color palette, this retro-inspired hotel is one of the cooler-looking options in the city. All rooms have cable and CD players, and deluxe rooms (only a little pricier than the standard ones) feature marble baths. $319

Bryant Park Hotel 40 W 40th St, between Fifth and Sixth aves ☎1-877/640-9300 or 212/869-0100, 🖥www.bryantparkhotel.com. This hotel shows off its edgy attitude in its stylish contemporary rooms, luxurious 70-seat film-screening room, and funky *Cellar Bar*, which is always filled with media types. (Skip the seizure-inducing intro on the hotel's website). $545

Casablanca 147 W 43rd St, between Sixth Ave and Broadway ☎1-888/922-7225 or 212/869-1212, 🖥www.casablancahotel.com. Geometric Moorish tiles, inlaid wood, and *Rick's Café* are all here in this theme hotel along with a daily wine-and-cheese reception and comp gym passes. While the décor is 1940s Morocco, the rooms all have up-to-date amenities. Two-night minimum on weekends. $349

Chambers Hotel 15 W 56th St, between Fifth and Sixth aves ☎1-866/204-5656 or 212/974-5656, ⓦwww.chambershotel.com. Designed by architect David Rockwell, this place houses over 500 original works of art in its gallery-sized hallways. The modern, tasteful rooms approximate a New York apartment, as do the mezzanine-level lounge spaces. Inside the *Chambers* is *Town*, a very good, if pricey, restaurant. $525

Edison 228 W 47th St, between Broadway and Eighth Ave ☎212/840-5000, ⓦwww.edisonhotelnyc.com. The most striking thing about the 1000-room *Edison* is its beautifully restored Art Deco lobby, built in the same style as Radio City Music Hall. The rooms, while not fancy, are clean and relatively new. Prices are quite reasonable for midtown. $195

Flatotel 135 W 52nd St, between Sixth and Seventh aves ☎1-800/352-8683 or 212/887-9400, ⓦwww.flatotel.com. A comfortable, stylish hotel in the heart of midtown highlighting clean lines and motifs inspired by architect Frank Lloyd Wright. For those not bothered by agoraphobia, check out the Sky Gym fitness center on the 46th floor. $369

Hampton Inn Times Square 851 Eighth Ave, between W 51st and 52nd sts ☎212/581-4100, ⓦwww.hamptoninn.com. While the facade has absolutely zero character, the hotel warms up slightly inside. Rooms, if not exacly trendy, are decorated in maroon, brown, and gold, with free in-room Internet access, coffee makers and movie channels. $349

Hilton Times Square 234 W 42nd St, between Seventh and Eighth aves ☎1-800/HILTONS or 212/840-8222, ⓦwww.hilton.com. This gorgeous property is housed in a 44-story tower, which yields awesome views in all directions. The neutral-toned rooms are good-sized, with attractive furnishings in blonde wood. Ask about packages or specials. $379

Hotel 41 at Times Square 206 W 41st St ☎1-877/847-4444 or 212/703-8600, ⓦwww.hotel41.com. With just 47 rooms, this boutique hotel blends classic and contemporary styles to pleasing effect. Rooms come with high-speed Internet access, Aveda bath products, free Internet and cappuccino, and satellite TV. $339

Hotel Grace 125 W 45th St, between Sixth and Seventh aves ☎212/354-2323, ⓦwww.room-matehotels.com. Until recently known as Hotel QT, this latest incarnation ups the extroversion. Guests have round-the-clock access to the spa and pool, and the kiosk stocked with candles and liquor is also the reception 'desk.' Rooms are ultra-modern (and pet friendly) but modest-sized, with platform beds. It takes some getting used to the darkish hallways, however. $249

Hudson 356 W 58th St, between Eighth and Ninth aves ☎1-800/444-4786 or 212/554-6000, ⓦwww.hudsonhotel.com. Once you get past the *Hudson*'s chartreuse-lit escalators and space-shuttle-esque bar, the rooms are surprisingly tasteful (though miniscule), and there's the added cache of a library and sky terrace. Rates are lower during the week than on weekends. $479

Iroquois 49 W 44th St, between Fifth and Sixth aves ☎1-800/332-7220 or 212/840-3080, ⓦwww.iroquoisny.com. Once a haven for rock bands, this elegant, reinvented boutique hotel has comfortable, tasteful rooms with Italian-marble baths and mahogany and suede headboards. The lounge is named for actor James Dean, one of the hotel's residents from 1951 to 1953. Some claim his room (#803) still retains an element of magic. $489

Jumeirah Essex House 160 Central Park S, between Sixth and Seventh aves ☎1-888/645-5697 or 212/247-0300, ⓦwww.jumeirahessexhouse.com. Formerly known as simply *Essex House*, this beautiful hotel has been restored to its original Art Deco splendor with a $90 million renovation. The best rooms have spectacular Central Park views, and despite the attentive service and marble lobby, the atmosphere is quite relaxed. $499

Le Parker Meridien 118 W 57th St, between Sixth and Seventh aves ☎212/245-5000, ⓦwww.parkermeridien.com. This hotel maintains a shiny, clean veneer, with comfortably modern rooms, a huge fitness center, rooftop swimming pool, and 24hr room service. Inquire about discounted weekend rates. $519

Mansfield 12 W 44th St, between Fifth and Sixth aves ☎1-800/255-5167 or 212/277-8700, ⓦwww.mansfieldhotel.com. One of the nicest little hotels in the city, the *Mansfield* manages to be both grand and intimate. A clubby library lounge, and live jazz during the week (not to mention free wi-fi and a gym), lends the place an affable air, conducive to simply wandering around. Rates are fair, especially considering the complimentary European breakfast and all-day cappuccino. $349

Marriott Marquis 1535 Broadway, at W 45th St ☎212/398-1900, ⊛www.nymarriottmarquis .com. It's worth dropping by here even if only to gawk at the split-level atrium and ride the glass elevators to New York's only revolving bar and restaurant. The hotel is well-designed for conference or convention guests, though the rooms themselves are modest for the high price. $429

Mayfair 242 W 49th St, between Broadway and Eighth Ave ☎1-800/556-2932 or 212/586-0300, ⊛www.mayfairnewyork.com. This boutique-style hotel, across the street from the St Malachay Actors' Chapel, has toile-wallpapered rooms, and a charming, old-fashioned feel. A nice touch is the preponderance of historic photographs on loan from the Museum of the City of New York. $199

Michelangelo 152 W 51st St, between Sixth and Seventh aves ☎1-800/237-0990 or 212/765-0505, ⊛www.michelangelohotel.com. A veritable palazzo on Broadway, this hotel, part of an Italian chain, features acres of marble. While no expense is spared in the luxurious "standard" rooms, suites come in Art Deco, Empire, or Country French – take your pick. Make sure to check out the special Internet rates. $445

Milford Plaza 700 Eighth Ave, between 44th and 45th sts ☎1-800/221-2690 or 212/869-3600, ⊛www.milfordplaza.com. Rooms are tiny and the atmosphere is impersonal in this *Ramada* hotel, but hordes of theater-goers still flock here for the "Lullabuy [sic] of Broadway" deals, which include theater tickets. Packages vary; best to call or book online. $249

Millennium Broadway 145 W 44th St, between Broadway and Sixth Ave ☎1-866/866-8086 or 212/768-4400, ⊛www.millenniumhotels.com. Black marble and modern Italian wall-to-ceiling artwork dominate the *Millennium Broadway* lobby; the sleek lines continue in the beautiful off-white bedrooms. Rates are high but justifiably so. $429

Muse 130 W 46th St, between Sixth and Seventh aves ☎1-877/NYC-MUSE or 212/485-2400, ⊛www.themusehotel.com. A small hotel in the center of the Times Square area,

Muse caters to Europeans. The slightly dark and off-putting lobby (it looks like the reception area at a brokerage house) contrasts with the airy rooms, done in bold black-and-white patterns. *The District* restaurant downstairs (seasonal American) is similarly confident; it's won kudos from the *New York Times*. $419

Novotel 226 W 52nd St, at Broadway ☎212/315-0100 or 1-800/NOVOTEL, ⊛www .novotel.com. This international chain hotel is large enough to offer a decent range of facilities while small enough to cultivate some character. The look is casual but sleek, featuring uncluttered wood with blue accents, and the food good (as you might expect from a French-owned establish-ment). $269

Paramount 235 W 46th St, between Broadway and Eighth Ave ☎212/764-5500, ⊛www .nycparamount.com. A former budget hotel renovated into a boutique bolt-hole by Ian Schrager (co-founder of *Studio 54*), the *Paramount* offers chic, closet-sized rooms. It also boasts a trendy (and sometimes raucous) bar. $279

🏃 **Park Savoy** 158 W 58th St, between Sixth and Seventh aves ☎212/245-5755, ⊛www.parksavoyhotel.com. Despite a somewhat chilly desk staff, the *Park Savoy* with its cozy rooms (all with private bath) is just a block from Central Park, which makes this hotel great value for the area. $185

🏃 **The Plaza** Fifth Ave at Central Park South ☎212/759-3000, ⊛www.theplaza.com. Silencing the naysayers, *The Plaza* has awakened from its two-year slumber with new owners and looking better than ever. The grand tradition of the hotel is still there in the Baccarat chandeliers (in the rooms, too) and 24-carat-gold fixtures, but now there's also a huge screen for your viewing pleasure, and a wireless flat-panel gadget that can turn on the DVD, dim the lights, and summon the floor butler. Needless to say, service is impeccable. $895

Salisbury 123 W 57th St, between Sixth and Seventh aves ☎212/246-1300, ⊛www.nycsalisbury.com. Good service, large (somewhat old-fashioned) rooms with kitch-enettes, and proximity to Central Park and Carnegie Hall are the attractions here. $319

Sanctuary 132 W 47th St, between Sixth and Seventh aves ☎1-800/388-8988 or 212/382-0600, ⊛www.sanctuaryhotelnyc.com. It takes a serious overhaul to make the jump from one to four stars, but that's what the Sanctuary set its sights on. The former plain *Portland Square* is now ultra-modern and trendy in both its common spaces and rooms. $350

Shoreham 33 W 55th St, between Fifth and Sixth aves ☏212/247-6700, ⊛www.shoreham hotel.com. The *Shoreham* is done up, or rather, down, in minimalist chic: a cool white marble lobby, blue wall accents, polished steel columns, and a black-clad, spiky-haired staff only emphasize the fact. The rooms are of average size, but there's a boisterous bar scene downstairs. $399

The Time 224 W 49th St, between Broadway and Eighth Ave ☏1-877/TIME NYC or 212/246-5252, ⊛www.thetimeny.com. *Tempus fugit* – and everything here reminds you of this fact, from the waist-level clock in the lobby to the hallways bedecked with Roman numerals (though the 24hr fitness center may help time stand still, for a bit…). Smallish rooms are tricked out with Bose sound systems, ergonomic work stations, and LCD screens. $299

Warwick 65 W 54th St, at Sixth Ave ☏1-800/223-4099 or 212/247-2700, ⊛www .warwickhotelny.com. Legendary newspaperman William Randolph Hearst commissioned the hotel in 1926, and stars of the 1950s and 1960s – including Cary Grant, Rock Hudson, the Beatles, Elvis Presley, and JFK – stayed here as a matter of course. Although the hotel has lost its showbiz cachet, the elegant lobby, restaurant, and cocktail lounge still make it a pleasant place to stay. The staff is helpful and quite friendly. $399

Wellington 871 Seventh Ave, at W 55th St ☏1-800/652-1212 or 212/247-3900, ⊛www .wellingtonhotel.com. Close to the cultural meccas of Carnegie Hall and Lincoln Center, the *Wellington* is very reasonably priced for this neck of town. Some of the traditionally-decorated rooms have kitchenettes. (And according to the staff, Borat did not sleep here…) $259

Westin New York at Times Square 270 W 43rd St at Eighth Ave ☏1-800/WESTIN-1 or 212/201-2700, ⊛www.westinnewyork.com. The copper-and-blue-glass high-rise seems a little out of place – it was designed by Miami architects – but it's nonetheless a welcome addition to the Times Square scene. The high-tech rooms have comfortable beds and sweeping views, while baths come with 5-speed double shower heads. $369

Upper East Side: north of E 59th Street

Franklin 164 E 87th St, between Lexington and Third aves ☏212/369-1000, ⊛www.franklin hotel.com. An apparent contradiction: how can one establishment win kudos as both "sexiest hotel" and "best bed and breakfast"? In any case, the quiet residential location makes up for its distance to the heart of the city, and the cheery rooms and baths fitted with Bulgari bath products prove very relaxing. $299

Mark 25 E 77th St, at Madison Ave ☏212/744-4300, ⊛www.themarkhotel.com. This hotel really lives up to its claims of sophistication and elegance. The lobby is decked out in Biedermeier furniture and sleek Italian lighting, and there's a pervasive sense of refinement in the plush guest rooms, restaurant, and invitingly dark bar. $655

Pierre 2 E 61st, at Fifth Ave ☏1-800/743-7734 or 212/940-8101, ⊛www.tajhotels.com. The *Pierre* is consistently named one of New York's top hotels. It was Salvador Dalí's favorite in the city, though the only surreal aspects today are the prices. If these

▲ The Pierre

You'll find fewer rooms, more amenities, and an emphasis on design at these intimate properties:

60 Thompson 60 Thompson St, between Spring and Broome sts; p.276

Alex 205 E 45th St, between Second and Third aves; p.280

Chambers 15 W 56th St, between Fifth and Sixth aves; p.282

Gansevoort 18 Ninth Ave, at W 13th St; p.276

Library 299 Madison Ave, at E 41st St; p.280

Mansfield 12 W 44th St, between Fifth and Sixth aves; p.282

Mercer 147 Mercer St, at Prince St; p.277

prohibit a stay, afternoon tea in the glorious frescoed *Rotunda* is highly recommended. $640

Sherry Netherland 781 Fifth Ave, between E 59th and 60th sts ☏ 212/355-2800, ⊛ www .sherrynetherland.com. If a large sum of money ever comes your way, rent a whole floor here and live-in permanently (many of the guests do) – the stunning views of Central Park are worth it. The service is excellent; the room service is by renowned restaurateur Harry Cipriani. $599

Wales 1295 Madison Ave, at E 92nd St ☏ 212/876-6000, ⊛ www.waleshotel.com. Just steps from "Museum Mile," this Carnegie Hill hotel has hosted guests for over a century. Rooms are attractive with antique details, thoughtful in-room amenities, and some views of Central Park. Complimentary bottled spring water and continental breakfast. $399

The Upper West Side: north of W 59th Street

Amsterdam Inn 340 Amsterdam Ave, at W 76th St ☏ 212/579-7500, ⊛ www.amsterdaminn .com. From the owners of the *Murray Hill Inn* (see p.278), the rooms here are fairly spare but clean, and the staff is friendly and helpful. A 16-story tower is going up next door and weekday construction will last into 2009, so plan for a full day of sightseeing... $139

Beacon 2130 Broadway, at W 75th St ☏ 212/787-1100, ⊛ www.beaconhotel.com. The *Beacon* is perfectly situated for strolling the gourmet markets and museums of the Upper West Side. While the rooms are comfortable and reasonably-sized (with kitchenettes), they probably won't win any style awards. $285

Lucerne 201 W 79th St, at Amsterdam Ave ☏ 1-800/492-8122 or 212/875-1000, ⊛ www .thelucernehotel.com. This beautifully restored 1904 brownstone, with its extravagant Baroque terracotta entrance, charming rooms, and accommodating staff, is just a block from the Museum of Natural History (see p.194) and close to the liveliest stretches of Broadway and Columbus Avenue. $300

Mandarin Oriental New York 80 Columbus Circle, W 60th St between Broadway and Columbus Ave ☏ 212/805-8800, ⊛ www .mandarinoriental.com. The pampering is on par with the astronomical rates at this entertainment-industry favorite. A plush palace of spacious, handsome rooms complete with Frette linens and floor-to-ceiling windows, the hotel offers both guests and diners spectacular views from the 35th floor *Lobby Lounge*. $855

Milburn 242 W 76th St, between Broadway and West End ☏ 1-800/833-9622 or 212/362-1006, ⊛ www.milburnhotel .com. Once past the classic-feel lobby, the rooms (all with kitchenettes) and suites are a little less showy but are on the large side for the neighborhood. And the presence of a library of children's books and videogame players make this welcoming and well-situated hotel great for families. $229

On the Ave 222 W 77th St, between Amsterdam and Broadway ☏ 1-800/509-7598 or 212/362-1100, ⊛ www.ontheave-nyc.com. With its stainless-steel sinks, minimalist baths and dark-wood bed platforms, *On the Ave* feels forward-looking yet somehow out of step. Though light on amenities, it is still clean, comfortable, and relatively inexpensive. $289

Apartment swapping

If you're coming to New York for more than a few nights, and you happen to own a place in your home city/country, the least expensive and most authentic accommodation option by far is **apartment swapping**. You'd be amazed at the number of New Yorkers who would like to get out of the city for a few days or weeks; what's more, your humble Dublin or Seattle flat may seem spacious and exotic to a Manhattanite. Don't be afraid to play up your dwelling's positive features – the mountain view or medieval church that you take for granted may be just what your swap-partner's doctor ordered – and to ask for pictures and references of the potential swap in return. One of the most reputable exchange organizations is **Home Exchange** (☎310/798-3864 or 1-800/877-8723, ⊛www.homeexchange.com).

Brooklyn

Marriott Brooklyn 333 Adams St, Brooklyn Heights ☎718/246-7000, ⊛www.marriott .com. A favorite among those doing business on Wall Street, this modern hotel features wired rooms, a 12,000-square-foot pool, and amazing views of the Brooklyn Bridge. Keep in mind that many of the rooms here are built more for business-traveler clientele comfort and ease of work, than for luxury. $279

Airport hotels

If your flight gets in at an ungodly hour, or if you have difficulty waking up in a timely manner, it may benefit your sanity to stay at one of the area's **airport hotels**. Usually comfortable and conveniently near the tarmac (though not always quiet), these offerings exist simply to ease the getting-to-the-airport stress associated with inconvenient traffic delays and hearing-impaired taxi drivers ("You wanted Newark? I thought you said JFK...").

JFK

DoubleTree 135–30 140th St, Queens ☎718/322-2300
Holiday Inn JFK 144–02 135th Ave, Queens ☎718/659-0200
Ramada Plaza JFK Building 144, Van Wyck Expressway S, Queens ☎718/995-9000

LaGuardia

Crowne Plaza LaGuardia 104–04 Ditmars Blvd, Queens ☎718/457-6300
LaGuardia Airport Hotel 100–15 Ditmars Blvd, Queens ☎718/426-1500
Sheraton LaGuardia East 135–20 39th Ave, Queens ☎718/460-6666

Newark

Courtyard 600 Rt 1–9 South off Rt 78, Newark ☎973/643-8500
Holiday Inn 160 Frontage Rd, Newark ☎973/589-1000
Marriott Airport Behind tower at the airport, Newark ☎973/623-0006

Hostels

Hostels are just about the only option for backpackers in New York. While they can vary greatly in quality, most are fine as long as you don't mind sleeping in a bunk bed and sharing a room with strangers (though if you're traveling in a group of four or six you can often book a room for yourselves).

Some hostels are affiliated with organizations that require you to be a member in order to stay, so be sure to ask when calling for a reservation. Although not all hostels require memberships, it's a good rule of thumb that the ones which do are generally cleaner, safer, and more affordable. For hostels that do not participate in the larger budget-travel community, always ask about safety, security, and locker availability before checking in and bunking down.

Hostels in New York are especially busy – and fairly rowdy – when the legions of summer backpackers descend on the city. The following is a small selection of the best hostels and YMCAs in the city, all of which have rooms for well under $100.

Big Apple Hostel 119 W 45th St, between Sixth and Seventh aves ☎212/302-2603, ⓦwww .bigapplehostel.com. You can't beat this hostel's Times Square location – it's easily the city's best budget pick. There's a secure luggage room, communal refrigerator, and even an outdoor deck with barbeque. All rooms have a/c and shared baths. Dorms $45, private double rooms $125–160, including tax.

Central Park Hostel 19 W 103rd St, at Central Park W ☎212/678-0491, ⓦwww.central parkhostel.com. Upper West Side hostel in a renovated five-story walk-up has dorm beds for 4, 6, 8, or 10 people, as well as private rooms. All rooms share clean bathrooms, and lockers are available (bring a padlock). Sheets and blankets are included, payment in cash or traveler's checks only; you must have a passport, or an international student or non–New York State ID. Dorms $28–45, private rooms $89–135, includes tax.

Chelsea Center Hostel 313 W 29th St, at Eighth Ave ☎212/643-0214, ⓦwww.chelseacenter hostel.com. This small, clean, safe, private hostel has beds for $35 (including tax), including sheets, blankets, and a light breakfast. Private rooms $100–140. Reservations are essential in high season. Cash only.

Chelsea International Hostel 251 W 20th St, between Seventh and Eighth aves ☎212/647-0010, ⓦwww.chelseahostel.com. A smart choice located in the heart of Chelsea. Share the clean, rudimentary rooms with 3 or 5 other people, or book a private double room. All guests must leave a $10 key deposit. No curfew; passport required. Dorms $28 ($32 with bath), private rooms $80, including tax.

Gershwin 7 E 27th St, between Fifth and Madison aves ☎212/545-8000, ⓦwww .gershwinhotel.com. This hostel/hotel is geared toward younger travelers, with Pop Art décor, a bar/cocktail lounge, and dormitories with 4, 6, or 10 beds per room. Reservations highly recommended. Dorm beds from $34, private rooms from $109.

Hostelling International-New York 891 Amsterdam Ave, at W 103rd St ☎212/932-2300,

ⓦwww.hinewyork.org. Dorm beds start at $29 (in 10-bed rooms); members pay a few dollars less per night. The massive facilities – 624 beds in all – include a restaurant, garden, games room (with a PlayStation 2), self-catering kitchen, TV room, and laundry. Reserve well in advance – this hostel is very popular, partly due to the range of scheduled activities and tours offered.

Jazz on the Park 36 W 106th St, at Central Park W ☎212/932-1600, ⓦwww.jazzonthepark.com. This groovy bunkhouse boasts a TV/games room, a café, and lots of activities, including live jazz on weekends, pub crawls, and iPod parties. Rooms sleep between 2 and 12 people, and are clean, bright, and have a/c. Reserve at least one week in advance. Dorms from $20, private double rooms with bath from $125.

Uptown Hostel 239 Lenox Ave, at W 122nd St ☎212/666-0559, ⓦwww.uptownhostel.com. Clean, comfortable beds in the heart of Harlem. Bunk rooms sleeping 4–6 people, singles, and doubles are available. Inquire about weekly rates at the kindly owner's annexed property. Dorms $20, singles $35, doubles $55.

Vanderbilt YMCA 224 E 47th St, between Second and Third aves ☎212/912-2500, ⓦwww.ymcanyc.org. Smaller and quieter than most of the hostels listed here, and neatly placed in midtown Manhattan, only five minutes' walk from Grand Central. Swimming pool, gym, and laundromat on the premises. All rooms have a/c and shared baths. Singles $85, bunk-bed doubles $95.

Wanderers Inn Hostel West 257 W 113th St, between Frederick Douglass and Adam Clayton Powell blvds ☎212/222-5602, ⓦwww .wanderersinn.com. Located close to Columbia and the Cathedral Church of St John the Divine, this renovated space features a backyard (with deck), kitchen, and Internet access. Dorm rooms have their own bathroom, but private rooms must share. Reception open 24hr. Passport required, no smoking and no curfew. Dorms $24, bunk and double rooms $80–90.

West Side YMCA 5 W 63rd St, at Central Park W ☎212/875-4100, ⓦ www.ymcanyc.org. This "Y" is steps from Central Park and housed in a landmark building that boasts pool tiles gifted from the King of Spain. It has two floors of rooms, an inexpensive restaurant, swimming pool, gym, and laundry. All rooms have a/c and semi-private or shared bathroom. Singles and bunk-bed doubles around $105.

Whitehouse Hotel of New York 340 Bowery, at Bond St ☎212/477-5623, ⓦ www .whitehousehotelofny.com. This is the only hostel in the city that offers private single and double rooms at dorm rates. Unbeatable prices combined with an ideal downtown location, and amenities such as a/c, ATMs, cable TV, and linens, make this hostel great value. Singles $28, doubles $54.

Bed and breakfasts

Staying at a **bed and breakfast** can be a good way of visiting New York at an affordable price. But don't go looking for B&Bs on the streets: most rooms – except for a few which we've found off the beaten track (listed below) – are let out via the following official agencies, which all recommend making your reservations as far in advance as possible, especially for the cheapest rooms. Rates run about $80–100 for a double, or $150 and up a night for a studio apartment. Don't expect to socialize with your temporary landlord/lady, either. In the case of a "hosted" room, chances are your space will be self-contained, and you'll hardly see them. Renting an "unhosted" apartment means that the owner won't be there at all. B&Bs are also your best bet in the outer boroughs, and especially in Brooklyn, where hotels are few and far between. There are quite a few to choose from, many of which are housed in Brooklyn townhouses and provide a welcome change to the corporate high-rise accommodations typically available in Manhattan.

B&B agencies

Affordable New York City ☎212/533-4001, ⓦ www.affordablenyc.com. Detailed descriptions are provided by this established network of 120 properties (B&Bs and apartments) around the city. B&B accommodation from $95 (shared bath) and $125 (private bath), unhosted studios $150–175, and one-bedrooms $175–230. Cash or traveler's checks only; four-night minimum. Very customer-oriented and personable staff.

Bed and Breakfast Network of New York ☎1-800/900-8134 or 212/645-8134, ⓦ www .bedandbreakfastnetny.com. Call at least one month in advance, and ask about weekly and monthly specials. Lists hosted doubles for $110–150.

City Lights Bed & Breakfast ☎212/737-7049, ⓦ www.citylightsbandb.com. There are more than 200 carefully screened B&Bs (and short-term apartment rentals) on this agency's books. Many of the hosts are involved in theater and the arts, which means there's a little more artistic flair to these accommodations than your run-of-the-mill variety. Hosted doubles are $80–175; unhosted apartments cost $135–300 and up per night depending on size. Hosts are paid directly. Three-night minimum stay.

CitySonnet ☎212/614-3034, ⓦ www.citysonnet .com. This small, personalized, artist-run B&B/short-term apartment agency offers accommodation all over the city, but specializes in Greenwich Village. Singles and doubles start at $135, private apartments for up to 3 guests go for $175–295 and unhosted artist lofts begin at $275.

Colby International 21 Park Ave, Eccleston Park, Prescot L34 2QY, UK ☎0151/292-2910, ☏292-2911, ⓦ www.colbyinternational.com. Guaranteed accommodation can be arranged from the UK. Book at least a fortnight ahead in high season for these excellent-value apartments (studios to 3-bedrooms $200–450) and B&B singles ($90) and doubles ($110–120).

Manhattan B&Bs

Inn at Irving Place 56 Irving Place, at E 17th St ☎1-800/685-1447 or 212/533-4600, ⓦ www .innatirving.com. Frequented by celebrities, this handsome pair of 1834 brownstones ranks as one of the most exclusive guesthouses in the city. It costs $325–645 a night to stay in one of the twelve rooms (or "residences") – each named for a famous architect, designer, or actor. The *Inn* also offers five-course high teas ($35 per person). **Inn on 23rd St 131 W 23rd St, between Sixth and Seventh aves ☏ 1-877/387-2323 or 212/463-0330, ⓦ www.innon23rd.com.** This family-run B&B is adorned with heirlooms and comfortable furniture in a series of theme quarters. Options like the 1940s Room, Maritime Room and Bamboo Room feature pillow-top mattresses and white-noise machines to block out any extraneous din. Hop on the M23 bus and you can explore the Chelsea art scene. Rooms start at $329.

New York Gisele's Bed and Breakfast 134 W 119th St, at Lenox Ave ☏ 212/666-0559, ⓦ www .nygiselebnb.com. A lovely old brownstone just north of Central Park in Harlem, this B&B features comfortable double rooms (shared bathrooms) for $110 a night for two people.

Brooklyn B&Bs

Akwaaba Mansion 347 MacDonough St, at Stuyvesant Ave, Bedford-Stuyvesant ☏ 718/455-5958, ⓦ www.akwaaba.com. A New York landmark, this Victorian mansion is one of a kind, featuring Afrocentric details like Daffodil rag dolls and Adrinkra fabrics. A tearoom, sunny porch, and Southern-style breakfast will make anyone feel right at home. In case you were wondering, the Ghanaian name translates as "welcome." The beautiful rooms go for $160 per night.

Baisley House 294 Hoyt St, between Union and Sackett sts, Carroll Gardens ☏ 718/935-1959, ⓦ www.virtualcities.com/ons/ny/n/nyn1901.htm. Another charming Victorian brownstone, this one dates from 1865. Singles $144, doubles $170–200, all with shared bath. There's a two-night minimum stay.

Bed & Breakfast on the Park 113 Prospect Park W, between 6th and 7th sts, Park Slope ☏ 718/499-6115, ⓦ www.bbnyc.com. A handsome 1892 limestone townhouse with views over Prospect Park. There are five double rooms with private baths ranging from $175–325 a night.

Union Street Bed & Breakfast 405 Union St, between Smith and Hoyt sts, Carroll Gardens ☏ 718/852-8406, ⓦ www.unionstbrooklynbandb .com. A four-room Victorian brownstone in a historic area. Singles $115, doubles $160 (three-night minimum).

Cafés, bakeries, and snacks

E ateries geared toward people on the go are omnipresent in New York. Travelers will be hard pressed to find an area that doesn't offer something in the way of a small meal; breads, pastries, pizzas, sandwiches, bagels, meats, cheeses, juices, ice creams, and vegetarian goodies are among the myriad comestible options available. Every neighborhood has several favorite haunts; this chapter details establishments good for breakfast, lunch, and snacks. See Chapter 25, "Restaurants," if you're in the mood for a larger, sit-down affair.

New York's **cafés** and **bakeries** have been greatly influenced by the city's diverse ethnic populations; American, French, and Italian establishments are the most visible throughout the city. Many of the more long-established cafés are in downtown Manhattan, and are perfect for lingering or just resting up between sights. A good number of them are quite European in feel – the grouping at the junction of Bleecker and MacDougal streets in the West Village is determinedly Left Bank, for example.

New York also has a number of **coffeehouses** and **tearooms** that provide fresh coffee and tea, fruit juices, pastries, and light snacks. There are **coffee shops** or **diners** on just about every block that serve cheap, decent breakfast specials. The more upscale midtown hotels are good places to stop for formal tea, too, if you can afford the prices they charge for the English country-house atmosphere they often try to contrive.

Specialty eating

We've highlighted particular types of snacks and lighter meal options and listed them in boxes on the following pages.

Bagels p.293
Breakfast: coffee shops and diners p.299
Bubble tea in Chinatown p.292
Ice cream p.302
Pizza by the slice p.300
Some atmospheric cafés p.296

Financial District and City Hall

Bakeries and cafés

Financier Patisserie 62 Stone St ☎ 212/344-5600. High-quality French pastry shop known for its signature almond cake, traditionally baked in the shape of a gold bar. Coffee, made-to-order salads, paninis, and soups accompany the cakes and assorted vienoisserie, all made daily on the premises. Also located in World Financial Center and at 35 Cedar St. Closed Sun.

Sandwiches and snacks

The Little Place 61 Warren St, at W Broadway ☎ 212/528-3175. Tiny, smartly priced Mexican joint known for its authentic egg dishes, tacos, and fajitas.
Plaza Food Court Foley Square. Two kiosks serve up salads ($5.95), pizza slices ($1.75), soups, and burritos, with plenty of outdoor seating facing Foley Square.

Tribeca and Soho

Bakeries and cafés

Balthazar Bakery 80 Spring St, between Crosby St and Broadway ☎ 212/965-1414. This bakery has wonderful breads (including a dark chocolate loaf) and pastries of all sorts. They also serve great home-made fizzy lemonade.
Bouley Bakery 130 W Broadway, on the corner of Duane St ☎ 212/964-2525. Wunderkind David Bouley's tiny bakery/café has truly great breads and baked goods, as well as reasonably priced sandwiches.
Once Upon a Tart 135 Sullivan St, between Houston and Prince sts ☎ 212/387-8869. A good place to come for a light lunch or to satisfy a sugar craving. The interior is a bit cramped, but intimate and oh-so-quaint.
Vesuvio Bakery 160 Prince St, between W Broadway and Thompson St ☎ 212/925-8248. Baking since 1920, this cute Italian bread store also sells a range of breakfast items (bagels from $1), cheesecake ($5), panini sandwiches ($8.50), wraps and salads ($6.50).

Sandwiches and snacks

🏃 **Hampton Chutney 68 Prince St, at Crosby** ☎ 212/226-9996. Don't let the name deceive you: this place is all about *dosas*, *uttapams* and naan breads, traditional South Indian fare, albeit with plenty of American ingredients. Orders are spiced up with a choice of fresh, home-made chutneys: cilantro, curry, mango, tomato, or peanut.
Pepe Rosso To Go 149 Sullivan St, between Houston and Prince sts ☎ 212/677-4555. Deservedly popular Italian take-out, offering cheap but imaginative pasta dishes (such as penne vodka with pancetta) and panini. Almost everything on the menu is under $10.
Soda Shop 125 Chambers St, between W Broadway and Church St ☎ 212/349-7553. Victorian décor adds to the old-time theme here, with egg creams, triple-thick ice cream shakes, and plenty of savory snacks and breakfasts from $4.50.

Chinatown

Bakeries and cafés

Fay Da Bakery 83 Mott St, at Canal St ☎ 212/791-3884. Chinatown is littered with Hong Kong–style bakeries, but this is one of the best, offering all the favorite sweet and savory buns – try the hot dog-like sausage or pork floss versions ($1), and the fresh mango or green-tea rice balls ($0.75).

Sandwiches and snacks

Chinatown Ice Cream Factory 65 Bayard St, between Mott and Elizabeth sts ☎ 212/608-4170. An essential stop after dinner, even though the wondrously unusual flavors are good any time. Specialties include green tea, ginger, almond cookie, and lychee.

Bubble tea in Chinatown

In the 1980s, the Taiwanese, who have always been at the cutting edge of Chinese tea culture, gave their traditional drink a contemporary twist: bubbles (actually pearl tapioca). Bubble tea eventually became a major fad all over Asia, and though the craze has eased somewhat, the following teahouses still do a steady trade in milk-added or fruit-flavored teas, enhanced with tapioca beads. These chewy beads, which come in white or purple-black, impart only a minor flavor, but they change the texture of the drink significantly. Be sure to sample some traditional nutty biscuits with your tea.

Green Tea Café 45 Mott St, between Bayard and Pell sts ☎212/693-2888

HSF 46 Bowery, between Canal and Bayard sts ☎212/374-1319

Tearrific 51 Mott St, between Bayard and Pell sts ☎212/393-9009

Uiui Bubble Tea 49 Bayard St, between Elizabeth St and the Bowery

Egg Custard King 76 Mott St, between Canal and Bayard sts ☎212/226-8208. Created in the 1940s (probably in Portuguese Macau), egg custard tarts (*dan tat* in Cantonese) are a major obsession in Hong Kong, and this small basement canteen is an easy introduction, with a variety of flavors for under $1.

Fong Inn Too 46 Mott St, between Bayard and Pell sts. This basic shop sells two delicious main dishes, primarily to the line of eager take-out customers: fried radish (or "turnip") cake ($1.50) and silky soft soy-bean pudding, served piping hot with sweet syrup ($0.75–2).

Laoshan Shandong Guotie 106 Mosco St, between Mulberry and Mott sts ☎212/693-1060. Identified simply by a "Fried Dumpling" sign in English, this hole-in-the-wall specializes in pan-fried dumplings characteristic of northern China, with the absolute bargain price of $1 for 5. Squeeze onto a bench inside or take-out.

Little Italy and Nolita

Bakeries and cafés

Bread 20 Spring St, between Mott and Elizabeth sts ☎212-334-1015. Stylish café specializing in creative baguette and panini sandwiches packed with high-quality meats and cheeses; highlights include the fresh sardines and tuna, and aged Italian salami.

Café Gitane 242 Mott St, between Prince and Houston sts ☎212/334-9552. Come here to brush up on your French and settle into a bowl of delicious café crème. For those looking for a bite to eat, excellent Moroccan-influenced food is also on offer. Chock-full of posers, but still one of the best cafés around.

Ceci-Cela 55 Spring St, between Mulberry and Lafayette sts ☎212/274-9179. Tiny French patisserie with tables in the back for those who want to linger, as well as a stand-up counter and bench out front designed for those who can't wait to devour their delectable baked goods. The almond croissants and *palmiers* (elephant-ear-shaped, sugar-coated pastries) are divine, as are the cocoa-dusted truffles.

Ciao Bella Gelato 285 Mott St, between Houston and Prince sts ☎212/431-3591. Heavenly take-out gelato and sorbet, some of the best in the city; the blood-orange sorbet is to die for and the coffee gelato equally delicious.

Ferrara's 195 Grand St, between Mott and Mulberry sts ☎212/226-6150. The best-known and most traditional of Little Italy's coffeehouses, this neighborhood landmark has been around since 1892. Try the cheesecake, cannoli, or, in summer, *granite* (Italian ices). Outdoor seating is available in warmer weather.

Sandwiches and snacks

Pinkberry 41 Spring St, between Mott and Mulberry sts ☎212/274-8696. This LA chain is known as "crackberry" for good reason, its non-fat, low-cal frozen yogurt creating a minor sensation on opening in New York in 2006. Choose from original, green tea, and coffee flavors, then pile on a vast range of fruit and nut toppings. One of eleven outlets in the city.

Ray's 27 Prince St, between Mott and Elizabeth sts ☎ 212/966-1960. While countless pizzerias in the city claim to be the "original *Ray's*," this Little Italy mainstay is perhaps the most distinctive of the bunch (and it's not a chain). The thick Sicilian slices ($2.75) are particularly good.

🏃 **Rice to Riches 37 Spring St, between Mott and Mulberry sts** ☎ 212/274-0008.

Rice pudding made hip and utterly irresistible, served up in this funky space in a variety of sweet flavors, from peanut butter and choc chip, to mango and cinnamon. Bowls start at $5.50. There are a few tables inside.

🏃 **Saigon Vietnamese Sandwich 369 Broome St, between Mott and Elizabeth sts** ☎ 212/219-8341. One of the best makers of Vietnamese sandwiches (known as *bánh mì*) in the city. The classic is made with a large chunk of French bread, and stuffed with grilled pork, sausage, and thinly sliced pickled vegetables, all for less than $5.

Lower East Side

Bakeries and cafés

Kossar's 367 Grand St, at Essex St ☎ 212/473-4810. A Jewish bakery. The *bialys* at *Kossar's* just may be the best in the city.

Teany 90 Rivington St, between Orchard and Ludlow ☎ 212/475-9190. Nice Lower East Side stop-off for a wide selection of teas and classic high-tea sandwiches, as well as vegan scones and baked beans on toast.

Yonah Schimmel's 137 E Houston St, between Forsyth and Eldridge sts ☎ 212/477-2858. The knishes, rounds of vegetable- or meat-stuffed dough, are baked fresh on the premises, as are the wonderful bagels. Patronized by a mixture of old men wisecracking in Yiddish and – on Sun, especially – young uptowners wading through the *New York Times*.

Bagels

Theories abound as to the **origin of the modern bagel**. Most likely, it is a derivative of the pretzel, with the word "bagel" coming from the German *biegen*, "to bend." Whatever their birthplace, it is certain that bagels have become a **New York institution**. Until the 1950s bagels were still handmade by Eastern-European Jewish immigrants in cellars scattered around New York's Lower East Side.

Modern-day bagels are softer and have a smaller hole than their ancestors – the hole made them easy to carry on a long stick to hawk on street corners. Their curiously chewy texture is a result of being boiled before they are baked. They are most traditionally (and famously) served with cream cheese and lox (smoked salmon). The last decade has witnessed the invention of such flavors as blueberry and cheese, which purists decry as reducing their revered bagel to a low-class muffin alternative.

Though bagels are now an American dietary staple, New Yorkers would say only a few places serve **the real thing**. Here is a list of some of the city's better bagelsmiths. (And if you prefer *bialys*, a drier and flatter bagel without a hole, head straight to *Kossar's*; see above).

Bagel Buffet 406 Sixth Ave, between W 8th and 9th sts ☎ 212/477-0448

Bagels on the Square 7 Carmine St, between Bleecker St and Sixth Ave ☎ 212/691-3041

David's Bagels 228 First Ave, between 13th and 14th sts ☎ 212/533-8766

Ess-A-Bagel 359 First Ave, at E 21st St ☎ 212/260-2252

H & H Bagels 2239 Broadway, at W 80th St ☎ 212/595-8000

Hot & Crusty 2387 Broadway, between 87th and 88th sts ☎ 212/496-0632

Sandwiches and snacks

Doughnut Plant 379 Grand St, between Essex and Clinton sts ☏212/505-3700, ⓦwww.doughnutplant.com. Serious (and seriously delicious) donuts; make sure to sample the seasonal flavors and glazes, including pumpkin and passion fruit.

Il Laboratorio del Gelato 95 Orchard St, between Broome and Delancey sts ☏212/343-9922. This shrine to cream and sugar serves up over 75 flavors, including fig, lavender, and malt.

The Pickle Guys 49 Essex St, at Grand St ☏212/656-9739. Come here to sate your craving for all things briny: pickles, peppers, and olives are only a few of the salty items displayed outside the store in huge barrels.

Russ & Daughters 179 E Houston St, between Allen and Orchard sts ☏212/475-4880. Technically, this store is known as an "appetizing." The original Manhattan gourmet shop, it was set up around 1900 to sate the appetites of homesick immigrant Jews with smoked fish, pickled vegetables, cheese, and bagels – it still does a great job delivering the goods.

🏃 **Vanessa's Dumplings 118A Eldridge St, between Grand and Broome sts.** This always busy Chinese eatery knocks out various combinations of steamed or fried pork, shrimp, and vegetable dumplings at the bargain price of $1 for 4 – the crispy sesame pancake with pork is just as addictive.

East Village

Bakeries and cafés

Cloister Café 238 E 9th St, between Second and Third aves ☏212/777-9128. This café is worth frequenting for its spacious garden dining area (with fountain) and collection of original stained-glass windows; stick with the coffee and desserts, as the rest of the food is a bit hit-and-miss. It's a popular late-night spot.

🏃 **De Robertis 176 First Ave, between E 10th and E 11th sts** ☏212/674-7137. A traditional Italian bakery/café that's been around since 1904. The old-New-York vibe is so good that the establishment has been featured in multiple Woody Allen flicks. Wonderful ricotta cheesecake and espresso.

Moishe's 115 Second Ave, at E 7th St ☏212/505-8555. Excellent prune danishes, *hamantashen*, seeded rye, and other kosher treats.

Veniero's Pasticceria & Café 342 E 11th St, between First and Second aves ☏212/674-7070. An East Village bakery and neighborhood institution since 1894, *Veniero's* desserts and décor are fabulously over-the-top. The ricotta cheesecake and home-made gelato are great in the summer.

Sandwiches and snacks

B & H Dairy 127 Second Ave, between E 7th St and St Mark's Place ☏212/505-8065. A tiny vegetarian luncheonette that serves home-made soup (try the split pea), latkes, and absolutely divine challah bread. You can also create your own juice combinations (carrot–beet, for example).

Crif Dogs 113 St Mark's Place, between First Ave and Ave A ☏212/614-2728. Hot-dog aficionados swear by these deep-fried, shiny wieners bursting with flavor, enjoyed Philly-steak style, smothered in cheese, or topped with avocado and bacon.

Juicy Lucy's 85 Ave A, between E 5th and 6th sts ☏212/777-5829. This very small and congested but congenial juice bar has a wide range of standard juices and yogurt-based smoothies, along with tofu chili dogs and other vegan treats.

🏃 **Liquiteria 170 Second Ave, at E 11th St** ☏212/358-0300. The smoothies here are by far the best in Manhattan (try the "Orangasm" or the "Reggae Rumba"). There are over 30 smoothie combos, and loads of supplement shots. You can also get delicious, healthy lunches like oatmeal with fresh fruit or organic PB&Js.

Mamoun's Falafel 22 St Mark's Place, between Third and Second aves. Despite the tatty, cheap-looking exterior, this is the best place for cheap, wholesome falafel in the city (it's one of three outlets), with filling portions for $2 and convenient late-night hrs.

Panya Bakery 10 Stuyvesant St, between Third Ave and E 9th St ☏212/777-1930. A tiny

Japanese take on the sandwich shop with some unique and yummy pastries – try the chocolate sponge cake with green-tea filling.

Pommes Frites 123 Second Ave, between E 7th St and St Marks Place ☎212/674-1234. Arguably the best fries in the city, with gooey, Belgian-style toppings available; try the rosemary garlic mayo or curry ketchup. Portions range from $4 to $7.50.

Veselka 144 Second Ave, corner of E 9th St ☎212/228-9682. East Village mainstay that offers fine home-made borscht (hot in winter, cold in summer), latkes, *pierogi*, and great burgers and fries. Open 24hrs.

Via Della Pace 48 E 7th St, between First and Second aves ☎212/253-5803. Dark and cozy East Village café with good Argentine pastas and sandwiches, plus a great selection of coffees and desserts. The tiramisu is excellent.

▲ Veselka

West Village

Bakeries and cafés

A Salt and Battery 112 Greenwich Ave, between Jane and Horatio sts ☎212/691-2713. Manhattan's only true chippie. It's an authentic enough affair, with decent battered fish, great chips, mushy peas, and mugs of tea, but it's also expensive – fish suppers cost a good $20. There's minimal counter seating; most get their fish to go.

Caffè Dante 79 MacDougal St, between Bleecker and Houston sts ☎212/982-5275. A morning stop-off for many locals since 1915. It's often jammed with NYU students and professors sipping cappuccinos, espressos, and caffè alfredo with ice cream.

Caffè Reggio 119 MacDougal St, between Bleecker and W 3rd sts ☎212/475-9557. This is one of the first Village coffeehouses, dating back to 1927, embellished with all sorts of Italian antiques, paintings, and sculpture. It's always crowded; in warm weather there are outdoor tables for people- or tourist-watching. Tennessee Williams sipped espresso here, and scenes from *Godfather II* were filmed inside.

Caffè Vivaldi 32 Jones St, between Bleecker and W 4th sts ☎212/691-7538. An old-fashioned Viennese-style coffeehouse with fireside coziness and a popular local venue for live music in the evenings, when it becomes more like a wine bar.

Dessert Truck E 8th St and University Place. Mobile pudding-station that knocks out delectable desserts like slow-baked cinnamon apples topped with cranberries, and chocolate bread pudding for just $5. Scoops of home-made ice cream are $1. Check out ⓦwww.desserttruck.com to peruse the menu. Open Tues–Sun 6pm till around 11pm or midnight.

Doma 17 Perry St, at Seventh Ave ☎212/929-4339. A corner window, good brews, and linger-all-day vibe make this a neighborhood favorite; it's the anti-*Starbucks*.

Grey Dog 33 Carmine St, between Bleecker and Bedford sts ☎212/462-0041. Casual, stay-all-afternoon café specializing in warm muffins and huge "Michigan-style" sandwiches. Try the awesome Philly cheese steak ($9.25) or light quiche with salad ($10.95). Opens at 6.30am weekdays and 7am weekends, making it perfect for an early breakfast.

Magnolia Bakery 401 Bleecker St, at W 11th St ☎212/462-2572. There are lots of baked goods on offer here, but everyone comes for the heavenly and deservedly famous multicolored cupcakes (celebrated in both *Sex and the City* and *Saturday Night Live*), $2.25 each. Lines can stretch around the block.

Marquet Patisserie 15 E 12th St, between Fifth Ave and University Place ☎212/229-9313. Thanks to its convenient location, ample tables, excellent menu, and low-key atmosphere, this is the perfect mid-Village place to warm up or cool down and rest your feet. There's an emphasis on café fare but they serve more substantial meals, too.

Tea & Sympathy 108 Greenwich Ave, between W 12th and 13th sts ☎212/807-8329. Self-consciously British tearoom, serving an afternoon high tea full of traditional staples like jam roly-poly, treacle pud, shepherd's pie, and scones. Perfect for British tourists feeling homesick.

Thé Adoré 17 E 13th St, between Fifth Ave and University Place ☎212/243-8742. A charming little tearoom on two floors. Downstairs is a counter with excellent pastries, Japanese scones and croissants; upstairs is a small café that serves baguette sandwiches and tasty bowls of soup. Daytime hrs only; closed Sun; generally closed Sat in Aug, but it varies, so call ahead.

Sandwiches and snacks

Bagel Buffet 406 Sixth Ave, between W 8th and 9th sts ☎212/477-0448. Wide selection of fillings and good-value bagel and salad platters for around $5. Open 24hrs.

Cones 272 Bleecker St, between Seventh Ave and Morton St ☎212/414-1795. Wonderful gelatos by two Argentine brothers. Flavors like tiramisu and rich chocolate attract long lines, especially on warm summer nights.

Elixir 523 Hudson St, between W 10th and Charles sts ☎212/352-9952. Casual, friendly joint where you can order juices, smoothies, and seasonal "elixirs" with health-promoting ingredients. Check out the "Femme," which blends peppermint, rosemary, nettle, and dandelion.

Faicco's Pork Store 260 Bleecker St, between Morton and Leroy sts ☎212/243-1974. This old-school Italian butcher serves some of the best-value sandwiches in the city, huge rolls of ham, sausage, and chicken cutlet with aged provolone from $6. Add a tangy *prosciutto* ball for $1.

Gray's Papaya 402 Sixth Ave at 8th St ☎212/260-3532. For a real New York experience, grab a crispy hot dog ($1.25) at this standing-room-only chain at this established rival of *Papaya Dog* down the road. The "papaya" refers to the fresh tropical fruit drinks also sold here (gimmicky, but delicious).

NY Dosa Washington Square S at Sullivan St. Thiru Kumar is one of New York's best loved street vendors, cooking up spicy South Indian vegan food and filling *dosas* at his tiny cart, all for under $10. NYU students start lining up here before noon. Weekdays only.

Peanut Butter & Company 240 Sullivan St, between Bleecker and W 3rd Sts ☎212/677-3995. Peanut butter in ways you never imagined. Try the "Elvis" – a grilled peanut butter and honey sandwich with bananas, or the slightly more adventurous "Spicy

Some atmospheric cafés

Coffee is big business in New York. While the profusion of retail chains like *Starbucks* has encroached upon the city's smaller mom-and-pop establishments, there are still a good number of atmospheric options much more worthy of your dollar.

Café Mozart 154 W 70th St, at Broadway ☎212/595-9797; p.300

Caffè Reggio 119 MacDougal St, between Bleecker and W 3rd sts ☎212/475-9557; p.295

De Robertis 176 First Ave, at 10th St ☎212/674-7137; p.294

Tea & Sympathy 108 Greenwich Ave, between W 12th and 13th sts ☎212/807-8329; above

Thé Adoré 17 E 13th St, between Fifth Ave and University Place ☎212/243-8742; above

Peanut Butter Sandwich," made with pineapple jam and grilled chicken. Sandwiches are $5–6.50.

Two Boots to Go West 75 Greenwich Ave, at W 11th St ⊤212/633-9096. Great thin-crust pizzas with a cornmeal dusting and Cajun flavor. Try a slice of the "Newman" (sopressata, sweet sausage, and ricotta) or the "Mrs (Emma) Peel" (round vegetable Sicilian). Also at 42 Ave A.

Waverly Restaurant 385 Sixth Ave, at Waverly Place ⊤212/675-3181. The *Waverly* is a comfy neighborhood diner. It's especially good for a late-night burger, a bacon and egg breakfast, or an egg cream.

Chelsea

Bakeries and cafés

Billy's Bakery 184 Ninth Ave, between 21st and 22nd sts ⊤212/647-9956. Opened by a former employee of *Magnolia Bakery*, though the rustic farmhouse interior is far less crowded and the cupcakes cheaper and just as scrumptious. Other highlights include a tangy Key Lime Pie.

Rafaella on Ninth 178 Ninth Ave, at 21st St ⊤212/741-3230. The main attraction at this local café is the gracious, antique ambience, enhanced by Victorian-style chairs, shabby sofas, and gilded antiques. Stick with coffee, as the food is not so great.

Sandwiches and snacks

Amy's Bread 75 Ninth Ave, between W 15th and 16th sts ⊤212/462-4338. You can find *Amy's* breads in fine stores citywide, but it's freshest here in the Chelsea Market. Their grilled-cheese sandwiches, made with chipotle peppers, are some of the best in the city.

Eleni's Cookies 75 Ninth Avenue (inside Chelsea Market) ⊤212/255-7990. This bright, pink-hued store is super-moist cupcake and cookie heaven; the Everything Cookie (combining cranberries, walnuts, and coconut) is virtually a meal in itself. It's also a great place for gifts.

F&B 269 W 23rd St, between Seventh and Eighth aves ⊤646/486-4441. Terrific European-influenced street food (namely gourmet hot dogs, bratwurst, and knockwurst, as well as salmon dogs and mouthwatering Swedish meatballs) at digestible prices. A good selection of veggie offerings as well.

Union Square, Gramercy Park, and the Flatiron District

Bakeries and cafés

Amai Tea & Bake House 171 Third Ave, between E 16th and 17th sts ⊤212/863-9630. Small but tranquil teahouse with a choice of 45 quality teas, from earthy oolongs to flowery jasmines. Green-tea cakes or lemongrass-ginger cookies make a perfect accompaniment (3 for $2).

City Bakery 3 W 18th St, between Fifth and Sixth aves ⊤212/366-1045. A good place to come for a filling lunch. Try the tortilla pie, the idiosyncratic pretzel croissant, or – for sweet tooths - the beer hot-chocolate with home-made marshmallow, so thick you'll need a fork.

Lady Mendl's 56 Irving Place, at E 17th St ⊤212/533-4600. Classic English high teas are the stock-in-trade of this small inn set in a handsome pair of brownstones. As per tradition, their five-course menus are served in the afternoon, complete with silver service and a tower of sandwiches ($35 per person).

News Bar 2 W 19th St, between Fifth and Sixth aves ⊤212/255-3996. Tiny, minimalist café with a very good selection of pastries and periodicals. It's a good spot to people-watch; many of the patrons are photographers and models.

Sandwiches and snacks

Eisenberg's Sandwich Shop 174 Fifth Ave, at 22nd St ⊤212/675-5096. A colorful luncheonette, this shop has been serving cheesy Reubens, great tuna sandwiches, matzohball soup, and old-fashioned fountain sodas at a well-worn counter since 1930.

Shake Shack Madison Square Park.
Danny Meyer's leafy food kiosk in the center of Madison Square Park has proved wildly popular since opening in 2004, with assorted office-workers, tourists, and foodies forming long lines for the perfectly grilled burgers and frozen-custard shakes. You can also buy beer and wine to sip outside, with everything around $5 or less.

Uncle Mo's Burrito & Taco Shop 14 W 19th St, between Fifth and Sixth aves ⊤212/727-9400. Authentic Mexican fare; these tortilla-wrapped goods (available for take-out) are some of the city's best.

Wichcraft 11 E 20th St, at Broadway. This gourmet sandwichery is a fine wallet-friendly lunch option. Tuck into a moist Sicilian tuna sandwich ($9) or one of their excellent veggie sides ($4).

Midtown East

Bakeries and cafés

Buttercup Bake Shop 973 Second Ave, between 51st and 52nd sts ⊤212/350-4144. This *Magnolia Bakery* off-shoot is similarly known for its 1950s-style comfort sweets, especially the moist cupcakes and banana pudding.

Ess-a-Bagel 831 Third Ave, at 51st St ⊤212/980-1010. Neighborhood residents swear by this shop, filled with all the lox, whitefish salad, and cream cheese you can possibly want. Go early, as the tables fill up quickly.

Sandwiches and snacks

Fresco by Scotto on the Go 40 E 52nd St, between Madison and Park aves

⊤212/935-3434. This welcoming Italian takeout spot serves up fresh pastas, home-made pizzas, and toothsome sandwiches.

Tea Box Takashimaya, 693 Fifth Ave, between 54th and 55th sts ⊤212/350-0180. Despite its location at the city's chicest Japanese department store (see p.390), this basement tearoom is very quiet. The small but pricey menu features both Asian and Western snacks – think bento boxes, soups, salads. A pot of tea here can be an elixir after a long day of shopping and sightseeing.

Viand 673 Madison Ave, at E 61st St ⊤212/751-6622. Affordable little chain coffee shop near Barney's serving rich brews, awesome turkey sandwiches, and all-around delicious snacks. Service is speedy and the prices sweet.

Midtown West

Bakeries and cafés

Algonquin Hotel lobby 59 W 44th St, between Fifth and Sixth aves ⊤212/840-6800. The archetypal American interpretation of the English drawing room, located in the airy, attractive lobby of the hotel by the same name (see p.345), and reeking of faux nineteenth-century robber-baron splendor.

La Maison du Chocolat 30 Rockefeller Concourse, 49th St between Fifth and Sixth aves ⊤212/265-9404. The French vibe here is palpable: the original *Maison* is in Paris. The two hot chocolates on the menu (and two iced in summer) are so thick you'll need a spoon to eat them (but they're not as sweet as you might expect). Their fruit plates, chock-full of market-fresh berries, grapefruit, and pineapple, are must-tastes too.

Little Pie Company 424 W 43rd St, between Ninth and Tenth aves ⊤212/736-4780. True to its name, the *Little Pie Company* serves pies to die for. The peach–raspberry, available only in summer, has earned quite a passionate following.

Poseidon Bakery 629 Ninth Ave, between W 44th and 45th sts ⊤212/757-6173. Known best for the phyllo dough hand-rolled on the premises and supplied to many of the city's restaurants, *Poseidon* also sells decadent *baklava*, strudel, cookies, spinach-and-meat pies, and assorted other sweet Greek pastries. Closed Sun and Mon.

Sandwiches and snacks

Brasserie Maison 1700 Broadway, at W 53rd St ⊤212/757-2233. This is a good place to linger over a coffee or a meal – a rarity in midtown. The menu offers a range of burgers, soups, salads, pastas, and average French-tinged brasserie standards (stick with the simpler items on the menu). Large outdoor seating area. Open 24hrs.

Cosmic Diner 888 Eighth Ave, at W 52nd St ☎212/333-5888. The perfect stop pre- or post-theater. All the usual suspects are here: burgers (from pizza to Texas to bison), hearty lumberjack pancakes, stuffed sandwiches, and yummy entrée salads.

Upper East Side

Bakeries and cafés

Café Sabarsky in the Neue Galerie 1048 Fifth Ave, at E 86th St ☎212/288-0665. Sumptuous décor that harkens back to Old Vienna fills the handsome parlor of the former Vanderbilt mansion. The menu reads like that of an upscale Eastern-European *Kaffeehaus*; it includes superb pastries, like Klimt torte and strudels, and small sandwiches, many made with cured meats.

Payard Patisserie & Bistro 1032 Lexington Ave, between 73rd and 74th sts ☎212/717-5252. This is real French pastry – buttery, creamy, and over the top. The cookies, cakes, and crème brûlée are made to the exacting standards of the very finest Parisian patisseries, and while it's a bit pricey it's also worth every dime. The café is separate from the main dining room, and is a civilized place to stop for tea, coffee, and something sweet.

Rohrs, M. 310 E 86th St, between Second and Third aves ☎212/608-6473. Coffee connoisseurs say this cozy spot serves one of the city's best brews. The company has been around since 1896, but their current digs are fairly new.

Serendipity 3 225 E 60th St, between Second and Third aves ☎212/838-3531. Adorned with Tiffany lamps, this long-established eatery and ice-cream parlor has been a favorite spot for sweet-sixteen parties and

▲ Café Sabarsky

New Yorkers are passionate about their pizza, but that's where agreement on the topic largely ends. There are many strongly held opinions when it comes to **defining a good slice**, and one man's mozzarella epiphany is often his neighbor's tasteless cardboard triangle. Fortunately, the city is home to restaurants that serve all kinds of delicious variations on the theme, from hunky pieces smothered in red sauce and dripping with cheese to cornmeal-dusted dough with gourmet toppings to authentic Neapolitan pizza with wafer-thin crusts. Here are some places to sample New York's myriad pizza possibilities:

Mariella Pizza 151 E 60th St, between Lexington and Third aves ☎212/319-5999; below

Patsy's Pizza 2287 First Ave, between 117th and 118th sts ☎212/534-9783; p.302

Ray's 27 Prince St, between Mott and Elizabeth sts ☎212/966-1960; p.293

Two Boots to Go West 75 Greenwich Ave, at Seventh Ave ☎212/633-9096; p.297

first dates for years. The frozen hot-chocolate, a trademarked and copyrighted recipe, is out of this world, and the wealth of ice cream offerings are a real treat, too.

Wildgreen Café 1555 Third Ave, at 88th St ☎212/828-7656. A small-town feel adds to the draw of this shop "where natural foods become gourmet." It's justly known for its muffins, salads, wraps, and juices.

Sandwiches and snacks

Alice's Tea Cup 156 E 64th St, at Lexington Ave ☎212/486-9200. For mommies and their little girls, *Alice's* hosts tea parties (reserve well ahead) and offers afternoon tea "all day, every day"! The place also does a brisk business with its menu of crêpes, egg dishes, and light and tasty sandwiches. Cupcakes are great too, and there are

(naturally) over 95 tea varieties on sale for you to take home. Other branches on W 73rd St and E 81st St.

Mariella Pizza 151 E 60th St, between Lexington and Third aves ☎212/319-5999. The fine, generously proportioned slices here are more like a full meal than a snack. A great spot to grab a bite while hoofing it around midtown.

Mitchell London 22A E 65th St, between Fifth and Madison aves ☎212/737-2850. The goods from caterer/restauranteur Mr. London are justifiably praised. Try the egg salad or turkey and brie sandwiches, with one of their unbelievably rich brownies for desert.

Tal Bagels 333 E 86th St, between First and Second aves ☎212/427-6811. The bagels may be a little too chewy, but the spread selection at this family institution is to die for, especially the smoked fish. Don't let the lines scare you; they move fast.

Upper West Side and Morningside Heights

Bakeries and cafés

Cafe on Broadway 2350 Broadway, at 86th St ☎212/496-4004. Bustling mini-diner on upper Broadway. It's good for the pick-what-you-want salads, or a flavored coffee and a danish.

Café Lalo 201 W 83rd St, between Amsterdam and Broadway ☎212/496-6031. Reminiscent of Paris, down to the cramped tables and inconsistent service. Try the "shirred" eggs (made fluffy with a cappuccino machine) with all sorts of herbs and other add-ins, or

the wonderful Belgian waffles. Great desserts, too.

Café Mozart 154 W 70th St, between Columbus Ave and Broadway ☎212/595-9797. This faded old Viennese coffeehouse serves rich tortes and apple strudel, among dozens of other cavity-inducing items.

Edgar's Café 255 W 84th St, between West End Ave and Broadway ☎212/496-6126. A pleasant coffeehouse with good (though expensive) desserts and light snacks, great hot cider in the winter, and well-brewed coffees and teas all the time. Named for Edgar Allan

Poe, who at one time lived a block or so farther east on 84th Street.

🏃 **Hungarian Pastry Shop 1030 Amsterdam Ave, between W 110th and 111th sts** ☎212/866-4230. This simple, no-frills coffeehouse is a favorite with Columbia University affiliates. You can sip your espresso and read Proust all day if you like (madeleines, anyone?); the only problem is choosing among the pastries, cookies, and cakes, all made on the premises. Open 'til at least 10pm every night.

Sandwiches and snacks

Barney Greengrass 541 Amsterdam Ave, between 86th and 87th sts ☎212/724-4707. The "sturgeon king" is an Upper West Side fixture; the deli (and restaurant) have been around since time began. The smoked-salmon section is a particular treat.

EJ's Luncheonette 447 Amsterdam Ave, between W 81st and 82nd sts ☎212/873-3444. This retro, family-friendly diner serves huge BLT sandwiches, excellent inexpensive chili, and the best Cobb salads in the city.

Gray's Papaya 2090 Broadway, at W 72nd St ☎212/799-0243. Open 24/7, this insanely popular hot-dog joint is an NYC institution, famous for their long-running "Recession Special": 2 dogs and a drink for $3.

Grom 2185 Broadway, at W 76th St ☎212/362-1837. You can cheer *Grom* for bringing authentic, bold-flavored *gelati* to the Big Apple (this is their first outpost outside Italy), or you can curse them for being the first frozen purveyor to break the $5 mark for one scoop.

Hampton Chutney 464 Amsterdam Ave, between 82nd and 83rd sts ☎212/362-5050.

Indian-influenced wraps (in *dosas*) or plates (on *uttapams*), big in both taste and size. At $10–12, they're also a buck or two more than a sandwich, but you can easily share if you're not too hungry. Of course, there's also a choice of chutney: cilantro, tomato, mango, curry, peanut, and, in season, pumpkin.

P&W Sandwich Shop 1030 Amsterdam Ave, between W 110th and 111th sts ☎212/222-2245. A luncher run by the people from the *Hungarian Pastry Shop* next door (see opposite), serving a few good Eastern-European specialties.

Popover Café 551 Amsterdam Ave, at 87th St ☎212/595-8555. Charming, casual eatery (decorated with stuffed bears) where the dishes come with the home-made touch. Best to go for breakfast, lunch, or brunch rather than dinner.

Tom's Restaurant 2880 Broadway, at 112th St ☎212/864-6137. The greasy-spoon diner – where *Seinfeld*'s Jerry, George, Elaine, and Kramer kvetched about nothing – is no great shakes food-wise, but the prices almost make up for the quality. Often filled with Columbia University students who come for the great breakfast deals (under $6) on weekday mornings.

Zabar's Café 2245 Broadway, at W 80th St ☎212/787-2000, ⊛www.zabars.com. Adjacent to the Upper West Side institution (where you can pick up all manner of comestibles, see p.400), this small spot is always crowded with locals and tourists. Best for the cheap, freshly prepared bagel-and-lox sandwiches, but everything's tasty: scones, panini sandwiches, soups, coffee drinks, frozen yogurt and smoothies.

Harlem and above

Bakeries and cafés

Café Amrita 301 W 110th St, between Manhattan Ave and Frederick Douglass Blvd ☎212/222-0683. If your ramble through Central Park leaves you at its northwest corner, sink into a leather chair at this roomy café for an excellent coffee or grilled sandwich.

M & G Diner 383 W 125th St, between Morningside and St Nicholas aves ☎212/864-7326. Ideally located for a filling breakfast (try the

pancakes) before a day of touring Harlem, this soul-food diner is also great for a plate of fried chicken before closing time – which sometimes never arrives.

New Leaf Café 1 Margaret Corbin Drive, Fort Tyron Park ☎212/568-5323. An airy, renovated 1930s building with views of Fort Tyron Park, the *New Leaf* offers fresh, very reasonably priced dishes like arugula-stuffed ravioli, mostly to visitors coming from the nearby Cloisters. Closed Mon.

Ice cream

There's a whole range of rich and delicious choices that fall under the great **"ice cream"** canopy in New York City. In recent years, ice-cream makers have become more creative, and there's a growing emphasis on fresh ingredients. Gelato, the dense Italian ice cream made with less air than its American counterpart, has entered the everyday lexicon, with sorbets, Italian "ices" (shaved ice with flavored syrups), and frozen yogurt following close behind as lighter options. The current craze is Tasti D-Lite, a low-calorie ice cream alternative available on almost every city block. As a departure from the chain-store ice creams (Ben & Jerry's, Häagen-Dazs) found in freezers everywhere, check out the following establishments:

Chinatown Ice Cream Factory 65 Bayard St, between Mott and Elizabeth sts ☎212/608-4170; p.291

Ciao Bella Gelato 285 Mott St, at Houston ☎212/431-3591; p.292

Cones 272 Bleecker St, between Seventh Ave and Morton St ☎212/414-1795; p.296

Dessert Truck E 8th St and University Place; p.295

Grom 2185 Broadway, at W 76th St ☎212/362-1837; p.301.

Patsy's Pizza 2287 First Ave, between 117th and 118th sts ☎212/534-9783. Legend has it that Frank Sinatra craved their thin-crust pies so badly he had them flown out to Hollywood. Around since the 1930s, this is one of the last vestiges of Italian Harlem. Unlike most of the old-fashioned thin-crust pie joints, they offer slices to go; pies start at $10.

Brooklyn

Fulton Ferry District and DUMBO

Almondine 85 Water St, near Main St ☎718/797-5026. Reasonably priced patisserie, run by a former *Le Bernadin* pastry chef with chocolatier Jacques Torres (below), that churns out all kinds of buttery, flaky treats, as well as sandwiches on crusty baguettes, soups, and quiches.

Brooklyn Ice Cream Factory 1 Water St, at the Fulton Ferry pier ☎718/246-3963. An old fireboat house contains the perfect reward for the walk across the Brooklyn Bridge: super-rich ice cream with toppings created by the pastry chef at the neighboring *River Café*. Closed Mon.

DUMBO General Store 111 Front St, at Washington and Adams sts ☎718/855-5288. DUMBO's best café, in an airy former art-supply store, has long rustic tables ideal for reading or conversation, and delicious panini and salads. Full breakfasts are served till 3pm every day, and at night (Mon–Sat) the place transforms into *Hecho en Dumbo*, a Mexican restaurant with superbly inventive small plates made with local and organic ingredients. Live music Fri & Sat.

Jacques Torres Chocolate 66 Water St ☎718/875-9772. Warm up in winter with the super-thick hot chocolate, enjoy a flaky *pain au chocolat*, or just pig out on truffles.

Brooklyn Heights

Montague Street Bagels 108 Montague St, at Hicks St ☎718/237-2512. Brisk service and fantastic, doughy bagels make this the perfect place to grab a snack before heading down to the Esplanade and parking yourself on a bench. Open 24hrs.

Tazza 311 Henry St, at Atlantic ☎718/243-0487. Right on the border with Cobble Hill, this likable *enoteca* serves Italian wines by the glass, espresso, sweets culled from the city's best bakeries, and particularly fine panini – try the fig and ricotta. Ample sidewalk seating in warm weather.

Fort Greene

Cake Man Raven Confectionery 708A Fulton St, at Hanson Place ☎718/694-CAKE. The Cake Man is best known for his stunning red velvet cake, which he has baked for everyone from Harry Belafonte to Spike Lee. You can also pick up a delicious coconut-cream pie and other sweets.

Habana Outpost 757 Fulton St, at S Portland ☎718/858-9500. The Brooklyn branch of the ever-popular NoLita institution *Café Habana* wears its green credentials on its sleeve: the place is solar powered and holds a weekend market on its outdoor dining patio with an emphasis on recycled products. Opt for a burrito or quesadilla with a side of sweet plantains and an ear of corn slathered with mayo, cheese, and lime. Closed Tues.

Cobble Hill and Carroll Gardens

D'Amico Foods 309 Court St, between Sackett and Degraw ☎718/875-5403. All sorts of Italian provisions, but best known for its espresso, served since 1948. Closed Sun.
Robin des Bois 195 Smith St, between Warren and Baltic ☎718/596-1609. Stop in at this antique-laden café/bar for a filling *croque monsieur* or the "Sherwood Special," a charcuterie selection served on a rustic wood board. A pretty garden out back continues the forest theme. Weekdays 4pm to midnight; weekends 11am to midnight.

Sweet Melissa Patisserie 276 Court St, at Douglass St ☎718/855-3410. For a snack to go, the home-made fruit tarts, cakes, cookies, and muffins crowding the narrow front counter here are hard to beat, but the creamy quiches and fancy sandwiches, like filet mignon on a baguette, hold their own, especially when enjoyed in the idyllic backyard garden. There's a larger branch (also with a garden) at 175 7th Ave, at 1st St, in Park Slope (☎718/502-9153).

Red Hook

Baked 359 Van Brunt St, at Dikeman St ☎718/222-0345. Relaxed neighborhood café that's been justly celebrated for its cookies, cakes, muffins, Rice Krispy treats, granola, and marshmallows, all made on the premises but found in cafès and shops throughout the Northeast.

Fairway Café 480–500 Van Brunt St, at Reed St ☎718/694-6868. You'll have to thread your way through the mammoth gourmet supermarket to get here, but it's well worth it for the wallet-friendly sandwiches (try the tender lobster roll), salads, and hot entrees, which you can eat on the back deck overlooking the water. Open daily 8am–8pm.

Park Slope and Prospect Heights

Chip Shop 383 Fifth Ave, at 6th St ☎718/832-7701. Upscale chippie beloved by UK expats as well as non-carb-conscious New Yorkers. Kid-friendly atmosphere. Another branch in Brooklyn Heights, 129 Atlantic Ave, between Clinton and Henry sts.
Cocoa Bar 228 Seventh Ave, between 3rd and 4th sts ☎718/499-4080. Slim neighborhood café right in the heart of the 7th Avenue scene, with a mix of twentysomethings tapping on laptops and moms with kids. Good, strong coffee with chocolatey pastries, spacious back garden, fine wine and beer selection, and free wi-fi. Open from 7 or 8am till 11pm or midnight daily.
Gorilla Coffee 97 Fifth Ave, at Park Place ☎718/230-3244. Punk-rock outpost serves the best (Fair Trade) java in the neighborhood, with strong, fresh drip coffee and expert espresso drinks topped off with perfect crema. Skip the pastries here and head down the street to *Blue Sky Bakery* (53 Fifth Ave) for a home-made, fruit-filled muffin.
Joyce Bakeshop 646 Vanderbilt Ave, at Park Place ☎718/623-7470. Welcome new spot on Prospect Heights' burgeoning main strip with fresh-baked sweet and savory scones, muffins, tarts–and croissants, with high tea served Tues–Fri noon–5pm. Closed Mon.
Press 195 195 Fifthth Ave, between Sackett and Union ☎718/857-1950. Thirty varieties of hot pressed sandwiches on home-made ciabatta, including several good vegetarian options, plus tasty salads, with a pretty backyard garden to boot.

Tom's 782 Washington Ave, at Sterling Place ☎718/636-9738. Brooklyn institution that's handily located just a few blocks from the Brooklyn Museum, with standard-issue diner fare and old-fashioned fountain drinks like lime rickeys and egg creams. Best, though, is the amiable vibe, with garrulous Tom and his whole family making you feel like a long-lost friend. Open Mon–Sat 6am–4pm. Closed Sun.

Bay Ridge

Hinsch's Confectionery 8515 Fifth Ave, between 85th and 86th sts ☎718/748-2854. A Bay Ridge icon, as famous for its ice cream (try the fresh strawberry syrup topping) and old-fashioned diner food as for its beautiful, unchanged luncheonette setting.

Coney Island

Nathan's 1310 Surf Ave, at Stillwell Ave, Coney Island ☎718/946-2202. Right there when you get off the subway, this is the home of the "famous Coney Island hot dog." Serving

▲ Nathan's, Coney Island

since 1916, *Nathan's* holds a nationally televised annual Hot Dog Eating Contest on July 4.

Queens

Astoria and Long Island City

Athens Café 32-01 30th Ave, at 32nd St, Astoria ☎718/626-2164. The place to see and be seen on 30th Ave. On warm days the prime sidewalk tables are packed full of young Greeks all nursing frappes – foamy, Greek-style iced coffees. It's also great for spinach pies and desserts.

🏃 **Djerdan 34-04 31st Ave, at 34th St, Astoria** ☎718/721-2694. Cheap and filling, *burek* – savory meat, spinach, or cheese pies, which go for $4 per slice – is

Williamsburg and Greenpoint

Bliss 191 Bedford Ave, between N 6th and N 7th sts ☎718/599-2547. Vegans can get their fix at this crunchy, no-meat, no-dairy spot. They even serve a full vegan breakfast. Others might find the fare a little bland.
Café Grumpy 193 Meserole Ave, at Diamond St ☎718/349-7623. Spacious Greenpoint outpost for the artsy set, with exposed brick walls, lots of light, expertly made espresso, granola, pastries, and pre-made vegetarian sandwiches.

🏃 **Egg 135 N 5th St, between Bedford Ave and Berry St** ☎718/302-5151. Highly regarded Southern-style breakfasts, including biscuits and gravy, served weekdays 7am–3pm, weekends 8am–2pm, with lunch served too on weekdays. The newly introduced dinner menu (Wed–Sun only) showcases belt-breaking comfort food like fried chicken, braised pork shank, and toasted pound cake topped with lemon custard and vanilla ice cream.
Supercore 305 Bedford Ave, between S 1st and S 2nd sts ☎718/302-1629. Standard hipster coffee hangout, with an added layer of Japanese cool – you can get some home-style *beni-tori* (chicken in ginger sauce over rice), as well as a cappuccino and a salmon and watercress sandwich.
Verb Café 218 Bedford Ave, at 5th St ☎718/599-0977. Wedged between a bookstore and a record shop, *Verb* was one of the first bohemian spots on Bedford, and still anchors the scene with an appropriately lackadaisical vibe, strong coffee, pastries, peanut-butter-and-banana sandwiches, and a reliably kickin' alt-rock soundtrack.

the specialty of this simple Balkan eatery, and a tasty alternative to pizza. Try the "special" version, drizzled with garlicky yogurt.
Omonia Café 32-20 Broadway, at 33rd St, Astoria ☎718/274-6650. Broadway's liveliest café is still a stronghold for Greek men poring over Hellenic newspapers during the day, but after dinner the international crowd is younger and more upbeat. Make sure to order a thick wedge of flaky, buttery, sticky-sweet *baklava*, the best of the desserts here. Open from 7am right

through to 3 or 4am the following day, every day.

Jackson Heights and Corona

Empanadas del Parque Café 56-27 Van Doren St, at 108th St, Corona ☎718/592-7288. The traditional Latin-American meat pie is given a gourmet spin at this celebrated place, with a veggie version stuffed with guava and cheese and a sweet one that comes with Nutella and sliced bananas. Nothing costs more than $2.

Shaheen Sweets 72-09 Broadway, Jackson Heights ☎718/476-6512. Stashed inside the vast *Roti Boti Restaurant* is this tidy sweets counter offering Pakistani treats like *gulabjam*, sweet dough balls soaked in syrup, and *kheer*, Pakistani-style rice pudding.

Flushing

Tai Pan Bakery 37-25 Main St, between 37th and 38th streets ☎718/461-8668. Snag a tray and a pair of tongs and get to work assembling your own Chinese carb feast from among the vast assortment of sweet (pineapple) and savory (roasted pork) buns, sugary doughnuts, and custard tarts in this chaotic and popular spot. There are a few hard-won tables.

The Bronx

The Feeding Tree 892 Gerard Ave, at 161st St ☎718/293-5025. Spicy jerk shrimp and chicken, curry goat stew, and other Jamaican specialties come with rice and beans, mixed vegetables, and sweet plantains at this friendly, no-frills fixture near Yankee Stadium. Cash only.

Staten Island

Ralph's Famous Italian Ices 501 Port Richmond Ave, at Catherine St ☎718/273-3675. In business since 1928, this beloved place has spawned a few franchises. Its unusual and wide selection of water ices (honeydew, root beer, and blueberry) and sherbets (spumoni, cremalata, and cannoli) have won many a heart and taste bud.

Restaurants

A large part of visiting New York City is experiencing not just the food but the **culture of dining**. As a port city, New York has long received the best foodstuffs from around the globe and, as a major immigration gateway, it continues to attract chefs who know how to cook all the world's cuisines properly, even exceptionally, as well as populations who know the real thing. Then there are the "foodies," locals who make it their business to seek out the best, most unique, and newest dining establishments in the city, and aren't shy about sharing the fruits of their labors. Travelers will soon find that restaurant-hopping is one of the city's most popular pastimes.

This chapter includes eateries that offer everything from fried chicken to foie gras (and sometimes both), though you should keep in mind that New York's culinary scene is extremely dynamic – even the most food-obsessed locals have a hard time keeping up. Restaurants are always opening and closing, and the establishment *du jour* can change in the blink of an eye; gastronomes and those on the prowl for something new turn to publications like *Time Out New York*, *New York* magazine, or the *New York Times'* Wednesday *Dining Out* section for the lowdown on what's good. More serious foodies dig a little deeper and look to sites on the Web, like Ⓦwww.chowhound.com, Ⓦwww.citysearch.com, and Ⓦwww.dailycandy.com, for opinions and leads on sizzling new chefs and gourmet hotspots. For travelers, the most important aspect of exploring the city's diverse culinary landscape, though, is having a sense of adventure – eating is one of the great joys of being in New York, and it would be a shame to waste time on the familiar.

Cuisines

American cooking is an umbrella term for a vast array of dishes. It includes such standards as steaks, burgers, fried chicken, and macaroni and cheese, but it also refers to menus that highlight local and seasonal ingredients, and recipes that draw on years of tradition as well as new culinary concepts. You'll find many American restaurants offering a rich array of regional specialties: everything from New England clam chowder and Cajun jambalaya to Southern grits and Southwestern barbecue ribs. **Continental** cuisine is generally a hybrid of American, Italian, and French influences, featuring pastas, meats, poultry, and fish or seafood in light sauces and a variety of nightly specials.

You'll encounter an astonishing range of **ethnic cuisines**. **Chinese** food, at its best in Chinatown but available all over the city, is comprised of familiar Cantonese dishes as well as spicier Sichuan and Hunan ones – most

We've highlighted particular types of restaurants and listed them in boxes in the text. We've also picked out a few favorites in the city, which is very hard to do; most of the places recommended in this chapter are exactly that – recommended – though this might give you an easy guide:

Favorites
Burgers p.308
Haute cuisine p.328
Pizza (by the pie) p.330
Quintessential New York p.320
Sushi p.310

Types
Brunch p.323
Restaurants with views p.325
Vegetarian restaurants p.311

restaurants specialize in one of the three. **Japanese** food runs the price gamut from super cheap to extremely expensive; there are a plethora of sushi establishments in the city. Other Asian cuisines are also in abundance, including **Indian** (best in Jackson Heights, Queens), **Indonesian**, **Korean**, **Thai**, and **Vietnamese**.

Italian cooking is widespread and not terribly expensive, especially if you stick to pizza or pasta. **French** restaurants tend to be pricier, although there are an increasing number of bistros and brasseries turning out less costly but authentic and reliable French dishes.

There is also a whole range of **Eastern European** restaurants – Russian, Ukrainian, Polish, and Hungarian – that serve well-priced, filling fare (emphasis on the filling), including *pierogi* (meat-, potato-, or cheese-stuffed dumplings). The historical legacy of **Jewish food**, meanwhile, is most obvious in the ubiquitous bagel, of which New York can be justly proud (see box, p.293), and which you'll typically find filled with cream cheese and lox.

Central and South American and **Caribbean** restaurants are a steadily growing presence in New York. The large, satisfying, frequently spicy meals on offer are often good deals.

While the **fusion** fad, combining influences and ingredients from different foreign cuisines (often Asian), has waned, there are still places featuring hybrids like Chinese–Peruvian and Japanese–Brazilian. Numerous **vegetarian** and **wholefood** eateries cater to any taste or health trend.

Financial District

Although the neighborhood is slowly becoming more residential, eating options in the Financial District remain geared to the great daily tide of commuters coming in and out of the city, a strange mix of take-out feeding troughs, kebab stalls (even on Wall Street), and overpriced power-lunch spots. New Yorkers tend to deem this part of town a culinary wasteland; we've included some places that prove the exception to that rule. Many restaurants close early and either have reduced hours or are closed on weekends.

American and Continental

Bridge Café 279 Water St, at Dover St ☎212/227-3344. You wouldn't guess from this café-restaurant's up-to-the-minute interior that it is the city's oldest surviving tavern, opening in 1847 (the building is 50 years older). The crab cakes are excellent, as is the list of microbrew beers. Entrees $20–30.

Church & Dey Millennium Hilton, 55 Church St, 3rd floor ☎212/312-2000. The immense dining room at this casual American brasserie overlooks the World Trade Center site. The menu includes first-rate regional favorites, as well as dishes like good old-fashioned meatloaf. The sea scallops with basil risotto cakes, and pecan pie are also standouts.

Delmonico's 56 Beaver St, at William St ☎212/509-1144. Many a million-dollar deal has been made at this 1837 landmark steakhouse (check out the pillars from Pompeii). Patrons tend to come more for its historic charms – including classic dishes like Lobster Newburg and Baked Alaska (which was invented here) – than its pricey porterhouses. Closed Sat.

Fraunces Tavern Restaurant 54 Pearl St ☎212/968-1776. The first floor of this historic building is one of downtown's best-kept secrets, a fine restaurant serving delicious crab cakes, pot roast and apple pie. The wood-paneled bar next door opens for drinks and more casual fare – the burger is pretty good.

Paris Café 119 South St ☎212/240-9797. Established in 1873, this old-fashioned bar and restaurant has played host to a panoply of luminaries, from Thomas Edison to Buffalo Bill. These days, the elegant square bar and tempting seafood specials still pull in a lively crowd, mostly tourists; entrees $15–25.

Steamer's Landing 375 South End Ave ☎212/432-1451. Outdoor terraces and great views of the Hudson make this a fine spot to enjoy dishes like the delicious seafood stew ($24), though it can get crowded during peak dining times.

French

Brasserie Les Halles 15 John St, between Broadway and Nassau St ☎212/285-8585. One of two *Les Halles* in New York, this French bistro serves "French Beef, American Style." The Rive Gauche fantasy of *Kitchen Confidential* chef Anthony Bourdain, the menu strives for authenticity but often ends up including over-the-top Gallic dishes, like escargots in garlic butter and duck confit shepherd's pie. Entrees $20–30.

Harry's Café 1 Hanover Square, at Pearl St ☎212/514-9454. Housed in the basement of historic India House and traditionally the haunt of Wall Street deal-makers, the newly revamped café serves lobster, burgers, and pastas, while the posher, pricier steakhouse gets rave reviews for its porterhouses and "Gilded Age" atmosphere.

Italian

Adrienne's Pizzabar 54 Stone St ☎212/248-3838. One of the better Italian restaurants downtown, though as with many places on Stone Street, service can be hit-and-miss. The food is fantastic; *nonna*-style square pizzas with crispy crust come in innovative combinations, but the crumbled sausage topping is especially tasty, and all the cheeses are extremely high quality.

Carmine's Bar and Grill 140 Beekman St, at Front St ☎212/962-8606. In business since 1903, this decently priced place specializes in Northern Italian–style seafood and exudes a comfortable, if run-down, ambience. Try a glass of the house wine and a bowl of linguini in clam sauce.

Scandinavian

Smorgas Chef Downtown 53 Stone St ☎212/422-3500. Established by Norwegian masterchef Morten Sohlberg, this fabulous restaurant dishes out traditional Scandinavian specials such as Swedish meatballs with lingonberry preserve, and Norwegian-style North Sea cod, as well as plenty of lighter lunch options. The outdoor tables and old-world feel enhance the European ambience.

Tribeca

While **Tribeca**'s enclave of very fine restaurants has long attracted Manhattan's "beautiful people," dining in this part of town can leave serious eaters hungry for both a better selection and quality. Most eating establishments are fairly upscale, and you often pay for the view, the overly decorated dining room, or the prospect of dining in famous company rather than the victuals. A bit of exploration will almost certainly turn up a delicious and decently priced meal, but you have to be willing to look for it.

American and Continental

Bread Tribeca 301 Church St, at Walker St ☎212/334-8282. During the day, this spot features a great selection of toothsome sandwiches served on crusty bread. At dinner, the fried fresh calamari ($12) and linguine with fresh clams ($19) get raves.

Bubby's 120 Hudson St, between Franklin and N Moore sts ☎212/219-0666. A relaxed place serving American comfort food, like matzoh-ball soup ($8) and pulled pork ($16). It's the pies, though, that really pull in the crowds – try a slice of the Key Lime ($6.95). The weekend brunch menu is very popular.

▲ Bubby's

City Hall 131 Duane St, between Church St and W Broadway ☎212/227-7777. With a nod toward old-time New York City, *City Hall* is all class, serving amazing steaks and always-fresh oysters.

Harrison 355 Greenwich St, at Harrison St ☎212/274-9310. Upscale version of an upstate country inn, with a smart cherry-wood dining room and a contemporary American menu that includes roasted monkfish with peanut potatoes, and pork chops with coco beans. The desserts are must-try: chocolate beignets with hazelnut sauce, and raspberry rhubarb crostata ($8–9). Entrees from $12.

Tribeca Grill 375 Greenwich St, at Franklin St ☎212/941-3900. The *Grill* is owned by Robert De Niro; no doubt some people come for a glimpse of the actor, though it's really the food – fine American cooking with Asian and Italian accents – they should be concentrating on. The setting is nice, too: an airy, brick-walled eating area around a central Tiffany bar. Entrees range $22–39.

Asian

Nobu 105 Hudson St, at Franklin St ☎212/219-0500. *Nobu*'s lavish woodland décor complements its superlative Japanese cuisine. Try the black cod with miso ($23) – one of the city's best dishes – and chilled sake served in hollow bamboo trunks. Prices are high (entrees from $28), and reservations hard to get; if you can't get in, try the adjacent *Next Door Nobu*.

Austrian

Danube 30 Hudson St, between Duane and Reade sts ☎212/791-3771. Old Vienna lives on: schnitzel is taken to heavenly heights at this opulent pastry-puff of a restaurant, part of the Bouley stable. It's expensive (entrees start at $30), but a terrific spot for an evening on the town. Closed Sun.

French and Belgian

Bouley 120 W Broadway, at Duane St ☎212/964-2525. Modern French food made from the freshest ingredients by celebrated chef Daniel Bouley. Popular with celebs, the prices are fairly steep (entrees from $38); soften costs by opting for one of the prix-fixe options (from $48).

Chanterelle 2 Harrison St, at Hudson St ☎212/966-6960. Some say that visitors to New York should live on stale bread, then spend all their money here. The haute French cuisine (options include roast asparagus with black truffles) is of the finest order, and the wines are so rare that patrons are advised to reserve a bottle ahead of time so that it can be properly decanted. Lunch entrees start at $25, but dinners are pricey ($98 and up).

Soho

Though best known for its posh boutiques and upscale galleries, a number of the city's top restaurants still make their home here – expect to pay top dollar for the more venerable hotspots. A pilgrimage to this area is especially warranted if you're looking for great fresh seafood.

American and Continental

Aquagrill 210 Spring St, at Sixth Ave ☎212/274-0505. The moderately expensive seafood at this cozy Soho spot is so fresh it's practically still flopping. The raw bar and Sunday brunch are excellent, yet not prohibitively priced. Oysters run around $2–3 a pop, clams $1.30–1.40.

Cupping Room Café 359 W Broadway, between Broome and Grand sts ☎212/925-2898. Snuggle in at this affordable American bistro for comfort food, but avoid visiting on weekends – the brunch line can stretch around the block. Good bets are the vast choice of salads ($14–19) or the juicy burgers ($10). Live music on Wed and Fri nights.

Mercer Kitchen *Mercer Hotel*, 99 Prince St, at Mercer St ☎2122/966-5454. This hip eatery, with ground-level café and basement

Petite Abeille 134 W Broadway, between Duane and Thomas sts ☎212/791-1360. *Tintin* comic books cover the walls at this nice little Belgian spot. It's notable for its $17 special of mussels, *pommes frites*, and a beer; on Wed the mussels are all-you-can-eat ($19.95). The menu also includes a fine selection of Continental drafts.

South Asian

Pakistan Tea House 176 Church St, at Reade St ☎212/240-9800. Great, cheap Pakistani tandooris, baltis, and curries. The staff will also create made-to-order flatbreads. Main dishes average $6–8.

Turkish

Turks & Frogs 458 Greenwich St, at Desbrosses St ☎212/966-4774. This authentic, red-walled Turkish restaurant has become a local favorite thanks to the excellent service, exotic, antique-laden interior, and exquisite food such as stuffed baby eggplants, creamy caviar, and feta cheese and lamb dumplings.

restaurant, entices hotel guests and scenesters alike with the casual creations of Jean-Georges Vongerichten, who makes ample use of his raw bar and wood-burning oven. Try the raw tuna and wasabi pizza (entrees from $16). Pricey, but a guaranteed good time.

Spring Street Natural Restaurant 62 Spring St, at Lafayette St ☎212/966-0290. Though not wholly vegetarian, this restaurant serves up freshly prepared health-food in a large, airy space. Try the "Mayan" eggs ($7.50), served with tortillas, black beans, and guacamole, for brunch. The heavy crowds hinder the service, which is invariably slow.

Tailor 525 Broome St, between Sullivan and Thompson sts ☎212/334-5182. This stylish restaurant-cum-cocktail lounge is worth a try for its inventive drinks and desserts as much as the main event: a menu of sweet and salty dishes perfect for nibbling (like grilled octopus with crunchy coffee). Finish off with a bazooka (vodka and "bubble-gum cordial"), or mango ravioli.

Asian

Blue Ribbon Sushi 119 Sullivan St, between Prince and Spring sts ☏212/343-0404. Though the sushi is excellent, the focus here is actually more on the outstanding raw bar, with a wide selection of oysters, littleneck clams, and other tempting bivalves. They don't take reservations and the lines for a table can be long, but never fear: the kitchen is open until 2am.

Cendrillon 45 Mercer St, between Broome and Grand sts ☏212/343-90123. This pan-Asian restaurant, run by a passionate Filipino couple, serves consistently exceptional food (try the vinegary *adobo*; $10–12), not to mention creative cocktails with rare fruits and spice infusions (from $10), and swoon-worthy desserts.

Kelley and Ping 127 Greene St, between Prince and Houston sts ☏212/228-1212. Sleek pan-Asian tearoom and restaurant that serves tasty bowls of noodle soup and other dishes at moderate prices. Dark wood cases filled with Thai herbs and cooking ingredients add to the informal, streetmarket-esque ambience.

Omen 113 Thompson St, between Prince and Spring sts ☏212/925-8923. Traditional Kyoto eatery with lovely decorative touches, including beautiful crockery and menus made from rice paper. Though named for its famous Udon noodle soup, it also serves by far the best sushi in the area (try the bluefin sashimi platter; $30), with a rotating seasonal menu and an extensive sake list. Salmon and fig ($27) and tuna tartare ($30) are also favorites. If you only go to one Japanese restaurant in New York, make it this one.

French

Balthazar 80 Spring St, between Crosby St and Broadway ☏212/965-1414. After years in operation, this is still one of the hottest restaurants in town. The tastefully ornate Parisian décor keeps your eyes busy until the food arrives; then all you can do is savor the fresh shellfish and exquisite pastries. A meal here is well worth the money. Entrees $17–37.

L'Ecole 462 Broadway, at Grand St ☏212/219-3300. Students of the French Culinary Institute serve up affordable French delights at *L'Ecole* – even the bread basket deserves reverence. The four-course prix-fixe menu is $39.95 per person for dinner, $26.50 for lunch (three courses); book in advance. Closed Sun.

Provence 38 MacDougal St, between Prince and Houston sts ☏212/475-7500. This very popular Soho bistro serves excellent seafood, including a delicious coquilles St Jacques. It features a lovely, airy eating area and a garden for the summer, as well as a waitstaff with thick French accents. Main dishes $18–27.

Raoul's 180 Prince St, between Sullivan and Thompson sts ☏212/966-3518. Sexy French bistro seemingly lifted from Paris. The food, especially the steak au poivre ($37) and the artichoke vinaigrette ($10), is wonderful – a fact your wallet won't let you forget. The service is great, too. Reservations recommended. Closed Aug.

Vegetarian restaurants

Angelica Kitchen 300 E 12th St, between First and Second aves ☏212/228-2909; p.317

Madras Mahal 104 Lexington Ave, between E 27th and 28th sts ☏212/684-4010; p.323

Souen 28 E 13th St, between University Place and Fifth Ave ☏212/627-7150; p.320

Spring Street Natural Restaurant 62 Spring St, at Lafayette St ☏212/966-0290; p.310

Italian

Mezzogiorno 195 Spring St, at Sullivan St
☏212/334-2112. This bright Soho restaurant is as much a place to people-watch as it is a place to eat. The good and inventive menu, including excellent pizzas ($14–16), great salads ($9–14), and *prosciutto* with caramelized pears ($15) make up for the slightly higher prices.

Chinatown

If you're after authentic (not to mention affordable) Chinese, Thai, or Vietnamese food, head for the bustling streets of **Chinatown**, where you can sample a little bit of everything. Weekends are especially busy, as New Yorkers come to this neighborhood for *dim sum* brunch, literally "your heart's delight" in Cantonese. Not surprisingly, the streets are lined with dumpling houses and Peking-duck window displays.

Chinese

Big Wong 67 Mott St, between Bayard and Canal sts ☏212/964-0540. This cheap, cafeteria-style Cantonese BBQ joint serves some of Chinatown's tastiest duck and congee (savory rice stew).

Excellent Dumpling House 111 Lafayette St, between Canal and Walker sts ☏212/219-0212. The dumplings at this busy Chinese restaurant are most certainly excellent – they come filled with meat or vegetables, or in soup – but they aren't the only things on offer; try the tasty fried scallion pancake. Prices are low enough to sample a number of dishes.

Golden Bridge Restaurant 50 Bowery, at Canal St ☏212/227-8831. This vast *dim sum* palace comes close to replicating the quality, atmosphere, and organized chaos of a Hong Kong restaurant, with trolleys loaded with dumplings, buns, and chicken's feet circling the tables.

Hop Kee 21 Mott St, at Mosco St ☏212/267-2729. Not much to look at (really a diner) but this aging Cantonese place has some of the best seafood in Chinatown, including sizzling stir-fried calamari and hard-shell crab. Also serves excellent pork and onion dumplings.

Hsin Wong Restaurant 72 Bayard St, between Mott and Elizabeth sts ☏212/925-6526. Best place to try mouthwatering *char siu* (seasoned barbecue pork; $4.25) and congee ($3). Usually full of Hong Kong regulars – a good sign.

New York Noodletown 28 Bowery, at Bayard St ☏212/349-0923. *Noodletown* is best during soft-shell crab season (May–Aug), when the crustaceans are crispy, salty, and delicious. The roast meats and soups are good year-round (try the baby pig on rice). Entrees $8–10.

Peking Duck House 28 Mott St, between Chatham Square and Pell St ☏212/227-1810. This chic and shiny-clean eatery dishes up – you guessed it – duck; the crispy fried birds are carved tableside. If you can ignore the shouts of the commanding owner, you're in for an amazing meal. Slightly pricier than the competition, but worth it.

Ping's Seafood 22 Mott St, between Chatham Square and Pell St ☏212/602-9988. While this Hong Kong–style seafood restaurant is good any time, it's most enjoyable on weekends for *dim sum*, when carts of tasty, bite-sized delicacies whir by every 30 seconds. This place offers superb bang for your buck.

Southeast Asian

Bo Ky 80 Bayard St, at Mott St ☏212/406-2292. The inexpensive noodle soups are very good at this cramped Chinese–Vietnamese eatery. The house specialty is a big bowl of rice noodles with shrimp, fish, or duck.

Nyonya 194 Grand St, between Mott and Mulberry sts ☏212/334-3669. The grub at this Malaysian restaurant is superb, and comes at wallet-friendly prices. Try the chicken curry, spicy squid, or clay-pot noodles. If you're in the mood for something sweeter, order some coconut milk – it's served chilled in the shell.

Pho Bang 157 Mott St, between Grand and Broome sts ☏212/966-3797. One of the most popular Vietnamese restaurants in the city, often packed with diners at weekends. The main event is *pho*, Vietnamese beef noodle soup, which comes in several varieties, but the crispy spring rolls and chicken curry are also excellent.

Pongsri 106 Bayard St, at Baxter St ☎212/349-3132. Patrons at this restaurant eat well-priced Thai food at long communal tables. The whole-fish dishes, crispy and spicy, are standouts.

Little Italy and Nolita

Mulberry Street is **Little Italy**'s main drag, and though often crowded with weekend tourists, the mostly Southern Italian eateries and carnival-like atmosphere can make for an entertaining dinner or dessert excursion. It's best not to have high culinary hopes for the neighborhood, however: Little Italy's many red-sauce restaurants are fair, but not great.

The **Nolita** strip at the north end of Little Italy is notable for its popular budget restaurants, which are often packed to the gills with aspiring fashionistas and film-industry hipsters.

Asian

Kitchen Club 30 Prince St, at Mott St ☎212/274-0025. This oddly integrated Japanese–Dutch eatery features an eclectic, if somewhat expensive, menu. Entrees include miso-marinated steak with huckleberries, and the dessert menu features Linzer torte; the sake list at the adjacent bar is also good.

Lovely Day 196 Elizabeth St, between Prince and Spring sts ☎212/925-3310. Frequented by the Soho/Lower East Side hipster set, this budget restaurant is jam-packed till closing. The Asian-leaning menu lists nicely priced pad thai, satays, and grilled pork chops with roasted apples.

Ethiopian

Ghenet 284 Mulberry St, between Houston and Prince sts ☎212/343-1888. This atmospheric and relatively inexpensive Ethiopian restaurant serves a changing menu of unusual spicy dishes that you eat with your hands and sop up with a cold, sponge-like bread. Utensils are available on request, though they seem vaguely frowned upon by the waitstaff.

Italian

Emilio's Ballato 55 E Houston, between Mulberry and Mott sts ☎212/274-8881. Serving by far the best Italian in the area, *Ballato* has a great low-key atmosphere, a spicy penne *arrabbiata*, tasty spaghetti *vongole*, and veal chops so tender they melt in your mouth.

▲ Lombardi's

Lombardi's 32 Spring St, at Mott St ☎212/941-7994. The oldest pizzeria in Manhattan, *Lombardi's* serves some of the best pies in town, including an amazing clam pizza; no slices, though. There's open-air dining upstairs.

Peasant 194 Elizabeth St, between Prince and Spring sts ☎212/965-9511. Patrons here should expect to pay $22–29 for self-consciously rustic and hearty grilled entrees, such as *osso buco* or grilled *branzino* (sea bass), served from an open kitchen with a wood-burning oven. Closed Mon.

Umberto's Clam House 178 Mulberry St, at Broome St ☎212/431-7545. Specializing in rich, Italian seafood for almost forty years, though the best dish is the simplest – linguine in white clam sauce ($20.95).

Latin American

Bar Bossa 232 Elizabeth St, between Prince and Houston sts ☎212/625-2340. The great ambience at this South American eatery complements the extremely yummy food, including tomato-laden *bruschette*, several outstanding fish dishes, and a very rich Guinness chocolate cake.

Café Colonial 276 Elizabeth St, at Houston St ☎ 212/274-0044. A low-key Brazilian café with good food. On weekends it's a top brunch spot for its omelets; at night go for the chicken Veracruz or the grilled

tilapia. Avoid the steaks; their cuts are not the best.

Café Habana 17 Prince St, at Elizabeth St ☎ 212/625-2001. Small and always crowded, this Cuban–South American eatery features some of the best skirt steak ($11.25) and fried plantains ($3) this side of Havana. They also have a take-out window next door that serves great *café con leche*.

Lower East Side

The trendy **Lower East Side**, once dominated by immigrant tenements and sweatshops, has turned into something of a culinary destination, with Stanton, Rivington, and **Clinton streets** as the main thoroughfares. You'll find some inviting gastronomic *boîtes* here, such as *WD-50*, that have garnered dedicated fans for their sophisticated and unusual menus. There are also some terrific little Latin *comedores*, along with some stalwart old-time joints selling Jewish and Eastern European delicacies.

American and Continental

Schiller's Liquor Bar 131 Rivington St, at Norfolk St ☎ 212/260-4555. Fairly high-end restaurant made up to look like a Prohibition-era speakeasy. Menu offerings are eclectic and self-consciously "American," including pan-fried trout and pork chops smothered in sautéed onions.

Shopsin's Essex St Market, 120 Essex St (no phone). Something of a New York institution, Kenny Shopsin ran his famously idiosyncratic diner in the West Village for years (no cell phones or parties of five), but was forced down here by high rents. His addictive creations – like peanut-butter-filled pancakes – have a loyal following.

Stanton Social 99 Stanton St, between Ludlow and Orchard sts ☎ 212/995-0099. Chandeliers, lizard-skin banquettes, and retro booths draw a young, hip crowd to this 1940s-inspired restaurant-cum-lounge bar. Food here is designed for sharing: try the zesty snapper tacos with mango salsa, or thick lobster rolls. Reserve or expect a long wait.

WD-50 50 Clinton St, between Rivington and Stanton sts ☎ 212/477-2900. To critics, this experimental *haute* spot crammed into a retrofitted corner *bodega* is either the future of gourmet food or the emperor's new clothes. Sample the creations of chef Wylie DuFresne, who "goes diva" with

unconventional entrees like venison tartare with edamame ice cream, then decide for yourself.

Chinese

Congee Village 100 Allen Street, between Delancey and Broome sts ☎ 212/941-1818. You'll see this Cantonese restaurant as you exit the rear of the tenement museum, a shrine to the eponymous fragrant, soupy rice dish served in numerous varieties, and a wide range of other Hong Kong favorites for less than $10.

Jewish

Katz's Deli 205 E Houston St, at Ludlow St ☎ 212/254-2246. *Katz's* overstuffed pastrami or corned beef sandwiches, doused with mustard and complemented by a side pile of pickles, should keep you going for about a week. The egg creams are also delicious. Don't lose your meal ticket or you'll be charged an arm and a leg.

Sammy's Roumanian Steakhouse 157 Chrystie St, at Delancey St ☎ 212/673-0330. This basement Jewish steakhouse offers much more than many customers are prepared for, including schmaltzy songs, delicious-but-heartburn-inducing food (complete with home-made *rugelach* and egg creams for dessert), and vodka chilled in blocks of ice.

Latin American

El Cibao 72 Clinton St, at Rivington St
⊕212/228-0873. El Cibao is the best of a
slew of Dominican restaurants on the Lower
East Side. The fare is hearty and
inexpensive; the sandwiches, particularly
the *pernil* (pork) toasted crisp in a sandwich
press, are great.

East Village

Over time, the **East Village**'s mix of radicals, professionals, and immigrants has
produced one of the most potent dining scenes in the city. While variety and
quality are high, the prices here are a good bit lower than you'll find elsewhere
in Manhattan. The range of culinary options makes dining in this neighborhood
exciting: you can peruse menus on Indian Row; sample dishes at the handful of
Ukrainian eateries; or go out on a limb and try something a little more off-beat,
like Afghani, Tibetan, or Persian cuisine. Most New Yorkers come to the East
Village for its American and Continental dining scene, which, while not as
exotic, is far and away the best of all.

American and Continental

Acme 9 Great Jones St, at Lafayette St
⊕212/420-1934. Come here for authentic
Southern and Cajun grub; the menu
features po-boys, corn bread, and
jambalaya. It's especially popular for
weekend brunch – the fried catfish filet with
two eggs is a local favorite.

**Five Points 31 Great Jones St, between Bowery
and Lafayette St** ⊕212/253-5700. Upscale
New American cuisine, including some of
the best brunch below 14th Street. Try the
slow-cooked pulled pork sandwich ($12.50)
or the banana-stuffed French toast ($9).

**Graffiti Food & Wine Bar 244 E 10th St,
between First and Second aves**
⊕212/677-0695. Pastry chef Jehangir Mehta
cooks up a fusion of Chinese, American,
and Indian flavors in this artsy space, with
just four tables and courses ranging $7–12:
chili pork dumplings, grapefruit confit, and
cumin eggplant wrap grace the menu.
Closed Mon.

**Mama's Food Shop 200 E 3rd St, between aves
A and B** ⊕212/777-4425. Enjoy whopping
portions of tasty and cheap homestyle
dishes like meatloaf, macaroni and cheese,
and a good selection of roasted
vegetables.

**Mermaid Inn 96 Second Ave, between E 5th and
6th sts** ⊕212/674-5870. This restaurant takes
its seafood seriously, serving simple and
fresh dishes in an elegant yet unpretentious
dining room (outdoor seating in summer).
The raw bar is excellent, and specials
change daily depending on the catch.

**Prune 54 E 1st St, between First and
Second aves** ⊕212/677-6221. With a
menu full of surprises, this Mediterranean
restaurant delivers one of the city's most
exciting dining experiences, serving dishes
like sweetbreads wrapped in bacon, seared
sea bass with Berber spices, and buttermilk
ice cream with pistachio puff-pastry. It's
pricey but not as expensive as you might
think (entrees from $19).

**Sarita's Mac & Cheese 345 E 12th St, between
Second and First aves** ⊕212/358-7912. Indulge
your macaroni and cheese cravings at this
homey joint, with ten creative varieties on
offer, blending cheddar, Gruyére, brie, and
goat's cheese with herbs and meats. Pick
your portion sizes: nosh, major munch–or
mongo ($4.25–12.50).

**Tasting Room 72 E 1st St, between First and
Second aves** ⊕212/358-7831. A longtime
foodie favorite for its casual fine dining.
While the ostensible purpose of the menu
here is to complement the enviable wine list
(hence the name), the food itself is definitely
worth going out of your way for: try the
braised pork tongue, the poached trout, or
the sautéed blowfish.

Asian

**Bond Street 6 Bond St, between Broadway and
Lafayette St** ⊕212/777-2500. Very hip, super-
suave Japanese restaurant on multiple stories
(there's a happening lounge on the ground
floor). The sushi is amazing, the miso-glazed
sea bass exquisite, and the steak a treat.
Entrees $18–32, sushi sets $20–28.

Dok Suni 119 First Ave, between E 7th and St Mark's Place ☎212/477-9506. Hip around the edges with great prices to boot, this is a fine bet (and longtime local favorite) for Korean home cooking, including *bibimbop* and *kim chee* rice. The only real drawbacks here are the metal chopsticks, which can retain heat and can be frustratingly slippery.

Elephant 58 E 1st St, between First and Second aves ☎212-505-7739. The menu at this eclectic East Village favorite features a delicious fusion of fairly priced Thai and French delicacies, including innovative fish specials and superb noodle dishes. Look for the bright blue-and-yellow awning.

Hasaki 210 E 9th St, at Stuyvesant St ☎212/473-3327. Some of the best sushi in the city is served at this popular but mellow downstairs cubby-hole. Sit at the bar and the chefs will try to tempt you with a variety of improvised dishes not found on the menu.

Jewel Bako 239 E 5th St, between Second and Third aves ☎212/979-1012. Come here for exotic Japanese delicacies, including a lot of sushi/sashimi offerings that you can't get elsewhere in New York – like live raw lobster (not for the faint of heart). A memorable dining experience, though very expensive. Closed Sun.

Momofuku Noodle Bar 171 First Ave, between E 10th and E 11th sts. Celebrated chef David Chang's first restaurant, where his simplest creations are still the best: silky steamed pork buns, laced with hoisin sauce and pickled cucumbers ($9), or steaming bowls of chicken and pork ramen noodles ($10).

SEA Thai 75 Second Ave, between E 4th and 5th sts ☎212/228-5505. This high-energy, basement Thai restaurant flaunts fab food at killer prices. Try the SEA Caesar salad ($3), the patpong green curry with shrimp ($8), or the pad thai ($8).

Shabu Tatsu 216 E 10th St, between First and Second aves ☎212/477-2972. Tasty, moderately priced Korean barbecue: choose a combination of meat or seafood platters, then cook them yourself right at your table.

Takahachi 85 Ave A, between E 5th and 6th sts ☎212/505-6524. Superior sushi at affordable prices. You'll probably have to wait for a table at dinner – they don't take reservations.

Tsampa 212 E 9th St, between Third and Second aves ☎212/614-3226. Absorb the Buddhist vibes at this Tibetan restaurant, adorned with prayer flags and giant images of the Dalai Lama. Vegetarians have plenty to choose from, with lots of fresh greens, barley soup, various noodles and *momo* (Tibetan dumplings), though there are also several meat dishes.

French

Casimir 103 Ave B, between E 6th and 7th sts ☎212/358-9683. This dark, spacious French bistro specializes in straightforward fare at decent prices. Try the filet mignon or the thick-cut pork chop, both excellent – and surprisingly well-priced – cuts of meat.

Indian

Brick Lane Curry House 343 E 6th St, between First and Second aves ☎212/979-2900. Smack in the heart of curry row, and hands down the best Indian in the East Village, thanks to its wide selection of traditional favorites, including some fiery *phaal* curries ($14–20).

Haveli 100 Second Ave, between E 5th and 6th ☎212/982-0533. Far superior to most of its neighbors on E 6th Street (with the notable exception of *Brick Lane*), this roomy Indian restaurant serves creative and well-executed classics (curries $10–12).

Italian

Frank 88 Second Ave, between E 5th and 6th sts ☎212/420-0202. A tiny neighborhood favorite, where basic, traditional American–Italian dishes are served at communal tables. It's packed every night with hungry locals. No credit cards.

Il Buco 47 Bond St, between Lafayette St and Bowery ☎212/533-1932. This antiques-filled Mediterranean eatery delivers authentic dishes from southern Europe with creative, wholesome flair. The wine cellar is alleged to have inspired Edgar Allan Poe's *The Cask of Amontillado*. It's quite expensive, and they don't accept credit cards (pastas $20–22, entrees $28–39).

Lavagna 545 E 5th St, between aves A and B ☎212/979-1005. This red-hued hideaway seduces East Villagers with potato-cheese gratin, pasta with sausage, and succulent pork dishes. It's been described by local regulars as perfect from beginning to end, and that includes the bill.

Supper 156 E 2nd St, between aves A and B ☎212/477-7600. Great little Italian restaurant with oversized, medieval-looking tables and benches. Try the "priest strangler" pasta (shaped like little nooses) with marinara and fresh ricotta. No reservations or credit cards.

Latin American

Boca Chica 13 First Ave, at E 1st St ☎212/473-0108. Authentic South American food, piled high and served with black beer or tropical drinks. It gets crowded, especially late at night and weekends, and the music is loud. Bring your dancing shoes and be ready to party.

Moroccan

Zerza 304 E 6th St, at Second Ave ☎212/529-8250. Authentic Moroccan restaurant serving superb tagines, *harira* soup, grilled meats, and decent cocktails to wash them down.

Check out the live belly-dancing on Fri and Sat evenings. Entrees $15–20.

Spanish

Xunta 174 First Ave, between E 10th and 11th sts ☎212/614-0620. This gem of a restaurant buzzes with hordes of young people, all perched on rum barrels, downing pitchers of *sangría*, and choosing from the dizzying tapas menu. You can eat (and drink) very well for around $25; the dates with bacon ($5.50) are especially tasty.

Vegetarian

Angelica Kitchen 300 E 12th St, between First and Second aves ☎212/228-2909. Vegetarian macrobiotic restaurant with various daily specials for a decent price. Patronized by a colorful downtown crowd and serving some of the best veggie food in Manhattan.

⑤

West Village

Restaurants in the **West Village** cater to the neighborhood's many and varied residents – everyone from students to celebrities – so the culinary scene is fairly diverse. You'll find loads of take-out spots and places with prix-fixe meals around New York University. Farther west, dining rooms get snazzier, menus more interesting, and prices higher, particularly along Seventh Avenue and into the Meatpacking District, where there's a preponderance of French bistros, and your *cassoulet* is often garnished with a sniffy attitude.

American and Continental

Blue Hill 75 Washington Place, between MacDougal and 6th sts ☎212/539-1776. One of the better restaurants in the West Village, lauded for the rustic American and New England fare, including parsnip soup and braised cod, made with seasonal upstate ingredients. Don't miss the rich chocolate bread pudding.

Corner Bistro 331 W 4th St, at Jane St ☎212/242-9502. A down-home pub with cavernous cubicles, paper plates, and maybe the best burger in town ($6.75). It's a long-standing haunt for West Village literary and artsy types, with a mix of locals and die-hard fans queuing up nightly for excellent and inexpensive grub and a chance to play the great jazz jukebox; don't be discouraged – the line moves quickly.

Gotham Bar & Grill 12 E 12th St, between Fifth Ave and University Place ☎212/620-4020. This

restaurant is generally reckoned to be one of the city's best New American restaurants; if you don't want to splurge on a full meal, at least go for a drink at the bar, where you can watch the beautiful patrons drift in. Maine lobster risotto is a highlight ($26).

Home 20 Cornelia St, between Bleecker and W 4th sts ☎212/243-9579. One of those rare restaurants that manages to pull off cozy with flair. The creative and reasonably priced American food is always fresh and tasty, though it may be a better deal at lunch (around $20 per person) than dinner ($30–40 per person). Try the fennel-crusted pork loin ($19).

Mary's Fish Camp 64 Charles St, at W 4th St ☎646/486-2185. Lobster rolls, bouillabaisse, and grilled whole fish adorn the menu at this small, noisy West Village spot. Go early, as they don't accept reservations and the line lasts into the night. Definitely one of the best seafood spots in the whole

RESTAURANTS | West Village

city – you can almost smell the salty air. Entrees $14–24. Closed Sun.

Pearl Oyster Bar 18 Cornelia St, between Bleecker and W 4th sts ☎212/691-8211. This upmarket version of a New England fish shack is best known for its lemony-fresh lobster roll (which featured in *The Sopranos*). You may have to fight for a table here, but the thoughtfully executed seafood dishes are well worth it. You won't shell out as much as you might expect.

▲ Pearl Oyster Bar

Perilla 9 Jones St, between Bleecker and W 4th sts ☎212/929-6868. The highly acclaimed restaurant of Harold Dieterle, winner of the first season of US TV series *Top Chef*, is an excellent place to enjoy the creations of a celebrity on the rise, without breaking the bank or waiting two years for a table. His clever menu includes dishes like spicy duck meatballs and grilled snowy grouper, with entrees around the $25 mark.

The Pink Teacup 42 Grove St, between Bleecker and Bedford sts ☎212/807-6755. A Southern soul-food institution in the heart of the Village, serving good smothered pork chops, cornbread, and anything fried for under $15. They do a good brunch and weekday lunch special ($7.50), too. No credit cards.

The Spotted Pig 314 W 11th St, at Greenwich St ☎212/620-0393. New York's first gastro-pub, courtesy of chef Mario Batali. The menu is several steps above ordinary bar food – think smoked haddock chowder and sheep's ricotta *gnudi* – and the wine list is excellent. Entrees $17–29, with lunch plates under $20.

Asian

Café Spice 72 University Place, between E 10th and 11th sts ☎212/253-6999. This popular, funky Indian eatery has an expansive and affordable menu of flavorful offerings; try the *dosas*. Be sure to ask for a booth, if you intend to have a conversation over dinner. Otherwise, it's too hard to hear over the din.

Chow Bar 230 W 4th St, at W 10th St ☎212/633-2212. This reasonably priced pan-Asian restaurant supplies a creative selection of dishes, like Shanghai lobster noodles ($23), and killer cocktails (from $12).

Fatty Crab 643 Hudson St, between Gansevoort and Horatio sts ☎212/352-3590. This laid-back but stylish Malaysian diner serves high-quality, authentic fare: the *kang kong* comes with perfect shrimp paste, the oyster omelet is Penang-style, and the bowls of glorious, finger-licking chili crab are worth the effort (and the mess). Expect to pay $12–20 per dish.

Tomoe Sushi 172 Thompson St, between Bleecker and Houston sts ☎212/777-9346. The nightly lines may look daunting, but there's a good reason to join them: this is some of the best, freshest sushi in Manhattan, and it's affordable, to boot. There are some seasonal dishes (like a softshell crab roll) on the menu, but the impossibly fresh fluke and other fish on offer is what draws the crowds – you can be sure the quality is superb.

Yama 38–40 Carmine St, between Bedford and Bleecker sts ☎212/989-9330. This intimate yet bustling Japanese restaurant serves great sushi, and everything else is tasty, too – try the "Sushi for Two" special, which could feed an army. In warm weather, see if you can get a table in the small garden out back.

Austrian

Wallse 344 W 11th St, at Washington St ☎212/352-2300. The Austrian fare offered here has been updated for the 21st century, and the dining room is adorned with Julian Schnabel canvases. The uniquely crafted menu features light-as-air schnitzel, frothy Riesling sauces, and fantastic strudels, and the wine list includes some notable rare vintages.

French and Belgian

Bar Six 502 Sixth Ave, between W 12th and 13th sts ⊤212/691-1363. Patrons flock to this small bistro for its hopping happy hour and inventive, reasonably priced French–Moroccan fare. There's outdoor seating in nice weather.

Café de Bruxelles 111 Greenwich Ave, at W 13th St ⊤212/206-1830. Taste the city's most delicious *frites* (served with home-made mayo) and mussels at this affordable Belgian establishment. There's also a nice selection of Belgian beers, including peach- and strawberry-infused brews.

Chez Brigitte 77 Greenwich Ave, between Bank and W 11th sts ⊤212/929-6736. Only a dozen people fit in this tiny restaurant at one time. The stews and roast-meat dinners go for under $10, and the simple menu features a number of other bargains as well, like the $5 Provençal omelet.

Cornelia Street Café 29 Cornelia St, between Bleecker and W 4th sts ⊤212/989-9319. As much American diner as French café, there is no more comfortable restaurant in NYC. The pastas, salads, and weekend brunch offerings are great, and the prices aren't bad either (entrees $8–14). Downstairs is a cabaret featuring occasional jazz, poetry, and performance art.

Italian

Arturo's Pizza 106 W Houston St, at Thompson St ⊤212/677-3820. Coal-oven pizzas (no slices) that may be the best in town. While-you-eat entertainment often includes live jazz, and there are a couple of outdoor tables on busy Houston Street.

Babbo 110 Waverly Place, between MacDougal St and Sixth Ave ⊤212/777-0303. Originally a coach house (converted into a tearoom in the 1920s, popular with the Roosevelt family), this super-high-end Italian is deservedly touted as one of the best in the city. Try the mint love-letters or goose-liver ravioli, or go for one of the expensive tasting menus ($69–75). You won't get a reservation less than two months in advance, so just show up and either eat at the bar or try for an open table along the window – they don't take reservations for those. Arrive around 5:30pm if you don't want to wait.

Extra Virgin 259 W 4th St, between Perry and Charles sts ⊤212/691-9359. This is more Mediterranean than Italian, featuring a range of seafood specials such as *branzino* in *romesco* sauce and lemon-crusted cod fillet, but also addictive gorgonzola fondue. Expect long waits at the weekend, when the street-side tables are crammed with homesick Europeans.

'ino 21 Bedford St, between Downing sts and W Houston sts ⊤212/989-5769. Duck in here for a satisfying and nicely priced meal; choose from a list of *bruschette*, *tramezzine* (a hearty cousin of the tea sandwich), and Italian wines. The sweet *coppa* ham sandwich with fiery hot peppers and *rucola* (arugula) is one of the best in the city, served with sugary roasted garlic cloves on the side.

John's Pizzeria 278 Bleecker St, between Sixth and Seventh aves ⊤212/243-1680. This full-service restaurant serves some of the city's most popular pizzas, thin with a coal-charred crust ($12–18). Be prepared to wait in line for a table; they don't do slices, and there is no take-out.

Lupa 170 Thompson St, between Bleecker and Houston sts ⊤212/982-5089. *Lupa* serves hearty, rustic Italian specialties such as *osso buco* (braised veal), and *gnocchi* with fennel sausage. Hint: go before 6.30pm and you'll have no problem getting a table.

Latin American

Day-O 103 Greenwich Ave, at W 12th St ⊤212/924-3161. A lively atmosphere and good, affordable food draw a young crowd to this Caribbean/Southern joint. Menu highlights include fried catfish, jerk chicken, and coconut shrimp. Stay away from the tropical drinks if you have a weak head/stomach – they are quite strong.

Mi Cocina 57 Jane St, at Hudson St ⊤212/627-8273. Come here for authentic Mexican food in an upscale setting; the spiced, meat-stuffed poblano chillis (*chiles en nogada*) are especially good. It's often packed, so be prepared to wait.

Tortilla Flats 767 Washington St, at W 12th St ⊤212/243-1053. This Mexican dive has great margaritas, a loud sound system, and plenty of kitsch, including hula-hoop contests. Be careful, it gets really crowded.

chickpea and spinach salad, and bargain lamb chops ($12).

Spanish

Sevilla 62 Charles St, at W 4th St ☎212/929-3189. A long-standing Village favorite, *Sevilla* is dark, fragrant (from garlic), and serves good, moderately priced food. Try the garlic soup, the fried calamari, and the large pitchers of strong *sangría*.

Middle Eastern

Moustache 90 Bedford St, between Grove and Barrow sts ☎212/229-2220. A small, cheap spot specializing in "pitzas" (pizzas of pita bread and eclectic toppings); also offers great hummus,

Vegetarian

Souen 28 E 13th St, between University Place and Fifth Ave ☎212/627-7150. This vegetarian and macrobiotic restaurant uses only organic produce, fish, shrimp, and grains. The food is likwise tasty enough to whet the appetites of meat-eaters.

Chelsea

Once characterized by retro diners and places to people-watch rather than eat, in recent years **Chelsea** has sprouted some respectable eating establishments that manage to please the palate as well as the wallet. There's a mosaic of cuisines – Thai, Creole, Mexican, Italian, and traditional American, among others – and atmospheres available, with something for just about everyone.

American and Continental

Cafeteria 119 Seventh Ave, at W 17th St ☎212/414-1717. Don't let the name fool you: *Cafeteria* may be open 24 hours and serve great chicken-fried steak, meatloaf, and macaroni and cheese, but it's nothing like a truckstop. Expect a smart all-white interior, gold-rimmed mirrors, and a fashionable clientele.

Cookshop 156 Tenth Ave, at 20th St ☎212/924-4440. Latest addition to the Marc Meyer stable, with ever-busy streetside tables and a menu of seasonal, contemporary American fare – dishes change frequently, but might include pheasant pasta, Idaho brook trout, and Vermont suckling pig. Set lunches ($25) and weekend brunches ($10–12) are the best deals.

Empire Diner 210 Tenth Ave, between W 22nd and 23rd sts ☎212/243-2736. With its gleaming chrome-ribbed Art Deco décor, this is one of Manhattan's original diners, still open 24hrs and still serving up plates of simple (if not much better than average) American comfort food. Prices can be a

bit high for the quality of the meal (entrees $13–16).

Hill Country 30 W 26th St, between Broadway and Sixth Ave ☎212/255-4544. Most authentic Texas barbecue joint in the city, with huge servings of moist, fatty brisket, roast pork, and peppery sausage brought in from Kreuz Market near Austin. Grab a table then order your meats (priced by the pound) and sides (such as mac and cheese) from the counters.

Moran's 146 Tenth Ave, at W 19th St ☎212/627-3030. You can get good swordfish and lobster (priced per pound) here, but it's the steaks and chops ($30–40) that are most impressive. The plush, stained-wood seating area is tasteful; try and get a table in the cozy back room, especially in winter, when the fireplace is roaring.

The Old Homestead 56 Ninth Ave, between W 14th and 15th sts ☎212/242-9040. Steak. Period. But really gorgeous steak, served in an almost comically old-fashioned walnut dining room by waiters in black vests. Expensive ($20–44), but portions are huge.

Park 118 Tenth Ave, between W 17th and 18th sts ☎212/352-3313. It's easy to

Ethnic New York

Historically a gateway to America, New York City can stake a fair claim to being the most ethnically diverse metropolis in the world. A remarkable third of today's Americans can trace their roots to Ellis Island, in New York Harbor, where their ancestors arrived during the nineteenth and early twentieth centuries. Many immigrants stayed in New York and built a life in the city, with the result that just about every ethnic community in the United States is now present here. As the largest city in America and its commercial hub, New York remains one of the principal magnets that draw people to the

Museum of Chinese in the Americas, Chinatown ▲

Yonah Schimmel Bakery, Lower East Side ▼

Fire hydrant, Little Italy ▼

Downtown Manhattan

New York City is in some ways a giant processing machine – it assimilates its newcomers, and then they move on to other parts of the city or country. Nowhere is this more evident than in downtown Manhattan, where neighborhoods settled by ethnic groups in the nineteenth century have long since become home to others. Recently bolstered by new immigration from mainland China and Vietnam, **Chinatown** is spilling over its traditional boundaries into nearby enclaves like Little Italy and the Lower East Side. Even though **Little Italy** now has only a handful of Italians, it's still riotously decorated with red, white, and green. Eastern European Jews settled the **Lower East Side** in the nineteenth century, but the city's Jewish population has dispersed over the last few decades, and the neighborhood has become increasingly Hispanic. Nonetheless, there are still remnants of the area's history: knish shops, and the odd synagogue or market in between Puerto Rican delis and Chinese restaurants. Just north of the Lower East Side is the **East Village**, where the city's Ukrainian population has traditionally resided. The neighborhood also features a tiny enclave of Indian restaurants, though the city's largest Indian community is in Jackson Heights, Queens.

Uptown Manhattan

Midtown Manhattan is resolutely WASPish and white, as is the Upper East Side until 100th Street, where it becomes gritty **El Barrio**, or **Spanish Harlem**, the city's largest Puerto Rican neighborhood. The **Upper West Side**, on the other side of Central Park, retains vestiges of its roots as the home of a large Jewish population. North of the park, **Harlem** is the most famous African-American community in the United States, enjoying something of a renaissance as its rows of beautiful brownstones are refurbished and big retailers snap up its commercial real estate. Still farther north, at the tip of Manhattan, lie **Washington Heights** and **Inwood**, thriving Hispanic neighborhoods with large Dominican populations.

▲ Lenox Lounge, Harlem

▼ Ukrainian Museum, East Village

Brooklyn

Today, many of New York's ethnic communities flourish in the outer boroughs. In Brooklyn, architecturally rich Bedford-Stuyvesant stands as the USA's largest Afro-American community outside of Chicago, and was once home to Weeksville, a black community established in the wake of the abolition of slavery. To the south lies **Crown Heights**, home to both the city's largest West Indian

Parades and festivals

New York's ethnic communities celebrate their heritage in parades and festivals held throughout the year. Most last a day, but some go for a week – or even a month. Visitors to New York will be hard-pressed to miss these events, as they often take over whole neighborhoods and main transportation arteries. Some of the best are:

Lunar (Chinese) New Year, the first full moon between Jan 21 and Feb 19 (see p.416)

St Patrick's Day Parade, March 17 (see p.417)

Greek Independence Day Parade, late March (see p.417)

National Puerto Rican Day Parade, second Sun in June (see p.419)

West Indian-American Day Parade and Carnival, Labor Day (see p.420)

Feast of San Gennaro, ten days in mid–Sept (see p.421)

▼ Chinese New Year

Korean food, Flushing ▲

Brighton Beach, Brooklyn ▼

population and a significant number of Hasidic Jews. Trendy **Williamsburg** is similarly divided, as hipster galleries established in the last few years vie for space with the area's long-standing Jewish population and a small but growing Latino community. Just north of Williamsburg, **Greenpoint** is quieter, with an older Polish population. At the southern end of the island, oceanside **Brighton Beach**, sometimes called "Little Odessa," boasts the largest community of Russian immigrants in the United States, and is worth a visit for its restaurants, with their glamorous, over-the-top entertainment.

Queens and the Bronx

Queens, the city's largest borough, is also the most ethnically varied. In **Astoria**, just across the East River from midtown Manhattan, you'll find the largest number of Greeks in the world (outside of Greece, of course). Large communities of South Americans and South Asians live in **Jackson Heights**, and are slowly moving south into **Sunnyside** and **Woodside**, historically Irish neighborhoods. **Flushing** is known as the city's second Chinatown, though Koreans, Malaysians, and Vietnamese also make up a sizeable percentage of the population, one which claims more than fifty percent of its make-up from Asian ancestry. While it lacks the readily identifiable architecture of its Manhattan cousin, it compensates with non-tourist-oriented restaurants offering a more authentic dining experience.

In the Bronx, **Belmont** is now home to more Italians than Little Italy, and the main drag, Arthur Avenue, bustles with salumerias, bakeries and Italian-American eateries, most of which, in common with Flushing, are more geared to the local community than the tourist dollar.

get lost in *Park*'s vast warren of rooms filled with fireplaces, geodes, and even a Canadian redwood in the middle of the floor. The garden is a treat. Pizza, pasta, catfish, and burgers ($12–18) fill the New American menu.

Red Cat 227 Tenth Ave, between W 23rd and 24th sts ☎212/242-1122. Superb service, a fine American–Mediterranean kitchen, and a warm atmosphere all make for a memorable dining experience at *Red Cat*. It's a big local favorite and popular for dates – book ahead.

Asian

Monster Sushi 158 W 23rd St, between Sixth and Seventh aves ☎212/620-9131, ⓦ www .monstersushi.com. "Monster" portions of sushi are on offer here (hence the name), though it's their creative rolls that are the real draw. Not the cheapest sushi in town (sets $17–20), but good. They have several other locations around Manhattan.

Royal Siam 240 Eighth Ave, between W 22nd and 23rd sts ☎212/741-1732. This reasonably priced Thai restaurant has come up with surprisingly flavorful renditions of the old standards.

French

La Lunchonette 130 Tenth Ave, at W 18th St ☎212/675-0342. Even though it's tucked away in a remote corner of Chelsea, this understated little restaurant is always packed with loyal patrons. The menu features the best of French country cooking, including steak *au poivre*, and lamb sausage with sautéed apples, though the specialty is slow-cooked *cassoulet*.

Paradou 8 Little W 12th St, between Greenwich and Washington sts ☎212/463-8345. This underrated Provençal-style French bistro is a far better (and more authentic) option than some of the more touristy places in the area. Great wines by the glass, and good prices.

Italian

Bottino 246 Tenth Ave, between W 24th and 25th sts ☎212/206-6766. One of Chelsea's most popular restaurants, *Bottino* attracts the in-crowd looking for authentic Italian food served in a slick, downtown atmosphere. The home-made leek tortellini (winter months only) is truly tantalizing. Pastas range $14–20, with meaty entrees a bit pricier at $18–30.

Chelsea Ristorante 108 Eighth Ave, between W 15th and 16th sts ☎212/924-7786. This brick-walled restaurant is as enjoyable for its relaxed and unpretentious ambience as it is for its northern Italian food.

Latin American

La Taza de Oro 96 Eighth Ave, between W 14th and 15th sts ☎212/243-9946. Come here for a tasty, filling Puerto Rican meal. Specials change daily, but are always served with a heap of rice and beans. Don't miss the delicious *café con leche*.

Maroon's 244 W 16th St, between Seventh and Eighth aves ☎212/206-8640. Memorable Caribbean and Southern food in a hot and hopping basement space. The cocktails are some of the best in blocks, and the prices are good, too.

Rocking Horse 182 Eighth Ave, between W 19th and 20th sts ☎212/463-9511. Wash down inventive Mexican cuisine with deliciously potent mojitos and margaritas from the bar. Try to keep track of the tab, if you can; drinks make the bill go up quickly.

Spanish

El Quijote 226 W 23rd St, between Seventh and Eighth aves ☎212/929-1855. *El Quijote* has changed very little over the years (it needed only a minimal makeover when it appeared in the 1996 film *I Shot Andy Warhol*, though the movie was set in 1968). It still serves decent *mariscos* and fried meats, but the bland paella should be avoided.

Union Square, Gramercy Park, and the Flatiron District

The neighborhoods of **Union Square**, **Gramercy Park**, and the **Flatiron District** are heavily trafficked, and are therefore prime spots for restaurants. Some of the city's best dining establishments are in this part of town, the finest of which have come to help define New American cuisine. There are also plenty of places to grab a cheap meal, but the neighborhood notables definitely lean toward upscale.

American and Continental

Blue Water Grill 31 Union Square W, at 16th St ⊤212/675-9500. All-round high-quality seafood restaurant. It's hard to go wrong here, whether you choose the grilled fish, caviar, or delicacies from the raw bar. Prices are commensurately high (entrees $26–34).

Chat 'n' Chew 10 E 16th St, between Fifth Ave and Union Square W ⊤212/243-1616. Come for large portions of standard American comfort food served in a colorful diner setting. Menu classics include macaroni and cheese, fried chicken, and yummy sweet-potato fries. It's a good budget option, with most orders under $10.

City Crab 235 Park Ave S, at E 19th St ⊤212/529-3800. This large and very popular eatery prides itself on its large selection of fresh East Coast oysters and clams. Most people come to consume great piles of these bivalves (and pints of ale). Roughly $20–30 per person for a full dinner.

Craft 43 E 19th St, between Broadway and Park Ave S ⊤212/780-0880. Very trendy (read: crowded) but otherwise quite relaxed place serving up some of New York's most inventive food. Popular dishes include roast foie gras, dayboat scallops, and tasty, sautéed wild mushroom sides.

🏃 **Gramercy Tavern 42 E 20th St, between Broadway and Park Ave S** ⊤212/477-0777. The neocolonial décor, exquisite New American cuisine, and perfect service make for a memorable meal at one of the city's best restaurants. The seasonal tasting menus are well worth the steep prices, but if you don't want to splurge, you can also drop in for a drink or more casual meal in the lively front room.

🏃 **The House 121 E 17th St, between Union Square and Irving Place** ⊤212/353-2121. One of the most romantic restaurants in the city, set in a gorgeous three-story carriage house built in 1854, with a fabulous sharing menu based around seasonal, New York State ingredients – the wine cellar is also top-notch.

Pure Food & Wine 54 Irving Place, between E 17th and 18th sts ⊤212/260-5454. Upscale, raw-food restaurant, where food is never heated to more than 118 degrees

Fahrenheit. Prepare for goat-cheese-stuffed squash blossoms and chilli lime tortilla wraps, for $20–30.

Union Square Café 21 E 16th St, between Fifth Ave and Union Square W ⊤212/243-4020. Choice California-style dining in a classy but comfortable atmosphere. No one does salmon like the chefs here, and the polenta with gorgonzola is incredible. Meals aren't cheap – prices average $100 and up for two – but the creative menu is a real treat.

▲ Union Square Café

Asian

Choshi 77 Irving Place, at E 19th St ⊤212/420-1419. Don't worry about wearing a T-shirt and jeans to this casual Japanese establishment. The fresh sushi is first-rate.

Jaiya Thai 396 Third Ave, between E 28th and 29th sts ⊤212/889-1330. The food at this affordable restaurant is red hot and delicious. Don't let the bland décor deceive you – when the menu says "medium spicy," expect to get your head blown off. The far tamer but decent pad thai goes for $10.

L'Annam 393 Third Ave, at E 28th St ⊤212/686-5168. Solid Vietnamese in a hip dining room. Good for a quick meal, as the service is quite fast. The $6.50 lunch specials can't be beat, but almost everything is under $10.

Republic 37 Union Square W, between 16th and 17th sts ☎212/627-7172. The pleasant décor, fast service, low prices, and serviceable noodle dishes at *Republic* make it a popular pan-Asian spot. The tasty dumpling appetizers are the best part.

French and Belgian

Brasserie Les Halles 411 Park Ave S, between E 28th and 29th sts ☎212/679-4111. *Les Halles* is a noisy, bustling, would-be Left Bank bistro – complete with carcasses dangling in a butcher's shop in the front. The menu includes rabbit, steak *frites*, and other staples, with entrees $13–30.

German

Rolf's 281 Third Ave, at E 22nd St ☎212/473-8718. An old-world feeling dominates this dark, chintz-covered East Side institution. The schnitzel and *sauerbraten* (marinated roast beef) are always good, but the best time to go is Christmas, when the restaurant is smothered in over-the-top Yuletide décor.

Indian

Curry in a Hurry 119 Lexington Ave, at E 28th St ☎212/683-0900. A local favorite, offering inexpensive and delicious buffet-style Indian food. You can eat well for around $10.
Madras Mahal 104 Lexington Ave, between E 27th and 28th sts ☎212/684-4010. This eatery is a kosher vegetarian's dream, but everyone else will like it, too. Curries are around $10.
Tabla Metropolitan Life Building, 11 Madison Ave, at E 25th St ☎212/889-0667. This restaurant's swanky, *nouveau* Indian fare is served in an elegant, glassed-in second-floor dining

Brunch

Weekend brunch is a competitive business in New York. The selections below (reviewed in more detail elsewhere) all offer a good weekend menu, sometimes for a price that includes a free cocktail or two – though offers of freebies are to be treated with suspicion by those more interested in the food than getting blitzed. Don't regard this as a definitive list: there are excellent brunch possibilities all over the city.

Downtown Manhattan
Acme 9 Great Jones St, at Lafayette St ☎212/420-1934; p.315
Balthazar 80 Spring St, between Broadway and Crosby St ☎212/965-1414; p.311
Bubby's 120 Hudson St, at N Moore St ☎212/219-0666; p.309
Cupping Room Café 359 W Broadway, between Broome and Grand sts ☎212/925-2898; p.310
Five Points 31 Great Jones St, between Bowery and Lafayette St ☎212/253-5700; p.315
Home 20 Cornelia St, between Bleecker and W 4th sts ☎212/243-9579; p.317

Midtown Manhattan
Brasserie Les Halles 411 Park Ave S, between E 28th and 29th sts ☎212/679-4111; p.323
Cafeteria 119 Seventh Ave, at W 17th St ☎212/414-1717; p.320

Uptown Manhattan
E.A.T. 1064 Madison Ave, between E 80th and 81st sts ☎212/772-0022; p.329
Sarabeth's 423 Amsterdam Ave, between W 80th and 81 sts ☎212/496-6280; p.331
Sylvia's Restaurant 328 Lenox Ave, between W 126th and 127th sts ☎212/996-0660; p.333

room. Start off with the duck samosas and move on to the pan-seared skate with baby artichokes and chickpeas. You'll likely be squeezed in among a horde of young banker types but the food is worth it. *Bread Bar at Tabla*, on the first floor, serves Indian tapas.

Italian

Enoteca I Trulli 122 E 27th St, between Lexington and Park aves T 212/481-7372. Just next to a lovely wine bar of the same name, this gourmet Italian restaurant features robust entrees like *orecchiette* (ear-shaped pasta) with rabbit *ragù* ($21), and roasted rack of lamb with fava-bean purée ($38). Service can be a bit stiff, but for dishes like these it's worth it.

Turkish

Turkish Kitchen 386 Third Ave, between 27th and 28th sts T 212/679-6633. Ruby-red walls and balconies lend a suitably exotic backdrop to this excellent Turkish restaurant,

with dishes such as tender lamb kebabs, and *tavuk pirzola* (chicken stuffed with green peppers and creamy cheese) starting at around $18.

Latin American

Coffee Shop 29 Union Square W, at 16th St T 212/243-7969. Reasonably priced fare (especially the turkey burgers) at this Brazilian establishment, though the staff can be a bit snooty at times. It's a solid lunch spot as well as a good late-night hangout; the kitchen is open until 5:30am Wed–Sat and they serve great *caipirinha* drinks.

Spanish

Casa Mono 52 Irving Place, at E 17th St T 212/253-2773. This eclectic tapas bar both challenges and enchants the palate with such dishes as pumpkin and goat cheese croquetas ($9) and mussels with cava and chorizo sausage ($15). The adjacent and sherry-heavy *Bar Jamón* (125 E 17th St; see p.347) is open until 2am daily.

Midtown East

Catering mostly to weekday office crowds, **Midtown East** overflows with restaurants, many of them nondescript and overpriced. You probably won't want to make the eateries in this neighborhood the focal point of too many excursions, but, that said, there are a few timeworn favorites in the area, such as the *Oyster Bar* in Grand Central Terminal and *Smith & Wollensky*.

American and Continental

Aquavit 65 E 55th St, between Madison and Park aves T 212/307-7311. Exquisite fish dishes abound at this superb Scandinavian restaurant, though the menu also features more exotic dishes, like reindeer. A meal here is a real treat, and it's priced accordingly. Reserve well ahead.
Comfort Diner 214 E 45th St, between Second and Third aves T 212/867-4555. One of the friendliest spots in town, this retro diner serves up hearty staples like meatloaf, fried chicken, and macaroni and cheese. It's a great place to fill up empty stomachs and rest weary toes.
El Rio Grande 160 E 38th St, between Lexington and Third aves T 212/867-0922. Long-established Murray Hill Tex-Mex place with a gimmick: you can eat Mexican, or if you prefer, Texan, by simply crossing the

"border" and walking through the kitchen. Personable and fun – and the margaritas are earth-shattering ($7 and up).
Four Seasons 99 E 52nd St, between Lexington and Park aves T 212/754-9494. The face of New York's fine dining for decades, this timeless Philip Johnson–designed restaurant delivers on every front. If you can't swing the grotesque prices of the dishes on the French-influenced American menu, go for a cocktail and peek at the famous pool room. Housed in the Seagram Building, it is much stuffier than other top restaurants in the city. Closed Sun.
The Modern 9 W 53rd St, inside the Museum of Modern Art T 212/333-1220. The highly-praised *Modern* seems elegant without trying too hard and without adding any unnecessary stuffiness. Fresh, seasonal ingredients are artfully combined to yield unexpected but wholly delicious dishes.

Chorizo-crusted codfish with white cocoa-bean puree and almond *panna cotta* with caviar and clams are just two of the unlikely options. Expensive.

Oyster Bar Lower level, Grand Central Terminal, at E 42nd St and Park Ave ☎212/490-6650. This wonderfully distinctive place is down in the vaulted dungeons of Grand Central. Midtown office-workers who pour in for lunch come to choose from a staggering menu – she-crab bisque, steamed Maine lobster, and sweet Kumamoto oysters top the list. Prices are moderate to expensive; you can eat more cheaply at the bar.

Smith & Wollensky 797 Third Ave, at E 49th St ☎212/753-1530. A grand, if clubby, steak-house, where waiters – many of whom have worked here for twenty years or more – serve you the primest cuts of beef imaginable. Quite pricey – you'll pay at least $40 per steak – but it's worth the splurge. Go basic with the sides and wines.

Asian

Hatsuhana 17 E 48th St, between Fifth and Madison aves ☎212/355-3345. *Hatsuhana* was one of the first restaurants to introduce sushi to New York many moons ago, and it's still going strong. Despite the spartan décor, this place is not at all cheap, so try to go for the midweek prix-fixe lunch.

Le Colonial 149 E 57th St, between Third and Lexington aves ☎212/752-0808. Colonial exploitation never looked as good as it does at this high-end homage to French Indochina, with its bamboo-fan interiors and excellent Vietnamese dishes like *choa tom* (grilled shrimp wrapped around sugar cane), *bo luc lac* (seared filet mignon, watercress,

and pickled onions), and *vit quay* (ginger-roast duck with tamarind sauce).

Vong 200 E 54th St, at Third Ave ☎212/486-9592. The best Southeast Asian food in midtown, served in a trendy dining room in the bowels of the appropriately named Lipstick Building (it's shaped like a lipstick cylinder). Great early-evening prix-fixe meals; don't miss the crab cakes or the rabbit entree.

French

La Grenouille 3 E 52nd St, between Fifth and Madison aves ☎212/752-1495. The *haute* French cuisine here has melted hearts and tantalized palates since 1962. All the classics are done to perfection, and the service is beyond gracious. Its prix-fixe lunch is $45, and dinner is $82 per person without wine.

Montparnasse 230 E 51st St, between Second and Third aves ☎212/758-6633. This French bistro, as authentic as you can find in NYC, has a devoted following and a $23 pre-theater dinner menu, an amazing deal. Try a traditional steak *frites* or red-wine-braised lamb shank.

Italian

Luna Piena 243 E 53rd St, between Second and Third aves ☎212/308-8882. One of the better Italian restaurants in a neighborhood awash in mediocre eateries. The food is filling and the service friendly, and there's an enclosed garden for warm summer evenings.

Naples 45 200 Park Ave, at E 45th St ☎212/972-7001. Named one of America's 10 greatest pizzas by American Heritage, the

Restaurants with views

This is a brief list of restaurants that draw patrons just for their views or location. The restaurants are covered in more detail in other sections; note that the quality of the views will almost invariably be reflected in the size of your bill.

Boat Basin Café W 79th St, at the Hudson River ☎212/496-5542; p.331

Boathouse Café Central Park Lake, east side, near E 72nd St entrance ☎212/517-2233; p.331

River Café 1 Water St, at Furman St on the East River, Brooklyn ☎718/522-5200; p.334

Tavern on the Green W 67th St, at Central Park W ☎212/873-3200; p.331

Terrace in the Sky 400 W 119th St, between Amsterdam Ave and Morningside Drive ☎212/666-9490; p.332

pies at this place are flavorful (with toppings like roasted vegetables, fennel, and *prosciutto di Parma*) and come with just the right amount of wood-burning-oven char. Also fish, chicken, steak, and pasta specialties.

Jewish

2nd Avenue Deli 162 E 33rd St, between Lexington and Third aves ☎212/689-9000. Even the *shiksas* love this place, a reincarnation of the family-run Jewish institution that closed in 2005. It's no longer on Second Ave, but the stuffed cabbage, pastrami-and matzoh-ball soup are as tasty as ever. It may seem expensive, but the sandwiches (around $20) are filling enough for two.

Mexican

Zarela 953 Second Ave, between E 50th and 51st sts ☎212/644-6740. If you've ever wondered what home-cooked Mexican food really tastes like, this festive restaurant is the place to go. It's noticeably more expensive than most Mexican places, but worth every cent.

Spanish

Solera 216 E 53rd St, between Second and Third aves ☎212/644-1166. Tapas and other Spanish specialties are served here in a stylish townhouse setting. As you'd expect from the surroundings and the ambience, it can be expensive, but it's one of the city's better Iberian eateries.

Midtown West

While many of Manhattan's best dining establishments are located downtown, manifold good meals await you in **Midtown West**. The eateries in Little Brazil (West 46th Street) serve up some excellent, if meat-heavy, dishes, while Restaurant Row (West 46th Street between Eighth and Ninth avenues) is a frequent stopover for theater-goers seeking a late-night meal. Cheaper (and often better) alternatives can be found along Ninth Avenue and farther west into Hell's Kitchen. Be advised that many restaurants in the Times Square area (not the ones we have included here) are overpriced and not of the highest quality.

Afghani

Ariana Afghan Kebab 787 Ninth Ave, between W 52nd and 53rd sts ☎212/262-2323. A casual neighborhood restaurant serving inexpensive kebabs (chicken, lamb, and beef) and vegetarian meals.

American and Continental

'21' Club 21 W 52nd St, between Fifth and Sixth aves ☎212/582-7200. This is simply one of New York's most enduring institutions – the city's Old Boys come here to meet and eat. There's a dress code, so wear a jacket and tie. Three-course early dinner prix-fixe menus are $40 per person in the *Bar Room*, which is a pretty good deal, considering most entrees (such as the chop, loin, and leg of Vermont lamb with crushed purple potatoes) go for $45 all on their own.
Bryant Park Grill 25 W 40th St, between Fifth and Sixth aves ☎212/840-6500. Most patrons come to this restaurant for its enviable location in leafy Bryant Park. Enjoy lovely

views from inside the spacious dining room or al fresco on the terrace. The food is prosaically standard upscale (Caesar salad, rack of lamb).
db Bistro Moderne City Club Hotel, 55 W 44th St, between Fifth and Sixth aves ☎212/391-2400. Famous chef-owner Daniel Boulud gives average Joes a chance to taste his creations at this bistro, which is decidedly more affordable than his other culinary shrines. A few items do toe the expense line, however, including the sublime $32 burger, layered with foie gras, black truffle, and short-rib meat.
HK 523 Ninth Ave, at W 40th St ☎212/947-4208. This shiny industrial eatery has lots of light and a smartly priced American and Mediterranean menu. Try the fresh grilled-calamari salad ($6.95).
Quality Meats 57 W 58th St, between Fifth and Sixth aves ☎212/371-7777. The front doors give the impression you're stepping into a meat locker – and you are, in a sense. Top-notch beef (and lots of it); in contrast to

many steakhouses, the appetizers and sides are well done, too.

Thalia 828 Eighth Ave, at W 50th St ☎212/399-4444. *Thalia* is a solid choice for imaginative, New American cuisine in the Theater District. The 5000-square-foot eating area is full of color and the prices aren't bad either. Try the "Thaliatelle" (pasta with rock shrimp, mussels, mushrooms, fava beans, tomatoes, pecorino, mint, and white wine; $19) or the skate with fine herb butter ($21).

Virgil's Real BBQ 152 W 44th St, between Sixth and Seventh aves ☎212/921-9494. *Virgil's*, one of New York's earliest entries in the BBQ game, is one of the few Times Square eateries that's not just for tourists. All the food groups – Memphis, Carolina, Texas, even Maryland (ham) – are well represented, and you'll likely be able to skip breakfast in the morning.

West Bank Café 407 W 42nd St, at Ninth Ave ☎212/695-6909. The menu here features some American dishes and some French dishes, all of which are delicious and not as expensive as you might think – entrees range $18–24. It's very popular with theater people, especially after performances.

Asian

Nobu 57 40 W 57th St, between Fifth and Sixth aves ☎212/757-3000. The northern branch of the famous Japanese gustatory palace. Tucked away in the middle of the block, *Morimoto*-lovers can still find their favorites here, and the black cod with miso ($24) is still to die for.

Pongsri Thai Restaurant 244 W 48th St, between Broadway and Eighth Ave ☎212/582-3392. This restaurant is popular with local businesspeople for its extensive and good-value lunch menu. The list of dinner options is massive.

Ruby Foo's 1626 Broadway, at W 49th St ☎212/489-5600. The best dining option in Times Square, *Ruby Foo's* has a wide-ranging Asian menu that includes everything from sushi platters to *dim sum* to Thai noodle dishes, all done surprisingly well. There's another branch at 2182 Broadway, at W 77th St (☎212/724-6700).

Shun Lee 43 W 65th St, at Columbus Ave ☎212/595-8895. The service and table settings here are strictly formal, but you should feel free to dress casually. This venerable local institution – conveniently

across the street from Lincoln Center – has top-notch Chinese food. Steer yourself toward the menu's many seafood delicacies.

Sugiyama 251 W 55th St, between Broadway and Eighth Ave ☎212/956-0670. Though you may want to take out a loan before dining at this superb Japanese restaurant, you're guaranteed an exquisite experience, from the enchanting *kaiseki* (chef's choice) dinners (from $52) to the regal service.

Won Jo 23 W 32nd St, between Broadway and Sixth Ave ☎212/695-5815. Budgeteers will like this "K-town" favorite for its excellent BBQ, wallet-friendly prices, and round-the-clock Korean menu. The service, however, could stand some improvement.

French

Aureole One Bryant Park, Sixth Ave between 42nd and 43rd sts ☎212/319-1660. *Aureole's* French-accented American food is unbelievably tasty and inventive. It's also quite expensive: the prix-fixe options bring the cost to $84 per head, or $115 for the five-course tasting menu. Stop by just for the show-stopping desserts (like the berry *millefeuille* with lavender *crème fraiche* and pistachio filo crisps), or the almost-affordable lunch special for $38.

Chez Napoleon 365 W 50th St, between Eighth and Ninth aves ☎212/265-6980. One of several authentic Gallic eateries that sprang up in this area during World War II, when it was a hangout for French soldiers. A friendly, family-run bistro, it continues to serve solid, high-quality food. Not cheap, though – bring plenty of cash.

Hourglass Tavern 373 W 46th St, between Eighth and Ninth aves ☎212/265-2060. This tiny French eatery on Restaurant Row features a three-course prix-fixe menu for $20. The gimmick is the hourglass above each table, the emptying of which means you're supposed to leave and make way for someone else. In reality, the glasses seem to last more than an hour, and to be only rarely enforced. Cash only.

🏃 **Le Bernardin 155 W 51st St, between Sixth and Seventh aves** ☎212/554-1515. The most storied seafood restaurant in the United States, serving incomparable new angles on traditional Brittany fish dishes in elegant surroundings. This is one dinner you'll never forget, though you may cry when the bill arrives.

Rue 57 60 W 57th St, at Sixth Ave ☎212/307-5656. This attractive brasserie is noisy inside and out (buses rumble by on 57th outside the often open windows) but worthwhile. Try the eggs Florentine (at brunch), the mini Kobe burgers or the potato-crusted salmon. And, surprise, it even offers decent sushi.

German

Hallo Berlin 626 10th Ave, between W 44th and W 45th sts ☎212/977-1944. Come to *Berlin* to enjoy all manner of German sausages and unusual ales in a pleasant bench-and-table beer-garden setting. At $15–20 for mains, the prices aren't bad.

Italian

Becco 355 W 46th St, between Eighth and Ninth aves ☎212/397-7597. Catering to the pre-theater crowd, *Becco* is most notable for its $23 *Sinfonia di Pasta*: the all-you-can-eat dinner with a choice of three pasta-and-sauce combinations.

Trattoria dell'Arte 900 Seventh Ave, at W 57th st ☎212/245-9800. Unusually nice restaurant for this stretch of midtown, with an airy interior, excellent service, and good food. Great, wafer-thin crispy pizzas, decent and imaginative pasta dishes from around $23, upscale items like the veal chop ($45) and snapper livornese, and a mouthwatering antipasto bar – all eagerly patronized by an elegant, out-to-be-seen crowd.

Jewish and Russian

Carnegie Deli 854 Seventh Ave, between W 54th and 55th sts ☎212/757-2245. The most generously stuffed sandwiches in the city are served by the rudest of waiters at this famous Jewish deli. Still, it's a must-have experience, if you can stand the inflated prices.

Petrossian 182 W 58th St, at Seventh Ave ☎212/245-2214. Pink granite and etched mirrors set the mood at this decadent Art Deco establishment, where champagne and caviar are the norm. That said, wow! is this place expensive. The most affordable option (sans caviar, sans champagne) is the $39 prix-fixe dinner.

Russian Tea Room 150 W 57th St, between Sixth and Seventh aves ☎212/581-7100. In its third incarnation, the restaurant has nowhere near the cachet of the original, but is nonetheless recommended (the stroganoff

and the chicken Kiev are faves). With appetizers from $15–20, and mains $30–40, you'll need plenty of dough.

Stage Deli 834 Seventh Ave, between W 53rd and 54th sts ☎212/245-7850. Genuine New York attitude and gigantic, overstuffed sandwiches ($14) are what's on the menu at this open-all-night rival to the better-known *Carnegie Deli*. The food (and the prices) are better here.

Uncle Vanya Café 315 W 54th St, between Eighth and Ninth aves ☎212/262-0542. Moderately priced Russian delicacies, comprising more than the obligatory borscht and caviar.

Latin American

Churrascaria Plataforma 316 W 49th St, between Eighth and Ninth aves ☎212/245-0505. Meat (the fare of choice) is served in this huge, open Brazilian dining room by waiters carrying swords stabbed with succulent slabs of grilled pork, chicken, and lots of beef. The $55 prix-fixe (your only option) covers all of these various grilled meats and more. Don't miss the addictive *caipirinhas* (Brazil's national drink).

Hell's Kitchen 679 Ninth Ave, between W 46th and 47th sts ☎212/977-1588. Lively atmosphere aided and abetted by six different kinds of frozen margarita and sophisticated renderings of Mexican cuisine. Start with the coriander tuna tostadas and move on to the red snapper in *chipotle* and corn broth. For dessert, the caramelized banana *empanadas* are unbeatable.

Emporium Brasil 15 W 46th St, between Fifth and Sixth aves ☎212/764-4646. *The* place to go on Little Brazil Street for *feijoada* (a stew of black beans with hunks of dried pork and pig parts) on Saturdays. Fairly casual during the day, it becomes a little classier for dinner.

Rough Guide favorites

Haute cuisine

Rosa Mexicano 61 Columbus Ave, between W 62nd and 63rd sts ☏212/977-7700. Right across from Lincoln Center, it's the perfect location for a post-opera meal. Try the guacamole, which is mashed at your table, and their signature pomegranate margaritas.

Upper East Side

Upper East Side restaurants mostly exist to serve a discriminating mixture of Park Avenue matrons and young professionals; many of the city's best Japanese and French restaurants call this area home. Otherwise, the cuisine here is much like that of the rest of Manhattan: a middling mixture of Asian, standard American, and reasonable Italian cafés. More and more family-oriented restaurants are popping up here all the time.

American and Continental

Atlantic Grill 1341 Third Ave, between E 76th and 77th sts ☏212/988-9200. Fresh seafood (think nori-wrapped salmon, teriyaki sea bass and crab cakes, as well as sushi and some nice salads) in a pleasant mid-upscale setting.

Barking Dog Luncheonette 1678 Third Ave, at E 94th St ☏212/831-1800. This diner-like place offers outstanding, cheap American food (like mashed potatoes and gravy). Kids will feel at home, especially with the puppy motif. Adults will appreciate the excellent Cobb salad.

E.A.T. 1064 Madison Ave, between E 80th and 81st sts ☏212/772-0022. Owned by restaurateur and gourmet grocer Eli Zabar, *E.A.T.* is expensive and crowded but the food is excellent, notably the soups, breads, ficelles, and Parmesan toast. The mozzarella, basil, and tomato sandwiches are fresh and heavenly.

Etats-Unis 242 E 81st St, between Second and Third aves ☏212/517-8826. This pocket-size, New American restaurant is perfect for an intimate evening on the town. There's a nicely curated wine list and menu to match. Pricey (entrees like panko-crusted crab cakes with mango, fennel, cilantro, and mint are in the $35 range) but a reasonable splurge.

Fred's at Barney's 660 Madison Ave, 9th floor, between E 60th and 61st sts ☏212/833-2200. Well-reviewed boutique store restaurant that doesn't feel like an afterthought. A bit pricey, but a comfortable place to relax between shopping for shoes and cosmetics.

King's Carriage House 251 E 82nd St, between Second and Third aves ☏212/734-5490. You'll feel as if you've been transported to the country at this romantic, converted carriage-house. With reliable Continental cuisine (such as *prosciutto*-wrapped quail), it's a fine place for an afternoon pick-me-up cup of tea or an unwind-me-down glass of wine.

Asian

Donguri 309 E 83rd St, between First and Second aves ☏212/737-5656. Sushi lovers won't want to miss this little five-table, family-run spot featuring some of the best bluefin tuna in town, as well as superb Kumamoto oysters, mushroom tempura, and broiled whitefish. There are only two seatings per night (7 & 9pm) and they tend to hustle out the early shift ASAP, so don't plan on lingering.

Pig Heaven 1540 Second Ave, between E 80th and 81st sts ☏212/744-4333. A good-value Chinese restaurant. The accent is on pork (it's decorated with images of pigs, and spare ribs are the featured items on the menu), but everything else is good, too.

Saigon Grill 1700 Second Ave, at E 88th St ☏212/996-4600. If you can put up with the hectic service and in-and-out attitude, then head here for affordable, well-executed Vietnamese dishes.

Sushi of Gari 402 E 78th St, between First and York aves ☏212/517-5340. Amiable neighborhood sushi shop with top-quality fish. The tasting menu is full of unusual offerings, including *toro* and pickled radish.

French

Café Boulud 20 E 76th St, between Madison and Fifth aves ☏212/772-2600. The muted but elegant interior of chef Daniel Boulud's second Manhattan eatery makes this an exceedingly pleasant place to savor his sublime concoctions (case in point:

Moroccan spiced duck). And save room (and $14!) for dessert!

Daniel 60 E 65th St, between Madison and Park aves ☎212/288-0033. Upscale and expensive fare from chef Boulud (again) – think black sea bass in Syrah sauce and "quartet of pig *provençale*." There's even an elaborate, seasonal, vegetarian prix-fixe menu ($105). One of the best French restaurants in New York City.

Le Refuge 166 E 82nd St, between Lexington and Third aves ☎212/861-4505. Quiet, intimate, and deliberately romantic old-style French restaurant in an old city brownstone. The bouillabaisse and other seafood dishes are delectable. Expensive but worth it; save trips here for special occasions. Closed Sun during the summer.

Indian and Middle Eastern

Dawat 210 E 58th St, between Second and Third aves ☎212/355-7555. One of the most elegant gourmet Indian restaurants in the city. The chicken *tikka masala* ($19) is superbly marinated and spiced. It can be a bit pricey – entrees average about $21.

Persepolis 1407 Second Ave, between E 74th and 75th sts ☎212/535-1100. One of the few places in New York City for Persian food, this is also one of the best. Smells of rose, cherry, and cardamom fill the dining room. It's affordable, too.

Rectangles 1431 First Ave, between E 74th and 75th sts ☎212/744-7470. Probably the best Middle Eastern food in the city, this Yemeni–Israeli restaurant features tasty standards like hummus, *baba ghanoush*, and a spicy chicken soup that can instantly cure the common cold.

Italian

Caffè Buon Gusto 236 E 77th St, between Second and Third aves ☎212/535-6884. The Upper East Side has no shortage of middling Italian restaurants, but the food at *Buon Gusto* is a notch better than its peers (and a notch lower in price). The penne vodka is excellent.

Carino 1710 Second Ave, between E 88th and 89th sts ☎212/860-0566. Family-run Upper East Side Italian joint, with low prices, friendly service, and good food. Two can eat here for under $30.

Rao's 455 E 114th St, between First and Pleasant aves ☎212/722-6709, ⊛www.raos.com. You must reserve waaaay in advance (it's only got 10 tables, and one seating a night), but if the stars are aligned, you can be part of the most authentic Italian dining experience in the city. (If not, there's always their mail order operation.) Cash only.

Eastern European

Beyoglu 1431 Third Ave, at 81st St ☎212/650-0850. *New York* magazine's fave place for *mezes* (the Turkish version of appetizers), and the doner kebabs and fish specials are super as well. Loud (the second floor is quieter), reasonably priced, and definitely filling.

Heidelberg 1648 Second Ave, between E 85th and 86th sts ☎212/628-2332. The atmosphere here is *mittel*-European kitsch, with gingerbread trim and waitresses in Alpine goatherd costumes. The food, though, is the real deal, featuring excellent liver-dumpling soup, *Bauernfrühstück* omelets, and pancakes (both sweet and potato). And they serve *Weissbier* the right way, too – in giant, boot-shaped glasses.

Latin American

Maya 1191 First Ave, between E 64th and 65th sts ☎212/585-1818. Excellent, high-end Mexican entrees are served in a large, colorful, and noisy dining room. The rock shrimp *ceviche*, chicken *mole*, and grilled dorado filet make this one of the best restaurants on the Upper East Side – and among the best Mexican spots in the whole city.

Taco Taco 1726 Second Ave, at E 90th St ☎212/289-8226. High-quality, super-cheap taco depot with some unconventional fillings (beef tongue and sautéed cabbage) in addition to the standards. The fish tacos are especially good.

Rough Guide favorites

Pizza by the pie
Arturo's Pizza West Village, p.319
John's Pizzeria West Village, p.319
Lombardi's Little Italy, p.313
Trattoria dell'Arte Midtown West, p.328
V&T Pizzeria Upper West Side, p.332

Vegetarian

Candle Café 1307 Third Ave, at 75th St
T212/472-0970. This vegan favorite does its
best to dress up all that tofu and seitan,
often with surprising results. Salads are a
standout, as are the soups and juices from
the "farmacy." Moderately priced.

Upper West Side and Morningside Heights

The **Upper West Side** is yuppie-residential, and the cuisine on offer is tailored
to local tastes. There are lots of generous burger joints, Chinese restaurants,
friendly coffee shops and delectable, if a bit pricey, brunch spots. You'll never be
at a loss for good, comforting dishes, but don't expect many memorable meals.

African

**Awash 947 Amsterdam Ave, between 106th and
107th sts** T212/961-1416. Ethiopian expats
flock to this brightly colored restaurant
offering sumptuous vegetarian and meat
combo platters ($11–17). Dig in with your
hands, but lay off the too-sweet honey wine.

American and Continental

**Boat Basin Café W 79th St, at the Hudson River
with access through Riverside Park** T212/496-
5542. An outdoor restaurant, the *Boat Basin*
is only open May through Sept. The informal
tables are covered in red-and-white-
checked cloths, and the food is standard –
burgers with fries, hot dogs, sandwiches,
and some more serious entrees like grilled
salmon – but inexpensive considering the
prime location. On weekend afternoons a
violin trio adds to the pleasant ambience.
**Boathouse Café Central Park Lake, at W 72nd St
entrance** T212/517-2233. A peaceful retreat
after a hard day's trudging around the Fifth
Avenue museums. You get great views of
the famous Central Park skyline and decent
American/Continental cuisine, but at very
steep prices. Closed Oct to March.
**Ouest 2315 Broadway, between W 83rd and
84th sts** T212/580-8700. This New American
restaurant has earned a loyal following for
its exceptional gourmet comfort-food, such
as braised beef short ribs with baby beets,
or the leg and loin of rabbit; there's also a
$33 three-course pre-theater menu
(weekdays only).
**Per Se 1 Central Park W, 10 Columbus Circle,
Time Warner Center** T212/823-9335.
Standard dishes are utterly transformed in
the $275 nine-course pre-fixe. Mushroom
soup becomes "Cappuccino of Forest
Mushrooms" and is served in a *café au lait*

cup; "Macaroni and Cheese" is the name
for a dish that includes poached lobster,
orzo, and a thin sliver of parmesan. Reservations accepted only by phone two
months prior to the day, and jackets are
required for men.
**Santa Fe 73 W 71st St, between Columbus Ave
and Central Park W** T212/724-0822. Upscale
Southwestern cuisine in lovely surroundings
– muted earth tones, large arrangements of
fresh flowers, and a cozy fireplace in the
bar. The food is first-rate; be prepared to
spend about $40 per person.
**Sarabeth's 423 Amsterdam Ave, between W 80th
and 81st sts** T212/496-6280. Best for brunch,
this country-style restaurant serves delectable baked goods and impressive omelets.
Expect to wait in line for a table, especially
for weekend brunch.
**Tavern on the Green Central Park W, between W
66th and 67th sts** T212/873-3200. This
fantastical, tacky tourist trap remains a New
York institution. The American and

▲ Tavern on the Green

Continental cuisine is dependable if not extraordinary, and during warmer months there's dancing Thursday evenings on the terrace.

Asian and Indian

Haru 433 Amsterdam Ave, between W 80th and 81st sts ☎212/579-5655. A solid stand-by in this part of town if you're craving sushi. It's extremely popular, so you should expect to wait for a table.

Hunan Park 154 W 72nd St, between Columbus and Amsterdam aves ☎212/724-4411. Some of the best Chinese food on the Upper West Side is served here, in a large, crowded room, with typically quick service and moderate prices. Try the spicy noodles in sesame sauce and the dumplings.

Rikyu 483 Columbus Ave, between W 83rd and 84th sts ☎212/799-7847. A wide selection of Japanese food, including sushi made to order. Inexpensive lunches and early-bird specials make this place a relative bargain.

Sapphire 1845 Broadway, between W 60th and 61st sts ☎212/245-4444. Capable Indian eatery conveniently located near the Time Warner Center. The Mon–Sat buffet lunch ($14) is a great deal.

French

Café des Artistes 1 W 67th St, between Columbus Ave and Central Park W ☎212/877-3500. Charming, fantastical restaurant with richly hued murals and an international menu; its $35 prix-fixe dinner is a good option for those on a budget.

Jean Georges Trump International Hotel, 1 Central Park W, between W 60th and 61st sts ☎212/299-3900. French fare at its finest, crafted by star chef Jean-Georges Vongerichten. The gracious service is a throwback to another, more genteel, era. With the meal starting at $150, it's definitely the place for a special occasion; for the more price-conscious, the front-room *Nougatine* has a prix-fixe summer brunch for $24. The wine list includes bottles ranging from $30 all the way to $12,000.

Picholine 35 W 64th St, between Broadway and Central Park W ☎212/724-8585. This French favorite always gets rave reviews, especially for its cheese plate. A terrific spot for a celebratory dinner.

Italian

Carmine's 2450 Broadway, between W 90th and 91st sts ☎212/362-2200. A family-style Southern Italian joint with big portions, big flavors, and a big personality. Though often packed to the rafters, it's a bit more civilized than the outpost in Times Square (200 W 44th St ☎212/221-3800).

Gennaro 665 Amsterdam Ave, between W 92nd and 93rd sts ☎212/665-5348. A tiny, bustling source of truly great Italian food. The excellent menu includes such moderately priced favorites as a warm potato, mushroom, and goat cheese tart, and braised lamb shank in red wine. Don't forget to save room for dessert. Open for dinner only. No credit cards.

Terrace in the Sky 400 W 119th St, between Amsterdam Ave and Morningside Drive ☎212/666-9490. Enjoy harp music, marvelous Mediterranean fare, and bird's-eye views of Morningside Heights from this romantic uptown spot.

V&T Pizzeria 1024 Amsterdam Ave, between W 110th and 111th sts ☎212/663-1708. Checked tablecloths and a low-key, down-home feel describes this pizzeria near Columbia University, with predictably college-aged patrons. Good and inexpensive.

Jewish and Eastern European

Artie's Delicatessen 2290 Broadway, between W 82nd and 83rd sts ☎212/877-2721. All the wise-cracking attitude of an old-timer, but the place is less than 10 years old. Best choices: knish dogs, corned beef, noodle pudding, potato pancakes, black-and-whites, and birthday cake. Don't forget the pickles!

Fine & Schapiro 138 W 72nd St, between Broadway and Columbus ☎212/877-2721. Long-standing Jewish deli that's open for lunch and dinner, serving delicious old-fashioned kosher fare. Great chicken soup.

Latin American

Café con Leche 424 Amsterdam Ave, at W 80th St ☎212/595 7000. This great neighborhood Dominican restaurant serves roast pork, rice and beans, and some of the hottest chilli sauce you've ever tasted. Cheap and very cheerful. Also at 726 Amsterdam Ave, between 95th and 96th sts.

Calle Ocho 446 Columbus Ave, between W 81st and 82nd sts ☎212/873-5025. Very tasty Latino fare, including *ceviche* (there's a wide selection priced $12–15) and *chimchuri* steak ($25) with yucca fries, served in an immaculately designed restaurant with a hopping lounge. The mojitos ($8) are as tasty and potent as any in the city.
La Caridad 2199 Broadway, at W 78th St ☎212/874-2780. This no-frills eatery – something of an Upper West Side institution – doles out Cuban and Chinese food to hungry diners (the Cuban is better than the Chinese). Expect to queue.

Middle Eastern

Turkuaz 2637 Broadway, at W 100th St ☎212/665-9541. Sip a glass of *raki* in *Turkuaz*'s cavernous dining room and linger over such Turkish delicacies as grape leaves stuffed with salmon cubes. There are some vegetarian options.

Vegetarian

Josie's 300 Amsterdam Ave, at 74th St ☎212/769-1212. Fresh, tasty, meatless dishes with an Asian twist, as well as organic chicken and seafood.

Harlem and above

While visitors to **Harlem** will find plenty of cheap Caribbean and West African eateries, it would be unthinkable not to try the soul food for which the area is justifiably famous. Whether it's ribs or fried chicken and waffles you're craving, you simply can't go wrong. Many of these restaurants are run by passionate chef-owners who pride themselves on their delicious, calorie-rich dishes.

American and Continental

Amy Ruth's 113 W 116th St, between Lenox Ave and Powell Blvd ☎212/280-8779. The honey-dipped fried chicken is more than enough reason to travel to this casual family restaurant. It gets busy after church on Sun.
Charles' Southern Style Kitchen 2841 Frederick Douglass Blvd ☎212/926-4313. Fried chicken is the specialty at this tiny Harlem spot, but the filling macaroni and cheese is equally good. There's a $10 open buffet Wed–Sun for $12, $14 after 4pm.
Dinosaur Bar-B-Que 646 W 131 St, between Broadway and Riverside Drive ☎212/694-1777. This convivial joint, an outpost of the original (in Syracuse, NY, of all places), seems authentic enough, with decent brisket and hot links, but it's especially known for its chicken wings (of all things). Live blues every Sat from 10pm onwards.
Londel's Supper Club 2620 Eighth Ave, between W 139th and 140th sts ☎212/234-6114. A little soul food, a little Cajun, a little Southern-fried food. This is an attractive, down-home place where you can eat upscale items like sautéed prawns ($23) or more common treats such as fried chicken and waffles ($14); either way, follow it up with some

sweet-potato pie. Jazz and R&B on Fri and Sat evenings at 8 and 10pm.
Sylvia's Restaurant 328 Lenox Ave, between W 126th and 127th sts ☎212/996-0660. The most well-known Southern soul-food restaurant in Harlem – so famous that Sylvia herself even has her own packaged-food line. While some find the barbecue sauce too tangy, the fried chicken is exceptional and the candied yams are justly celebrated. Also famous for its Sunday gospel brunch, but be prepared for a long wait.

Caribbean

Caridad Restaurant 4311 Broadway, at W 191st St ☎212/781-1880. In the heart of Washington Heights, this place serves mountains of Dominican food at cheap prices. Try the *mariscos*, the specialty of the house, with lots of *pan y ajo* (thick slices of French bread grilled with olive oil and plenty of garlic). Be sure to go with an appetite.
La Fiesta Restaurante 3797 Broadway, between 157th and 158th sts ☎212/281-2886. There's not much atmosphere here, but it doesn't matter much, since you'll likely be busy devouring a hearty platter of roasted goat ($9) or downing the pork or beef tripe soup ($6.50).

Sisters **47 E 124th St, between Park and Madison aves** ⊤212/410-3000. Spicy, inexpensive Caribbean classics like jerk chicken, goat curry, callaloo, and oxtail stew in an unassuming diner. Best for lunch or an early dinner, as the favorite dishes start selling out as the evening wears on.

Brooklyn

Over the past several years **Brooklyn** has turned into a seriously food-centric borough, with dozens of ambitious new restaurants cropping up in rapidly gentrifying neighborhoods like Park Slope, Boerum Hill, Fort Greene, and Williamsburg. Eateries here tend to be more relaxed and cheaper than comparable spots in Manhattan, though there are plenty of places where you can splurge if you want to. As elsewhere, local and organic foods dominate the most progressive menus. Ethnic restaurants flourish in other parts of the borough, from the long-established mom-and-pop Italian spots in Carroll Gardens to the flashy new Russian supperclubs in Brighton Beach.

Fulton Ferry District and DUMBO

Five Front 5 Front St, at Old Fulton St ⊤718/625-5559. Friendly, relaxed bistro with a pressed tin ceiling, long wooden bar, and beautiful back garden that's good at any time of day or night but particularly pleasant for weekend brunch, with dishes like goat-cheese scramble with smoked salmon ($15) and challah French toast ($14). Closed Tues.

Grimaldi's 19 Old Fulton St, between Water and Front sts ⊤718/858-4300. People line up down the sidewalk for the delicious, thin, and crispy pizza pies, legendary throughout the city. Lunchtime is a better bet for avoiding crowds. Cash only.

River Café 1 Water St, between Furman and Old Fulton sts ⊤718/522-5200. You can get better food for the price (or even cheaper) in New York, but *River Café* is more about the romantic atmosphere and spectacular views of the Brooklyn Bridge. The prix-fixe dinner, with dishes like foie gras and rock lobster, costs $95 per person for three courses, $115 for six, excluding wine. There's also a prix-fixe Sunday brunch. Lunch (Mon–Sat) is à la carte but still pricey.

Superfine 126 Front St, between Jay and Pearl sts ⊤718/243-9005. *Superfine*'s ever-changing menu has a fresh, Mediterranean bent, with lots of big salads, and Sunday brunch features *huevos rancheros* with New Mexican green chillis ($8.50), a nod to the chef's Southwestern roots. Dinner entrees $13–22. Closed Mon.

Brooklyn Heights

Heights Café 84 Montague St, at Hicks St ⊤718/625-5555. Near the Esplanade and with lots of sidewalk seating, this mainstay offers a pleasant environment for lunch – sandwiches and wraps run about $10 – or for an early drink and appetizer of steamed mussels or fried calamari. For a full dinner, though, you can do better elsewhere.

Henry's End 44 Henry St, at Cranberry St ⊤718/834-1776. Neighborhood bistro with a loyal following for its hearty if somewhat old-fashioned fare and laid-back atmosphere. Mains run from $18.95 for chicken breast with goat cheese and fig jam to $25.95 for steak *au poivre*. Not a good choice for vegetarians at any time of year, it's known for its wild-game festival, which runs from Oct to Feb. Dinner only.

Waterfalls 144 Atlantic Ave, at Henry St ⊤718/488-8886. Middle-Eastern specialties with a Syrian touch, touted by many as the best in the city, and certainly the finest on Atlantic Avenue. Try the vegetarian platter ($12), which offers a taste of all the veggie appetizers, from *baba ghanoush* (eggplant dip) to falafel. Open daily noon–10pm.

Waterfront Ale House 155 Atlantic Ave, between Clinton and Henry sts ⊤718/522-3794. This inexpensive and friendly old-style pub serves good spicy chicken wings, ribs, burgers, and killer Key Lime Pie. Open Sun–Thurs noon–11pm, Fri & Sat noon–midnight.

Downtown Brooklyn

Junior's 386 Flatbush Ave, at DeKalb Ave ☎718/852-5257. Open 24hr and with enough lights to make it worthy of Vegas, *Junior's* offers everything from chopped-liver sandwiches to ribs to a full cocktail bar. Most of it is just so-so – the real draw is the cheesecake, for which the place is justly famous. The servings are mammoth.

▲ Junior's

Fort Greene

🏃 **Locanda Vini e Olii 129 Gates Ave, at Cambridge Place** ☎718/622-9202. Gorgeous, inventive Italian fare served in a restored pharmacy, all gleaming dark wood and glass. Duck *papardelle*, fluffy *gnocchi*, and even beef tongue in parsley sauce may show up on the menu. Very affordable (mains $12–26) and worth the walk to the far reaches of Fort Greene (aka Clinton Hill). Reservations recommended. Closed Mon.

Loulou 222 Dekalb Ave, between Adelphi and Clermont sts ☎718/246-0633. Reliably delicious and inexpensive French fare, with a dinner menu that can be heavy on seafood (the female half of the husband-and-wife ownership team hails from Brittany), and very good brunch (think lots of Nutella). Entrees ($15–20) are two-for-the-price-of-one on Thursdays; live guitar music Tues and Fri.

Thomas Beisl 25 Lafayette Ave, between Ashland Place and St Felix St ☎718/222-5800. Directly across the street from BAM (see p.225), this recreated Viennese café is just elegant enough to set the tone for a pre-show dinner. Rich beef-cheek goulash ($16), sauerkraut-and-trout crêpes ($8), fantastic desserts, and a year-round patio are all highlights. It's open for lunch, too.

Boerum Hill and Carroll Gardens

🏃 **Bar Tabac 128 Smith St, at Dean St** ☎718/923-0918. High-spirited French bistro with an all-French wine list and well-turned-out, generously portioned staples like *moules frites* ($14.95), onion soup, and *steak frites* ($19.95). Live music on weekends, sidewalk tables in warm weather, and great brunch to boot. Open daily from 10am to 1am or 2am.

Café LULUc 214 Smith St, at Baltic St ☎718/625-3815. Wide-ranging, crowd-pleasing, French-influenced menu offering everything from *croque monsieur* ($8) to *coq au vin* ($14.50) for dinner, with plenty of pastas and grilled-fish dishes in between. Breakfasts are a particularly good deal, with eggs Benedict, pancakes, or French toast for only $7 apiece. Open 8am–12:30am daily; cash only.

Frankies 457 Spuntino 457 Court St, at Luquer St ☎718/403-0033. Co-chefs Frank and Frank revive and refine Italian-American favorites on the south side of Carroll Gardens. Home-made pastas ($13–17) are the way to go, coupled with a fresh salad of seasonal greens and a few crostini. Enjoy your meal on the breezy garden patio out back. Cash only.

The Grocery 288 Smith St, between Sackett and Union sts ☎718/596-3335. Loyal fans are obsessed with this place, one of the most expensive in the area (entrees $26–28). The owners combine seasonal ingredients in simple but satisfying ways (whole boneless trout with cornbread and ramp stuffing, for instance). Reservations recommended, though the garden is unreserved. Closed Sun.

Red Hook

🏃 **The Good Fork 391 Van Brunt St, between Coffey and Van Dyke sts** ☎718/643-6636. This sliver of a restaurant with exposed brick and thrift-store décor turns out terrific fare with a focus on local ingredients. The changing menu is New American with Asian flourishes, as per the Korean-style grilled skirt-steak with *kim chee* rice and a fried egg ($19). Dinner only; reservations recommended. Closed Mon.

Park Slope and Prospect Heights

Al Di Là 248 Fifth Ave, at Carroll St ☏718/783-4565. Venetian country cooking at its finest at this husband-and-wife-run trattoria. Standouts include beet and ricotta ravioli (with poppy seeds), *saltimbocca*, and the daily risotto. Early or late, expect at least a 45min wait (they don't take reservations). Dinner only; closed Tues.

▲ Al Di Là

Beast 638 Bergen St, at Vanderbilt Ave ☏718/399-6855. Trendy newcomer with a Gothic feel – lots of dark wood and iron chandeliers – turns out inventive, generously portioned tapas with a Mediterranean twist, like grilled kielbasa with French lentils ($8) and beer-braised short ribs ($13), with lots of good veggie options as well. A popular brunch is served Sat & Sun 11am–3pm.

Bonnie's 278 5th Ave ☏718/369-9527. Casual, fun-loving diner that's great for its juicy Cajun-spiced burgers and impressive beer list. As the owners are natives of western New York, *Bonnie's* also serves up big plates of sticky Buffalo chicken wings. Sit at the bar to watch the short-order cook sweat or take a rickety table in back. Lunch and dinner daily.

Rose Water 787 Union St, at Sixth Ave ☏718/783-3800. Intimate Mediterranean–American bistro, serving excellent seasonal dishes with flavorful accents, including a

three-course market-menu dinner Mon–Thurs for $27. Excellent brunch, too.

Bay Ridge

Agnanti Meze 7802 Fifth Ave, at 78th St ☏718/833-7033. Come to the bigger branch of the Astoria, Queens, favorite (see p.338) for exceptionally fresh Greek food.

Nouvelle 8716 Third Ave, at 87th St ☏718/238-8250. A former executive chef of *Nobu* (see p.309) runs this flashy pan-Asian lounge, favored by locals for its miso-marinated cod and melt-in-your-mouth sashimi.

Coney Island

Gargiulo's 2911 W 15th St, between Surf and Mermaid aves ☏718/266-4891. A gigantic, noisy, century-old family-run Coney Island restaurant famed for its large portions of hearty Neapolitan food. Most pasta dishes are $10–15, most meat and seafood dishes $15–20. Closed Tues.

Totonno's Pizzeria Napolitano 1524 Neptune Ave, between 15th and 16th sts ☏718/372-8606. The coal-oven-fired pies at this ancient, no-frills spot inspire devotion among pizza lovers for their sweet, fresh mozzarella and crispy crust. Try the half-bianca, half-margherita ($17.95). No slices; cash only. Closed Mon & Tues.

Brighton Beach

Café Glechik 3159 Coney Island Ave, between Brighton Beach Ave and 10th St ☏718/616-0494. A refreshing break from the flashier places in the neighborhood, this *tchotchke*-laden Ukrainian restaurant is known for its dumplings – *pelmeni* and *vareniki* – as well as its borscht, stews, and stuffed cabbage, all at bargain prices. Cash only.

Primorski 282 Brighton Beach Ave, between 2nd and 3rd sts ☏718/891-3111. One of the best of Brighton Beach's Russian hangouts, with a huge menu of authentic Russian dishes, including blintzes, stuffed cabbage, and chicken Kiev. Dinner entrees are $10–20; for the best deal, drop by for the $10 prix-fixe lunch. Live dance music every evening, though it's altogether less glitzy than *Rasputin*.

Rasputin 2670 Coney Island Ave, at Ave X ☏718/332-8333. Though most people come for the way-over-the-top, Vegas-style entertainment, including scantily clad dancers doing cheesy floor routines, the food here is actually outstanding, with banquet fare starting at $65 a person. One of the truly great "only in New York" experiences. Open Fri–Sun 8pm–3am.

Williamsburg

Bamonte's 32 Withers St, at Union Ave ☎718/384-8831. Red-sauce restaurants abound in NYC, but this is one of the legends, serving traditional Italian-American dishes like handmade giant cheese ravioli since 1900. Closed Tues.

Diner 85 Broadway, at Berry St ☎718/486-3077. This groovy eatery in a Pullman diner-car has a tiny menu of upscale American grub (grass-fed burgers, roasted chicken, fantastic fries), along with a dozen varieties of Champagne. The kitchen is open till midnight. Closed Mon.

DuMont 432 Union Ave, at Devoe St ☎718/486-7717. Top-notch bistro whose sensitive restoration of the old-timey space (tin ceiling, tiled floor) is matched by the well-edited menu. Try the signature salad of *haricots verts*, pecans, Danish blue cheese, and bacon ($9) with the signature burger ($12.50), and if it's warm out, ask for a seat in the back garden. The tiny offshoot *DuMont Burger*, 314 Bedford Ave (between 1st and 2nd), offers burgers (including a chickpea variety), a few simple salads, and fries, to be taken out or devoured at the high wooden counter.

Fette Sau 345 Metropolitan Ave, at Havemeyer St ☎718/963-3404. Worthy newcomer to NYC's barbecue scene, with an industrial-chic vibe anchored by the industrial-strength Southern Pride smoker. Order your meat by the pound (beef brisket $15, flank steak $20), tack on a couple of sides, and wash it all down with a glass of small-batch whiskey or bourbon. Open till 2am weeknights, 4am weekends.

Peter Luger Steak House 178 Broadway, at Driggs Ave ☎718/387-7400. Catering to carnivores since 1887, *Peter Luger* may just be the city's finest steakhouse. The service is surly and the décor plain, but the porterhouse steak – the only cut served – is divine. Old-school sides like creamed spinach are just a distraction. Cash only; expect to pay at least $60 a head. Reservations required.

SEA 114 N Sixth St, at Berry St ☎718/384-8850. A favorite of Williamsburg's stylish-yet-cash-strapped set, this enormous restaurant centered around a skylit reflecting pool serves Thai food at attractive prices (noodles and curries are only $9). A DJ gives the place a clublike ambience at night, but during the day it's quite serene.

Greenpoint

Old Poland Bakery and Restaurant 190 Nassau Ave, at Humboldt St ☎718/349-7775. Cheap and delicious Polish food as served in the old country. The atmosphere is nil, and service can be curt, but the pork shank with mashed potatoes and vegetables will definitely fill you up.

Paloma 60 Greenpoint Ave, between Franklin and West sts ☎718/349-2400. Comfortable, arty neighborhood bistro with something for everyone on its short-but-sweet "urban American" menu, including a pumpkin-stuffed poblano pepper for vegetarians ($14) and a grass-fed burger for carnivores ($9). Tasty brunch, too. Closed Mon.

The Queen's Hideaway 222 Franklin St, at Green St ☎718/383-2355. There's Led Zeppelin on the vintage turntable and plenty of cast-iron skillets in the closet-sized kitchen of this idiosyncratic restaurant. The menu changes nightly, but you can count on some sort of pork dish, amazing-black bean fritters, and barbecue on Tues. Vegetarians will have a bit of a hard time. Closed Mon.

Queens

The most ethnically diverse of all the boroughs, **Queens** offers some of the city's best opportunities to sample a wealth of authentic foreign flavors, from Bosnian and Greek to Brazilian and Colombian to Szechuan and Thai. Though most places listed here are easily accessible by subway, it can take up to 45 minutes to get to some of them from Manhattan, so plan accordingly.

Long Island City and Astoria

🏃 **Agnanti Meze 19-06 Ditmars Blvd, Astoria**
☎718/545-4554. Specializing in Greek *meze* – small plates for snacking – this restaurant overlooks Astoria Park. Don't miss the "specialties from Constantinople" section of the menu, with goodies like *bekri-meze*, wine-soaked cubes of tender meat. There's a second location in Bay Ridge, Brooklyn (see p.336).

Kabab Café 25-12 Steinway St, Astoria
☎718/728-9858. The culinary highlight of Steinway Street's "Little Egypt," this tiny, velvet-swathed den is the domain of Chef Ali, who lavishes patrons with traditional Middle Eastern goodies (smoky *baba ganoush*, lighter-than-air falafel) as well as his own creations – don't miss the honey-glazed duck. Ask the prices of off-the-menu specials if you're on a budget – they can be shockingly high. Closed Mon.

Lounge 47 47-10 Vernon Blvd, Long Island City
☎718/937-2044. This funky restaurant and bar with a gorgeous back patio offers spruced-up American basics like mac and cheese with rosemary crumb topping ($9) and juicy hamburgers, as well as more international morsels like Indian pakora and a lamb sandwich with spicy *chipotle* mayo spread ($10). Brunch served Sat & Sun noon–4pm.

Malagueta 25-35 36th Ave, Astoria ☎718/937-4821. Refined (but reasonably priced) Brazilian cuisine served in a simple whitewashed corner space. If you want to spice up the *moqueca de camarão* (shrimp in coconut milk), ask for a side of hot *molho* sauce. Come Sat for *feijoada* ($15), Brazil's national dish, a black-bean clay-pot stew served with collard greens and rice. Closed Mon.

Taverna Kyclades 33-07 Ditmars Blvd, Astoria
☎718/545-8666. Friendly, popular Greek *taverna* specializing in seafood – try the grilled calamari or broiled scallops. Start with a selection of dips, including the garlic-yogurt-cucumber *tzatziki*. Dessert, a traditional Greek custard, is on the house. Entrees $12–20.

Tournesol 50-12 Vernon Blvd, Long Island City
☎718/472-4355. Warm French bistro in Hunters Point, steps from the Vernon Blvd #7 stop and an easy walk from PS 1. Staples are steak *frites* and garlicky *escargots* are reliably good, the wine list is small but well chosen, and brunch is very tasty. Mains $13–18.

🏃 **Uncle George's 33-19 Broadway, Astoria**
☎718/626-0593. This 24hr joint serves simple, ultra-cheap Greek food on red-checked tablecloths. Go for the roasted half-chicken with lemon potatoes or the *spanakopita* (spinach pie), with a carafe of *retsina*. Most entrees are under $10.

Sunnyside and Woodside

🏃 **Spicy Mina 64-23 Broadway, Woodside**
☎718/205-2340. Absolutely the best Indian and Bangladeshi food in all five boroughs – the samosa *chaat* appetizer, the Bengali-style mustard fish, and the *daal* fry (split peas) are exceptionally good. Be prepared for a wait, as the eponymous Mina cooks entirely from scratch.

Sripraphai 64-13 39th Ave, Woodside
☎718/899-9599. Truly authentic Thai food that puts anything in Manhattan to shame – sweet, sour, (very) spicy, and astoundingly cheap. Try the "drunken" noodles with beef and basil ($7) or a whole steamed striped bass with ginger, chilli, and lime ($16.50), along with staples like papaya salad and lemongrass soup. An outdoor patio is open in the summer. Closed Wed.

Jackson Heights

Jackson Diner 37-47 74th St, between 37th and Roosevelt aves ☎718/672-1232. Manhattan foodies make regular pilgrimages to this famous Indian restaurant, which produces outstanding versions of classics like tandoori chicken, goat curry, and shrimp *biryani*. If you love spicy food, don't miss the *vindaloo*. Entrees $10–24. Cash only.

La Pequeña Colombia 83-27 Roosevelt Ave, at 84th St ☎718/478-6528. Literally "Little Colombia," this simple spot doles out inexpensive but filling *empanadas* (meat pies) and *arepas* (corn cakes) along with a gut-busting "Mountain Platter" – ground beef and rice with fried egg, rice, pork rind, and plantains ($11) – and other specialties. Try the fruit drinks, such as *maracuya* (passion fruit) or *guanabana* (soursop).

Flushing

San Soo Kap San 38-13 Union St ☎718/359-0123. Korean barbecue over real charcoal – a rarity these days (though some dishes are made over gas – ask first). Also serves excellent *bibimbop* (beef, vegetables, and

egg over rice in a hot stone bowl).
Open 24hrs.
Spicy and Tasty 39-07 Prince St ☏718/359-1601. Tea-smoked duck is the signature dish

at this Sichuan specialist, regarded by many as the finest in NYC; prepare yourself for plenty of spicy noodle dishes as well. Open till 3am.

The Bronx

In the **Bronx**, and the whole of the city, Belmont is *the* place to taste old-school Italian–American "red sauce" cuisine, while City Island's family establishments specialize in fresh-caught seafood, best enjoyed on warm summer evenings when the waterside dining is at its most scenic.

South Bronx

Sam's 596–598 Grand Concourse, at 150th St ☏718/665-5341. About a ten-minute walk from Yankee Stadium, *Sam's* makes for a tasty, cheap pre-game meal, whether you want American soul food or Caribbean standards: chicken comes roasted, jerked, fried, smothered, or barbecued. Closes at 7pm on Tues and Wed.

Belmont

Dominick's 2335 Arthur Ave, at 187th St ☏718/733-2807. All you would expect from a Belmont neighborhood Italian: communal family-style seating, hearty food, and (usually) low prices – sometimes hard to gauge, as there's no printed menu or written check. Just tell your server what you're in the mood for and listen closely. Cash only. Closed Tues.
Roberto Restaurant 603 Crescent Ave, between Arthur Ave and Hughes St ☏718/733-9503. Not quite so stuck in a time warp as other

Belmont favorites, *Roberto* is renowned for its rich pastas, served with style on giant platters or, sometimes, baked in foil. Chef's specials are always the best option. Entrees ($15–28) are big enough to share. Closed Sun.

City Island

Le Refuge Inn 586 City Island Ave, at Cross St ☏718/885-2478. A romantic getaway at a historic B&B, this place might be a little frilly for some, but the French-inflected menu, with dishes like bouillabaisse, is a nice change from standard City Island fare. Prix-fixe brunch, lunch, and dinner are $25, $45, and $50 respectively. Cash only; closed Mon. Reservations recommended.
Lobster Box 34 City Island Ave, at Rochelle St ☏718/885-1952. Don't mess around with appetizers or sides at this City Island old-timer at the south end of the island – lobster fried, broiled, or steamed is the way to go ($29–41); prices are a little lower at lunch (no lunch on Sun).

Staten Island

Staten Island is so far out of the way that you won't be heading there just for the food. But if you're here sightseeing, you can end your day with a romantic dinner in a garden, or with a quality helping of schnitzel.

Aesop's Tables 1233 Bay St, at Maryland Ave ☏718/720-2005. The leafy back garden is a main attraction at this whimsical Mediterranean restaurant, situated directly across from the Alice Austen House. Entrees head north of $25; thriftier souls should opt for the house-special meatloaf, with wild boar sausage ($16), or the steamed mussels ($11). Dinner-only Tues–Sat; closed Mon.
Denino's Tavern 524 Port Richmond Ave, at Hooker Place ☏718/442-9401. A Staten Island favorite since 1937, serving pizza with a

slightly thicker, chewier crust than most brick-oven joints in the city. *Ralph's Famous Italian Ices* (p.305) is right across the street, making dessert a no-brainer. Cash only.
Killmeyer's Old Bavaria Inn 4254 Arthur Kill Rd, at Sharrotts Rd ☏718/984-1202. A full-tilt German beer garden near the south end of the island, complete with schnitzel, *sauerbraten*, and giant steins of beer, and live oompah music outside on the weekends. Entrees ($15–20) are large enough to feed two.

Drinking

he **bar scene** in New York City is quite eclectic, with a broader range
of places to drink than in most American cities, and prices to suit most
pockets. Bars generally open their doors at noon and close them in the
early hours of the morning – 4am at the latest, when they have to close
by law. In a basic bar you'll pay around $6–7 for a pint of beer "on tap" (also
referred to as "on draft"). At the other end of the spectrum are the city's plush
hotel and rooftop bars (see box, p.345), where **prices** tend to start at around
$15 per drink. Keep an eye out for "happy hour" bargains and two-for-one
drink deals. Wherever you go, you'll be expected to tip a buck per drink.

The most obvious drink choice is typically **beer**. You'll see the usual American
standards – Budweiser, Sam Adams, etc – alongside such European staples as
Stella Artois and Heineken pretty much everywhere. Bars with bigger selections
often feature real ales on tap and **microbrews** from across the country. Try
some of the **local brews**: the *Brooklyn Brewery* does a fine range of beers in all
styles (lager, pilsner, wheat, and so on; see p.351), as do newcomers **Sixpoint
Craft Ales** and **Greenpoint Beer Works**, both also from Brooklyn. The
Harlem Brewing Company produces Sugar Hill Golden Ale; and the *Blue
Point Brewery*, on Long Island, does several excellent seasonal ales.

Wine demands a better-filled wallet than beer does. When in a restaurant or
bar, expect a 100 percent mark-up (at least!) on the cost of a bottle. There are
a couple of points of potential confusion for overseas visitors when it comes
to **liquor**. Bear in mind that whether you ask for a drink "on the rocks" or
not, you'll most likely get it poured into a glass filled with ice; if you don't
want it like this ask for it "straight up." Also, American shots are approximately
double the size of British and European shots, meaning you get more bang
for your buck.

When **buying your own liquor or wine**, you'll need to find a liquor store
– supermarkets only sell beer. You must be over age 21 to buy or consume
alcohol in a bar or restaurant, and it's against the law to drink alcohol on the
street. Note that some bars insist **you show photo ID** to get in (even if you
look well over 21), so make sure you carry some. Also by law, all NYC bars must
serve **nonalcoholic drinks**, though you shouldn't expect to pay less for them;
sodas, juices, and sparkling waters often sell for the same price as beer.

The bar scene

New York's watering holes are much more interesting below 14th Street than
above. Some of the best establishments are located in the **East Village**, the **West
Village**, **NoLita**, **Soho**, and the western reaches of the **Lower East Side**.

There's a decent mix of **midtown** drinking spots, though bars here tend to be geared to tourists and an after-hours office crowd and, consequently, can be pricey and rather dull (there are a few notable exceptions). The **Upper East Side** is home to quite a few raucous sports and Irish bars, while the **Upper West Side** has a serviceable array of bars, although most tend to cater to Columbia University students and more of a clean-cut yuppie crowd. Farther uptown, the bars of **Harlem**, while not numerous, offer some of the city's most affordable jazz in a relaxed environment (see p.355 for more jazz clubs).

Check out the scene in the outer boroughs if you can, where bars range in feel from neighborly to über-hip. **Williamsburg** is an easy ride from Manhattan on the L-train and the best place if you're short of time. Other areas to try are **Park Slope** and the collective of **Boerum Hill**, **Cobble Hill**, and **Carroll Gardens** (known as Bococa), especially along Smith Street; head out to **Fort Greene** if this still feels too tame.

The listings that follow are grouped, approximately, according to the chapter divisions outlined in the Guide. Bear in mind that many places double as bar and restaurant, and you may therefore find them listed not here but in the previous chapter, "Restaurants." For ease of reference, however, all specifically **gay and lesbian bars** are gathered together in "Gay and lesbian New York," Chapter 29.

The Financial District and City Hall area

The Beekman 15 Beekman St, between Nassau and William sts ☎212/732-7333. This Wall Street landmark's great selection of more than twenty draught beers is complemented by frequent live music.

Jeremy's Alehouse 228 Front St, at Peck Slip ☎212/964-3537. *Jeremy's* stands in the shadow of the Brooklyn Bridge and the nearby South Street Seaport, serving well-priced pints of beer (there are 15 or so to choose from) and excellent fish dishes. The fried clams ($7.95) get rave reviews.

Rise at the Ritz-Carlton Hotel, 2 West St, 14th floor, Battery Park ☎212/344-0800. Try this plush hotel lounge for swanky sunset drinks, tiered trays of gourmet tapas, and unsurpassed views of the Statue of Liberty.

Tribeca and Soho

Bubble Lounge 228 W Broadway, between Franklin and White sts ☎212/431-3433. Swanky place to pop a cork or two. There's a long list of Champagnes and sparklers, but beware the skyrocketing tabs.

Ear Inn 326 Spring St, between Washington and Greenwich sts ☎212/226-9060. "Ear" as in "Bar" with half the neon "B" chipped off. This historic pub, a stone's throw from the Hudson River, opened in 1890 (the building dates from 1817). Its creaky (and some claim, haunted) interior is as cozy as a Cornish inn, with a good mix of beers on tap and basic, reasonably priced American food.

Fanelli 94 Prince St, at Mercer St ☎212/226-9412. Established in 1872, *Fanelli* is one of the city's oldest bars. Relaxed and informal, it's a favorite destination of the not-too-hip after-work crowd.

Grace 114 Franklin St, between Church St and W Broadway ☎212/343-4200. *Grace* teems with old-school class – there's a 40ft mahogany bar. It's a nice place for a cocktail; try a Pimm's Cup.

Greenwich Street Tavern 399 Greenwich St, at Beach St ☎212/334-7827. Friendly neighborhood bar, refreshingly unpretentious for this part of town, with a solid menu of snack food, easy-going (generally male) clientele, and beers for $3 in happy hour (Wed & Thurs 5–7pm).

Kenn's Broome Street Bar 363 W Broadway at Broome St ☎212/925-2086. Open since 1972 but set in an aging 1825 Federal-style house, this comfortable bar offers 15 real ales (eight drafts), from Harpoon Winter Warm to Flying Dog Pale Ale (they also have Stella on tap), and decent burgers from $8.

Knitting Factory Tap Bar 74 Leonard St, between Church St and Broadway ☎212/219-3006. The street-level bar is fun, but the cozy downstairs taproom is where things really hum, with numerous draft microbrews and free live music – usually some out-there form of jazz – that usually gets going after 11pm. (For details on the jazz venue, see "Nightlife," p.354.)

Puffy's Tavern 81 Hudson St, between Harrison and Jay sts ☎212/766-9159. This small dive serves cheap booze without a single ounce of attitude, rare in this area. The cool jukebox specializes in old 45s.

The Room 144 Sullivan St, between Houston and Prince sts ☎212/477-2102. Dark, homey two-room bar with exposed brick walls and comfortable couches. No spirits, but an impressive array of domestic and international beers.

Toad Hall 57 Grand St, between W Broadway and Wooster St ☎212/431-8145. With a pool table, good service, and excellent bar snacks, this stylish alehouse is a little less hip and a little more of a local hangout than some of its neighbors.

Chinatown, Little Italy, and Nolita

Mulberry Street Bar 176-1/2 Mulberry St, between Broome and Grand sts ☎212/226-9345. Though it looks like a backroom hangout from *The Sopranos*, it's actually a friendly local dive-bar open to all. Formerly known as *Mare Chiaro*, the wooden bar, subway tile floor and pressed tin roof have barely changed since it opened in 1908.

Pravda 281 Lafayette St, between Prince and Houston sts ☎212/226-4944. This chic Russian lounge serves stiff vodka drinks and hard-boiled eggs for snacking. Now that its heyday has passed, there are fewer crowds, and hence a more relaxed vibe, but it's still a great place. Try the coconut vodka.

Room 18 18 Spring St, at Elizabeth St ☎212/219-2592. Somehow, this inexpensive, romantic, Asian tapas bar has remained under the radar for years. Sound choice for a date – the exotic cocktails (think pomegranate mojitos and grape Martinis) are always fabulous.

Sweet & Vicious 5 Spring St, between Bowery and Elizabeth St ☎212/334-7915. A neighborhood favorite, *Sweet & Vicious* is the epitome of rustic chic, with exposed brick, lots of wood, and antique chandeliers. The back garden is just as cozy as the inside bar.

Lower East Side

Back Room 102 Norfolk St, between Delancey and Rivington sts ☎212/677-9489. With a hidden, back-alley entrance, this former speakeasy was reputedly once a haunt of gangster Meyer Lansky. To find it, walk down the metal steps and through to the back of the building.

Barramundi 67 Clinton St, between Stanton and Rivington sts ☎212/529-6900. Though the interior is just fine, it's *Barramundi*'s magical, fairy-lit garden that's the real selling point. Come early, as the garden closes at 10pm.

Barrio Chino 253 Broome St, at Orchard St ☎212/228-6710. Don't be confused by the Chinese lanterns or drink umbrellas here –

the owner's specialty is tequila, and there are a dozen brands to choose from. Shots are served with a traditional *sangría* chaser, made from a blend of tomato, orange, and lime juices.

Delancey Lounge 168 Delancey St, at Clinton St ☎212/254-9920. Williamsburg hipsters meet Lower East Side chic at this rooftop lounge. Things can get frisky in the basement, which pulsates with loud music.

Happy Ending Lounge 302 Broome St, between Eldridge and Forsyth sts ☎212/334-9676. This former erotic massage parlor has been reborn as an exceptionally cool bar and club, with the original tiled sauna rooms downstairs converted to cozy booths. Drinks $8–12.

King Size Bar 21 Essex St, between Canal and Hester sts ☏212/995-5464. This ironically-named bar certainly isn't big, but the DJ plays old-school hip-hop and the exposed-brick walls are adorned with some eye-catching graffiti art. Drinks $3–12.

Kush 191 Chrystie St, between Stanton and Rivington sts ☏212/677-7328. Beguiling Moroccan bar with live music, excellent, salty bar snacks, and even belly dancing. Exempt from the smoking ban, *Kush* offers hookah pipes.

Libation 137 Ludlow St, between Stanton and Rivington sts ☏866/216-1263. A sexy lounge spanning two floors. It's a bit eclectic, with $10 cocktails, an American tapas menu, and DJs spinning '80s, hip-hop, and everything in between.

Magician 118 Rivington St, between Essex and Norfolk sts ☏212/673-7881. Dark and sedate, couples come here as much for the intimate atmosphere as for the drinks, which are all of average price.

Max Fish 178 Ludlow St, between Houston and Stanton sts ☏212/529-3959. Local hipsters come here in droves, lured by the unpretentious but arty vibe and the jukebox which, quite simply, rocks any other party out of town. Cheap beers, too.

East Village

7B 108 Ave B, at E 7th St ☏212/473-8840. A quintessential East Village hangout, *7B* has often been used as the sleazy set in films and commercials. It features deliberately mental bartenders, cheap pitchers of beer, and one of the best punk and rock'n'roll jukeboxes in the Village.

Angel's Share 8 Stuyvesant St, between E 9th St and Third Ave ☏212/777-5415. This serene, candlelit haven is a great date spot: it's kept deliberately romantic by the entry rules –

Karaoke

Despite the potential to make participants both hoarse and more than a little embarrassed, **karaoke** is still going strong in New York. If you have the guts (and the stamina) to join in, these places will all give you a memorable night:

Arlene's Grocery 95 Stanton St, between Orchard and Ludlow sts ☏212/358-1633. For something completely different, check out their punk and heavy metal karaoke. Every Monday night at 10pm (free) a live band backs anyone willing to get up and give it their all, wailing tunes from the Ramones to Guns 'N' Roses.

Asia Roma 40 Mulberry St, between Worth and Bayard sts ☏212/385-1133. Despite the fact that this is one of the few places in the city where you can sing for free (though you'll need to buy food and drinks), it's often devoid of crowds (and atmosphere). Good to practice that rendition of *Cry Me a River*, though.

MBC Music Box 25 W 32nd St, between Broadway and Fifth Ave ☏212/967-2244. This Little Korea spot has twelve sound-proofed rooms for private tune-filled parties. Choose from very long song lists.

Planet Rose 219 Ave A, between E 13th and 14th sts ☏212/353-9500. The funky living room dècor and casual atmosphere here should ease any stage fright. Most singers don't even get attention.

Sing Sing Karaoke 81 Ave A, between E 5th and 6th sts ☏212/674-0700. A little divey but fun, though the drinks are expensive. Fifteen rooms in which to sing to your heart's content.

Winnie's 104 Bayard St, between Mulberry and Baxter sts ☏212/732-2384. Tiny Chinatown bar where the most dedicated New Yorkers go to belt out a few tunes. It's pretty seedy, but nowhere else in the city will you find such a social hodgepodge united in a common cause: bad singing.

parties larger than four will not be admitted. The cocktails are reputed to be some of the best in the city. Can be hard to find: walk into the *Village Yokocho* complex, up the stairs to the *Gyu-ya* restaurant and look for the door on the left.

Bar Veloce 175 Second Ave, between E 11th and 12th sts ☎212/260-3200. Tiny, slick wine bar fit for the Mod Squad, with excellent hors d'oeuvres and a fine wine list; look for the Vespa parked out front.

Bourgeois Pig 111 E 7th St, between First Ave and Ave A ☎212/475-2246. The decadent Versailles theme at this funky wine bar, replete with wall-sized mirrors, chandeliers, and crimson satin couches, is backed by an extensive cocktail menu (using just wines, beers, and Champagne), including bubbly served in silver punch bowls (from $12).

Burp Castle 41 E 7th St, between Second and Third aves ☎212/982-4756. A delightfully weird place: the bartenders wear monks' habits, choral music is piped in, and you are encouraged to speak in tones below a whisper. Oh, and there are over 550 different types of beer.

Cozy Cafe 43 E 1st St, between First and Second aves ☎212/475-0177. Comfortable sofas and soft pillows make this subterranean Middle Eastern hookah bar all the more relaxing. Belly dancers Fri and Sat nights.

Croxley Ales 28 Ave B, between E 2nd and 3rd sts ☎212/253-6140. This top-notch sports bar smells strongly of BBQ wings and has a great selection of 30 draft and 75 bottled brews, all reasonably priced. Countless TVs are tuned into all the night's big games.

d.b.a. 41 First Ave, between E 2nd and 3rd sts ☎212/475-5097. A beer-lover's paradise, *d.b.a.* has at least 60 bottled beers, 14 brews on tap, and an authentic hand-pump. Garden seating (with a small smoking section) is available in the summer.

Decibel 240 E 9th St, between Second and Third aves ☎212/979-2733. A rocking atmosphere (with good tunes) pervades this beautifully decorated, underground sake bar. The inevitable wait for a wooden table will be worth it, guaranteed.

Grassroots Tavern 20 St Mark's Place, between Second and Third aves ☎212/475-9443. This wonderful, roomy, underground den has cheap pitchers, baskets of popcorn for a buck, an extended happy hour, and at least three of the

manager's pets roaming around at all hours of the day or night.

Hi Fi 169 Ave A, between E 10th and 11th sts ☎212/420-8392 Formerly a live-music venue, this spot has been stripped of its stage, but is still great for music, featuring an mp3 jukebox with over 19,000 albums. Great-looking hipster boys and girls pack this place, drinking hard pretty much every night of the week.

Holiday Cocktail Lounge 75 St Mark's Place, between Second and First aves ☎212/777-9637. Unabashed dive with a mixed bag of customers, from old-world grandfathers to young professionals, and a bona-fide character (more or less) tending bar. Auden and Sinatra were both regulars here, and it's supposed to have inspired Madonna's first big hit.

KGB 85 E 4th St, at Second Ave ☎212/505-3360. On the second floor, this dark bar is set in what was the HQ of the Ukrainian Communist Party in the 1930s. Better known now for its marquee literary readings and the Kraine Theater in the basement (see p.362).

Lakeside Lounge 162 Ave B, between E 10th and 11th sts ☎212/529-8463. The owners, a local DJ and a record producer, have stocked the *Lakeside* jukebox with old rock, country, and R&B records. Live performers frequently pack into one small corner.

Manitoba's 99 Ave B, between E 6th and 7th sts ☎212/982-2511. Run by Dick Manitoba, lead singer of the punk group The Dictators, the kickin' jukebox and rough-and-tumble vibe at this spot make it a favorite among East Villagers who really just like to drink.

McSorley's Old Ale House 15 E 7th St, between Second and Third aves ☎212/473-9148. Yes, it's touristy and often full of local frat boys, but you'll be drinking in history along with your beer at this cheap, landmark bar: *McSorley*'s served its first brew in 1854. Try the turkey sandwich with hot mustard; it's one of the best bar snacks in the city.

Sophie's 507 E 5th St, between aves A and B ☎212/228-5680. Inexpensive draft beer and oh-so-cheap mixed drinks make this bar one of the most popular East Village hangouts. The crowd around the pool table can get very raucous.

St Dymphna's 118 St Marks Place, between First Ave and Ave A ☎212/254-6636. With a tempting, filling menu and some of the city's best Guinness, this snug Irish watering-hole is a favorite among young East Villagers.

The Sunburnt Cow 137 Ave C, between E 8th and 9th sts ☎212/529-0005. *The Sunburnt Cow* is like nothing else in the neighborhood. The popular Aussie bar uses wooden stumps for stools and has lighting designed to resemble sunsets. Cocktails are decidedly strong.

Temple Bar 332 Lafayette St, between Bleecker and Houston sts ☎212/925-4242. One of the most discreet and romantic spots for a drink downtown, this sumptuous, dark lounge evokes the glamour of the early 1940s. They take their Martinis very seriously; the guacamole appetizer is the best dish on the short snack menu.

Von 3 Bleecker St, between Bowery and Lafayette St ☎212/473-3039. Like an old pair of jeans, this wine-and-beer-only bar is comfortable (and welcoming) through and through. The prices are pretty nice, too.

Zum Schneider 107–109 Ave C, at E 7th St ☎212/598-1098. A German beer-hall (and indoor garden) with a mega-list of brews and *wursts* from the Fatherland. It can be a bit packed with frat-boy types; in the early evening, though, the old-world vibe is sublime.

West Village

55 Bar 55 Christopher St, between Sixth and Seventh aves ☎212/929-9883. A gem of an underground dive-bar that's been around since the days of Prohibition, with a great jukebox, congenial clientele, and live jazz music seven nights a week.

Hotel bars

When you're feeling fabulous in New York, there's no better place to go for a Martini, Cosmo, or mojito than a **hotel bar**. These posh watering-holes are for the well-bred and well-maintained. Expensive drink in hand, sink back into a comfy banquette and watch the parade of foreign dignitaries, royalty, well-groomed businesspeople, media celebs, chic socialites, and mysterious strangers conducting important affairs. The experience will be worth the price ($16 and up).

The Bar *Four Seasons Hotel*, 57 E 57th St, between Madison and Park aves ☎212/758-5757

Bemelmans Bar *The Carlyle Hotel*, 35 E 76th St, at Madison Ave ☎212/744-1600

The Blue Bar *The Algonquin Hotel*, 59 W 44th St, between Fifth and Sixth aves ☎212/840-6800

Cellar Bar *Bryant Park Hotel*, 40 W 40th St, between Fifth and Sixth aves ☎212/642-2260

Church Lounge *Tribeca Grand Hotel*, 2 Ave of the Americas, at White St ☎212/519-6600

Grand Bar *SoHo Grand Hotel*, 310 W Broadway, between Grand and Canal sts ☎212/965-3000

King Cole Bar *St Regis Hotel*, 2 E 55th St, between Fifth and Madison aves ☎212/339-6721

North Square Lounge *Washington Square Hotel*, 103 Waverly Place, at Washington Square Park ☎212/254-1200

Salon de Ning *Peninsula Hotel*, 700 Fifth Ave, at E 55th St ☎212/956-2888

Thom's Bar *60 Thompson*, 60 Thompson St, between Broome and Spring sts ☎212/219-2000

View Restaurant & Lounge *The Marriott Marquis*, 1535 Broadway, at W 45th St ☎212/929-2243

Wet Bar *W Court Hotel*, 130 E 39th St, at Lexington Ave ☎212/592-8844

Whiskey Blue *The W*, 541 Lexington Ave, between E 49th and 50th sts ☎212/407-2947

Blind Tiger Ale House 281 Bleecker St, at Jones St. This wood-paneled pub is the home of serious ale connoisseurs, with 28 rotating drafts, a couple of casks, and loads of bottled beers – they also serve cheese plates from *Murray's* (see p.399). The prime location means it tends to get packed.

The Dove 288 Thompson St, between Bleecker and W 3rd sts ⊤212/254-1435. Filled with the post-college crowd, this subterranean bar is always chilled. Jazzy happy hours evolve into upbeat late nights.

Fat Black Pussycat 130 W 3rd St, between Sixth Ave and MacDougal St ⊤212/533-4790. This lively pub is an NYU favorite, with popular happy hours (weekdays 4–8pm), plenty of cozy wooden booths, darts and billiards. The pub's original location on MacDougal St is where Bob Dylan allegedly wrote *Blowin' in the Wind*.

Fiddlesticks 54–58 Greenwich Ave, at Perry St ⊤212/463-0516. Don't be put off by the Irish kitsch here. Not only is the owner the real deal, but the Guinness is poured well and there are Gaelic lessons and Quiz Night every week.

Kettle of Fish 59 Christopher St, at Seventh Ave ⊤212/414-2278. This basement bar is a great escape from the scene on Seventh Avenue, with plenty of real ales (including Sixpoint), a no-nonsense staff and mix of sports fans, tourists, and students. The original *Kettle* on MacDougal St was a legendary Beat hangout.

Minetta Tavern 113 MacDougal St ⊤212/475-3850. This time-warped ex-speakeasy is a great place for a drink to start your night, with aging photos on the walls and wood-paneled dining room beyond the bar. William S. Burroughs would treat an invariably broke Jack Kerouac to dinner here.

Other Room 143 Perry St, between Washington and Greenwich sts ⊤212/645-9758. The cozy-cool atmosphere, excellent drink menu, and "way-west" location of this wine-and-beer bar have guaranteed it a special place in locals' hearts.

Peculier Pub 145 Bleecker St, between LaGuardia Place and Thompson St ⊤212/353-1327. Local bar popular with NYU students. The establishment's main claim to fame is the number of beers it sells – more than 500 in all, with examples from just about any country you can think of.

West West Side Highway, at W 11th St ⊤212/242-4375. Design-forward cement floors, Moderne furniture, and exceptional bartenders make this monochromatic bar/cocktail lounge a happening place to watch the sun set over the Hudson River.

White Horse Tavern 567 Hudson St, at W 11th St ⊤212/243-9260. A Greenwich Village institution, opening in 1880: Dylan Thomas supped his last here before being carted off to the hospital with alcohol poisoning, while Norman Mailer and Hunter S. Thompson were also regulars. The beer and food are cheap and palatable, and outside seating is available in the summer.

Chelsea

Elmo 156 Seventh Ave, between W 19th and 20th sts ⊤212/337-8000. Chelsea has been a trendy neighborhood for years, and nothing captures that better than this swanky spot, where hot socialites drink cocktails and little is cheap.

Half King 505 W 23rd St, between Tenth and Eleventh aves ⊤212/462-4300. This popular Irish pub is owned by a small group of writers/artists and features good food and regular literary events. They've been known to book some heavy hitters, like Sebastian Junger (one of the owners) and Michele Wucker.

Hiro Ballroom in the Maritime Hotel, 371 W 16th St, at Ninth Ave ⊤212/242-4300. Chic, spacious indoor/outdoor lounge in one of the city's latest (and most successful) architectural conversions, decked out like a Hong Kong nightclub in the 1940s. Live bands and guest DJs provide entertainment Thurs–Sun.

Hogs & Heifers 859 Washington St, at W 13th St ⊤212/929-0655. "Hogs" as in the burly motorcycles parked outside; "heifers" as in, well, ladies. Though officially there's no more bar dancing (Julia Roberts was famously photographed doing so), those bold enough to venture into this rough-and-tumble Meatpacking District joint can still drink to excess.

Marquee 289 Tenth Ave, between 26th and 27th sts ⊤646/473-0202. Everyone's a celebrity of some sort at *Marquee*, one of the hottest velvet-rope spots in town. Dress for success and make sure your paycheck cleared.

Peter McManus Café 152 Seventh Ave at 19th St. Unlike many Irish pubs in the city, this is the real deal, moving to this location in 1936 and since appearing in episodes of *Seinfeld* and *Law & Order*. The worn oak bar adds character, along with the tasty in-house McManus Ale and two old-style telephone booths inside.

Trailer Park Lounge 271 W 23rd St, between Seventh and Eighth aves ☎212/463-8000. In a neighborhood full of clout and pout, anything goes here. They serve margaritas by the pitcher.

Union Square, Gramercy Park, and the Flatiron District

Bar Jamón 125 E 17th St, at Irving Place ☎212/253-2773. A superb place to sip on sherry and nosh on Spanish tapas. Be forewarned though: there are only 14 stools. Closed Mon.

Belmont Lounge 117 E 15th St, between Union Square and Irving Place ☎212/533-0009. Oversized couches, dark cavernous rooms, and an outdoor garden reel in a continuous stream of twenty-something singles. The strong drinks help liven things up.

Cibar 56 Irving Place, between E 17th and 18th sts ☎212/460-5656. The strong, innovative cocktails, elegant décor and pretty, well-tended herb garden make this cozy hotel bar the place of choice for a tryst.

No Idea 30 E 20th St, between Broadway and Park Ave S ☎212/777-0100. This bizarre palace of inebriation has something for everyone, from $5 pints of mixed drinks to a pool room, TV sports, and even a drink-for-free-if-your-name's-on-the-wall night. Check the website, ⓦwww.noideabar.com, to see if your first name is coming up.

Old Town Bar & Grill 45 E 18th St, between Broadway and Park Ave S ☎212/529-6732.

This atmospheric Flatiron District bar is popular with publishing types, photographers, and the staff of the *New York Observer*. Originally opened in 1892, much of the creaking interior is original, including the rickety dumbwaiter and fine mahogany bar.

Pete's Tavern 129 E 18th St, at Irving Place ☎212/473-7676. Open since 1864, this former speakeasy now trades unashamedly on its history, which has included such illustrious patrons as O. Henry, who allegedly wrote the short story *The Gift of the Magi* in his regular booth here.

Revival 129 E 15th St, between Irving Place and Third Ave ☎212/253-8061. Walk down the stairs and into this friendly narrow bar with great outdoor seating in the backyard. Popular with fans waiting for concerts at Irving Plaza around the block.

Underbar at the W Union Square Hotel, 201 Park Ave S (entrance on E 17th St) ☎212/358-1560. A fashionable meatmarket hotel bar for beautiful people. Red-velvet ropes keep out the riff-raff and the ill-dressed.

Midtown East

Campbell Apartment southwest balcony in Grand Central Terminal ☎212/953-0409. Once home to businessman John W. Campbell, who oversaw the construction of Grand Central, this majestic space – built to look like a Florentine palace – was sealed up for years. Now, after a snappy refit by designer Nina Campbell, it's one of New York's most distinctive cocktail bars. Go early, bring a chunk of cash, and don't wear sneakers.

FUBAR 305 E 50th St, between First and Second aves ☎212/872-1325. Midtown isn't known for its dive-bar scene, so it's no wonder that

FUBAR is the coolest around; it even challenges those in the Village. Great daily happy hours and $5 margarita pints on Wed (4–8pm).

Le Colonial 149 E 57th St, between Lexington and Third aves ☎212/752-0808. The upstairs bar of this Vietnamese restaurant is decked out in opulent Asian style, with red velvet chairs, teak tables, and aging photos of Saigon. Try the specialty cocktails; Le Colonial is a mix of gin, cassis and raspberry (average drinks $16).

Lever House 390 Park Ave, at E 53rd St ☎212/888-2700. This NYC power-drinking stalwart is in a 1950s landmark. The interior strikes a balance between retro and futuristic; though this is primarily a posh restaurant, it's worth a look and a Martini or two at the white-glass bar – you never know who you'll rub elbows with here.

Midtown West

Hudson Bar in the Hudson Hotel, 356 W 58th St, between Eighth and Ninth aves ☎212/554-6000. Philippe Starck mixes French Rococo décor and modern lighting here, with spectacular results. Drinks are fun: try the lemongrass cocktails. The high prices reflect the tourist/banker clientele, though it can be hard to get in – it's one of those places.
Jimmy's Corner 140 W 44th St, between Broadway and Sixth Ave ☎212/221-9510. The walls of this long, narrow corridor of a bar, owned by ex-fighter/trainer Jimmy Glenn, are a virtual boxing hall of fame. You'd be hard-pressed to find a more characterful dive anywhere in the city – or a better jazz/R&B jukebox.

▲ Jimmy's Corner

Landmark Tavern 626 Eleventh Ave, at W 46th St ☎212/757-8595. Off-the-beaten-path but long-established Irish tavern (open since 1868) with great Guinness and a tasty menu of pub food such as shepherd's pie and fish and chips – the Irish soda bread is baked fresh every day.
MObar in the Mandarin Oriental, 80 Columbus Circle, at W 60th St between Ninth Ave and Broadway ☎212/805-8826. On the 35th floor of the *Mandarin Oriental*, this *boîte* is a cozy alternative to the hotel's main lobby lounge, with a shiny nickel bar and leather seating;

P.J. Clarke's 915 Third Ave, at E 55th St ☎212/317-1616. Friendly bartenders serve thirty varieties of wine (12 by the glass) and a moderate selection of beers at *P.J. Clarke's*, one of the city's most famous watering holes. The bar is casual, though there is a pricey restaurant out back.

try over 20 wines by the glass and cocktails that will surely put a dent in your wallet.
P.J. Carney's 906 Seventh Ave, between 57th and 58th sts ☎212/664-0056. Despite the historic pedigree (this tiny bar was established in 1927) and a straggle of loyal locals, *Carney's* is crammed most nights with tourists and sports fans. The beer and pub food isn't bad, though; consider for an afternoon pit-stop between midtown and the park.
Rudy's 627 Ninth Ave, between W 44th and 45th sts ☎212/974-9169. One of New York's cheapest, friendliest, and liveliest bars, a favorite with local actors and musicians. *Rudy's* offers free hot dogs, a backyard that's great in the summer, and some of the cheapest pitchers of beer in the city ($9).
Russian Vodka Room 265 W 52nd St, between Broadway and Eighth Ave ☎212/307-5835. As you might expect, they serve 53 different types of vodka here, as well as their own fruit-flavored and sublime garlic-infused concoctions. Office workers mingle with Russian and Eastern European expats; you'll be laughed out of the bar if you ask for a mixer.
Stitch 247 W 37th St, between Seventh and Eighth aves ☎212/852-4826. A loud sports bar serving a mostly after-work commuter crowd, within stumbling distance of all Madison Square Garden events. Large plasma TV above the bar, with others scattered about. Decent pub fare and upstairs lounge. Happy hour runs daily till 7pm ($6 cocktails).
Stout 133 W 33rd St, between Sixth and Seventh aves ☎212/629-6191. With more than 20 excellent beers on tap, 125 of them by the bottle, and an equally expansive menu, this Irish-theme pub is another great after-work, pre-MSG option.

Upper East Side

American Trash 1471 First Ave, between E 76th and 77th sts ☏212/988-9008. Don't let the name put you off: this self-styled "professional drinking establishment" has a friendly bar staff, a pool table, a sing-along jukebox, a photo booth, and a happy hour dedicated to getting you pleasantly intoxicated.

Auction House 300 E 89th St at Second Ave ☏212/427-4458. This is a cozier, smarter alternative to the frat-boy pubs that dominate this part of town, with two quiet candlelit rooms decked out like Victorian parlors. Perfect for couples.

Bar Coastal 1495 First Ave at E 78th St ☏212/288-6635. This surf-themed bar is a loud but fun place to experience the area's notorious frat-boy rep. Plasma screens show nonstop sports, the dartboard and pool table are always in use and the menu of "atomic" bar food (such as buffalo chicken wings smothered in blue cheese) helps soak up the beer.

Metropolitan Museum of Art 1000 Fifth Ave, at E 82nd St ☏212/535-7710. It's hard to imagine a more romantic spot to sip a glass of wine and kick off the evening (bars close at 8.30pm Fri & Sat), whether on the *Roof Garden Café* (open May–Oct), which has some of the best views in the city, or in the *Balcony Bar* overlooking the Great Hall.

Stir 1363 First Ave at E 73rd St ☏212/744-7190. Funky lounge bar and popular date venue, with comfy sofas and seductive pillows making another stark contrast to the mainly sports bar territory around here. It becomes more club-like later on, with plenty of dancing, and the bar food and cocktails (especially the margaritas) are excellent.

Subway Inn 143 E 60th St, at Lexington Ave ☏212/223-8929. This neighborhood dive bar, across from Bloomingdale's, has been serving customers since 1937, and is great for a late-afternoon beer.

Upper West Side

Dead Poet 450 Amsterdam Ave, between W 81st and 82nd sts ☏212/595-5670. You'll wax poetical and then drop dead if you stay for the duration of this sweet Irish pub's happy hour: it lasts 4–8pm and offers draft beer at $3 a pint (on Tues it's $4 all night). The backroom has armchairs, books, and a pool table.

Ding Dong Lounge 929 Columbus Ave, between 105th and 106th sts ☏212/663-2600. This punk bar with a DJ and occasional live bands attracts a vibrant mix of graduate students, neighborhood Latinos, and stragglers from the nearby youth hostel. Daily happy hour 4–8pm, with $3 draft beer and $4 cocktails.

Dublin House Tap Room 225 W 79th St, between Broadway and Amsterdam Ave

☏212/874-9528. This lively Upper West Side Irish pub, which pours a very nice Black & Tan, is dominated at night by the young, inebriated, and rowdy.

Prohibition 503 Columbus Ave, at W 84th St ☏212/579-3100. Stylish bar and lounge with funky décor (check out the lamps suspended in wine bottles) and live music every night (usually funk and jazz). The back room is always much quieter, and the house-made Martinis are spectacular.

Yogi's 2156 Broadway, between 75th and 76th sts ☏212/873-9852. This small neighborhood dive is a real throwback, with (predominantly male) regulars slumped at the long bar and a Western feel (Johnny Cash and Hank Williams rule the jukebox). Cheap beer.

Harlem

The Den 2150 Fifth Ave between 131st and 132nd sts ☏212/234-3045. Great place to start or end your night in Harlem: a stylish bar with exposed brick walls and live jazz, open-mic nights and excellent DJs at the weekend. Try the Cuervo Gold Supa Fly or Wu Wu Tang cocktails. The $21 Sunday brunch (noon–5pm) is also worth checking out. Happy hour Mon–Fri 5–7pm.

MoBay Uptown 17 W 125th St, between Fifth and Lenox aves ☏212-876-9300. This restaurant and lounge is great for live gospel, jazz, R&B, and reggae, with Harlem's very own Sugar Hill beer served at the bar, along with

Harlem mojitos. The food ranges from Southern soul food to Caribbean specials like curry goat.

Showmans 375 W 125th St, at Morningside Ave ☎212-864-8941. This small, long-established blues, jazz, and gospel music haunt is often packed with Harlemites and, increasingly, tourists. Jazz shows

Tues–Thurs at 8.30pm, Fri and Sat at 10.30pm; no cover charge.

Striver's Lounge 2611 Frederick Douglass Blvd, at W 139th St ☎212/491-4422. Just west of Strivers Row, this bar-cum-soul food restaurant comes alive at night with jazz, R&B, and poetry open-mic nights (Wed 9pm). The food's also worth the trip.

Downtown Brooklyn

Floyd 131 Atlantic Ave, between Clinton and Henry sts, Brooklyn Heights ☎718/858-5810. Tricked out with antique couches and comfy leather chairs, the main draws here are the cheap draft beers (includes Brooklyn Lager), popular indoor bocce court, and live English Premier League games.

Hideout 266 Adelphi St at DeKalb Ave, Fort Greene ☎718/855-3010. This former garage has been transformed into a smart wood-and-brick bar lined with just 25 stools, where the friendly staff pours various home-made cocktails such as the blackberry *caipirinha* and the snow mosquito – note that the only beer on the menu is the pricey Grimbergen ($9).

Moe's 80 Lafayette Ave at S Portland Ave, Fort Greene ☎718/797-9536. Vintage furniture and candles set the tone at this two-level bar,

with a young, eclectic clientele and two-for-one happy hour (daily 3–7.30pm). Perfect for pre- or post-BAM drinks (p.361).

Stonehome Wine Bar 87 Lafayette Ave, between S Portland Ave and S Elliot Place, Fort Greene ☎718/624-9443. Stylish wine bar with the added bonus of backyard patio, perfect for spring and summer evenings (and smokers). The bar itself is a gorgeous, curving, cherry-wood masterpiece, and the carefully crafted wine list is impressively long.

Superfine 126 Front St, between Jay and Pearl sts, DUMBO ☎718/243-9005. Awesome split-level bar is, with an orange-felt pool table, a "superfine" drink list and the occasional live band. Also does decent Mediterranean food (see p.334).

South Brooklyn

Bar Great Harry 280 Smith St, at Sackett St, Carroll Gardens ☎718/222-1103. Essential stop on any Carroll Gardens pub crawl, with a vast list of Belgian beer and microbrews (12 on tap and 70 in bottles). Prices range $5 to $8.

Brooklyn Inn 148 Hoyt St, at Bergen St, Boerum Hill ☎718/625-9741. Locals – and their dogs – gather at this convivial

▲ Brooklyn Inn

favorite with high ceilings, a solid wood bar imported from Germany in the 1870s, and friendly staff. Great place for a daytime buzz or shooting pool in the back room.

Jakewalk 282 Smith St, at Sackett St, Carroll Gardens ☎347/599-0294. Neighborhood wine bar decked out in orange and gold, with an impressive 50 wines by the glass (from $5) to sample (along over with 100 whiskeys and specialty cocktails). Be sure to order one of the 40 cheeses to go with your drink, sourced from the nearby gourmet deli.

Sunny's 253 Conover St, between Beard and Reed sts, Red Hook ☎718/625-8211. Red Hook is a long trek from Manhattan, but if you're exploring the area during the day, make sure you grab at least one drink at this pub by the river. Open, on-and-off, since 1890, it's an old-school dive with $4 bottle beers and loyal regulars. Expect erratic opening hours, swing bands, and impromptu jam sessions.

Park Slope

The Gate 321 Fifth Ave, at 3rd St ☏718/768-4329. An extensive array of beers and an outdoor patio lure Park Slopers to this roomy, congenial staple of the Fifth Avenue bar scene.

Union Hall 702 Union St, between Fifth and Sixth aves ☏718/638-4400, ⓦunionhallny.com. Vast bar, restaurant, and live music venue, with a library-like interior of bookshelves, fireplaces, and sofas near the bar, and two wildly popular bocce courts (arrive early to get a game). The basement hosts bands 3–4 times a week – check out the website for the schedule.

Williamsburg

Barcade 388 Union St, between Powers and Ainslie sts ☏718/302-6464. This former metal-work shop is crammed with old-fashioned arcade games (think Donkey Kong), each of which take the original 25 cents per game. The beers are good too, with an excellent choice of 25 brews on tap ($5).

Brooklyn Brewery 1 Brewers Row, 79 N 11th St, Williamsburg ☏718/486-7422. New York's best-known microbrewery, open every Fri night only (6–11pm), for "happy hour" (beers $3). See box, p.243, for more on brewery tours.

Pete's Candy Store 709 Lorimer St, between Frost and Richardson sts ☏718/302-3770. This terrific little spot was once a real candy store. There's free live music every night, poetry on Thursdays, comedy Mondays, Bingo Tuesdays, and pub quiz Wednesdays.

Radegast Hall 113 N 3rd St, at Berry St ☏718/963-3973. This Austro-Hungarian *biergarten* is fairly authentic, a spacious wooden beer-hall serving steins of foamy German brews. The dining room serves great food and is popular with families, while the beer garden attracts the serious boozers.

Spuyten Duyvil 359 Metropolitan Ave at Havemeyer St ☏718/963-4140. Beer lovers should make for this popular pub, stocking over 100 bottled brands (mostly potent Belgian brews), six on tap, and a rotating selection of cask-pulled ales.

Queens

Bohemian Hall and Beer Garden 29-19 24th Ave, between 29th and 30th sts, Astoria ☏718/721-4226. This old Czech bar is the real deal, catering to old-timers and serving a good selection of pilsners, as well as other hard-to-find brews. In back, there's a very large beer garden, complete with picnic tables, trees, burgers, and sausages, and a bandshell for polka groups. Great fun in good weather, and well worth the trip from Manhattan.

Harry's at Water Taxi Beach 2 Borden St, at 2nd St, Long Island City. No phone; ⓦwww.watertaxibeach.com. The sand may be imported from Jersey, but the festive spirit is real at this summertime phenomenon with smashing views across the East River to the UN. Cheap beers and grilled food are served up from a tiki hut at least five days a week – it's often closed Mon and Tues – with a small cover charge for dance parties on weekend nights.

The Bronx

Yankee Tavern 161st St, at Gerard Ave ☏718/292-6130. Since 1923, this has been the "original sports bar." Everyone wears their pinstripes on their sleeves in this dive. Yankees employees blow off steam here after games – they're suits by the taps. Be sure to buy them a round – after a day of The Boss's tirades, they'll need it.

Nightlife

A s the city that never sleeps, New York is undeniably a **nightlife** hotspot. Bars don't start to fill up until 11pm, if not later, and clubs look like empty rooms until midnight or 1am. Even confirmed early birds should try to stay out late at least a few times during their stay, as the city's legendary energy is most obvious when most other cities have bedded down for the night.

Since the early 2000s, New York's **live music** scene has been undergoing a post-punk and garage-rock revival, fueled by bands from the East Village, the Lower East Side, and Williamsburg in Brooklyn. On any night of the week you take your pick from several good clubs in these neighbourhoods, and are sure to hear something exciting. The city also continues to set the standard in jazz, with a number of venues where you can hear the most popular contemporary performers.

Though the city's **nightclubs** have largely recovered from a string of closures and police raids that occurred in the winter of 2006, West Chelsea bore the brunt of the crackdown and is no longer the nerve center of the city's club scene. You'll find the action much more spread out, with the Lower East Side, Tribeca, the East and West Village and even Brooklyn offering as many venues as the Meatpacking District, now the city's premier, if slightly overrated, nightlife hub. Depending on what events are being thrown that night, you can count on hearing virtually any kind of music, no matter the club: very few slavishly devote themselves to one style.

Whatever you're planning to do after dark, remember to **carry ID** at all times to prove you're over 21 – you'll likely be asked by every doorman. Note that some venues do not even allow under-21s to enter, let alone drink – call to check if you're concerned.

The sections that follow provide accounts of the pick of the city's venues. Since the music and club scenes are constantly changing, it's a good idea to get up-to-date info once you hit the ground. The listings magazine *Time Out New York* is pretty reliable; you can pick up the current week's issue for a few bucks from virtually any newsstand. Otherwise, grab a freesheet like *The Village Voice* (Ⓦwww.villagevoice.com) or *The Onion* (whose cultural listings are excellent). These can be found on street corners in self-serve newspaper boxes, as well as in many music stores; all of them contain detailed **listings** for most scenes.

Rock, pop, and eclectic music

New York's **rock scene** currently leans heavily toward garage- and indie-rock, with bands like Interpol, The Bravery, The Strokes, The Rapture, and the Yeah

YeahYeahs leading the charge. Foreign acts – especially British bands – invariably play the city as a tryout before they set about "cracking" America; whatever band is hot in the UK's weekly *NME* music magazine will probably be playing NYC soon.

As for **venues**, rising rents have forced many smaller and medium-sized places to close or decamp to Brooklyn (especially Williamsburg) and New Jersey. Most of the best performance spaces are still in Manhattan, though; there's a large cluster of exceptionally good venues in the East Village and Lower East Side.

Large venues

Beacon Theatre 2124 Broadway, at W 74th St Ⓣ212/496-7070, Ⓦwww.beacontheatrenyc .com. This beautifully restored theater caters to a more mature rock and pop crowd, hosting everyone from George Michael to Radiohead. Scorsese's 2008 movie of a Rolling Stones concert, *Shine a Light*, was filmed here. Tickets $50–300.

Hammerstein Ballroom 311 W 34th St, at Ninth Ave Ⓣ212/564-4882, Ⓦwww .mcstudios.com. This grand 1906 building has seen many incarnations: it's been an opera house, a vaudeville hall, and a Masonic temple, and it now hosts indie and rock bands. Capacity is 3600, but the sound system and acoustics are of high enough quality that most seats are pretty good. Tickets $50 and up.

Madison Square Garden Seventh Ave, at W 32nd St Ⓣ212/465-6741, Ⓦwww.thegarden.com. New York's principal big stage, the Garden hosts not only hockey and basketball games but also a good portion of the stadium rock and pop acts that visit the city. Seating capacity is 20,000-plus, so the arena's not exactly the most soulful place to see a band – but for big names, it's the handiest option.

Radio City Music Hall 1260 Sixth Ave, at 50th St Ⓣ212/247-4777, Ⓦwww.radiocity.com. Not the prime venue it once was; it occasionally hosts a terrific concert, but for the most part its schedule is clogged with cutesy tribute shows and schlocky musicals. The acoustics are flawless and the building itself has a great sense of occasion – it seems to inspire the artists who play here to put on a memorable show.

▲ Radio City Music Hall

Roseland Ballroom 239 W 52nd St, at Broadway Ⓣ212/247-0200, Ⓦwww.roselandballroom .com. This historic ballroom opened in 1919 and was once frequented by Adele and Fred Astaire, among others. Although now a ballroom-dancing school, several times per month it turns into a concert venue, putting on big names in rock and pop. Tickets $10–50.

Mid-sized and small venues

Arlene's Grocery 95 Stanton St, at Ludlow St Ⓣ212/473-9831, Ⓦwww.arlenesgrocery.net. An intimate, erstwhile *bodega* (hence the name) that hosts nightly gigs by local, reliably good indie bands. Regularly patronized by musicians, talent scouts, and open-minded rock fans. Go on

Mon nights after 10pm for punk and heavy metal karaoke, when you can sing along with a live band. Cover $10 or less for most shows.

Barbès 376 9th St at 6th Ave, Park Slope, Brooklyn ☎718/965-9177, **ⓦwww.barbesbrooklyn.com.** Bar and intimate backroom performance space that hosts jazz but also readings and film screenings (check the website). Suggested donation $10 for all events.

The Bitter End 147 Bleecker St, at Thompson St ☎212/673-7030, **ⓦwww.bitterend.com.** Young MOR bands in an intimate club setting, mostly folky rockers in the Dylan mold. A catalogue of the famous people who've played the club is posted by the door – it's a pretty long list. Cover is usually $8–12, but some gigs are free, and there is a two-drink minimum.

Bowery Ballroom 6 Delancey St, at Bowery ☎212/533-2111, **ⓦwww.boweryballroom.com.** No attitude, great acoustics, and even better views have earned this site praise from both fans and bands. Major labels test their up-and-comers here, so it's a great place to catch the Next Big Thing of any genre. Highly recommended. Tickets $13–16.

▲ Bowery Ballroom

The Fillmore NY at Irving Plaza 17 Irving Place, at E 15th St ☎212/777-6800, **ⓦwww.irvingplaza.com.** Once home to Off-Broadway musicals (hence the dangling chandeliers and blood-red interior), *Irving Plaza* now features an impressive array of rock, electronic, and techno acts. The main room has wildly divergent acoustics; stand toward the back on the ground floor for the truest mix of sound. Tickets usually range $20–50.

Knitting Factory 74 Leonard St, between Church St and Broadway ☎212/219-3055, **ⓦwww.knittingfactory.com.** While this intimate downtown space is known for its avant-garde jazz, you can hear all other kinds of aural experimentation here too, everything from art rock to electronica. Tickets $5–25.

The Living Room 154 Ludlow St, between Stanton and Rivington sts ☎212/533-7235, **ⓦwww.livingroomny.com.** Comfortable couches (hence the name) and a friendly bar make for a relaxed setting in which to hear local, low-key folk and acoustic rock. Shows usually range $10–20, with a one-drink minimum.

Maxwell's 1039 Washington, at 11th St, Hoboken, New Jersey ☎201/798-0406, **ⓦwww.maxwellsnj.com.** This neighborhood rock club hosts up to a dozen bands a week, including some big indie names. This is one of the best places to check out the tri-state scene. Brave the PATH train (or a cab ride) out to Jersey, and you won't regret it. Tickets $7–25.

Mercury Lounge 217 E Houston St, at Essex St ☎212/260-7400, **ⓦwww.mercuryloungenyc.com.** Dark, Lower East Side mainstay features a mix of local, national, and international rock and pop acts. It's owned by the same crew as the *Bowery Ballroom*, and is similarly used as a trial venue by major labels for up-and-coming artists. Tickets $10–20.

Music Hall of Williamsburg 66 N 6th St, at Kent, Williamsburg ☎718/486-5400, **ⓦwww.musichallofwilliamsburg.com.** A large performance space with excellent acoustics, set in an old factory. One of Brooklyn's really great venues and another in the *Bowery Ballroom* stable – expect the same kind of acts. From 6pm until the opening band starts, all drinks and draft beer are $3. Tickets $10–20.

NuBlu 62 Ave C, at 4th St ☎212/979-9925, **ⓦwww.nublu.net.** This bar – marked only by a small blue light above the door – is owned by the mavens who run the record label of the same name. Jamming jazz and funk bands from their roster regularly play in the front room. No cover.

Pianos 158 Ludlow St, at Rivington St
T 212/505-3733, W www.pianosnyc.com.
There's no cover to get in the door at this
converted piano factory (hence the name),
but to get into the tiny back room – where
the music is – you'll need to fork out extra
($5–15). The sound system's a standout,
and the endless roster of mostly rock bands
(expect four choices nightly) means the
place is usually packed. Drink prices are
somewhat high, and the line to get in
habitually long.
**Rockwood Music Hall 196 Allen St, between
Houston and Stanton sts** T 212/477-4155,
W www.rockwoodmusichall.com. Seven nights
of live music draw hordes of locals to this
tiny space. Though there are no bad seats,
it's a good idea to come early – it's often
packed.
**SOB's (Sounds of Brazil) 204 Varick St, at W
Houston** T 212/243-4940, W www.sobs.com.
Premier place to hear hip-hop, Brazilian,
West Indian, Caribbean, and world music

acts within the confines of Manhattan.
Vibrant and danceable, with a high quality
of music. Shows most nights; times and
ticket prices vary according to the
performer.

**Southpaw 125 Fifth Ave, between
Sterling Place and Douglass St, Park
Slope** T 718/230-0236, W www.spsounds
.com. Brooklyn's premier live venue, with
5000 square feet of space and a wide range
of acts and DJs from almost every genre.
Admission varies, but is rarely more than
$10–12, while a cab from lower Manhattan
costs around $10–15.

**Village Underground 130 W 3rd St, at
Sixth Ave** T 212/777-7745,
W www.thevillageunderground.com. Tiny
basement performance space that is one of
the most intimate and innovative clubs
around. Big names have been known to
crash the party: Guided by Voices and the
late RL Burnside have both appeared,
among others. Cover $7–15.

Jazz

Jazz in New York has seen a bit of a resurgence in the last ten years. The last
decades of the twentieth century saw the city's clubs go through a rough patch,
but new owners are now breathing life into older venues, and the establishment
of a clutch of performance spaces in the late 1990s has helped reinvigorate the
scene. There are more than forty locations in Manhattan that present jazz
regularly. You'll find the best of these clubs in the West Village and Harlem,
though midtown venues have steadily been improving in quality; there are also
a few fine sites in Chelsea and the East Village.

To find out **who's playing**, check the usual sources, notably the *Village
Voice* (W www.villagevoice.com) and *Time Out New York* (W www.timeoutny
.com); other good jazz rags are the monthlies *Hothouse* (W www.hothouse
jazz.com), a free magazine available at venues and hotels, and *Down Beat*
(W www.downbeat.com).

Price policies vary from club to club, but most places have a hefty cover ($20–
50) and a minimum charge for food and drinks. An evening out at a major club
will cost at least $25 per person, $40–50 per person if you'd like to eat. Piano
bars – smaller and often more atmospheric – come cheaper; some have neither
an admission fee nor a minimum, though expect to pay inflated drink prices.

Jazz venues

Birdland 315 W 44th St, at Ninth Ave
T 212/581-3080, W www.birdlandjazz
.com. Not the original place where Charlie
Parker played, but nonetheless an established supper club that plays host to some
big names. Sets nightly at 9 and 11pm.
Music charge of $20–50; at a table, you'll

need to spend a minimum of $10 or more
on food or drink, while at the bar, the cover
includes your first drink.
**Blue Note 131 W 3rd St, between Sixth Ave
and MacDougal St** T 212/475-8592, W www
.bluenotejazz.com. Open since 1981, this jazz
institution regularly hosts top international
performers, with the likes of Sarah Vaughan,
Dizzy Gillespie, and Oscar Peterson making

lauded appearances over the years. Tickets usually range $15–25. Note that Blue Note Records is totally separate.

Café Carlyle in The Carlyle Hotel, 35 E 76th St, at Madison Ave ☎212/744-1600, ⊛www .thecarlyle.com. This intimate, dressy spot was home to legendary crooner Bobby Short, and Woody Allen still plays clarinet here most Mon nights in the fall, winter, and spring; it's a chic, Upper East Side scene, and well worth the ticket price. $30–60 cover, no minimum.

Iridium Jazz Club 1650 Broadway, at W 51st St ☎212/582-2121, ⊛www .iridiumjazzclub.com. Contemporary jazz performed seven nights a week in a Surrealist décor described as "Dolly meets Disney." The nonagenarian godfather of electric guitar Les Paul plays every Mon. Cover $25–50, $10 food and drink minimum; Sun jazz brunch.

▲ Iridium Jazz Club

Jazz at Lincoln Center 33 W 60th St, at Columbus Circle ☎212/258-9800, ⊛www .jazzatlincolncenter.org. There are three different spaces at this venue in the Time Warner Center. The two larger auditoria, Rose Hall and Allen Room, are nice, but the smallest one is the pick of them all: the 140-seater *Dizzy's Club Coca-Cola*. It has panoramic views, a speakeasy-style atmosphere, and inventive programming.

Jazz Standard 116 E 27th St, at Park Ave S ☎212/576-2232, ⊛www.jazzstandard.net. A spacious underground room with great sound and even better performers has earned this club high praise and a loyal clientele. Sets daily 7.30pm and 9.30pm, Fri & Sat extra set at 11.30pm. Cover $20–30; all with $10 minimum.

Joe's Pub 425 Lafayette St, at Astor Place ☎212/539-8777, ⊛www.joespub.com. Stylishly classic bar in Joe Papp's Public Theater

attracts a hipper crowd than many jazz/cabaret spots; there are performances seven days a week, ranging from Broadway songbooks to readings from the *New Yorker*'s fiction issues. Mon nights are often given over to a big name from Broadway in solo concert. $12–25.

Lenox Lounge 288 Malcolm X Blvd, at 124th St ☎212/427-0253, ⊛www.lenoxlounge.com. Entertaining Harlem since the 1930s, this renovated, historic jazz lounge has an over-the-top Art Deco interior (check out the Zebra Room), and features three sets nightly. Known more for contemporary riffs than traditional jazz standards. Cover $20, with a $16 drink minimum at weekends.

Louis 649 649 E 9th St between aves B and C ☎212/673-1190. With no cover and live performances seven nights a week, *Louis 649* is a must if you love jazz. Mon and Thurs are lively, and weekends get downright hectic. They serve gourmet bottled beer and a number of excellent vintages, but no cocktails.

Smoke 2751 Broadway, at 106th St ☎212/864-6662, ⊛www.smokejazz.com. This Upper West Side joint is a real neighborhood treat, with plush couches, lavish chandeliers, and a retro, upscale feel. Sets start at 9, 11pm, and 12.30am; stop by for happy hour and $5 cocktails daily 5–8pm. Cover varies.

Village Vanguard 178 Seventh Ave, at 11th St ☎212/255-4037, ⊛www.villagevanguard.com. A NYC jazz landmark, the *Village Vanguard* celebrated its seventieth anniversary in 2005. There's a regular diet of big names. Mon–Thurs admission is $30, while Sat & Sun entry is $35; both tickets include a $10 drink credit.

Zinc Bar 90 W Houston St, at LaGuardia Place ☎212/477-8337, ⊛www.zincbar.com. Great jazz venue with strong drinks and a loyal bunch of regulars. The blackboard above the entrance announces the evening's featured band. Cover is $8 with a one-drink minimum (two at the tables). Hosts both new talent and established greats, with an emphasis on Latin American rhythms.

Nightclubs

New York's **nightlife** has come a long way since its decadent, devil-may-care disco years. The city's after-dark party places are now corporate businesses, with many megaclubs, like *Pacha*, for example, part of multi-city chains and others, such as *Bungalow 8*, the haunt of celebrity wannabes with a stringent door policy that favours the young, rich, and beautiful. Happily, plenty of unpretentious clubs remain, especially in the Lower East Side, though venues shift and change, opening and closing according to finances, fashion, and the enforcement of anti-drug laws.

In terms of what you can expect to find at a club, New York's DJs rely on a varied diet of **house music, electro-house and techno**, though there's a growing cadre of inventive hip-hop, retro soul, indie rock, and Latin-jazz venues. As in any large city, **illegal drugs** are a part of clubbing here – expect door searches to be thorough, and heavy penalties if you're caught with any kind of banned substance. That said, alcohol fuels New York's nightlife just as much as ecstasy does, so staying legal doesn't mean you'll be left out of the fun. Regarding **dress codes**, New York is a casual kind of town where clubs are concerned – unless noted in our reviews, you can usually turn up in smart-casual dress and be fine. If you arrive at a club before midnight, expect a longish wait till the dance floor gets going: nothing really starts to happen until after midnight.

Below is a list of the current hot venues, plus a few perennials; of course, since clubs come and go constantly, it's important to check up-to-date info with one of the free magazine/newspapers like the *Village Voice*, or pick up a copy of *Time Out New York*. Fliers are always the best way to hear about the latest nightspots: see the list of record stores on p.400 for places to pick them up.

Apt 419 W 13th St, at Ninth Ave ⓣ212/414-4245, ⓦwww.aptwebsite.com. Tucked behind an unmarked doorway, this well-hidden bar/club is known for its inventive, eclectic DJ roster (including iPod-powered DIY nights). There are two spaces: a lounge-like upstairs room and a sleek, wood-paneled downstairs bar. Cover $10.

Cielo 18 Little W 12th St, at Ninth Ave ⓣ212/645-5700, ⓦwww.cieloclub.com. Expect velvet rope-burn at this super-exclusive see-and-be-seen place: there's only room for 250 people. Though run by Nicolas Matar, a former DJ at Ibiza's legendary *Pacha* club, it's the Mon-night reggae and dub party from François K that most people talk about. Cover $10–20; the sound system is amazing.

Club Shelter 150 Varick St, at Vandam St ⓣ646/862-6117, ⓦwww.clubshelter.com. Big but friendly venue harking back to the heyday of Chicago house with an excellent sound system. Soulful house guru Timmy Regisford spins on Sat. No dress code. Cover $15–20.

Lotus 409 W 14th St, at Tenth Ave ⓣ212/243-4420, ⓦwww.lotusnewyork.com. This rocking basement bar/club plays deep house and soul from 11pm onwards. The club's reputation is based on their Fri- and Sat-night parties, but these are strictly for a designer-dressed crowd. Cover $20, free if you dine at the Asian fusion restaurant upstairs (min $25 per person).

Love 40 W 8th St, at MacDougal St ⓣ212/477-5683, ⓦwww.musicislove.net. This West Village club hosts some of the hottest nights in the city, from drum'n'bass to house and hip-hop, with an awesome sound system and a regular line-up of top international DJs – check the website first, though, to see what's on. Cover is usually $15.

Otto's Shrunken Head 538 E 14th St ⓣ212/228-2240, ⓦwww.ottosshrunkenhead.com. This East Village joint is hard to pigeonhole; a tiki bar that hosts live indie and punk rock bands, as well as some of the most popular club nights on the island. Dark Water at 10pm on Tues features rock, industrial, 1980s, and Goth music, while Thurs spotlights new ska, reggae, dub, and rocksteady. Weekends also see a host of rock/punk parties – check the website for details. Usually no cover.

Pacha 618 W 46th St ⓣ212/209-7500, ⓦwww.pachanyc.com. The New York outpost of the chain of Ibiza superclubs. Sprawling over 30,000 square feet, and featuring a spine-tingling high-tech sound system, three floors, palm trees, and mosaic mirrors, this is the place for a big, corporate club experience, and a generally non-local clientele – expect big, sweaty crowds. Cover $30.

Sapphire Lounge 249 Eldridge St, at Houston St ℡212/777-5153, ⓦwww.sapphirenyc.com. DJ bar and lounge, with an arty, sleazy, sexy vibe, created by the dark lights and enhanced by the moody Lower East Side regulars. The programming is inventive, offering music of almost every genre on different nights, from reggae to hip-hop to breakbeat – as a plus, it's open every night of the week, and the cover is usually minimal ($5–12).

Spy 17 W 19th St, at Fifth Ave ℡212/352-2001, ⓦwww.spyclubnyc. This space changes names frequently, but retains the same ownership. The party always comes here, ranging from rock to disco to hip-hop. The kitchen is open late to fuel you for the dance floor. Drinks aren't cheap and neither is the $25–30 weekend cover.

Stanton Public 17 Stanton St between Bowery and Chrystie St, ⓦwww. www.stantonpublic .com. Another bar doubling as indie dance club, with DJs spinning Brit Pop Sat nights, 1980s, punk, electro, and indie on Fri, with two floors and over 17 beers on tap. Happy hour 4–8pm, and entry is normally free.

Stonewall Inn 53 Christopher St, at Seventh Ave ℡212/463-0950, ⓦwww.thestonewallinnnyc .com. The gay civil-rights movement began outside this club in the late 1960s and it doesn't look like it's changed much since. The patrons haven't changed much either, though the latest pop music invades Thursday nights during the weekly dance party, keeping things more or less fresh and current. The crowd is mostly tourists and men, but everyone is made to feel welcome.

Studio B 259 Banker St, between Calyer St and Meserole Ave, Greenpoint ℡718/389-1880, ⓦclubstudiob.com. Hip Brooklyn club with a massive dance floor for live bands and DJ nights, as well as a cozy back room sporting leather sofas, red curtains, and Baroque chandeliers. Beer is cheap ($6) but hours and cover varies – check the website before trekking over there.

Sullivan Room 218 Sullivan St, at Bleecker St ℡212/252-2151, ⓦwww .sullivanroom.com. Hidden basement club for serious dancing. Fri and Sat, popular with students from nearby NYU, are good for house music. The only downside: two bathrooms for the whole place. Thurs–Sat 10pm–4am. Cover $10–15.

The performing arts
and film

"**P**erforming arts**" is really an all-encompassing title for New York's legion of cultural offerings. While many travelers tend automatically to think of the glittery Broadway productions housed on and around Times Square, locals will inform you that such a heading also includes more experimental Off-Broadway theater companies, as well as comedy clubs, cabarets, dance troupes, and the opera, to name but a few of the city's options.

Prices for live performances vary wildly: expect to pony up $150 for a night at the opera, while Shakespeare is performed for free in Central Park every summer. The high prices of many shows can be off-putting; see the box on p.360 for some tips on how to see Broadway blockbusters on a budget.

The silver screen is just as important a part of New York's arts scene as its live performances are. New York gets the first run of most American **films** as well as many foreign ones, often long before they open in Europe (or the rest of America). There's also a very healthy arthouse and revival scene.

Listings for the arts can be found in a number of places. The most useful sources are the clear and comprehensive listings in *Time Out New York*, the free *New York Press*, and the "Voice Choices" section of the free *Village Voice*. Fancier events are usually touted in *New York* magazine's "Agenda" section, "Goings On About Town" in the *New Yorker*, and both Friday's "Weekend" and Sunday's "Arts and Leisure" sections of the *New York Times*. You'll find specific Broadway listings in the free *Official Broadway Theater Guide*, available at theater and hotel lobbies.

If you want to plan your itinerary before you leave home, websites such as ⓦwww.newyork.citysearch.com and ⓦwww.timeoutny.com have information on arts events in New York. You can also check the useful sites ⓦwww.nytheatre.com, ⓦwww.broadway.com, and ⓦwww.offbroadwayonline.com for up-to-date info on both major Broadway shows and local theater listings. The best sites from which to purchase tickets are ⓦwww.telecharge.com and ⓦwww.ticketmaster.com.

Theater

Theater venues in the city are referred to as being "**Broadway**," "**Off-Broadway**," or "**Off-Off-Broadway**." These groupings don't necessarily mean

Tickets for Broadway shows can cost as much as $125 for orchestra seats at the hottest shows, and as little as $25 for day-of-performance rush tickets (often standing room only) for some of the long-runners; check listings magazines for availability. Off-Broadway's best seats are cheaper than those on Broadway, averaging $30–70. Off-Off-Broadway tickets should rarely set you back more than $25.

The best places to go for bargains are the **TKTS booths** (☎212/221-0885, ⊛www .tdf.org), which offer cut-rate, day-of-performance tickets for many Broadway and Off-Broadway shows. Expect to pay half the face value, plus a $2.50 service charge (cash or travelers' checks only). The booth at Duffy Square, located at Broadway between 45th and 47th streets is open Mon–Sat 3–8pm plus 10am–2pm for Wed and Sat matinees, and 11am–7pm for all Sunday performances; there's another outlet near the South Street Seaport at the corner of Front and Water streets (near the rear of 199 Water St). There's also a new TKTS office in Downtown Brooklyn at 1 Metro Tech Center, open Mon–Fri 11am–6pm.

If you're prepared to pay full price for tickets, you can, of course, go directly to the theater (or the theater website) or call one of the following **ticket sales agencies**. **Telecharge** (☎1-800/432-7250 or 212/239-6200, ⊛www.telecharge.com) and **Ticketmaster** (☎1-800/755-4000 or 212/307-4100, ⊛www.ticketmaster.com) sell Broadway tickets over the phone; note that no show is represented by both these agencies. **Ticket Central at Playwrights Horizon Theater** (416 W 42nd St, between Ninth and Tenth aves ☎212/279-4200; daily noon–8pm) sells tickets to many Off-Broadway theaters. Expect a $5–7 surcharge per ticket. When buying tickets, always ask where your seats are located, as once you get to the theater and find yourself in the last row of the balcony, it's too late (for most seating plans, check ⊛www.playbill.com).

a theater's address is physically on or off Broadway; instead they represent a descending order of ticket prices, production polish, elegance, and comfort. In theory at least, the further off-Broadway and down the price scale you go, the more innovative productions are.

Although **Broadway** shows have diversified somewhat of late, they remain predominantly grandiose tourist-magnet musicals, packing in the biggest crowds and boasting the biggest-name stars. A recent trend has been megahit musicals adapted from movies, including multiple Tony Award–winners *Hairspray* and *Spamalot* – a popular theatrical rendition of *Monty Python and the Holy Grail*. The majority of Broadway theaters are located in the blocks just east or west of Broadway (the avenue) between 41st and 53rd streets, conveniently near the larger Times Square tourist hotels.

A bit less glitzy is **Off-Broadway**, the best place to discover new talent and adventurous new American drama and musicals. Off-Broadway theaters are home to lower-budget social and political dramas, satire, ethnic plays, and repertory – in other words, anything that can make money without having to fill a huge hall each night (most of these theaters seat between 100 and 500). Lower operating costs also mean that Off-Broadway often serves as a forum to try out what sometimes ends up as a big Broadway production.

Off-Off-Broadway is the fringe of New York's theater world. Off-Off venues (often with fewer than 100 seats) aren't bound by union regulations to use professional actors, and shows range from shoestring productions of the classics to outrageous and experimental performance art. Prices range from free to cheap, and the quality can vary from execrable to electrifying. Frankly, there's a lot more of the former than the latter, so it's best to use weekly reviews as your guide.

We've picked out a smattering of reliable Off- and Off-Off venues (the Broadway theaters generally book whatever shows they can, and therefore don't offer a consistent type of production).

Off-Broadway

Astor Place Theater 434 Lafayette St, at Astor Place ☎212/254-4370. Showcase for exciting work since the 1960s, when Sam Shepard's *The Unseen Hand* and *Forensic and the Navigators* had the playwright himself playing drums in the lobby. For the last fifteen years, however, the theater has been the home of the comically absurd but very popular performance artists Blue Man Group (ⓦwww.blueman.com).

Atlantic Theater Company 336 W 20th St, at Eighth Ave ☎212/645-8015, ⓦwww .atlantictheater.com. As you'd expect from a theater founded by David Mamet and William H. Macy, this place is known for accessible, intelligent productions of modern dramatic classics, works by everyone from Harold Pinter to Martin McDonagh. The ATC also runs an acting school nearby on 16th Street, and you can sometimes catch student performances here, too.

Barrow Street Theatre 27 Barrow St, at Seventh Ave S ☎212/243-6262. This small theater inside a landmark West Village building was once the long-term home of Off-Broadway favorite the Drama Dept. That company has been replaced by a more profit-minded organization, which is generating artistically excellent but more commercially viable productions, like The Civilians' production of *Gone Missing*.

🏃 **Brooklyn Academy of Music** 30 Lafayette Ave, Brooklyn ☎718/636-4100, ⓦwww .bam.org. Despite its name, Brooklyn Academy of Music (usually referred to as BAM) regularly presents theatrical productions on its three stages, often touring shows from Europe and Asia. Every autumn BAM puts on the Next Wave festival of large-scale performance art (see p.421). Not so much Off-Broadway as Off-Manhattan, but well worth the trip.

City Center 131 W 55th St, at Seventh Ave ☎212/581-1212, ⓦwww.citycenter.org. This large, midtown venue is best known for its Encores! series. These readings and studio performances usually run for one weekend only, and are designed to revive long-forgotten or overlooked musicals, from Gilbert & Sullivan to modern dance. It's also home to the Manhattan Theater Club (ⓦwww.mtc-nyc.org), which deals in serious new theater featuring major American actors. Many productions eventually transfer to Broadway; see them here first, though prices aren't that much cheaper.

New World Stages 340 W 50th St, between Eighth and Ninth aves ☎212/239-6200. Five stages, actually, with good sightlines, ranging in size from 200 to 500 seats. Several productions that debuted here have grown into small-scale hits.

Orpheum Theater 126 Second Ave, between 7th St and St Mark's Place ☎212/477-2477. One of the East Village's biggest theaters, once known for hosting David Mamet and other influential new American shows, but more recently the home of the percussion group Stomp. Wheelchair-accessible.

Playwrights Horizons 416 W 42nd St, at Ninth Ave ☎212/564-1235, ⓦwww.playwrights horizons.org. This well-respected drama-centric space is located smack in the center of Times Square, though its mission remains the same as it was when it was founded in a YMCA in 1971 – championing works by undiscovered playwrights. They also get top-line actors.

🏃 **The Public Theater** 425 Lafayette St ☎212/539-8500, ⓦwww.publictheater .org. Founded by Broadway legend Joe Papp as the Shakespeare Workshop, The Public Theater is the city's primary presenter of the Bard's plays. In the summer, the Public produces the free Shakespeare in the Park series at the open-air Delacorte Theater in Central Park (see p.158). For most of the year, though, this major Off-Broadway institution delivers thought-provoking and challenging productions from new, mostly American, writers.

Vivian Beaumont Theater and the Mitzi E. Newhouse Theater Lincoln Center, Broadway, at W 65th St ☎212/239-6200, ⓦwww.lct.org. Technically Broadway theaters, these stages are far enough away from Times Square in distance and, usually, quality, to qualify as Off. A great place to see stimulating new work by playwrights like Tom Stoppard and John Guare.

Westside Theatre 407 W 43rd St, between Ninth and Tenth aves ☎212/315-2244, ⊛www .westsidetheatre.com. Two small theaters, known for productions of Shaw, Wilde, and Pirandello. The downstairs one has wheelchair access.

Off-Off-Broadway and performance-art spaces

Dixon Place 258 Bowery, at Stanton St, 2nd floor ☎212/219-0736, ⊛www.dixonplace.org. Very popular small venue dedicated to experimental theater, dance, and literary readings.

The Drilling Company 107 W 82nd St ☎212/877-0099, ⊛www.drillingcompany.org. Third home of Lower East Side performance group, formerly known as Ludlow Ten, that's best known for producing the summer-long Shakespeare in the Park(ing Lot) series of free performances at the Municipal Parking Lot at Broome and Ludlow.

The Flea 41 White St, at Church St ☎212/226-2407. Cutting-edge drama space run by Jim Simpson, Sigourney Weaver's husband. The program stretches from performance art and drama to acrobatics. Though many of the actors here are not professionals, the quality remains impressively high.

Franklin Furnace Archive 80 Hanson Place #301, at Portland Ave, Brooklyn ☎718/398-7255, ⊛www.franklinfurnace.org. An archive dedicated to installation work and performance art, the Franklin Furnace has launched the careers of performers as celebrated and notorious as Karen Finley and Eric Begosian. Performances take place at various downtown locations – check the website or call for updated schedules.

Here 145 Sixth Ave, at Spring St ☎212/647-0202, ⊛www.here.org. A very open-minded, intriguing space supporting experimental fare from both new artists and established performers like Suzanne Vega. Puppetry and performance art are special strengths.

Kraine 85 E 4th St, between Second and Third aves ☎212/777-6088, ⊛www.horsetrade.info. This 99-seat East Village theater is home to twelve different residential companies and is mostly known for presenting unusual comedies. Another plus for this budget space is the raked seating, which makes for good sightlines. It's in the basement of the same building as artsy *KGB*, a bar known for its author readings (see p.344).

La Mama E.T.C. (Experimental Theater Club) 74A E 4th St, at Second Ave ☎212/475-7710, ⊛www.lamama.org. The mother of all Off-Off venues, founded almost 50 years ago. A real gem with four different auditoria, La Mama is known for politically and sexually charged material as well as visiting dance troupes from overseas. For raw amateur performances, check out The Galleria space a few blocks away.

New York Theater Workshop 79 E 4th St, at Second Ave ☎212/460-5475, ⊛www.nytw.org. An eminent experimental workshop that often chooses cult hit shows and has presented plays by Tony Kushner, Susan Sontag, and Paul Rudnick; best known these days as the place the global musical megahit *Rent* was first shown to the public.

Ontological-Hysteric Theater St Marks Church, 131 E 10th St, at Second Ave ☎212/420-1916, ⊛www.ontological.com. Produces some of the city's best radical shows; especially famous for the work of independent theater legend Richard Foreman.

Performing Garage 33 Wooster St, at Grand St ☎212/966-3651, ⊛www.thewoostergroup.org. The famous Wooster Group (which includes Willem Dafoe) performs regularly in this Soho space. Tickets are like gold dust (very hard to come by), but the effort to find them is worth it.

P.S. 122 150 First Ave, at 9th St ☎212/477-5288, ⊛www.ps122.org. A converted school in the East Village that is perennially popular for its jam-packed schedule of revolutionary performance art, dance, and one-person shows in its two theaters.

▲ P.S. 122

St Ann's Warehouse 38 Water St, Brooklyn ☎718/254-8779, ⊛www.artsatstanns.org. Housed in a hulking industrial space, St Ann's is in a part of DUMBO relatively far from the subway (see p.222). Brave the walk, though, as the main stage is consistently impressive for both drama and music – there are Broadway tryouts here and musicians like Lou Reed often play *intime* sets. There's also a café and gallery space in the entrance.

Theater for the New City 155 First Ave, at 10th St ☎212/254-1109, ⓦwww.theaterforthenewcity.net. This major performance venue is best known as the site where Sam Shepard's Pulitzer Prize–winning *Buried Child* premiered in 1978. It's still churning out fine drama through its emerging-playwrights program. TNC also performs outdoors for free at a variety of venues throughout the summer and hosts the Lower East Side Festival of the Arts at the end of May.

Tribeca Performing Arts Center 199 Chambers St, at Greenwich St ☎212/220-1460, ⓦwww.tribecapac.org. TriPac, as it's known, is owned by the Community College of Manhattan, a fact reflected in its programming: mostly high-end local theater and dance groups, plus kids' workshops and multicultural events. It's also known for fine jazz performances.

Classical music and opera

New Yorkers take their **classical music and opera** seriously. Long lines form for anything popular, many concerts sell out, and summer evenings can see a quarter of a million people turning up in Central Park for free performances by the New York Philharmonic. Tickets can be somewhat easier to come by for performances by the city's top-notch chamber-music ensembles (most of the patrons are members of the city's geriatric crowd).

Opera venues

Amato Opera Theater 319 Bowery, at 2nd St ☎212/228-8200, ⓦwww.amato.org. This Bowery venue presents an ambitious and varied repertory of classics performed by up-and-coming young singers and conductors. The Opera in Brief series on Sat mornings (Sept–May) is enchanting for kids. Performances at weekends only, Sept–May.

Juilliard School 60 Lincoln Center Plaza, at 65th St ☎212/799-5000, ⓦwww.juilliard.edu. Located right next door to the Met (see below), Juilliard students often perform under the direction of a famous conductor, usually for low ticket prices.

Metropolitan Opera House Lincoln Center, Columbus Ave, at 64th St ☎212/362-6000, ⓦwww.metopera.org. More popularly known as the Met, New York's premiere opera venue is home to the world-renowned Metropolitan Opera Company from Sept to late April. Tickets are expensive (up to $295) and can be well-nigh impossible to snag, though 175 (cheap) standing-room tickets, priced between $20 and $30, for each performance go on sale at 10am every Sat for the following week's show. The limit is one ticket per person, and the line has been known to form at dawn.

The New York State Theater Lincoln Center, 65th St, at Columbus Ave ☎212/870-5570, ⓦwww.nycopera.com. This is where the New York City Opera plays David to the Met's Goliath. Its wide and adventurous program varies wildly in quality depending on the production (check out a *NY Times* review before purchasing) – some quite creative, others boringly mediocre – but seats go for less than half the Met's prices.

Concert halls

92nd Street Y Kaufman Concert Hall 1395 Lexington Ave, at 92nd St ☎212/996-1100, ⓦwww.92y.org. This wood-panelled space is especially welcoming since performers are usually available to chat or mingle with the audience after shows. Great line-up of chamber music and solo events.

The Alice Tully Hall Lincoln Center, Broadway and W 65th St ☎212/721-6500. A smaller Lincoln Center hall for the top chamber orchestras, string quartets, and instrumentalists. The weekend chamber series are deservedly popular, though the crowd is composed almost exclusively of the 65-and-over set. Prices similar to those in Avery Fisher (see below).

Avery Fisher Hall Lincoln Center, Broadway and W 65th St ☎212/875-5030,

@ www.lincolncenter.org. The permanent home of the New York Philharmonic. Ticket prices for the Philharmonic range $12–50. The open rehearsals (9.45am on concert days) are a great bargain; tickets are about $15. Avery Fisher also hosts the very popular annual Mostly Mozart Festival in August.

Bargemusic Fulton Ferry Landing, Brooklyn ☏718/624-4061, @ www .bargemusic.org. Chamber music in a wonderful river setting on a moving barge below the Brooklyn Bridge. Thurs through Sat 8pm, Sun 4pm. Tickets are $35, $20 for full-time students.

Brooklyn Academy of Music 30 Lafayette Ave, Brooklyn ☏718/636-4100, @ www.bam.org. The BAM Opera House is the perennial home of Philip Glass operatic premieres and Laurie Anderson performances. It also hosts a number of contemporary imports from European and Chinese companies, often with a large modern-dance component.

▲ Brooklyn Academy of Music

Carnegie Hall 154 W 57th St, at Seventh Ave ☏212/247-7800, @ www.carnegiehall.org. The greatest names from all schools of music have performed here, from Tchaikovsky (who conducted the hall's inaugural concert) to Toscanini to Gershwin

to Billie Holiday. The tradition continues, and the stunning acoustics – said to be the best in the world – lure big-name performers (such as Renée Fleming and Katya Labèque) at sky-high prices. Check website for up-to-date admission rates and schedules. To learn more about the building itself, head to the Rose Museum on the 2nd floor here.

Cathedral of St John the Divine 1047 Amsterdam Ave, at 112th St ☏212/662-2133, @ www.stjohndivine.org. A magnificent Morningside Heights setting that hosts occasional classical and New Age performances. Also home to the Early Music Foundation (@ www.earlymusicny.org), which performs scores from the eleventh through the eighteenth centuries.

Lehman Center for the Performing Arts 250 Bedford Park Blvd, Bronx ☏718/960-8833, @ www.lehmancenter.org. First-class concert hall drawing the world's top performers, as varied as alumni of the Bolshoi Ballet and Ladysmith Black Mambazo.

Merkin Concert Hall 129 W 67th St, at Broadway ☏212/501-3330, @ www .merkinconcerthall.org. This intimate and adventurous venue in the Elaine Kaufman Cultural Center is a great place to hear music of any kind. Plays host to the New York Guitar Festival in January.

Symphony Space 2537 Broadway, at 95th St ☏212/864-5400, @ www .symphonyspace.org. The Symphony Space has a varied performance schedule, from "ground-breaking, style-crashing" new classical to jazz. It's especially known for its World Music Institute, and its kid-oriented weekend shows.

Town Hall 123 W 43rd St, at Sixth Ave ☏212/840-2824, @ www.the-townhall-nyc .org. This midtown hall has an unusual history: it was designed by Stanford White (the mastermind of the original Madison Square Garden) and commissioned by suffragettes as a protest-friendly space. One of the egalitarian innovations in the design was the omission of any box seats in order to provide better acoustics and sightlines from every seat in the house. As for programming, it's best known for an eclectic policy – from its Sunday Afternoon Opera series to Cole Porter celebrations to klezmer music.

Dance

As favorites like Bill T. Jones, Mark Morris, and Savion Glover continue to show, **dance** – especially experimental or avant-garde performance – is still surging in popularity in New York. The city has five major ballet companies, dozens of modern troupes, and untold thousands of soloists; all performances are listed in broadly the same periodicals and websites as music and theater, though you might also want to pick up *Dance Magazine* (Ⓦwww.dancemagazine.com) for extra specifics. The official dance season runs from September through January and April through June.

The following is a list of some of the major dance venues in the city, though a lot of the smaller, more esoteric companies and solo dancers also perform at spaces like Dixon Place and P.S.122, listed on p.362 under Off-Off Broadway. Dance fans should also note that the annual Dance on Camera Festival (Ⓣ212/727-0764, Ⓦwww.dancefilmsassn.org) of dance films takes place over three weekends at the Walter Reade Theater at Lincoln Center in January.

92nd Street Y Harkness Dance Center 1395 Lexington Ave, at 92nd St Ⓣ212/415-5500, Ⓦwww.92y.org. Hosts performances and discussions, often for free.

Brooklyn Academy of Music 30 Lafayette St, Brooklyn Ⓣ718/636-4100, Ⓦwww.bam.org. America's oldest performing-arts academy is still one of the busiest and most daring dance producers in New York. In the autumn, BAM's Next Wave festival features the hottest international attractions in avant-garde dance and music, and each spring since 1977 BAM has hosted the annual DanceAfrica Festival, America's largest showcase for African and African-American dance and culture.

City Center 131 W 55th St, at Seventh Ave Ⓣ212/581-1212, Ⓦwww.citycenter.org. This large, midtown venue hosts some of the most important troupes in modern dance, including the Paul Taylor Dance Company, the Alvin Ailey American Dance Theater, and

---

Free summer concerts

Concert prices just keep getting higher, but in summer there are often budget-priced or free alternatives.

Lincoln Center Out-of-Doors (Ⓣ212/875-5108, Ⓦwww.lincolncenter.org) hosts a varied selection of daily free performances of music and dance events on the plaza throughout the summer.

Bryant Park (Ⓣ212/768-4242, Ⓦwww.bryantpark.org) is home to free Broadway and Off-Broadway musical performances during the summer (one weekday lunchtime; check schedules), as well as short pop concerts staged by the TV show *Good Morning America* early on Friday mornings.

SummerStage Festival (Ⓣ212/360-2777, Ⓦwww.summerstage.org) in Central Park puts on an impressive range of free concerts of all kinds of music throughout the summer; performances take place at the Rumsey Playfield (near the 72nd St and Fifth Ave entrance). A highlight here is the occasional Wednesday-night performance of Verdi by the **New York Grand Opera**. **New York Philharmonic's Concerts in the Park** (Ⓣ212/875-5709, Ⓦwww.nyphilharmonic.org) is a series of concerts and fireworks displays that turns up all over the city and the outer boroughs in July. Similarly, there's the **Met in the Parks** series (Ⓣ212/362-6000, Ⓦwww.metopera.org) in June and July.

For other free classical music and jazz performances, try the **Washington Square Music Festival** (Ⓣ212/252-3621, Ⓦwww.washingtonsquaremusicfestival.org) on Tuesdays at 8pm throughout July, or the **Celebrate Brooklyn Festival** (Ⓣ718/855-7882, Ⓦwww.celebratebrooklyn.org) at Prospect Park Bandshell in Brooklyn, on July and August weekends.

the American Ballet Theater. Also puts on the September Fall for Dance Festival.

Cunningham Studio 55 Bethune St, at Washington St ⓣ212/255-8240, ⓦwww .merce.org. The home of the Merce Cunningham Dance Company stages performances once a week by emerging modern choreographers, usually on Fri and Sat nights.

Dance Theater Workshop 219 W 19th St, at Seventh Ave ⓣ212/924-0077, ⓦwww.dtw.org. Founded in 1965 as a choreographers' collective to support emerging artists in alternative dance, DTW is now housed in a multimillion-dollar building. There's a mid-sized main stage, an art gallery, and smaller workshop spaces, all of which boast more than 175 performances from nearly 70 artists and companies each season. The relaxed, friendly vibe and reasonable ticket prices (from $15–25) haven't changed.

Danspace Project St Mark's-Church-in-the-Bowery, 131 E 10th St, at Second Ave ⓣ212/674-8194, ⓦwww.danspaceproject.org. Experimental contemporary dance, with a season running from Sept to June in one of the more beautiful performance spaces.

The Joyce Theater 175 Eighth Ave, at 19th St ⓣ212/242-0800, ⓦwww.joyce.org. The Joyce is one of the best-known downtown dance venues. It hosts short seasons by a wide variety of acclaimed dance troupes such as Pilobolus, the Parsons Dance Company, and Momix. The Joyce also gives perform-ances at their Soho space, a former

firehouse (155 Mercer St, at Prince St ⓣ212/431-9233).

Juilliard Dance Workshop 155 W 65th St, at Broadway ⓣ212/799-5000, ⓦwww.juilliard .edu. The dance division of the Juilliard School often holds free workshop perform-ances, and each spring six students work with six composers to present a Composers and Choreographers concert.

Lincoln Center's Fountain Plaza 65th St at Columbus Ave ⓣ212/875-5766, ⓦwww.lincolncenter.org. Open-air venue for the enormously popular Midsummer Night Swing, where each night you can learn a different dance style en masse (everything from polka to rockabilly) and watch a performance – all for $15. Tickets go on sale at 5.45pm the night of the show; the season runs June–July.

Metropolitan Opera House Lincoln Center, 65th St at Columbus Ave ⓣ212/362-6000, ⓦwww .metopera.org. Home of the renowned American Ballet Theater (ⓦwww.abt.org), which performs at the Opera House from early May into July. Prices for ballet at the Met range from $295 for the best seats at special performances to $15 or so for standing-room tickets, which go on sale the morning of the performance.

New York State Theater Lincoln Center, 65th St at Columbus Ave ⓣ212/870-5570, ⓦwww .lincolncenter.org. Lincoln Center's other major ballet venue is home to the revered New York City Ballet (ⓦwww.nycballet.com), which performs for a nine-week season each spring.

Cabaret and comedy

New York is one of America's **comedy** capitals, and there are several major clubs that feature professional performers, some of whom you'll recognize from television and film. There are also a good number of alternative comedy venues in downtown Manhattan that eschew the standard "comedy routine" fare for zanier "conceptual" comedy. Most mainstream clubs have shows every night, with two or more on weekends; it's usual to be charged a cover plus a two-drink minimum fee.

Cabaret has cooled off a bit of late, but there are still a couple of top venues where you can see some truly amazing stuff from the likes of Woody Allen, Elaine Stritch, and Eartha Kitt.

The list below represents the best-known comedy and cabaret venues in town, but performances can also be found at a multitude of bars, clubs, and art spaces all over the city. Check *Time Out New York* and the *Village Voice* for the fullest and most up-to-date listings.

Comedy clubs

Carolines 1626 Broadway, at 49th St
℡212/757-4100, ⒲www.carolines.com. Even
after 25 years, *Carolines* still books some of
the best stand-up acts in town; this is
where most of the biggest names perform.
Cover $15–30 Sun–Thurs, $25–40 Fri and
Sat. Two-drink minimum. Also has a
"supper lounge," *Comedy Nation*,
downstairs.

**Chicago City Limits Theater 318 W 53rd St,
at Eighth Ave** ℡212/888-5233, ⒲www
.chicagocitylimits.com. The oldest improvisa-
tion theater in New York. $15 admission
with a two-drink minimum.

**Comedy Cellar 117 MacDougal St, at Bleecker
St** ℡212/254-3480, ⒲www.comedycellar.com.
Popular Greenwich Village comedy club
now in its third decade. It's a good late-
night hangout. $10–15 cover plus two-drink
minimum.

Comic Strip Live 1568 Second Ave, at 81st St
℡212/861-9386, ⒲www.comicstriplive.com.
Famed showcase for stand-up comics and
young singers going for the big time. Cover
$15–20 plus two-drink minimum.

Dangerfield's 1118 First Ave, at 61st St
℡212/593-1650, ⒲www.dangerfields.com.
Vegas-style new-talent showcase founded
by Rodney Dangerfield. $15–20 cover with,
unusually, no minimum drink charge.

**Gotham Comedy Club 208 W 23rd St, between
Seventh and Eighth aves** ℡212/367-9000,
⒲www.gothamcomedyclub.com. A swanky
comedy venue in Chelsea, highly respected
by New York media types and those who
scout up-and-coming comics. Cover
$10–30 plus two-drink minimum.

**Stand-Up New York 236 W 78th St, at
Broadway** ℡212/595-0850, ⒲www
.standupny.com. Upper West Side all-ages
forum for established comics, many of
whom have appeared on *Leno* and
Letterman. Hosts the Toyota Comedy
Festival in June. Cover $12–16 plus two-
drink minimum – you're required to arrive a
half-hour before showtime, so call or
check the website for the night's schedule
before arriving.

🏃 **Upright Citizens Brigade Theater 307 W
26th St, between Eighth and Ninth aves**
℡212/366-9176, ⒲www.ucbtheater.com.
Consistently hilarious sketch-based and
improv comedy, seven nights a week.
You can sometimes catch *Saturday Night
Live* cast members in the ensemble.
Cover $5–8.

Cabarets

**Café Carlyle inside Carlyle Hotel, 35 E 76th St,
at Madison Ave** ℡212/744-1600, ⒲www
.thecarlyle.com. Though long-term resident
musician Bobby Short may have passed
away, there's still ample reason to come
here – it's where Woody Allen plays
clarinet every Mon, and divas like Eartha
Kitt and Elaine Stritch drop by for a week's
residency. If you don't want to eat (the
food's expensive and unexciting),
standing at the bar is just as fun – though
it's still a pricey night out. Cover $60–100,
jacket required.

Don't Tell Mama 343 W 46th St, at Ninth Ave
℡212/757-0788, ⒲www.donttellmamanyc.com.
Lively and convivial Midtown West piano bar
and cabaret featuring rising stars and
singing waitresses. Cover free–$20, two-
drink minimum.

Duplex 61 Christopher St, at Seventh Ave
℡212/255-5438, ⒲www.theduplex.com. West
Village cabaret popular with a boisterous
gay and tourist crowd. Barbra Streisand and
Lea Delaria have performed here (though
not together), and Off-Off-Broadway shows
like *Nunsense* played here in their infancy.
Has a rowdy piano bar downstairs and a
cabaret room upstairs. Open 4pm–4am.
Cover free–$20 plus two-drink minimum.

🏃 **Joe's Pub 425 Lafayette St, between
Astor Place and 4th St** ℡212/539-8500,
⒲www.publictheater.org. The hipper, late-
night arm of the Joseph Papp Public
Theater, this is one of the sharpest and
most popular music venues in the city, with
a wide range of cabaret acts nightly, from
Broadway crooner Donna McKechnie to
Norwegian folk icon and Hardanger fiddle
virtuoso Annbjørg Lien, and everything else
in between.

🏃 **The Oak Room at the Algonquin Hotel, 59
W 44th St, between Fifth and Sixth aves**
℡212/419-9331, ⒲www.algonquinhotel.com.
A site with some history (it has introduced
luminaries like Diana Krall and Michael
Feinstein), and perhaps the best place for
cabaret, though it's also an expensive
ticket. Cover $60–75, with mandatory
seating for dinner ($70) early Fri and Sat
shows. Sun show (brunch) is a relatively
reasonable $65.

Film

The locals grumbled when ticket prices in the city broke the $10 barrier in 2004, and despite continued increases – a show currently costs around $12 – New York is still a movie-lover's dream. There are plenty of state-of-the-art **movie theaters** all over the city; most are multiscreen complexes, and have all the charm of large airports, but they also have the advantages of superb sound, luxurious seating, and perfect sightlines. This is even the case for Times Square's cinemas, which in the past have tended to be small and noisy but now are typified by the towering megaplexes on 42nd Street.

For listings, your best bets are *Time Out New York* or freebies like the *Village Voice*; otherwise, check the local papers on Fridays, when the papers publish new reviews and schedules for the following week. For accurate showtimes, and to book a ticket in advance, call ☎212/777-FILM or check Ⓦwww.fandango.com and Ⓦwww.moviefone.com. Despite the per-ticket surcharge of around $1.50, it's often worth booking ahead: hot new releases usually sell out on opening weekend among the cutthroat New York cinema crowd. Since there's no reserved seating it often pays to get tickets to a must-see show in advance.

New York used to be one of the best cities in the world to see **old movies**, but the cinema landscape has changed considerably in recent years. Most of the old repertory houses that showed a regular menu of scratchy prints of old chestnuts and recent favorites have gone. In their place have sprung up an impressive selection of museums and revival houses. These new venues show an imaginatively programmed series of films – retrospectives of particular directors and actors, series from different countries, and programs of specific genres. In the case of visitors, what you get to see is a matter of chance: if you're lucky your trip may coincide with a retrospective of your favorite director or movie heart-throb.

We've highlighted our pick of New York's best movie theaters below, divided into those showing first-run mainstream and indie fare, and the venues that specialize in revivals and more obscure and experimental flicks, though the list is by no means exhaustive.

First-run movies

AMC Empire 25 234 W 42nd St, at Eighth Ave ☎212/398-3939. One of the few skyscraper multiplexes: 25 screens, all with stadium seating, soaring upward. Though it's usually crowded on weekends, it offers a decent mix of mainstream and arthouse films, and even has its own restaurant.

AMC Loews Lincoln Square & IMAX 1998 Broadway, at 68th St ☎212/336-5020. More and more mainstream films are being converted to IMAX technology and are being re-released on the huge screens here in high resolution just months after their original theatrical debuts. Worth checking out for sci-fi spectaculars, if nothing else. Oh, and the venue has 12 other first-run theaters besides, though it's often bedlam.

BAM Rose Cinemas 30 Lafayette Ave, at Ashland Place, Brooklyn ☎718/636-4100, Ⓦwww.bam.org. There are four screens at BAM's film site. The programming is mostly one or two current films mixed with a couple of classics or rarities; the year-round BAMcinématek series usually offers the most interesting choices.

Clearview's Ziegfeld 141 W 54th St, between Sixth and Seventh aves ☎212/765-7600. Sitting on the site of the old Ziegfeld Follies (hence the name), this midtown movie palace with its massive screen (one of the biggest in the country) is the place locals come to for an old-fashioned cinema experience. Numerous film premieres also take place here.

Regal Battery Park 11 102 North End Ave ☎212/945-3418. One great reason to visit: its out-of-the-way siting means it's possibly the quietest multiplex around.

Regal Union Square 14 850 Broadway, at 13th St ☎212/253-6266. Stadium seating venues in a great location.

Indies and foreign

Angelika Film Center 18 W Houston St, at Mercer St ☎212/995-2000, ⓦwww .angelikafilmcenter. Six-screen arthouse venue, with a rather overhyped reputation – screens are tiny, and the subway tends to rumble by at inopportune moments, rattling the subterranean rooms. Still, it's one of the few surviving venues for smaller films in the city.

IFC Center 323 Sixth Ave, at W 3rd St ☎212/924-7771, ⓦwww.ifccenter.com. One of the newest independents, with three screens, new indies, foreign and documentaries, and popular midnight shows. Features a much larger screen and a better sound system than you'll find at most other arthouses.

Landmark Sunshine Cinema 143 E Houston St, at First Ave ☎212/330-8182, ⓦwww .landmarktheatres.com. When this former Yiddish vaudeville house opened as a cinema in 2001, it quickly seized the Angelika's crown as the best place to see indie films, thanks to larger screens, better seating, and a less threadbare building.

Lincoln Plaza 1886 Broadway, at 62nd St ☎212/757-2280. This six-screen theater is as close as the Upper West Side gets to an arthouse venue. While it plays an occasional smaller mainstream Hollywood picture, it's known for acclaimed foreign and independent films.

Paris Fine Arts 4 W 58th St, at Fifth Ave ☎212/688-3800. An old-fashioned cinema (there's even a balcony) that specializes in foreign films as well as well-reviewed mainstream fare.

Revivals

Anthology Film Archives 32 Second Ave, at 2nd St ☎212/505-5181, ⓦwww.anthologyfilm archives.org. A bastion of experimental filmmaking. Programs of mind-bending abstraction, East Village grunge flicks, and

---

Film festivals and seasonal screenings

There always seems to be some **film festival** or other running in New York. The granddaddy of them all, the **New York Film Festival**, starts at the end of September and runs for two weeks at Lincoln Center. It's well worth catching if you're in town, though tickets for the most popular films can sell out very quickly. If you're determined to see something, watch the reviews in the *New York Times* each morning – when movies are panned, there's usually a cluster of people trying to sell off their tickets outside the theater that night. More info: ⓦwww.filmlinc.com.

See Chapter 33, "Parades and festivals," for info on the larger filmfests; here's a list of some of the smaller, but still worthwhile, festivals and seasonal screenings:

Asian American Film Festival ⓦwww.asiancinevision.org; July

Bryant Park Summer Film Festival (free; outdoor screenings of old Hollywood favorites on Mon nights at sunset) ⓦwww.bryantpark.org; June–August

GenArt Film Festival of American Independents ⓦwww.genart.org; April

Human Rights Watch International Film Festival ⓦwww.hrw.org; June

Margaret Mead Festival (anthropological films at the Museum of Natural History) ⓦwww.amnh.org; October or November

New Fest: Lesbian & Gay Film Festival ⓦwww.newfestival.org; June

New York Jewish Film Festival at Lincoln Center ⓦwww.filmlinc.com; January

River Flicks at Chelsea Piers (free screenings of cult crowd-pleasers) ⓦwww .hudsonriverpark.org; July–August

Socrates Sculpture Garden Film Festival (free screenings of classics every Wed starting at sunset in Long Island City, Queens) ⓦwww.socratessculpturepark.org; July–August

Tribeca Film Festival ⓦwww.tribecafilmfestival.org; late April to early May

auteur retrospectives all rub shoulders here. Tickets $8.

Chelsea Classics at the Clearview Chelsea, 260 W 23rd St, between Seventh and Eighth aves ☎212/691-5519. Thursday nights belong to campy classics (more often than not starring Joan Crawford and/or Bette Davis). Introduced by the blonde "lady" with green streaks, Hedda Lettuce. Tickets $6.50.

Film Forum 209 W Houston St, at Sixth Ave ☎212/727-8110, ⊛www.filmforum .org. The cozy three-screen Film Forum has an eccentric but famously popular program of new independent movies, documentaries, and foreign films, as well as a repertory program specializing in silent comedy, camp classics, and cult directors. All in, one of the best alternative spaces in town.

The Museum of Modern Art 11 W 53rd St, at Fifth Ave ☎212/708-9480, ⊛www.moma.org. MoMA is famous among local cinephiles for its vast collection of films, its exquisite programming, and its regular audience of cantankerous senior citizens. The movies themselves range from Hollywood screwball comedies to hand-painted Super 8. Tickets $10.

Museum of the Moving Image 35th Ave, at 36th St, Astoria, Queens ☎718/784-0077, ⊛www.ammi.org. The AMMI is usually well worth a trip out to Queens, either for the pictures – which are often serious director

retrospectives and silent films, with a strong emphasis on cinematographers – or for the cinema museum itself (see p.249 for review). Although the place is currently undergoing renovation through the end of 2009, films will continue to screen in Queens and Manhattan locations (call ☎718/784-0077 for schedule).

Symphony Space 2537 Broadway, at 95th St ☎212/864-5400, ⊛www.symphonyspace.org. A varied and often surprising program of festivals (including one for shorts), special director's series and weekend double features.

Two Boots Pioneer Theater 155 E 3rd St, at Ave A ☎212/254-3300, ⊛www.twoboots.com. Sun nights are for short films, Tues for rarely seen and underrated gems, and the rest of the week is devoted to themed program-ming throughout the year. Tickets $10.

Walter Reade Theater Lincoln Center, 165 W 65th St, at Broadway ☎212/875-5600, ⊛www .filmlinc.com. Programmed by the Film Society of Lincoln Center, the Walter Reade is simply the best place in town to see great films. This beautiful, modern theater has perfect sightlines, a huge screen, and impeccable acoustics. The emphasis is on foreign films and the great auteurs; it's also home to many of the city's festivals (see box, p.369). Tickets $11.

Literary events and readings

New York has long been viewed as a **literary mecca**. The city's proliferation of competitive bookstores means that you can see someone performing wordy wonders any night of the week. (For recommendations on specific stores, see Chapter 31, "Shopping," and see Chapter 33, "Parades and festivals," for book festivals.)

92nd Street Y Unterberg Poetry Center 1395 Lexington Ave ☎212/415-5500, ⊛www.92y.org. Quite simply, the definitive place to hear all your Booker, Pulitzer, and Nobel prize–winning favorites, as well as many other exciting new talents. Name almost any American literary great – from Tennessee Williams to Langston Hughes – and they've probably appeared here; expect the current line-up to be just as blockbusting. Additional programs are held at 92Y Tribeca (200 Hudson St, at Canal St).

Barnes & Noble The city's numerous B&Ns host a surprisingly diverse range of readings

almost every night of the week. See p.387 for store locations and contact details; the Union Square branch generally gets the highest-profile authors and events.

Half King 505 W 23rd St, at Tenth Ave ☎212/462-4300, ⊛www.thehalfking.com. Large, divey bar owned by macho author Sebastian Junger (*The Perfect Storm*): it's not surprising, then, that most Monday nights are devoted to free readings by a big-name contemporary author – Jerry Stahl and Edna O'Brien have both appeared. On other occasions there's an intriguing program centered on great

Poetry slams and readings

Poetry and story slamming is a literary version of freestyle rapping, in which performers take turns presenting stories and poems (often mostly or entirely improvised) on stage. At their best, slams can be thrilling, raw, and very funny (not to mention competitive – many feature a judges' panel). We've pulled out the three best places to sample New York slams, including the eatery where it all began, the *Nuyorican Poets Café*.

Bowery Poetry Club 308 Bowery, at Houston St ℡212/614-0505, ⊛www .bowerypoetry.com. A combination café/bar/bookstore with a small stage at the back, this community-focused space is owned by Bob Holman, who used to run *Nuyorican* (see below). There are occasional big names on stage, but it's mostly impressively enthusiastic amateurs. The space is quite busy, with several different events (even the nonliterary: drag king/queen bingo? BadAss Burlesque?) in the course of an evening.

The Moth (at Storyville Center for the Spoken Word) 330 W 38th St, between Ninth and Tenth aves ℡212/742-0551, ⊛www.themoth.org. Offbeat literary company that's known for its story slams – open-mic nights where amateurs vie for a five-minute on-stage storytelling spot. There's also the yearly Moth Ball (Nov) that sends the funds raised from ticket sales to local charities. Though most events take place at the Moth's home base here, there are also sporadic offshoots round town – check the website for schedules.

Nuyorican Poets Café 236 E 3rd St, between aves B and C ℡212/505-8183, ⊛www.nuyorican.org. Alphabet City's *Nuyorican* remains one of the most talked-about performance spaces in town. Its poetry slams are what made it famous, but there are also theater and film-script readings, occasionally with well-known downtown stars.

magazine writing read by a group of journalists. Check the calendar on the site for schedules.

KGB 85 E 4th St ℡212/505-3360, ⊛www .kgbbar.com. Grubby but welcoming little bar that hosts free readings every Sun and Tues, though there are readings (everything from poetry to non fiction to items like "Kinky Jews' Evening of Jewish Lit-Erotica") most other nights as well. To read here is a prestigious honor; expect to see top names, like Michael Cunningham. Call or check the

website for up-to-date schedules. The building also houses the Kraine Theater (p.362).

Symphony Space 2537 Broadway, at 95th St ℡212/864-5400, ⊛www.symphonyspace.org. The highly acclaimed Selected Shorts series, in which actors read the short fiction of a variety of authors (everyone from James Joyce to David Sedaris), usually packs the Symphony Space theater; Bloomsday on Broadway, a one-day celebration of James Joyce's *Ulysses*, is in its 27th year.

Gay and lesbian New York

here are few places in America – indeed in the world – where **gay culture** thrives as it does in New York. Open gays and lesbians are considered mainstream here – so much so that the city is one of the few places that Republican administrations avidly court gay voters. By some estimates, about twenty percent of New Yorkers identify themselves as gay or lesbian; when you add in bisexual and transgender individuals, the figure climbs even higher – as it does when you take into account the number of gay visitors who come to New York each day.

The largely liberal orientation of New York politics has been generally beneficial to the gay community since the 1969 riots at the *Stonewall Bar* marked the onset of the gay-rights movement (see box, p.109). Nonetheless, significant issues still remain hotly disputed, **marriage equality** most of all. While the New York State Supreme Court ruled gay marriage illegal in 2006, with former governor Eliot Spitzer's promises of equality derailed upon his resignation, Spitzer's replacement, David Patterson, has vowed to continue the movement toward gay marriage (and all its associated benefits, like survivorship rights and access to family health-care plans). The city passed domestic-partner legislation, affecting both gay and heterosexual couples, in 1998, but with the bill's limited scope, many same-sex couples have opted for Vermont civil unions and Canadian marriages, even though they were not recognized here. But it seems that may be about to change: in May 2008, Governor Patterson issued a directive that required state agencies to recognize same-sex marriages officiated elsewhere as valid in New York.

The rights of **transgender** individuals are also contentious – New York City has a 2002 law prohibiting discrimination on the basis of gender identity or expression, but transgender people are commonly prevented from using public bathrooms. Within the New York City gay community itself, today's major battles revolve largely around the nihilistic practice of "barebacking" (having unprotected sex with strangers), as well as gay-identity issues within the African-American community, where homophobia is surprisingly prevalent (though by no means omnipresent).

Socially, gay men and lesbians are fairly visible in the city, and while it's not recommended that gay couples hold hands in public before checking out the territory, there are a few **neighborhoods** where the gay community makes up the majority of the population. **Chelsea** (especially Eighth Ave between 14th and 23rd sts), the **East Village/Lower East Side**, and Brooklyn's **Park Slope** are the largest of these, and have all but replaced the West Village as gay New York's hub. A strong gay presence still lingers in the vicinity of **Christopher Street** in the West Village, but it's in Chelsea that gay male socializing is most ubiquitous and open. Lesbians will find large communities in laid-back Park Slope and around East Houston Street. Other neighborhoods with a strong gay and lesbian presence are Morningside Heights (Columbia University's college town), Queens' Astoria, and Brooklyn's Prospect Heights (mainly residential), DUMBO, and Williamsburg. All of the city's alternative communities come together in major events like **Pride Week** in late June (Pride Month), which includes a rally, Dyke March, Dyke Ball, Brooklyn Pride, Black Pride, innumerable parties, and the infamous (if commercialized and sweltering) **Lesbian & Gay Pride Parade** (see p.419).

Several free weekly **newspapers and magazines** serve New York's gay community: *Gay City News* (Ⓦ www.gaycitynews.com), *New York Blade* (Ⓦ www.nyblade.com), *Next* (for men; Ⓦ www.nextmagazine.net), *HX* (for men; Ⓦ www.hx.com), and *GO NYC* (for women; trans-friendly; Ⓦ www .gonycmagazine.com). (*Next* includes an extremely handy map in each issue.) You'll find these at the LGBT Community Services Center (see below), at street-corner boxes, bars, cafés, lesbian and gay bookstores, and occasionally at newsstands, where glossy national mags such as *Out, POZ, Girlfriends, Diva, MetroSource*, and others are also available. The listings in *Time Out New York* are helpful as well. If you're looking for a date, some action, or just people to party with while you're here, post a personal (or respond to someone else's) on craigslist (free; Ⓦ newyork.craigslist.org), the popular online message-board. Other useful resources are listed throughout this chapter.

Resources

The Audre Lorde Project 85 S Oxford St, Brooklyn ☎ 718/596-0342, Ⓦ www.alp.org. Center for LGBT people of color.

Callen-Lorde Community Health Center 356 W 18th St, between Eighth and Ninth aves ☎ 212/271-7200, Ⓦ www.callen-lorde.org. LGBT medical center and clinic. A good place to seek privacy-sensitive medical attention, with sliding price plan based on income.

Gay Men's Health Crisis (GMHC) 119 W 24th St, between Sixth and Seventh aves ☎ 212/367-1000, Ⓦ www.gmhc.org. Despite the name, this incredible organization – the oldest and largest not-for-profit AIDS organization in the world – provides testing, information, and referrals to everyone: gay, straight, and transgender.

The Lesbian, Gay, Bisexual & Transgender Community Services Center 208 W 13th St, west of Seventh Ave ☎ 212/620-7310, Ⓦ www .gaycenter.org. The Center – which celebrated its 25th year in 2008 – houses well over a hundred groups and organizations, sponsors workshops, parties, 12-step programs, movie nights, guest speakers, youth services, programs for parents, and lots more. Even the bulletin boards are fascinating.

SAGE: Senior Action in a Gay Environment 305 Seventh Ave, at 27th St, 6th floor ☎ 212/741-2247, Ⓦ www.sageusa.org. Support and activities for gay seniors. Most activities take place at the Center, at 208 W 13th St (see above), where the group maintains another small office.

Sylvia Rivera Law Project ☎ 212/337-8550, Ⓦ www.srlp.org. Legal services and organization for transgender and intersexed individuals.

Accommodation

The following places to stay are friendly to gays and lesbians and convenient for the scene. The prices at the end of each listing represent the lowest price for a double in high season, excluding taxes.

Chelsea Pines Inn 317 W 14th St, between Eighth and Ninth aves ☎1-888/546-2700, ⓦwww .chelseapinesinn.com. Housed in an old brownstone on the Greenwich Village/Chelsea border, this hotel offers clean, comfortable, "shabby chic" rooms. Guests are mostly gay. Best to book in advance. $160

Colonial House Inn 318 W 22nd St, between Eighth and Ninth aves ☎212/243-9669, ⓦwww .colonialhouseinn.com. You won't mind that this B&B is a little worn around the edges – its attractive design and contributions to the GMHC make for a feel-good experience. Only deluxe rooms include en-suite bathrooms, while some rooms have refrigerators and fireplaces. Expanded continental breakfast. $110

Hotel 17 255 E 17th St, between Second and Third aves ☎212/475-2845, ⓦwww.hotel17ny .com. Woody Allen's *Manhattan Murder Mystery* was filmed here, and the 120 rooms have been tastefully redone, though some of them still share baths. In a good neighborhood, too. $150

Incentra Village House 32 Eighth Ave, between 12th and Jane sts ☎212/206-0007, ⓦwww .incentravillage.com. Some of the eleven Early American–look studios in this residential neighborhood townhouse come with kitchenettes; there are also two suites, one with access to a private garden. Three-night cancellation policy and three-night minimum stay at weekends. $169

Arts and culture

There's always a good amount of gay and gay-friendly performance and visual art on in New York, much of it in mixed venues: check the listings in the *Village Voice*, *Time Out New York*, and the free papers noted in the introduction to this chapter. You'll only be able to scratch the surface of New York's gay scene on a brief visit. If you're here for a longer trip, and are so inclined, check out "out" sports teams and women's self-defense organizations, which provide a terrific opportunity to meet people. Contact the LGBT Community Services Center for more information (see p.373).

Center for Lesbian and Gay Studies CUNY Graduate Center, 365 Fifth Ave, between 34th and 35th sts ☎212/817-1955, ⓦwww.clags .org. Fascinating talks and seminars featuring luminaries such as Judith Butler. Particular attention is paid to international, transgender, and disability studies.

Lesbian Herstory Archives 484 14th St, Park Slope, Brooklyn ☎718/768-DYKE, ⓦwww .lesbianherstoryarchives.org. Original materials on dyke life, mostly throughout the past century. Old-school and inspiring. Open a few hours a day Sat–Wed on a variable schedule, so call ahead or visit the website for times.

Leslie-Lohman Gay Art Foundation 26 Wooster St, between Grand and Canal sts ☎212/ 431-2609, ⓦwww.leslielohman.org. The Foundation maintains an archive and permanent collection of lesbian and gay art,

with galleries open to the public during shows. Tues–Sat noon–6pm.

MIX (the New York Lesbian and Gay Experimental Film/Video Festival) ☎212/742-8880, ⓦwww.mixnyc.org. This celebrated annual festival, which takes place in Nov, offers politically radical and technically avant-garde films.

Museum of Sex 233 Fifth Ave, at 27th St ☎212/689-6337, ⓦwww.mosex.org. Provocative explorations of sex throughout history; plenty of LGBT material, plus talks and workshops. Admission $14.50; ages 18 and up only.

National Archive of LGBT History/The Pat Parker/Vito Russo Center Library at the LGBT Community Services Center (see p.373) ☎212/620-7310. Terrific, interesting archive of gay life in America, and a lending library with 12,000 titles. The archive is open Thurs

6–8pm, and also by appointment Sun (afternoons) and Mon–Wed (evenings).
New Festival (aka New York Lesbian and Gay Film Festival) ⊤212/571-2170, ⓦwww .newfestival.org. This not-to-be-missed annual festival kicks off Pride Month (also known as June).
New York City Gay Men's Chorus ⊤212/344-1777, ⓦwww.nycgmc.org. Wildly popular 250-member gay men's choral group that has sung with Cyndi Lauper and other famous names at major venues like Carnegie Hall. Call or check website for concert schedule and membership information. Parent organization Big Apple Performing Arts handles three other gay-themed choral groups as well.

Cafés and restaurants

Many restaurants in Chelsea and the Village (both West and East) are either gay-owned or operated, and most of those that don't have a specific agenda welcome gay travelers. The spaces listed below are all perennial favorites, though the list is by no means exhaustive; a short conversation with a shop owner or fellow traveler will likely turn up a host of other dining options, in addition to those included in the Chelsea, East Village, and West Village sections of Chapter 25 (Restaurants).

Bluestockings 172 Allen St, between Stanton and Rivington sts ⊤212/777-6028. Fair-trade café and lefty bookstore that functions as an informal center of the lesbian and bi community. Hosts Dyke Knitting Circle, as well as readings, performances, meetings, and screenings.
Cafeteria 119 Seventh Ave, at W 17th St ⊤212/414-1717. Don't let the name fool you: *Cafeteria* may be open 24hrs and serve great meatloaf, and macaroni and cheese, but it's no truckstop. It's more like a transplanted Miami Beach café: the modern, plastic-accented interior is always packed with beautiful diners and a sexy waitstaff.
Cowgirl 519 Hudson St, at W 10th St ⊤212/633-1133. Genial eatery with a Texas/Western theme. It's big on burger-and-bbq offerings, and hosts a sometimes lively bar scene among the kitschy décor.
East of Eighth 254 W 23rd St, between Seventh and Eighth aves ⊤212/352-0075. Excellent dishes with a variety of influences; crabcakes, upscale pork loin, pizza and pasta sit alongside matzoh-ball soup, tapas from the Caribbean, Vietnamese spring rolls, Oaxacan guacamole, and Middle Eastern *meze*. Reasonably priced.
Manatus 340 Bleecker St, between Christopher and W 10th sts ⊤212/989-7042. Laid-back and comfortable diner on one of the Village's more active streets.
Petite Abeille 466 Hudson St, between Barrow and Grove sts ⊤212/741-6479. Charming, tiny spot specializing in omelets, grilled sandwiches, and French and Belgian favorites. Locals enjoy the *moules marinières* ($17) and the *croque madame* ($11).
Tea Lounge 837 Union St, between Sixth and Seventh aves, Park Slope, Brooklyn ⊤718/789-2762. Spacious café, and the de facto headquarters of a community of gays and lesbians, tea aficionados (it offers about 60 varieties) and knitters. One of two Slope locations; there's another in Cobble Hill (Brooklyn).

Bars

Gay men's bars cover the spectrum from relaxed pubs to hard-hitting clubs full of glamour and attitude. Most of the more-established places are in Greenwich Village and Chelsea, and along Avenue A in the East Village. Park Slope in Brooklyn and the East Village are the centers of the **lesbian** universe, while dyke bars and club nights are cropping up at a crazy rate in Chelsea and along Hudson Street in the West Village. (Things used to tend to get raunchier as one headed farther west to the bars and cruisers of the wild West Side

Highway, but the area has largely been tamed; the famed Meatpacking District has transitioned from transgendered streetwalker turf to upwardly mobile baby-stroller playland.) In Brooklyn, Williamsburg has become a major hotspot for young, hip, mixed LGBT club nights. Check local weeklies for current listings.

Mainly for men

Barracuda 275 W 22nd St, between Seventh and Eighth aves ☎212/645-8613. A favorite spot in New York's gay scene, and pretty laid-back for Chelsea. Two-for-one happy hour 4–9pm during the week, crazy drag shows, and a look that changes several times a year.

The Boiler Room 86 E 4th St, between First and Second aves ☎212/254-7536. Used to be one of the hottest bars in the city but now it's really just a local NYU bar with a pool table. While still a good hangout (mostly gay but with some lesbian presence), don't expect any atmosphere; it's always got the look of a retiree's garage during the summer.

Brandy's Piano Bar 235 E 84th St, between Second and Third aves ☎212/744-4949. Handsome uptown cabaret/piano bar with a crazy, mixed, and generally mature clientele. Definitely worth a visit.

The Cock 29 Second Ave, between E 1st and 2nd sts ☎212/777-6254. The popular phrase "hot mess" is perhaps the best way to sum up *The Cock* (they prefer "from bitch to butch" or "from glitter to gutter"). Trashy, sexy, and – entirely depending on your way of thinking – fun.

The Dugout 185 Christopher St, at Weehawken St ☎212/242-9113. Right by the river, this West Village hangout with a pool table and video games is the place to go for cheap beers… or bears (the Metrobears social group holds regular Friday-evening pub nights).

The Eagle 554 W 28th St, between Tenth and Eleventh aves ☎646/473-1866. The place for leather-bar fans, with a super-cool industrial feel and bi-level, multi-room layout, plus an open roof terrace that's inevitably the most packed part of the bar. Dress code some nights.

Eastern Bloc 505 E 6th St, between aves A and B ☎212/777-2555. Think high-class dive bar with a vaguely Russian motif. Drink specials every night, go-go boys on the weekends. Go early for a chilled-out neighborhood crowd, and later for the East Village mob scene.

Excelsior 390 Fifth Ave, between 6th and 7th sts, Park Slope, Brooklyn ☎718/832-1599. The amusingly versatile jukebox, friendly rather than overtly cruisy clientele, and two outside spaces make this Brooklyn's best bar for guys.

g 223 W 19th St, between Seventh and Eighth aves ☎212/929-1085. Nearly as stylish as its "guppie" clientele, this deservedly popular lounge also features a different DJ every night of the week.

GYM 167 Eighth Ave, between 17th and 18th sts ☎212/337-2439. Casual, friendly, non-scene hangout that features large-screen TVs, video games, pool table, and smokers patio. Rare sports bar where you can actually watch a game.

Marie's Crisis 59 Grove St, between Seventh Ave S and Bleecker St ☎212/243-9323. Well-known cabaret/piano bar popular with tourists and locals alike. Features old-time singing sessions nightly. Often packed, always fun.

Metropolitan 559 Lorimer Ave, at Metropolitan Ave, Brooklyn ☎718/599-4444. "Hipster" hangout sans (much) attitude. Every other Sat hosts 80s night.

Phoenix 447 E 13th St, between Ave A and First Ave ☎212/477-9979. This relaxed East Village pub is much loved by the so-not-scene boys who live there, and other guys who just want reasonably priced drinks and a fun crowd.

Rawhide 212 Eighth Ave, at 21st St ☎212/242-9332. Hell-bent for leather, Chelsea's Rough Rider Room is a popular stand-by – it's been here literally forever and still draws a good (but aging) crowd seven nights a week. Opens at 10am for those who like beer for breakfast. Closes late, too.

Stonewall 53 Christopher St, between Waverly Place and Seventh Ave S ☎212/488-2705. Yes, that *Stonewall*, site of the seminal 1969 riot, mostly refurbished and flying the pride flag like they own it – which, one could say, they do. Bingo, DJs, drag variety shows, and comedy nights; call ahead to see what's on.

Therapy 348 W 52nd St, between Eighth and Ninth aves ☎212/397-1700. Sleek bar/lounge geared to Midtowners and the post-work drinking crowd. DJ sets (weekends) and drag shows, washed down with signature cocktails that keep up the psychological theme like the Gender Bender (citron vodka, lemonade, and watermelon juice) and the Anorexic (rum and diet Red Bull in a Splenda-rimmed glass).

Vlada 331 W 51st St, between Eighth and Ninth aves ⊤212/974-8030. Really, another Russian-leaning gay bar? This one couldn't be more different: it's in Midtown West, with a decidedly posh and trendy feel. Infused vodka is the house specialty: the fifteen options range from cherry to tarragon.

Mainly for women

Cubbyhole 281 W 12th St, at W 4th St ⊤212-243-9041. This welcoming, kitschy, small but famous West Village dyke bar is something

of a required stopover, since it's been here forever.

Ginger's 363 Fifth Ave, between 5th and 6th sts, Park Slope, Brooklyn ⊤718/788-0924. The best dyke bar in New York is this dark, laid-back Park Slope joint with a pool table, outdoor space, and plenty of convivial company.

Henrietta Hudson 438 Hudson St, at Morton St ⊤212/924-3347, ⊛www.henriettahudsons .com. Laid-back in the afternoon but brimming by night, especially on weekends, this is the top lesbian place in Manhattan. Weekly theme nights.

Clubs

Gay and lesbian **club nights** in New York (often held weekly at nondenominational nightspots) can be some of the most outrageous in the world. Check *Time Out New York*, *HX* (⊛www.hx.com), and *GO NYC* (⊛www.gonyc magazine.com) for up-to-date info. The clubs and nights listed below have stood the test of time; all have their coveted cabaret license, so go forth and dance.

Don Hill's 511 Greenwich St, at Spring St ⊤212/219-2850, ⊛www.donhills.com. An open-to-all-up-for-anything place, where you will find Britpop drag queens, mod rock dominatrixes, and mohawked Johnny Rotten wannabes. Pole dancers and porn complete the vibe.

Escuelita 301 W 39th St, at Eighth Ave ⊤212/631-0588. This is one of the city's very best gay clubs, and also popular with the crowd from New Jersey. The Latino-flavored party is all about kitsch, dress-up, salsa, cruising, and drag. Thurs through Sun, 18 and up.

The Monster 80 Grove St, at Sheridan Square ⊤212/924-3558. Large, campy bar with

drag cabaret, piano, and downstairs dance floor. Very popular, especially with tourists, yet has a strong "neighborhood" feel. Every night brings something else, from amateur and professional go-go boys to Latin grooves and a Sunday tea dance (5.30pm).

Splash 50 W 17th St, between Fifth and Sixth aves ⊤212/691-0073, ⊛www.splashbar.com. Large (10,000 sq ft), loud club with all the trimmings: smoke, lights, and go-go boys on pedestals. Basement lounge. Open daily; cover charge $20 after 10pm on weekends.

The Web 40 E 58th St, between Park and Madison aves ⊤212/308-1546. Spacious dance club for the gay Asian population.

Sex

A number of delightful and perfectly legal sex ("play") parties and establishments have sprung up throughout the city. Some are invitation-only; some welcome LGBT men and women to play in the same space; many are BDSM-oriented. Alcohol is not served at any.

Bear Hunt ⊛www.bearhuntnyc.com. Weekly get-together for the chubby, the hairy, and those who appreciate them. Non-discretionary door; showers and refreshments offered.

New York Renegades ⊛www.nyrenegades.com. Hard-core gay men's BDSM organization that hosts play parties, bar nights, and retreats.

S.O.S. (Society of Spankers) 250 W 26th St ⊛www.paddlesnyc.com/sos. The original NYC spanking party, every other Thurs ($25).

SPAM 210 Fifth Ave, at Union St, Brooklyn ⊤718/789-4053. Monthly Park Slope play party for the entire LGBT community. Underwear only. Usually fourth Sat each month; admission is $20 for men, $10 for women.

Submit 253 E Houston St, between aves A and B ☎718/789-4053, ⓦwww.submitparty.com. This trendy, hot-and-heavy S&M girl party

welcomes novices, voyeurs, serious players, and anyone who can't afford such good play equipment. Demos and theme nights abound. Women and trans only, 18 and over.

Religion

There are numerous **gay religious organizations** in New York; many of these have regular meetings and services at the LGBT Community Services Center (see p.373).

Congregation Beth Simchat Torah 57 Bethune St, at Washington St ☎212/929-9498, ⓦwww.cbst.org. LGBT synagogue with Fri 8.30pm and Sat 10am Shabbat services, plus larger services (Fri 7pm) at the Church of the Holy Apostles in Chelsea, 296 Ninth Ave, at 28th St (☎212/807-6799).

Dignity New York ☎646/418-7039, ⓦwww.dignityny.org. Large, gay Catholic

organization that holds numerous events, including services on Sun at 7.30pm at St John's Episcopal Church, 218 W 11th St, at Waverly Place.

Metropolitan Community Church 446 W 36th St, between Ninth and Tenth aves ☎212/629-7440, ⓦwww.mccny.org. Services each Sun at 9am and 7pm.

Shops

Babeland 94 Rivington St, between Orchard and Ludlow sts ☎212/375-1701; also 43 Mercer St, between Grand and Broome sts ☎212/966-2120, ⓦwww.babeland.com. Superlative, sophisticated feminist (and queer) sex-toy store, perhaps the best in the nation. Sex workshops fill up quickly.

▲ Babeland

The Leather Man 111 Christopher St ☎212/243-5339. Leather accessories, clothes, and the like.

Nasty Pig 265A W 19th St, between Seventh and Eighth aves ☎212/691-6067. Home-grown fetish store with a friendly attitude.

Nickel 77 Eighth Ave, at 14th St ☎212/242-3203. Housed in an old bank building, this men-only spa also sells hair and skin care products from various companies.

The Oscar Wilde Memorial Bookshop 15 Christopher St, between Sixth and Seventh aves ☎212/255-8097. An unbeatable selection of gay-and-lesbian-themed books and a major community spot.

Rainbows & Triangles 192 Eighth Ave, between 19th and 20th sts ☎212/627-2166. Another good source for fiction and nonfiction as well as coffee-table pictorial books. The store carries T-shirts, "adult" gear and videos, candles, CDs, cards, and seasonal gifts too.

Universal Gear 140 Eighth Ave, between 16th and 17th sts ☎212/206-9119. Stylish garb for gays, and a huge underwear selection.

Commercial galleries

A rt, especially contemporary art, is big in New York. Although the city is frankly no longer the center of the world art scene – the twentieth century, with artists like Willem De Kooning, Jackson Pollock, Mark Rothko, Andy Warhol, Ellsworth Kelly, and Agnes Martin all living in the city, was really the city's creative heyday – there's still plenty here to interest contemporary-art lovers. There are several hundred **galleries** in New York, covering a wide range of aesthetics, cultural viewpoints, and styles; most of the prominent ones are in Soho and Chelsea. Even if you have no intention of buying, many of these high-profile galleries are well worth a visit, as are some of the alternative spaces, run on a nonprofit basis and less commercial than mainstream galleries.

Broadly speaking, Manhattan galleries fall into five main areas: the **Upper East Side** in the 60s and 70s for antiques and the occasional (minor) Old Master; **57th Street** between Sixth and Park avenues for important modern and contemporary names; **Soho** for established artists; **Chelsea** for the trendy and up-and-coming; and **Tribeca** for more experimental displays.

Some of the most vibrant gallery scenes in the city are to be found outside Manhattan, however, in **DUMBO** and **Williamsburg** (in Brooklyn) and the neighborhood of **Long Island City** (Queens). Recently, Williamsburg has "done a Soho" and become almost as expensive as downtown Manhattan in terms of housing, pushing less-established artists farther out to Greenpoint and Bushwick. There are still lots of spaces, though, and a few worthwhile galleries are listed if you want to check out what's going on in the independent world of art in New York City.

Several of the city's more exclusive galleries are invitation-only, but most accept walk-ins (although sometimes with a bit of attitude). Pick up a copy of the *Gallery Guide* (Ⓦ www.galleryguide.org) – available upon request in the

Art tours

One of the best ways to see the top galleries in the city is through an art tour. Here are a couple of your best bets:

Art Entrée 48–18 Purves St, Queens ℡718/391-0011, Ⓦ www.artentree.com. This excellent Long Island City–based company provides studio, gallery, museum, architecture, and public art tours throughout NYC. Note that they're personalized, and therefore, expensive.

New York Gallery Tours 526 W 26th St, Manhattan ℡212/946-1548, Ⓦ www .nygallerytours.com. First-rate tours of Chelsea's galleries, including $20 Saturday visits to the neighborhood's "eight most fascinating shows," as well as $300 group tours for up to 12 people, available any day of the week.

larger galleries – for listings of current shows and each gallery's specialty. The weekly *Time Out New York* offers broad listings of the major commercial galleries. Admission is almost always free; the galleries that do charge a fee are considered a bit tacky.

Listed below are some of the more interesting exhibition spaces in Manhattan and elsewhere. Opening times are roughly Tuesday through Saturday 10am to 6pm, but note that many galleries have truncated summer hours and are closed during August. The best time to gallery-hop is on weekday afternoons; the absolute worst time is on Saturday, when out-of-towners flood into the city's trendier areas to do just that. Openings – usually free and easily identified by crowds of people drinking wine from plastic cups – are excellent times to view work, eavesdrop on art-world gossip, and even eat free food. A list of openings appears, again, in the *Gallery Guide*.

Tribeca and Soho galleries

14 Sculptors Gallery 332 Bleecker St, Suite K35 ☎212/966-5790, Ⓦwww.14sculptors.com. Just as the name implies, an exhibition space formed by fourteen diverse sculptors to display noncommercial figurative and abstract contemporary art. Open by appointment only.
The Drawing Center 35 Wooster St ☎212/219-2166, Ⓦwww.drawingcenter.org. Presents shows of contemporary and historical works on paper, from emerging artists to the sketches of the Great Masters.
Louis Meisel 141 Prince St ☎212/677-1340, Ⓦwww.meiselgallery.com. Specializes in

Photorealism – past shows have included Richard Estes and Chuck Close – as well as Abstract Illusionism (owner Meisel claims to have invented both terms). Also exhibits saucy American pin-ups.
O K Harris 383 W Broadway ☎212/431-3600, Ⓦwww.okharris.com. Named for a mythical traveling gambler, O K is the gallery of Ivan Karp, a cigar-munching champion of Super-Realism. One of the first Soho galleries and, although not as influential as it once was, still worth a look.

Chelsea galleries

The galleries listed below are housed in independent spaces, but there are also several large **warehouses** in this neighborhood that hold multiple galleries and are worth exploring as a group, if you have time.

303 Gallery 525 W 22nd St ☎212/255-1121, Ⓦwww.303gallery.com. 303 Gallery shows works in a comprehensive range of media by fairly well-established contemporary artists.
Allen Sheppard Gallery 530 W 25th St ☎212/989-9919. One of the most interesting painter galleries in the district, this space exhibits great stuff from the likes of David Konigberg, Willy Lenski, and Sonya Sklaroff.
Barbara Gladstone Gallery 515 W 24th St ☎212/206-9300, Ⓦwww.gladstonegallery.com. Paintings, sculpture, and photography by hot contemporary artists like Matthew Barney and Rosemarie Trockel.
Edward Thorp 210 Eleventh Ave, 6th floor ☎212/691-6565, Ⓦwww.edwardthorpgallery.com. Mainstream contemporary American,

South American, and European painting and sculpture. Highlights of their roster include painter Matthew Blackwell and sculptor Deborah Butterfield.
Feature 5276 Bowery ☎212/675-7772, Ⓦwww.featureinc.com. This former Chicago gallery tends toward briefly exhibiting fairly cerebral modern artists (such as the controversial Richard Kern of "New York Girls" fame) rather than extensively highlighting a select few.
Gagosian Gallery 555 W 24th St ☎212/741-1111, Ⓦwww.gagosian.com. A stalwart fixture on the New York scene, the Gagosian features both modern and contemporary works, including pieces by artists like Damien Hirst, David Salle, Eric Fischl, Richard Serra, and photographer Alec Soth,

who's made a big mark of late. There's also a branch uptown, at 980 Madison Ave.

Gavin Brown's Enterprise 620 Greenwich St ⊤212/627-5258. An ultra-hip space featuring the young, cool, and fearless of the mixed-media art world.

Greene Naftali 508 W 26th St, 8th floor ⊤212/463-7770, ⓦwww.greenenaftaligallery.com. A wide-open, airy gallery noted for its top-notch large group shows and conceptual installations. Very cool stuff.

Lehmann Maupin 540 W 26th St ⊤212/255-2923, ⓦwww.lehmannmaupin.com. Shows a range of established international and American contemporary artists working in a wide range of media, among them Tracey Emin, Juergen Teller, and Gilbert & George. Also showcases diverse new talent.

Mary Boone Gallery 541 W 24th St ⊤212/752-2929, ⓦwww.maryboonegallery.com. An extension of Boone's uptown gallery (745 Fifth Ave; see p.382), this Chelsea space has facilities for large-scale works and installations by the up-and-coming darlings of the

▲ Mary Boone Gallery

art world. At least a couple of the artists nurtured by Boone – David Salle and Julian Schnabel – have achieved superstar status.

Matthew Marks Gallery 522 W 22nd St ⊤212/243-0200, ⓦwww.matthewmarks.com. The centerpiece of Chelsea's art scene, Matthew Marks shows pieces by such well-known minimalist and abstract artists as Cy Twombly and Ellsworth Kelly. They also have nearby branches at 523 W 24th St and 521 W 21st St.

Paula Cooper 521 & 534 W 21st St ⊤212/255-1105. An influential gallery that shows a wide range of contemporary painting, sculpture, drawings, prints, and photographs, particularly minimalist and conceptual works, and even has a recording label, Dog w/a Bone.

Robert Miller 524 W 26th St ⊤212/366-4774, ⓦwww.robertmillergallery.com. Exceptional shows of twentieth-century artists (Lee Krasner, Joan Nelson, and Bernar Venet, to name but a few). This is one of New York's true big-gun galleries.

Sikkema Jenkins 530 W 22nd St ⊤212/929-2262, ⓦwww.sikkemajenkins.com. This somewhat controversial space often features exhibits with a definite political slant. Recently they've been focusing on illustration.

Sonnabend 536 W 22nd St ⊤212/627-1018, ⓦwww.sonnabendgallery.com. A top gallery featuring painting, photography, and video from contemporary American and European artists. Regular exhibitions from the likes of Robert Morris and Gilbert & George.

Sperone Westwater 415 W 13th St ⊤212/999-7337, ⓦwww.speronewestwater.com. High-quality European and American painting and works on paper. Artists have included Francesco Clemente, Frank Moore, and Susan Rothenberg.

Team Gallery 83 Grand St ⊤212/279-9219, ⓦwww.teamgal.com. Beautiful, voyeuristic, and cutting-edge work by artists such as Tracey Emin and Genesis P-Orridge is shown here.

Upper East Side galleries

Gemini G.E.L. at Joni Moisant Weyl 980 Madison Ave, 5th floor ⊤212/249-3324, ⓦwww.joniweyl.com. Etchings and contemporary graphics, with some vintage prints; has shown works by Roy

Lichtenstein and Robert Rauschenberg. By appointment only.

Knoedler & Co 19 E 70th St ⊤212/794-0550, ⓦwww.knoedlergallery.com. Renowned, nearly ancient gallery specializing in postwar and contemporary art, particularly the New York School. Shows some of the best-known names in twentieth-century art, such as Stella, Rauschenberg, and Fonseca. **Leo Castelli 18 E 77th St** ☎ 212/249-4470, ⓦ www.castelligallery.com. One of the original dealer-collectors, Castelli was instrumental in aiding the careers of Rauschenberg and Warhol, and this gallery offers big contemporary names at high prices.

Galleries on West 57th Street and around

Marlborough New York 40 W 57th St ☎ 212/541-4900, ⓦ www.marlboroughgallery .com. Internationally renowned gallery showing top modern and contemporary artists and graphic designers. Recent shows have included well-known sculptors Jacques Lipchitz and Tom Otterness. Has branches in Chelsea and abroad.
Mary Boone 745 Fifth Ave, at 57th St, 4th floor ☎ 212/752-2929, ⓦ www.maryboonegallery .com. Mary Boone was Leo Castelli's protégée, and her gallery specializes in installations, paintings, and works by up-and-coming European and American artists, as well as established artists already

involved with the gallery. The Mary Boone now also has an interesting branch in Chelsea (p.381).
Pace Wildenstein 32 E 57th St ☎ 212/421-3292, ⓦ www.pacewildenstein.com. This celebrated gallery exhibits works by most of the great modern American and European artists, from Picasso to Calder to Noguchi and Rothko. Recent shows have included Diane Arbus and Agnes Martin. Also has a good collection of prints and African art. Two Chelsea satellites located at 534 W 25th St (☎ 212/929-7000) and 545 W 22nd St (☎ 212/989-4258) specialize in edgier works and large installations.

DUMBO and Brooklyn Heights galleries

DUMBO Arts Center 30 Washington St, DUMBO ☎ 718/694-0831, ⓦ www.dumboartscenter.org. A huge warehouse space dedicated to showing innovative new group work in five to six shows yearly. The self-proclaimed origin and center of DUMBO's art scene.
The Rotunda Gallery 33 Clinton St, Brooklyn Heights ☎ 718/875-4047, ⓦ www.brooklynx .org/rotunda. This mixed-media, not-for-profit exhibition space features work by Brooklyn-based contemporary artists.

Smack Mellon Gallery 92 Plymouth St, DUMBO ☎ 718/834-8761, ⓦ www.smackmellon.org. An interesting space that displays multidiscipli-nary, high-tech work by artists who have for the most part flown under the radar of art critics and spectators.
UrbanGlass 647 Fulton St (enter at 57 Rockwell Place around the corner), DUMBO ☎ 718/625-3685, ⓦ www.urbanglass.org. Small but amazing glass gallery attached to the studio of the same name.

Williamsburg galleries

Front Room 147 Roebling St ☎ 718/782-2556, ⓦ www.frontroom.org. One of the neighbor-hood's best galleries and also a popular performance-art space. Best place to get a good first sense of the local scene.
Pierogi 177 N 9th St ☎ 718/599-2144, ⓦ www .pierogi2000.com. This former workshop mounts fascinating installations of various kinds. It is noted in the art world for its traveling "flatfiles," a collection of folders

containing the work of 600 or so artists, stored clinically and provocatively in metal, sliding cabinets.
WAH (Williamsburg Art and Historical Center) 135 Bedford St ☎ 718/486-6012, ⓦ www .wahcenter.net. Beautiful, fascinating multimedia arts center, with a focus on painting and sculpture. Sat & Sun noon–6pm. See p.243.

Alternative spaces

The galleries listed above (at least those in Manhattan) are part of a system designed to channel artists' work through the gallery spaces and, eventually, into the hands of collectors. While initial acceptance by a major gallery is an important rite of passage for an up-and-coming artist, it shouldn't be forgotten that this system's philosophy is based on making money for gallery owners, who normally receive fifty percent of the sale price. For an artist's work to be noncommercial in these spaces is perhaps an even greater sin than being socially or politically unacceptable.

The galleries included below, often referred to as **alternative spaces**, provide a forum for the kind of risky and non-commercially viable art that many other galleries may not be able to afford to show. Those mentioned here are at the cutting edge of new art in the city.

Incidentally, a train ride of about 90 minutes will bring you to Dia: Beacon (Riggio Galleries), a sprawling assortment of contemporary works housed in a 300,000-square-feet space in a former printing warehouse on the banks of the Hudson River. See the listing below for details.

Apex Art 291 Church St ⓣ 212/431-5270, ⓦ www.apexart.org. A nonprofit exhibition space that invites dealers, artists, writers, critics, and international art-world bodies to act as curators and mount idea-based shows, along with lectures and associated events.

Art in General 79 Walker St ⓣ 212/219-0473, ⓦ www.artingeneral.org. Experimental, nonprofit gallery with multimedia exhibits and performances, and an emphasis on multicultural themes.

Artists Space 38 Greene St, 3rd floor ⓣ 212/226-3970, ⓦ www.artistsspace.org. One of the most respected alternative spaces, with frequently changing theme-based exhibits, film screenings, videos, installations, and events. In over thirty years of existence, Artists Space has presented the work of thousands of emerging artists.

Dia: Beacon 3 Beekman St, Beacon, NY ⓣ 845/440-0100, ⓦ www.diabeacon.org. Managed by the Dia Art Foundation, the collection features such great contemporary artists as Dan Flavin, Richard Serra, Robert Smithson, and Andy Warhol (his mega-scale *Shadows* resides here). Admission is $10 ($7 for seniors and students).

Exit Art 475 Tenth Ave ⓣ 212/966-7745, ⓦ www.exitart.org. A hip crowd frequents this huge alternative gallery, now located in Hell's Kitchen. It favors big installations, up-and-coming, multimedia, and edgy cultural and political subjects. Nice café, too.

New York Earth Room 141 Wooster St ⓣ 212/989-5566, ⓦ www.earthroom.org. An incredible permanent exhibit by Walter de Maria, featuring a room filled, as the name suggests, with masses of dirt. Managed by Dia, which also oversees "The Broken Kilometer" exhibit at 393 W Broadway; both exhibits are closed during the summer

PS122 Gallery 150 First Ave ⓣ 212/228-4249, ⓦ www.ps122gallery.org. Nonprofit gallery, affiliated with a high-profile experimental performance space that highlights emerging artists.

White Columns 320 W 13th St, enter on Horatio St ⓣ 212/924-4212, ⓦ www.whitecolumns.org. White Columns focuses on emerging artists, and is considered very influential. Check out the fascinating, ever-changing group shows.

Shopping

Retail junkies beware: shops are one of New York's killer attractions. The city is the undisputed commercial capital of America, especially in fashion. There are flagship stores for every major brand, both ubiquitous (H&M) and exclusive (Versace), so you can stock up just as easily on a designer leather clutch as you can a pair of tennis socks. In between all the big names, you'll also find dozens of quirky local boutiques and bazaars worth seeking out. We've sifted through the best that the city has to offer and presented our pick of Manhattan's retail wonders below.

Practicalities

Opening hours in midtown Manhattan are roughly Monday through Saturday 9am to 6pm, with a later closing time (usually) on Thursday. Downtown shops (Soho, Tribeca, the East and West villages, the Lower East Side) tend to stay open later, at least until 8pm and sometimes until about midnight; bookstores especially are often open late. Most stores are open Sunday as well, but with abbreviated hours. Chinatown's shops and stalls are open all day, every day, while the stores that serve workers in the Financial District stick to nine-to-five office hours, and are usually shuttered on Saturday and Sunday. These places excepted, expect retail establishments to be most crowded on weekends, especially in Soho and midtown.

Credit cards are widely accepted: even the smallest shops usually take American Express, MasterCard, or Visa. An 8.375 percent **sales tax** will be added to your bill for all purchases except clothing and footwear. The city tax on these items was rolled back at the end of 2007, but you still have 4.375 percent of state and municipal taxes to deal with.

Finally, wherever you're shopping, **be careful**. Manhattan's crowded, frenzied stores are ripe territory for pickpockets and bag-snatchers.

Beauty and cosmetics

All department stores stock the main brands of beauty products (as does Century 21, often at a deep discount – see p.395), but if you're looking for hard-to-find cosmetics lines, here are the best options.

Aveda 233 Spring St, between Sixth Ave and Varick St ☎212/807-1492. New-agey cosmetics company specializing in plant-extract-based shampoos, conditioners, and skincare; some locations also have a spa where you can sign up for pricey treatments. Call for more locations.

C.O. Bigelow Apothecary 414 Sixth Ave, between 8th and 9th sts ☎212/473-7324. Established in 1882, C.O. Bigelow is one of the oldest apothecaries in the country – and that's exactly how it looks, with the original Victorian shopfittings still in place. Specializing in lesser-known and European beauty brands, this is the place to come for beauty and cosmetic items that you can't find elsewhere in the city.

Kiehl's 109 Third Ave, between 13th and 14th sts ☎212/677-3171, ⒲www.kiehls.com. Decorated with aviation and motorcycle memorabilia, this 150-year-old pharmacy sells its own range of natural-ingredient-based classic creams, oils, etc. Known for giving out plenty of samples to customers, whether you're buying or not. Lots of celebs swear by this stuff, especially the patented Crème de Corps body lotion.

Lush 1293 Broadway, between 33rd and 34th sts ☎212/564-9120, ⒲www.lush.com. Cosmetics and beauty products made from fresh fruits, vegetables, and oils. Popular items include the water-soluble "bath bombs," chunks of specialty soap that the staff cuts for you from large bricks, and

thick facial cleansers the consistency of chocolate mousse.

MAC 113 Spring St, between Greene and Mercer sts ☎212/334-4641; also 175 Fifth Ave, at 22nd St ⒲www.maccosmetics.com. MAC is known for both its high-quality, non-animal-tested cosmetics and its HIV/AIDS fundraising (pick up a Viva Glam lipstick to donate). Quite popular with models and celebs.

Ray's Beauty Supply 721 Eighth Ave, at 45th St ☎212/757-0175, ⒲www.raybeauty.com. This ramshackle store supplies most of the city's hairdressers with their potions and props. Something of an "industry insider" place, but the public is welcome. The low prices make it worth a detour.

Ricky's 590 Broadway, between Houston and Prince sts ☎212/226-5590; 267 W 23rd St, between Seventh and Eighth aves ☎212/206-0234. New York's haven for the overdone, the brash, and the OTT (think drag-diva favorites and plenty of lurid wigs). Stocks cool brands like Urban Decay and Tony & Tina as well as a house line of products. Additional locations (sixteen of them) around the city.

Sephora 555 Broadway, between Prince and Spring sts ☎212/625-1309; also 597 Fifth Ave, at E 48th St ☎212/980-6534, ⒲www.sephora .com. "Warehouse" of perfumes, make-up, and body-care products all lined up alphabetically so everything's easy to find and you don't have to pester any sales people. Call for additional locations.

Shopping categories

Zitomer 969 Madison Ave, at 76th ☎212/737-5561. A venerable pharmacy that has transformed itself into a full-blown mini-department store, Zitomer serves the beauty and cosmetic needs of the Fifth-Avenue gentry. Stocked to the gills with every brand and item imaginable.

Salons and spas

Antonio Prieto 127 W 20th St, between Sixth and Seventh aves ☎212/255-3741. One of the top hair salons in town, Antonio Prieto requires reservations at least a month in advance. Prieto himself is only in town part-time, but his trained stylists are equally outstanding, not least with hair extensions.

Astor Place Hair Designers 2 Astor Place, at Broadway ☎212/475-9854. If you're caught short in the city and need a cheap haircut, try this local institution, a unisex barbershop with dozens of haircutters sprawled about three floors. Trims $14 and up.

Bliss 568 Broadway, 2nd floor, between Houston and Prince sts ☎212/219-8970, ⊛www .blissworld.com. Top-notch spa with massage, facial, nail, and wax services. There's a bevy of beauty potions waiting for you to purchase as you depart, including the spa's own popular lotions and the full line of Crème de la Mer skin products. There are two other spas at 12 W 57th St between Fifth and Sixth aves, and inside the W Hotel at 541 Lexington Ave at 49th St (use the number above for an appointment at any location).

John Frieda 30 E 76th St, at Madison Ave ☎212/327-3400; also 825 Washington St, between Gansevoort and Little W 12th sts ☎212/675-0001. An excellent, highly-rated (and quite expensive) hair salon that's also home to the city's top celebrity stylist, Serge Normant, and colorist, Harry Josh.

🏃 Jin Soon 56th E 4th St, between Second Ave and the Bowery ☎212/473-2047. Small, soothing Japanese hand-and-foot spa. It's great for mani-and pedicures.

Ling 191 Prince St, at Sullivan St ☎212/982-8833. The city's most talked-about facial spa, located in the heart of Soho. Call for additional locations.

Sally Hersberger 425 W 14th St, between Ninth and Tenth aves ☎212/206-8700. Stylist to stars like Sarah Jessica Parker, Sally Hersberger reigns supreme among New York's hair pros. She's in town about half the time, but her entire staff is trained in "the Hersberger method." Good spot for star gazing.

Soho Sanctuary 119 Mercer St, between Prince and Spring sts ☎212/334-5550. One of the best spas in the city, with a steam room, a sauna, and a full range of services. Eminently relaxing, and women-only.

Stephen Knoll 625 Madison Ave, between 58th and 59th sts, 2nd floor ☎212/421-0100. Knoll made his name as Cindy Crawford's stylist in the 1990s and is still one of New York's very finest. He's in the salon year-round, so there's a decent chance you can book an appointment with him personally.

Books

New York is something of a literary mecca. All the major publishing houses have an office in the city, and there are more independent booksellers here than in most other parts of America. Dedicated bibliophiles will be in heaven, surrounded by shops that run the gamut from clever and focused (Partners & Crime, see p.388) to quirky and expansive (St Mark's Bookshop, see opposite). Quick literary fixes can be easily taken care of, too – superstores like Barnes & Noble are omnipresent in New York.

General interest and new books

🏃 Book Culture 536 W 112th St, between Broadway and Amsterdam Ave ☎212/865-1588. Formerly Labyrinth Books, the largest independent bookstore in the city boasts a fine selection of literary (especially international) fiction and academic texts for local Columbia students and faculty.

Corner Bookstore 1313 Madison Ave, at 93rd St ☎212/831-3554. Upscale bookstore with an excellent literature selection and a chilled-out atmosphere.

McNally Robinson 52 Prince St, between Mulberry and Lafayette sts ☎212/274-1160.

This Canadian book chain has gained a foothold in the heart of Manhattan with its prime Soho location. Great service, and the staff here is friendly too.

Posman Books inside Grand Central Terminal, 42nd St and Vanderbilt Ave ☎212/983-1111. A friendly, relatively roomy spot to kill some time while you're waiting for that train.

St Mark's Bookshop 31 Third Ave, at 9th St ☎212/260-7853, ⓦwww.stmarksbookshop .com. The best-known independent bookstore in the city, with a good selection of titles on contemporary art, politics, feminism, the environment, and literary criticism, as well as more obscure subjects. Good postcards, too, and stocked full of radical and art magazines. Open until midnight.

Shakespeare & Co 939 Lexington Ave, at 69th St ☎212/570-0201; also 716 Broadway, at Washington Place ☎212/529-1330; 137 E 23rd St, at Lexington Ave ☎212/505-2021; and 1 Whitehall St, at Broadway ☎212/742-7025; ⓦwww.shakeandco.com. New and used books, both paper and hardcover. Great for fiction and psychology. There's also a branch at the Brooklyn Academy of Music (see p.225).

Three Lives & Co 154 W 10th St, at Waverly Place ☎212/741-2069, ⓦwww.threelives.com. Excellent literary bookstore that has an especially good selection of works by and for women, as well as general titles. There's an excellent reading series in the fall, which has previously hosted the likes of Anne Rice and Jane Smiley.

Second-hand books

Argosy Bookstore 116 E 59th St, at Park Ave ☎212/753-4455, ⓦwww.argosybooks.com. Unbeatable for rare books, Argosy also sells clearance books and titles of all kinds, though the shop's reputation means you may find mainstream works cheaper elsewhere.

Housing Works Used Books Café 126 Crosby St, between Houston and Prince sts ☎212/334-3324, ⓦwww.housingworks.com. The Housing Works has a good selection of very cheap books. With a small espresso and snack bar and comfy chairs, it's a great place to spend an afternoon. They're fairly paranoid about shoplifting; check your purses and backpacks at the door. Proceeds benefit AIDS charity.

🏃 **Strand Bookstore** 828 Broadway, at 12th St ☎212/473-1452; also an annex at 95 Fulton St, at Gold St ☎212/732-6070, ⓦwww .strandbooks.com. Yes, it's hot and crowded, and the staff seems to resent working there, but with "18 miles of books" and a stock of more than 2.5 million titles, this is the largest discount book operation in the city – and one of few survivors in an area once rife with second-hand bookstores. There are recent review copies and new books for half price in the basement; older books go for anything from 50¢ up.

▲ Strand Bookstore

West Sider Books 2246 Broadway, at 80th St
ⓣ212/362-0706. Used and out-of-print
books, especially art, illustrated, and antique
children's titles. Watch out for overpriced
works – there are a few.

Special-interest bookstores

Art and architecture

MoMA Design Store 81 Spring St, at Crosby
ⓣ646/613-1367. Contemporary art books
galore.

Unoppressive, Non-Imperialist Bargain Books
34 Carmine St, between Bleecker and Bedford
sts ⓣ212/229-0079. Arty overstock amongst
a hodgepodge of travel guides, biographies,
children's pop-up books, and spiritual titles
also here.

Urban Center Books 457 Madison Ave, at 50th
St ⓣ212/935-3592, ⓦwww.urbancenterbooks
.org. Architectural-book specialists with a
very helpful staff.

Comics and sci-fi

Forbidden Planet 840 Broadway, at 13th St
ⓣ212/473-1576, ⓦwww.fpnyc.com. Science
fiction, fantasy, horror fiction, graphic
novels, and comics. Great for its large
backlist of indie and underground comics,
they also hawk T-shirts and the latest sci-fi
toys and collectibles.

Jim Hanley's Universe 4 W 33rd St, between
Fifth Ave and Broadway ⓣ212/268-7088,
ⓦwww.jhuniverse.com. Some swear by this
23-year-old space that offers mainstream
issues from the big leagues (DC, Marvel) as
well as graphic novels, manga, small
pressings and collectibles. Authors, illustra-
tors and comic-related media types (Neil
Gaiman, Mr. Tarantino, director Guillermo
Del Toro) have often stopped by to discuss
their work. Staff is knowledgable and tries
extra hard to please. Open daily.

St Mark's Comics 11 St Mark's Place, between
Second and Third aves ⓣ212/598-9439. Tons
of comic books, including some underground editions; well known for their huge
stock. Action figures, cards, and a whole
room of back issues.

Crime and mystery

The Mysterious Bookshop 58 Warren St
ⓣ212/587-1011, ⓦwww.mysteriousbookshop
.com. The founder of this store started the
Mysterious Press (now owned by Warner
Books). The shop sells mysteries of every

kind, from classic detectives to just-
published titles, and also trades in some
first editions and "Sherlockiana."

Partners & Crime 44 Greenwich Ave, at Charles
St ⓣ212/243-0440, ⓦwww.crimepays.com.
Crime novels. Also home to the Cranston
and Spade Theater Co, which performs
classic 1940s radio scripts on the first
Saturday night of every month (tickets $5).

International and foreign Language

Kinokuniya Bookstore 1073 Sixth Ave, between
40th and 41st sts ⓣ212/765-7766, ⓦwww
.kinokuniya.com/ny. The largest Japanese
bookstore in New York, with English books
on Japan, too.

Librairie de France 610 Fifth Ave, in the
Rockefeller Center Promenade ⓣ212/581-8810,
ⓦwww.frencheuropean.com. Small space
housing a wealth of French and Spanish
books, a shop with 8000 dictionaries of
more than 100 languages, and a department of listen-and-learn language books,
records, and tapes. Located in Rockefeller
Center since 1935.

Rizzoli 31 W 57th St, between Fifth and Sixth
aves ⓣ212/759-2424. Manhattan branch of
the prestigious Italian bookstore chain and
publisher. They specialize in European publications, and have a good selection of
foreign newspapers and magazines along
with art books of all sorts.

Russian Bookstore 21 174 Fifth Ave, between
22nd and 23rd sts ⓣ212/924-5477. All books,
all in Russian, all the time. For curiosity's
sake, worth a trip even for a non-speaker.

Religion and spirituality

East West Books 78 Fifth Ave, at 13th St
ⓣ212/243-5994. Bookstore with a mind,
body, and spirit slant. Eastern religions,
New Age, and health and healing.

J. Levine Judaica 5 W 30th St, at Fifth Ave
ⓣ212/695-6888, ⓦwww.levinejudaica.com.
The ultimate Jewish bookstore. Closed Sat.

Logos Bookstore 1575 York Ave, at 83rd St
ⓣ212/517-7292. Christian books and gifts.

West Side Judaica 2412 Broadway, at 88th St
ⓣ212/362-7846. Books about Judaism, with
funky menorahs for sale on the side.
Closed Sat.

Miscellaneous

Biography Bookshop 400 Bleecker St, at 11th St
ⓣ212/807-8655. Venerable Greenwich Village
corner bookstore focusing exclusively on

letters, diaries, memoirs, autobiographies, and, of course, biographies.

Bluestockings 172 Allen St, at Stanton St ⊤212/777-6028. New and used titles, but only those authored by or related to women. Cozy, well-stocked, collective-style store in what was once a dilapidated crack house; nice café, too.

Books of Wonder 18 W 18th St, between Fifth and Sixth aves ⊤212/989-3270, ⊛www .booksofwonder.com. A heavenly collection of kid lit.

Center for Book Arts 28 W 27th St, at Sixth Ave, 3rd floor ⊤212/481-0295, ⊛www .centerforbookarts.org. Not so much a bookstore as a space dedicated to the art of bookmaking. Hosts regular readings and workshops – fascinating stuff.

Complete Traveller Antiquarian Bookstore 199 Madison Ave, at E 35th St ⊤212/685-9007. An extensive collection of rare travel tomes, including the entire Baedekers series (the first "modern age" guides), WPA Guides, old

books on NYC and maps galore. You can also find other (non-travel) first pressings and vintage children's books here.

Drama Bookshop 250 W 40th St, between Seventh and Eighth aves ⊤212/944-0595, ⊛www.dramabookshop.com. Theater books, scripts, and publications on all manner of drama-related subjects.

Kitchen Arts & Letters 1435 Lexington Ave, at 94th St ⊤212/876-5550. Cookbooks and books about food; run by a former culinary editor.

Revolution Books 146 W 26th St, between Sixth and Seventh aves ⊤212/691-3345, ⊛www .revolutionbooksnyc.org. New York's major left-wing bookstore and contact point, even more important now that, to Revolution and many of the nation's citizens, "critical thinking is under assault." A wide range of political and cultural titles and periodicals. More significantly, a place for healthy discourse: almost every night the store holds screenings, salons, or other events.

Department stores and malls

Barneys, Bergdorf Goodman, and Saks Fifth Avenue are among the world's most famous (and most beautiful) **department stores** – each of their buildings is a landmark in itself. In general, the status of department stores in America is not what it once was; the last decades of the twentieth century were particularly tough, as specialty outlets swallowed up business. The department stores that have survived this transition, especially those in New York, have tweaked their offerings to provide fewer essentials and more luxuries (Macy's is a rare exception).

Barneys New York 660 Madison Ave, at 61st St ⊤212/826-8900, ⊛www.barneys.com. Mon–Fri 10am–8pm, Sat 10am–7pm, Sun 11am–6pm. Barneys has been considered the trendiest New York department store for over a decade now, and shows no sign of weakening, with exclusive rights to sell Balenciaga and other top lines. It's a temple to designer fashion, and the best place to find cutting-edge labels or next season's hot item. The Co-op section, focusing on younger styles, was such a hit that the powers that be opened several standalone Barneys Co-op stores.

Bergdorf Goodman 754 Fifth Ave, at 57th St ⊤212/753-7300. Mon–Fri 10am–8pm, Sat 10am–7pm, Sun noon–6pm. Make sure you come here, even if it's only to ogle the windows, which approach high art. With in-house tailoring, superb service, the most

comprehensive cosmetics department known to humankind and superior hair, nail, and brow salons, Bergdorf's is the store of choice for many New Yorkers. It has exclusive rights to lines by Yves Saint Laurent and Chloe, among others. The men's store is across Fifth Avenue.

Bloomingdale's Lexington Ave, at 59th St ⊤212/705-2000, ⊛www.bloomingdales.com. Mon–Fri 10am–8.30pm, Sat 10am–7pm, Sun 11am–7pm. When an Upper East Side matron dies, "Bloomies," not "Rosebud," is most likely the last word on her lips. Out-of-towners flock here for its famed "classiness," though local power-shoppers are more likely to view it as a bit of a frumpy has-been. It does still have the atmosphere of a large, bustling bazaar, packed with concessionaires offering perfumes and designer clothes.

Henri Bendel 712 Fifth Ave, between 55th and 56th sts ℡212/247-1100 or 1-800/HBENDEL. Mon–Sat 10am–8pm, Sun noon–7pm. More gentle in its approach than the biggies, this store's refinement is thanks in part to its classic reuse of the Coty perfume building, with windows by René Lalique. There's an array of top-shelf make-up at street level and gorgeous designer clothing – with price tags certain to send your blood pressure soaring – upstairs. The powder rooms appear designed for royalty.

Jeffrey 449 W 14th St, at Tenth Ave ℡212/206-1272. Opened in the 1990s, Jeffrey is a relative newcomer to New York's department-store scene. The all-white emporium is set squat in the middle of the city's cutting-edge Meatpacking District, and features offerings from trend-setting lines like Boudicca and Tess Giberson. The brand-new sheen has worn off in recent years (and the service has become much friendlier).

Macy's 151 W 34th St, on Broadway at Herald Square ℡212/695-4400 or 1-800/289-6229, Ⓦwww.macys.com. Mon–Thurs 10am–9.30pm, Fri & Sat 9am–10pm, Sun 11am–8.30pm. With two buildings, two million square feet of floor space, and ten floors (four for women's garments alone), Macy's is, quite simply, the largest department store in the world. Given its size, it's not the hotbed of top fashion it ought to be: most merchandise is of mediocre quality (particularly the jewelry).

The real reason to come here is The Cellar, the housewares department in the basement. It's arguably the best in the city.

Saks Fifth Avenue 611 Fifth Ave, at 50th St ℡212/753-4000, Ⓦwww.saks.com. Mon–Fri 10am–8pm, Sat 10am–7pm, Sun noon–7pm. Since 1924, the name Saks has been virtually synonymous with style. No less true today, the store has updated itself to carry the merchandise of all the big designers, while still retaining its reputation for quality. The ground floor can be a bit like Grand Central terminal as multiple salesgirls assault you with drive-by perfume sprays, but they stock top cosmetic lines (like Armani) that you can't find elsewhere in the city.

Takashimaya 693 Fifth Ave, between 54th and 55th sts ℡212/350-0100. This beautiful Japanese department store is a Manhattan mainstay, offering a scaled-down assortment of expensive merchandise simply displayed and exquisitely wrapped. The café, The Tea Box, on the lower level, has an assortment of teapots and loose teas.

Time Warner Center 10 Columbus Circle, at 60th St ℡212/823-6300, Ⓦwww.shopsatcolumbus circle.com. Gleaming mega-mall that anchors the city's massive Time Warner headquarters. It's known for its upscale eateries, large Whole Foods grocer, and branches of Sephora, J. Crew, and Benetton. Also houses Lincoln Center's snazzy venue, Jazz at Lincoln Center.

Electronic and video equipment

The sole reason to buy **electronic and video equipment** in New York is if you are visiting from Europe, where such merchandise is more expensive. Tech-heads can brave the risky discount shopping on Sixth and Seventh avenues north of Times Square in the 50s for cameras, stereos, and MP3 players; there's another cluster of camera stores in midtown along Fifth and Sixth avenues between 30th and 50th streets. The motto here is *caveat emptor*: know what you want or expect a hard sell for more expensive equipment than you need. It's much easier to head for the meccas of B&H or J&R, where merchandise is not only cheap, but reliable as well.

B&H Photo Video 420 Ninth Ave, between 33rd and 34th sts ℡212/444-6615 or 1-800/606-6969. For film, cameras, and specialty equipment; knowledgeable sales staff will take the time to guide you through a buying decision. Excellent used-goods selection upstairs. Closed Sat and Jewish holidays.

Bang & Olufsen 952 Madison Ave, at 75th St ℡212/879-6161, Ⓦwww.bang-olufsen.com. Incredibly good, high-quality audio and some video equipment, all in sleek, modern Danish design. Call for other locations.

Harvey Electronics 2 W 45th St, at Fifth Ave ℡212/575-5000, Ⓦwww.harveyonline.com.

Top-of-the-line electronics equipment, sold by experts. Closed weekends.

J&R Music and Computer World 15–23 Park Row, between Beekman and Ann sts ☎212/238-9000, ⓦwww.jr.com. You'll find a good selection (for decent prices) of stereo and computer equipment at this strip of stores down by City Hall, as well as home appliances and CDs. If you can plug it in, they sell it here – and often at the cheapest prices in the city.

Fashion: accessories

Agent Provocateur 133 Mercer St, at Prince St ☎212/965-0229. New York outpost of the saucy, sexy, luxury lingerie line, co-owned by Joe Corre, son of avant-garde designer Vivienne Westwood. Think frills, bows, and lashings of lace.

Alain Mikli Optique 986 Madison Ave, between 76th and 77th sts ☎212/472-6085. The French king of eyewear. This is the *only* place to go for high-end fashionable frames. Treat yourself – you won't regret it.

Kate Spade 454 Broome St, at Prince St ☎212/274-1991. Boxy, high-quality fabric bags that were all the rage in the late 1990s. Get yourself one now that they're out of vogue and you may be doing yourself a favor – the "retro" Kate Spade craze is only a matter of time.

Me & Ro 241 Elizabeth St, between Houston and Prince sts ☎917/237-9215, ⓦwww.meandrojewelry.com. The hottest, most distinctive jeweler in Manhattan, with tasteful modernist designs worth going out of your way for. Some items are quite expensive, but you can get really nice earrings here for a reasonable price.

Robert Marc 551 Madison Ave, between 55th and 56th sts ☎212/319-2000. Exclusive New York distributor of frames by the likes of Lunor and Kirei Titan; also sells Retrospecs, restored antique eyewear from the 1890s to the 1940s. Very expensive and very hot. Call for other locations.

Selima Optique 59 Wooster St, at Greene St ☎212/343-9490; also 899 Madison, at 72nd ☎988-6690. Owner Selima Selaun stocks her own line of girly, groovy specs, alongside favorites from well-known designers like Dior and Kata.

The Diamond District

The strip of 47th Street between Fifth and Sixth avenues is known as the **Diamond District**. At street level are dozens of retail shops and more than twenty specialist marts known as "exchanges" – combined they sell more jewelry than any other area in the world. There are separate dealers for different gems, gold, and silver – even dealers who will string your beads for you, appraisers, and "findings" stores where you can pick up the basic makings of do-it-yourself jewelry, like chains and earring posts. Some jewelers trade only among themselves; some sell retail; and others do business by appointment only. Most shops are open Monday through Saturday 10am to 5.30pm, though a few close on Friday afternoon and Saturday for religious reasons, and the standard vacation time is from the end of June to the second week in July.

It is very important that you shop armed with some information. Research what you are looking for and be as particular as possible. If at all feasible, it's always better to go to someone who has been specifically recommended to you. For a listing of all the district's vendors, shopping tips, and the "Buyers Bill of Rights," visit ⓦwww .diamonddistrict.org.

If you want to get your sparklies graded or appraised, try the Gemological Institute of America at 580 Fifth Ave, 2nd floor (☎1-800/366-8519), or the Universal Gemological Laboratory at 71 W 47th St, suite 204 (☎212/921-3324).

Fashion: clothing

New York is one of the five nerve centers of the global fashion industry, though the emphasis here is on sportswear rather than couture. In addition to hot local designers, you'll find boutiques for just about every major designer on the planet, with prices significantly lower than in European cities or Tokyo.

As such, **clothes shopping** here is a feast for any fashionista; if you are prepared to search the city with sufficient dedication you can find just about anything. We've divided this section into five categories: **boutiques and trendy labels**, where you can pick up local big names or one-offs; **chain stores**, Manhattan flagships of well-known American retail names; **designer stores**; **discount stores**, like legendary low-priced designer palace Century 21, where you can snag big names at deep discounts; and **vintage and thrift**, including the increasingly popular (and browse-worthy) resale or consignment stores, where owners sell off last season's barely worn outfits.

Boutiques and trendy labels

American Apparel 712 Broadway, at 8th St ☎646/383-2258, ⓦwww.americanapparel.net. Guaranteed sweatshop-free, 100% PC tees and other items from LA. Worth checking out as much for the endless colors, low prices, and sharp cut as for their ethics.

Calypso St Barth's 407 Broome St, at Lafayette St ☎212/941-6100. Forget black; color is the name of the game here. Vibrant fashions imbued with a rich hippie aesthetic – think string bikinis at $75 a pop. There are several other branches, specializing in jewelry and accessories, on the same block.

Clothing and shoe sizes

Women's dresses and skirts
American	4	6	8	10	12	14	16	18
British	8	10	12	14	16	18	20	22
Continental	38	40	42	44	46	48	50	52

Women's blouses and sweaters
American	6	8	10	12	14	16	18
British	30	32	34	36	38	40	42
Continental	40	42	44	46	48	50	52

Women's shoes
American	5	6	7	8	9	10	11
British	3	4	5	6	7	8	9
Continental	36	37	38	39	40	41	42

Men's suits
American	34	36	38	40	42	44	46	48
British	34	36	38	40	42	44	46	48
Continental	44	46	48	50	52	54	56	58

Men's shirts
American	14	15	15.5	16	16.5	17	17.5	18
British	14	15	15.5	16	16.5	17	17.5	18
Continental	36	38	39	41	42	43	44	45

Men's shoes
American	7	7.5	8	8.5	9.5	10	10.5	11	11.5
British	6	7	7.5	8	9	9.5	10	11	12
Continental	39	40	41	42	43	44	44	45	46

DDC Lab 427 W 14th St, at Ninth Ave ⊤212/414-5801. The designer-denim label's flagship store, stocking finessed, highly finished jeans as well as experimental knitwear made from high-tech fabrics.

Intermix 1003 Madison Ave, at 77th St ⊤212/249-7858; also 125 Fifth Ave, at 19th St ⊤212/533-9720; and 98 Prince St, between Mercer and Greene sts ⊤212/966-5303. Trendy boutiques for the working-girl fashionista, and a flat-out fun place to shop. A wide assortment of brands both high and low, and an admittedly confusing merchandise layout – they're called "intermix" for a reason.

⚡ Kirna Zabête 96 Greene St, between Prince and Spring sts ⊤212/941-9656. The best of the downtown shops, this is a concept store that stocks hand-picked highlights from capsule collections of Rick Owens, Proenza Schouler, Chloe, Ghesquiere, and other icons *du jour*. The great vibe and service here have kept the store in business for over 15 years.

Opening Ceremony 35 Howard St, between Broadway and Lafayette ⊤212/219-2688. Concept store that stocks foreign brands you can't find elsewhere in the US, including London's Topshop. Plans are afoot to add lines from other unavailable designers from Milan and Tokyo.

Patricia Field 302 Bowery, between Bleecker and E Houston sts ⊤212/966-4066. Touted as the founder of Manhattan's most inventive clothing store, Pat Field was one of the first NYC vendors of "punk chic"; her recent renaissance came as the *tour de force* costumier behind Carrie Bradshaw's outfits in *Sex and the City*. This store has plenty of her wild designs at reasonable prices, as well as wacky accessories.

Scoop 1275 Third Ave, at 73rd St ⊤212/535-5577. Every season is cruise season at this lively fashion outpost for youngish Upper East Side girls. There's a bit of a bubblegum, Paris Hilton vibe to the place, but it's well stocked with the latest designs from a dozen different labels.

Seize Sur Vingt 243 Elizabeth St, at Prince St ⊤212/343-0476. James and Gwendolyn Jurney offer exquisite old-school men's shirts at their store – and for $50 more will run up a bespoke version specially for you. They also have a small selection of suits and crisp boxer-shorts.

TG-170 170 Ludlow St, between Houston and Stanton sts ⊤212/995-8660. Small, unique store featuring emerging local designers. It's a good spot for very cool bargain-priced items from the up-and-coming. Highly recommended.

Triple 5 Soul 290 Lafayette St, between Houston and Prince sts ⊤212/431-2404. The city's top skategear shop also stocks a healthy supply of popular men's & ladies' hip-hop gear.

Unis 226 Elizabeth St, at Prince St ⊤212/431-5533, ⊛www.unisnewyork.com. Designer Eunice Lee offers skinny T-shirts, slouchy jeans, and slimfit sweaters in muted colors that are part Britpop revival, part Tokyo teen.

Designer stores

We've listed all the outlets for the major **designer labels** – no big-name brand worth its cashmere would be without a Manhattan outpost, so the choice is enormous. As a general rule, internationally known design houses are concentrated uptown on Fifth Avenue in the 50s and on Madison Avenue in the 60s and 70s. The newer, younger designers are found downtown in Soho, NoLita, the East and West villages, and Tribeca.

202 75 Ninth Ave, inside Chelsea Market, between 15th and 16th sts ⊤212/421-7720. Everything's understated and elegant, though the knitwear is the standout here, in designer Nicole Farhi's most recent venture mixing fashion and food (the original Upper East Side store is now closed). The front of the shop holds a café with tasty sandwiches and plates (and french toast on the weekend); it's a favorite place for fashionistas to refuel on black coffee.

agnès b 103 Greene St, at Prince St (women and men) ⊤212/925-4649; also 13 E 16th St, at Fifth Ave (women) ⊤212/741-2585; and 1063 Madison Ave, between 80th and 81st sts (women) ⊤212/570-9333. Pared-down classic Parisian chic, all clean lines and fresh air, with unexpected bursts of color.

Alexander McQueen 417 W 14th St, between Ninth and Tenth aves ⊤212/645-1797. Theatrical but flattering and well-cut clothes for women. His stablemate at the Gucci group,

ALEXANDER MCQUEEN

▲ Alexander McQueen

Stella McCartney, has a store a few
doors down.

Anna Sui 113 Greene St, at Prince St
ⓣ212/941-8406. Funky, thrift-store-inspired
clothes for girly girls.

🏃 **Balenciaga** 542 W 22nd St, between 10th
and 11th aves ⓣ212/206-0872. The
high-glamour designs of Nicolas Ghesquiere
have brought this eminent Italian house
back to the very top of high fashion, with
prices to match. Unique fabrics and unpar-
alleled attention to detail in each piece make
this the designer of choice for those who
can afford it.

Burberry's 131 Spring St, at Green St
ⓣ212/925-9300; also 9 E 57th St, at Fifth
Ave ⓣ212/355-6314. Their classic plaids
and tweeds are still available, but these
days they're on the back burner in favor
of hot designer Christopher Bailey's
more up-to-date offerings. Their women's
coats are among the world's most
sought-after.

🏃 **Calvin Klein** 654 Madison Ave, at 60th St
ⓣ212/292-9000. Sleek, minimalist
sportswear from the master of classic
American fashion.

🏃 **Chloe** 850 Madison Ave, at 70th St
ⓣ212/717-8220. Industry watchers
predicted the demise of this line when Stella
McCartney departed, but her former partner
Phoebe Philo has this brand flying higher
than ever with one stunning collection after
another, including the hottest bag to come
out in years (the Paddington).

Christian Dior 21 E 57th St, at Madison Ave
ⓣ212/931-2950. John Galliano amps up the
glamour here with his show-stopping

designs, though they still haven't given him
the couture line he craves.

Comme des Garçons 520 W 22nd St, at Tenth
Ave ⓣ212/604-9200. Japanese designer Rei
Kawakubo's avant-garde line has a stunning
showcase in this Chelsea store – worth
stopping to see even if you don't plan to
buy any clothes.

DKNY 655 Madison Ave, at 60th St ⓣ212/223-
3569; also 420 W Broadway, between Spring
and Prince sts ⓣ646/613-1100. Donna
Karan's younger, cheaper line has two
concept-store locations in the city, selling
accessories and homewares for the "DKNY
lifestyle" alongside clothes.

Dolce & Gabbana 825 Madison Ave, at 69th St
ⓣ212/249-4100. Both the diffusion and
designer lines by this Italian duo offer
studded, showy clothes – just make sure
you're thin enough to slip into them.

Donna Karan 819 Madison Ave, at 69th St
ⓣ1-866/240-4700. Subtle clothes in
understated shades guaranteed to flatter
any figure.

Giorgio Armani 760 Madison Ave, at 65th St
ⓣ212/988-9191. Splash out on one of
Armani's legendary deconstructed suits.

Gucci 725 Fifth Ave, at 54th St ⓣ212/826-2600;
also 840 Madison Ave, at 70th St ⓣ212/717-
2619. Tom Ford may be gone, but his
revamping of this classic label has had a
lasting effect. Cutting-edge leather accessories and retro-cool clothes for a new
generation.

Hermes 691 Madison Ave, at 62nd St
ⓣ212/751-3181. More than just scarves for
your mother and ties for your dad; check
out the clothes designed by camera-shy
Martin Margiela.

Issey Miyake 802 Madison Ave, between 67th
and 68th sts ⓣ212/439-7822. Come here for
classic, arty separates – there's also a
branch stocking his micro-pleated
womenswear, Pleats Please, at 128
Wooster St, at Prince St (ⓣ212/226-3600).

J. Lindeberg 126 Spring St, at Greene St
ⓣ212/625-9403. The namesake line of the
designer who launched Diesel, aimed at
anyone who wants to channel his inner
rockstar. There's also a smallish
womenswear selection.

John Varvatos 122 Spring St, at Greene St
ⓣ212/965-0700. Boxy, though flattering
casualwear and suits, plus his highly
successful line of leather Converse
sneakers.

Krizia 769 Madison Ave, at 66th St ☏212/879-1211. Pick up a lightweight linen suit or a floaty sundress or two here.

Marc Jacobs 163 Mercer St, between Houston and Prince sts ☏212/343-1490. Marc Jacobs rules the New York fashion world like a Cosmopolitan-sipping colossus. Women from all walks of life come here to blow the nest egg on his latest "it" bag or pair of boots. Check out his second line, Marc by Marc, at 403 Bleecker St, at 11th St (☏212/924-0026).

Marni 161 Mercer St, between Houston and Prince sts ☏212/343-3912. Get here before prices go completely through the roof – this relative newcomer from Milan has already been anointed "the new Prada" by fashion editors everywhere. The tops here are especially exquisite, with an emphasis on bright colors and unique patterns.

Miu Miu 100 Prince St, at Greene St ☏212/334-5156; also 831 Madison Ave, at 70th St ☏212/249-9660. Miuccia Prada's fun, often bizarre, diffusion line; note that both stores only stock the women's collection.

Paul Smith 108 Fifth Ave, at 16th St ☏212/627-9770. Excellent, sophisticated menswear, often employing eccentric, eye-catching color combinations.

Philosophy di Alberta Ferretti 452 W Broadway, at Prince St ☏212/460-5500. Summery clothes for that sun-soaked long lunch in the Tuscan hills.

Polo Ralph Lauren 867 Madison Ave ☏212/606-2100 and **Polo Sport Ralph Lauren** 888 Madison Ave ☏212/434-8000; both between 71st and 72nd sts. The master of all things preppy: buy a blazer here and make like you're money.

Prada 575 Broadway, at Prince St ☏212/334-8888. The jaw-dropping flagship store designed by Rem Koolhaas is as much of a sight as Miuccia's deservedly famous clothes.

Stella McCartney 429 W 14th St, at Tenth Ave ☏212/255-1556. More of the same stuff she produced at Chloe – uniforms for "it" girls slumming downtown. Her fellow Gucci-group designer Alexander McQueen is close by (see p.393).

Valentino 747 Madison Ave, at 65th St ☏212/772-6969. Wall-to-wall glamorous gowns.

Versace 647 Fifth Ave, at 52nd St ☏212/317-0224. Loud, brassy, red-carpet-worthy clothes for those who like to enter a room with an exclamation mark.

Yohji Yamamoto 103 Grand St, at Mercer St ☏212/966-9066. Huge boutique in south Soho selling fragrances, clothes, and shoes, all in Japanese avant-garde designs.

Yves Saint Laurent 855 Madison Ave, at 71st St ☏212/988-3821. Sexy, oh-so-French separates for men and women.

Zero 225 Mott St, between Prince and Spring sts ☏212/925-3849. Much-celebrated local designer Maria Cornejo's NoLita boutique features the best of her cutting-edge fashions, which tend toward a simple color palette and some unconventional cuts.

Discount stores

Century 21 22 Cortlandt St, at Broadway ☏212/227-9092, ⊛www.c21store.com. The granddaddy of designer discount department stores, where all the showrooms send their samples to be sold at the end of the season, usually at 40 to 60 percent off retail prices – the richest pickings are in July and Jan. A limited number of dressing rooms, so buy what you want and return whatever doesn't fit.

Daffy's 1311 Broadway, at 34th St, Herald Square ☏212/736-4477. Name-brand clothes at discount prices for men, women, and children. Specializes in Italian designers like Les Copian. Five other locations in Manhattan; call for details.

Loehmann's 101 Seventh Ave, between 16th and 17th sts ☏212/352-0856, ⊛www.loehmanns.com. New York's best-known department store for designer clothes at knockdown prices, especially glamorous evening-wear. No refunds and no exchanges after 30 days.

Syms 42 Trinity Place, at Rector St ☏212/797-1199; also 400 Park Ave, at 54th St ☏212/317-8200. "Where the educated consumer is our best customer" – the stock's a bit stuffier than elsewhere, so plan on picking up a suit for work or a classic white blouse.

Woodbury Common Premium Outlet Mall 498 Red Apple Court, Central Valley, New York State ☏845/928-4000, ⊛www.premiumoutlets.com. Dedicated bargain-hunters should hop on a bus from Port Authority Terminal (see p.23) for the 1hr ride north of the city to this designer-label discount-outlet mall. There are factory stores from Gucci, Chanel, Versace, Catherine Malandrino, D&G, Diane Von Furstenberg, and Dior – and that's just for starters – though you'll mostly find discards and leftovers from the previous season.

Vintage, second-hand, and thrift stores

Aside from the standout shops we've listed below, there's a heavy concentration of thrift and vintage stores in the Lower East Side, especially around Ludlow and Rivington streets. Don't be surprised to find a famous designer (or one of their minions) rifling through the racks in this area – they're probably searching about for inspiration for their next collection.

Amarcord 84 E 7th St, at First Ave ℡212/614-7133. This place is a real find. The owners make regular trips through their home country of Italy in search of discarded Dior, Gucci, Yves Saint Laurent, and so forth from the 1940s onward. Things aren't too expensive, especially considering all the pieces are in mint condition. Their shop at 252 Lafayette St, between Prince and Spring sts ℡212/431-4161 carries menswear.

Andy's Chee-pees 18 W 8th St, between Fifth Ave and Macdougal ℡212/420-5980. The place to go for those all-American bowling shirts, pump-attendant tees, and beat-up denimwear.

Cheap Jack's 303 Fifth Avenue, at 31st St ℡212/777-9564. Not as cheap as it once was, but still a good and comprehensive source of used clothing and accessories.

Cherry 19 Eighth Ave, at Jane St ℡212/924-1410. Everything from vintage Halston cocktail dresses to swing-era chiffon gowns, with an especially large selection of 60s mod clothing. High-end, but cheaper than Resurrection (see opposite).

Domsey's 431 Broadway, Williamsburg, Brooklyn ℡718/384-6000. Discreetly embedded along the East River's decrepit warehouse district, this five-story thrift store sells everything from boutique pieces to boot-camp salvage… by the pound! Plan to rifle ruthlessly and expect good rewards as a result.

Edith Machinist 104 Rivington St, at Ludlow St ℡212/979-9992. Extremely popular with the trendy vintage set, this used-clothing emporium holds some amazing finds (particularly shoes) for those willing to sift through the massive stock.

Gabay's Outlet 225 First Ave, at E 14th St ℡212/254-3180. An East Village store crammed with remaindered merchandise (Marc Jacobs, YSL, and the like) from midtown's department stores.

Housing Works Thrift Shop 143 W 17th St, between Sixth and Seventh aves ℡212/366-0820; **also 306 Columbus Ave, at 75th St** ℡212/579-7566; **and 202 E 77th St, at Third Ave** ℡212/772-8461. Upscale thrift stores where you can find second-hand designer pieces in very good condition. All proceeds benefit Housing Works, an AIDS social-service organization.

INA 101 Thompson St, at Prince St ℡212/941-4757; **also 21 Prince St, at Elizabeth St** ℡212/334-9048; **and 208 E 73rd St, at Second Ave** ℡212/249-0014. Designer resale shop usually crammed with end-of-season, barely worn pieces by hot designers. Fair prices make it by far the best second-hand store in the city. The men's store is at 262 Mott St, at Prince St (℡212/334-2210).

Marmalade 172 Ludlow St, between Houston and Stanton sts ℡212/473-8070. Great spot for mid-range vintage fare, from funky T-shirts to Valentino pumps. Prices are reasonable and there are always some unique items.

Michael's: The Consignment Shop 1041 Madison Ave, at 79th St, 2nd floor ℡212/737-7273. Bridal wear as well as slightly used designer women's clothing from names like Ungaro, Armani, and Chanel.

Reminiscence 50 W 23rd St, between Fifth and Sixth aves ℡212/243-2292. Designed to evoke your memories of the 1980s everything-with-palm-trees phase. It carries funky new and used clothes for men and women – expect plenty of Hawaiian shirts, tie-string overalls, and tube tops – in addition to period-relevant tchochkes.

Resurrection 217 Mott St, at Spring St ℡212/625-1374, ⊛www.resurrectionvintage.com. Hands down the best high-end place for vintage clothing in the city, with first-class Pucci and Halston classics from the 60s through to the 80s. The prices are very high, but it's still worth it just to check out the Pucci gowns and python Dior jackets.

Screaming Mimi's 382 Lafayette St, between E 4th and Great Jones sts ℡212/677-6464, ⊛www.screamingmimis.com. One of the most well-established lower-end second-hand stores in Manhattan. Vintage clothes, including lingerie, bags, shoes, and housewares at reasonable prices.

At the beginning of each fashion season, designers' and manufacturers' showrooms are still full of leftover merchandise from the previous season. These pieces are removed via informal sample sales, which kick off in October and run through March, though there are usually a few in April and May. You'll always save at least fifty percent off the retail price, though you may not be able to try on the clothes and you can never return them. Always take plenty of cash with you; some sales will not accept credit cards. The best way to find out what sales are coming up is to check the current issues of *Time Out New York* (ⓦ www.timeoutny.com) and *New York* magazine (ⓦ www.newyorkmetro.com). You can also sign up for the free regular emails issued by **Charlie Suisman's MUG** (ⓦ www.manhattanusersguide.com), **Clothing Line** (ⓦ www.clothingline.com), or **Daily Candy** (ⓦ www.dailycandy.com). If you're a really determined bargain-hunter, or just want to spend your entire time in New York sample-sale shopping, consider subscribing to the **S&B Report** (published monthly for $75/year; ⓦ www.lazarshopping.com).

Tokio 7 64 E 7th St, between First and Second aves Ⓣ 212/353-8443. Attractive second-hand and vintage designer consignment items; known for its flashy, eccentric selection – think plenty of Gaultier, Moschino, and McQueen – rather than boring, basic black.

What Comes Around Goes Around 351 W Broadway, between Broome and Grand sts Ⓣ 212/343-9303, ⓦ www.wcaga.com. Established and well-loved downtown vintage store. Popular with magazine stylists borrowing pieces for shoots.

Fashion: shoes

Most department stores carry two or more shoe salons – one for less expensive brands and one for finer shoes. **Barneys** and **Loehmann's** are both known for their selection of high-end footwear, while the greatest concentration of bargain shoe shops can be found in the Village on West 8th Street, between University Place and Sixth Avenue, and on Broadway below West 8th Street.

Shoes on Sale is the largest shoe sale open to the public, with more than 50,000 pairs of shoes. It is held each year around the second week in October, in a tent in Central Park, at Fifth Avenue and 60th Street. Check the newspapers or visit ⓦ www.ffany.org for details.

Alife 161 Bowery, between Delancey and Broome sts Ⓣ 212/219-3505. Sneaker nirvana, with an entire wall filled with limited-edition Adidas, Pumas, and lesser-known brands.
Camper 125 Prince St, at Wooster St Ⓣ 212/358-1842. Cult Spanish footwear with springy soles; some are based on eccentric takes on the bowling shoe.
Jimmy Choo 645 Fifth Ave, at 51st St Ⓣ 212/593-0800. Popular British designer has a huge Manhattan following for his high-heeled, high-priced, high-quality shoes.
John Fluevog 250 Mulberry St, at Prince St Ⓣ 212/431-4484. Innovative designs for a walk about town – most styles are casual but quirky, with buckles or brightly colored detailing.

Jutta Neumann 158 Allen St, between Stanton and Rivington sts Ⓣ 212/982-7048. Her custom-designed, super-comfy sandals are all the rage downtown, and she also sells popular leather handbags.
Kenneth Cole 610 Fifth Ave at 49th St Ⓣ 212/373-5800. Classic and contemporary shoes and beautiful bags in excellent full-grain leather. Call for more locations.
Manolo Blahnik 31 W 54th St, at Fifth Ave Ⓣ 212/582-3007. World-famous strappy stilettos – good for height (of fashion), hell for feet. More popular than ever thanks to Carrie Bradshaw and company in *Sex and the City*.
Nine West 675 Fifth Ave, at 53rd St Ⓣ 212/319-6893. Immensely popular

designer look-alikes, often with good seasonal reductions. Call for other locations.

Otto Tootsi Plohound 273 Lafayette St, at Prince St ☎212/431-7299; and 137 Fifth Ave, at 20th St ☎212/460-8650. If you want to run with a trendy crowd, these shoes will help: the best place to browse a range of brands, from Prada loafers to DSquared sneakers.

🏃 **Sigerson Morrison 28 Prince St, at Mott St ☎212/219-3893.** Kari Sigerson and

Miranda Morrison make timeless, simple, and elegant shoes for women. A required pilgrimage for shoe worshippers. The location just round the corner, Belle, 242 Mott St, at Prince St (☎212/941-5244), stocks their popular line of handbags.

Steve Madden 41 W 34th St, between Fifth and Sixth aves ☎212/736-3283. Very popular copies of up-to-the-minute styles, well loved for their ability to take on New York's "shoe-killing" streets.

Flea markets and craft fairs

New York **flea markets** are outstanding for funky and old clothes, collectibles, lingerie, jewelry, and crafts; there's also any number of odd places – parking lots, playgrounds, or maybe just an extra-wide bit of sidewalk – where people set up to sell their wares, especially in spring and summer.

Annex/Hell's Kitchen Flea Market 39th St, between Ninth and Tenth aves. Sat & Sun 10am–6pm. ☎212/243-5343. This is the fastest-growing fair in New York, with 170 vendors selling regular and retro antiques, furniture, vintage clothes, and bric-a-brac. Two other locations at 26–37 and 112 W 25th St.

Green Flea I.S. 44 Columbus Ave, at 77th St. Sun 10am–6pm, and Greenwich Ave and Charles St. Sat 11am–7pm. Two of the best and largest markets in the city: antiques and collectibles, desks and chests, textiles, vintage

clothing, haberdashery and hot sauces, plus a farmers' market (Columbus location).

Malcolm Shabazz Harlem Market 52 W 116th St, at Fifth Ave. Daily 10am–8pm ☎212/987-8131. Bazaar-like market, with an entrance marked by colorful fake minarets. A dazzling array of West African cloth, clothes, jewelry, masks, Ashanti dolls, and beads. Also sells leather bags, music, and Black Pride T-shirts.

Noho Market Broadway, at 4th St. Sat & Sun 10am–7pm. House music, jewelry, clothes, woven goods from South America, New Age paraphernalia and the like.

Food and drink

Food is a New York obsession – hence the proliferation of **gourmet groceries** and **specialty markets** across the city. For general snacking and late-night munchies, there's usually a 24-hour corner shop (referred to as a "bodega" by residents) within a few blocks' walk of anywhere.

Note that New York State's liquor-licensing laws mean that supermarkets and bodegas can only sell beer, and wine and spirits are only available in liquor stores. In either place, you'll need to be 21 to buy (and be able to prove it with a photo ID if asked). An added wrinkle is that the laws also preclude liquor-store owners from opening seven days a week, so most – though not all – are shut on Sundays.

🏃 **Agata & Valentina 1505 First Ave, at 79th St ☎212/452-0690.** The top gourmet grocer in town, with fresh pastas made on the premises, an enviable deli and cheese counter, a variety of pricey delicacies, and an outstanding butcher.

Balducci's 81 Eighth Ave, at 14th St ☎212/741-3700. Resident in a grand old former bank

with ultra-high ceilings, Balducci's is the rare gourmet store where you can sit down and enjoy some of your purchases (seating is upstairs, toward the back). Excellent prepared foods, and a notably comprehensive selection of cheeses.

Barney Greengrass 541 Amsterdam Ave, at 86th St ☎212/724-4707. "The Sturgeon King" is an Upper West Side smoked-fish institution, trading since 1908. You can sit down, or take your brunch makings to go.

Chelsea Market 75 Ninth Ave, at 15th St ☎212/243-6005, ⓦwww.chelseamarket.com. A complex of eighteen former industrial buildings, among them the old Nabisco Cookie Factory. A true smorgasbord of stores, including Amy's Bread, Bowery Kitchen Supply, the Fat Witch Bakery, Imports from Marrakech, The Green Table, Morimoto, the Ronnybrook Dairy, Hale & Hearty Soups, and the Manhattan Fruit Exchange.

Dean & Deluca 560 Broadway, between Prince and Spring sts ☎212/226-6800. One of the original big neighborhood food emporia. Beautiful quality fruit and veggies and top-notch prepared foods. Very chic, very Soho, and not at all cheap. They also have several other locations throughout the city.

Economy Candy 108 Rivington St, at Essex St ☎212/254-1832. A candy shop on the Lower East Side, selling tubs of sweets, nuts, and dried fruit at low prices.

Essex Street Covered Market Essex St, between Rivington and Delancey sts. Mon–Sat 8am–7pm. ☎212/388-0449. Here, a kosher fish market, Latino grocers, Saxelby Cheesemongers, Roni-Sue's Chocolates, and a Chinese greenmarket all live under one roof, reflecting the diversity of the neighborhood.

Euro Market 30–42 31st St, between 30th and 31st aves, Astoria ☎718/545-5569. Well - stocked deli, dozens of varieties of olives and soft drinks, and foodstuffs (and candies) from both edges of the continent and every-where in between.

Fairway 2127 Broadway, at 74th St ☎212/595-1888, ⓦwww.fairwaymarket.com.

Long-established Upper West Side grocery that many locals find better value than the more famous Zabar's (see p.400). The operation has its own farm on Long Island, so the produce is always fresh, and the range in some items is enormous. Fantastic organic selection upstairs.

Li-Lac 40 Eighth Ave, at Jane St ☎212/924-2280. Li-Lac's delicious chocolates have been handmade since 1923. One of the city's best treats for those with a sweet tooth – try the fresh fudge or hand-molded Lady Liberties and Empire States.

🏃 **Murray's Cheese Shop 257 Bleecker St, at Sixth Ave** ☎212/243-3289, ⓦwww.murrayscheese.com. More than 300 fresh cheeses and excellent panini sandwiches,

▲ Murray's Cheese Shop

Greenmarkets

Several days each week, long before sunrise, hundreds of farmers from Long Island, the Hudson Valley, and parts of Pennsylvania and New Jersey set out in trucks to transport their fresh-picked bounty to New York City, where they are joined by bakers, cheesemakers, and other artisans at **greenmarkets**. These are run by the city authorities, roughly one to four days a week, and are busiest from June through September. Usually you'll find apple cider, jams and preserves, flowers and plants, maple syrup, fresh meat and fish, pretzels, cakes and breads, herbs, honey – just about anything and everything produced in the rural regions around the city – not to mention occasional live-worm composts and basil ice cream.

To find the greenmarket nearest to you, call ☎212/788-7476 or visit ⓦwww.cenyc.org; the largest and most popular is held in Union Square, at E 17th St and Broadway, year-round on Mon, Wed, Fri & Sat from 8am to 6pm.

all served by a knowledgeable staff. Saturday afternoons feature free tastings and occasionally, tours of the cheese caves in the cellar (call ahead). Online, check out the "Cheese Blog."

Porto Rico Importing Company 201 Bleecker St, at Sixth Ave ⊤212/477-5421. An astounding 110 coffees (their specialty) and 140 varieties of tea on offer. Rumor has it that the house blends are as good as many of the more expensive coffees.

Russ & Daughters 179 E Houston St, at Orchard St ⊤212/475-4880. Technically, this store is known as an "appetizing" – the original Manhattan gourmet shop, set up around 1900 to sate the appetites of homesick immigrant Jews, selling smoked fish, pickled vegetables, cheese, and bagels. This is one of the oldest and best.

Sahadi 187 Atlantic Ave, between Clinton and Court sts, Brooklyn Heights ⊤718/624-4550. Fully stocked Middle-Eastern grocery store selling everything from Iranian pistachios to creamy home-made hummus.

Titan 25–56 31st St, between Astoria Blvd and 20th St, Queens ⊤718/626-7771. Olympic-sized store for comestible Greek goods,
including imported feta cheese, yogurt, and stuffed grape leaves.

Vintage New York 482 Broome St, at Wooster St ⊤212/226-9463; also 2492 Broadway, at 93rd St ⊤212/721-9999. This New York State–based winery is one place where you'll be able to pick up a bottle on Sundays. It's worth stopping by at other times to try the tasting bar, where you can sample 5 different vintages for as little as $15.

Warehouse Wines and Spirits 735 Broadway, between 8th St and Waverly Place ⊤212/982-7770. The top place to get a buzz for your buck, with a wide selection and frequent reductions on popular lines.

Zabar's 2245 Broadway, at 80th St ⊤212/787-2000, ⓦwww.zabars.com. The apotheosis of New York food-fever, Zabar's is still the city's pre-eminent gourmet shop. Choose from an astonishing variety of cheeses, olives, meats, salads, freshly baked breads and croissants, and prepared dishes. Upstairs, shop for shiny kitchen and household implements to help you put it all together at home. Avoid weekend afternoons, when the tour buses pull up outside and turn a visit to the modest-sized store into Dante's seventh circle of hell.

Music

The age of **music stores** is fading fast, sadly, as retailers, both chain and independent, struggle with both online vendors and the rise of the download-hungry iPod generation. Of the large chains, only the Virgin Megastore and J&R Music remain (unless you count the Circuit City and Best Buy electronics stores), and over 80 shops in Manhattan and Brooklyn have bit the dust since 2003. Nevertheless, many excellent **independent record stores** survive in pockets in the East and West villages, with particularly cheap used bargains available around St Mark's Place. Especially popular are small stores dedicated to various permutations of electronica, and venerable jazz–record stores with great LP selections that have been around for decades.

Academy 12 W 18th St, between Fifth and Sixth aves ⊤212/242-3000; also 415 E 12th St ⊤212/780-9166; and 96 N 6th St, Brooklyn ⊤718/218-8200, ⓦwww.academy-records.com. Used, rare and/or hard to find titles are the Academy's forte.

Etherea 66 Ave A, at 5th St ⊤212/358-1126. Specializing in indie rock and electronica, both domestic and import, on CD and vinyl, this is one of the best shops in the city. Good used selection and sweet, obsessive staff.

Fat Beats 406 Sixth Ave, at 8th St, 2nd floor ⊤212/673-3883. The name says it all: it's *the* source for hip-hop on vinyl in New York City.

Generation Records 210 Thompson St, at Bleecker St ⊤212/254-1100. The focus here is on hardcore, metal, and punk with some indie. New CDs and vinyl upstairs, used goodies downstairs. It also gets many of the imports the others don't have, plus fine bootlegs. A ginger giant tabby and feline cohorts Reed and Lulu act as cat security squad.

Halcyon 57 Pearl St, at Water St, Dumbo, Brooklyn ⊤718/260-WAXY, ⓦwww.halcyonline.com. A trusted source for dance music, but offers stuff ranging from jazz to techno. It now carries drum'n'bass and import titles from defunct yet revered Lower East Side store Breakbeat Science, now an online-only operation. Radio shows, listening parties, and a general air of music-nerd community make this a top pick.

House of Oldies 35 Carmine St, at Bleecker St ☎212/243-0500, Ⓦwww.houseofoldies.com. Just what the name says – oldies but goldies of all kinds. Vinyl only.

J&R Music World 23 Park Row, at Beekman St ☎212/238-9000. Downtown's family-owned, home-grown music retailer, with a knowledgeable staff and reasonable prices. Check out the company's adjacent stores that offer computer equipment and electronics (see p.391).

Jazz Record Center 236 W 26th St, between Seventh and Eighth aves ☎212/675-4480, Ⓦwww.jazzrecordcenter.com. The place to come for rare or out-of-print jazz LPs from the dawn of recording through the bebop revolution, avant-jazz, and beyond. They also have rare books, videos, and memorabilia.

Kim's 6 St Mark's Place, at Second Ave ☎212/598-9985. Extensive selection of new and used indie obscurities on CD and vinyl, some very cheap. Esoteric videos upstairs. Expect the staff to have a serious attitude problem.

Other Music 15 E 4th St, at Broadway ☎212/477-8150, Ⓦwww.othermusic.com. This homespun place is an excellent spot for "alternative" CDs, both old and new, that can otherwise be hard to find. Stocking less indie on vinyl than it once did, and now leaning toward experimental and electronica, the store retains the same ever-friendly and knowledgeable staff.

Sound Fix 110 Bedford St, Williamsburg, Brooklyn ☎718/388-8090, Ⓦwww .soundfixrecords.com. Friendly, well-stocked store, specializing in indie rock; the website features album reviews and the store often hosts (free) in-store appearances and listening parties.

Virgin Megastore 1540 Broadway, at 45th St ☎212/921-1020; also 52 E 14th St, at Union Square ☎212/598-4666. The last of the big-time brick-and-mortar music stores?

Westsider Records 233 W 72nd St, at Broadway ☎212/874-1588. Specializes in rare LPs.

Specialty stores

The shops below are either offbeat and interesting to visit or sell useful items that are cheaper in New York than elsewhere.

ABC Carpet and Home 888 Broadway, at 19th St ☎212/473-3000. Six floors of antiques and country furniture, knick-knacks, linens, and, of course, carpets. The grandiose, museum-like setup is half the fun. Wander through to garner decorating ideas.

De La Vega Gallery Store 102 St Marks Place, at 13th St ☎212/876-8649, Ⓦwww.delavega international.com. Home gallery for Harlem's only (self-proclaimed) "graffiti artist, painter, photographer, educator, activist, thinker," whose catchy sayings and simple drawings City residents sometimes wake to find in chalk on the sidewalks. The store sells T-shirts, prints, and other memorabilia.

Dinosaur Designs 250 Mott St, at Prince St ☎212/680-3523. Chunky resin homewares and jewelry from Australia in a dazzling palette of bright reds, greens, blues, yellows, and violets. The bold bangles are best-sellers.

Exit 9 64 Ave A, at 4th St ☎212/228-0145, Ⓦwww.shopexit9.com. Quirky, kooky emporium of kitsch, stocking soaps, bags, cards, and various other offbeat goodies – great for last-minute gifts.

Flight 001 96 Greenwich Ave, at 12th St ☎212/989-0001. The best place for bags in the city, from Mandarina Duck to Freitag, plus a stylish selection of travel accessories (alarm clocks, candles, specialty mini-toiletries) and books.

Maxilla & Mandible 451 Columbus Ave, between 81st and 82nd sts ☎212/724-6173. Natural history made entertaining, with coyote skulls, butterflies (and scorpions) under glass, hollowed-out ostrich eggs, polished shells, and anatomical charts. It's not just for show – the (background) staff consists largely of serious scientists. Perhaps not for the squeamish.

MoMA Design Store 81 Spring St, at Crosby ☎646/613-1367. The Museum of Modern Art's retail wing, this shop holds a host of super-stylish housewares, modish knick-knacks, and contemporary art books.

Moss 150–152 Greene St, at Houston St
☎1-866/888-6677. By far the premier shop
for top-quality designer home accessories
and furniture. Owner Murry Moss is a design
guru, and his playland of a store offers
everything from wacky but expensive
furniture (think sofas made from corrugated
cardboard) to more affordable but still
super-stylish salt and pepper shakers.

Mxyplyzyk 125 Greenwich Ave, at 13th St
☎212/989-4300, ⓦwww.mxyplyzyk.com.
Don't let the weird name put you off (for the
record, it's pronounced "Mixee-plizz-ik," and
is named for a character in a 1930s
Superman comic); this is a housewares and
gift shop, with sleek table-top and bath
products as well as stationery, watches,
and sundries.

New York Yankees Clubhouse Shop 393
Fifth Ave, between 36th and 37th sts

☎212/685-4693. In case you want that "NY"
logo on all your clothing…

Paper Presentation 23 W 18th St, between Fifth
and Sixth aves ☎212/463-7035. Perhaps the
most comprehensive paperie in the city,
with hand-made and unique wrapping
papers, stationery, fountain-pen ink, presentation folders, cards and gifts.

Utrecht Art Supplies 111 Fourth Ave, between
11th and 12th sts ☎212/777-5353. The brand
has a 40-year hold on the NYC art market.
Carries all manner of paints and brushes,
printmaking supplies, drawing materials
(charcoal to crayons), along with portfolios
in which to carry the finished products.

Village Chess Shop 230 Thompson St, at W 3rd
St ☎212/475-8130. Every kind of chess set
for every kind of pocketbook. Usually
packed with people playing and contem-
plating their next move. Open until 11pm.

Sporting goods

There are quite a number of sporting-goods outlets in the city – from cookie-
cutter chain stores to mom-and-pop cycle shops to multistory sneaker
pleasure-domes. Check them out for merchandise as well as for their wealth of
information about sports in and around the city.

Bicycle Renaissance 430 Columbus Ave, at 81st
St ☎212/724-2350, ⓦwww.bicyclerenaissance
.com. A classy place with competitive prices,
custom-bike building, and usually, same-day
service. Specialized and Cannondale bikes,
and Carrera and Pinarello frames in stock.

BLADES Board & Skate 120 W 72nd St, at
Amsterdam Ave ☎212/787-3911; also 659
Broadway, between Bleecker and Bond sts
☎212/477-7074. Rent or buy rollerblades,
snowboards, and the like. Handy for
Central Park.

Eastern Mountain Sports (EMS) 591 Broadway,
at Houston St ☎212/966-8730. Top-quality
merchandise covering almost all outdoor
sports, including skiing and kayaking.

Mason's Tennis Mart 56 E 53rd St, at Park Ave
☎212/755 5805. New York's last remaining
tennis specialty store – they let you try out
all rackets.

Niketown 6 E 57th St, at Fifth Ave ☎212/891-
6453. You can enter this five-floor sneaker

temple through an atrium in Trump Tower, or
through the front entry lined with b-ball
court hardwood. Then, you can join the
masses and purchase Nike clothing and
accessories at full price. To try your own
hand at color coordination, design your own
super-high-end sneakers with Nike iD: sign
up for an appointment beforehand with a
"Studio Design Consultant" at ☎212/891-
6454, Mon–Fri 10am–7pm.

Paragon Sporting Goods 867 Broadway, at 18th
St ☎212/255-8036. Family-owned, with three
levels of general merchandise, stocking
nearly everything you'll need for most
sports.

Super Runners Shop 1337 Lexington Ave, at
89th St ☎212/369-6010; also 360 Amsterdam
Ave, at 77th St ☎212/787-7665; and 1246 Third
Ave, at 72nd St ☎212/249-2133. Experienced
runners work at all three locations; co-
owner Gary Muhrcke won the first NYC
Marathon in 1970.

Sports and outdoor activities

I f measured by sheer number of teams and the coverage they are given, New York ranks as the number-one **sports** city in America. TV stations cover most regular-season games and all post-season games in the big four American team sports – **baseball**, **football**, **basketball**, and **ice hockey**. Baseball is a vital part of New York culture; even tepid sports fans have some allegiance to either the Yankees or the Mets. Tickets can often be hard to find (some are impossible – it all depends on what team is in town) and most don't come cheap. Nothing compares to the chill of the arena, the smell of the grass, and the anxiety of pre-game introductions, but if you don't get a chance to see this slice of Americana in person, there are always **sports bars** – establishments with free-flowing beer, king-sized television screens, and their own special kind of rabid fans (see the box on p.409 for listings).

Many **participatory activities** in the city are either free or fairly affordable, and take place in all kinds of weather. New Yorkers are passionate about **jogging** – there are plenty of places to take a scenic run – and you can **swim** at local pools or borough beaches. However, even with the help of the Parks Department (☎311, ⓦwww.nycgovparks.org) it can be hard to find facilities for some sports (like tennis), especially if you are not a city resident. To this end, many New Yorkers spend between $40 and $100 (or more) a month to be members of private **health clubs**; you can usually get a free trial week at one of the major ones (the Ys, New York Sports Clubs, Crunch, Bally's, etc), particularly if you use the address where you are staying in New York.

Baseball

In the early 1840s, the New York Knickerbocker Club played "base ball" near Madison Square in Manhattan, before moving to Elysian Fields, across the Hudson River in Hoboken, New Jersey. There, on June 26, 1846, they laid down the basic rules (the "Knickerbocker Rules") of the game of **baseball**, as it is played to this day.

For half a century, New York was home to three Major League Baseball (MLB) teams: the New York Giants and the Brooklyn Dodgers, who represented the National League, and the **New York Yankees**, who represented the American League. Additionally, in the years before MLB was integrated, the Negro League had several notable teams based in the city.

Minor-league baseball

Attending a minor-league baseball game is great fun. Not only do you get the chance to see up-and-coming players compete with those hanging on for one last shot at The Show, but the crowds are smaller, the seats are better and tickets much cheaper. 1999 saw the birth of the first new baseball franchise in New York in several decades: the minor-league **Staten Island Yankees** (☎718/720-9265, ⓦwww.siyanks.com; tickets $5–13), who play in the Class A New York–Penn League (June–Sept). They can be seen at the Richmond County Bank Ballpark at St George, within walking distance of the Staten Island ferry terminal.

After a 43-year absence, baseball returned to Brooklyn in 2001 in the form of the **Brooklyn Cyclones** (☎718/449-8497, ⓦwww.brooklyncyclones.com; tickets $7–15), an affiliate of the Mets that play in the same New York–Penn League as the Staten Island Yankees. The beautiful, oceanside stadium is at the former Steeplechase Park in Coney Island.

The almost–decade between 1947 and 1956 was the golden age of baseball in New York, with the Yankees steamrolling their opponents and larger–than–life, heroic competitors like Mickey Mantle, Joe DiMaggio, and Jackie Robinson playing for the Dodgers. This period ended abruptly in 1957, when the Giants and Dodgers bolted to California at the end of the season – though the city has mostly forgotten the Giants, many Brooklyn residents are still scarred by the loss of the Dodgers. New York was bereft of a National League franchise until the **Mets** arrived at the Polo Grounds in 1962, moving two years later to Shea Stadium in Flushing, Queens.

The MLB **season** lasts for the better part of the year: Spring Training exhibition games occur in March, the **regular season** runs from April to the end of September, and the post-season series takes place in October.

Yankee Stadium

Yankee Stadium, the Bronx home of the New York Yankees, has witnessed more than a few awe-inspiring moments since Babe Ruth christened it with a home run on opening day in 1923. Certain images from the stadium, recycled over and over, have become iconic in American sports history: Babe Ruth tiptoeing daintily around the bases after yet another majestic moonshot; Joe DiMaggio's phenomenal 56-game hitting streak and his effortless grace in centerfield; Mickey Mantle's awesome power; and the dying Lou Gehrig's farewell to the game on July 4, 1939, when he declared himself "the luckiest man on the face of the earth."

Though baseball is (justly) the stadium's most famous activity, other sports have seen their moment in the sun here as well. On June 22, 1938, black heavyweight champion Joe Louis knocked out Hitler's National Socialist hero Max Schmeling in the first round. In (American) football, "the greatest game ever played" took place at Yankee Stadium in December 1958 between the New York Giants and the Baltimore Colts. The televised championship game went into a dramatic overtime period, indirectly helping popularize the sport across the country.

After more than 85 years, though, Yankee Stadium was becoming outdated, with limited amenities for players and fans alike, and in 2009 the **New Yankee Stadium** will open just north of the old location, between 161st and 164th streets. Part of a larger Bronx redevelopment project that also includes a hotel, a conference center, and a school, construction is scheduled to be finished for the beginning of the 2009 season.

New York Yankees

Reciting the achievements of the **Yankees** (also known as "The Bronx Bombers") over the decades can get tedious. They are the team with the most World Series titles (through 2007, they boast 26), and they have been in the playoffs for 45 of the last 86 seasons: an almost unheard-of success rate for major-league sports.

If possible, try to catch a game when the Boston Red Sox are in town. The long-running rivalry between the teams' fans – originating in 1920, when former Red Sox star pitcher Babe Ruth was traded to the Yankees – makes for an exciting time. The other great games to try for are the "Subway Series," when the Bombers face their cross-town rivals, the Mets, in June interleague play. The players on both teams are seemingly unphased by the series, but it makes for high drama among their divided fans. For more on the Bombers, see the box on p.258. For details on buying **tickets**, which start at $14 for the bleachers and range well over $200 for the best seats, see p.410.

New York Mets

The **Mets** have often been regarded as the ugly bridesmaids of the city, and despite a much-hyped rebirth in 2006, with a change in management and the addition of Hall of Fame pitcher Pedro Martínez and former Yanks bench coach Willie Randolph, the team was eventually defeated by St Louis in the National League Championship Series. In 2007, things seemed to fall apart again; the Mets became the first team in baseball history to blow a lead of seven or more games, the second worst collapse ever.

Like their Bronx rivals, the Mets move to a **new stadium** in 2009: **Citi Field** in Willets Point, Queens. For **tickets** ($5–117), see p.410.

Football

The **National Football League (NFL) regular season** stretches from September through the end of December. New York's teams are the **Jets** and the **Giants**; both play at **Giants Stadium**, part of the Meadowlands Sports Complex in New Jersey. Plans for a new stadium in Manhattan were finally defeated in 2005, and both teams are expected to move to the **New Meadowlands Stadium** in 2010, presently under construction near the current complex. Tickets for both teams are always officially **sold out** well in advance, but you can often pick up tickets (legally) from secondary-broker websites such as ⓦwww.ticketliquidator.com. Prices fluctuate according to supply and demand.

New York Giants

In 2008, the **Giants** defeated the New England Patriots in Super Bowl XLII in one of the biggest upsets in NFL history, propelling the team (and especially quarterback **Eli Manning**) to superstar status. Since 1925, the **Giants** have won four NFL and two previous Super Bowl championships (1987 and 1991). Due to the length of the waiting list for season tickets (incredibly long), the **Giants** (ⓣ201/935-8222, ⓦwww.giants.com) actually encourage current ticket-holders to sell their unused seats to people farther down on the list; you have to join the waiting list (by mail) to have a shot at these tickets. For details on Giants Stadium and buying tickets ($70 and up), see p.410.

New York Jets

Founded in 1960 as part of an upstart American Football League, the **Jets** (☏516/560-8200, ⓦwww .newyorkjets.com), originally known as the Titans, currently play at the Giants Stadium in New Jersey and will share the New Meadowlands Stadium with the Giants in 2010.

The Jets' 16–7 Super Bowl III victory in 1969 (following the 1968 regular season) earned respect for the fledgling AFL and set the stage for the creation of the National Football League as it is today. As with the Giants, secondary websites offer the best deals on **tickets**, which can go for as low as $20, depending on the game (see p.410).

Professional basketball

The **National Basketball Association (NBA) regular season** begins in November and runs through the end of April. The two professional teams in the New York area are the **New York Knicks** (Knickerbockers), who play at Madison Square Garden, and the **New Jersey Nets**, whose current venue is the Izod Center at the Meadowlands Sports Complex in New Jersey, though the team may relocate to Brooklyn in 2010. There is also a women's professional team in New York, the WBNA **Liberty**. Tickets to see them play are fairly easy to come by, though the team is growing in popularity.

New York Knicks

It's not easy being a **Knicks** (ⓦwww .nba.com/knicks) fan. Madison Square Garden is one of the ugliest structures in North America; their last championship win was way back in 1973 (though the Knicks consistently make the playoffs); and after all that, tickets are expensive and virtually impossible to come by.

For details on Madison Square Garden and buying tickets (cheapest seats $10–$70), see p.410.

New Jersey Nets

The **Nets** (ⓦwww.nba.com/nets/) began life in 1967, as the New Jersey Americans. Led by the legendary Julius Irving (Dr J), they won two championships (1974 and 1976) while playing on Long Island before joining the NBA. Runs in 2006 and 2007 resulted in second-round defeats, but the 2007-2008 season proved to be the worst of the decade. Nets tickets are easier to come by than for the Knicks, owing to the comparative

difficulty of getting to their New Jersey arena. This may change, though, if the Nets move to the **Barclays Center** in Brooklyn (part of the Atlantic Yards project; see p.226), for the 2010 season.

For details on the Izod Center and buying tickets ($10–210), see p.410.

New York Liberty

The Women's National Basketball Association (WNBA) season opens when the NBA season ends and runs through the summer to its playoffs in September. The league jumped off in 1997, with the New York team, the **Liberty**, finishing as runners-up for the title; despite making the playoffs almost every year (including 2007), and appearing in four finals, the Liberty has yet to win the championship. Games are at Madison Square Garden, and prices low compared with those for the Knicks. You can usually get a ticket; call ☏1-877/ WNBA-TIX, go to ⓦwww.wnba .com/liberty, or pick some up at MSG. **Ticket prices**: $10–64.50.

College basketball

The **college basketball** season begins in November and ends with "March Madness," in which conference tournaments are followed by a 65-team tournament to select a national champion. The national tournament may be the most exciting, eagerly anticipated sporting event in the US.

Madison Square Garden (℡212/465-6741, Ⓦwww.thegarden.com and Ⓦwww.bigeast.org) hosts pre-season tournaments and the Big East Conference tournament. Metropolitan-area colleges pursuing hoop dreams include Long Island, Stony Brook, Columbia, Seton Hall, and St John's universities.

Ice hockey

There are two professional hockey teams in New York: the **Rangers**, who play at Madison Square Garden, and the **Islanders**, whose venue is the Nassau Coliseum on Long Island. In addition, the **New Jersey Devils** play out at the Prudential Center in Newark. All three compete in the Atlantic Division of the Eastern Conference of the **National Hockey League (NHL)**. The **regular season** lasts throughout the winter and into early spring, when the playoffs take place.

New York Rangers

One of the six original NHL teams, the **Rangers** (℡212/465-6000, Ⓦwww.newyorkrangers.com) were founded in 1926 and won the Stanley Cup – awarded to the winner of the playoffs – three times in the following fifteen years. According to hockey lore, giddy from their 1940 playoff-finals victory over the Toronto Maple Leafs, the Madison Square Garden owners paid off their $3 million mortgage and celebrated by burning the deed in Lord Stanley's cup – an act of desecration that provoked a curse upon the franchise and its fans. The Rangers ended their 54-year championship drought in 1994, but this was followed by another long period of mediocre performances – since making the playoffs in 2006 and 2007, the team finally looks set for a sustained period of success.

Ticket prices: $40–254; for details on Madison Square Garden and buying tickets, see p.410.

New York Islanders

Founded in 1972, the **Islanders** (℡1-800/882-ISLES, Ⓦwww.newyorkislanders.com) were fortunate enough to string together their four Stanley Cups in consecutive years (1980–83) and thus qualify as a bona fide hockey dynasty. Since then, however, it's been mostly downhill, though they did make the playoffs in 2004 and 2007.

Ticket prices: $19–120; for details on Nassau Coliseum and buying tickets, see p.410.

New Jersey Devils

The nomadic **New Jersey Devils** franchise (W www.newjerseydevils .com) was founded in 1974 as the Kansas City Scouts, and moved to New Jersey (after a brief stint as the Colorado Rockies in Denver) in 1982.

A succession of mediocre seasons was interrupted when the Devils beat the heavily favored Detroit Red Wings in four straight games to win the 1995 Stanley Cup. They regained the Cup in 2003, but lost it to the Philadelphia Flyers in the first round of the 2004 playoffs. In 2008 (their first season at the Prudential Center in Newark), the Devils were beaten by arch rivals New York Rangers in the first round of the playoffs.

Ticket prices: $19–349; for details on the Prudential Center and buying tickets, see p.410.

Soccer

The game of **soccer** (European football) continues to grow in popularity in America, especially with the much-hyped arrival of David Beckham at the Los Angeles Galaxy in 2007. Though soccer coverage is not as extensive in the US as it is abroad, it's not too hard to catch on TV and in sports bars (see box opposite).

The **New York Red Bulls** (T 201/583-7000, W www.redbull.newyork .mlsnet.com), who play at Giants Stadium in New Jersey, are the metropolitan area's Major League Soccer representatives. They won the Eastern Division title in 2000 and got as far as the playoff semifinals; their performance since has often been less than stellar. The Bulls are expected to move to the purpose-built **Red Bull Park**, in Harrison, New Jersey, in late 2009. The MLS **season** runs April through November.

Ticket prices: $15–64; for details on buying tickets, see p.410.

Horse racing

The two busiest **horse-racing** tracks in the area are the **Aqueduct Race Track** and the **Belmont Race Track**, both with thoroughbred racing.

Aqueduct (T 718/641-4700, W www.nyra.com/index_aqueduct.html) in Ozone Park, Queens, has racing from October through December, and again from January through April. **Belmont** (T 516/488-6000, W www.nyra.com), in Elmont, Long Island, is home to the Belmont Stakes (June), one of the three races in which three-year-olds compete for the **Triple Crown**. Belmont is open April through July and September through October. Admission at Aqueduct ranges from $1 to $5 depending on where you park and sit; Belmont ranges $2 to $7. Valet parking costs $4 at Aqueduct and $6 at Belmont.

Off-track betting

To **place a bet** anywhere other than the track itself, find an **OTB (Off-Track Betting)** office. There are plenty around the city; call

T 212/221-5200 or check W www .nycotb.com for locations. You need an established account to place an Internet or phone bet: to set one up, use the website or call T 1-800/OTB-8118.

40/40 Club 6 W 25th St at Broadway ⓣ212/989-0040, ⓦthe4040club.com. Jay-Z's towering, two-level sports bar is probably the smartest place you'll ever watch the game, with six cream-colored leather swing chairs, suspended from the ceiling, Italian marble floors, and fifteen 60-inch LCD flat-screen TVs. After the game, the whole thing becomes a thumping R&B and hip-hop club.

The Central Bar 109 E 9th St, between Third and Fourth aves ⓣ212/529-5333, ⓦcentralbar.8m.com. Warm, friendly Irish bar showing European football alongside American games.

ESPN Zone 1472 Broadway, at W 42nd St ⓣ212/921-3776, ⓦespnzone.com /newyork. ESPN-affiliated sports bar/restaurant, where you can catch the action from one of 278 screens (even in the bathroom), assuming you can get in.

Jimmy's Corner 140 W 44th St, between Broadway and Sixth Ave ⓣ212/221-9510. See p.348 for review.

Kinsdale Tavern 1672 Third Ave, at 93rd St ⓣ212/348-4370. Upper East Side Irish sports bar.

Mickey Mantle's 42 Central Park S, between Fifth and Sixth aves ⓣ212/688-7777. Perhaps the city's most famous sports bar, packed with memorabilia; it's hard to tell which is more bland, though, the food or the décor.

Ship of Fools 1590 Second Ave, between 82nd and 83rd sts ⓣ212/570-2651. No matter what the game, the amiable owner at this Upper East Side postgrad hangout will try to put it up for you on one of their 42 satellite TVs (13 big ones). The bar grub is better than expected.

Stitch 247 37th St, between Seventh and Eighth aves ⓣ212/852-4826, ⓦwww .stitchnyc.com. See p.348 for review.

To watch racing in comfort, try *The Inside Track* (run by OTB) at 991 Second Ave, at 53rd St (ⓣ212/752–1940), or OTB's two other tele-theaters, the *Winner's Circle*, 515 Seventh Ave, at 38th St (ⓣ212/730–4900), and *O'Neill's Seaport Restaurant*, 170 John St, at Water St (ⓣ212/344–5959), with food, drink, schmoozing, and wagering on the premises.

Tennis

The **US Open Championships**, held each September at the National Tennis Center in Flushing Meadows–Corona Park, in Queens, is the top US tennis event of the year. In 1997, the Flushing complex opened a new center court, the Arthur Ashe Stadium. Tickets go on sale the first week or two of June at the Tennis Center's box office (ⓣ718/760-6200, ⓦwww.usta.com), open Monday through Friday 9am–5pm and Saturday 10am–4pm. Promenade-level seats at the stadium cost $22–80 (better seats can cost several hundred dollars) for evening games, while day-passes start at $48. If they are sold out, keep trying up to the day of the event because corporate tickets are often returned. Tickets for the big matches are incredibly difficult to get – you can either take a chance with scalpers, secondary-ticket websites, or try your luck at the Will Call window for people who don't show up.

Tickets and venues

Tickets for most sporting events can be booked ahead with a credit card through Ticketmaster (☎212/307-7171, ⓦwww.ticketmaster.com) and collected at the gate, though it's cheaper – and of course riskier for popular events – to try to pick up tickets on the night of the event. You can also call or go to the stadium's box office and buy advance tickets. If the box office has sold out, try one of the numerous Internet brokers that sell **secondary tickets** (tickets that are resold by agencies or individuals); prices are set according to supply and demand, so can be cheaper or substantially more, depending on the importance of the game and the seats. Try ⓦwww.ticketliquidator.com, ⓦwww.stubhub.com, or ⓦwww.razorgator.com.

Scalping (reselling a ticket, usually on the day of the event outside the arena, at an inflated price) is illegal, and with the explosion of secondary websites, virtually redundant. If all else fails, simply catch the action on the big screen in a sports bar.

Citi Field 126th St and Roosevelt Ave, Willets Point, Queens ☎718/507-8499, ⓦmets.mlb .com. The new home of the Mets is due to open April 2009. Take #7 train, direct to Willets Point. Box office Mon–Fri 9am–6pm, Sat, Sun & holidays 9am–5pm.

Madison Square Garden Seventh Ave, between 31st and 33rd sts ☎212/465-6741, ⓦwww .thegarden.com. Take #1, #2, #3, #A, #C, or #E to 34th St–Penn Station. Box office Mon–Fri 9am–6pm, Sat 10am–6pm.

Meadowlands Sports Complex containing both Giants Stadium and Izod Center, off routes 3, 17, and New Jersey Turnpike exit 16W, East Rutherford, New Jersey ☎201/935-8500, ⓦwww .meadowlands.com. Regular buses from Port Authority Bus Terminal on 42nd St and Eighth Ave. Box office open for all arenas Mon–Sat 11am–6pm.

Nassau Coliseum 1255 Hempstead Turnpike, Uniondale ☎516/794-9303, ⓦwww.nassau coliseum.com. Not very accessible other than by car. If you don't have your own

transportation, take the Long Island Railroad to Hempstead, then bus #N70, #N71, or #N72 from Hempstead bus terminal, one block away. Another option, which may be safer at night, is to catch the LIRR to Westbury and take a cab (5–10min ride) to the stadium. Box office Mon–Fri 9.30am–4.45pm.

Prudential Center 165 Mulberry St, between Edison Place and Lafayette St, Newark ☎973/757-6000, ⓦwww.prucenter.com. The home of the New Jersey Devils is just two blocks from Newark Penn Station, easily accessible by NJ Transit, Amtrak, and PATH trains from Manhattan.

Yankee Stadium 161st St and River Ave, South Bronx ☎718/293-6000, ⓦyankees.mlb.com. Subway #C, #D, or #4 direct to 161st St Station. Box office Mon–Fri 9am–5pm. The new Yankee Stadium should be open in April 2009, just to the north. Get to the game early and visit Monument Park, where all the Yankee greats are memorialized.

Participatory activities

Beaches

New York's **beaches** aren't worth a trip to the city in and of themselves, but they can be a cool summer escape from Manhattan. Most are only a MetroCard ride away.

Brooklyn

Brighton Beach #B and #Q trains to Brighton Beach. Technically the same stretch as

Coney Island Beach, but less crowded and populated mainly by the local Russian community. Boardwalk vendors sell ethnic snacks.

Coney Island Beach at the end of half a dozen subway lines: fastest is the #D train to Stillwell Ave. After Rockaway (see opposite), this is NYC's most popular bathing spot, jam-packed on summer weekends. The Atlantic here is only moderately dirty and there's a good, reliable onshore breeze.

Queens

Jacob Riis Park #2 and #5 trains to Flatbush Ave, then #Q35 bus. Good sandy stretches and very pristine. Some parts are popular with gay men. Nude bathing, once popular here, is no longer permitted.

Rockaway Beach #A and #C trains to any stop along the beach. Forget California: this seven-mile strip is where hundreds of thousands of New Yorkers come to get the best surf around – surf so good that the Ramones even wrote a song about it. Best beaches are at 9th St, 23rd St, and 80–118th sts.

Bicycling

New York has over 100 miles of **cycle paths**; those in Central Park, Riverside Park, and the East River Promenade are among the nicest. Two sources have done an excellent job of providing specific cycling routes and maps, laws and regulations, and other relevant info: the bike advocacy organization Transportation Alternatives (☎212/629-8080, Ⓦwww.transalt.org), which has some good maps, and the New York City Department of City Planning (Ⓦhome2.nyc.gov/html/dcp/html/bike/home.shtml), which has a wealth of information available as part of their BND (Bicycle Network Development) project. You'll find extensive (and downloadable) bike maps for all five boroughs, in addition to information on how to use mass transit in planning your bike ride. By law, you must wear a helmet when riding your bike on the street. Most bike stores rent bicycles by the day or hour. Refer to the *Yellow Pages* or websites such as Ⓦwww.bikenewyork.org for a list of rental shops.

Here are some clubs and resources for cycling enthusiasts:

Bicycle Habitat 244 Lafayette St ☎212/431-3315, Ⓦbicyclehabitat.com. Known for an excellent repair service, they also offer rentals, tune-ups, and advice.

Critical Mass Ⓦwww.critical-mass.org. A grassroots movement whose main agenda is to promote cycling as an alternate means of transportation. Group rides are organized on the last Friday of the month. Place and time decided last minute. Be sure to check the website.

Five Borough Bike Club ☎212/932-2300 ext 115, Ⓦwww.5bbc.org. This club organizes rides throughout the year, including the Montauk Century, where riders can chose routes varying between 65 and 140 miles from New York to Montauk, Long Island.

New York Cycle Club ☎212/828-5711, Ⓦwww.nycc.org. This 1400-member club offers many rides.

Boating

Downtown Boathouse Hudson River Pier 40, Pier 96, Clinton Cove at 56th St, and 72nd St ☎646/613-0740 (status) or 613-0375 (general information), Ⓦwww.downtownboathouse.org. Free kayaks and canoes available May–Oct weekends 9am–6pm.

Loeb Boathouse East Side of Central Park, between 74th and 75th sts ☎212/517-2233, Ⓦwww.centralparknyc.org. Rowboats and kayaks for rent March–Oct, daily 10am–5pm. Rates are $12 for the first hour, $3 per additional 15 minutes, plus $30 deposit. Bikes for $9–15/hr.

Bowling

300 New York Chelsea Piers Lanes, W 23rd St and Hudson River ☎212/835-2695, Ⓦwww.300newyork.com. AMF runs a 40-lane alley that morphs into a laser-lit, Day-Glo alternate universe called Xtreme Bowling Wed–Sun 5pm till close (nobody under 21 allowed without an adult after 9pm, although kids are the ones who would most enjoy it). Open Mon–Thurs & Sun 9am–11pm, Fri & Sat 9am–2am; $8 per game per person Mon–Fri 9am–5pm, $9 Sat & Sun 9am–5pm; $10 Xtreme Bowling (Sun–Thurs), $11 (Fri & Sat). $6 shoe rental.

Bowlmor Lanes 110 University Place, between 12th and 13th sts ☎212/255-8188, Ⓦwww.bowlmor.com. Long-established, large disco/bowling alley with a bar and shop. Open Mon & Thurs 11am–2am, Tues & Wed 11am–1am, Fri & Sat 11am–3.30am, Sun 11am–midnight. Mon–Thurs $9.45 per game per person before 5pm, $10.95 evenings; Fri & Sat $10.95 before 5pm, $12.95 evenings, Sun $10.95. $6 shoe rental.

Fishing

Sometimes the amount of concrete in New York can make you forget that the city is actually surrounded by water, much of it teeming with fish. Call the New York State Department of Health's Center for Environmental Health Information line (T 1-800/458-1158) for the latest tips on clean water and if you should toss your catch in the frying pan or back into the current.

Big City Fishing Pier 46 (West Village), Pier 84 (Midtown West) T 212/627-2020. Hudson River Park Trust runs this free program every summer weekend, providing free fishing rods, reels, and bait (as well as instruction) on a first-come, first-served basis, with a half-hour limit when others are waiting. Common species caught include the American eel, striped bass, black sea bass, fluke, and snapper – all fish are returned to the river at the end of the day.

New York Harbor Sportfishing T 201/725-6755, W www.nyharborfishing.com. Reliable local outfit run by Captain Joe Shastay, with more than 1900 charters in 26 years. Rates start at $680 for four hours.

Golf

Manhattan has no **public golf courses**, though there is a four-level driving range at Chelsea Piers (T 212/336-6400). Recommended among those in the outer boroughs are the following, all of which are subject to low and generally standardized prices (though you need your own clubs); full information is available at W www.nycparks.org. The fee for 18 holes on weekdays before noon is $33.25, and $28.75 thereafter; the weekend rate is $41 all day. Non-residents must pay an additional fee of $8.

Dyker Beach Golf Course 86th St and 7th Ave, Dyker Heights, Brooklyn T 718/836-9722. Often noted for its striking views of the Verrazano Narrows, Dyker is also convenient, right near the 86th Street stop on the #R train.

Central Park, Chelsea Piers, and Hudson River Park

Central Park is, at 843 acres, the center of the city's recreational life, from croquet to chess to soccer to socializing to sunning to swimming. Joggers, in-line skaters, walkers, and cyclists have the roads to themselves on weekdays 10am–3pm and 7–10pm and all day on weekends and holidays. It is not recommended that you hang out in the park too long after the sun goes down; at any rate, it is closed during the wee hours. To find out what is going on where and when, call T 212/310-6600 or look at W www.centralparknyc.org. You can also pick up a calendar of events or directory in the park. See Chapter 14, "Central Park," for more information.

Chelsea Piers W 23rd St and the Hudson River (between 17th and 23rd sts) T 212/336-6666, W www.chelseapiers.com. It features a year-round outdoor driving range, a track, the largest rock-climbing wall in the Northeast (as well as a smaller one for kids), basketball courts, a health club, indoor sand volleyball courts, and more. You can also join the crew of the *Adirondack* and the *Imagine*, two beautiful 78-foot wooden schooners, which sail from Pier 62. During the two-hour sail of lower New York Harbor, passengers can take the wheel, help hoist the sails, or just enjoy the surroundings. Boats operate May–Oct Wed 3.30pm, Thurs & Fri 1pm & 3.30pm, Sat 4.30pm, Sun 1pm, 2pm, 3.30pm, 4.30pm; $40, includes drinks; T 646/336-5270, W www.sail-nyc.com.

Hudson River Park T 212/533-7275, W www.hudsonriverpark.org. Twenty years in the planning, Hudson River Park is a massive redevelopment of the west-side waterfront from Battery Park to 59th St. The park links the Battery City Esplanade with Midtown, landscaping 550 acres of river, shoreline, and old piers along the way; the final sections of the park (Tribeca and Chelsea segments) should be open by 2010. Fishing is possible, and any number of sports facilities have already opened or are in the works.

Split Rock Golf Course & Pelham Golf Course
870 North Shore Rd, Pelham, Bronx ☎718/885-1258. Split Rock is considered the most challenging course in the city. Pelham, right next door, is somewhat easier.

Van Cortlandt Park Golf Course Van Cortlandt Park S and Bailey Ave, Bronx ☎718/543-4595. The oldest 18-hole public golf course in the country.

Health and fitness: pools, gyms, and baths

You can join one of the city's **recreation centers** (☎212/447-2020, ⓦwww.nycparks.org) for $50–75 per year (ages 18–54), $10 (seniors), or free (under 18). All have gym facilities; some hold fitness and other classes, and most have an indoor and/or outdoor pool.

Riverbank State Park W 145th St and Riverside Drive ☎212/694-3600. Beautiful facility built on top of a waste refinery in Harlem. Despite the strange location, it has great tennis courts, an outdoor track, an ice-skating rink (Nov–March), and several indoor facilities including a skating rink and Olympic-sized pool. Park admission is free; pool is $2, seniors and ages 4–15 $1, physically challenged free.

Russian & Turkish Baths 268 E 10th St ☎212/473-8806 or 674-9250, ⓦwww.russian turkishbaths.com. A neighborhood landmark that's still going strong, with steam baths, sauna, and an ice-cold pool, as well as a massage parlor and a restaurant. Free soap, towel, robe, slippers, etc. Admission $30, additional fee for massages and other extras. Open Mon, Tues, Thurs & Fri noon–10pm, Wed 10am–10pm, Sat 9am–10pm, Sun 8am–10pm; men only Sun opening until 2pm; women only Wed opening until 2pm; co-ed otherwise (shorts are mandatory).

Horse riding

Jamaica Bay Riding Academy 7000 Shore Parkway, Brooklyn ☎718/531-8949, ⓦwww .horsebackride.com. Trail riding, both Western and English, around the eerie landscape of Jamaica Bay. $37 for a guided 45min ride; lessons $85 for one hour.

Kensington Stables 51 Caton Place at E 8th St, Prospect Park, Brooklyn ☎718/972-4588, ⓦwww.prospectpark.org. Horses and classes available for rides along Prospect Park's 3.5-mile bridle path for $30/hr, daily 10am–sunset. Private lessons are $50/hr.

Ice-skating

New York's freezing winter weather makes for good **ice-skating**. The best rinks are in Central and Prospect parks; don't try skating on a lake, as the ice can be deceptively thin.

Lasker Rink 110th St, Central Park ☎212/534-7639, ⓦwww.centralparknyc.org. This lesser-known ice rink is at the north end of the park, and used as a pool in summer. Much cheaper than the Wollman Rink, though less accessible – both rinks are now owned by Donald Trump. Nov–March $4.50, under 12 and seniors $2.25, skate rental $4.75.

Rockefeller Center Ice Rink between 49th and 50th sts, off Fifth Ave ☎212/332-7654. It's a quintessential New York scene, lovely to look at but with long lines and high prices. $10–14, under 12 and seniors $7.50–8.50, rentals $8.

Sky Rink Pier 61 ☎212/336-6100, ⓦwww .chelseapiers.com. Ice-skate year-round at this indoor rink at Chelsea Piers. Mon–Fri 1.30–5.20pm, Sat & Sun 1–3.50pm; $12.50, youth and seniors $10. Rentals $7.

Wollman Rink 62nd St, Central Park ☎212/439-6900, ⓦwww.wollmanskatingrink.com. Lovely rink, where you can skate to the marvelous, inspiring backdrop of the lower Central Park skyline – incredibly impressive at night. $9.50–12, under 12 $4.75–5, seniors $4.75–8.25. Rentals $5. There's also a Wollman Rink in Brooklyn's Prospect Park ($5, children & seniors $3, rental $6; ⓦwww.prospectpark.org).

▲ Wollman Rink, Central Park

New York City Marathon

Every year on the first Sunday in November 37,000 runners come to New York to run the **New York City Marathon**. Along with the competitors come the fans: on average, two million people turn out each year to watch the runners try to complete the 26.2-mile course, which starts in Staten Island, crosses the Verrazano Narrows Bridge and passes through all the other boroughs before ending at the *Tavern on the Green* in Central Park. The race is taken very, very seriously, although not with the solemnity usually awarded to home baseball games.

If you are a runner, you can try to take part, but beware: the competition is fierce before the race even starts. Not everyone who submits the necessary entry forms is chosen to participate; race veterans (who have run fifteen or more New York Marathons), qualified New York Road Runners Club (NYRRC) members who have completed at least nine official races during the calendar year, and those who have applied and been rejected for the last three NYC marathons receive guaranteed entry, which can also be (completely legitimately) procured for you by a travel agent in your home country. Many athletes with disabilities participate as well; the wheelchair champion in 2006 set a record time of 1:29:22. Obtain forms from ⓦwww .nycmarathon.org or the NYRRC. Applications must be sent before May 1 for that year's race (US lottery applications June 1), and you must be at least 18 years old on race day.

Jogging and running

Jogging is still very much the number-one fitness pursuit in the city. The most popular venues are Central Park, Hudson River Park, and the Battery City Esplanade. A favorite circuit in Central Park is the 1.57 miles around the reservoir; just make sure you jog in the right direction – counterclockwise. For company on your runs, contact the New York Road Runners Club (ⓣ212/860-4455, ⓦwww.nyrrc.org), which sponsors many races and fun runs per year, including the Frostbite 10 Mile (Jan) and the Brooklyn Half-Marathon (April or May), plus numerous other events for runners.

Pool

Along with bars and nightclubs, a good option for an evening in Manhattan is to play **pool**, not only in dingy yet serious halls, but also in gleaming bars where well-heeled yuppies mix with the regulars. A number of sports, dive, and gay and lesbian bars have pool tables as well, though these are often much smaller than regulation size. Snooker fans will also find a few tables throughout the city.

Amsterdam Billiards 85 Fourth Ave, at E 11th St ⓣ212/995-0333, ⓦamsterdambilliardclub .com. Very popular, upscale Union Square billiards club with 26 tables. They serve liquor and beer along with bar food. Mon–Fri noon–4am, Sat & Sun 11am–3am; $5.50–$9.50/hr.

Slate 54 W 21st St, between Fifth and Sixth aves ⓣ212/989-0096, ⓦwww.slate-ny.com. Extremely gentrified two-story sports-bar-like Chelsea hall (over 30 tables) that serves better-than-average food and has well-kept facilities. Go during the day when it's less crowded, or noon–3pm weekdays when lunch is free. Sun–Thurs noon–3am, Fri & Sat noon–4am; $7/hr.

Rock climbing

Manhattan's skyline is the Himalayas of cityscapes, and while many have tried (illegally) scaling the city's skyscrapers, the concrete jungle is also full of difficult (and sanctioned) climbing routes. Chelsea Piers has one of the nicest climbing walls in the city (and the largest); see p.114 for more information. Visit ⓦwww.climbnyc .com for the latest on climbing gyms in the city.

City Climbers Club ⓣ212/974-2250, ⓦwww
.cityclimbersclub.com. Their website has all the
info you need on bouldering in Central Park,
indoor rock gyms, and people looking for
climbing buddies, and the yearly membership
($250) or daily passes ($15) are a fraction of
what they cost elsewhere. The club's
climbing wall and headquarters at the 59th
Street Rec Center will be closed for renovation through 2009 and 2010 – check the
website for news about alternative venues.
Manhattan Plaza Health Club 482 W 43rd St,
between Tenth and Ninth aves ⓣ212/974-2250,
ⓦwww.mphc.com. Climbing gym with 5000
square feet of climbing surface, including a
cave with a 40ft lead roof, two 20ft squeeze
chimneys, and a 160ft bouldering route. Day
pass $20. Mon, Thurs–Sun noon–10pm,
Tues & Wed 7am–10pm.

Tennis

There's not a great deal of court space
in New York, so finding an affordable
one can be tough. For information on
all city courts, including those in
Central Park (see below), go to
ⓦwww.nyc.gov/parks.
Central Park Tennis Courts ⓣ212/360-8133.
Their $100 permit (seniors $20, under-17s
$10) which runs from April through Nov,
provides access to all municipal courts in
the five boroughs. Once you have a permit
you can reserve a court 30 days in advance
($7) or just turn up and wait.

Yoga

New York is a great place to try
yoga for the first time, with classes
offered throughout the day at scores
of locations. You'll find all difficulty levels and numerous styles;
like much of the Western world,
the ancient practice has a large
following in fitness clubs where it
tends to be regarded as just another
gym class (with aerobic hybrids like
Yogalates), but there are plenty of
traditional forms like *jivamukti*, and
classes where breathing is more
important than how many calories
you burn. Yoga studios will also be
able to tell you where to practice
martial arts and Pilates. If you intend
to take a number of sessions, you
may want to purchase a New York
Yoga PassBook, an excellent deal
at $75 for 300 sessions at name
workshops throughout the city and
suburbs (ⓣ212/808-0765, ⓦwww
.health-fitness.org/ny.html). From
spring through fall, many outdoor
classes are free; check *Time Out New
York* or websites such as ⓦnewyork
cityyoga.com for listings.
Om Yoga 6/F, 826 Broadway, between E 13th
and E 12th sts ⓣ212/254-9642, ⓦwww
.omyoga.com. Many classes for beginners,
plus more advanced workshops. Includes
meditation. $18 per session, $28 two intro-
ductory classes, $1 mat rental.
Yoga Center of Brooklyn 474 Smith St, at 9th St
ⓣ718/858-4554, ⓦwww.brooklynyoga.com.
Carroll Gardens center offering strenuous
classes at all levels and in different styles,
informed by ideas of wellness and spiritu-
ality. $16 per session.

Parades and festivals

N ew York City takes its numerous **parades and festivals** extremely seriously. They are often political or religious in origin, but as in most of the world, whatever their official reason for existing, they are generally just an excuse for music, food, and dance. Almost every large ethnic group in the city holds an annual get-together, often using Fifth Avenue as the main drag. In general, it is a big mistake to drive, take a taxi, or ride the buses anywhere near these events.

Chances are, your stay will coincide with at least one festive happening. For more details and exact dates of the events listed below, phone ☎1–800/NYC-VISIT or go to ⓦwww.nycvisit.com. Also look at listings in the *Village Voice*'s "Voice Choices," *New York Magazine*'s "Agenda," *Time Out New York*'s "Around Town" sections, and in the *New York Times*' "Weekend Arts" section, published every Friday.

January

Outsider Art Fair (mid-Jan ☎212/777-5218, ⓦwww.sanfordsmith.com): Leading dealers of outsider, primitive, visionary, and intuitive art exhibit their collections at the Mart, 7 W 34th St, at Fifth Ave.

New York Jewish Film Festival (mid–late Jan ☎212/496-3809 or 875-5600, ⓦwww.filmlinc .com or ⓦwww.thejewishmuseum.org): Screenings of complex, provocative Jewish films with an international bent, as well as some rare oldies. Most films are shown at Lincoln Center's Walter Reade Theater.

Lunar (Chinese) New Year (first full moon between Jan 21 and Feb 19 ⓦwww .explorechinatown.com): A noisy, joyful occasion celebrated for two weeks along and around Mott Street in Lower Manhattan, as well as in Sunset Park, Brooklyn, and Flushing, Queens. The chances of getting a meal without a reservation anywhere in Manhattan's Chinatown during this time are slim.

Martin Luther King Jr Day Tributes (third Mon ☎718/636-4100, ⓦwww.bam.org): City-wide celebration honoring Dr King's contribution to civil rights and African-American heritage. The free talks and performances at the Brooklyn Academy of Music are the day's most notable occurrences.

Restaurant Week (late Jan–early Feb ☎212/484-1200, ⓦwww.restaurantweek.com): For about ten weekdays, you can get prix-fixe three-course lunches at some of the city's finest establishments for $25, or three-course dinners for $35. This can be quite a savings at restaurants like *Aquavit* and *Nobu*, though the limited menus don't always show off the cuisine at its best, and you must make reservations months in advance for the most desirable places. Also in July.

In various sections of the city on weekend afternoons in the spring, summer, and fall, **street fairs** close a stretch of several blocks to traffic to offer pedestrians T-shirts, curios, and gut-busting snacks like sausage sandwiches and fried dough. Unfortunately, once you've seen one, you've seen them all, as the vendors are rarely neighborhood-specific. You'll find the most local flavor at the raucously tacky Feast of San Gennaro (see p.421), which could be called the prototypical street fair. Heading to the outer boroughs often yields more character too – you might happen across *lucha libre* (Mexican wrestling) along with the usual fare.

Street fairs are usually listed in *Time Out New York* and neighborhood newspapers. Smaller block parties, sponsored by community groups rather than business organizations, are more intimate affairs, generally with one sidestreet closed to cars, kids performing, politicos popping in to shake hands, and everyone taking part in a huge pot-luck meal. They're typically not advertised, however, so consider yourself lucky to stumble on one.

February

Westminster Kennel Club Dog Show (mid-Feb ☎212/213-3165, ⓦwww.westminsterkennelclub.org): Second only to the Kentucky Derby as the oldest continuous sporting event in the country, this show at Madison Square Garden welcomes 2500 canines competing for best in breed, along with legions of fanatic dog-lovers.

March

St Patrick's Day Parade (March 17 ☎212/484-1222, ⓦwww.saintpatricksdayparade.com): Based on an impromptu march through the Manhattan streets by Irish militiamen on St Patrick's Day in 1762, this parade is a draw for every Irish band and organization in the US and Ireland, and it's impressive for the sheer mobs of people – no cars or floats are allowed. Parade organizers have long prohibited gay and lesbian groups from marching, but they have a vocal presence on the sidelines. Starting around 11am at St Patrick's Cathedral on Fifth Ave (following 8.30am Mass), it heads uptown to 86th St.

Greek Independence Day Parade (late March ☎718/204-6500, ⓦwww.greekparade.org): Not as long or as boozy as St Pat's, more a patriotic nod to the old country from floats of pseudo-classically dressed Hellenes. When Independence Day (March 25) falls in the Orthodox Lent, the parade is shifted to April or May. It usually kicks off from 60th St and Fifth Ave and runs up to 79th St.

New Directors, New Films (late March to early April ☎212/875-5638, ⓦwww.filmlinc.com): Lincoln Center and MoMA present this two-week series, one of the city's best, but rarely surrounded by hype. Films range from the next indie hits to obscure, never-to-be-seen-again works of genius, and the majority of the filmmakers are from other countries. Tickets go on sale several weeks before the beginning of the festival, and films with a lot of buzz will sell out.

April

New York Underground Film Festival (early April ☎212/505-5110, ⓦwww.nyuff.com): Experimental video, fringy political documentaries, animated shorts, and more at this catch-all, way-out-of-the-mainstream event at the Anthology Film Archives, 32 Second Ave, at 2nd St.

Easter Parade (Easter Sun ☎212/360-8111, ⓦwww.nycgovparks.org): Evoking the old fashion parade on the city's most stylish avenue, hundreds of people promenade up Fifth Ave, from 49th to 57th streets, in elaborate, flower-bedecked Easter bonnets. There's also usually an "Eggstravaganza," a free children's festival including an egg-rolling contest, on the Lower Forty Acres in Central Park.

Tribeca Film Festival (late April to early May ⓣ212/941-2400, ⓦwww.tribecafilmfestival.org): Launched in 2002, this glitzy two-week fest presents an admirable mix of soon-to-be-blockbusters and indie work, including shorts and international films. Purchase tickets well in advance.

May

Sakura Matsuri: Cherry Blossom Festival (early May ⓣ718/623-7200, ⓦwww.bbg.org): Music, art, dance, traditional fashion, and sword-fighting demonstrations celebrate Japanese culture and the brief, sublime blossoming of the Brooklyn Botanic Garden's 200 cherry trees. Free with garden admission.

Five Boro Bike Tour (early May ⓣ212/932-2453, ⓦwww.bikenewyork.org): Cars are banished from the route of this 42-mile ride through all five boroughs, and some 30,000 cyclists take to the streets.

Ukrainian Festival (mid-May ⓣ212/674-1615): This weekend festival sees East 7th St – between Second and Third aves – filled with marvelous Ukrainian costumes, folk music and dance, plus foods and traditional crafts like egg-painting.

Fleet Week (end of May ⓦwww.cnrma.navy.mil/fleetweek): The boisterous annual welcome of sailors from the US, Canada, Mexico, and the UK, among others, with ceremonies at the Intrepid Sea, Air & Space Museum.

Summer outdoor fun

Summer arts programs are nice treats for those who stay in the city through the muggiest months. As most of these shows are free or at least very cheap, they're swarmed with fun-seeking New Yorkers – plan on arriving very early to stake out a picnic spot on the grass, and book tickets ahead when possible.

Bryant Park Summer Film Festival (mid-June to mid-Aug ⓣ212/512-5700, ⓦwww.bryantpark.org): Each Monday night picnickers watch classic films like *Breakfast at Tiffany's* on the lush lawn of Bryant Park. Get there very early, and bring a blanket.

Celebrate Brooklyn (June–Aug ⓣ718/855-7882, ⓦwww.celebratebrooklyn.org): One of New York's longest-running free music series, at the band shell in Prospect Park; great Latin performances, among others; $3 donation requested.

Midsummer Night Swing (July ⓣ212/875-5766, ⓦwww.lincolncenter.org): In Lincoln Center's Damrosch Park, West 62nd St at Amsterdam Ave, every Tuesday through Saturday evening, learn a different dance en masse each night to the rhythm of live swing, mambo, merengue, samba, or country. Lessons at 6.30pm, music and dancing at 7.30pm. $15.

New York Philharmonic (June–Aug ⓣ212/875-5656, ⓦwww.newyorkphilharmonic.org): See p.159.

River to River Festival (June–Sept ⓦwww.rivertorivernyc.com): Big-name performers in pop and world music and dance take the stage in Battery Park, the World Financial Center, and elsewhere in Lower Manhattan; free.

Rooftop Films (June–July ⓣ718/417-7362, ⓦwww.rooftopfilms.com): Set on factory roofs and in public parks in Brooklyn and Manhattan, this movie series offers nifty backdrops for watching hip indie shorts; $9.

Shakespeare in the Park (June–Aug ⓣ212/539-8500, ⓦwww.publictheater.org): See p.159.

SummerStage (June–Aug ⓣ212/360-2777, ⓦwww.summerstage.org): See p.159.

Salute to Israel Parade (late May or early June ☎ 212/245-8200, ⓦ www.salutetoisrael.com): This celebration of Israeli independence attempts to display unity within New York's ideologically and religiously diverse Jewish community. On Fifth Ave, between 57th and 79th sts, rain or shine.

June

Museum Mile Festival (first Tues evening ☎ 212/606-2296, ⓦ www.museummilefestival .org): On Fifth Ave from 82nd to 105th sts. Nine museums, including the Museum of the City of New York, the Cooper Hewitt, the Guggenheim, the Neue Galerie, and the Met, are open free 6–9pm, and the street is closed down for a massive block party.

American Crafts Festival (early June ☎ 973/746-0091, ⓦ www.craftsatlincoln.org): Over two weekends in June, entertainment and food accompany four hundred juried displays at Lincoln Center.

National Puerto Rican Day Parade (second Sun ☎ 718/401-0404, ⓦ www.nationalpuertorican dayparade.org): The largest of several buoyant Puerto Rican celebrations in the city: seven hours of bands, flag-waving, and baton-twirling from 44th to 86th sts on Fifth Ave, with an estimated two million people in attendance.

Affordable Art Fair (mid-June ☎ 212/255-2003, ⓦ www.aafnyc.com): Four days of art sales for which everything is priced less than $10,000, held at the Metropolitan Pavilion, 135 W 18th St.

JVC Jazz Festival (mid-June ☎ 212/501-1390, ⓦ www.festivalnetwork.com): The jazz world's top names appear at Carnegie Hall, *Le Poisson Rouge*, and other venues around the city.

Mermaid Parade (first Sat on or after June 21 ☎ 718/372-5159, ⓦ www.coneyislandusa.com): At this outstanding event, participants dress like mermaids, fish, and other sea creatures, and saunter through Coney Island, led by assorted offbeat celebs. A Mermaid Ball with burlesque entertainment follows.

Pride Week (third or fourth week of June ☎ 212/807-7433, ⓦ www.nycpride.org): The world's biggest lesbian, gay, bisexual, and transgender Pride event kicks off with a rally in Bryant Park and ends with a march down Fifth Ave, a street fair in Greenwich Village, and a huge last-night dance.

Dyke March (fourth Sat ☎ 212/479-8520, ⓦ www.nycdykemarch.org): This technically illegal march rallies a diverse group of lesbian and bisexual women, from young-sters to topless grannies, at Bryant Park, to protest discrimination.

Washington Square Music Festival (June–July ☎ 212/252-3621, ⓦ www.washingtonsquare musicfestival.org): Since 1953, a series of classical, jazz, and big-band concerts, every Tues night, at this outdoor venue (rain space is NYU's Frederick Loewe Theatre, 35 W 4th St).

July

Independence Day (July 4 ☎ 212/494-4495): The fireworks above the East River are visible from all over Manhattan, but the best places to view them are the South Street Seaport (where live rock bands accompany the display), the Esplanade in Brooklyn Heights, or the waterfront in Greenpoint or Williamsburg, starting at about 9pm. The crowds are unimaginable, especially on FDR Drive below 42nd St, which is closed to cars. If you do come here, know that there are no restrooms in the area, nor any kind of refreshment vendors.

New York City Tap Festival (early July ☎ 646/230-9564, ⓦ www.atdf.org): This week-long festival features hundreds of tap dancers who perform and give workshops.

Bastille Day (Sun closest to July 14 ☎ 212/355-6100, ⓦ www.fiaf.org): Celebrate with the Alliance Française and notable French restaurants on 60th St, between Lexington and Fifth aves.

Asian American International Film Festival (mid-July ☎ 212/989-1422, ⓦ www .asiancinevision.org): New films from Asia and the Asian diaspora, held at the Asia Society, 725 Park Ave, at 70th St.

Antiques-lovers can find plenty of treasures in New York; these are only a few of the city's notable annual expos.

Winter Antiques Show (late Jan ☎718/292-7392, ⓦwww.winterantiquesshow.com): Foremost American antiques show takes over the Park Avenue Armory, Park Ave and 67th St, for one week; $20 per day.

New York Antiquarian Book Fair (early April ☎212/944-8291, ⓦwww.abaa.org): Collection of rare books, letters, drawings, etc, held at the Park Avenue Armory. Get free appraisals of up to five items on "Discovery Day"; $15 admission per day.

WFMU Record Fair (late Oct or early Nov ☎201/521-1416 ext 225, ⓦwww.wfmu .org): Everything from ancient 78s to 1980s hip-hop is up for grabs in this celebration of vintage vinyl at the Metropolitan Pavilion, 125 W 18th St; $6 admission per day.

Pier Antiques Show (mid-Nov ☎212/255-0020, ⓦwww.stellashows.com): Largest metropolitan antiques fair, including vintage clothing, on piers 92 and 94, Twelfth Ave and 55th St; $15 admission per day.

Restaurant Week (mid-July): See p.416.

Festa del Giglio (mid-July ☎718/384-0223, ⓦwww.olmcfeast.com): Havemeyer St between N 8th and N 11th sts in Williamsburg is taken over by this ten-day Catholic street festival, which centers around a procession of a giant wooden boat and a figure of St Paulinus on an 85-foot tower.

Mostly Mozart (late July to late Aug ☎212/875-5766, ⓦwww.lincolncenter.org): More than forty concerts and Mozart-themed events at Lincoln Center, in the longest-running indoor summer festival in the US.

August

Harlem Week (all month ☎212/862-8473, ⓦwww.harlemdiscover.com): What began as a week-long festival around Harlem Day on Aug 20 has stretched into a month of African, Caribbean, and Latin performances, lectures, and parties; some events in July, Sept, and Oct, too.

Hong Kong Dragon Boat Festival (first weekend in Aug ☎718/767-1776, ⓦwww.hkdbf-ny.org): Flushing Meadows Corona Park is the site of this highly competitive race of 38-foot-long sculls; live entertainment, an arts and crafts market, and a dumpling-eating contest round out the weekend.

New York International Fringe Festival (mid–late Aug ☎212/279-4488, ⓦwww.fringenyc.org): With more than two hundred companies performing at various downtown venues, this cutting-edge series is the biggest for performance art, theater, dance, puppetry, and more, offering the chance to see the hit shows before they move to bigger stages.

HOWL! Festival of East Village Arts (late Aug ☎212/505-2225, ⓦwww.howlfestival.com): Eight days devoted to the Beats and other neighborhood heroes, with an Allen Ginsberg Poetry Fest, a Charlie Parker jazz jam, and the great drag extravaganza Wigstock; in and around Tompkins Square Park.

September

West Indian–American Day Parade and Carnival (Labor Day ☎718/467-1797, ⓦwww.wiadca .com): Brooklyn's largest parade, modeled after the carnivals of Trinidad and Tobago, features music, food, dance, floats with enormous sound systems, and scores of steel-drum bands – not to mention more than a million attendees.

Broadway on Broadway (mid-Sept ☎212/869-1890, ⓦwww.broadwayonbroadway.com): Free performances featuring songs by casts of the major Broadway musicals, culminating in a shower of confetti; held in Times Square.

Feast of San Gennaro (ten days in mid-Sept ☎212/226-6427, ⓦ www.sangennaro.org)**: Since 1927, the festival has celebrated the patron saint of Naples along Mulberry St and its environs in Little Italy, with a cannoli-eating contest, midway games, and tasty things to eat. In three parades (the largest is Sept 19, the saint's day), a San Gennaro statue is carried through the streets with donations pinned to his cloak.

African–American Day Parade (late Sept ☎212/384-3080, ⓦ www.africanamerican dayparade.org)**: Drum lines, step-dancers, politicians, the Boys Choir of Harlem, and other participants march through Harlem from 111th St and Adam Clayton Powell Blvd to 142nd St, then east toward Fifth Ave, in the largest black parade in America.

DUMBO Art Under the Bridge Festival (late Sept ☎718/694-0831, ⓦ www.dumboartscenter.org /festival)**: More than 200 resident artists show their work in open studios, bands perform, and bizarre installations fill the streets in the stylish waterfront neighborhood in Brooklyn.

New York Film Festival (late Sept to mid-Oct ☎212/875-5600, ⓦ www.filmlinc.com)**: One of the world's leading film festivals unreels at Lincoln Center; tickets can be very hard to come by, as anticipated art hits get their debuts here.

October

Pulaski Day Parade (early Oct ⓦ www .pulaskiparade.com)**: On Fifth Ave, for the celebration of Polish heritage.

New Yorker Festival (early Oct ⓦ festival .newyorker.com)**: Literary, music, and film celebrities hobnob on stage with *New Yorker* editors, writers, and cartoonists at this three-day festival, held at venues throughout the city. Tickets sell out quickly; sign up online for the Festival Wire to get advance notification of events by email.

Columbus Day Parade (second Mon ☎212/249-9923, ⓦ www.columbuscitizensfd.org)**: On Fifth Ave between 49th and 79th sts, 35,000 marchers commemorate Italian-American heritage and the day America was put on the map. Parallel events celebrate the heritage of American Indians and other native peoples.

New York City Wine & Food Festival (mid-Oct ⓦ www.nycwineandfoodfestival.com)**: The Food Network and *Food & Wine* magazine team up to present the city's biggest food festival, with big-name television and cookbook personalities giving talks and demonstrations, and Meatpacking District restaurants hosting specially priced dinners. Tickets are expensive, but the proceeds go to charity.

Open House New York (mid-Oct ☎212/991-6469, ⓦ www.ohny.org)**: For one weekend, take tours of more than 175 landmark buildings, ecofriendly structures, and other remarkable architectural spaces in all five boroughs, most of which are usually closed to the public.

Village Halloween Parade (Oct 31 ⓦ www .halloween-nyc.com)**: In America's largest Halloween celebration, starting at 7pm on Sixth Ave at Spring St and making its way up to 23rd, you'll see spectacular costumes, giant puppets, bands, and any other bizarre stuff New Yorkers can muster. Get there early for a good viewing spot; marchers (anyone in costume is eligible) line up at 6:30pm. (A tamer children's parade usually takes place earlier that day in Washington Square Park.)

▲ Village Halloween Parade

Next Wave Festival (Oct–Dec ☎718/636-4100, ⓦ www.bam.org)**: Consistently excellent experimental arts festival at the Brooklyn Academy of Music, bringing the likes of Pina Bausch and Laurie Anderson to the stage in elaborate productions since 1981.

Macy's Parade Inflation Eve

See Mickey Mouse and the other characters being inflated the night before **Macy's Thanksgiving Day Parade**. It's not as crowded as on parade day, and you can experience something not broadcast to every home in America. The giant nylon balloons are set up on West 77th and 81st streets between Central Park West and Columbus Avenue at the American Museum of Natural History. Wander around the feet of these giants and watch them gradually take shape.

November

New York City Marathon (first Sun ☎212/423-2249, ⓦwww.ingnycmarathon.org): Some 37,000 runners from all over the world – from the Kenyan champs to regular folks in goofy costumes – assemble for this high-spirited 26.2-mile run on city pavement through the five boroughs. One of the best places to watch is Central Park South, almost at the finish line.

Veterans Day Parade (Nov 11 ☎212/693-1476): The United War Veterans sponsor this annual event on Fifth Ave from 23rd to 59th sts. Ceremony at 10.15am, salute and parade at 11am.

Macy's Thanksgiving Day Parade (Thanksgiving Day ☎212/494-4495, ⓦwww.macysparade.com): A made-for-TV extravaganza, with big corporate floats, dozens of marching bands from around the country, and Santa Claus's first appearance of the season. Some two million spectators watch it along Central Park W from 77th St to Columbus Circle,

and along Broadway down to Herald Square, 9am–noon.

Rockefeller Center Christmas Tree Lighting (late Nov ☎212/632-3975, ⓦwww.rockefellercenter.com): Switching on the lights on the enormous tree in front of the ice rink begins the holiday season, in a glowing moment sure to warm even the most Grinch-like heart. The crowds, however, can be oppressive.

African Diaspora Film Festival (late Nov–early Dec ☎212/864-1760, ⓦwww.nyadff.org): Films from throughout the world, by and about people of African descent, are shown at several Manhattan venues.

Holiday Train Show (late Nov to mid-Jan ☎718/817-8700, ⓦwww.nybg.org): Model trains and trolleys thread their way across the Brooklyn Bridge and through a twinkling New York City, complete with the Empire State Building and Yankee Stadium.

December

Hanukkah Celebrations (usually mid-Dec): During the eight nights of this Jewish feast, a menorah-lighting ceremony takes place at Brooklyn's Grand Army Plaza (☎718/778-6000), and the world's largest menorah is illuminated on Fifth Ave near Central Park (☎212/736-8400).

Kwanzaa (mid-Dec ☎212/568-1645, ⓦwww.africanfolkheritagecircle.org): Celebrations city-wide, including a story-telling show by the African Folk Heritage Circle in Harlem.

New Year's Eve in Times Square (Dec 31 ☎212/768-1560, ⓦwww.timessquarenyc.org): Several hundred thousand revelers party in the cold and well-guarded streets – a crowd-management nightmare, so take the subway and get where you're going early. Elsewhere in the city, you can choose from alcohol-free singles bashes, all-out clubbing, a four-mile midnight group run in Central Park, or calmer activities, like meditation marathons.

Kids' New York

New York can be quite a wonderful place to bring **children**. Obvious attractions like museums, theaters, skyscrapers, ferry rides, and all the diversions of Central Park will certainly thrill them, but a visit with kids may also give you reason to appreciate the simpler pleasures of the city, from watching street entertainers to introducing your youngsters to strange foods and fascinating neighborhoods like Chinatown. The city is full of high-caliber free events aimed at children, especially in the summer; puppet shows, garden plantings, cultural celebrations, park festivals, and storytelling hours at local bookstores are all excellent ways to entertain. Many museums and theaters also feature specific children's programs. Following are details on some attractions especially appealing to kids, but make sure to phone ahead for specific times, etc, to avoid any disappointment.

General advice

For a **listing** of what's available when you're in town, see the detailed NYC*kids*ARTS Cultural Calendar (free; Ⓦwww.nyckidsarts.org). *Time Out New York* (and the extra-specialized *TONY Kids*), the *Village Voice*, and websites such as Ⓦwww.gocitykids.com are also valuable resources. A solid directory of family-oriented events all around the city is available through NYC & Co., the convention and visitors bureau, 810 Seventh Ave between 52nd and 53rd streets (Mon–Fri 8.30am–6pm, Sat & Sun 9am–5pm; ℡212/484-1222, Ⓦwww.nycvisit.com).

Once in the city, your main problem won't be finding stuff to do with your kids, but transporting them all. Though some natives navigate the streets and subway stairs with strollers, most prefer to keep infants and even toddlers conveniently contained in a backpack or front carrier – ultimately a much better way of getting around with small children. Indeed, many attractions do not accommodate strollers, though some will keep yours temporarily while you visit – call ahead for details. Most sights, restaurants, and stores, however, are at the very least quite tolerant of children.

Subways are the fastest way to get around and are perfectly safe – don't worry about bringing your smallest children aboard; in fact, the kids will probably get a kick out of them, crowds, noise, and all. Buses are slower, but antsy or bored kids can stare through the large windows at the hustle and bustle outside. As a bonus, children under 44 inches (112cm) ride free on the subway and buses when accompanied by an adult.

Finally, if all else fails, or if you want some quiet time to enjoy the city's more mature offerings, just hire a **babysitter** (see box, p.424).

Babysitting

The **Babysitters' Guild**, 60 E 42nd St (☎212/682-0227, ⓦwww.babysittersguild .com), offers childcare services with carefully selected staff, most of whom have teaching and nursing backgrounds. Fees (for one kid) are $25 an hour, four hours minimum, plus $4.50 to cover transportation ($10 after midnight), and "extra" children are $5 additional per hour. It's $5 extra for one of the multilingual sitters (sixteen foreign languages are represented in all). The organization is fully licensed and bonded. Book as far in advance as you can.

Check ⓦwww.gocitykids.com for many more childcare options.

Museums

You could spend an entire holiday just checking out the city's many **museums**, almost all of which contain something fascinating for kids. The following is a brief overview of the ones that tend to evoke special enthusiasm. See the appropriate Guide chapters for more details on these and other museums.

American Museum of Natural History and the Rose Center for Earth and Space

Central Park W at 79th St ☎212/769-5100, ⓦwww.amnh.org. Daily 10am–5.45pm, Rose Center until 8.45pm on first Fri of month. IMAX shows 10.30am–4.30pm, every hour on the half-hour daily 10.30am–4.30pm. Suggested donation $15, children $8.50, students/seniors $11 (includes the Rose Center). Special exhibits and IMAX additional charge; combination packages available.

One of the best museums of its kind, this enormous complex is filled with fossils, gems, meteorites, and other natural objects (more than 34 million in all). Your first stop should be the **Fossil Halls**, where you'll find towering dinosaur skeletons and interactive computer stations that are sure to please all ages. Other halls are dedicated to more contemporary beasts: a full-scale herd of elephants dominates the **Akeley Hall of African Mammals**, a 94-foot-long blue whale hangs over the **Milstein Hall of Ocean Life**, and the **Hall of Biodiversity** offers a multimedia recreation of a Central African rain forest. In the winter, the **Butterfly Conservatory** is a sure bet for younger children. Weekends bring special events for families, including very young kids.

Just across from the Hall of Biodiversity lies the **Rose Center for Earth and Space**, which features the Space Theater, the Big Bang Theater (in which the beginning of the universe is recreated every half-hour), and the lavish **Hayden Planetarium**, among other awesome attractions.

Brooklyn Children's Museum

145 Brooklyn Ave, at St Mark's Ave ☎718/735-4400, ⓦwww.brooklynkids.org. Call for hours and suggested donation.

Founded in 1899, this was the world's first museum designed specifically for children. It's full of authentic ethnological, historical, and technological artifacts with which kids can play, plus live animals, including a 17-foot-long Burmese python. The museum's space – it's largely underground – creates a cool atmosphere; a new street-level wing with an emphasis on "green" learning is scheduled to open in late 2008.

Children's Museum of Manhattan

212 W 83rd St, between Broadway and Amsterdam Ave ☎212/721-1234, ⓦwww .cmom.org. Tues–Sun 10am–5pm; $9, seniors $7, under age 1 free.

This terrific participatory museum, founded in 1937, has five floors full of imaginative displays that involve a lot of clambering around. Older children can produce their own television shows in the Media Center, and exhibits often have a hip edge – Andy Warhol's kid-friendly art, for instance. Highly recommended for children ages 1–12.

Children's Museum of the Arts

182 Lafayette St, between Broome and Grand sts ☎212/274-0986, ⓦ www.cmany.org. Wed–Sun noon–5pm, Thurs until 6pm; $9, pay what you wish Thurs 4–6pm; under 1 year free.
At this gallery, children are encouraged to look at different types of art and then create their own with paints, paper, clay, fabric, and other simple media. Holiday special events are particularly interesting – African mask-making for Kwanzaa, for example. Admission includes various dance, movie, and music programs on weekends.

Intrepid Sea, Air & Space Museum

Pier 86, W 46th St at Twelfth Ave ☎212/245-0072, ⓦ www.intrepidmuseum.org. Call for hours and admission fees.
Even non-military-minded kids will be impressed by the massive scale of this aircraft-carrier-cum-museum – not to mention the huge collection of airplanes and helicopters. The site, recently renovated, now includes a 15,000-sq-ft space for hands-on learning, in which children can climb a cargo net, experience (via computer) life on a ship, and (for older kids or adults) simulate aircraft launches.

Museum of the City of New York

1220 Fifth Ave, at 103rd St ☎212/534-1672, ⓦ www.mcny.org. Tues–Sun 10am–5pm; suggested donation $9, students & seniors $5, families $20; free Sun 10am–noon and for children under 12.
The "New York Toy Stories" exhibit showcases dollhouses, old-fashioned toys, and fantasy objects from the museum's 10,000-item collection, like the Stettheimer dollhouse that includes a miniature art gallery inside. Kids will also have fun identifying the city's landmarks, depicted in paintings in the picture gallery.

New York City Fire Museum

278 Spring St, between Hudson and Varick sts ☎212/691-1303, ⓦ www.nycfiremuseum.org. Tues–Sat 10am–5pm, Sun 10am–4pm; suggested donation $5, students and seniors $2, under 12 $1.
A sure hit with the preschool crowd, this space pays pleasing homage to New York City's firefighters. On display are fire engines

▲ New York City Fire Museum

from yesteryear (horse-drawn and steam-powered), helmets, dog-eared photos, and a host of motley objects on three floors of a former fire station. A neat and appealing display, even though it's not full of interactive doodads.

New York Hall of Science

111th St, at 46th Ave, Flushing Meadows–Corona Park, Queens ☎718/699-0005, ⓦ www.nyhallsci.org. July & Aug Mon–Fri 9.30am–5pm, Sat & Sun 10am–6pm; Sept–June Tues–Thurs 9.30am–2pm, Fri 9.30am–5pm, Sat & Sun 10am–5pm; $11, students & children $8; free Sept–June Fri 2–5pm & Sun 10–11am.
Housed in a glowing blue tower built for the 1964–65 World's Fair, this is one of the top science museums in the country. A highlight is the outdoor Science Playground (open March–Dec; an additional $4), where kids can clamber around as they learn about scientific principles. Located in Queens, the Hall of Science makes for a good day-trip combined with a visit to the Queens Zoo or the nearby Queens Museum of Art.

New York Transit Museum

Old subway entrance at Schermerhorn St and Boerum Place, Brooklyn ☎718/694-1600, ⓦ www.mta.info/mta/museum. Tues–Fri 10am–4pm, Sat & Sun noon–5pm; $5, children & seniors $3. Also: Transit Museum Gallery and Store at Grand Central Terminal, open daily; free.
Housed in an abandoned 1930s subway station, this museum offers more than a hundred years of transportation memorabilia, including old subway cars and buses dating back to the turn of the nineteenth century. Frequent activities for kids include underground tours, workshops, and an annual bus festival – all best for younger school-kids. It's a quick hop on the subway,

but if you don't want to go to Brooklyn, at least stop in to the museum's annex at Grand Central in Manhattan, which has its own rotating exhibits.

South Street Seaport Museum

12 Fulton St T 212/748-8600, @www.southstseaport.org. **April–Oct Tues–Sun 10am–6pm, Nov–March Fri–Sun 10am–5pm all galleries; Mon 10am–5pm Schermerhorn Row Galleries only; $10; seniors and students $8; $5 children 5–12.**

South Street Seaport's dock is home to a small fleet of historic ships which kids are welcome to tour, including a nicely preserved 1893 fishing schooner, a merchant vessel with a towering mast, and a hard-working harbor tugboat. With some planning, you may even be able to go out on one of the crafts for a harbor tour (summers only). The museum building itself will seem staid in comparison to the boats.

Staten Island Children's Museum

Snug Harbor Cultural Center, 1000 Richmond Terrace, Staten Island T 718/273-2060, @www.statenislandkids.org. **June–Aug Tues–Sun 10am–5pm, Sept–May Tues–Sun noon–5pm; $5, grandparents free Wed.**

This is a good way to round off a trip on the Staten Island ferry; the #S40 bus runs from the ferry terminal. Expect, among other things, giant chess sets, a small-scale playhouse complete with costumes, a great exhibit about bugs that includes a human-size anthill, and an outdoor play area on the water where kids can sail boats and learn about oysters.

Sights and entertainment

Brooklyn Botanic Garden

900 Washington Ave T 718/623-7200, @www.bbg.org. **March–Oct Tues–Fri 8am–6pm, Sat, Sun & holidays 10am–6pm; Nov–Feb Tues–Fri 8am–4.30pm, Sat, Sun & holidays 10am–4.30pm; $8, students & seniors $4, free Tues, Sat before noon, Nov–Feb weekdays; seniors free Fri.**

This gorgeous landscape behind the Brooklyn Museum of Art is very child-friendly, with giant carp in the ponds and ducks to chase around. Kids will enjoy the City Farmers and KinderGarden programs, and parents can drop in for the flower-arranging classes (dried and silk), garden tutorials, tours, and yoga sessions. Families crowd the place for seasonal events like the Cherry Blossom Festival in late April.

Bronx Zoo

Bronx River Parkway at Fordham Rd T 718/367-1010, @www.bronxzoo.org. **April–Oct Mon–Fri 10am–5pm, Sat, Sun & holidays 10am–5.30pm; Nov–March daily 10am–4.30pm; $15, seniors $13, children 3–12 $11. Rates are reduced during the winter. Pay what you wish on Wed, parking $10.**

The largest urban zoo in America, with thrilling permanent exhibits – check out Wild Asia (summer only), the lush rainforest of JungleWorld, and the Congo Gorilla Forest. Kids can watch penguins being fed, get up close with Siberian tigers, or ride a giant bug on an insect-themed carousel. Highly recommended for an all-day excursion, particularly in spring, when many baby animals are born. Be prepared for small additional fees once inside; check website for "bad weather bargains" and other specials.

Central Park

Central Park provides year-round, sure-fire entertainment for the younger set. In the summer it becomes one giant playground, with activities ranging from storytelling to rollerblading to boating. Highlights include the nature exhibits at **Belvedere Castle**, in mid-park at 79th St; the surprisingly fast **Carousel**, at 64th St, a vintage model salvaged from Coney Island; **Central Park Zoo**, Fifth Ave at 64th St, where youngsters will be delighted at the singing bronze animals on the musical clock at the entrance to the Tisch Children's Zoo; **Loeb Boathouse**, east side at 74th St, where you can rent rowboats; and ice-skating at **Wollman Rink**, east side at 63rd St. For more detailed information on these and other sights, see Chapter 14, "Central Park."

New York Aquarium

Surf Ave at W 8th St, Coney Island, Brooklyn T 718/265-FISH, @www.nyaquarium.com.

June–Aug Mon–Fri 10am–6pm; weekends until 7pm; rest of the year closing times vary from 4.30pm to 5.30pm; $12, under 12 $9 & seniors $10.

Although it dates to 1896, the aquarium has very modern-looking exhibits dedicated to jellyfish and sea horses, along with 8000 other underwater animals. Open-air sea-lion shows and feedings – shark, penguin, sea otter, and walrus – are held several times daily. This is also the site of the famous Coney Island boardwalk and amusement park – older children and teens will find it a good spot to people-watch.

New York Botanical Garden

Bronx River Parkway at Fordham Rd, Bronx (across from the Bronx Zoo) ☎718/817-8700, ⓦwww.nybg.org. **Tues–Sun, Mon & holidays 10am–6pm; $20, students & seniors $18, under 12 $7; parking $12.**

One of America's foremost public gardens,

with an enormous conservatory showcasing a rainforest and other types of ecosystems, plus the 12-acre Everett Children's Adventure Garden, which includes several mazes. Prices above are for the entire complex; tickets that entitle you to the grounds only are available for $6, in case you want to just take your baby to a green spot for a discreet nap.

Sony Wonder Technology Lab

550 Madison Ave, at 56th St ☎212/833-8100, ⓦwww.sonywondertechlab.com. **Tues–Sat 10am–5pm; free.**

Sony's gee-whiz exhibit space emphasizes the marvels of the digital age, and although it's a bit corporate-slick, tech-minded kids will enjoy creating their own video games and trying out TV editing, among other computer-driven activities. This is a hugely popular attraction, so make reservations (no fee) up to three months in advance; same-day tickets are sometimes available as well.

Shops: toys, books, and clothes

Bank Street Bookstore 610 W 112th St, at Broadway ☎212/678-1654, ⓦwww.bankstreet books.com. The first floor of this store – affiliated with Bank Street College of Education – is filled with children's books and games, while the second floor is devoted to nonfiction books and educational materials. Frequent special events and afternoon story hours with big names like E.L. Konigsburg and Hilary Knight, of *Eloise* fame.

Books of Wonder 18 W 18th St, between Fifth and Sixth aves ☎212/989-3270, ⓦwww .booksofwonder.com. Showpiece kids' bookstore, with a great Oz section, plus story hour on Sun at noon and author appearances Sat in the spring and fall.

Dylan's Candy Bar 1011 Third Ave, at 60th St ☎646/735-0078. Kids will catch a sugar high just walking in the door of this stylish shop devoted to all things sweet. The selection is almost paralyzing, with everything from a rainbow of gummy candy to retro favorites like Charleston Chews.

F.A.O. Schwarz 767 Fifth Ave, at 58th St ☎212/644-9400, ⓦwww.fao.com. This multi-story toy emporium features an on-site ice-cream parlor, a whole wing dedicated to Legos, and the legendary danceable floor

piano featured in the 1988 film *Big*. Very popular (and very expensive), but a less frenzied experience than the plasticky Toys 'R' Us in Times Square.

Metropolitan Museum Store 15 W 49th St ☎212/332-1360, ⓦwww.metmuseum.org/store. The third floor of the shop is devoted to arty children's toys, many of which highlight pieces in the museum's collection.

Red Caboose 23 W 45th St, between Fifth and Sixth aves, lower level ☎212/575-0155. A unique shop specializing in models, particularly trains and train sets.

Space Kiddets 26 E 22nd St, between Park Ave and Broadway ☎212/420-9878, ⓦwww .spacekiddets.com. Show your baby's musical taste with a CBGB onesie or a David Bowie tee from this funky clothes shop that stocks infant through pre-teen sizes; vintage toys can be found at the shop around the block (46 E 21st St).

Tannen's Magic Studio 45 W 34th St, Suite 608, between Fifth and Sixth aves ☎212/929-4500, ⓦwww.tannens.com. Your kids will never forget a visit to the largest magic shop in the world, with nearly 8000 props, tricks, and magic sets. The staff is made up of magicians who perform free shows throughout the day.

Theater, circuses, and other entertainment

The following is a highly selective roundup of **cultural activities** that might be of interest to children. As always, find out more by checking the listings in the *New York Times* (which publishes its calendar of youth activities in the arts section on Fri) and magazines such as *Time Out New York Kids*. Note too that the Brooklyn Museum and the Met, among other museums, often have events for children, as do many bookstores.

BAMfamily Brooklyn Academy of Music, 30 Lafayette Ave ☎718/636-4100, ⬤www.bam .org. This periodic series presents public performances for families on weekends, as well as the international BAMkids Film Festival each March.

Barnum & Bailey Circus Madison Square Garden ☎212/465-6741, ⬤www.ringling.com. This large touring circus arrives in New York on a mile-long train in mid-March and stays for about three weeks. The real highlight is before the circus starts, when the elephants are escorted from the rail yards in Queens to the west side of Manhattan – usually around midnight, but the sight is worth staying up for. Keep an eye on local papers for the precise date and route.

Big Apple Circus Lincoln Center ☎212/721-6500, ⬤www.bigapplecircus.org. Small circus that performs in a tent in Damrosch Park next to the Met, from late Oct to early Jan. Tickets $40–80, or $15–33 for matinees.

Manhattan Children's Theatre 52 White St ☎212/226-4085, ⬤www.manhattanchildrens theatre.org. $20, inquire for children's prices. Classic plays, fairy tales, and musicals, plus some new works.

New York with teens

For many teenagers, the sights and sounds of New York (paired with a little well-placed down-time) will be fascinating enough, particularly if they have certain obsessions (movies, Buddhism, soccer, indie rock, pizza – anything, really) easily satisfied by the city. If your adolescent travel companions need something a little extra, try wandering around the East Village (particularly along St Mark's Place and in Tompkins Square Park, longtime punk hangouts that have softened enough to be edgy but not alarming), or throw in some strategic shopping on the streets of Chinatown and on Broadway in neighboring Soho, especially in the inexpensive teen clothing stores – H&M (515 and 558 Broadway ☎212/343-2722) and Yellow Rat Bastard (483 Broadway ☎1-877/YELL-RAT), among others, plus numerous cut-rate sneaker and shoe stores. Independent record stores abound in the East and West villages, and crafty types can head to Knit New York (307 E 14th St ☎212/387-0707, ⬤www .knitnewyork.com), a friendly store-café that also offers knitting classes. Obscure theme restaurants such as *Ninja New York* (25 Hudson St ☎212/274-8500), *Jekyll and Hyde Club* (1409 Sixth Ave ☎212/541-9505, and the smaller *Pub* at 91 Seventh Ave South in Greenwich Village ☎212/989-7701), and the unbelievable sweet shop Economy Candy (108 Rivington St ☎1-800/352-4544) should successfully occupy all but the most jaded teenage traveler, as will the Hip Hop Look at NY tours of the Bronx ($58; ☎212/714-3527, ⬤www.hushtours.com), run by scene veterans.

Some teens will also get a kick out of walking around the NYU and Columbia campuses (see p.105 and p.200) and imagining themselves as students in a few years (older ones who are serious about applying can even arrange interviews). Teens can also get free makeovers at Sephora (1500 Broadway, in Times Square ☎212/944-6789, ⬤www.sephora.com; plus eight other locations in Manhattan), Bloomingdale's, and other upscale make-up counters. They can watch skateboarding stunts in the city's skate parks (Chelsea Piers has the best) or enjoy the thrill of trapeze classes (see opposite). With a high-school ID, they're eligible for $5 tickets to hundreds of films, museums, and performances through High 5 Tickets (☎212/445-8587, ⬤www.highfivetix.org).

New Victory Theater 209 W 42nd St, at Broadway ☎646/223-3020, ⓦwww .newvictory.org. The city's first theater for families, located in a grand old renovated Times Square space, presents a rich mix of theater, music, dance, storytelling, film, and puppetry, in addition to pre- and post-performance workshops. Affordable shows (most tickets $10–30) run 1–2hr. In keeping with the cultural calendar that much of the city runs on, the theater is dark (no performances) during the summer.

Streb Laboratory for Action Mechanics (S.L.A.M.) 51 N 1st St, Williamsburg, Brooklyn ☎718/384-6491, ⓦwww.strebusa.org. MacArthur-grant-winning choreographer Elizabeth Streb has developed a dynamic, physical dance style she calls Pop Action – go for one of the company's inspiring performances in its raw Brooklyn warehouse, or sign kids up for the week-long S.L.A.M. Summer Camps in July. The space also offers trampoline work, trapeze fun, and basic tumbling.

Trapeze School New York Hudson River Park at Canal St and 518 W 30th St ☎917/797-1872, ⓦnewyork.trapezeschool.com. Two-hour classes on the flying trapeze, for ages 6 and up, start at $67 (including a one-time $22 registration fee) and include an amazing view over the Hudson River from high atop the rig. Parents must accompany children – but if this seems too daunting, you can just go sit in the park and watch the intrepid high-flyers practice their moves. Classes run year-round (a heated tent is set up in the winter); book well in advance.

KIDS' NEW YORK | Theater, circuses, and other entertainment

Contexts

Contexts

History

To Europe she was America, to America she was the gateway of the earth. But to tell the story of New York would be to write a social history of the world.

H.G. Wells

Early days and colonial rule

Long before the arrival of European settlers, New York was inhabited by several Native American tribes; the **Algonquin** tribe was the largest and most populous in the area that is now New York City. Although descendants of the Algonquins and other tribes still live on Long Island's Shinnecock reservation, the appearance of Europeans in the sixteenth century essentially destroyed their settled existence, bringing an end to Native American life as it had existed here for several thousand years.

Giovanni da Verrazano was the first explorer to discover Manhattan. An Italian in the service of French king Francis I, he had set out to find the Pacific's legendary Northwest Passage, but like his countryman Christopher Columbus, had been blown off-course into what would become New York Harbor in 1524. Verrazano returned to France to woo the court with tales of fertile lands and friendly natives, but it was nearly a century before the powers of Europe were tempted to follow him.

In 1609 **Henry Hudson**, an Englishman employed by the **Dutch East India Company**, landed at Manhattan, sailing his ship, the *Half-Moone*, upriver as far as Albany. Hudson found that the route did not lead to the Northwest Passage, which he, too, had been commissioned to discover – but in charting its course for the first time he gave his name to the mighty river. Returning home, Hudson was persuaded to embark on another expedition, this time under the British flag. He arrived in Hudson Bay in the dead of winter, the temperature below freezing and his mutinous crew doubting his ability as a navigator; he, his son, and several loyal sailors were set adrift in a small boat on the icy waters where, presumably, they froze to death.

British fears that they had lost the upper hand in the newly discovered land proved justified when the Dutch established a trading post at the most northerly point on the river that Hudson had reached, **Fort Nassau**, and quickly seized the commercial advantage. In 1624, four years after the Pilgrims had sailed to Massachusetts, thirty families left Holland to become New York's first European settlers, most sailing up to Fort Nassau. But a handful – eight families in all – stayed behind on a small island they called Nut Island because of the many walnut trees there: today's Governors Island. The community slowly grew as more settlers arrived, and the little island became crowded; the **settlement of Manhattan**, taken from the Algonquin Indian word *Manna-Hata* meaning "Island of the Hills," began when families from Governors Island moved across the water.

The Dutch gave this new outpost the name **New Amsterdam**, and in 1626 the Dutch West India Company sent over **Peter Minuit** to govern the small community. Among his first, and certainly more politically adroit, moves was to buy the whole of Manhattan Island from the Native Americans for trinkets worth sixty guilders (about $25 today); the other side of this anecdote is that the Native Americans Minuit bought the island from didn't even come from Manhattan.

As the colony slowly grew, a string of governors succeeded Minuit, the most famous of them **Peter Stuyvesant** – "Peg Leg Pete," a seasoned colonialist from the Dutch West Indies who'd lost his leg in a scrape with the Portuguese. Under his leadership New Amsterdam doubled in size, population, and fortifications, with an encircling wall (today's **Wall Street** follows its course) and a rough-hewn fort on what is now the site of the Customs House built to protect the settlement from the encroaching British. Stuyvesant also built himself a farm (a *bouwerij*, in Dutch) nearby, giving Manhattan's Bowery district its name.

Meanwhile, the **British** were steadily and stealthily building up their presence to the north. They asserted that all of America's east coast, from New England to Virginia, was theirs, and in 1664 Colonel Richard Nicholls was sent to claim the lands around the Hudson for King Charles II. To reinforce his sovereignty, Charles sent along four warships and enough troops to land on Nut and Long islands. Angered by Stuyvesant's increasingly dictatorial leadership and the high taxes levied by the Dutch West India Company, the Dutch settlers refused to defend the colony against the British. Captain Nicholls' men took New Amsterdam, renamed it **New York** in honor of Charles II's brother, the Duke of York, and started what was to be a hundred-odd years of British rule, a period interrupted only briefly in 1673 when the Dutch once more gained, then lost, power in the region.

Revolution

By the 1750s the city had reached a population of 16,000, spread roughly as far north as Chambers Street. As the community grew, it also operated increasingly independently of the British, but England reasserted control in 1763, when France conceded sovereignty over most of explored North America. Within a year the British had riled colonists by imposing punitive taxes and requisitioning private dwellings and inns. Skirmishes between British soldiers and the insurrectionist **Sons of Liberty** culminated in January 1770 with the fatal stabbing of a colonist in New York City. A few weeks later, the **Boston Massacre** saw British troops open fire on taunting protesters, killing five and fanning the revolutionary flames.

New York did not play a large role in the **War of Independence**, due to several decisive defeats in the fall of 1776, first in Brooklyn in the vicinity of Prospect Park, then in Westchester County (the Bronx), with the British pushing the Americans ever northward. Though the Patriots were under the command of George Washington himself, the campaign was a disaster, ending with the routing of three thousand American troops at Fort Washington (near today's George Washington Bridge), and the occupation of the city by the British for the remainder of the war.

Lord Cornwallis's **surrender** to the Americans in October 1783 marked the end of the Revolutionary War, and a month later New York was finally liberated. Washington – an infinitely sharper commander now than he was in the early days of the conflict – was there to celebrate, riding in triumphal procession down Canal Street and saying farewell to his officers at **Fraunces Tavern**, a facsimile of which stands at the end of Pearl Street. Soon after, New York became the fledgling nation's capital, and, on April 30, 1789, Washington its first president. The seat of the federal government was transferred to the District of Columbia a year later.

Immigration and civil war

In 1790 the first official census of Manhattan numbered the population around 33,000. Business and trade were steadily increasing, with the forerunner of the New York Stock Exchange created under a buttonwood tree on Wall Street in the early 1800s and ferry service established between New York and Albany, and between Brooklyn and Manhattan, a few years later.

In 1825, the completion of the **Erie Canal** (running from the Hudson River across the state to the Great Lakes) opened up internal trade and increased demand for cheap labour. The first waves of **immigrants**, mainly **Irish** and **German**, began to arrive in the mid-nineteenth century, the former forced out by famine, the latter by the failed revolutions of 1848–49. Though traders grew wealthy, the city could not handle the arrival of so many people all at once: epidemics of yellow fever and cholera were common, exacerbated by poor water supplies, unsanitary conditions, and the poverty of most of the newcomers, not least in the Lower East Side where two of the largest communities – **Italians** and **Eastern Europeans** (many of them Jewish) – shared one of the most notorious slum areas of its day.

When the **Civil War** broke out in 1860, New York sided with the Union (North) against the Confederates (South). While the city saw little hand-to-hand fighting, it was fertile ground for much of the liberal thinking that had informed the war. In 1863, an unjust **conscription law** provoked the draft riots, with impoverished New Yorkers (especially Irish immigrants) burning buildings, looting shops, and lynching African-Americans; more than a thousand people were killed. A sad addendum to the war was the assassination of Abraham Lincoln in 1865.

The late nineteenth century

After the Civil War, New York began to assume the mantle as the wealthiest and most influential city in the nation by dint of its skilled immigrant workers, distribution networks, and financial resources. Broadway developed into the main thoroughfare, with grand hotels, restaurants, and shops catering to the rich; newspaper editors **William Cullen Bryant** and **Horace Greeley** respectively founded the *Evening Post* and the *Tribune*; and the city became a magnet for intellectuals, with **Washington Irving** and **James Fenimore Cooper** among notable residents. **Cornelius Vanderbilt** controlled a vast shipping and railroad empire from here, and **J.P. Morgan**, the banking and investment wizard, was instrumental in organizing financial mergers, creating the nation's first major corporations.

The latter part of the nineteenth century was in many ways the city's golden age: elevated railways (**Els**) sprang up to transport people quickly and cheaply around the city; **Thomas Edison** lit the streets with his new electric lightbulb, powered by the nation's first commercial power plant, on Pearl Street; and in 1883, the **Brooklyn Bridge** was unveiled. In 1898, New York City – formerly just Manhattan – assumed its current size by officially incorporating Brooklyn, Staten Island, Queens, and the part of Westchester County known as the Bronx.

All this expansion stimulated the city's cultural growth. **Walt Whitman** eulogized the city in his poems and **Henry James** recorded its manners and mores in novels like *Washington Square*. Along Fifth Avenue, **Richard Morris Hunt** built palaces for the wealthy robber–barons who had plundered Europe's collections of fine art – collections that would eventually find their way into the newly opened **Metropolitan Museum**.

Turn-of-the-century development

In 1898, boosted by the first wave of Asian immigrants, New York's population topped three million for the first time, making it the largest city in the world. Nearly half its residents were foreign-born, with **Ellis Island**, the depot that processed arrivals, handling two thousand people a day. Many immigrants worked in sweatshops for the city's growing, notoriously exploitative garment industry. Although workers began to strike for better pay and conditions, it took the **Triangle Shirtwaist Factory** fire (see p.106) to rouse public and civic conscience; within months the state passed 56 factory-reform measures, and unionization spread through the city.

On the upside of New York's capitalist expansion, the early 1900s saw some of the city's wealth going into adventurous new architecture. In Soho classical facades were mass-produced from **cast iron**, and the **Flatiron Building** of 1902 announced the arrival of what was to become the city's trademark – the skyscraper. **Stephen Crane**, **Theodore Dreiser**, and **Edith Wharton** all wrote stories about the city, and in 1913 the **Armory Exhibition** of paintings by Picasso, Duchamp, and others caused a sensation. Skyscrapers pushed ever higher, and in 1913 a building that many consider the *ne plus ultra* of the genre, downtown's **Woolworth Building**, was completed. **Grand Central Terminal** also opened that year, celebrating New York as the gateway to the continent.

The war years and the Depression: 1914–45

As New York benefited from the trade and commerce generated by World War I, there was – perhaps surprisingly – little conflict between the various European communities crammed into the city, and few attacks on Germans.

Prohibition was passed in 1920 in an attempt to sober up the nation, but New York paid little heed. Under the helm of **Mayor Jimmy Walker**, who was quoted as saying, "No civilized man goes to bed the same day he wakes up," the city entered the Jazz Age. Writers as diverse as **Damon Runyon**, F. **Scott Fitzgerald**, and **Ernest Hemingway** portrayed the excitement of the times, and musicians such as **George Gershwin** and **Benny Goodman** packed nightclubs with their new sound. Bootleg liquor ran freely in speakeasies all over town. The **Harlem Renaissance** soared to prominence with writers like **Langston Hughes** and **Zora Neale Hurston**, and music from **Duke Ellington**, **Cab Calloway**, and **Billie Holiday**.

The **Wall Street Crash** of 1929, however, brought the party to an abrupt end. On October 24, known as "**Black Tuesday**," sixteen million shares were traded in a panicked sell-off; five days later, the New York Stock Exchange collapsed, losing $125 million ($1.5 billion in today's dollars). Millions lost their savings;

banks, businesses, and industries shut their doors. By 1932 approximately one in four New Yorkers was out of work, and shantytowns, known as "Hoovervilles" (after then–President Hoover, widely blamed for the Depression), had sprung up in Central Park to house the jobless and homeless.

Surprisingly, during this period three of New York's most beautiful skyscrapers were built – the **Chrysler Building** in 1930, the **Empire State** in 1931 (though it stood near-empty for years), and in 1932 **Rockefeller Center** – but this impressive spate of construction was of little immediate help to those in Hooverville, Harlem, or other depressed parts of the city. It fell to **Fiorello LaGuardia**, Jimmy Walker's successor, to run the crisis-strewn city. He did so with stringent taxation, anti-corruption, and social-spending programs that won him the approval of the city's citizens. Simultaneously, President Roosevelt's **New Deal** supplied funds for roads, housing, and parks, the latter undertaken by controversial Parks Commissioner **Robert Moses**. Under LaGuardia and Moses, the most extensive public-housing program in the country was undertaken; the Triborough, Whitestone, and Henry Hudson bridges were completed; fifty miles of new expressway and five thousand acres of new parks were designed and built; and, in 1939, the airport in Queens that still bears the legendary mayor's name was opened.

The country's entry into **World War II** in 1941 saw New York take on a top-secret role: the **Manhattan Project**, wherein scientists at Columbia University performed the experiments crucial to the creation of the first atomic weapon.

The postwar years

After World War II, New York regained its top-dog status in the fields of finance, art, and communications, both in America and the world, its intellectual and creative community swollen by European refugees. The city was the obvious choice as the permanent home of the **United Nations Organization**: lured by Rockefeller-donated land on the east side of Manhattan, the UN started construction in 1947, and the completion of the complex instigated the rapid development of midtown Manhattan.

But even as the city, like the rest of the country, experienced a postwar boom, uniquely urban pressures were building. Immigrants from Puerto Rico and elsewhere in Latin America once more crammed East Harlem, the Lower East Side, and other poor neighborhoods, as did blacks from poor rural areas. Racial disturbances and riots started flaring up in what had for two hundred years been one of the more liberal of American cities. One response to the problem was a general exodus of the white middle-classes – the **Great White Flight** as the media labeled it – out of New York. Between 1950 and 1970 more than a million families left the city. Things went from bad to worse during the 1960s with **race riots** in Harlem and Bedford-Stuyvesant in Brooklyn.

The **World's Fair** of 1964 was a white elephant to boost the city's international profile, but on the streets the calls for civil liberties for blacks and withdrawal from Vietnam were, if anything, stronger than in most of the rest of the country. What few new buildings went up during this period seemed willfully to destroy much of the best of earlier traditions. In particular, the eyesore that is **Madison Square Garden**, built on the site of the grand old Neoclassical **Pennsylvania Station**, is still lamented as one of the city's worst architectural blunders.

The 1970s and 1980s

Manhattan reached **crisis point** in 1975 as companies, along with their employees, began leaving the city, lured by cheap land and low taxes in the suburbs. Even after municipal securities were sold, New York ran up a debt of millions of dollars. Essential services, long shaky due to underfunding, were ready to collapse. Ironically, the mayor who oversaw this fiasco, **Abraham Beame**, was an accountant.

Three things saved the city: the **Municipal Assistance Corporation**, which was formed to borrow the money the city could no longer get its hands on; the 1978 election of **Edward I. Koch** as mayor, a man whose tough talking helped reassure jumpy corporations; and, in a roundabout way, the plummeting of the dollar on the world currency market following the rise of oil prices in the 1970s. This last factor, combined with cheap transatlantic airfares, brought European tourists into the city en masse for the first time: with them came money for the city's hotels and service industries.

The city's slow reversal of fortunes coincided with the completion of two face-saving building projects: the former **World Trade Center** was a gesture of confidence by the Port Authority of New York and New Jersey, which financed it; and the 1977 construction of the **Citicorp Center** added modernity and prestige to its environs on Lexington Avenue. The era is also renowned for its raucous nightlife: starting in the mid-1970s, singles bars sprang up all over the city, gay bars proliferated in the Village, and disco was king. The impossible-to-get-into **Studio 54** was an internationally known hotspot, where drugs and illicit sex were the main events off the dance floor.

The real-estate and stock markets boomed during the 1980s, ushering in another era of Big Money; fortunes were made and lost overnight and big Wall Street names, like **Michael Milken**, were thrown in jail for insider trading. A spate of construction gave the city more eye-catching, though not necessarily well-loved, architecture, notably **Battery Park City**, and master builder **Donald Trump** provided glitzy housing for the super-wealthy. The stock market dip in 1987 started yet another downturn, and Koch's popularity waned. In 1989, he lost the Democratic mayoral nomination to **David Dinkins**, a 61-year-old black ex-marine who went on to beat Republican Rudolph Giuliani, a hard-nosed US attorney, in a hard-fought election. Even before the votes were counted, though, pundits forecast that the city was beyond any mayoral healing.

New York slipped, hard and fast, into a **massive recession**: in 1989 the city's budget deficit ran at $500 million. Of the 92 companies that had made the city their base in 1980, only 53 remained, the others having moved to cheaper pastures; and one in four New Yorkers was officially classed as poor – a figure unequaled since the Depression. By the end of 1990, the city's budget deficit had reached $1.5 billion; creditors were less than amused.

The 1990s: the Giuliani years

Throughout 1991 the effects of these financial problems on the city's ordinary people became more and more apparent: homelessness increased; some public schools became no-go zones with armed police and metal detectors at the gates; and a garbage-workers' strike left piles of rubbish rotting on the streets. Worse yet, a number of serious racial incidents and riots throughout his term contradicted Dinkins' pet phrase "gorgeous mosaic" for describing the city's multicultural make-up. In 1993 New York, traditionally a Democratic city, wanted a change and saw it in **Rudolph Giuliani** – the city's first Republican mayor in 28 years.

The voters were rewarded: Giuliani's first term ushered in a dramatic upswing in New York's prosperity. A *New York Times* article described 1995 as "the best year in recent memory for New York City." The pope even came to town and called New York "the capital of the world." The city's reputation flourished, with remarkable decreases in crime and a revitalized economy that helped spur the tourism industry to some of its best years ever.

Giuliani emerged as a very proactive mayor, and one quite happy to take credit for reducing crime – making the city streets and its subways safe – and the bloated city bureaucracy. While he made enemies among progressives for gutting rent stabilization laws and providing massive tax-breaks to corporations for moving to or remaining in the city (even as he reduced payments to the poor), Giuliani was handily re-elected to a second term in 1997. The city's economy continued to grow, and a series of civic improvements, including the cleaning up of Times Square, the renovation of Grand Central Terminal, and the influx of chain stores into Harlem, ensued.

Several high-profile incidents involving shocking allegations of **police brutality** marred Giuliani's second term, but these issues would all be superseded by events that would shock the city – and cause the locals to lean on Giuliani once more.

2000 and beyond

As if the dot-com bust in the spring of 2001 weren't hobbling enough, New York City was hit by the worst terrorist attack of the modern era on **September 11, 2001**. The story is now horribly familiar: two hijacked planes crashed into the Twin Towers of the World Trade Center, and, as the flaming fuel melted their steel frames, the towers collapsed. In all, 2750 people, including 343 firefighters, were killed in the catastrophe.

Over the next nine months, workers carted off 1.5 million tons of steel and debris, and by March 2002 the site was clear, well ahead of schedule (some would later ask if the job was perhaps done too quickly: several thousand Ground Zero workers continue to have chronic breathing problems as a result of not wearing ventilators and not following other environmental precautions at the site). So assured was his guidance throughout the ordeal that if Rudolph Giuliani had been able to run again, he most certainly would have won in a landslide. The law, however, precluded him from running for a third term – he set his sights on the presidency instead – and so on January 1, 2002, businessman **Michael Bloomberg** replaced him as mayor.

Though he had no prior political experience, Bloomberg, also a Republican, proved himself an able leader, using his corporate know-how to shore up the city's shaky finances – the city ended the 2006 fiscal year with a $6.1 billion budget surplus – and reorganize the school system. One of the mayor's most controversial acts was to follow California's lead and **ban smoking** in bars, clubs, and all restaurants in 2003. Bar owners, naturally, fought the move, but it turned out to be good for business: patrons seem to drink more and stay longer in a smoke-free environment, and smokers have gotten used to lighting up outside. In 2004 Bloomberg handily won re-election to a second term, during which he signed a law banning "trans-fats" in New York restaurants, pushed through a plan to replace the city's 13,000 taxicabs with hybrid vehicles by 2012, and proposed a congestion pricing scheme to reduce traffic in Manhattan similar to the one in London. Only the last plan has met with significant resistance, mainly from upstate legislators and outer-boroughs commuters.

Not until the fall of 2007 did the economy begin to slump once more, as Wall Street registered heavy losses connected to the subprime mortgage crisis. Yet unlike previous downturns, New York's real-estate market remained robust well into 2008, with the weak dollar – and the city's continued cachet – attracting foreign investors like never before. For tourists and culture vultures, completion of major renovations at the **Metropolitan Museum of Art** and the **Morgan Library** came as good news, as did the opening of the **New Museum of Contemporary Art** on a formerly bleak stretch of Bowery.

The 2008 presidential election season ended up as a disappointment for both Giuliani and the state's junior senator, **Hillary Rodham Clinton**, who lost their bids for the Republican and Democratic nominations, respectively. Bloomberg, who formally dropped out of the Republican Party and declared himself an Independent in 2007, toyed with the idea of a run for the White House but decided against it – for now. Instead, in 2008 the mayor commissioned a poll to see if New Yorkers would consider abolishing term limits to allow him to run again. Despite approving of the mayor's work in office, New Yorkers wanted term limits to remain. According to his aides, Bloomberg will comply with their wish, leaving City Hall at the end of 2009.

Books

Since the number of books about or set in New York is so vast, what follows is necessarily selective – use it as a place to begin further sleuthing.

Essays, memoirs, and narrative nonfiction

Djuna Barnes *New York*. This collection of newspaper stories – from 1913 to 1919 – looks mostly at out-of-the-way characters and places. Highly evocative of the times.

Anatole Broyard *Kafka was the Rage: A Greenwich Village Memoir*. Readable, if somewhat slight and occasionally misogynistic account of "bohemian" 1940s Greenwich Village life.

Josh Alan Friedman *Tales of Times Square*. Expanded in 2007, the book chronicles activities on and around the square between 1978 and 1984, pornography's golden age, documenting a culture under siege of impresarios, pimps, and 25-cent thrills.

Phillip Lopate (ed) *Writing New York*. A massive literary anthology of both fiction and nonfiction writings on the city, with selections by authors from Washington Irving to Tom Wolfe.

Federico García Lorca *Poet in New York*. The Andalusian poet and dramatist spent nine months in the city around the time of the 1929 Wall Street Crash. This collection of over thirty poems reveals his feelings on loneliness, greed, corruption, racism, and mistreatment of the poor.

Frank McCourt *'Tis*. In the follow-up memoir to the phenomenon *Angela's Ashes*, McCourt relates life in NYC – concentrating on his time teaching in the public-school system – once he's left Ireland behind.

Joseph Mitchell *Up in the Old Hotel*. Mitchell's collected *New Yorker* essays are works of sober, if manipulative, genius, definitively chronicling NYC characters and situations with a reporter's precision and near-perfect style.

Jan Morris *Manhattan '45*. Morris's best piece of writing on Manhattan, reconstructing New York as it greeted returning GIs in 1945. Effortlessly written, fascinatingly anecdotal, and marvelously warm about the city.

Georges Perec and Robert Bober *Ellis Island*. A brilliant, moving, original account of the "island of tears": part history, part meditation, and part interviews. Some of the stories are heartbreaking (between 1892 and 1924 there were 3000 suicides on the island), and the pictures are even more so.

History, politics, and society

Herbert Asbury *The Gangs of New York*. First published in 1928, this fascinating telling of the seamier side of New York is essential reading. Full of historical detail, anecdotes, and character sketches of crooks, the book describes New York mischief in all its incarnations and locales.

Edwin G. Burrows and Mike Wallace *Gotham: A History of New York City to 1898*. Enormous and encyclopedic in its detail, this is a serious history of the development of New York, with chapters on everything from its role in the Revolution to reform movements to its racial make-up in the 1820s.

Robert A. Caro *The Power Broker: Robert Moses and the Fall of New York*. Despite its imposing length, this brilliant and searing critique of New York City's most powerful twentieth-century figure is one of the most important books ever written about the city and its environs. Caro's book brings to light the megalomania and manipulation responsible for the creation of the nation's largest urban infrastructure.

George Chauncey *Gay New York: The Making of the Gay Male World 1890–1940*. Definitive, revealing account of the city's gay subculture.

Kenneth T. Jackson (ed) *The Encyclopedia of New York*. Massive, engrossing, and utterly comprehensive guide to just about everything in the city. Did you know, for example, that Truman Capote's real name was Streckford Persons?

Roger Kahn *The Boys of Summer*. This account of the 1950s Brooklyn Dodgers by a Beat writer who covered them is considered one of the classic baseball reads.

John A. Kouwenhoven *Columbia Historical Portrait of New York*. Interpreting the evolution of the city in visual terms (with illuminating captions accompanying the illustrations), this opus is monumental, fascinating, and definitive.

David Levering Lewis *When Harlem Was in Vogue*. Much-needed account of the Harlem Renaissance, a brief flowering of the arts in the 1920s and 1930s that was suffocated by the dual forces of the Depression and racism.

Jonathan Mahler *The Bronx Is Burning: 1977, Baseball, Politics, and the Battle for the Soul of a City*. Incredible portrait of the city as it was in the late 1970s, weaving together Yankee Reggie Jackson's conflicts with manager Billy Martin, the duel between Mario Cuomo and Ed Koch, the birth of punk rock, the hunt for serial killer Son of Sam, the blackout and looting, and more.

Legs McNeil and Gillian McCain *Please Kill Me*. An oral history of punk music in New York, artfully constructed by juxtaposing snippets of interviews as if the various protagonists (artists, financiers, impresarios) were in a conversation. Sometimes hilarious, often quite bleak.

Luc Sante *Low Life: Lures and Snares of Old New York*. This chronicle of the city's seamy side between 1840 and 1919 is a pioneering work. Full of outrageous details usually left out of conventional history, it reconstructs the day-to-day life of the urban poor, criminals, and prostitutes with shocking clarity.

Gay Talese *Fame and Obscurity*. Talese deftly presents interviews with New York City's famous (Sinatra, DiMaggio, etc) and its obscure (bums, chauffeurs, etc), offering not only a window into the heart of NYC, but that of human existence.

Jennifer Toth *Mole People*. A creepy sociological study of the people who live below NYC streets, in the dark reaches of the subway tunnel system. You may never again ride the subway without your face plastered to the window looking for signs of human life.

Art, architecture, and photography

Lorraine Diehl *The Late Great Pennsylvania Station*. The anatomy of a travesty. How could a railroad palace, modeled after the Baths of Caracalla in Rome, stand for only fifty years before being destroyed? The pictures alone warrant the price.

Horst Hamann *New York Vertical.* This beautiful book pays homage to the New York skyscraper, and is filled with dazzling black-and-white vertical shots of Manhattan, accompanied by witty quotes from famous and obscure folk.

Jane Jacobs *The Death and Life of Great American Cities.* Landmark 1961 screed authored by Robert Moses' nemesis, and railing against urban over-planning.

David McCullough *Great Bridge: The Epic Story of the Building of the Brooklyn Bridge.* The story of the father-and-son Roebling team who fought the laws of gravity, sharp-toothed competitors, and corrupt politicians to build a bridge that has withstood the test of time and become one of NYC's most noted landmarks.

Jacob Riis *How the Other Half Lives.* Photojournalism reporting on life in the Lower East Side at the end of the nineteenth century. Its original publication in 1890 awakened many to the plight of New York's poor.

Stern, Gilmartin and Mellins/ Stern and Gilmartin, Massengale/ Stern and Mellins, Fishman *New York 1900/1930/1960.* These three exhaustive tomes, subtitled "Metropolitan Architecture and Urbanism," contain all you'll ever want or need to know about architecture and the organization of the city.

N. White and E. Willensky (eds) *AIA Guide to New York.* The definitive contemporary guide to the city's architecture – witty, immensely informative, and opinionated – and useful as an on-site reference.

Other guides

Richard Alleman *The Movie Lover's Guide to New York.* More than two hundred listings of corners of the city with cinematic associations: TV and film locations, stars' childhood homes and final resting places, and more. Interestingly written, painstakingly researched.

Federal Writers' Project *The WPA Guide to New York City.* Originally written in 1939 and recently reissued, this detailed guide offers a fascinating look at life in New York City when the Dodgers played at Ebbets Field, a trolley ride cost five cents, and a room at the

Plaza was $7.50. A surprising amount of description remains apt.

Rob Grader *The Cheap Bastard's Guide to New York City.* If the title doesn't immediately turn you off, this frequently updated guide is the book for you.

Andrew Roth *Infamous Manhattan.* A vivid and engrossing history of New York crime, revealing the sites of Mafia hits, celebrity murders, nineteenth-century brothels, and other wicked spots, including a particularly fascinating guide to restaurants with dubious, infamous, or gory pasts.

Fiction

Julia Alvarez *How the Garcia Girls Lost Their Accents.* Four Latina sisters are uprooted from their privileged life in the Dominican Republic to the Bronx in this compelling look at the modern immigrant experience.

Paul Auster *The New York Trilogy: City of Glass, Ghosts and The Locked Room.* Three Borgesian investigations into the mystery, madness, and murders of contemporary NYC.

James Baldwin *Another Country*. Baldwin's best-known novel, tracking the feverish search for meaningful relationships among a group of 1960s New York bohemians.

Lawrence Block *When the Sacred Ginmill Closes*. Tough to choose between Block's hard-hitting Matthew Scudder suspense novels, all set in the city; this might be the most compelling, with Hell's Kitchen, downtown Manhattan, and far-flung parts of Brooklyn expertly woven into a dark mystery.

Truman Capote *Breakfast at Tiffany's*. Far sadder and racier than the movie, this novel is a rhapsody to New York in the early 1940s, tracking the dissolute youthful residents of an uptown apartment building and their movements about town.

Caleb Carr *The Alienist*. This 1896-set thriller evokes old New York to perfection. The heavy-handed psychobabble grates at times, but the story line (the pursuit of one of the first serial killers) is still involving. Best for its descriptions of New York as well as saliva-inducing details of meals at long-gone restaurants.

Stephen Crane *Maggie: A Girl of the Streets*. 1893 melodrama about a girl growing up in a Lower East Side slum. Although luridly overdescribed, *Red Badge of Courage* author Crane was deservedly acclaimed for his groundbreaking naturalism; the fictional counterpart to Riis's work.

Don DeLillo *Underworld*. Following the fate of the baseball hit out of the park to win the 1951 pennant for the New York Giants, DeLillo's sprawling novel offers a counterhistory of twentieth-century America. His luminous prose is spellbinding even when the story feels faintly ridiculous.

Ralph Ellison *Invisible Man*. The definitive, if sometimes long-winded, novel of what it's like to be black and American, using Harlem and the 1950s race riots as a backdrop.

Oscar Hijuelos *Our House in the Last World*. A warmly evocative novel of a Cuban immigrant's life in New York from before the war to the present day.

Chester Himes *The Crazy Kill*. Himes wrote violent, fast-moving, and funny thrillers set in Harlem; this and *Cotton Goes to Harlem* are among the best.

Henry James *Washington Square*. Skillful and engrossing examination of the mores and strict social expectations of genteel New York society in the late nineteenth century.

Sue Kaufman *Diary of a Mad Housewife*. Recently reissued, this is a classic dissection of 1960s New York, satirically chronicling the antics of a group of social climbers along with the disintegration of a marriage.

Jonathan Lethem *Motherless Brooklyn*. Brooklyn author sets this quirky suspense novel in Cobble Hill and its environs, where a Tourette's sufferer tries to track down his boss's killer. See also his subsequent *The Fortress of Solitude*, which treats childhood and gentrification with great wit and sensitivity.

Mary McCarthy *The Group*. Eight Vassar graduates making their way in the New York of the Thirties. Sad, funny, and satirical.

Alice McDermott *Charming Billy*. Billy is a poetry-loving drunkard from Queens, looking to bring his Irish love over to New York City. National Book Award winner.

Jay McInerney *Bright Lights, Big City*. A trendy, "voice of a generation" book when it came out in the 1980s, it made first-time novelist McInerney a household name. The story follows a struggling New York writer in his job as a fact-checker at an important literary magazine (a thinly disguised *New Yorker*), and from one cocaine-sozzled nightclub to another. Still amusing.

Emma McLaughlin and Nicola Kraus *The Nanny Diaries: A Novel*. A delicious and nimble comic novel, culled from the authors' own experiences nannying to the wealthy families of the Upper East Side; later made into an entertaining film with Scarlett Johansson.

Dorothy Parker *Complete Stories*. Parker's stories are, at times, surprisingly moving, depicting New York in all its glories, excesses, and pretensions with perfect, searing wit.

Richard Price *Lush Life*. With perfect pitch for the language of the streets, Richard Price tells the sprawling story of the murder of a bartender on today's Lower East Side, a place where struggling writers, old Jewish immigrants, drug dealers, cops, and club kids uneasily coexist.

Judith Rossner *Looking for Mr Goodbar*. A disquieting book, tracing the life – and eventual demise – of a female teacher in search of love in volatile and permissive 1970s New York.

Henry Roth *Call It Sleep*. Roth's novel traces the awakening of a small immigrant child to the realities of life among the slums of the Jewish Lower East Side. Read more for the evocations of childhood than the social comment.

Suze Rotolo *A Freewheelin' Time: A Memoir of Greenwich Village in the Sixties*. Bob Dylan's formative years in the Village are recounted by his smart and sensitive girlfriend of four years, Suze Rotolo, who also talks about her own artistic pursuits and her family's devotion to communism.

Paul Rudnick *Social Disease*. Hilarious, often incredible send-up of Manhattan night-owls. Very New York, very funny.

J.D. Salinger *The Catcher in the Rye*. Salinger's gripping novel of adolescence, following Holden Caulfield's sardonic journey of discovery through the streets of New York. A classic.

Hubert Selby, Jr *Last Exit to Brooklyn*. When first published in Britain in 1966, this novel was tried on charges of obscenity. Even now it's a disturbing read, evoking the sex, immorality, drugs, and violence of Brooklyn in the 1960s with fearsome clarity.

Betty Smith *A Tree Grows in Brooklyn*. A classic, and rightly so – a courageous Irish girl learns about family, life, and sex against a vivid prewar Brooklyn backdrop. Totally absorbing.

Rex Stout *The Doorbell Rang*. Stout's Nero Wolfe is perhaps the most intrinsically "New York" of all the literary detectives based in the city, a larger-than-life character who, with the help of his dashing assistant, Archie Goodwin, solves crimes from the comfort of his sumptuous midtown brownstone. Wonderfully evocative of the city in the 1940s and 1950s.

Lauren Weisberger *The Devil Wears Prada*. A satirical snapshot of New York's cutthroat magazine world, this *roman à clef* from *Vogue* editor Anna Wintour's former assistant is pleasant enough, but the film version with Meryl Streep is even better.

Edith Wharton *Age of Innocence*. A withering, deftly drawn picture of New York high society at the turn of the twentieth century and how rigid social convention keeps two sensitive, ill-fated lovers apart. See also Wharton's astounding *House of Mirth* and her classic stories *Old New York*.

Tom Wolfe *Bonfire of the Vanities*. Set all around New York City, this sprawling novel skewers 1980s status-mongers to great effect.

New York on film

With its skyline and rugged facades, its mean streets and swanky avenues, its electric energy and edgy attitude, New York City is a natural-born movie star. From the silent era's cautionary tales of young lovers ground down by the metropolis, through the smoky location-shot *noirs* of the 1940s, right through to the Lower East Side indies of the past twenty years, New York has probably been the most filmed city on earth.

What follows is a selection not just of the best New York movies but the most New York of New York movies – movies that capture the city's atmosphere, pulse, and style; movies that celebrate its diversity or revel in its misfortunes; and movies that, if nothing else, give you a pretty good idea of what you're going to get before you get there.

Ten great New York movies

Breakfast at Tiffany's (*Blake Edwards, 1961*). The most charming and cherished of New York movie romances, starring Audrey Hepburn as party girl Holly Golightly. Hepburn and George Peppard run up and down each other's fire escapes and skip along Fifth Avenue, taking in the New York Public Library and that jewelry store.

Do the Right Thing (*Spike Lee, 1989*). Set over 24 hours on the hottest day of the year in Brooklyn's Bed-Stuy – a day on which the melting pot reaches boiling point – Spike Lee's colorful, stylish masterpiece moves from comedy to tragedy to compose an epic song of New York.

King Kong (*Merian C. Cooper and Ernest B. Schoedsack, 1933*). *King Kong* paints a vivid picture of Depression-era Manhattan, and gives us the city's most indelible movie image: King Kong straddling the Empire State Building and swatting at passing planes.

Manhattan (*Woody Allen, 1979*). This black-and-white masterpiece, one of the truly great eulogies to the city, details the self-absorptions, lifestyles, and romances of middle-class intellectuals, to the tune of a Gershwin soundtrack.

On the Town (*Gene Kelly and Stanley Donen, 1949*). Three sailors get 24 hours' shore leave in NYC and fight over whether to see the sights or chase the girls. Starring Gene Kelly, Frank Sinatra, and Ann Miller flashing her gams in the Museum of Natural History, this was the first musical taken out of the studios and onto the streets. Smart, cynical, and satirical with a bunch of terrific numbers.

On the Waterfront (*Elia Kazan, 1954*). Few images of New York are as unforgettable as Marlon Brando's rooftop pigeon coop at dawn and those misty views of the New York Harbor (actually shot just over the river in Hoboken), in this unforgettable story of long-suffering longshoremen and union racketeering.

Shadows (*John Cassavetes, 1960*). Cassavetes' debut film is a New York movie *par excellence*: a New Wave melody about jazz musicians, young love, and racial prejudice, shot with bebop verve and jazzy passion in Central Park, Greenwich Village, and even the MoMA sculpture garden.

Sweet Smell of Success (*Alexander Mackendrick, 1957*). Broadway as a nest of vipers. Gossip columnist Burt Lancaster and sleazy press-agent Tony Curtis eat each other's tails in this snappy, cynical study of showbiz corruption. Shot on location and mostly at night, in steely black and white, Times Square and the Great White Way never looked so alluring.

Taxi Driver (*Martin Scorsese, 1976*). A long night's journey into day by the great chronicler of the city's dark side. Scorsese's New York is hallucinatorily seductive and thoroughly repellent in this superbly unsettling study of obsessive outsider Travis Bickle (Robert De Niro).

West Side Story (*Robert Wise and Jerome Robbins, 1961*). Sex, singing, and Shakespeare in a hyper-cinematic Oscar-winning musical (via Broadway) about rival street gangs.

Modern New York

The 25th Hour (*Spike Lee, 2002*). Lee stacks his film (based on an excellent first novel by David Benioff) with an impressive cast, headed by Ed Norton as a drug dealer on the last day before he goes to prison, ricocheting round between friends and lovers. Bleak, but gripping.

Bad Lieutenant (*Abel Ferrara, 1992*). Nearly every movie by Ferrara, from *Driller Killer* to *The Funeral*, deserves a place in a list of great New York movies, but this, above all, seems his own personal *Manhattan*: a journey through the circles of Hell with Harvey Keitel as a depraved Dante.

The Cruise (*Bennett Miller, 1998*). A documentary portrait of a true New York eccentric, Timothy "Speed" Levitch, a Dostoyevskian character with a baroque flair for language and an encyclopedic knowledge of local history, who takes puzzled tourists on guided "cruises" around the city, on which he rails against the tyranny of the grid plan and rhapsodizes about "the lascivious voyeurism of the tour bus."

In America (*Jim Sheridan, 2003*). Sheridan and his two daughters wrote this autobiographical tale of an immigrant Irish family arriving in New York in the 1980s, and even in its bleakest moments, the tenderness and intimacy of the story is enchanting.

Kids (*Larry Clark, 1995*). The best New York summer movie since *Do the Right Thing*, and just as controversial. An overhyped but affecting portrait of a group of amoral, though supposedly typical, teenagers hanging out on the Upper East Side, in Washington Square Park, and in the Carmine Street swimming pool on one muggy, mad day.

Little Odessa (*James Gray, 1995*). Tim Roth plays the prodigal son returning to Brooklyn in this somber, beautifully shot story of the Russian mafia in Brighton Beach and Coney Island.

Roger Dodger (*Dylan Kidd, 2002*). A self-important advertising exec (Campbell Scott) takes his nephew (Jesse Eisenberg) on an alcohol-fueled tour of the city in search of sex, plumbing the depths of his own depravity. Extremely witty, if hard to watch.

Six Degrees of Separation (*Fred Schepisi, 1993*). Brilliant, enthralling adaptation of John Guare's acclaimed play which uses the story – a young black man (Will Smith) turns up at a rich Upper East Side apartment claiming to be the son of Sidney Poitier – as a springboard for an examination of the great social and racial divides of the city.

Smoke (*Wayne Wang, 1995*). A clever, beguiling film scripted by novelist Paul Auster, which connects a handful of stories revolving around Harvey Keitel's Brooklyn cigar store. A companion film, *Blue in the Face*, has a looser, more improvisational feel.

Unmade Beds (*Nicholas Barker, 1998*). This poignant, occasionally hilarious, and beautifully stylized documentary about four single New Yorkers looking for love in the personal columns, visualizes the city as one endless Edward Hopper painting, full of lonely souls biding time in rented rooms.

New York past

The Age of Innocence (*Martin Scorsese, 1993*). The upper echelons of New York society in the 1870s brought gloriously to life. Though Scorsese restricts most of the action to drawing rooms and ballrooms, look out for the breathtaking matte shot of a then-undeveloped Upper East Side.

Basquiat (*Julian Schnabel, 1996*). Haunting portrait of the artist as a young (doomed) man, rising from spray-painting graffiti and living in a box in a Lower East Side park to taking the New York art world by storm in the early 1980s. David Bowie plays a sensitive Andy Warhol.

The Crowd (*King Vidor, 1928*). "You've got to be good in that town if you want to beat the crowd." A young couple try to make it in the big city but are swallowed up and spat out by the capitalist machine. A bleak vision of New York in the 1920s, and one of the great silent films.

The Godfather Part II (*Francis Ford Coppola, 1974*). Flashing back to the early life of Vito Corleone, Coppola's great sequel recreated the Italian immigrant experience at the turn of the century, portraying Corleone quarantined at Ellis Island and growing up tough on the meticulously recreated streets of Little Italy.

The Last Days of Disco (*Whit Stillman, 1998*). About the most unlikely setting for Stillman's brand of square WASPy talkfests would be the bombastic glittery bacchanals that were *Studio 54* in its late-1970s heyday, which is what makes this far more enjoyable than the same season's overly literal and melodramatic *54* (*Mark Christopher, 1998*).

Little Fugitive (*Morris Engel and Ruth Orkin, 1953*). A Brooklyn 7-year-old, tricked into believing he has killed his older brother, takes flight to Coney Island where he spends a day and a night indulging in all its previously forbidden pleasures. This beautifully photographed time capsule of 1950s Brooklyn influenced both the American indie scene and the French New Wave.

Pollock (*Ed Harris, 2000*). From a cramped Manhattan apartment to the barren nature of the Hamptons, abstract artist Jackson Pollock drips on canvases and battles his wife (Oscar-winner Marcia Gay Harden), fame, and drink. Harris is powerful in the title role.

Radio Days (*Woody Allen, 1987*). Woody contrasts reminiscences of his loud, vulgar family in 1940s Rockaway with reveries of the golden days of radio and the glamour of Times Square.

Saturday Night Fever (*John Badham, 1977*). What everybody remembers is the tacky glamour of flared white pantsuits and mirror-balled discos, but *Saturday Night Fever* is actually a touching and believable portrayal of working-class youth in the 1970s, Italian-American Brooklyn, and the road to Manhattan.

Summer of Sam (*Spike Lee, 1999*). The dark summer of 1977 – the summer of the "Son of Sam" killings, a blistering heatwave, power blackouts, looting, arson, and the birth of punk – provides the perfect backdrop for Lee's sprawling tale of paranoia and betrayal in an Italian-American enclave of the Bronx.

New York comedy and romance

Annie Hall (*Woody Allen, 1977*). Oscar-winning autobiographical comic romance, which flits from reminiscences of Alvy Singer's childhood living beneath the Coney Island Cyclone, to life and love in uptown Manhattan, is a valentine both to ex-lover co-star Diane Keaton and to the city. Simultaneously clever, bourgeois, and very winning.

Men in Black (*Barry Sonnenfeld, 1997*). One of the most wittily imaginative Manhattan movies portrays the city as a haven for a brave new wave of immigration, with Tommy Lee Jones and Will Smith keeping watch for extraterrestrials and the future of the universe hanging in the balance in a MacDougal Street jewelry store.

Miracle on 34th Street (*George Seaton, 1947*). The perfect antidote to all the nightmares and mean streets of New York films, *Miracle* opens during Macy's annual Christmas parade, where a kindly old gentleman with a white beard offers to replace the store's inebriated Santa.

The Out-of-Towners (*Arthur Hiller, 1969*). If you have any problems getting into town from the airport take solace from the fact that they can be nothing compared to those endured by Jack Lemmon and Sandy Dennis – for whom everything that can go wrong does go wrong – in Neil Simon's frantic comedy.

Quick Change (*Howard Franklin and Bill Murray, 1990*). The "change" is cash stolen from a bank. The "quick" of the title is ironic: though the robbery was easy, it's fleeing the city that proves difficult, as Bill Murray and his cohorts are delayed by cops, other crooks, and regular, eccentric New Yorkers. One of Murray's best efforts.

The Seven Year Itch (*Billy Wilder, 1955*). When his wife and kid vacate humid Manhattan, Mitty-like pulp editor Tom Ewell is left guiltily leching over the innocent TV-toothpaste temptress upstairs – Marilyn Monroe, at her most wistfully comic. The sight of her pushing down her billowing skirt as she stands on a subway grating (at Lexington Ave and 52nd St) is one of the era's and the city's most resonant movie images.

So This is New York (*Richard Fleischer, 1948*). A bomb on its initial release, this rarely shown but edgy and innovative comedy plants three Midwesterners amongst the sharpies and operators of 1930s New York. The voiceover by star Henry Morgan (an Indiana salesman thoroughly unimpressed by the big city) is sublimely sarcastic.

Stranger than Paradise (*Jim Jarmusch, 1984*). Only the first third of this, the original slacker indie, is set in New York, but its portrayal of Lower East Side lethargy is hilariously spot-on. The film's downtown credentials – John Lurie is a jazz saxophonist with the Lounge Lizards, Richard Edson used to drum for Sonic Youth, and Jarmusch himself is an East Village celebrity – are impeccable.

Tootsie (*Sidney Pollack, 1982*). Tired of being rejected in audition after audition, a struggling actor (comic turn for Dustin Hoffman) dons a wig and woman's attire to win a prize role on an afternoon soap. Great script, with a memorable scene set in the *Russian Tea Room*.

New York nightmares

The Addiction (*Abel Ferrara, 1995*). A simple trip home from the college library turns into a living nightmare for Lili Taylor when she's bitten by a vampiric streetwalker on Bleecker Street and transformed into a blood junkie cruising the East Village for fresh kill.

After Hours (*Martin Scorsese, 1985*). Yuppie computer programmer Griffin Dunne inadvertently ends up on a nightlong odyssey into the Hades of downtown New York, a journey that goes from bad to worse to awful as he encounters every kook south of 14th Street. Amazing footage of pre-gentrified Soho.

American Psycho (*Mary Harron, 2000*). This stylized adaptation of the Bret Easton Ellis novel succeeds largely due to Christian Bale, pulling off some blacker-than-black comedy in his role as a securities trader consumed by designer labels, the ladder of success, and Huey Lewis lyrics.

Escape from New York (*John Carpenter, 1981*). In the then-not-too-distant future (1997, in fact), society has given up trying to solve the problems of Manhattan and has walled it up as a lawless maximum-security prison from which Kurt Russell has to rescue the hijacked US president. Ludicrous but great fun.

Jacob's Ladder (*Adrian Lyne, 1990*). Tim Robbins gets off the subway in Brooklyn but discovers himself locked inside a deserted station… and then his troubles really begin as his Vietnam-induced hallucinations turn the city into one hell of a house of horrors.

The Lost Weekend (*Billy Wilder, 1945*). Alcoholic Ray Milland is left alone in the city with no money and a desperate thirst. The film's most famous scene is his long trek up Third Avenue (shot on location) trying to hawk his typewriter to buy booze, only to find all the pawn shops closed for Yom Kippur.

Marathon Man (*John Schlesinger, 1976*). Innocent, bookish Dustin Hoffman runs for his life all over Manhattan after he's dragged into a conspiracy involving old Nazis and tortured with dental instruments. ("Is it safe?") Shot memorably around the Central Park Reservoir and Zoo, Columbia University, the Diamond District, and Spanish Harlem.

Requiem for a Dream (*Darren Aronofsky, 2000*). A jagged and harrowing adaptation of Hubert Selby's novel about a band of junkies' descent into insanity amidst their cold, gray Coney Island surroundings.

Rosemary's Baby (*Roman Polanski, 1968*). Mia Farrow and John Cassavetes move into their dream New York apartment and think they have problems with nosy neighbors – but that's just until Farrow gets pregnant and hell, literally, breaks loose. Arguably the most terrifying film ever set in the city.

The Taking of Pelham One Two Three (*Joseph Sargent, 1974*). Just when you thought it was safe to get back on the subway. A gang of mercenary hoods hijacks a train on its way through midtown and threatens to start killing one passenger per minute if their million-dollar ransom is not paid within the hour.

The Warriors (*Walter Hill, 1979*). The Coney Island Warriors ride to the Bronx for a meeting with all of New York's gangs; when the organizer is killed, the Warriors are unjustly blamed and have to navigate their way back to their home turf. Old-school subway graffiti, distinctive gang costumes, and a pervading sense of nighttime paranoia all contribute to this original cult film.

The mean streets

American Gangster (*Ridley Scott, 2007*). Russell Crowe is utterly convincing as the New York detective trying to bring down drug kingpin Frank Lucas (Denzel Washington), who built a heroin empire in the 1970s by mixing violence and family values. Washington's a bit too sweet to shoot a rival point-blank on a crowded sidewalk, but the directing is first-rate.

A Bronx Tale (*Robert De Niro, 1993*). An overlooked film with depth and heart. In a 1960s Bronx, Calogero witnesses a traffic accident and its aftermath at the hands of a local gangster, Sonny (Chazz Palminteri). Over the next several years, his loyalties to his bus-driver father (De Niro) are tested as he is seduced by Sonny's glamorous world. Great soundtrack.

Carlito's Way (*Brian De Palma, 1993*). Sumptuously filmed story of a Puerto Rican gangster (Al Pacino) trying to go straight – it plays somewhat by the numbers, but is notable for its unfashionably tragic story-arc and lively evocation of the 1970s disco- and salsa-club scenes.

The French Connection (*William Friedkin, 1971*). Plenty of heady Brooklyn atmosphere in this sensational Oscar-winning cop thriller starring Gene Hackman, whose classic car-and-subway chase takes place under the Bensonhurst Elevated Railroad.

Gangs of New York (*Martin Scorsese, 2002*). Sprawling, overlong, but impressive historical yarn, detailing the bitter immigrant rivalries and gang warfare that dogged early Manhattan settlement.

Goodfellas (*Martin Scorsese, 1990*). Vibrant and nuanced tale, based on the true story of a mob turncoat; another in a fine series of Scorsese New York stories. Seduced by the allure of the Mafia from a young age, Brooklyn native Henry Hill (a fine Ray Liotta) recounts 25 years of crime, his rise through the ranks, and decision to turn on his brethren.

King of New York (*Abel Ferrara, 1990*). Glossy pre-Giuliani saga in which Christopher Walken (having entirely too much fun) plays a crime boss trying to take over the entire city.

Mean Streets (*Martin Scorsese, 1973*). Scorsese's brilliant breakthrough film breathlessly follows small-time hood Harvey Keitel and his volatile, harum-scarum buddy Robert De Niro around a vividly portrayed Little Italy before reaching its violent climax.

Midnight Cowboy (*John Schlesinger, 1969*). The odd love story between Jon Voight's bumpkin hustler and Dustin Hoffman's touching urban creep Ratso Rizzo plays out against both the seediest and swankiest of New York locations. The only X-rated film to receive an Oscar for Best Picture.

Naked City (*Jules Dassin, 1948*). A crime story that views the city with a documentarist's eye. Shot on actual locations, it follows a police manhunt for a ruthless killer all over town toward an unforgettable chase through the Lower East Side and a shoot-out on the Williamsburg Bridge.

Prince of the City (*Sidney Lumet, 1981*). Lumet is a die-hard New York director, and this is his New York epic. A corrupt narcotics detective turns federal informer to assuage his guilt, and Lumet takes us from drug busts in Harlem to the cops' suburban homes on Long Island, to federal agents' swanky pads overlooking Central Park.

Superfly (*Gordon Parks Jr, 1972*). Propelled by its ecstatic Curtis Mayfield score, this blaxploitation classic about one smooth-looking drug dealer's ultimate score is best seen today for its mind-boggling fashion excess and almost documentary-like look at the Harlem bars, streets, clubs, and diners of thirty-odd years ago. Also see Parks' *Shaft*, released a year earlier.

New York song and dance

42nd Street (*Lloyd Bacon, 1933*). One of the best films ever made about Broadway – though the film rarely ventures outside the theater. Starring Ruby Keeler as the young chorus girl who has to replace the ailing leading lady: she goes on stage an unknown and, well, you know the rest.

Fame (*Alan Parker, 1980*). Set in Manhattan's High School for the Performing Arts, the film may be a gawky musical, but in its haphazard, sentimental, ungainly way it still manages to capture some of the city's agony and ecstasy.

A Great Day in Harlem (*Jean Bach, 1994*). A unique jazz documentary that spins many tales around the famous Art Kane photograph for which the cream of New York's jazz world assemble on the steps of a Harlem brownstone one August morning in 1958. Using home-movie footage of the event and present-day interviews, Bach creates a wonderful portrait of a golden age.

Guys and Dolls (*Joseph L. Mankiewicz, 1955*). The great Broadway musical shot entirely on soundstages and giving as unlikely a picture of Times Square hoodlums (all colorfully suited sweetie-pies) as was ever seen. And a singing and dancing Marlon Brando to boot.

Hair (*Milos Forman, 1979*). Film version of the counterculture musical turns Central Park into a hippie paradise for the hirsute, charismatic (and very young) Treat Williams and his fellow Aquarians. Laced with humor, it's got a spectacular opening sequence, with choreography (including dancing police horses) by Twyla Tharp.

New York, New York (*Martin Scorsese, 1977*). Scorsese's homage to the grand musicals of postwar Hollywood, reimagined for the post-Vietnam era.

Travel
store

Visit us online

www.roughguides.com

Information on over 25,000 destinations around the world

- **Read** Rough Guides' trusted travel info
- **Access** exclusive articles from Rough Guides authors
- **Update** yourself on new books, maps, CDs and other products
- **Enter** our competitions and win travel prizes
- **Share** ideas, journals, photos & travel advice with other users
- **Earn** points every time you contribute to the Rough Guide community and get rewards

BROADEN YOUR HORIZONS

NOTES

NOTES

Small print and Index

A Rough Guide to Rough Guides

Published in 1982, the first Rough Guide – to Greece – was a student scheme that became a publishing phenomenon. Mark Ellingham, a recent graduate in English from Bristol University, had been travelling in Greece the previous summer and couldn't find the right guidebook. With a small group of friends he wrote his own guide, combining a highly contemporary, journalistic style with a thoroughly practical approach to travellers' needs.

The immediate success of the book spawned a series that rapidly covered dozens of destinations. And, in addition to impecunious backpackers, Rough Guides soon acquired a much broader and older readership that relished the guides' wit and inquisitiveness as much as their enthusiastic, critical approach and value-for-money ethos.

These days, Rough Guides include recommendations from shoestring to luxury and cover more than 200 destinations around the globe, including almost every country in the Americas and Europe, more than half of Africa and most of Asia and Australasia. Our ever-growing team of authors and photographers is spread all over the world, particularly in Europe, the USA and Australia.

In the early 1990s, Rough Guides branched out of travel, with the publication of Rough Guides to World Music, Classical Music and the Internet. All three have become benchmark titles in their fields, spearheading the publication of a wide range of books under the Rough Guide name.

Including the travel series, Rough Guides now number more than 350 titles, covering: phrasebooks, waterproof maps, music guides from Opera to Heavy Metal, reference works as diverse as Conspiracy Theories and Shakespeare, and popular culture books from iPods to Poker. Rough Guides also produce a series of more than 120 World Music CDs in partnership with World Music Network.

Visit www.roughguides.com to see our latest publications.

Rough Guide travel images are available for commercial licensing at www.roughguidespictures.com

Rough Guide credits

Text editor: Brendon Griffin
Layout: Anita Singh
Cartography: Jasbir Sandhu
Picture editor: Nicole Newman
Production: Rebecca Short
Proofreader: Jan McCann, Diane Margolis
Cover design: Chloë Roberts
Photographer: Susannah Sayler, Angus Oborn, Nelson Hancock
Editorial: **London** Ruth Blackmore, Alison Murchie, Andy Turner, Keith Drew, Edward Aves, Alice Park, Lucy White, Jo Kirby, James Smart, Natasha Foges, Róisín Cameron, Emma Traynor, James Rice, Emma Gibbs, Kathryn Lane, Christina Valhouli, Monica Woods, Mani Ramaswamy, Joe Staines, Peter Buckley, Matthew Milton, Tracy Hopkins, Ruth Tidball; **New York** Andrew Rosenberg, Steven Horak, AnneLise Sorensen, Ella Steim, Anna Owens, Sean Mahoney, Paula Neudorf; **Delhi** Madhavi Singh, Karen D'Souza
Design & Pictures: **London** Scott Stickland, Dan May, Diana Jarvis, Mark Thomas, Chloë Roberts, Sarah Cummins, Emily Taylor; **Delhi** Umesh Aggarwal, Ajay Verma, Jessica Subramanian, Ankur Guha, Pradeep Thapliyal, Sachin Tanwar, Nikhil Agarwal

Production: Vicky Baldwin
Cartography: **London** Maxine Repath, Ed Wright, Katie Lloyd-Jones; **Delhi** Jai Prakash Mishra, Rajesh Chhibber, Ashutosh Bharti, Rajesh Mishra, Animesh Pathak, Karobi Gogoi, Alakananda Bhattacharya, Swati Handoo, Deshpal Dabas
Online: **London** George Atwell, Faye Hellon, Jeanette Angell, Fergus Day, Justine Bright, Clare Bryson, Áine Fearon, Adrian Low, Ezgi Celebi, Amber Bloomfield; **Delhi** Amit Verma, Rahul Kumar, Narender Kumar, Ravi Yadav, Debojit Borah, Rakesh Kumar, Ganesh Sharma
Marketing & Publicity: **London** Liz Statham, Niki Hanmer, Louise Maher, Jess Carter, Vanessa Godden, Vivienne Watton, Anna Paynton, Rachel Sprackett, Libby Jellie, Holly Dudley; **New York** Geoff Colquitt, Nancy Lambert, Katy Ball; **Delhi** Ragini Govind
Manager India: Punita Singh
Reference Director: Andrew Lockett
Operations Manager: Helen Phillips
PA to Publishing Director: Nicola Henderson
Publishing Director: Martin Dunford
Commercial Manager: Gino Magnotta
Managing Director: John Duhigg

Publishing information

This eleventh edition published January 2009 by
Rough Guides Ltd,
80 Strand, London WC2R 0RL
345 Hudson St, 4th Floor,
New York, NY 10014, USA
14 Local Shopping Centre, Panchsheel Park,
New Delhi 110017, India
Distributed by the Penguin Group
Penguin Books Ltd,
80 Strand, London WC2R 0RL
Penguin Group (USA)
375 Hudson Street, NY 10014, USA
Penguin Group (Australia)
250 Camberwell Road, Camberwell,
Victoria 3124, Australia
Penguin Group (Canada)
195 Harry Walker Parkway N, Newmarket, ON,
L3Y 7B3 Canada
Penguin Group (NZ)
67 Apollo Drive, Mairangi Bay, Auckland 1310,
New Zealand

Cover concept by Peter Dyer.
Typeset in Bembo and Helvetica to an original design by Henry Iles.
Printed in China
© Martin Dunford 2009
No part of this book may be reproduced in any form without permission from the publisher except for the quotation of brief passages in reviews.
480pp includes index
A catalogue record for this book is available from the British Library.
ISBN: 978-1-84836-039-6

Help us update

We've gone to a lot of effort to ensure that the eleventh edition of **The Rough Guide to New York City** is accurate and up to date. However, things change – places get "discovered", opening hours are notoriously fickle, restaurants and rooms raise prices or lower standards. If you feel we've got it wrong or left something out, we'd like to know, and if you can remember the address, the price, the hours, the phone number, so much the better.

Please send your comments with the subject line "**Rough Guide New York City Update**" to ©mail@roughguides.com. We'll credit all contributions and send a copy of the next edition (or any other Rough Guide if you prefer) for the very best emails.

Have your questions answered and tell others about your trip at
Ⓦcommunity.roughguides.com

Acknowledgements

Shea Dean would like to thank her editor, Brendon, for his sharp wit and sharp eye throughout the editing process; Ella Steim and Andrew Rosenberg of Rough Guides, for the great assignment; and Marc, for making life in Brooklyn such an adventure.

Stephen Keeling Thanks to consummate blogger and all-round New York expert Victor Ozols, Seth Fineberg for East Village tips and punk history, the Brooklyn Brewery for Friday nights, the kind staff at the Met, Brendon Griffin for his judicious editing, Andrew Rosenberg and Ella Steim at Rough Guides, and finally Tiffany Wu, whose love and support, as always, made this possible.

Todd Obolsky Many thanks to Ella Steim at RG, Matt Carstensen, Francisca Ovalle at NYC & Company, Trey Ditto, Marissa Anshutz, Olivia Cuervo, Kate Sheleg at Central Park Conservancy, Amy Schmidt, and Michael Luruc.

The editor would like to thank Shea, Stephen, and Todd for all their time, talent and effort, as well as Ella Steim, Steven Horak, AnneLise Sorensen, Martin Dunford, Andrew Rosenberg, Nicole Newman, Anita Singh, Katie-Lloyd Jones, Róisín Cameron, Jasbir Sandhu, Umesh Aggarwal, Rebecca Short, Chloë Roberts, Diane Margolis and Jan McCann.

Readers' letters

Thanks to all the readers who have taken the time to write in with comments and suggestions (and apologies if we've inadvertently omitted or misspelt anyone's name):

Cassie Berkowitz, Patti Bordoni, Evan Camp, Alan Davison, Irvine Devitt, Tim Everaerts, Damian Jensen, Sarah Johnson, Bern Marcowitz, Jessica Mizerak, Periklis Polyzoidis, Siobhan Scanlan, Jan & Sue Szuszkiewicz, Sarah Tallent, Shorey Walker, Joanna Woodcock.

Photo credits

All photos © Rough Guides except the following:

Cover
Front picture: Statue of Liberty Mural
  © StockAB/Alamy
Back picture: Manhattan street scene
  © Scott Stickland

Things not to miss
03 Halloween Parade © Demetrio Carrasco/
  Rough Guides
12 Boucher Gallery, Frick Museum © Frick
  Museum
15 MOMA Garden © Timothy Hursley/MOMA
18 New York Mets v New York Yankees © Jim
  McIsaac/Getty Images

New York architecture color section
Empire State Building © Nicole Newman

Ethnic New York color section
West Indian-American Day Carnival and Parade
  © Joe Kohen/WireImage/Getty
Chinese dragon, Chinese New Year Parade
  © DK images

Black and whites
p.91 Lower East Side Tenement Museum
p.141 The Museum of Modern Art, designed by
  Yoshio Taniguchi © Timothy Hursley/MOMA
p.260 Bronx Zoo © Julie Larsen Maher/WC

SMALL PRINT

Selected images from our guidebooks are available for licensing from:
ROUGHGUIDESPICTURES.COM

Index

Map entries are in color.

I

INDEX

Map symbols

maps are listed in the full index using colored text

– – –	Chapter boundary		🕯	Lighthouse
—— --	Provincial boundary		⊞	Hospital
⬤5⬤	Interstate		⊠	Post office
⟨5⟩	US highway		@	Internet access
⊂5⊃	State highway		🕯	Lighthouse
⟩:::::::⟨	Tunnel		🏛	Monument
— —	Ferry route		✡	Synagogue
—•—	Railway		✦	Buddhist temple
▲	Peak		⚘	Cemetery
✈	International airport		╄	Church (town maps)
⊠	Gate		⬭	Stadium
Ⓜ	Subway station		▬	Building
⬥	Point of interest		⊞	Cemetery
ⓘ	Tourist office		▦	Park/forest
⟙	Gardens		▦	Beach

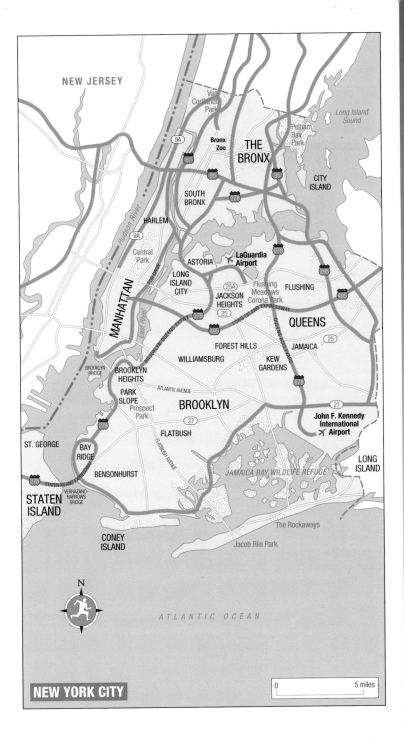

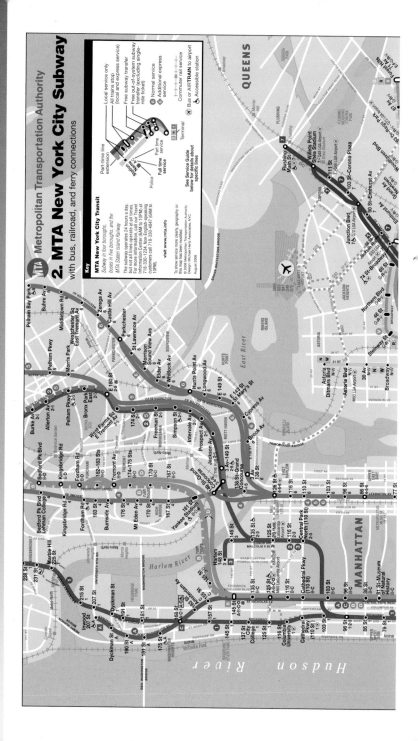

2. MTA New York City Subway

Metropolitan Transportation Authority

with bus, railroad, and ferry connections

Key

MTA New York City Transit

*Subways in four boroughs,
buses in five boroughs, and the
MTA Staten Island Railway*

The subway operates 24 hours a day,
but not all lines operate at all times.
For more information, call our Travel
Information Center (6AM to 10PM) at
718-330-1234. Non-English-speaking
customers call 718-330-4847 (6AM to
10PM).

visit www.mta.info

To show service more clearly, geography on
this map has been modified.
© 2008 Metropolitan Transportation Authority
Design: Michael Hertz Associates, NYC

August 2008

- Part time line
  extension
- Local service only
- All trains stop
  (local and express service)
- Free subway transfer
- Free out-of-system subway
  transfer (excluding single-
  ride ticket)
- ◆ Normal service
- ◇ Additional express
  service
- Full time
  service
- Part time
  service
- Commuter rail service
- ✈ Bus or AIRTRAIN to airport
- ♿ Accessible station

See Service Guide
below for details about
specific lines

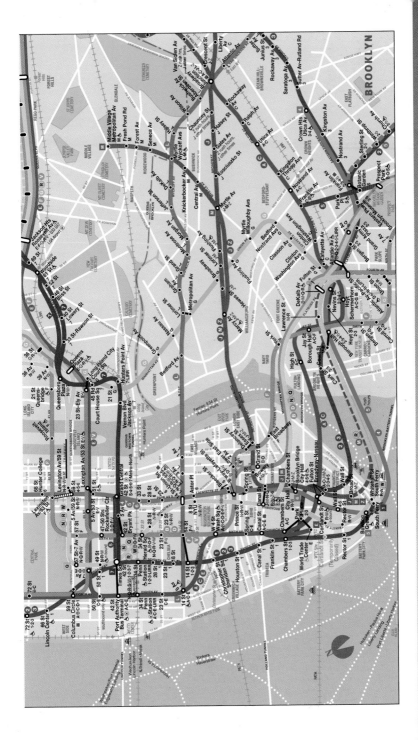

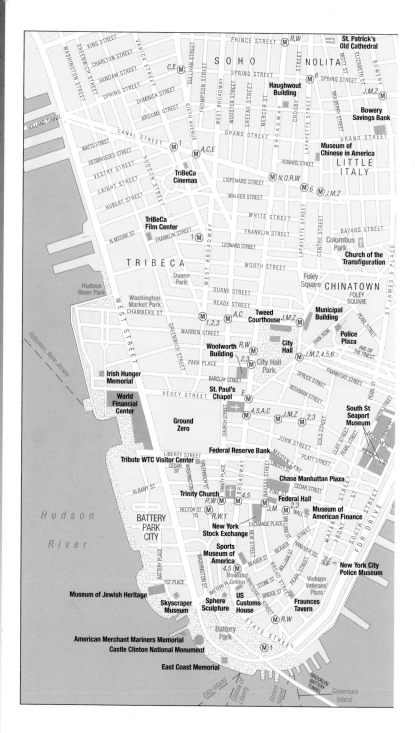

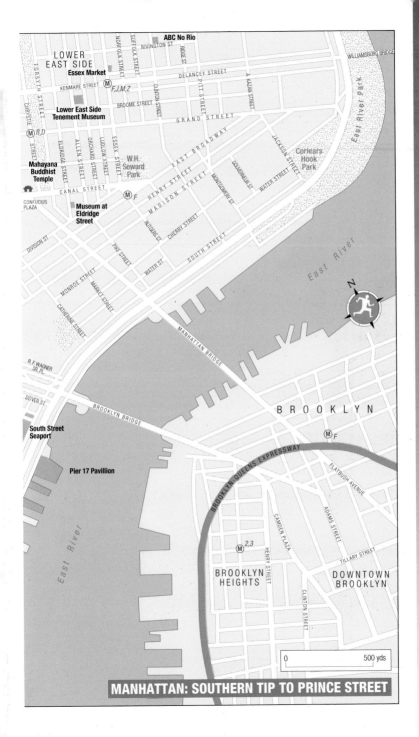

MANHATTAN: SOUTHERN TIP TO PRINCE STREET

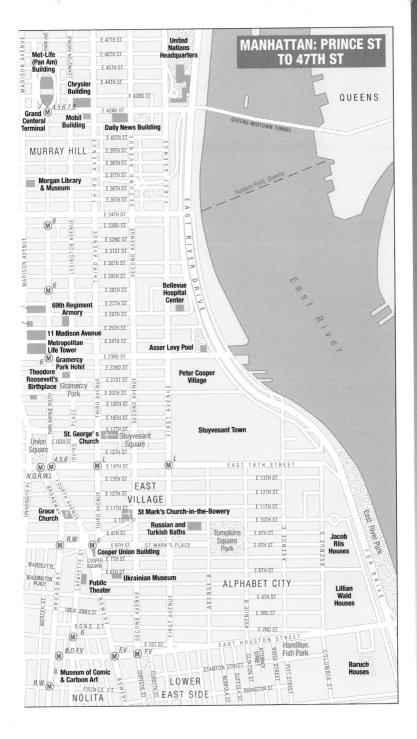

MANHATTAN: PRINCE ST TO 47TH ST

QUEENS

QUEENS MIDTOWN TUNNEL

Hunters Point, Queens

East River

United Nations Headquarters

E 47TH ST
E 46TH ST
E 45TH ST
E 44TH ST
E 43RD ST
E 42ND ST
E 40TH ST
E 39TH ST
E 38TH ST
E 37TH ST
E 36TH ST
E 35TH ST
E 34TH ST
E 33RD ST
E 32ND ST
E 31ST ST
E 30TH ST
E 29TH ST
E 28TH ST
E 27TH ST
E 26TH ST
E 25TH ST
E 24TH ST
E 23RD ST
E 22ND ST
E 21ST ST
E 20TH ST
E 19TH ST
E 18TH ST
E 17TH ST
E 16TH ST
E 15TH ST
E 14TH ST
E 13TH ST
E 12TH ST
E 11TH ST
E 10TH ST
E 9TH ST
E 8TH ST
E 7TH ST
E 6TH ST
E 4TH ST
E 3RD ST
E 2ND ST

EAST 14TH STREET
E 13TH ST
E 12TH ST
E 11TH ST
E 10TH ST
E 9TH ST
E 8TH ST
E 6TH ST

Met-Life (Pan Am) Building
Chrysler Building
Grand Central Terminal
Mobil Building
Daily News Building
MURRAY HILL
Morgan Library & Museum
69th Regiment Armory
11 Madison Avenue
Metropolitan Life Tower
Gramercy Park Hotel
Theodore Roosevelt's Birthplace
Gramercy Park
St. George's Church
Union Square
Stuyvesant Square
EAST VILLAGE
Grace Church
St Mark's Church-in-the-Bowery
Russian and Turkish Baths
Cooper Union Building
Public Theater
Ukrainian Museum
Museum of Comic & Cartoon Art

Bellevue Hospital Center
Asser Levy Pool
Peter Cooper Village
Stuyvesant Town
Tompkins Square Park
ALPHABET CITY
Jacob Riis Houses
Lillian Wald Houses
Hamilton Fish Park
Baruch Houses
East River Park

FDR DRIVE

NOLITA
LOWER EAST SIDE

MADISON AVENUE
PARK AVE
LEXINGTON AVENUE
THIRD AVENUE
SECOND AVENUE
FIRST AVENUE
EAST RIVER DRIVE

PARK AVENUE SOUTH
IRVING PLACE
FOURTH AVENUE
UNIVERSITY PL
BROADWAY
LAFAYETTE ST
COOPER SQUARE
SECOND AVENUE
FIRST AVENUE
AVENUE A
AVENUE B
AVENUE C
AVENUE D

WAVERLEY PL
WASHINGTON PLACE
MERCER ST
GREAT JONES ST
BOND ST
BOWERY
CHRYSTIE ST
FORSYTH ST
ELDRIDGE ST
ALLEN ST
ORCHARD ST
LUDLOW ST
ESSEX ST
NORFOLK ST
SUFFOLK ST
CLINTON ST
ATTORNEY STREET
RIDGE STREET
PITT STREET
COLUMBIA ST

EAST HOUSTON STREET
STANTON STREET
RIVINGTON ST
PRINCE ST

4,5,6,7,S
6
6
6
4,5,6
N,Q,R,W,L
L
L
R,W
6
B,D,F,V
F,V
F,V
R,W

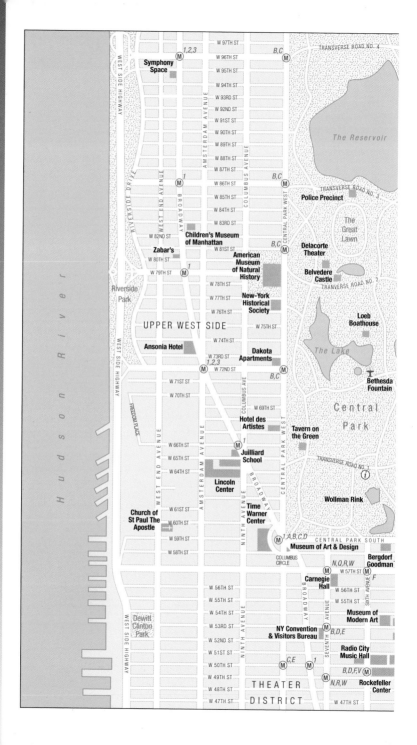

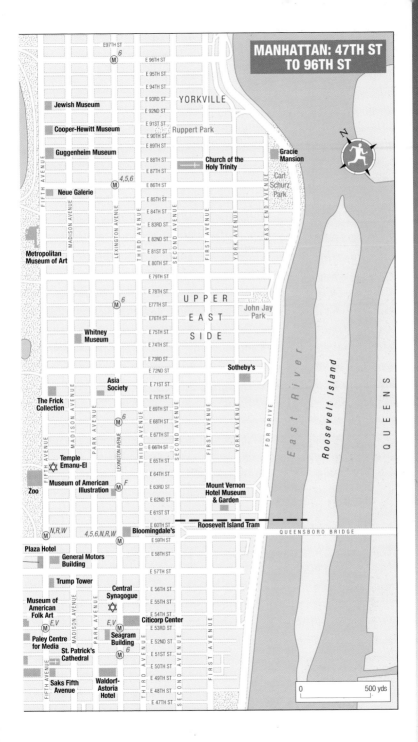

E97TH ST
6
E 96TH ST
E 95TH ST
E 94TH ST
E 93RD ST   YORKVILLE
Jewish Museum   E 92ND ST
E 91ST ST   Ruppert Park
Cooper-Hewitt Museum   E 90TH ST
E 89TH ST
Guggenheim Museum E 88TH ST
E 87TH ST   Church of the   Gracie
4,5,6   E 86TH ST   Holy Trinity   Mansion
Neue Galerie   E 85TH ST   Carl
Schurz
E 84TH ST   Park
E 83RD ST
E 82ND ST
Metropolitan   E 81ST ST
Museum of Art   E 80TH ST
E 79TH ST

E 78TH ST   U P P E R
6   E 77TH ST   John Jay
E 76TH ST   E A S T   Park
Whitney   E 75TH ST
Museum   E 74TH ST   S I D E
E 73RD ST
E 72ND ST   Sotheby's

Asia   E 71ST ST
Society   E 70TH ST
The Frick   E 69TH ST
Collection   6   E 68TH ST
E 67TH ST
E 66TH ST
Temple   E 65TH ST
Emanu-El   E 64TH ST
Museum of American F   E 63RD ST   Mount Vernon
Zoo   Illustration   E 62ND ST   Hotel Museum
E 61ST ST   & Garden
N,R,W   E 60TH ST   Roosevelt Island Tram
4,5,6,N,R,W   Bloomingdale's   QUEENSBORO BRIDGE
E 59TH ST
Plaza Hotel   E 58TH ST
General Motors
Building   E 57TH ST

Trump Tower   E 56TH ST
Central   E 55TH ST
Museum of   Synagogue
American   E 54TH ST
Folk Art   E.V   Citicorp Center
E.V   E 53RD ST
Paley Centre   Seagram   E 52ND ST
for Media   Building   E 51ST ST
St. Patrick's   6   E 50TH ST
Cathedral   E 49TH ST
Saks Fifth   Waldorf-   E 48TH ST
Avenue   Astoria   E 47TH ST
Hotel

East River   Roosevelt Island   QUEENS

FIFTH AVENUE   MADISON AVENUE   PARK AVENUE   LEXINGTON AVENUE   THIRD AVENUE   SECOND AVENUE   FIRST AVENUE   YORK AVENUE   EAST END AVENUE   FDR DRIVE

N

0   500 yds

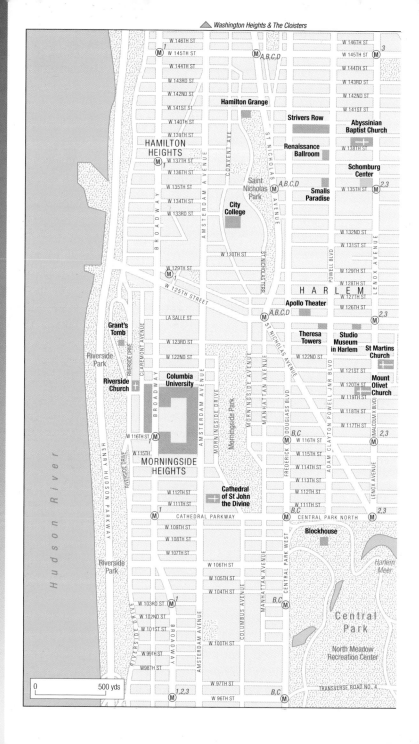